THE ENCYCLOPEDIA
OF THE
COLD WAR

A Political, Social, and Military History

THE ENCYCLOPEDIA
OF THE
COLD WAR

A Political, Social, and Military History

VOLUME IV: S–Z

Dr. Spencer C. Tucker
Volume Editor

Dr. Priscilla Roberts
Editor, Documents Volume

Dr. Paul G. Pierpaoli, Jr.
Associate Editor

Dr. Timothy C. Dowling
Mr. Gordon E. Hogg
Dr. Priscilla Roberts
Assistant Editors

PERSONAL PERSPECTIVE FOREWORD BY
John S. D. Eisenhower

ABC-CLIO

Santa Barbara, California   Denver, Colorado   Oxford, England

Cataloging-in-Publication Data is on file with the Library of Congress

ISBN: 978-1-85109-701-2   ebook: 978-1-85109-706-7

12   11   10   09   08   1   2   3   4   5   6   7   8

This book is also available on the World Wide Web as an ebook.
Visit abc-clio.com for details.

ABC-CLIO, Inc.
130 Cremona Drive, P.O. Box 1911
Santa Barbara, California 93116–1911

This book is printed on acid-free paper ⊗ .
Manufactured in the United States of America

Contents

List of Entries

List of Maps

General Maps

EAST CENTRAL EUROPE, 1945

SWEDEN

DENMARK
Copenhagen

55°N

*Baltic
Sea*

LATVIA S.S.R.

(RUSSIAN
S.S.R.)

LITHUANIA
S.S.R.

RUSSIAN S.S.R.

N

WEST
GERMANY

Berlin

EAST
GERMANY

BELORUSSIAN S.S.R.

POLAND

Warsaw

SOVIET UNION

50°N

Prague

Danube

CZECHOSLOVAKIA

UKRAINIAN S.S.R.

Dnieper R.

Vienna

AUSTRIA

Budapest

HUNGARY

MOLDOVIAN S.S.R.

45°N

ROMANIA

Belgrade

Bucharest

Danube R.

*Black
Sea*

YUGOSLAVIA

*Adriatic
Sea*

ITALY
Rome

Sofia
BULGARIA

Tirane

ALBANIA

40°N

Ankara

*Tyrrhenian
Sea*

GREECE

*Aegean
Sea*

TURKEY

*Ionian
Sea*

Athens

35°N

--- 1947 International boundaries

········· Allied Military Sector boundaries

*Mediterranean
Sea*

0   100   200 mi

0   100   200 km

15°E   20°E   25°E   30°E

xxvi

GLOBAL DIVISIONS AT THE HEIGHT OF THE COLD WAR, 1962

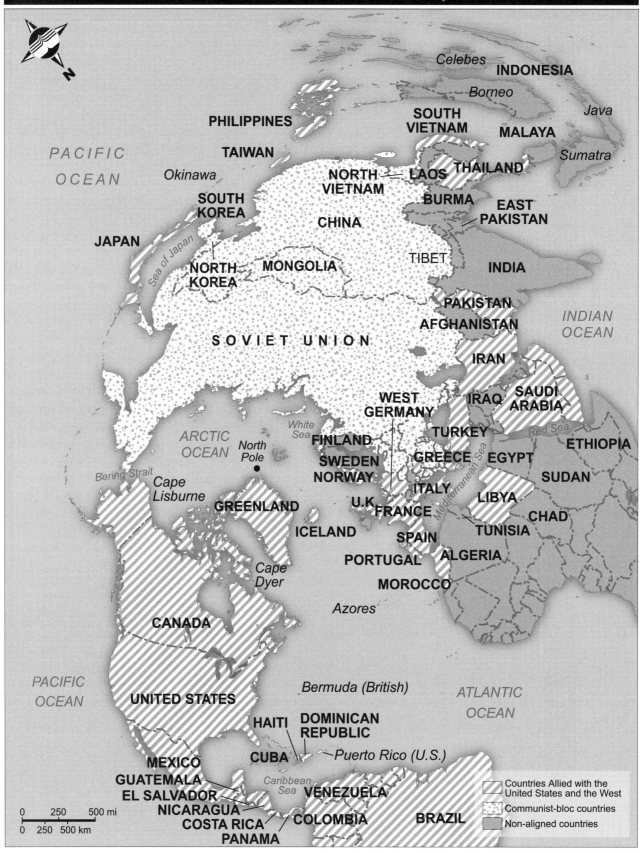

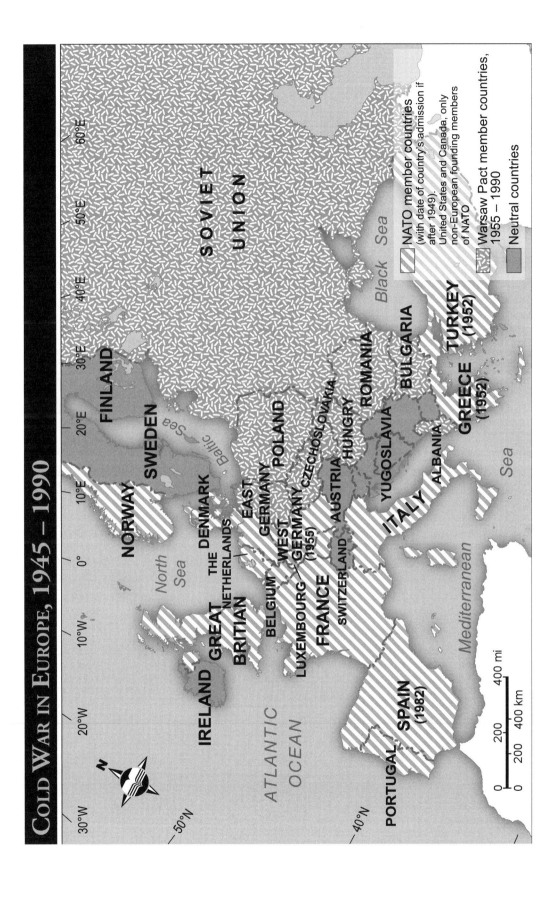

Cold War in Europe, 1945 – 1990

NATO member countries
(with date of country's admission if after 1949).
United States and Canada, only
non-European founding members
of NATO

**Warsaw Pact member countries,
1955 – 1990**

Neutral countries

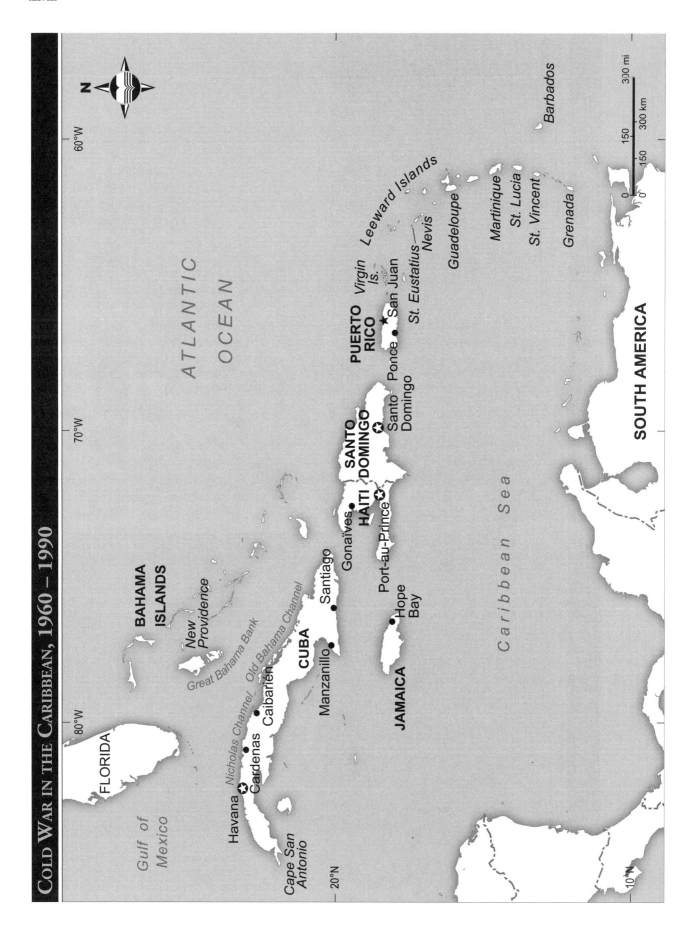

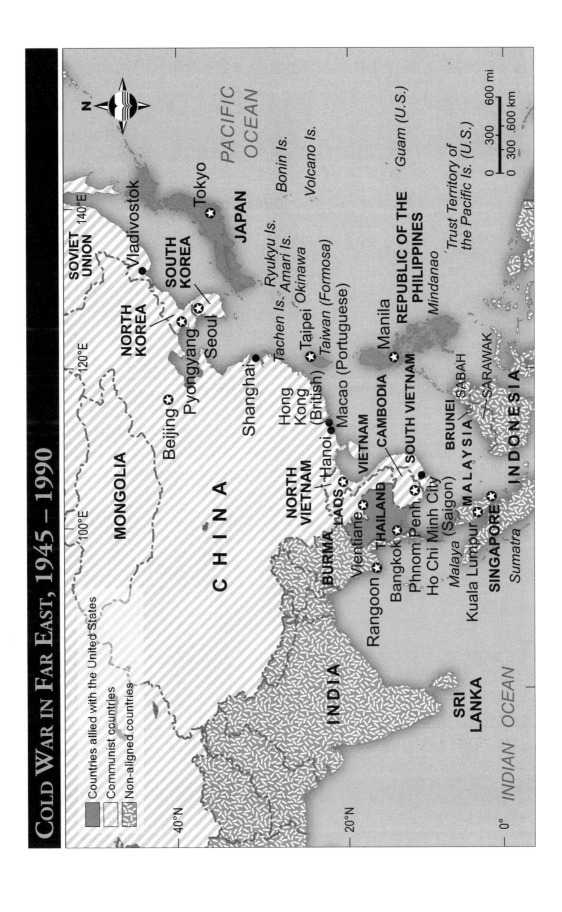

COLD WAR IN FAR EAST, 1945 – 1990

Countries allied with the United States
Communist countries
Non-aligned countries

Cold War in Middle East, 1945 – 1990

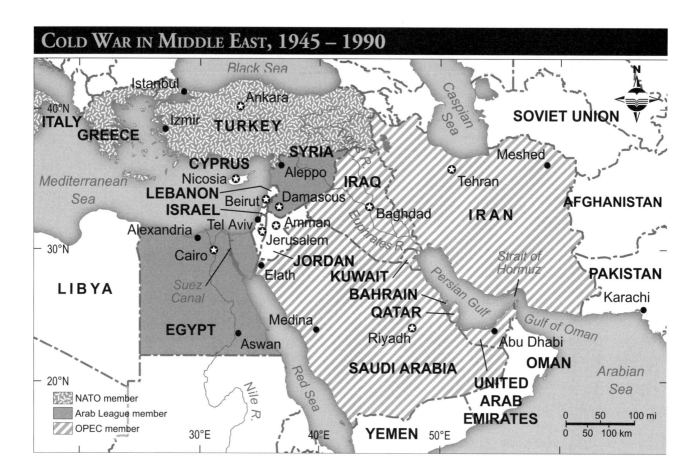

NATO member
Arab League member
OPEC member

EAST CENTRAL EUROPE, 1992

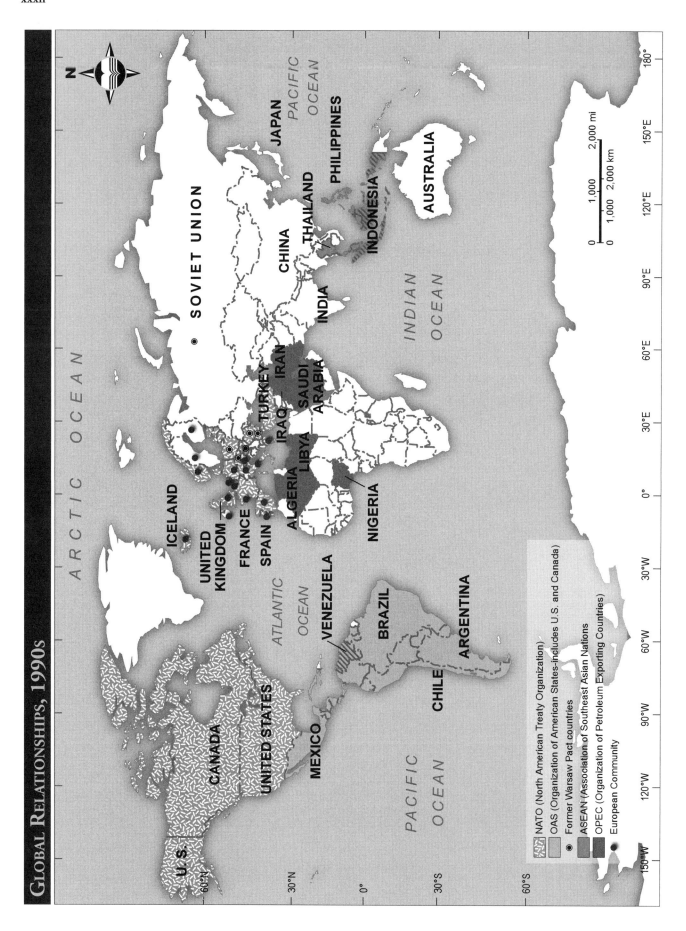

GLOBAL RELATIONSHIPS, 1990s

N

ARCTIC OCEAN

SOVIET UNION

JAPAN

PACIFIC OCEAN

CHINA

PHILIPPINES

THAILAND

ICELAND

INDONESIA

UNITED KINGDOM

TURKEY

IRAN

INDIA

AUSTRALIA

FRANCE

IRAQ

SAUDI ARABIA

SPAIN

LIBYA

ALGERIA

INDIAN OCEAN

ATLANTIC OCEAN

NIGERIA

VENEZUELA

BRAZIL

ARGENTINA

CHILE

MEXICO

UNITED STATES

CANADA

U.S.

PACIFIC OCEAN

60°N

30°N

0°

30°S

60°S

150°W   120°W   90°W   60°W   30°W   0°   30°E   60°E   90°E   120°E   150°E   180°

NATO (North American Treaty Organization)
OAS (Organization of American States–includes U.S. and Canada)
Former Warsaw Pact countries
ASEAN (Association of Southeast Asian Nations)
OPEC (Organization of Petroleum Exporting Countries)
European Community

0   1,000   2,000 mi
0   1,000   2,000 km

S

Saar

A coal-rich state in the Federal Republic of Germany (FRG, West Germany) bordering France and Luxembourg, historically a region of contested sovereignty between France and Germany. In the eighteenth century, the Saar region was partially in France and partially within two German principalities. The 1797 Treaty of Campo Formio transferred the entire area to France, but the 1815 Treaty of Paris following the Napoleonic Wars transferred the area to Bavaria and Prussia.

The Saar's extensive coal deposits led to industrial development following German unification in 1871. After World War I, the Saar was placed under the administration of the League of Nations for a period of fifteen years, with France to receive its coal production during that period to compensate France for the deliberate destruction of its coal mines by retreating German troops. At the end of the fifteen-year period, Saarlanders were to vote on their future. In a plebiscite held in January 1935, 90 percent of voters in the Saar opted to return to Germany.

After World War II the Saar passed under French military administration, and in 1947 the French set up an autonomous government for the region. In a plebiscite that year, the voters of the Saar approved economic unification with France, and a customs union went into effect in 1948. The other Western powers recognized this arrangement, much to the chagrin of West German leaders. France was obliged to give ground, however, for the 1954 Paris Pacts that provided for West German rearmament and its integration into the North Atlantic Treaty Organization (NATO) also provided for a compromise settlement of the Saar question. To the relief of the Germans, the Saar was declared to be autonomous rather than politically integrated into France. However, it was to remain economically integrated with France for fifty years. But Saar voters threw a monkey wrench into this arrangement by rejecting it in October 1955.

The 1952 European Coal and Steel Community (ECSC), which marked the movement toward the European Economic Community (EEC), and West Germany's integration into the Western alliance eased French concerns over the future of the Saar. As a result of the 1956 Franco-German Agreement, the Saar became a West German territory on 1 January 1957. Although the customs union with France was dissolved in July 1959, France was granted the right to exploit the Saar's Warndt coalfields until 1981.

Bernard Cook

See also
European Coal and Steel Community; European Economic Community; European Integration Movement; France; Germany, Federal Republic of
References
Cowan, Laing Gray. *France and the Saar, 1680–1948*. New York: Columbia University Press, 1950.
Freymond, Jacques. *The Saar Conflict, 1945–1955*. New York: Praeger, 1960.
Staerk, Dieter. *Das Saarlandbuch*. Saarbrücken: Minerva-Verlag Thinnes and Nolte, 1985.

Sadat, Anwar (1918–1981)

Egyptian nationalist leader, vice president (1966–1970), and president (1970–1981) of Egypt. Born on 25 December 1918

Anwar Sadat, president of Egypt from 1970 until his assassination in 1981. Sadat is remembered for his part in concluding the 1979 Camp David Peace Treaty between Egypt and Israel. (Jimmy Carter Library)

in Mit Abu al-Kum, Egypt, one of thirteen children, Anwar Sadat attended the Royal Egyptian Military Academy, from which he graduated in 1938 as a second lieutenant. His first posting was in the Sudan, where he met Gamal Abdel Nasser, fellow nationalist and future Egyptian president. Stemming from their mutual disdain of British colonial rule, Sadat and Nasser helped form the secret organization that would eventually be called the Free Officers Group, comprised of young Egyptian military officers dedicated to ending British rule and ousting King Farouk II. During World War II, Sadat was jailed for conspiring with the Axis powers to expel British forces from Egypt.

Sadat was an active participant in the 23 July 1952 coup against King Farouk engineered by the Free Officers Group. Farouk abdicated and left Egypt on 26 July 1952. When Egypt was declared a republic in June 1953, Major General Mohammad Naguib became its president, and Nasser became vice president. In October 1954, after an attempt on Nasser's life, Naguib was removed from office, while Nasser consolidated his power. In February 1955 Nasser became prime minister and seven months later became president. Sadat, meanwhile, served loyally under Nasser, acting as his chief spokesman and one of his closest personal confidants and advisors.

In 1964 Sadat became vice president of Egypt and then president upon Nasser's death in September 1970. When Sadat became president, Egypt's relationship with the Soviet Union, once robust, was showing signs of serious strain. At the time of his death, in fact, Nasser had been moving away from the Soviet Union. Part of the reason for this had been the reduction in equipment that the Soviets were willing to sell to Egypt. On 18 July 1972, Sadat ordered all Soviet advisors to leave the country, to be followed by pilots and other army technicians.

On 6 October 1973, Sadat led Egypt, along with Syria, into a war with Israel with the goal of reclaiming the Sinai Peninsula lost in the 1967 Six-Day War. Although Egypt was defeated in the war, initial military successes and Sadat's determination earned him great respect among his people and lifted the morale of the nation, which had been badly shaken by Nasser's heavy-handed rule and economic difficulties. At war's end, the United States and the Soviet Union both were concerned about the balance of power in the Middle East and thus negotiated a cease-fire agreement that was generally favorable to Egypt, allowing Sadat to claim a victory of sorts.

Realizing that only the United States could elicit any substantive concessions from Israel, Sadat completely severed relations with the Soviet Union in March 1976 and began working with the Americans toward a peace settlement with the Israelis. In a courageous move, Sadat became the first Arab leader to officially visit Israel in November 1977, meeting with Prime Minister Menachem Begin and even addressing the Israeli Knesset. In September 1978, Sadat signed the Camp David Accords, ushering in a comprehensive peace agreement with Israel. The accords were highly unpopular in the Arab world, however, especially among fundamentalist Muslims.

Although the Camp David Accords were, in the long run, beneficial for Egypt, many in the Arab world saw them as a great betrayal and viewed Sadat as a traitor. In September 1981, Sadat's government cracked down on extremist Muslim organizations and radical student groups, in the process arresting more than 1,600 people. Sadat's strong-arm tactics angered many in the Arab community and only exacerbated his problems, which included economic stagnation and charges that he had quashed dissident voices through force.

On 6 October 1981, Sadat was assassinated in Cairo while reviewing a military parade commemorating the Yom Kippur War. His assassins were radical fundamentalist army officers who belonged to the Islamic Jihad organization, which had bitterly denounced Sadat's peace overtures with Israel and his suppression of dissidents the month before. Sadat was succeeded in office by Hosni Mubarak.

Dallace W. Unger Jr.

See also

Arab-Israeli Wars; Begin, Menachem; Camp David Accords; Carter, James Earl, Jr.; Egypt; Farouk II, King of Egypt; Nasser, Gamal Abdel

References

Beattie, Kirk J. *Egypt during the Sadat Years.* New York: Palgrave, 2000.

Finklestone, Joseph. *Anwar Sadat: Visionary Who Dared.* Portland, OR: Frank Cass, 1996.

Hirst, David, and Irene Beeson. *Sadat.* London: Faber and Faber, 1981.

Sadat, Anwar. *In Search of Identity: An Autobiography.* New York: Harper and Row, 1978.

See also

Canada; Pearson, Lester Bowles

References

Bercuson, David J. *Blood on the Hills: The Canadian Army in the Korean War.* Toronto: University of Toronto Press, 1999.

Pickersgill, J. W. *My Years with Louis St. Laurent: A Political Memoir.* Toronto: University of Toronto Press, 1975.

Thomson, Dale C. *Louis St. Laurent, Canadian.* Toronto: Macmillan, 1967.

Saint-Laurent, Louis Stephen (1882–1973)

Canadian Liberal Party politician, minister of justice and attorney general (1941–1946, 1948), minister of external affairs (1946–1948), and prime minister (1948–1957). Born on 1 February 1882 in Compton, Quebec, Louis Saint-Laurent graduated from St. Charles College with a BA degree in 1902 and from Laval University with a law degree in 1905. He worked as a lawyer during 1905–1914, at which time he became a law professor at Laval University. He was actively involved in establishing the Canadian Bar Association and became Canada's preeminent expert on constitutional law.

Saint-Laurent entered Parliament in 1941 as a Liberal Party representative, and his second career as a politician proved as successful as his first. After holding a succession of important cabinet posts during 1941–1948, he was elected prime minister on 15 November 1948. He was not afraid of controversy and made many hard political decisions, the most difficult being Canada's participation in the Korean War (1950–1953).

Saint-Laurent was a fierce proponent of peace in the post–World War II era. In June 1950, when the United States urged United Nations (UN) involvement in Korea, Saint-Laurent was extremely hesitant to see Canada involved. At first he refused to act, but eventually he agreed to commit Canadian troops to the fight. Yet while soldiers were deployed, Saint-Laurent actively encouraged his secretary of state for external affairs, Lester B. Pearson, to continue efforts to settle the Korean War by diplomacy. Eventually, due in no small part to Canadian mediation efforts in the UN, a truce was signed in July 1953. Similarly, Saint-Laurent and Pearson were instrumental in ending the 1956 Suez Crisis, earning Pearson the Nobel Peace Prize. Domestically, the Saint-Laurent government followed progressive policies, creating new social welfare programs and expanding existing ones.

By 1957, however, Canadians sensed that the Liberal Party had grown stale, and it lost the 1957 elections. Saint-Laurent resigned his office in June 1957 and largely retired from politics. He died in Quebec City on 25 July 1973.

Maurice Williams and Takaia Larsen

Sakhalin Island

Pacific island located about 50 miles to the east of the mouth of the Amur River in the Soya Straits, just north of the northern tip of Japan and off the southeastern coast of Russia. Sakhalin Island is about 30,500 square miles in area and had a 1945 population of some 560,000 people.

Since the nineteenth century, both Japan and Russia have contested sovereignty over Sakhalin. The Japanese established settlements in southern Sakhalin in the late 1700s, and the Russians arrived in 1853. Two years later, when Japan and Russia opened diplomatic relations, they agreed that both nations might retain settlements on the island. In 1875, Japan abandoned its claims to Sakhalin because it had become difficult to oppose the Russians. Following Japan's defeat of Russia in the Russo-Japanese War of 1904–1905, however, Japan acquired full rights to southern Sakhalin and took the entire island after the 1917 Russian Revolution. Japan handed over to the Soviet Union control of Sakhalin north of the 50th Parallel as part of their normalization of diplomatic relations in 1925. Japan retained extensive rights to exploit oil, coal, timber, and other natural resources in the Soviet half of the island.

When the Soviet Union entered the war against Japan just days before the end of the Pacific conflict, the Red Army launched fierce attacks against the western coast of Sakhalin on 16 and 20 August 1945. Following conclusion of a local cease-fire on 23 August, the Soviets prohibited Japanese citizens on Sakhalin from leaving the island. Many were forced into hard labor on the island or in Siberia, and it was not until 1949 that they were all released.

As part of the price to get the Soviet Union into the war against Japan, at the February 1945 Yalta Conference the Western Allies had agreed to Soviet acquisition of all of Sakhalin. Although the 1951 San Francisco Peace Treaty with Japan confirmed the abandonment of Japanese claims on southern Sakhalin and the Kurile Islands, the transfer of those to the Soviet Union was not prescribed in the treaty. The Soviet Union, however, refused to sign the treaty. In October 1956, Japanese Prime Minister Hatoyama Ichirō visited Moscow and signed the Japan-Soviet Joint Declaration. This formally ended the state of war between the two nations but did not resolve the territorial dispute over the Kuriles and southern Sakhalin. The Soviet Union rejected the Japanese request to return to Japan the so-called Northern Territories of the Kuriles and Sakhalin, and the issue was put off.

The Soviets have held that Sakhalin Island is essential to securing their nation's southeastern flank, and this is the reason that they made such a desperate effort in August 1945 to take southern Sakhalin. The Sea of Okhotsk also became much more vital for military purposes following the development of submarine-launched ballistic missiles (SLBMs), and Soviet forces on Sakhalin were reinforced in the 1970s and 1980s. The Sea of Okhotsk was the most secure area for the Soviet nuclear missile submarine fleet, because all of the straits into the sea were under Soviet control. More generally, the Soviets felt less secure during this period because of ongoing tensions with China and strengthened security cooperation between the United States and Japan. For many years, the Japanese government feared that Soviet forces might invade northern Hokkaido Island on the Soya Straits to complete their enclosure of the Sea of Okhotsk. During the Cold War, Japan invested heavily in defenses on northern Hokkaido, which lay only a few miles south of Sakhalin.

In September 1983, Soviet aircraft shot down Korean Airlines (KAL) Flight 007 near Sakhalin. Currently, the issue of Sakhalin and the Kuriles remains a stumbling block to smoother relations between Japan and Russia.

Nakayama Takashi

See also

Japan; Japan, Armed Forces; Kurile Islands; San Francisco Peace Treaty; Territorial Changes after World War II

References

Nakayama Takashi. *1945-nen Natsu Saigo no Nisso-sen* [The Summer of 1945: The Last Russo-Japanese War]. Tokyo: Chuokoronshinsha, 2001.

Stephan, John J. *Sakhalin: A History.* New York: Clarendon, 1971.

U.S. Department of Defense. *Sea of Okhotsk, Soviet Union, Ostrov Sakhalin including the Tatar Strait.* Washington, DC: DMA/Combat Support Center/DOA, 1994.

Sakharov, Andrei Dmitrievich (1921–1989)

Soviet nuclear scientist, dissident, and human rights activist. Born on 21 May 1921 in Moscow, the son of a physics professor, Andrei Sakharov studied physics at Moscow University during 1939–1942 and at the Lebedev Institute of the Soviet Academy of Sciences during 1945–1947 under the eminent theoretical physicist Igor Tamm. Sakharov earned his doctorate in 1947 and joined the Soviet nuclear weapons program in 1948, working in a special group then headed by his mentor.

Dissident Soviet physicist Andrei D. Sakharov, father of the Soviet hydrogen bomb, upon learning that he was awarded the 1975 Nobel Peace Prize. (Bettmann/Corbis)

Spearheaded by Sakharov, Tamm's group produced the first Soviet hydrogen bomb, successfully tested in August 1953, a development that greatly intensified the nuclear arms race with the United States. For his contributions to the development of the hydrogen bomb, Sakharov received both the Lenin and Stalin Prizes and earned election as a full member of the Soviet Academy of Sciences in 1953.

Sakharov's participation in the Soviet nuclear weapons program lasted nearly twenty years. Initially, he believed that his work was of vital importance to the global balance of power. However, over time he grew uneasy with what he characterized as moral problems inherent in his work, and he became disillusioned with the Soviet system, specifically the absence of civil liberties and the secrecy surrounding science, culture, and technology.

Beginning in the late 1950s, Sakharov called on the Soviet regime to ban atmospheric testing of nuclear weapons. In the early to mid-1960s, he moved on to criticize the continuing influence of the erroneous theories of T. S. Lysenko on Soviet genetics and to protest Soviet leader Leonid Brezhnev's tentative first steps toward rehabilitating the legacy of Soviet dictator Josef Stalin. Sakharov ultimately crossed the Rubicon to full dissident in 1968, when his essay "Reflections on Progress, Peaceful Coexistence, and Intellectual Freedom" appeared in the Western press. This extended essay, also known as the Sakharov Memorandum, warned of the dangers, including thermonuclear annihilation, that threatened humanity. He also pushed for reconciliation between socialist and capitalist nations, advocated democratic freedoms in the Soviet Union, denounced collectivized agriculture, and called for a careful reexamination of the Stalin era. In response, the Brezhnev regime removed Sakharov from the Soviet nuclear weapons program and stripped him of all privileges to which he had been entitled as a member of the Soviet Nomenklatura.

In the summer of 1969, Sakharov became a senior researcher at the Lebedev Institute, but his primary concerns for the remainder of his life were human rights and the democratization of the Soviet Union. In 1970, he and fellow physicist Valeri Chalidze established the Moscow Human Rights Committee, which advocated freedom of speech, the full implementation of the Soviet constitution, and monitored violations of the law and the constitution including the arrests of dissidents by the Soviet regime. Sakharov's efforts in the name of human rights earned him the Nobel Peace Prize in 1975, making him the first Soviet citizen to garner the award, although he was not permitted to leave the Soviet Union to claim it.

Although the Soviet Komitet Gosudarstvennoi Bezopasnosti (KGB) harassed Sakharov and threatened him with prosecution, he remained a free man until 1980 when, in the wake of his criticisms of the 1979 invasion of Afghanistan and with the 1980 Moscow Olympics approaching, the Brezhnev regime exiled him to Gorky, a military-industrial city closed to foreigners. There Sakharov remained until December 1986, when Soviet leader Mikhail Gorbachev, as part of his policy of glasnost, freed him, allowing him and his wife Yelena Bonner to return to Moscow and resume his scientific endeavors.

In 1989, the Soviet Academy of Sciences selected Sakharov to serve as a deputy in the newly established Congress of People's Deputies, the first democratically elected national legislative body to sit in Russia since the Bolshevik Revolution. There Sakharov proved to be an outspoken critic of Gorbachev, constantly pushing him to carry his political and economic reforms further. Sakharov died of a heart attack in Moscow on 14 December 1989.

Bruce J. DeHart

See also

Bonner, Yelena Georgievna; Brezhnev, Leonid; Glasnost; Gorbachev, Mikhail; Hydrogen Bomb; Human Rights; Nomenklatura; Nuclear Arms Race; Peace Movements; Soviet Union

References

Bailey, George. *Galileo's Children: Science, Sakharov and the Power of the State.* New York: Arcade Publishing, 1990.

Lourie, Richard. *Sakharov: A Biography.* Hanover, NH: University Press of New England, 2002.

Sakharov, Andrei. *Memoirs.* Translated by Richard Lourie. New York: Knopf, 1990.

Salan, Raoul Albin-Louis (1899–1984)

French Army officer and bitter opponent of the dismantlement of France's colonial empire. Born in Roquecourbe (Tarn) near Toulouse on 10 June 1899, Raoul Salan was admitted to the French military academy at Saint-Cyr in August 1917 during World War I but was immediately sent to the front in France. He returned to Saint-Cyr after the war and graduated in August 1919. He then served in Algeria, Morocco, the Middle East, and Indochina.

At first loyal to Vichy following the defeat of French forces by the Germans in June 1940, Salan later rallied to the Free French Resistance in 1943 and, as a colonel in command of a regiment, took part in the liberation of metropolitan France. In 1945 he was posted to French Indochina, where he commanded French forces in northern Indochina, accompanying Vietnamese nationalist leader Ho Chi Minh to France and the July 1946 Fontainebleau Conference. In April 1952, Salan assumed command of all French forces in Indochina, holding that post until January 1953 when he became inspector general of land forces in France. He accompanied French Army commander General Paul Ely on a fact-finding tour to Indochina in June 1954 and then returned there with Ely when the latter was named high commissioner and commander in chief of French forces (July–October 1954). The French military defeat in the Battle of Dien Bien Phu in May 1954 was a clarion call for Salan, who believed that there could be no defeats for the French colonial empire, a conviction shared by many of his fellow officers.

During January–May 1955, Salan commanded the reserve army in France and was a member of the Supreme War Council. In November 1956 he was dispatched to Algeria as commander in chief of French forces there with the rank of general of the army. At the time, France was heavily engaged in fighting anticolonial forces in Algeria. Salan initially supported General Charles de Gaulle's ascension to power in May 1958 and the establishment of the French Fifth Republic. That December, de Gaulle, who mistrusted Salan, removed him from command.

In 1959 Salan retired to Algeria. When he realized that de Gaulle was prepared to grant Algeria independence, he allied himself with the anti–Algerian independence movement Algérie française (French Algeria). On 22 April 1961, Salan was one of four French generals to foment a military coup attempt in Algeria. Known as the Generals' Putsch, it failed after three days, and Salan went underground to lead the Secret Army Organization (OAS) in a brutal campaign of terror against the French government in both Algeria and France. That July he was sentenced in absentia to death for treason.

Arrested in Spain in April 1962, Salan was returned to France and tried a month later. Found guilty, he was sentenced to life imprisonment. He was released in May 1968 under a governmental amnesty. In 1982, President François Mitterrand restored Salan's military rank along with his pension. Salan died in Paris on 3 July 1984.

Cezar Stanciu

See also

Algerian War; Decolonization; De Gaulle, Charles; Dien Bien Phu, Battle of; Indochina War

References

Horne, Alistair. *A Savage War of Peace: Algeria, 1954–1962.* New York: Viking, 1977.

Salan, Raoul. *Le Sens d'un Engagement, 1899–1946.* Paris: Presses de la Cité, 1970.

———. *Indochine Rouge: Le Message d'Ho Chi Minh.* Paris: Presses de la Cité, 1975.

———. *Mémoires: Fin d'un Empire, "Le Viet-Minh Mon Adversaire" October 1946–October 1954.* Paris: Presses de la Cité, 1954.

Salazar, António de Oliveira (1889–1970)

Portuguese political leader and dictator. Born on 28 April 1889 in the village of Vimeiro, near the town of Santa Comba Dão, Portugal, António Salazar grew up a conservative Catholic. Educated at the University of Coimbra, he became a professor of political economy there. He was elected to the Portuguese Chamber of Deputies but soon withdrew because he considered it to be a futile exercise. In 1926, in order to end chronic political instability in Portugal (there had been forty cabinets since the overthrow of the monarchy in 1910), the Portuguese military seized power. Salazar was then briefly minister of finance. Recalled to the same post in 1928, he received the full authority that he demanded and in short order had placed Portuguese finances on a firm foundation. Over the next few years he gradually increased his power until in 1932 he became premier of an authoritarian government. From that point, he dominated Portuguese affairs until 1968.

Under a new constitution ratified in a 1933 referendum, Salazar reorganized Portugal as a corporative unitary republic rather than a pluralist state. A national assembly, elected by heads of families, served as the legislative body. A corporative chamber advised the assembly on social and economic matters and represented syndicates of various corporations. The Catholic Church also had widespread influence. Salazar's National Union party was the political voice of the so-called Estado Novo (New State), which combined eighteenth-century enlightened despotism with Christian morality, but also had both fascist and democratic trappings. This system came to be known as clerical fascism and subsequently became a model for the Nationalists in Spain and for Austria.

Profoundly religious, Salazar was also an ascetic and a bachelor. Unlike most dictators, he lived frugally on a modest salary and was utterly uninterested in the accumulation of personal wealth. He also remained virtually unknown to his people. While he admired fascism and supported the Nationalist side in the Spanish Civil War, he also intensely disliked Adolf Hitler and the Nazis and maintained diplomatic relations with Portugal's long-standing ally, Great Britain. As with Francisco Franco in Spain, Salazar appreciated the German war against communism but, unlike Franco, kept his country strictly neutral during World War II until, under British and U.S. pressure, he agreed in October 1943 to lease bases in the Azores. These proved vital to the Allies in the Battle of the Atlantic. Nonetheless, Salazar maintained that the nation was neutral, and Portugal profited from selling goods to both sides.

Portugal emerged from the war in a much better position than Spain, was readily admitted to the United Nations (UN), and was invited to join the North Atlantic Treaty Organization (NATO). Although Portugal was a police state, Salazar always tried to preserve some of the elements of a democratic façade. Unfortunately for his country, however, he refused to allow economic modernization, believing that it would place traditional Portuguese values at risk, and the resultant economic stagnation led many Portuguese to emigrate. In his last years in power, Salazar was increasingly forced to devote substantial financial and military resources to maintaining Portuguese control over its overseas empire, especially in Africa. An injury in 1968 led to a disabling stroke, forcing him to yield power to Marcelo Caetano, who began reforms. Salazar died in Lisbon on 27 July 1970.

Spencer C. Tucker

See also

Caetano, Marcelo Jose das Neves; Franco, Francisco; Portugal; Spain

References

Garnier, Christine. *Salazar: An Intimate Portrait.* New York: Farrar, Straus, 1954.

Georgel, Jacques. *Le salazarisme: Histoire et bilan, 1926–1974.* Paris: Cujas, 1981.

Kay, Hugh. *Salazar and Modern Portugal.* New York: Hawthorn, 1970.

San Francisco Peace Treaty (8 September 1951)

Treaty signed by Japan and forty-eight other nations in San Francisco, California, on 8 September 1951 formally terminating the state of war between Japan and the other signatories and restoring full sovereignty to Japan. The treaty went into force on 28 April 1952.

On 17 March 1947, General Douglas MacArthur publicly proposed an early peace treaty with Japan. However, differing attitudes among the European powers, the United States, the Soviet Union, and China over how best to approach such a treaty ultimately led to the postponement of any international conference on the subject.

Meanwhile, growing tensions between the Soviet Union and the United States enhanced Japan's political and strategic importance, leading the Americans to embark on a mission to reconstruct Japan both economically and politically. In light of growing tensions with the Soviet Union, together with the October 1949 communist victory in the Chinese Civil War, U.S. policymakers, particularly those in the Pentagon, argued for the need to maintain U.S. military bases in Japan. Consequently, the United States became increasingly inclined to end its occupation of Japan.

The Americans made substantial moves toward securing a peace settlement after John Foster Dulles was appointed consultant to the State Department in April 1950. Dulles, with nonpartisan domestic support, initiated negotiations with other Allied countries beginning in September 1950. Meanwhile, the outbreak of the Korean War in June 1950 added urgency to these peace negotiations.

The terms for the peace treaty drafted by the United States in late 1950 were seen as lenient and were consequently opposed by the Soviet Union, Australia, New Zealand, and the Philippines. While no compromise could be reached with the Soviet Union, U.S. policymakers persuaded the other states to accept the treaty's nonpunitive principles. The final draft of the treaty was jointly prepared by the United States and Great Britain.

The peace conference opened on 4 September 1951 in San Francisco and was attended by fifty-two nations. The treaty itself was signed by representatives of forty-nine nations, including Japan, on 8 September. Although their representatives were in attendance, the Soviet Union, Poland, and Czechoslovakia refused to sign the treaty.

The treaty stipulated Japan's abandonment of all territories acquired since 1895, including Korea, Taiwan, the Kurile Islands, and southern Sakhalin and its adjacent islands. American provisional control of the Ryukyu and Bonin islands was permitted, with an agreement to obtain ultimate authorization of the U.S. administration under a United Nations (UN) trusteeship. The document also established Japan's liability for payment of war reparations and drew attention to Japan's fragile economic situation. Later that same day, the United States and Japan also signed a security treaty.

Kuniyoshi Tomoki

See also
Dulles, John Foster; East Asia; Japan; Kurile Islands; Okinawa; United States–Japan Security Treaty; Yoshida Shigeru
References
Dunn, Frederick S. *Peace-Making and the Settlement with Japan.* Princeton, NJ: Princeton University Press, 1963.

Yoshitsu, Michael M. *Japan and the San Francisco Peace Settlement.* New York: Columbia University Press, 1983.

Sandinistas

Nicaraguan revolutionary movement and political party that toppled the dictatorship of Anastasio Somoza in 1979 and ruled Nicaragua during the 1980s.

After 1960, Somoza's restrictions on political opposition combined with the success of revolutionary movements in Cuba and elsewhere emboldened a group of activists to challenge his hold on power. Led by Carlos Fonseca, Tomás Borge, and Silvio Mayorga, the Frente Sandinista de Liberación Nacional (FSLN, Sandinista National Liberation Front) began its operations in Nicaragua's largest cities. The Sandinistas took their name from Augusto César Sandino (1895–1934), who led a nationalist rebellion against the U.S. military occupation of Nicaragua in the 1920s and early 1930s until his assassination by the U.S.-created Guardia Nacional (National Guard) enabled Somoza to seize control.

Designed as an urban guerrilla force, the FSLN had little impact. The corruption of the Somoza regime, however, helped sustain its organizational efforts. Shifting from urban to rural districts, the organization survived military defeats and factionalism well into the 1970s. In 1975, the group split into three organizational lines. The Prolonged Popular War faction (GPP), under the direction of Fonseca, Borge, and Henry Ruíz, led the effort to mobilize the population for war against the dictatorship. A second faction, led by Luis Carrión, Jaime Wheelock, and Carlos Núñez, focused on organizing workers and the urban underclass. A third group that would form the core of the Sandinistas' political force after 1979 built connections with business groups and other political opposition forces.

Somoza steadily lost popular support during the 1970s, and his reactionary policies helped the Sandinistas build their base and expand military operations. In 1974 the FSLN sponsored the formation of the United People's Movement (MPU), which linked unions, university students, and church-affiliated groups with their struggle. After 1977, the Sandinistas coordinated their campaigns with allied groups. Attacks against symbols of the Somoza regime, highlighted by the occupation of the National Palace and an ensuing prisoner exchange in 1978, demonstrated the FSLN's capabilities while it continued to build popular support.

International pressure and dwindling support from President Jimmy Carter's administration led Somoza to choose exile before defeat, and on 19 July 1979 the Sandinistas occupied Managua and took command of the government. The splits in the movement did not initially affect the Sandinistas'

Sandinistas patrol outside Managua, Nicaragua, on 22 July 1979. The Sandinistas seized power three days earlier. (Patrick Chauvel/Sygma/Corbis)

efforts. After declaring the unification of the movement's factions in 1979, the FSLN outlined its plans for the political, social, and economic transformation of Nicaragua. Nationalism, agrarian reform, progressive social reforms, universal medical care, and popular education clearly showcased the government's socialist orientation.

The Carter administration briefly offered humanitarian assistance to the Sandinistas, but domestic political pressure from conservatives forced the administration to end aid in 1980. The staunchly anticommunist President Ronald Reagan treated the Sandinistas much more harshly. In 1981 the Reagan administration engineered the end of financial support from international lending agencies and authorized the Central Intelligence Agency (CIA) to coordinate a counterrevolutionary movement in Nicaragua.

In 1982, with nearly $20 million from the United States, the Contra rebels began military operations against the Sandinista government. Launching small-scale raids from Honduras and Costa Rica, the Contras created an ongoing military challenge that sapped Sandinista resources. Nevertheless, the Sandinistas organized a government structure that allowed them to dominate the political process. A national directorate controlled the political process, the FSLN created youth groups and neighborhood committees to expand its base, and corpo-

rate bodies coordinated the political life of students, workers, and professionals.

Internationally, the Sandinistas counted on immediate support from Cuba and the Soviet Union. The Sandinista leadership chose to affiliate with the Socialist International rather than the Moscow-dominated Comintern. Harassed by Contra incursions and placed under a U.S. trade embargo that affected economic relations with its neighbors, the Sandinistas came to rely more and more upon economic and military aid from their communist allies.

Increasingly isolated, the Nicaraguan economy performed poorly under the Sandinistas. Inflation, shortages, and meager productivity hindered the government's efforts to diversify and expand the economy. Ultimately, the flagging economy undermined the Sandinistas' many ambitious social projects. Defense programs interfered with the agrarian reform program and exacerbated prickly government relations with the Miskito Indians in eastern Nicaragua.

In 1984, the U.S. Congress passed the Boland Amendment, which forbade further Contra funding. The Reagan administration skirted the restriction by illegally selling weapons to Iran as a way of generating funds for Contra operations. While revelations of these extralegal maneuvers rocked the Reagan administration, the Contra war continued.

To bring legitimacy to their regime, the Sandinistas organized national elections in 1984. Splits in the opposition forces allowed the Sandinistas to use their organizational strength to great effect. Daniel Ortega won election as president, and the Sandinistas worked to preserve their revolution's achievements, seeking international assistance in their ongoing conflict with the United States. In 1984, the International Court of Justice ruled that American actions in Nicaragua violated international laws but had no effect on U.S. policy. Latin American efforts to negotiate a peace settlement bore no fruit until 1989. Led by Costa Rican President Oscar Arias Sánchez, the 1989 Central American Peace Initiative brought about a final settlement. Under the plan, the Contras would disarm and the Sandinistas would authorize a national election, scheduled for February 1990.

Opposition forces united behind candidate Violeta Barrios de Chamorro, the widow of a leading opponent of the Somoza dictatorship who had been assassinated in 1978. Poor economic conditions and factionalism among the Sandinistas allowed the United Nicaraguan Opposition movement to capture the presidency and a majority of the seats in the National Congress. The Sandinistas' 1990 electoral defeat left the movement weakened and divided. Out of power, Sandinista leaders have recast their movement as a political party that competes effectively in local and national elections.

Daniel Lewis

See also
Contras; Iran-Contra Affair; Latin America, Popular Liberation Movements in; Reagan, Ronald Wilson; Somoza Debayle, Anastasio
References
Brentlinger, John. *The Best of What We Are: Reflections on the Nicaraguan Revolution.* Amherst: University of Massachusetts Press, 1995.
Gilbert, Dennis. *Sandinistas: The Party and the Revolution.* New York: Blackwell, 1988.

Saragat, Giuseppe (1898–1988)

Italian socialist politician, vice premier (1954–1957), and president (1964–1971) of the Republic of Italy. Born in Turin on 19 September 1898, Giuseppe Saragat served in the Italian Army in World War I and then studied economics at the University of Turin. In 1922 he joined the Italian Socialist Party (PSI).

Saragat entered the PSI Directorate in 1925, but the next year he went into exile, first in Austria and then in France, to escape Benito Mussolini's fascist dictatorship. Saragat returned to Italy in 1943 to participate in the Resistance and was arrested in November 1943 by the Germans but escaped. He became minister without portfolio in the Ivanoe Bonomi

government in 1944. In late 1945 Saragat was appointed ambassador to Paris and in 1946 was elected to the Constituent Assembly, becoming its president.

In the chaos of Italian politics unleashed by the Cold War, Saragat's vision of democratic socialism clashed with the decision of PSI leader Pietro Nenni to keep the party allied with the Communist Party. In January 1947 Saragat broke from the PSI and established his own party, which eventually became the Social Democratic Party (PSDI). This new political force developed a pro-Western political orientation, allied itself with the Christian Democrats, and entered the government, yet it remained a minor—albeit important—element of Italian politics. During 1954–1957, Saragat served as vice premier in the Mario Scelba and Antonio Segni governments.

The PSDI remained at odds with the PSI until the end of the 1950s. After 1956, however, the two parties began a rapprochement that culminated in a temporary reunification during 1966–1969 and the so-called Opening to the Left, namely the return of the PSI to the government and in its gradual detachment from the communists. Saragat's 1964 election to the presidency was a symbol of this new political climate. After his term expired in 1971, he became a life member of the Italian senate. He died in Rome on 11 June 1988.

Leopoldo Nuti

See also
Italy; Nenni, Pietro
References
Delzell, Charles F. *Italy in the Twentieth Century.* Washington, DC: American Historical Association, 1980.
Di Scala, Spencer. *Nenni to Craxi: Renewing Italian Socialism.* Oxford: Oxford University Press, 1988.

Sartre, Jean-Paul (1905–1980)

French philosopher, novelist, playwright, and social and literary critic. Born in Paris on 21 June 1905, Jean-Paul Sartre studied philosophy at the École Normale Supérieure, from which he graduated in 1929, the same year he met his lifelong companion Simone de Beauvoir, who became well known as a feminist writer and philosopher. During 1929–1930 Sartre served as an officer with a French military meteorological unit, and during most of the 1930s he taught at lycées in Paris and Le Havre.

Sartre's first novel, *La Nausée* (Nausea), published in 1938, caused an immediate sensation. Influenced by German phenomenological philosophy, the novel laid bare the human condition by embracing the idea that human life has no inherent purpose. At the beginning of World War II, Sartre served in the army and fought in the 1940 campaign for France. Captured by the Germans, he was sent to several prisoner-of-war camps, including Stalag XIID, where he produced his play

Bariona. Released in 1941, he wrote for the French Resistance during 1941–1944.

In 1945 Sartre founded with Beauvoir the journal *Les Temps Modernes.* A year later he published "Existentialism and Humanism," perhaps his most influential and widely read essay on existentialist philosophy. From 1945, he traveled extensively to lecture and write, becoming more politically active beginning in the 1950s. He refused to accept the 1964 Nobel Prize for Literature, arguing that to do so would compromise his political autonomy.

From the mid-1950s, Sartre was continually involved with leftist political causes. His efforts dealt with issues ranging from the lack of affordable housing in France to torture in Algeria and to the American war in Vietnam. While never a member of the Communist Party (he eschewed formal political allegiances), he evolved into a neo-Marxist who saw promise particularly in Maoism. His slide toward communism ultimately led to the painful end of his friendship with fellow existentialist Albert Camus. In 1960 Sartre reconciled the tenets of existentialism with those of classical Marxism in his *Critique of Dialectical Reason.* In 1960 he also signed the "Declaration on the Right to Insubordination in the War in Algeria" (also known as the "Manifesto of the 121") supporting Algerian independence and in 1966 was a member of fellow philosopher Bertrand Russell's International War Crimes Tribunal.

Sartre continued to write voluminously and, increasingly, about politics. He was the editor of *La Cause du Peuple* (1970), *Tout* (1970–1974), *Révolution* (1971–1974), and *Libération* (1973–1974) and was the founder, along with Maurice Clavel, of the Liberation news service in 1971. In failing health, Sartre began to lose his eyesight in 1975 and by the end of his life was completely blind. He died in Paris on 15 April 1980.

Andrew J. Waskey

See also
Camus, Albert; France; Prague Spring; Russell, Bertrand
References
Cohen-Solal, Annie. *Sartre: A Life.* Translated from the French by Anna Cancogni. New York: Pantheon, 1987.
Flynn, Thomas R. *Sartre and Marxist Existentialism: The Test Case of Collective Responsibility.* Chicago: University of Chicago Press, 1992.
Greene, Norman N. *Jean-Paul Sartre: The Existentialist Ethic.* Westport, CT: Greenwood, 1980.

Satō Eisaku (1901–1975)

Japanese politician and prime minister (1964–1972). Born on 27 March 1901 in Tabuse-chō in the Yamaguchi Prefecture, Satō Eisaku graduated from the law school of Tokyo Imperial University in 1924. He then entered the Ministry of Railways, serving there until 1948. In 1947 he was appointed permanent undersecretary of the Ministry of Railways but served in this post for just thirteen months. In 1948 he became chief cabinet secretary in the second Yoshida Shigeru government. Satō was chairman of the Policy Affairs Research Council of the Liberal Party in 1949 when he was elected to the Lower House of the Diet.

Satō held ministerial posts in the third and fourth Yoshida governments, including minister of the post office (1951–1952) and minister of construction (1952–1953). In 1953 he became director general of the Liberty Party (which merged with the Democratic Party in 1955 to become the Liberal Democratic Party), but he was forced to resign the position because of a ship-building company scandal during the fifth Yoshida cabinet in 1954. Satō subsequently became minister of finance during 1958–1960 under Prime Minister Kishi Nobusuke, Satō's elder brother by adoption.

In October 1964 Satō succeeded Ikeda Hayato as prime minister. During his seven years in office, Satō signed the 1965 Japan-Korea Treaty restoring normal diplomatic relations between the two countries and regaining control for Japan of the Ogasawara Islands in 1968. Although U.S. troops and bases remained on Japanese soil, Satō managed to negotiate a reversion of Okinawa to Japanese sovereignty in 1972.

Satō was less successful in establishing closer ties to either the Soviet Union or the People's Republic of China (PRC). Public outrage over his agreement to allow U.S. troops to remain on Okinawa ultimately forced his resignation in November 1972. He was awarded the Nobel Peace Prize in 1974 for his antinuclear diplomacy, an award that caused considerable controversy. Satō died in Chiyodaku, Tokyo, on 3 June 1975.

Kiichi Nenashi

See also
Fukuda Takeo; Japan; Okinawa
References
Lafeber, Walter. *The Clash: A History of U.S.-Japan Relations.* New York: Norton, 1997.
Reischauer, Edwin, O. *The Japanese Today: Change and Continuity.* Tokyo: Tuttle, 1988.
Schaller, Michael. *Altered States: The United States and Japan since the Occupation.* Oxford: Oxford University Press, 1997.

Saudi Arabia

Middle Eastern nation located on the Arabian Peninsula. The Kingdom of Saudi Arabia, founded in 1932, covers 756,981 square miles, nearly three times the area of the U.S. state of Texas, and had a 1945 population of some 3.5 million people. Saudi Arabia borders Jordan, Iraq, and Kuwait to the north; the Persian Gulf, Qatar, and the United Arab Emirates to the east; Oman and Yemen to the south; and the Red Sea to the west. It has been dominated by its ruling family, the House of Saud, for all of its modern history. King Ibn Saud, the founding monarch, ruled until his death in 1953. All succeeding kings have been his sons (he had more than fifty). The House of Saud has historical ties to the leadership of the Wahhabi sect of Islam, and as a result Saudi Arabian law and society are based on strict Muslim customs.

The role of Ibn Saud in Saudi Arabia cannot be overstated. The state grew inexorably as a result of his domination of the Arabian Peninsula in the early twentieth century as the Ottoman Empire declined. After the end of World War I, he consolidated his position and became king in 1925. The realm was renamed the Kingdom of Saudi Arabia seven years later. The fortunes of the kingdom were transformed with the discovery of petroleum in the 1930s.

American oil companies (Chevron in particular) played the leading role in oil exploration and formed a partnership with the Saudi monarchy, paying royalties for the right to extract and ship Saudi oil. The importance of oil during World War II enhanced the Saudi-U.S. relationship, and in 1944, the Arab-American Oil Corporation (ARAMCO) was formed. President Franklin D. Roosevelt helped to cement the growing relationship when he met with Ibn Saud on an American destroyer in 1945. The Saudi monarchy thus maintained close economic and strategic ties to the United States throughout the remainder of the century.

Because of the growing strategic importance of the Middle East and its oil reserves to Cold War geopolitics, both the United States and the Soviet Union sought increased influence in the region. The Soviets endorsed the rise of secular, socialist, Arab nationalist regimes in Egypt, Iraq, and Syria, and Soviet military assistance was crucial to these nations in their ongoing struggle with Israel after its founding in 1948. The United States countered these Soviet moves by tightening its ties to the royal regimes in Iran and Saudi Arabia.

In 1962 civil war broke out in Yemen as a nationalist faction supported by Egyptian President Gamal Abdel Nasser sought to overthrow the royal government there. Despite previous rivalries with the ruling house of Yemen, the Saudis gave financial support and military assistance to the Yemeni monarchy. Egypt and Saudi Arabia thus confronted each other directly in the conflict. The devoutly Muslim House of Saud opposed the rise of secular, socialist Arab nationalism and refused to tolerate the spread of Nasser's Pan-Arabism in the region. In addition, the respective affiliations of Egypt and Saudi Arabia with the Soviet Union and the United States made the Yemeni Civil War a regional theater of Cold War confrontation.

The Israeli issue greatly complicated U.S.-Saudi relations. The Saudis objected to the 1948 formation of Israel, opposed the displacement of Palestinian Arabs, and played a minor military role in the first Arab-Israeli War (1948). The Saudis would contribute significant funds to Palestinian causes until the 1991 Persian Gulf War.

Despite its vehement opposition to Israel, the Saudi government nonetheless maintained tepid relations with Arab nationalist regimes in Syria, Egypt, Iraq, and Jordan, Israel's principal enemies. Thus, Saudi Arabia did not participate in the Arab-Israeli wars of 1956, 1967, and 1973. However, as American support for Israel increased after the 1967 Six-Day War, the Saudis sought to influence American policy. This conflict laid the foundation for the 1973 oil embargo.

Saudi oil was largely controlled by American oil companies until the early 1970s. At that point, the House of Saud negotiated the gradual takeover of ARAMCO by Saudi interests. By 1973, the transfer of control had begun. When Egypt and Syria attacked Israel in October 1973, prompting the Yom Kippur War, Saudi Arabia's King Faisal obtained U.S. President Richard Nixon's assurances of American nonintervention. The Israelis suffered severe reversals in the opening stages of the conflict, however, which prompted Nixon to send U.S. military aid to Israel on 19 October. The next day, working through the Organization of Petroleum Exporting Countries (OPEC), the Saudi government implemented an oil embargo directed at the United States. The embargo made the United States vulnerable to an economic recession, and American fuel prices rose 40 percent during the five months of the crisis. Even after the embargo ended, oil prices remained high for the rest of the decade.

Saudi Arabia emerged from the crisis as the clear leader of OPEC and with renewed respect in the Arab world. Massive increases in oil revenues (from $5 billion in 1972 to $119 billion in 1981) transformed Saudi Arabia into an affluent, urbanized society with generous government subsidies and programs for its citizens and no taxation. The U.S.-Saudi relationship eventually recovered and remained close. Indeed, Saudi Arabia often used its influence in OPEC to keep oil prices artificially low from the mid-1980s to late 1990s.

Such policies, however, had a downside. When oil prices dipped dramatically during 1981–1985, the Saudi economy plunged into recession, presenting the government with significant domestic unrest. A similar scenario was played out in the late 1990s. This time the Saudis acted aggressively, hiking oil prices in 2000 and 2001 to right their foundering economy. Continuing close ties between Washington and Riyadh also played a major role in the 1991 Persian Gulf War, as Saudi Arabia was used as a staging area for U.S. troops during Operation DESERT STORM.

Despite the considerable power that the Saudis wielded in international relations beginning in the 1970s and the tremendous increase in wealth as a result of oil revenues, the House of Saud maintained strict control over Saudi society, culture, and law. Saudi Arabia remained an absolute monarchy until

Supertankers loading oil in Saudi Arabia for shipment abroad. (Corel)

1992, when the royal family promulgated the nation's first constitution.

Robert S. Kiely

See also

Arab-Israeli Wars; Arab Nationalism; Fahd, King of Saudi Arabia; Faisal, King of Saudi Arabia; Middle East; Nasser, Gamal Abdel; Organization of Petroleum Exporting Countries

References

Hourani, Albert. *A History of the Arab Peoples.* Cambridge: Harvard University Press, 1991.

Lacey, Robert. *The Kingdom.* New York: Harcourt Brace Jovanovich, 1982.

Lewis, Bernard. *The Middle East.* New York: Scribner, 1997.

Wynbrandt, James. *A Brief History of Saudi Arabia.* New York: Checkmark Books, 2004.

Savimbi, Jonas Malheiro (1934–2002)

Angolan rebel nationalist leader, founder of the National Union for the Total Independence of Angola (UNITA) movement, and guerrilla tactician. Born in Munhango, Bie Province, on 3 August 1934, Jonas Savimbi was purposely vague and evasive about his early life, claiming a PhD from the University of Lausanne, Switzerland. He may have spent two years in Portugal as a medical student. In 1966 he founded UNITA, a political movement dedicated to securing independence for that Portuguese colony. He fought a guerrilla war first against the Portuguese and then against the pro-Soviet, Marxist Angolan government, in the process surviving more than a dozen assassination attempts.

The Angolan nationalists fighting Portugal's colonial rule were the left-wing Popular Movement for the Liberation of Angola (MPLA), led by Agostinho Neto, and Savimbi's UNITA. After Angola won independence in 1975, Neto came to power with the explicit support of the Soviet Union and Cuba. Savimbi immediately turned his sights on the MPLA government, plunging the new nation into a horrific civil war. Both South Africa and the United States supplied UNITA with arms and weapons.

Among the African leaders who openly supported Savimbi were Felix Houphouet-Boigny of Ivory Coast and Mobutu Sese Seko of Zaire. Others were more discrete in their aid but nevertheless maintained diplomatic and commercial ties with UNITA. Savimbi began to score victories against the MPLA in the late 1980s. By 1990, in fact, his forces controlled almost half of Angola. The Angolan government negotiated a cease-fire with UNITA in 1991. The following year, Savimbi lost a questionable presidential election, and the civil war was reinvigorated, with periodic breaks, for another decade. Despite United Nation (UN) condemnatory sanctions and embargoes and international recognition of the popularly elected government in Luanda, Savimbi persisted, financing UNITA mainly through illicit sales of diamonds.

The United States and the Soviet Union used Angola as a proxy during the Cold War, while Savimbi used the Cold War to portray himself as a warrior against communism. With the Cold War ended along with the apartheid regime in South Africa, he continued the civil war, becoming a virtual international pariah with no major patrons. Savimbi died in battle in Lucusse on 22 February 2002. Just six weeks after his death, UNITA rebels signed a cease-fire, which ended the long civil war. Savimbi's struggle resulted in the deaths of more than a million people and the displacement of 2 million others.

John H. Barnhill

See also

Africa; Africa, Soviet Interventions in; Africa, U.S. Interventions in; Mobutu Sese Seko; Namibia

References

Bridgland, Fred. *Jonas Savimbi*. St. Paul, MN: Paragon, 1986.
Windrich, Elaine. *The Cold War Guerrilla*. Westport, CT: Greenwood, 1992.

Scandinavia

A region in the North Atlantic and Baltic Sea area strategically divided between East and West during the Cold War and that displayed a low degree of Cold War tensions and a high degree of internal cohesion. Scandinavia comprised the North Atlantic Treaty Organization (NATO) member states of Iceland, Norway, and Denmark (with Greenland and the Faeroe Islands) as well as neutral Sweden and Finland.

Finland was able to maintain a democratic and capitalist system despite its special ties to the Soviet sphere. Finland in particular and Scandinavia in general can thus be considered anomalies in the predominantly bipolar world of the Cold War. In spite of partial submission to the logic of the Cold War, the Scandinavians never really abandoned the bridge-building approach to international relations that they had pursued in the immediate postwar years. The superpowers in their turn were willing to relax their confrontation in this region and to grant some rather extraordinary exceptions.

Scandinavian nations shared many mutual historical and cultural ties, although Finnish is not a Scandinavian language. Finland was a grand duchy under the Russian tsars during 1809–1917 but is nonetheless an integral part of the Scandinavian community. In the Scandinavian languages, and similarly in Finnish, this community is designated with the term "Norden" ("the North"), whereas the term "Scandinavia" in these languages is ambiguous and might exclude Finland, Iceland, and Denmark. Therefore, the terms "Norden" and "Nordic" are often used instead of "Scandinavia" and "Scandinavian" in the comprehensive sense described above.

Despite their attempts to establish a common policy of neutrality at the end of the 1930s, the Scandinavian countries were unable to escape the harsh realities of World War II. Finland was attacked by the Soviet Union and ended up as an ally of Nazi Germany, while Denmark and Norway were attacked and occupied by Germany. Denmark's North Atlantic territories (which at that time also included Iceland) were controlled by Great Britain and the United States during the war. Only Sweden was able to retain its neutrality. These different historical experiences were fundamental to understanding the future orientation of these countries.

In the case of Finland, which in its turn had attacked the Soviet Union and had been forced to conclude an armistice in 1944, additional compulsion came into operation. In regard to Denmark and Norway, small parts of these countries were liberated by Soviet forces in 1945, and citizens of both countries felt uneasy about their presence until they departed in 1945–1946. Norway also came under Soviet pressure to participate in a common defense of the Svalbard (Spitzbergen) Archipelago in these years.

Denmark and Norway were in a position to pursue a policy of bridge building after World War II and adhered to this policy until the spring of 1948. The election of Norwegian Foreign Minister Trygve Lie as the first secretary-general of the United Nations (UN) in early 1946 was an acknowledgment of this effort. In the meantime, Sweden actively tried to improve its strained relations with the Soviet Union while maintaining nonalignment. This effort paid dividends in April 1953 when Swedish diplomat Dag Hammarskjöld was elected as the second secretary-general of the UN. Except for Finland, Scandinavian governments decided to participate in the 1947 Marshall Plan, but they also displayed some discomfort with having to take a stand in the Cold War.

The discomfort of nonalignment, however, became ever more pressing as the Cold War deepened. In particular, the February 1948 communist coup in Czechoslovakia was viewed as a signal to seek some sort of security arrangement beyond the framework of the UN. Furthermore, the fact that Finland was forced to conclude a Treaty of Friendship, Cooperation and Mutual Assistance with the Soviet Union in April 1948 raised fears of the possible Sovietization of Scandinavia. In Norway, which shared a border with the Soviet Union, but also in Denmark, there were signs of near hysteria in the spring of 1948.

Against this background, and in order to prevent diverging security paths among the three Scandinavian core countries, Swedish Foreign Minister Östen Undén suggested an outwardly neutral defense pact to Norway and Denmark in May

1948. Such an arrangement was seriously considered in the latter part of 1948 but collapsed in January 1949 because of irreconcilable differences between Norway and Sweden. While the Swedes insisted on independence from other military alignments, the Norwegians sought security guarantees from the West. The Danish government would have joined either configuration and, with a low-profile approach to foreign policy deeply rooted in its political culture, would even have preferred a bilateral defense union with Sweden over a more comprehensive Western arrangement. For strategic reasons, however, this solution did not appeal to the Swedes.

Thus, Denmark and Norway as well as Iceland were among the founding members of NATO in April 1949, while Sweden continued its policy of armed neutrality. The Swedish stance was also meant as a deliberate disincentive aimed at the Soviets so that the latter would not toy with the status of Finland. Even in the security policy of the Scandinavian NATO members, elements of neutrality or disengagement in the superpower conflict were preserved. Iceland placed the Keflavik Military Base at the disposal of the United States but did not establish any military forces of its own. Denmark and Norway built up their own defense rather slowly, and they accepted neither nuclear weapons nor foreign bases on their territory. The only exception was Greenland, where the Thule Military Base set up during World War II remained an American asset. On the other hand, the Danish government excluded from NATO military activity the island of Bornholm, the easternmost outpost of Denmark in the Baltic Sea, except as a listening post.

During the Korean War, Sweden, Denmark, and Norway contributed a hospital ship, field hospitals, and medical personnel. Since the UN's first peacekeeping operation in Suez in November 1956, all the Scandinavian countries except Iceland have been among major contributors to UN peacekeeping missions.

In recent years, new archival evidence has made it evident that Scandinavian involvement in the Cold War was deeper than contemporary actors admitted at the time. Contrary to its declared nonnuclear policy, for example, the Danish government gave the United States free rein to deploy nuclear weapons in Greenland. Even more remarkable is that allegedly neutral Sweden throughout the Cold War maintained rather elaborate security arrangements with the Western alliance that were kept secret. It is characteristic of the peculiar position of Scandinavia that while such conduct did occur, all parties involved, including the Soviet Union, contributed to the silence. Moreover, political relations with the Western powers, especially relations between Sweden and the United States, were characterized by a certain degree of aloofness. The support of the Scandinavian states for international law and the belief in the superiority of the Scandinavian welfare state contributed to the image of Scandinavia as representing a third

(and perhaps better) way to deal with the political, economic, and military exigencies of the Cold War.

Inter-Scandinavian cooperation consolidated the image of communality in the region and helped to establish a picture of unique security arrangements. In part to compensate for their different security policy orientation, the Scandinavian countries created the Nordic Council as a common parliamentary institution in 1952. They also closely cooperated in the framework of the UN, thereby frequently acting as mediators between East and West and increasingly between North and South. In 1955, the Soviet Union permitted Finland to become a member of the Nordic Council and of the UN. From then on, Scandinavian mutual cooperation helped Finland to retain a Western profile in spite of its foreign policy dependency on Moscow. The self-declared Finnish policy of neutrality was only at times acknowledged by the Soviet Union and has to be seen as a move in a game about sovereignty, not as corresponding to neutrality in the conventional sense of the word.

Tensions increased in Scandinavia in the 1970s and 1980s over external developments, one sign of which was the widely publicized incidents of Soviet submarines in Swedish waters. In this period, the considerable East-West military buildup began to threaten the status of Scandinavia as a quiet corner. There was some discussion of reviving proposals for a Nordic nuclear weapons–free zone, which had been considered in the 1960s, but nothing came of it.

Domestic developments in Scandinavia in the Cold War period were characterized by various peculiarities. Scandinavian countries were long regarded as representing a type of universal welfare state with a large public sector. They have all also been characterized as dominated by strong reformist social democratic parties as well as by a fragmented bourgeois camp and strong agrarian parties. Moreover, they have had a uniquely high degree of trade unionization, with up to 80 percent of the workforce, even white-collar workers, being organized in unions. Nonetheless, the capitalist and socialist sectors worked together with a high degree of consensus during the entire period of the Cold War.

Economically, in the Cold War the Scandinavian countries ranked among the most prosperous nations of the world, but there were characteristic time lags and substantial differences in economic structure. Sweden entered the postwar period with its industrial plan intact, with accelerated growth and an ever more pronounced tendency toward big business, unique for a country of its size. Denmark, for many years closest to Sweden among the Scandinavian states in terms of wealth, had a completely different economic structure based on agriculture and small-scale food industries. Finland was handicapped because of its lack of participation in the Marshall Plan and the reparations that it had to pay to the Soviet Union. A substantial portion of the Finnish workforce relo-

Swedish citizens protesting the international policies of the Soviet Union during the visit of a Soviet warship to Göteborg, Sweden, 8 June 1974. (Bettmann/Corbis)

cated to Sweden during the first decades of the Cold War. Not until the 1980s did Finland approach its Scandinavian neighbors economically or in regard to its welfare programs.

Norway has been characterized by its small industries. It owes its present status as one of the richest countries in the world per capita to the oil production in the North Sea begun in the 1970s. Finally, despite some attempts of diversification, Iceland has been largely dependent on fishery, which left that country economically vulnerable and placed it at the forefront of the fight for the extension of exclusive economic maritime zones.

Given these differences in economic structure, attempts in the 1950s and 1960s to establish closer economic collaboration and a customs union among the Scandinavian countries were doomed to failure. In part because of welfare state nationalism and in part because of nonalignment in the Cold War, the Scandinavian countries were hesitant to participate in the European Integration Movement. Only Denmark, which was heavily dependent on the export of agricultural products

to the Federal Republic of Germany (FRG, West Germany) and Great Britain, became a member of the European Community following a referendum in 1972. While the Norwegian elites were also in favor of accession, 53.5 percent of the population rejected such a move in the same year. Thus, while Denmark left the European Free Trade Association (EFTA) in favor of the European Community (EC), Norway remained in the EFTA, with Sweden and Iceland among the other members. Finland was an associated member of the EFTA, but not until 1986 did the Soviet Union allow Finland to join the organization as a regular member.

Norbert Götz

See also
Denmark; Faeroe Islands; Finland; Finlandization; Greenland; Hammarskjöld, Dag; Iceland; Karelia; Labor Movements; Lie, Trygve; Norway; Porkkala; Svalbard; Sweden
References
Ausland, John C. *Nordic Security and the Great Powers.* Boulder, CO: Westview, 1986.

Berner, Örjan. *Soviet Policies toward the Nordic Countries.* Lanham, MD: University Press of America, 1986.

Götz, Norbert. "'Norden': Structures That Do Not Make a Region." *European Review of History* 10(2) (2003): 323–341.

Hanhimäki, Jussi M. *Scandinavia and the United States: An Insecure Friendship.* New York: Twayne, 1997.

Lundestad, Geir. *America, Scandinavia and the Cold War.* Oslo: Universitetsforlaget, 1982.

Sundelius, Bengt, ed. *Foreign Policies of Northern Europe.* Boulder, CO: Westview, 1982.

Tunander, Ola. *Cold Water Politics: The Maritime Strategy and Geopolitics of the Northern Front.* London: Sage, 1989.

Wendt, Frantz. *Cooperation in the Nordic Countries.* Stockholm, Sweden: Almqvist and Wiksell, 1981.

Scheel, Walter (1919–)

Federal Republic of Germany (FRG, West Germany) minister for development aid (1961–1966), foreign minister and vice chancellor (1969–1974), and president (1974–1979). Born in Solingen on 8 July 1919, Walter Scheel began his career as a bank trainee. He served in the German military during World War II and became a solicitor in Düsseldorf in 1948.

A member of the Free Democratic Party (FDP), Scheel entered the Diet of his native state of North Rhine–Westphalia in 1950 and served in the Bundestag during 1953–1974. He was also a member of the European Parliament during 1958–1969. In November 1961, Chancellor Konrad Adenauer appointed Scheel minister for economic cooperation, later retitled minister for development aid. Together with fellow FDP ministers, he resigned his post in October 1966 to protest tax increases proposed by Chancellor Ludwig Erhard.

Scheel was elected FDP chairman in January 1968 and became foreign minister and vice chancellor in the Willy Brandt government on 21 October 1969. A strong supporter of Ostpolitik, Scheel helped normalize relations with the Soviet Union and Poland and recognized the German Democratic Republic (GDR, East Germany) with the 1972 Basic Treaty on mutual relations, which marked the end of the Hallstein Doctrine. He was elected president on 15 May 1974. During his tenure, he proved to be an indefatigable promoter of closer European cooperation. Scheel retired from politics in June 1979.

Bert Becker

See also
Adenauer, Konrad; Brandt, Willy; Erhard, Ludwig; Genscher, Hans-Dietrich; German Democratic Republic; Germany, Federal Republic of; Hallstein Doctrine; Ostpolitik

References
Banchoff, Thomas. *The German Problem Transformed: Institutions, Politics, and Foreign Policy, 1945–1995.* Ann Arbor: University of Michigan Press, 1999.

O'Dochartaigh, Pól. *Germany since 1945.* Houndsmill, UK, and New York: Palgrave Macmillan, 2004.

Scheel, Walter. *Walter Scheel im Gespräch mit Jürgen Emgert: Erinnerungen und Einsichten.* Stuttgart: Hohenheim, 2004.

Webb, Adrian. *Germany since 1945.* London and New York: Longman, 1998.

Schlesinger, Arthur Meier, Jr. (1917–2007)

Prominent U.S. historian, presidential advisor, and commentator on American political and cultural life. Born in Columbus, Ohio, on 15 October 1917, Arthur Schlesinger was the son of a distinguished historian. After study during 1934–1942 at Harvard University, from which he earned his doctorate in history, he served in the Office of War Information during 1942–1943 and in the Office of Strategic Services (OSS) during 1943–1945.

In 1946 Schlesinger won the Pulitzer Prize for his book *The Age of Jackson* (1945). A history professor at Harvard during 1946–1961, his interest and expertise in American politics led him to consult for President Harry S. Truman's administration and to engage in the political and cultural battles of his times, including participation in the foundation of Americans for Democratic Action (ADA) in 1947 and in the activities of the Congress for Cultural Freedom. Schlesinger's magisterial three-volume work *The Age of Roosevelt* (1957–1960) offered important insights into the New Deal era.

A strong New Deal liberal, Schlesinger actively campaigned for Democratic presidential nominee Adlai Stevenson in 1952 and 1956 and threw his support behind John F. Kennedy in 1960. In 1961, Kennedy appointed Schlesinger special assistant for Latin American affairs. He became part of Kennedy's inner circle and was deeply involved in initiatives such as the Alliance for Progress and in Italo-American relations.

Following Kennedy's 1963 assassination, Schlesinger returned to teaching and taught at the City University of New York during 1966–1994. He remained a close friend of the Kennedy family, continued to write prolifically on a wide range of issues, and provided a liberal perspective on American political life. Schlesinger died on 28 February 2007 in New York City.

Leopoldo Nuti

See also
Alliance for Progress; Kennedy, John Fitzgerald; Stevenson, Adlai Ewing, II

References
Depoe, Stephen P. *Arthur M. Schlesinger, Jr., and the Ideological History of American Liberalism.* Tuscaloosa: University of Alabama Press, 1994.

Diggins, John Patrick, ed. *The Liberal Persuasion: Arthur Schlesinger, Jr., and the Challenge of the American Past.* Princeton, NJ: Princeton University Press, 1997.

Schlesinger, Arthur M., Jr. *A Life in the 20th Century: Innocent Beginning, 1917–1950.* Boston: Houghton Mifflin, 2000.

Schlesinger, James Rodney (1929–)

U.S. director of the Central Intelligence Agency (CIA) during February–July 1973, secretary of defense during 1973–1975, and secretary of energy during 1977–1979. Born in New York City on 15 February 1929, James Schlesinger attended public schools before enrolling at Harvard, where he earned a doctorate in economics in 1956. He taught at the University of Virginia during 1956–1963, and during 1963–1969 he worked for the RAND Corporation, a think tank.

Following Richard M. Nixon's 1968 election as president, Schlesinger took a position with the Bureau of the Budget, and in 1971 Nixon named him chairman of the Atomic Energy Commission. In February 1973 Nixon appointed Schlesinger director of the CIA, but he stayed only five months before being confirmed as defense secretary that July.

Schlesinger's tenure at the Department of Defense coincided with a tense and troubled time in modern American history. The Vietnam War was winding down, and the Watergate scandal had already begun to engulf the Nixon administration. Schlesinger tried to maintain high defense budgets at a time of economic stagnation, when Congress was intent on trimming military spending. His efforts to increase defense spending were largely unsuccessful. He also sought to keep pace with the Soviets in terms of strategic nuclear weapons. Generally known as a hawkish hard-liner, he had doubts about the efficacy of détente, the warming of relations between the United States and the Soviet Union.

The most controversial part of Schlesinger's time in office came during the October 1973 Yom Kippur War. When several Arab countries launched a surprise attack against Israel, the Jewish state requested American military assistance. According to Secretary of State Henry Kissinger, Schlesinger delayed sending war matériel to Israel in U.S. aircraft for fear of offending Arab nations, a charge that Schlesinger has strenuously denied. This led to a permanent rift between the two men, and Kissinger thereafter worked assiduously to push Schlesinger out of the administration.

Following Nixon's resignation in August 1974, Schlesinger stayed on in President Gerald Ford's cabinet. However, Schlesinger's insistence on more defense appropriations and his disagreements with Kissinger led Ford to relieve Schlesinger of his post in November 1975. Schlesinger returned to public life in October 1977 when President Jimmy Carter, a Demo-

crat, named him to be the first secretary of energy. At the time, the United States was still reeling from the 1973–1974 energy crisis, and Carter was determined to implement a cohesive energy policy to wean America off oil imports. By 1979, however, Carter was unhappy with Schlesinger's efforts to handle the second energy crisis, precipitated by the 1979 Iranian Revolution and hostage crisis. Carter replaced Schlesinger in July 1979.

Schlesinger has remained active in politics, writing books and lecturing mostly on military and defense issues.

Justin P. Coffey

See also

Arab-Israeli Wars; Bush, George Herbert Walker; Carter, James Earl, Jr.; Central Intelligence Agency; Détente; Ford, Gerald Rudolph; Kissinger, Henry; Nixon, Richard Milhous; RAND Corporation

References

Greene, John Robert. *The Limits of Power: The Nixon and Ford Administrations.* Bloomington: Indiana University Press, 1992.

Schlesinger, James R. *America at Century's End.* New York: Columbia University Press, 1989.

Schmidt, Helmut (1918–)

Federal Republic of Germany (FRG, West Germany) minister of the interior (1961–1965), minister of defense (1969–1972), minister of economic affairs (1972–1974), and chancellor (1974–1982). Born on 23 December 1918 in Hamburg, Helmut Schmidt saw combat in the German Army during World War II before being taken prisoner by British forces late in the conflict. During 1945–1949, he studied economics at the University of Hamburg, earning a doctorate.

Schmidt joined the Social Democratic Party (SPD) in 1946 and was a civil servant in the state government of Hamburg beginning in 1949. He served in the Bundestag during 1953–1962 and in 1961 was appointed minister of the interior, a position he held until 1965. As such, Schmidt earned the reputation of a man of action after successfully coordinating relief efforts during the disastrous 1962 floods.

In 1965, however, Schmidt reentered the Bundestag and served the SDP in a number of leadership positions. Chancellor Willy Brandt appointed him defense minister in October 1969. When Brandt's minister for economic affairs and finance resigned under duress in July 1972, Schmidt took on that position. He soon gained critical acclaim for his economic policies. Upon the fall of the Brandt government, Schmidt became chancellor on 16 May 1974. He continued the Brandt coalition government and was reelected in 1976 and again in 1980.

During his tenure in office, Schmidt was confronted with the increasing threat of terrorism. Violent attacks of by the Red Army Faction, a far-leftist extremist group, against officials

Helmut Schmidt, chancellor of the Federal Republic of Germany (FRG, West Germany), speaking to the press at the Massachusetts Institute of Technology in Boston, 27 May 1983. Schmidt was at MIT to give the commencement address. (Bettmann/Corbis)

and politicians during 1974–1977 put the chancellor under enormous pressure to find solutions to combat this extremism without compromising constitutional liberties. Schmidt's popularity reached its zenith in October 1977 when West German forces freed all ninety-one hostages aboard a German jetliner hijacked by Palestinian terrorists in Somalia.

In foreign affairs, Schmidt managed to combine support for West European integration with further rapprochement with the East. He and French President Valéry Giscard d'Éstaing are generally regarded as the political architects of the 1979 European Monetary System, the precursor of the European Currency Unit (ECU) and of the euro currency.

Regarding the German Democratic Republic (GDR, East Germany), Schmidt continued the Ostpolitik of his predecessors. The chancellor's state visit to East Germany in December 1981 raised expectations of a closer rapprochement but resulted in little progress on contentious issues. The downturn in U.S.-Soviet relations had already begun to affect Schmidt's policy options by the late 1970s, however. After the North

Atlantic Treaty Organization (NATO) decided in 1979 to deploy new nuclear missiles, mainly in West Germany, by late 1983 and to pursue Intermediate-Range Nuclear Forces (INF) reduction negotiations in the interim, Schmidt's support of these proposals not only adversely affected his negotiations with Soviet leader Leonid Brezhnev in June 1980 but also caused a domestic backlash in Germany. Nationwide antinuclear protests ultimately sparked the creation of the Green Party as a new political force.

When Schmidt demonstrated little understanding of or tolerance for the peace activists and environmentalists, many Germans saw him as being out of touch. His political decline accelerated when a dispute with Free Democratic Party (FDP) Chairman Hans-Dietrich Genscher ensued over a program to reduce unemployment, which led to the resignation of the four FDP ministers in September 1982. After the Bundestag passed a vote of no confidence against the chancellor in favor of the Christian Democratic Union (CDU) leader Helmut Kohl on 1 October 1982, Schmidt resigned. In 1983 he became co-editor of the weekly magazine *Die Zeit* and in 1985 a member of its managing board, actively committing himself to writing on political topics.

Bert Becker

See also
Brandt, Willy; Brezhnev, Leonid; Genscher, Hans-Dietrich; German Democratic Republic; Germany, Federal Republic of; Giscard d'Éstaing, Valéry; Honecker, Erich; Kohl, Helmut; Scheel, Walter

References
Banchoff, Thomas. *The German Problem Transformed: Institutions, Politics, and Foreign Policy, 1945–1995.* Ann Arbor: University of Michigan Press, 1999.
Nicholls, Anthony James. *The Bonn Republic: West German Democracy, 1945–1990.* London and New York: Longman, 1997.
O'Dochartaigh, Pól. *Germany since 1945.* Houndsmill, UK, and New York: Palgrave Macmillan, 2004.
Schmidt, Helmut. *Men and Powers: A Political Perspective.* Translated by Ruth Heim. New York: Random House, 1989.
Schwelien, Michael. *Helmut Schmidt: Ein Leben für den Frieden.* Hamburg: Hoffman und Campe, 2003.
Sommer, Theo. "Helmut Schmidt." Pp. 439–456 in *Die deutschen Kanzler: Von Bismarck bis Kohl,* edited by Wilhelm von Sternburg. Frankfurt am Main: Fischer Taschenbuch Verlag, 1994.
Webb, Adrian. *Germany since 1945.* London and New York: Longman, 1998.
Wiegrafe, Klaus. *Das Zerwürfnis: Helmut Schmidt, Jimmy Carter und die Krise der deutsch-Amerikanische Beziehungen.* Berlin: Propyläen, 2005.

School of the Americas

U.S. military facility that trained Latin American militaries and police forces in counterinsurgency techniques during the Cold War. The School of the Americas opened in 1946 as the U.S. Army Caribbean School at Fort Amador in the Panama Canal Zone. The school was part of the larger U.S. Cold War containment strategy for Latin America that included the 1947 Rio Pact, the Organization of American States (OAS), and President Harry S. Truman's Point Four Program.

After World War II, Latin American militaries looked to the United States to supply the training for their national armed forces, replacing former French, Italian, and German military advisory groups. Particularly in the Caribbean region that included Central America, the Caribbean islands, and northern South America, the U.S. military sought to centralize its instruction of Latin American officers at a single location in the Panama Canal Zone. Initially, most of the training at the Caribbean Army School was in conventional warfare, unit exercises, and equipment maintenance. The school also taught police surveillance and antiriot techniques. Fear of Soviet subversion of Latin American labor movements and indigenous socialist parties became a prime concern for U.S. policymakers in the 1950s. Thus, American instructors trained Latin American armies more for internal repression, the crushing of possible procommunist coups, and the monitoring and suppression of leftist dissenters.

Following the successful 1959 Cuban Revolution, American concerns over communist penetration of the Western Hemisphere heightened, as did worries over the efficacy of leftist guerrilla movements championed by Ernesto "Che" Guevara and other Fidelistas. Guevara's activities unnerved U.S. military officials, who had watched a ragtag group of Cuban radicals defeat a 50,000-man Cuban Army that had been trained and equipped by the United States. Under the aegis of President John F. Kennedy's administration, counterinsurgency doctrine received greater emphasis in U.S. military strategy. In 1963 Kennedy vastly expanded the U.S. Army Caribbean School, renaming it the U.S. Army School of the Americas, and deployed the 8th Special Forces Group to the Canal Zone to serve as instructors. The institution greatly increased the variety of its training programs that now concentrated on counterinsurgency, civic action, crowd control, psychological warfare, and anticommunist ideology.

Critics of the School of the Americas assert that during this period the school began its policy of training officers in the techniques of interrogation, torture, kidnapping, assassination, and paramilitary terror tactics to be used in thwarting communist insurgencies. From 1946 through the 1990s, the school graduated nearly 60,000 officers. The school became a target of attack from Panamanian nationalists who saw the facility as a violation of U.S.-Panamanian treaties that approved American military bases within the Canal Zone for canal defense only, not for the continent-wide repression of dissent. In 1967, Bolivian units trained at the School of the Americas helped track down and kill Guevara. During the 1960s, trainees from the school participated in six different counterinsurgency campaigns against leftist guerrillas in Latin America.

In the 1980s, the School of the Americas came under even sharper scrutiny from human rights groups for its contribution to the U.S.-backed counterinsurgency wars in El Salvador, Guatemala, and Nicaragua. Human rights advocates such as Father Roy Bourgeois traced numerous atrocities committed against Central American civilians back to commanders and units trained by U.S. Green Berets at the School of the Americas. Links between graduates of the school and right-wing death squads also abounded. Critics increasingly referred to the institution as a "School for Assassins" or the "School for Dictators." Indeed, the school's alumni included Panamanian drug trafficker and dictator Manuael Noriega, Salvadoran death squad leader Roberto D'Aubuisson, Argentine military junta leader Leopoldo Galtieri, and Bolivian dictator Hugo Bánzer Suárez. Opposition to the school grew so vociferous that in 1984 the Pentagon agreed to withdraw the School of the Americas from the Canal Zone and transfer it to Fort Benning, Georgia, where it continues operating to this day under the new name of the Western Hemisphere Institute for Security Cooperation.

Michael E. Donoghue

See also
Americas; Communist Revolutionary Warfare; Latin America, Communist Parties in
References
Barber, Willard Foster. *Internal Security and Military Power: Counterinsurgency and Civic Action in Latin America*. Columbus: Ohio State University Press, 1966.
Calvert, Peter. *Revolution and International Politics*. London: Pinter, 1996
Nelson-Pallmeyer, Jack. *School of Assassins: The Case for Closing the School of the Americas and for Fundamentally Changing U.S. Foreign Policy*. Maryknoll, NY: Orbis, 1997.

Schriever, Bernard Adolf (1910–2005)

U.S. Air Force (USAF) general, commander of the Air Research and Development Command (ARDC)/Air Force Systems Command (AFSC) during 1959–1966, and key leader in the development of USAF missile and space capabilities. Born in Bremen, Germany, on 14 September 1910, Bernard Schriever immigrated to the United States with his parents in 1917. He graduated from Texas A&M University in 1931 and secured a U.S. Army commission. He earned an MA degree in aeronautical engineering from Stanford University in 1942.

Schriever was initially commissioned in the field artillery but then entered the U.S. Air Corps, earning his wings in June 1933. Prior to World War II, he served as a pilot and engineering maintenance officer. During the war, he flew B-17s in the Pacific theater and served in a number of staff positions, which led to duty at the U.S. Army Air Forces headquarters after the war. He continued to serve in staff positions related to science and research and development. He was promoted to brigadier general in June 1953.

In June 1954, Schriever became assistant to the commander of ARDC and commander of the Western Development Division with responsibility for the intercontinental ballistic missile (ICBM) program. He was promoted to major general in December 1955. He supervised the production of the first three classes of ICBMs: Atlas, Titan, and Minuteman. His responsibilities expanded into the USAF space program, which he also guided to success with the DISCOVERY/CORONA system. He moved up to command the ARDC in 1959 as a lieutenant general and remained in charge when the ARDC became the AFSC in April 1961. He was promoted to full general on 1 July 1961.

Schriever retired in April 1966 and was active as a consultant. He also founded the Urban Systems Associates. Often called the father of the air force missile and space programs, he was honored when Falcon Air Force Base outside Colorado Springs, Colorado, was renamed for him in 1998. Schriever died in Washington, D.C., on 20 June 2005.

Jerome V. Martin

See also

CORONA Program; United States Air Force

References

Frisbee, John L., ed. *Makers of the United States Air Force.* Washington, DC: U.S. Government Printing Office, 1987.

Spires, David N. *Beyond Horizons: A Half Century of Air Force Space Leadership.* Washington, DC: U.S. Government Printing Office, 1998.

Schröder, Gerhard (1910–1989)

Federal Republic of Germany (FRG, West Germany) minister of the interior (1953–1961), foreign minister (1961–1966), and minister of defense (1966–1969). Born in Saarbrücken on 11 September 1910, Gerhard Schröder earned his doctorate in law from the University of Bonn in 1934. He began his career as an assistant at the Kaiser Wilhelm Institute for Foreign and International Private Law, was a law clerk in 1936, and became a self-employed lawyer in Berlin in 1939.

Immediately after World War II, Schröder worked for the provisional government in the North Rhine Province of the British military occupation government, but in 1947 he established himself as a lawyer in Düsseldorf. A member of the Christian Democratic Union (CDU), he entered the Bundestag in September 1949. In his second cabinet, Chancellor Konrad Adenauer appointed Schröder minister of the

Dr. Gerhard Schröder, minister of the interior of the Federal Republic of Germany (FRG, West Germany), 1959. (Bettmann/Corbis)

interior in October 1953. He served in that post until November 1961. During his tenure, he pushed for a national emergency law, which was enacted only after acrimonious debates in 1968.

In Adenauer's fourth cabinet, Schröder became foreign minister in November 1961, a position he held until October 1966. An unabashed Atlanticist, he promoted closer ties with the United States, which was the major reason for his long-running quarrel with Adenauer. Schröder agreed, however, with both Adenauer and Chancellor Ludwig Erhard on the goals of enlarging the European Economic Community (EEC) and strengthening collaboration within the North Atlantic Treaty Organization (NATO). Regarding the Soviet bloc, Schröder showed some willingness to modify the Hallstein Doctrine and to allow a gradual thaw in relations with Eastern Europe in economic matters, which he described as the "policy of movement." West German industrial interests strongly supported Schröder's attempt to open relations with Soviet satellites, resulting in the opening of trade missions in four Eastern capitals during 1963–1964.

During December 1966–October 1969, Schröder served as minister of defense. During 1969–1980, he was chairman of the foreign committee of the Bundestag. Schröder died on 31 December 1989 in Kampen, Germany.

Bert Becker

See also
Adenauer, Konrad; Erhard, Ludwig; Germany, Federal Republic of; Hallstein Doctrine
References
Ash, Timothy Garton. *In Europe's Name: Germany and the Divided Continent.* New York: Random House, 1993.
Banchoff, Thomas. *The German Problem Transformed: Institutions, Politics, and Foreign Policy, 1945–1995.* Ann Arbor: University of Michigan Press, 1999.
Eibl, Franz. *Politik der Bewegung: Gerhard Schröder als Aussenminister, 1961–1966.* Munich: R. Oldenbourg, 2001.
Gray, William Glenn. *Germany's Cold War: The Global Campaign to Isolate East Germany, 1949–1969.* Chapel Hill: University of North Carolina Press, 2003.
Schröder, Gerhard. *Decision for Europe.* London: Thames and Hudson, 1964.

Schumacher, Kurt (1895–1952)

Federal Republic of Germany (FRG, West Germany) Social Democratic Party (SPD) politician and proponent of German unification. Born on 13 October 1895 in Kulm, Germany, Kurt Schumacher enlisted in the German Army at the outbreak of World War I and was severely wounded in December 1914. Beginning in 1915, he studied law and economics, receiving his doctorate from Münster University in 1920.

Schumacher joined the SPD in 1918 and served as editor of its newsletter during 1920–1924. He was elected to the Württemberg Diet in 1924, serving until 1931, and to the Reichstag in 1930, serving until 1933. He was imprisoned much of the time during 1933–1944 because of his opposition to Nazi rule.

In 1945, Schumacher became a driving force in the recreation of the SPD, proving to be a staunch opponent of the merging of the party with the German Communist Party (KPD). The October 1946 merger agreement reached with Otto Grotewohl, chairman of the German Democratic Republic (GDR, East German) SPD, confirmed Schumacher's status as the leading SPD politician in Germany's western occupation zones. After the fusion of the SPD and KPD in the Soviet occupation zone, which brought the Socialist Unity Party (SED) into being, Schumacher was elected chairman of the SPD for West Germany and West Berlin. A member of the Parliamentary Council since 1948, he supported the founding of West Germany but repeatedly stressed its provisional character.

Schumacher's campaign to become the first West German president ended unsuccessfully in the September 1949 elections. As a member of the Bundestag (lower house of parliament) since 1949 and especially as opposition leader of the SPD group, he became one of the strongest critics of Chancellor Konrad Adenauer, whose policy of integrating West Germany into the Western bloc was regarded by Schumacher as the main obstacle to Germany's reunification. Schumacher called Adenauer "the chancellor of the Allies" during a parliamentary debate in November 1949 and was excluded from a subsequent session. Schumacher not only opposed the dismantling of Ruhr industry and the agreements on the Saar region but also fought against the entry of West Germany into the European Council and against the founding of the European Steel and Coal Community. In spring 1952, he regarded the so-called Stalin Note, a Soviet propaganda proposal to reunite Germany, as an important step forward, but Adenauer rejected Schumacher's demand to consider it seriously. Schumacher died in Bonn on 20 August 1952.

Bert Becker

See also
Adenauer, Konrad; Germany, Federal Republic of; Grotewohl, Otto
References
Banchoff, Thomas F. *The German Problem Transformed: Institutions, Politics, and Foreign Policy, 1945–1995.* Ann Arbor: University of Michigan Press, 1999.
Childs, David. *From Schumacher to Brandt: The Story of German Socialism, 1945–1965.* Oxford and Frankfurt: Pergamon, 1966.
Edinger, Lewis J. *Kurt Schumacher: A Study in Personality and Political Behavior.* Stanford, CA: Stanford University Press, 1965.
Merseburger, Peter. *Die schwierige Deutsche, Kurt Schumacher: Eine Biographie.* Stuattgart: Deutsche Velags-Anstalt, 1995.
Moeller, Robert G., ed. *West Germany under Construction: Politics, Society, and Culture in the Adenauer Era.* Ann Arbor: University of Michigan Press, 1997.

Schuman, Robert (1886–1963)

French finance minister (1945–1947), premier (1947–1948), foreign minister (1948–1952), justice minister (1955–1958), and founder of the European Coal and Steel Community (ECSC). Born on 26 June 1986 in Luxembourg, the son of a French Lorrainer and his Luxembourg wife, Robert Jean-Baptiste Nicolas Schuman grew up in Luxembourg, speaking Luxembourgeois, French, and German fluently. A brilliant student, he also learned Greek, Latin, and English at the academically rigorous Atheneum. He then studied law at the universities of Bonn, Berlin, and Munich, where he again excelled, and in 1910 he began to practice law in Metz. During World War I he fought in the German Army, and when Germany's defeat returned Alsace-Lorraine to France, he remained in Metz, specializing in German legal problems, especially those arising from the region's repeated transfers.

An austere bachelor and a devout Roman Catholic, in 1904 Schuman joined the ultra-Catholic student organization Unitas and became a leading Catholic layman. He was well versed in religious literature, and his pronounced social conscience and commitment to democracy made him a prominent founder of France's Christian Democrat political movement. In 1919 he joined the Catholic Popular Democratic Party and won election to the French Chamber of Deputies, remaining there for forty years. When Germany invaded France in 1940, he refused to join Marshal Henri Philippe Pétain's collaborationist Vichy government but instead returned to Alsace-Lorraine, where his public condemnation of German expulsions of French residents brought his arrest. Escaping the Gestapo, Schuman participated in wartime resistance propaganda efforts, helping to found the Mouvement républicain populaire (MRP, Popular Republican Movement), France's Christian Democratic party.

As French governments rapidly succeeded each other after liberation in 1944, Schuman spent two years as finance minister and seven months as premier before serving as foreign minister from 1948 to 1952. His heritage, liberal Catholicism, and democratic outlook all guided his dedicated efforts to encourage West European reconciliation. Working closely with Jean Monnet, on 9 May 1950 Schuman issued the Schuman Declaration, a public appeal to other European nations to create the ECSC, which evolved into the European Economic Community (EEC) in 1957 and subsequently the European Union (EU). By integrating key sectors of the French, German, Italian, and Benelux economies, the ECSC greatly reduced the possibility of future European hostilities.

From 1955 to 1958 Schuman was French justice minister and from 1955 to 1961 president of the European Movement. In 1958 he became the first president of the European Parliamentary Assembly in Strasbourg, France, retiring in 1961. Schuman died at Scy-Chazelles, Lorraine, France, on 4 September 1963. In the early twenty-first century, he was under serious consideration for beatification as a Roman Catholic saint.

Priscilla Roberts

See also
European Coal and Steel Community; European Economic Community; European Integration Movement; European Parliament; European Union; France; Monnet, Jean; Monnet Plan; Schuman Plan

References
Dell, Edmund. *The Schuman Plan and the British Abdication of Leadership in Europe.* New York: Oxford University Press, 1995.
Kipping, Matthias. *Zwischen Kartellen und Konkurrenz: Der Schuman-Plan und die Ursprünge der Europäischen Einigung, 1944–1952* [Between Cartels and Competition: The Schuman Plan and the Origins of European Unification, 1944–1952]. Berlin: Duncker and Humblot, 1996.
Lejeune, René. *Robert Schuman: Père de l'Europe 1886–1963; La politique, chemin de sainteté.* Paris: Fayard, 2000.
Poidevin, Raymond. *Robert Schuman: Homme d'État, 1886–1963.* Paris: Imprimerie Nationale, 1986.
Rochefort, Robert. *Robert Schuman.* Paris: Cerf, 1968.

Schuman Plan

Proposal announced on 9 May 1950 by French Foreign Minister Robert Schuman whereby France and Germany would pool their coal and steel industries. The plan was designed to eliminate eighty years of Franco-German rivalry, which had contributed to two world wars. It also marked the first step toward West European political and economic integration.

Schuman and Jean Monnet, France's leading proponent of European integration, argued that the Schuman Plan would transform intra-European relations in numerous ways. First, Franco-German production of heavy industry would necessitate joint control of the mineral-rich Ruhr and Saar regions, the geographical bone of contention between France and Germany. A basis of trust would thus be created between the French, who still feared another attack by Germany, and the Germans, who were concerned about permanent dismemberment by a vengeful former enemy.

Second, the successful implementation of the Schuman Plan would essentially solve the German problem by forcing the Federal Republic of Germany (FRG, West Germany) to surrender much of its sovereignty in favor of integration into a larger European community. It was hoped that such an arrangement would stanch German militarism in the future. Yet Schuman and Monnet assured Germany that should the plan go forward, it would serve as the first step toward a mutual defense pact that would assuage its fears of permanent disarmament. This would later be proposed as the European Defense Community (EDC).

Third, the plan symbolized European integrationists' vision of a supranational organization that would transcend the nationalism they believed had stoked two world wars. Politically, therefore, Western Europe would become unified. Finally, the Schuman Plan could ultimately establish an economic bloc rivaling the United States and the Soviet Union.

Informed of the proposal on 8 May 1950, German Chancellor Konrad Adenauer agreed that the Schuman Plan was based on equal rights for both nations and removed the Saar question from traditional Franco-German rivalry. He quickly wrote the French foreign minister and pledged that he would strongly urge West Germany's Bundestag (lower house of parliament) to approve the plan. Within days, the United States and Italy declared their approval, with the Benelux countries (Belgium, the Netherlands, and Luxembourg) not far behind. After nearly a month of negotiations, the British signed off on it, and on 3 June 1950 a joint communiqué was issued announcing mutual acceptance of the plan. On 18 April 1951, France, West Germany, Italy, and the Benelux countries signed the Schuman Treaty, thereby creating the European Coal and Steel Community (ECSC).

Chris Tudda

See also
Adenauer, Konrad; European Coal and Steel Community; European Defense Community; Monnet, Jean; Saar; Schuman, Robert
References
Duchêne, François. *Jean Monnet: The First Statesman of Interdependence.* New York: Norton, 1994.
Fransen, Fredric J. *The Supranational Politics of Jean Monnet: Ideas and Origins of the European Community.* Westport, CT: Greenwood, 1996.
Gillingham, John. *Coal, Steel and the Rebirth of Europe, 1945–1955: The Germans and the French from the Ruhr Conflict to Economic Community.* New York: Columbia University Press, 1991.
Hitchcock, William I. *France Restored: Cold War Diplomacy and the Quest for Leadership in Europe, 1944–1954.* Chapel Hill: University of North Carolina Press, 1998.
Monnet, Jean. *Memoirs.* Garden City, NY: Doubleday, 1978.

Schweitzer, Albert (1875–1965)

Medical missionary, musician, theologian, and philosopher. Born in Kaysersberg, Upper Alsace (French territory then occupied by Germany), on 14 January 1875, the eldest son of a Lutheran pastor, Albert Schweitzer studied music and became an accomplished organist. In 1899 he was awarded a doctorate in philosophy by the University of Strasbourg. He remained at the university as a professor and administrator until 1913. In 1906 he published *The Quest of the Historical Jesus,* which dealt with the major scholarly writings on Jesus Christ, and *The Art of German and French Organ Builders and Players.* He also produced the widely used performance edition of Bach's organ works (1912–1914).

In 1905 Schweitzer began medical studies at the University of Strasbourg with the aim of becoming a mission doctor. In 1913 he received his medical degree and set out for Lambarene, Gabon, in French Equatorial Africa. There he founded the Albert Schweitzer Hospital to treat the inhabitants of that area. Although the hospital and his treatment methods were often criticized by outsiders as being colonial, Schweitzer continued to operate the hospital and treat thousands of African patients. He also continued to study philosophy and took a keen interest in world problems.

In 1923 Schweitzer wrote *Kulturphilosophie* (Philosophy of Civilization), setting forth his personal philosophy of the reverence for life, an ethical system based on the mutual respect of all living things. He used this philosophy to guide not only his hospital work but also his everyday life. He would later expound on it via several philosophical and theological publications.

Albert Schweitzer was a German theologian and philosopher who is known for his missionary medical work in Africa. He wrote many books on his studies of music and philosophy and was awarded the 1952 Nobel Prize for Peace. (Arthur William Heintzelman/Library of Congress)

In 1952, Schweitzer was awarded the Nobel Peace Prize. From the 1950s on, he spoke out against nuclear weapons and urged world leaders to stop nuclear weapons testing. Schweitzer died at Lambarene on 4 September 1965.

Carrie A. Lewis

See also
Africa; Nobel Peace Prize
References
Brabazon, James. *Albert Schweitzer.* Syracuse, NY: Syracuse University Press, 2000.
Cousins, Norman. *Albert Schweitzer's Mission.* New York: Norton, 1985.

Seabed Treaty (18 May 1972)

Treaty opened for signature in London, Moscow, and Washington, D.C., on 11 February 1971 forbidding the placement of any weapon of mass destruction on any seabed. The treaty entered into force on 18 May 1972, when it had been ratified by more than twenty-five nations.

By the 1960s, technological advances in weaponry raised concerns that nations might attempt to place nuclear weapons or other weapons of mass destruction on the seabed, or ocean floor. On 18 December 1967, the United Nations (UN) set up a committee to study means to ensure that the seabed was reserved for peaceful purposes. On 18 March 1969, the Soviet Union presented a draft treaty that called for the complete demilitarization of the seabed beyond a 12-mile national coastal limit. The U.S. government, which considered underwater listening devices as essential to U.S. defense, wanted only to ban the placement of weapons of mass destruction on the seabed. On 22 May 1969, the United States submitted a draft treaty calling for a prohibition on the placement of nuclear weapons and other weapons of mass destruction on the seabed beyond a 3-mile limit. Upon the announcement of the draft, U.S. President Richard Nixon declared that an agreement on the prohibition of weapons of mass destruction on the ocean floor would "prevent an arms race before it has a chance to start."

Following prolonged talks, the two sides managed to agree on a joint draft treaty that greatly resembled the original U.S. proposal. On 7 October 1969, the draft was submitted to the Conference of the Committee on Disarmament (CCD), a UN standing committee. The joint draft was then discussed and revised within both the CCD and the UN, and on 7 December 1970 the UN General Assembly approved a final draft by a vote of 104 to 2 (with El Salvador and Peru dissenting), with 2 abstentions (Ecuador and France).

The Seabed Treaty prohibits emplacement of nuclear weapons or other weapons of mass destruction on the seabed as well as launch installations or storage facilities (but not listening cables and similar nonweapon devices). The treaty allows signatories to undertake verification using their own means or within the framework established by the UN. The extent of territorial waters, at that time unclear in international law, was also a subject of much discussion. In the treaty, a 12-mile limit is used to define the seabed area and, hence, the application of the treaty.

The eleven-article treaty was officially called the Treaty on the Prohibition of the Emplacement of Nuclear Weapons and Other Weapons of Mass Destruction on the Seabed and the Ocean Floor and in the Subsoil Thereof. It entered into force on 18 May 1972 when the United States, the United Kingdom, the Soviet Union, and twenty-two other nations had ratified it. By 2004, sixty-six nations had taken that step.

The treaty is in many ways similar to the Antarctic Treaty (23 June 1961), the Outer Space Treaty (10 October 1967), and the Latin American Tlatelolco Treaty (25 April 1969), all of which sought to prevent the deployment of nuclear weapons in certain defined areas.

Gudni Jóhannesson

See also
Arms Control; Outer Space Treaty; Tlatelolco Treaty

References
Luard, Evan. *The Control of the Sea-Bed: Who Owns the Resources of the Oceans?* Rev. ed. London: Heinemann, 1977.
Seaborg, Glenn T., with Benjamin S. Loeb. *The Atomic Energy Commission under Nixon: Adjusting to Troubled Times.* New York: St. Martin's, 1993.
United Nations. *Report of the Committee on the Peaceful Uses of the Sea-Bed and the Ocean Floor beyond the Limits of National Jurisdiction.* New York: United Nations, 1973.
United States Arms Control and Disarmament Agency. *International Negotiations on the Seabed Arms Control Treaty.* Washington, DC: U.S. Government Printing Office, 1973.

Securitate

Established in 1945, Romania's secret police service, popularly known as the Securitate, went under the official title of Departamentul Securității Statului (DSS, Department of State Security) during 1978–1989 and was allied with the Departamentul de Informații Externe (DIE, Department of External Information), the main foreign intelligence service. Upon the fall of the Romanian communist regime in December 1989, the Securitate was proportionately the largest secret police force in Eastern Europe.

In April 1945, Petru Groza, Romania's Moscow-appointed prime minister, signed an order establishing the Serviciul Special de Informații (SSI, Special Information Service) to replace the World War II Siguranța. Initially directed by agents from the Soviet People's Commissariat for Interior Affairs (NKVD), the SSI dealt with both foreign and domestic intelligence, while military intelligence fell to the Army General Staff under Soviet Military Intelligence (GRU). Under Interior Minister Teohari Georgescu and Securitate head Lieutenant General Gheorghe Pintilie, the SSI was renamed the Direcția Generală a Securității Poporului (DGSP, General Directorate for People's Security) in 1948. Expansions in 1949 included setting up special security troops and a militia to replace the police and gendarmerie, and, in 1950, a Directorate for Labor Units to oversee some 180,000 inmates of concentration camps throughout Romania. In 1951, a body for foreign intelligence was set up in the renamed Direcția Generală a Securității Statuliu (DGSS, General Directorate of State Security). Throughout these changes, Alexandru Drăghici, who controlled both the Ministry of the Interior (1953–1965) and the short-lived Ministry of State Security, maintained a firm grip on the Securitate. The 1964 withdrawal of Soviet counselors marked the agency's increasing independence from Moscow. Following the 1965 death of party leader Gheorghe Gheorghiu-Dej, Nicolae Ceaușescu continued a nationalist line, purging NKVD agents and deposing Pintilie and Drăghici. The DIE became a separate body in 1972, and in 1978, the DGSS, now known as the DSS, was reorganized in nine directorates. As Romania's primary foreign intelligence organization, the DIE worked closely with the Ministry of the Interior, the Securitate, and the Directorate for Military Intelligence (DIA). The 1978 defection of DIE deputy director Lieutenant General Ion Pacepa led to a major purge of personnel and, upon his debriefing by U.S. Central Intelligence Agency (CIA) agents, the cooling of Romanian-U.S. relations.

Moreover, the December 1989 overthrow of Ceauşescu highlighted the Securitate's weakness. Although it is uncertain to what extent Securitate forces were primarily responsible for violence before and immediately after Ceauşescu's overthrow, allegations persist that former Securitate agents have retained powerful positions, particularly in the Ministry for Foreign Trade and in private import-export businesses.

Anna M. Wittmann

See also

Ceauşescu, Nicolae; Dr|ghici, Alexandru; Espionage; Gheorghiu-Dej, Gheorghe; Groza, Petru; Komitet Gosudarstvennoi Bezopasnosti; Romania

Reference

Deletant, Dennis. *Ceauşescu and the Securitate: Coercion and Dissent in Romania, 1965–1989.* New York: Sharpe, 1995.

Security and Cooperation in Europe, Conference on (1973–1990)

Multinational and multiphase discussions dealing primarily with the diminishment of East-West tensions in Europe and human rights issues. The Conference on Security and Cooperation in Europe (CSCE) first convened on 3 July 1973 and was attended by thirty-five European and North American states. The CSCE provided critical momentum for sweeping political and social changes in the Soviet bloc that would significantly influence the end of the Cold War.

The Soviets, seeking formal recognition of their post–World War II borders, had sought a European security conference since 1954. West European countries had resisted such a conference, concerned that it might strengthen the Soviets' international position and potentially divide the Western alliance. By the late 1960s, however, widespread public interest in reducing East-West antagonism led West European governments to reconsider their position. Moreover, the Soviet Union removed a significant obstacle to the conference by indicating that it would not oppose American or Canadian participation.

The outcome was a complex, drawn-out period of diplomacy divided into four phases: the Helsinki Consultations to determine the timing and agenda of the conference from 22 November 1972 to 8 June 1973, the six-day meeting of foreign ministers formally launching the CSCE from 3 July to 8 July 1973, the principal negotiations of the Geneva stage from 29 August 1973 to 21 July 1975, and the final summit from 30 July 1975 to 1 August 1975 during which representatives from the thirty-five states convened in Helsinki and signed the Helsinki Final Act.

The CSCE negotiations centered around four so-called baskets of issues. The first dealt with ten principles guiding relations in Europe, including the inviolability of frontiers, the territorial integrity of states, and the peaceful settlement of disputes. The first basket also incorporated confidence-building measures such as advanced notification of military troop maneuvers. The second basket addressed economic, scientific, and technological cooperation among CSCE states, while the third concentrated on humanitarian issues such as the reunification of families, improved working conditions for journalists, and increased cultural exchanges. The fourth basket focused on follow-up procedures.

The fourth basket extended the CSCE by stipulating that a follow-up meeting be held in 1977 in Belgrade, Yugoslavia, to assess the progress made toward fulfilling the terms of the Helsinki Final Act. The principal accomplishment of the Belgrade meeting (4 October 1977–9 March 1978) was the initiation of a process of review whereby countries that did not meet the terms of the Helsinki agreement, particularly its human rights provisions, could be held publicly accountable. Such reviews were held in a number of subsequent meetings that became known as the Helsinki Process. Despite the value of the follow-up meetings, however, some policymakers were concerned that the often acrimonious nature of the review process threatened the central goal of the CSCE, namely the reduction of tensions in Europe.

The Madrid review meeting (11 November 1980–9 September 1983) made little further progress in decreasing East-West tension or improving human rights, largely because of external events such as the imposition of martial law in Poland in December 1981 and the Soviet downing of KAL Flight 007 on 1 September 1983. The Vienna meeting from 11 November 1986 to 19 January 1989 produced significant accomplishments related to human rights issues, especially the right of people to emigrate, religious tolerance, the upholding of the rights of national minorities, and the removal of restrictions on foreign broadcasting. The Vienna meeting exemplified how the CSCE successfully linked human rights with other elements of East-West relations, and the agreement there to hold a conference on human rights in Moscow signaled the extent to which the Helsinki Process had encouraged and facilitated progress on these issues in states such as the Soviet Union.

The emphasis on the protection of human rights, as pursued by the North Atlantic Treaty Organization (NATO) and the neutral and nonaligned countries through the Helsinki Process, ultimately paved the way for the political and social transformations in Eastern Europe that marked the end of the Cold War. The CSCE summit meeting in Paris (19–21 November 1990) recognized, for the first time, the fundamental political and social changes that had occurred in Europe in the fifteen years since the signing of the Helsinki Final Act. In Paris, the leaders of the CSCE nations, including a now-reunified Germany, signed the Charter for a New Europe, recognizing the end of confrontation in Europe and, as the charter proclaimed, a new era of "democracy, peace, and unity."

Beyond the influential review meetings, the CSCE encouraged regular East-West engagement, forging connections that bridged some of the deep divisions in Europe with targeted discussions on issues such as scientific cooperation, the peaceful settlement of disputes, and security in the Mediterranean. These talks, known as experts' meetings, maintained connections between Western and Eastern countries. In addition, neutral and nonaligned CSCE signatories often played an important role in brokering compromises between the two sides.

Sarah B. Snyder

See also
Détente; Europe, Eastern; Europe, Western; Helsinki Final Act; Human Rights; KAL Flight 007

References
Korey, William. *The Promises We Keep: Human Rights, the Helsinki Process, and American Foreign Policy.* New York: St. Martin's/Institute of East-West Studies, 1993.

Thomas, Daniel C. *The Helsinki Effect: International Norms, Human Rights, and the Demise of Communism.* Princeton, NJ: Princeton University Press, 2001.

Sendero Luminoso
See Shining Path

Service, John Stewart (1909–1999)

U.S. Foreign Service officer and one of the so-called Old China Hands. Born in China to missionary parents on 8 August 1909, John Service grew up in Sichuan Province, attended high school in Shanghai, and studied art history at Oberlin College in Ohio. He returned to China in 1922 and, following a brief time in banking, joined the American Foreign Service. When the Japanese entered Beijing, he helped escort Americans to safety. Assigned to the new Guomindang (GMD, Nationalist) capital at Congqing as a political officer in 1941, his task was to gather information on all Chinese political parties and factions, including the communists. Service knew China well and had great insight regarding events there.

In the communist witch-hunt hysteria of the early Cold War period, Senator Joseph R. McCarthy attacked Service and other China Hands, including John Carter Vincent, John Paton Davies, and Oliver Edmund Clubb. Accused of being soft on communism, Service had in fact reported truthfully on corruption in Jiang Jieshi's Nationalist government. Service had also predicted a civil war that would lead to a communist victory if things were not changed.

Contrary to the charges made by the far Right, the China Hands did not welcome communism. They simply urged that U.S. pressure be brought to bear on Jiang and, failing that, advocated a policy of American neutrality in what was an inevitable civil conflict. Had their advice been heeded, the United States would probably have been able to maintain diplomatic relations with China. Certainly the charge that Service and other Foreign Service officials "lost" China was patently ridiculous. The Chinese themselves accomplished that.

In February 1950, Senator McCarthy specifically charged Service with being "a known associate and collaborator with communists." Although Service was subsequently cleared by a Senate committee, a Loyalty Review Board named by President Harry S. Truman said that there was "reasonable doubt as to his loyalty," and Secretary of State Dean G. Acheson dismissed Service the same day. In 1956 the U.S. Supreme Court ruled 8–0 (one justice took no part in the case) that the board had no right to review the State Department's findings and that Acheson had no right to dismiss him. Service then rejoined the State Department, retiring from an obscure post in the Liverpool, England, consulate in 1962.

Service then earned a master's degree at the University of California, Berkeley, and became library curator of its Center for Chinese Studies. With the 1970s thaw in relations between the United States and the People's Republic of China (PRC), Service visited China, even meeting with Chinese Prime Minister Zhou Enlai in 1971. Service also published several books on China. He died in Oakland, California, on 3 February 1999.

Spencer C. Tucker

See also
Acheson, Dean Gooderham; Jiang Jieshi; McCarthy, Joseph Raymond; Truman, Harry S.; Zhou Enlai

References
Kahn, E. J., Jr. *The China Hands: America's Foreign Service Officers and What Befell Them.* New York: Viking, 1975.

Service, John S. *Lost Chance in China: The World War II Despatches of John S. Service.* Edited by Joseph W. Esherick. New York: Random House, 1974.

U.S. Foreign Service officer John Stewart Service, whose career was ruined as a result of false accusations against him. (Bettmann/Corbis)

Sétif Uprising (8 May 1945)

An anticolonial uprising in Algeria that signaled the start of a liberation movement culminating in Algerian independence in 1962. On 8 May 1945, as much of the world celebrated the end of World War II in Europe, riots broke out among the Berber population of the city of Sétif in the Department of Constantine in Algeria. It began as just another victory parade, which had been approved by the French authorities.

Because 8 May was a market day, it attracted many Berbers from around the city who nursed long-standing grievances with the European settlers over the seizure of their ancestral lands. While marchers did carry posters proclaiming the Allied victory, there were also placards calling on Muslims to unite against the French for the release of nationalist leader Ahmed Messali Hadj and death to Frenchmen and Jews. Early in the parade a French plainclothes policeman pulled a revolver and shot to death a young marcher carrying an Algerian flag. This touched off a bloody rampage, often referred to as the Sétif Massacre.

Muslims attacked Europeans and their property, and violence quickly spread to outlying areas. The French authorities then unleashed a violent crackdown that included Foreign Legionnaires and Senegalese troops, tanks, air force planes, and even naval gunfire from a cruiser in the Mediterranean Sea. Settler militias and local vigilantes supported the authorities and took a number of prisoners from jails and executed them. Major French military operations lasted two weeks, while smaller actions continued for a month. An estimated 4,500 Algerians were arrested, of whom 99 were sentenced to death and another 64 were given life imprisonment. Casualty figures remain in dispute. At least 100 Europeans died. The official French figure of Muslim dead was 1,165, but this is certainly too low, and figures as high as 10,000 have been cited.

In March 1946 the French government announced a general amnesty and released many of the Sétif detainees, including moderate nationalist leader Ferhat Abbas, although his Friends of the Manifesto and Liberty political party was dissolved. The fierce nature of the French repression of the uprising was based on a perception that any leniency would be interpreted as weakness and only encourage further unrest.

The Sétif Uprising, which was not followed by any meaningful French reform, drove a wedge between the two communities in Algeria. Europeans now distrusted Muslims, and the Muslims never forgave the violence of the repression. French authorities did not understand the implications of this and were thus caught by surprise when a rebellion began in Algeria in November 1954.

Thomas D. Veve and Spencer C. Tucker

See also
Abbas, Ferhat; Algeria; Algerian War; Anticolonialism; Messali Hadj, Ahmed

References
Aron, Robert. *Les Origines de la guerre d'Algérie: Textes et documents contemporaine.* Paris: Fayard, 1962.
Gordon, David C. *The Passing of French Algeria.* London: Oxford University Press, 1966.
Horne, Alistair. *A Savage War of Peace: Algeria, 1954–1962.* New York: Viking, 1977.
Smith, Tony. *The French Stake in Algeria, 1945–1962.* Ithaca, NY: Cornell University Press, 1978.
Tucker, Spencer C. "The Fourth Republic and Algeria." Unpublished doctoral diss., University of North Carolina at Chapel Hill, 1965.

Shehu, Mehmet (1913–1981)

Albanian military leader and premier of Albania (1954–1981). Born in Corush in southern Albania on 10 January 1913, Mehmet Shehu graduated from the American Vocational School in Tirana in 1932 with a degree in agriculture. He also briefly attended the Naples Military Academy in Italy before being expelled for his communist sympathies. During the Spanish Civil War (1936–1939), he served in the International Brigades on the Republican side. Like many soldiers who fought for the Republican cause, he spent time in French internment camps, remaining there until 1942.

Shehu returned to Albania in 1942 and joined Enver Hoxha's military operations against the Italians, Germans, and noncommunist partisans. Shehu became a brigade commander in 1941 and was promoted to division command that same year. In 1943 he was elected a member of the Albanian Communist Party's Central Committee. The following year he became a member of the Albanian provisional government.

After the end of World War II, Shehu received advanced military training in Moscow and was named Albanian Army chief of staff in July 1946. Together with Hoxha, Shehu vociferously opposed Albania's incorporation into Yugoslavia. Hoxha removed him from office in December 1947, appar-

ently under pressure by Coci Xoxe, leader of the pro-Yugoslav faction. Shehu was politically rehabilitated in 1948 and led the infamous purges of the Albanian Communist Party during 1948–1951.

A member of the Central Committee and Politburo beginning in 1948, during 1949–1954 Shehu served as deputy chairman of the Council of Ministers, minister of internal affairs, and head of the Albanian police. He became prime minister in 1954 and was then subordinate in Albania only to Hoxha.

Shehu significantly shaped both Albanian foreign and domestic policy, including helping to create the Albanian-Chinese alliance in 1961 that lasted until the mid-1970s. Domestically, he helped collectivize agriculture, nationalize industry, and institute universal health care and education. From the mid-1970s on, however, he came to oppose Hoxha's policy of increasing Albania's isolationism and self-sufficiency. In 1981 the power struggle between Hoxha and Shehu was resolved with Shehu's death, allegedly a suicide, in Tirana on 17 December 1981. Many believe that it was in fact a political assassination ordered by Hoxha, who claimed that Shehu was an agent of the U.S., Soviet, and Yugoslav governments.

Robert N. Stacy

See also
Albania; Europe, Eastern; Hoxha, Enver

References
O'Donnell, James S. *A Coming of Age: Albania under Enver Hoxha.* Boulder, CO: East European Monographs, 1999.
Pipa, Arshi. *Albanian Stalinism: Ideo-Political Aspects.* Boulder, CO: East European Monographs, 1990.

Sherman, Forrest Percival (1896–1951)

American admiral and chief of naval operations. Born in Merrimack, New Hampshire, on 30 October 1896, Forrest Sherman graduated second in his United States Naval Academy class of 1917 and saw convoy escort service in World War I. He soon switched to naval aviation and thereafter remained a strong advocate for naval airpower. In May 1942 during World War II, he earned command of the aircraft carrier *Wasp*. While in support of the Guadalcanal campaign, he lost the *Wasp* to a Japanese submarine in September 1942. He survived the career blemish and was named chief of staff to Admiral John H. Towers, commander of the Pacific Fleet's air arm. Sherman then joined Admiral Chester Nimitz's staff as head of the War Plans Division.

Sherman made a substantial contribution to the navy's Cold War role. Promoted to vice admiral in December 1945, he served as deputy chief of naval operations under Nimitz during 1945–1947 and urged the navy to adopt a balanced force capable of global reach. Sherman served as the navy's representative during negotiations that helped unify the military services under the Defense Department in 1947. He advocated a permanent American naval presence in the Mediterranean Sea to counter Soviet moves in the Balkans. In December 1947, he assumed command of the U.S. Sixth Task Fleet in the Mediterranean.

Sherman was named chief of naval operations on 2 November 1949 in the wake of the disaster of the Revolt of the Admirals and began the task of restoring naval morale. He proved himself a powerful chief and began to carve out a strong role for the navy in the Cold War. He backed the carrier task force as central to the navy's Cold War mission and saw the need for future supercarriers. He also supported the expansion of the navy to meet other traditional missions, such as anti-submarine warfare, and saw a place for nuclear-powered vessels in the navy's future.

Sherman became the dominant member among the Joint Chiefs of Staff (JCS). With the outbreak of the Korean War, he was a reluctant supporter of Douglas MacArthur's Inchon operation but convinced the JCS to endorse the plan. He supported President Harry S. Truman's decision to remove MacArthur from Korean command. Still serving as chief of naval operations, Sherman died in Naples, Italy, on 22 July 1951 while on a diplomatic mission concerning U.S. North Atlantic Treaty Organization (NATO) basing rights.

Thomas D. Veve

See also
Clifford, Clark McAdams; Johnson, Louis Arthur; Korean War; MacArthur, Douglas; National Security Act; Norstad, Lauris; North Atlantic Treaty Organization, Origins and Formation of; Radford, Arthur William

References
Barlow, Jeffrey G. *Revolt of the Admirals: The Fight for Naval Aviation, 1945–1950.* Washington, DC: Naval Historical Center, 1994.
Palmer, Michael A. *Origins of the Maritime Strategy: American Naval Strategy in the First Postwar Decade.* Washington, DC: Naval Historical Center, 1988.
Reynolds, Clark G. "Forrest Percival Sherman, 2 November 1949–22 July 1951." Pp. 208–232 in *The Chiefs of Naval Operations,* edited by Robert W. Love Jr. Annapolis, MD: Naval Institute Press, 1980.

President Eduard Shevardnadze of Georgia, photographed during his meeting with Secretary of Defense William Cohen at the Pentagon, 17 July 1997. (U.S. Department of Defense)

Shevardnadze, Eduard (1928–)

Soviet foreign minister (1985–1990, 1991), chairman of the Georgian State Council (1992–1995), and president of Georgia (1995–2003). Born on 25 January 1928 in the Georgian village of Mamati, Eduard Shevardnadze graduated from the Party School of the Communist Party Central Committee in 1951 and from the Kutaisi Pedagogical Institute in 1959. He then became an instructor for the Komsomol (Communist Union of Youth). Joining the Communist Party in 1948, he rose quickly through its ranks. He became a member of the Georgian Supreme Soviet in 1959.

During 1961–1964 Shevardnadze served as a party regional secretary, and during 1964–1965 he was deputy minister of internal affairs for Georgia. He became minister of internal affairs of Georgia in 1965, a post he held until 1972. During this period, Shevardnadze reformed Georgian agriculture, creating new incentives for farmers and boosting production. He was also responsible for firing and imprisoning hundreds of officials in his fight against bureaucratic corruption, earning him the reputation of a merciless opponent of corruption and inefficiency. He also forced government officials to give up properties that they had attained through bribery and other illegal means. He firmly believed that the Soviet economy would never move forward if corruption continued to plague the system.

In 1972, Shevardnadze was appointed first secretary of the Georgian Communist Party, a post he occupied until 1985. There too he continued his fight against corruption. He became a member of the Central Committee of the Communist Party of the Soviet Union (CPSU) in 1976. In 1977 Soviet authorities conducted a series of crackdowns against human rights activists, jailing many of the movement's top figures. Shevardnadze's Georgian government participated in the crackdowns, and among those jailed was Zviad Gamsakhurdia, who in May 1991 would become the first democratically elected president of the independent Republic of Georgia. In 1978, Shevardnadze was promoted to candidate member status of the Soviet Politburo, which functioned as the central policymaking and governing body of the CPSU. That same year he was awarded the Order of Lenin for his honesty, integrity, and political courage.

In 1985, new Soviet leader Mikhail Gorbachev appointed Shevardnadze minister of foreign affairs after the resignation of Andrey Gromyko. Shevardnadze also became a full member of the CPSU Politburo. As foreign minister, he played an important role in ending the Cold War. He reformed Soviet foreign policymaking, implementing Gorbachev's policies. These included withdrawing from Afghanistan, developing new arms control strategies, establishing ties with Israel, negotiating German reunification, and allowing for the democratization of Eastern Europe. Shevardnadze rejected all aid requests by communist leaders in Eastern Europe when revolutions and democratization swept their countries, allowing for a smooth and relatively bloodless transition to democracy in the region.

These actions, however, made Shevardnadze many enemies in Moscow. Nonetheless, he adhered to a strict policy of liberalization, which gradually separated him from Gorbachev's incrementalist policy of preserving a socialist system. Because of these differences and growing criticism from Communist Party hard-liners, Shevardnadze resigned his post in December 1990 and warned that the nation was headed toward dictatorship. Following his resignation, an unsuccessful coup by communist hard-liners in August 1991 seemed to prove that Shevardnadze's prediction was correct. He returned to the post of foreign minister in November 1991 but resigned together with Gorbachev in December when the Soviet Union was officially dissolved.

In March 1992, Shevardnadze became head of an interim Georgian government following the ouster of President Gamsakhurdia. In 1995, Shevardnadze survived an assassination attempt and that same year was elected president of the Republic of Georgia by a comfortable margin. He survived a second assassination attempt in 1998. In 2000 he won a controversial presidential election that was immediately followed by accusations of vote rigging. In November 2003, Shevardnadze was forced to resign the presidency after huge demonstrations showed that he had lost much of his political clout.

Arthur M. Holst

See also
Georgia; Glasnost; Gorbachev, Mikhail; Gromyko, Andrey; Perestroika; Soviet Union

References
Ekedahl, Carolyn McGiffert, and Melvin A. Goodman. *The Wars of Eduard Shevardnadze*. University Park: Pennsylvania State University Press, 1997.
Shevardnadze, Eduard. *The Future Belongs to Freedom*. New York: Free Press, 1991.

Shigemitsu Mamoru (1887–1957)

Japanese diplomat and foreign minister (1943–1946, 1954–1957). Born in Ōita Prefecture on 29 July 1887, Shigemitsu Mamoru graduated from Tokyo University in 1911. He then joined the Foreign Ministry and served as an advisor to the Japanese delegation to the 1919 Paris Peace Conference and as consul general in Shanghai. He joined other Japanese diplomats after the conference in arguing for a more forceful Japanese foreign policy.

Shigemitsu was counselor to the Foreign Ministry during 1920–1924, chief secretary to the embassy in China during 1925–1927, and consul general in Shanghai during 1927–1930. In 1931 he became Japanese minister to China. Following the Manchurian Incident that same year, he sought direct talks with China rather than see the matter referred to the League of Nations. In April 1932 he was badly wounded (losing a foot) in an assassination attempt by a Korean nationalist.

As deputy foreign minister during 1933–1936, Shigemitsu devoted himself to Japan's relations with China. Resigning over the failure of his hard-line approach, he was subsequently Japanese ambassador to the Soviet Union (1936–1938), Great Britain (1938–1941), and the Wang Jingwei government in China during 1942. Shigemitsu opposed the Tripartite Military Pact that bound Japan to Germany and Italy.

Shigemitsu became foreign minister in the cabinet headed by Tōjō Hideki in 1943 and remained in that post in the subsequent Koiso Kuniaki and Higashikuni Naruhiko cabinets. As such, Shigemitsu signed the World War II capitulation agreement aboard the U.S. battleship *Missouri* on 2 September 1945. The next year, he was arrested and detained as a Class A war criminal. Sentenced to seven years in Sugamo Prison, he was released in 1950.

Shigemitsu was elected to the Japanese Diet in 1952. In 1954 he assumed the posts of both deputy prime minister and foreign minister in the Hatoyama Ichirō cabinet. In this post, Shigemitsu worked to restore diplomatic relations between Japan and the Soviet Union and to gain Japanese entry into the United Nations (UN), both of which occurred in 1956. Shigemitsu died in Yugawara in Kanagawa Prefecture on 26 January 1957.

Tomoyuki Takemoto and Spencer C. Tucker

See also
Hatoyama Ichirō; Japan
References
Shigemitsu Mamoru. *Japan and Her Destiny: My Struggle for Peace.*
    Edited by F. S. G. Piggott, translated by Oswald White. New York:
    E. P. Dutton, 1958.
Takeda, Tomoki. *Shigemitsu Mamoru To Sengo Seiji* [Mamoru
    Shigemitsu and Postwar Politics]. Tokyo: Yosikawa Kobunkan,
    2002.
Watanabe, Yukio. *Shigemitsu Mamoru: Shanghai Jiken Kara
    Kokuren Kamei Made* [From the Shanghai Incident to UN
    Affiliation]. Tokyo: Chuo Koron Shinsha, 1996.

Shining Path

Rural-based guerrilla organization founded in Peru and operational since 1980. Conceptually, Sendero Luminoso (Shining Path) developed in Peru during the 1960s. First established at a Peruvian regional university, the group was the result of frustration with a corrupt and unresponsive political system and the ambition of intellectuals to put theory into practice. Shining Path's key leader was Abimael Guzmán Reynoso, who headed the School of Education at the University of San Cristobal de Huamanga. During the 1960s, Guzmán, also known as "Chairman Gonzalo," recruited a core group of like-minded activists. They distinguished themselves from other Marxist groups by promoting a Maoist line of thought and action that reflected the split in the Cominform between the Soviet Union and China.

The adoption of a Maoist line, which Guzmán labeled "Marxist-Leninist–Maoist-Gonzalo Thought," fit Peru well, for its peasant population remained sizable and isolated from political affairs. As Shining Path developed, its leaders developed a strategy of action that involved the mobilization of the peasantry in a revolutionary struggle against international and domestic "oppressors of the people."

The organization used its strength among the student population to dominate university administrations into the 1970s. Graduates of the School of Education sought positions in rural schools, where they used their classrooms to develop community connections for Shining Path. Guzmán and other leaders deepened their connections with China and soon expanded their field operations beyond the university. The failure of government reforms, in particular land redistribution and rural economic development programs, convinced the Shining Path hierarchy that the revolutionary potential of the peasantry was as yet underdeveloped.

Believing that they could serve as a catalyst for a rural revolution that would expand and strangle the urban centers of capitalist exploitation, Shining Path's leaders launched its first military operation in 1980, working to create centers of revolutionary activity throughout the Andean highland region.

Shining Path reorganized peasant communities and extracted cash and material goods from "liberated" and other communities by force.

Peru's civilian governments initially proved incapable of meeting Shining Path's challenge. The election of President Alberto Fujimori in 1990, however, changed that. Fujimori suspended constitutional government and launched an ambitious campaign against Shining Path and other guerrilla organizations then in operation in other parts of Peru. His government also requested help and received aid from the United States to train the military and police forces in anti-guerrilla tactics. The United States provided additional support for campaigns against cocoa production, which increased the presence of security forces in rural areas. In addition, the Peruvian government trained and equipped peasant forces to separate Shining Path from its popular peasant base.

The Fujimori administration's war against Shining Path achieved success rather quickly. Peruvian forces captured Guzmán in 1992, and a series of subsequent antiguerrilla campaigns destroyed Shining Path's military capabilities. While still nominally active, Shining Path no longer represents a significant challenge to the Peruvian government.

Daniel Lewis

See also
Cominform; Latin America, Popular Liberation Movements in;
    Peru; Sino-Soviet Split
References
Masterson, Daniel. *Militarism and Politics in Latin America: Peru
    from Sanchez Cerro to "Sendero Luminoso."* Westport, CT:
    Greenwood, 1991.
Palmer, David Scott, ed. *Shining Path of Peru.* 2nd ed. New York:
    St. Martin's, 1994.

Shultz, George Pratt (1920–)

U.S. secretary of labor (1969–1970), secretary of the treasury (1972–1974), and secretary of state (1982–1989). Born in Englewood, New Jersey, on 13 December 1920, George Shultz was the son of a New York businessman. He majored in economics at Princeton University and graduated in 1942. He then joined the U.S. Marine Corps, serving in the Pacific theater as an artillery officer and ending World War II as a captain. After demobilization, in 1949 Shultz obtained a doctorate in industrial economics from the Massachusetts Institute of Technology, where he subsequently taught industrial relations, and then in 1957 began teaching at the University of Chicago.

Under Republican President Richard Nixon, Shultz served successively as secretary of labor (1969–1970), the first director of the Office of Management and Budget (1970–1972), and secretary of the treasury (1972–1974). He resigned in

March 1974 to become vice president of the Bechtel Corporation, an international construction company, where he remained until 1982.

In June 1982 Shultz became Republican President Ronald Reagan's second and last secretary of state, replacing the forceful but divisive Alexander M. Haig and adopting a low-key, nonconfrontational style. Even so, Shultz's cautious readiness to negotiate arms control agreements with the Soviet Union brought repeated clashes with the more hawkish secretary of defense, Caspar Weinberger, who favored major increases in weapons systems.

Shultz's tenure in office saw the emergence in 1985 of Mikhail Gorbachev as Soviet general secretary. Gorbachev was a conciliatory leader who became increasingly committed to reducing his country's international military commitments and improving U.S.-Soviet relations. Shultz, initially somewhat skeptical and inclined to discountenance the more optimistic Reagan's readiness in his 1986 Reykjavík meeting with Gorbachev to consider abolishing all nuclear weapons, nonetheless negotiated the 1987 Intermediate-Range Nuclear Forces (INF) Treaty, designed to remove all such weapons from Europe. In 1988 the Soviets also concluded an agreement to withdraw all their forces from Afghanistan, where they had been at war since 1979 with U.S.-backed mujahideen guerrillas.

From the time Shultz took office, initiatives to resolve or at least ease the entrenched disputes dividing between Israel and its Arab opponents after Israel's June 1982 invasion of Lebanon were one of his major preoccupations. Except in Afghanistan, the warming in U.S.-Soviet relations had relatively little impact on the nearly intractable Middle Eastern situation. Shultz drafted the September 1982 Reagan Plan envisaging partial Israeli withdrawal from occupied territory in return for Arab acceptance and respect for Israeli security interests, proposals that the Israeli government strongly rejected. Throughout his years in office, Shultz repeatedly but unsuccessfully tried to broker similar schemes. In December 1988 he prevailed upon Palestine Liberation Organization (PLO) leader Yasir Arafat to renounce the use of terrorism, a stance enabling the United States to open direct talks with the PLO, but Arafat failed to force his more radical followers to respect this stance, and within a year the U.S.-PLO talks broke down.

Shultz was a determined opponent of international terrorism and of governments, including those of Libya and Iran, that sponsored such tactics. After a suicide bomber from the Iranian-sponsored radical Islamic Hezbollah group attacked the barracks of the U.S. Marine Corps peacekeeping force in Beirut, Lebanon, in October 1983, killing 241 American servicemen, Shultz began to press Reagan to respond forcefully to such attacks on Americans. Shultz supported the use of force as well as military and economic sanctions, not just against individual terrorists but also against states that sponsored terrorism. He applauded Reagan's readiness in 1985 to employ military personnel to capture Palestinian hijackers of the American cruise ship *Achille Lauro* and to mount bombing raids on Libya in April 1986.

Shultz opposed and was therefore deliberately left in ignorance of efforts by National Security Advisor Robert McFarlane and others based in the Reagan White House to sell arms to the fundamentalist Islamic regime in Iran and surreptitiously use the proceeds to fund the activities of anticommunist Contra guerrillas in Nicaragua. The ensuing scandal, which broke in 1986, damaged but did not destroy Reagan's presidency, and his final years in office saw further incremental warming in U.S.-Soviet relations, which came to full fruition under his successor, George H. W. Bush.

Shultz retired at the end of Reagan's presidency and became a senior fellow at the conservative Hoover Institution in Palo Alto, California. In retirement he has written lengthy memoirs.

Priscilla Roberts

See also

Afghanistan; Afghanistan War; Arafat, Yasir; Arms Control; Bush, George Herbert Walker; Gorbachev, Mikhail; Haig, Alexander Meigs, Jr.; Iran; Iran-Contra Affair; Lebanon, U.S. Interventions in; Libya; Nixon, Richard Milhous; Palestine Liberation Organization; Reagan, Ronald Wilson; Reagan Doctrine; Terrorism; Weinberger, Caspar

References

Brands, H. W. *Into the Labyrinth: The United States and the Middle East, 1945–1953.* New York: McGraw-Hill, 1994.

Fitzgerald, Frances. *Way Out There in the Blue: Reagan, Star Wars, and the End of the Cold War.* New York: Simon and Schuster, 2000.

Laham, Nicholas. *Crossing the Rubicon: Ronald Reagan and US Policy in the Middle East.* Aldershot, UK: Ashgate, 2004.

Martin, David C., and John Walcott. *Best Laid Plans: The Inside Story of America War against Terrorism.* New York: Harper and Row, 1988.

Matlock, Jack F., Jr. *Reagan and Gorbachev: How the Cold War Ended.* New York: Random House, 2004.

Oberdorfer, Don. *From the Cold War to a New Era: The United States and the Soviet Union, 1983–1991.* Baltimore: Johns Hopkins University Press, 1998.

Quandt, William B. *Peace Process: American Diplomacy and the Arab-Israeli Conflict since 1967.* Washington, DC: Brookings Institution and University of California Press, 1993.

Shultz, George P. *Turmoil and Triumph: My Years As Secretary of State.* New York: Scribner, 1993.

Woodward, Bob. *Veil: The Secret Wars of the CIA, 1981–1987.* New York: Simon and Schuster, 1987.

Sihanouk, Norodom (1922–)

King (1941–1954), prime minister (1955–1960), head of state (1960–1970, 1975–1978, 1991–2004) of Cambodia. Born

Norodom Sihanouk was king of Cambodia from 1941 to 1955 and again from 1993 to 2004, and was also prime minister, head of state, and president. He tried, with only mixed results, to keep Cambodia neutral throughout the regional and civil conflicts that raged in Southeast Asia during his lifetime. (Library of Congress)

on 31 October 1922 in Phnom Penh to Cambodian King Norodom Suramarit and Queen Sisowath Kosawak, Norodom Sihanouk was educated in French primary schools in Indochina and spent two years studying at the French Cavalry and Armored School at Saumur, France, during 1946–1948. In November 1941 he became King of Cambodia. In 1945 while Cambodia was still under Japanese occupation, he proclaimed his country independent from French colonial rule. When the French returned after the Japanese surrender, however, they attempted to reassert control by minimizing Sihanouk's influence. He soon realized that only by championing independence from France could he maintain his popularity and power.

When the 1954 Geneva Conference formally granted Cambodian independence and called for free elections, Sihanouk abdicated the throne the next year in favor of his father. Sihanouk subsequently won a referendum and became prime minister in March 1955. Immensely popular among the peasantry, he strongly championed neutrality as the war in Vietnam escalated. Following his father's death in 1960, Sihanouk was again named head of state but was not granted the title of king.

Alternately taking sides with the People's Republic of China (PRC) and the United States, he tried to prevent the war in the neighboring Republic of Vietnam (RVN, South Vietnam) from spilling over into his country, but he was largely unsuccessful as Democratic Republic of Vietnam (DRV, North Vietnam) forces transited through Cambodia into South Vietnam, and they and the Viet Cong used eastern Cambodia as a sanctuary.

Frustrated in his efforts to keep Cambodia neutral, in 1968 Sihanouk restored relations with the United States and in 1970 secretly agreed to permit the Americans to bomb communist sanctuaries. At the same time, he attempted to block the growing influence of the communist Khmer Rouge.

While out of the country in March 1970, Sihanouk was ousted by a coup led by General Lon Nol. Sihanouk fled to Beijing, where he lived in exile. Following the 1975 Khmer Rouge takeover, he returned to Cambodia and became the symbolic head of state, while dictator Pol Pot remained the power behind the throne. In 1976 Sihanouk was placed under house arrest, but he escaped to China in 1978 when the Vietnamese invaded Cambodia. He unsuccessfully attempted to forge an alliance with the Khmer Rouge and others to oppose the new Vietnamese-imposed Cambodian regime. When Vietnam withdrew in 1989 and a peace treaty sponsored by the United Nations (UN) went into effect in 1991, he returned to Cambodia, where he was reinstated as king and Cambodian president, although his political power was limited. Sihanouk abdicated in October 2004 in favor of his son, Norodom Sihamoni.

Arne Kislenko and James H. Willbanks

See also
Cambodia; Cambodia, Vietnamese Occupation of; Khmer Rouge; Lon Nol; Pol Pot; Vietnam

References
Chandler, David P. *The Tragedy of Cambodian History: Politics, War and Revolution since 1945.* New Haven, CT: Yale University Press, 1991.
Kamm, Henry. *Cambodia: Report from a Stricken Land.* New York: Arcade, 1998.
Osborne, Milton. *Sihanouk: Prince of Light, Prince of Darkness.* Honolulu: University of Hawaii Press, 1994.

Sinai War
See Suez Crisis

"Sinews of Peace" Speech (March 1946)
Speech given by Sir Winston Churchill, viewed by many historians as the opening rhetorical salvo of the Cold War, in

which the term "iron curtain" was coined. On 5 March 1946 Churchill, who had been Britain's wartime prime minister, presented his "Sinews of Peace" address—also referred to as the "Iron Curtain" speech—at Westminster College in Fulton, Missouri. Churchill's comments strongly denounced Soviet aggression in Eastern Europe and warned that the Western powers must once again gird themselves for a potential conflict.

In October 1945 President Harry S. Truman forwarded an invitation from the president of Westminster College to Churchill, who had been defeated in the British elections of July 1945, to speak at that institution. Churchill accepted in November. He arrived in Washington, D.C., on 2 March and joined Truman on a three-day train trip to Missouri; the excursion had been Churchill's idea.

Churchill and Truman were cheered by some 30,000 people en route between Jefferson City and Fulton. More than 2,000 faculty, students, and invited guests filled the gymnasium at Westminster College on 5 March, a friendly audience for both Churchill and Truman.

In his speech, Churchill reviewed the history of the twentieth century with special emphasis on the period since the 1930s. He also painted a rather bleak and disappointing picture of Soviet behavior since the Allied victory over Germany a year earlier. Churchill argued that Soviet expansionist policies had drawn an "iron curtain" between Eastern and Western Europe. To counter the Soviets' threat to world peace, Churchill called for a mutual defense agreement among noncommunist states. He also called attention to the longstanding "special relationship" between the United States and Britain.

The speech had considerable impact. Americans and West Europeans were alerted to the new Soviet threat, and their governments appeared ready to respond to the challenge. Because of Churchill's Cassandra-like role in warning against appeasement in the 1930s and his defiance of Adolf Hitler in World War II, his remarks struck a responsive chord, although Truman was at the time noncommittal.

Churchill gave other speeches in Zurich, Strasbourg, Boston, and The Hague. These hugely successful speeches revitalized a political career that seemed to have ended in July 1945. His rhetorical success as leader of the opposition sustained his leadership of the Conservative Party and prepared the way for his political comeback in 1951. It also confirmed his constancy as an opponent of communism.

William T. Walker

See also

Attlee, Clement Richard, 1st Earl; Churchill, Winston; Truman, Harry S.; United Kingdom

References

Gilbert, Martin. *Churchill: A Life.* New York: Holt, 1991.
Harbutt, Fraser J. *The Iron Curtain: Churchill, America, and the Origins of the Cold War.* New York: Oxford University Press, 1986.
Muller, James W., ed. *Churchill's "Iron Curtain" Speech Fifty Years Later.* Columbia: University of Missouri Press, 1999.
Ramden, John. *Man of the Century: Winston Churchill and His Legend since 1945.* New York: Columbia University Press, 2003.
Thompson, Kenneth W. *Winston Churchill's World View: Statesmanship and Power.* Baton Rouge: Louisiana State University Press, 1983.

Singapore

Southeast Asian nation. The Republic of Singapore, covering just 267 square miles, is one the smallest nations in the world. Strategically located off the southern tip of the Malay Peninsula, it is composed of the main island of Singapore along with fifty-eight nearby islands between the South China Sea and the Indian Ocean. Singapore's 1945 population was roughly 1 million people. Its deep-water anchorage makes it a valuable harbor, and records dating from the third century BC suggest that even then it was the main port between the Indian Ocean and the South China Sea. A number of Asian and European empires controlled Singapore for 1,500 years, ending with British rule that began in 1819. By 1832 Singapore was the capital of the Straits Settlement. In 1867 it became a Crown colony. By World War I it was a thriving, multicultural city and a powerful fortress, heralded as "the Gibraltar of Asia."

World War II changed that. Japanese forces overran British defenses on Singapore in February 1942, and the loss of Singapore signaled the beginning of the end of Britain's empire. The British recaptured the city-state in 1945 and established a military government, but the war had unleashed nationalist sentiments. Many Singaporeans favored autonomy, especially after 1946 when the British prepared a federation of Malay states for independence while Singapore remained a colony. British and Malay leaders worried that equal representation for all ethnic groups in Malaya would favor the well-organized and entrepreneurial Chinese, especially in Singapore, where they made up 60 percent of the population.

The Malayan Emergency (1948–1960) exacerbated these concerns and delayed Singapore's independence. In 1959 Singapore was finally granted self-government, but Britain retained control of foreign affairs and defense. In Singapore's first general election that same year, the People's Action Party (PAP) won a landslide victory. It has remained in power ever since. PAP leader Li Guangyao completely dominated Singapore's politics, governing as prime minister until 1990. Consequently, much about Cold War Singapore revolves around Li.

Li's first major challenge came in 1963, when Britain ceded Singapore to the reconstituted Federation of Malaysia. Indonesia and Malaysia nearly went to war. Malaysia's prime minister, Tunku Abdul Rahman, skillfully averted war, but many Malay leaders wanted to break the Chinese hold on Singapore and were unwilling to extend equal representation to the Chinese in Malaysia. In 1964, race riots made for even more tension. However, the main source of contention between Singapore and Malaysia was money. Li's laissez-faire economic policies were antithetical to Malaysia's managed economy, designed to favor Malays. Moreover, within the union Singapore collected and retained taxes but sent 40 percent annually to Malaysia. After much negotiation and artful diplomacy, Singapore separated peacefully from Malaysia and became a wholly independent country in August 1965.

Li quickly set the agenda for Singapore's independence. He was deeply committed to free enterprise and took full advantage of Singapore's diverse, well-educated, and industrious residents. He encouraged foreign investment and built modern transportation systems and urban housing developments. Singapore became the second most active port in the world. It also grew into a major international airline hub. By the 1980s, Singapore diversified into a major financial center and high-technology manufacturer, making it one of Asia's economic "four dragons," alongside Taiwan, Hong Kong, and South Korea. Annual growth rates ranged between 8 and 11 percent for three decades, while per capita yearly income reached $12,000 by 1990, the fourth highest in Asia. With fewer than 4 million people, its gross domestic product (GDP) hit $75 billion by 1994. High life expectancies and literacy rates also distinguished Singapore. This success was all the more remarkable given the republic's lack of natural resources and its almost complete dependency on food, and even water, importation.

In foreign relations, Singapore was firmly in the Western camp until the mid-1970s, when it pursued a more neutral course. In 1967 it became a founding member of the pro-Western Association of Southeast Asian Nations (ASEAN). It also hosted British military bases until 1971 and then entered into the Five Power Defense Agreement with Britain, Australia, New Zealand, and Malaysia until 1975. Li was also a close friend to the United States and a vigorous supporter of the American war in Vietnam.

At the same time, Li worried about alienating the communist powers, particularly the People's Republic of China (PRC). Although deeply anticommunist, Li realized that the PRC was becoming a major regional, if not global, power. He believed that Singapore's Chinese population could potentially assist in integrating the PRC into the world community. Still, he avoided aggravating delicate relationships with nearby Malaysia and Indonesia. Both endured serious communist insurgencies connected to their Chinese communities, and consequently both viewed the PRC with suspicion. Accordingly, Singapore did not recognize the PRC until 1976, and only after both its neighbors had done so.

Ostensibly a democracy, Singapore was and still is criticized for its somewhat authoritarian character. Lee and the PAP ruled with a firm hand. There was little toleration of opposition parties, and the media was heavily controlled. Lee justified this by portraying Singapore as a Chinese state surrounded by distrustful Malays. He also claimed that Britain's declining posture in Asia left Singapore vulnerable. In addition, he argued that a stable society was needed to build the economy. The most controversial manifestation of Lee's paternalism was the Internal Security Act, which gave the government extraordinary authority to quash dissent. Whereas some point to Singapore's harsh laws and see a very low crime rate, others point to laws against chewing gum or not flushing toilets and see a dictatorship. Opposition to Lee did surface, but popular support for the PAP remained above 60 percent.

Lee resigned in 1990 and left the PAP in 1992, replaced by his deputy, Goh Chok Tong. In 2005 Lee remained a senior minister and was regarded as the senior statesman of Southeast Asia. Similarly, despite what some condemn as its ruthless efficiency, Singapore is widely considered to be a great Cold War success story.

Arne Kislenko

See also

Indonesia; Li Guangyao; Malayan Emergency; Malaysia; Rahman, Tunku Abdul; Southeast Asia

References

Chew, Ernest C. T. *A History of Singapore.* Singapore: Oxford University Press, 1991.

Lee, Kuan Yew. *From Third World to First: The Singapore Story, 1965–2000.* New York: HarperCollins, 2000.

Tarling, Nicholas, ed. *The Cambridge History of Southeast Asia,* Vol. 2, part 2. Cambridge: Cambridge University Press, 1999.

Turnbull, C. M. *A History of Singapore.* 3rd ed. Singapore: Oxford University Press, 2006.

Yahuda, Michael. *The International Politics of the Asia-Pacific, 1945–1995.* London: Routledge, 1996.

Singer, Ernő

See Gerő, Ernő

Sinn Féin

Irish political party advocating republicanism and opposition to British control. Newspaper editor and ardent Irish nationalist Arthur Griffith is usually credited with establishing Sinn Féin (roughly translated as "Ourselves" or "We Ourselves") in 1905. Griffith believed that by boycotting the British House of Commons, the Irish Parliamentary Party could reestablish

Irish independence. He also championed Irish cultural and economic independence.

Griffith's message attracted many Irishmen and Irishwomen, most of them radicals, who were frustrated by the failure of Westminster-based politics to advance Irish nationalism. The Sinn Féin League (its title until 1908) grew rapidly, often by absorbing other radical groups. It did not impress Irish Parliamentary Party leader John Redmond, however. After his party's candidate defeated Sinn Féin's first parliamentary candidate in 1908, he dismissed the group as "a temporary adhesion of isolated cranks."

Sinn Féin opposed Irish enlistments into the British Army during World War I but had nothing to do with the 1916 Easter Rebellion. The British government believed otherwise because of the group's radical reputation and undeniable influence on Irish politics, and London referred to the revolt as the "Sinn Féin Rebellion."

In late 1917, Sinn Féin became what the British thought it was a year earlier: the political arm of Irish republicanism. With Eamon De Valera, one of the surviving leaders of the Easter Rebellion, as its president, Sinn Féin quickly became a well-organized and effective national political party but did not became more popular than the long-established Irish Parliamentary Party until the 1918 Conscription Crisis, sparked by the British government's threat to impose a military draft on Ireland. In December 1918, Sinn Féin won 73 of Ireland's 105 Westminster seats and, as Griffith had exhorted, refused to go to London. Instead, the elected members of Parliament established the Dáil Éireann as the legitimate government of the Irish Republic proclaimed in 1916.

Sinn Féin supporters carry banners during a march in Birmingham to protest against internment in Ulster and the British police's alleged harassment of the Irish community, 7 October 1973. (Hulton-Deutsch Collection/Corbis)

Irish republicanism—and its political and military institutions, Sinn Féin and the Irish Republican Army (IRA), respectively—split over the 1921 Anglo-Irish Treaty. Led by De Valera, the antitreaty forces walked out of the Dáil and into civil war. These republicans, however, did not accept their 1923 defeat at the hands of the protreaty republicans, who adopted the name Cumann na Gaedheal (Legion of the Gaels) for their faction, which controlled the Irish Free State's government. Convinced that both the Irish Free State and Northern Ireland were illegitimate, Sinn Féin declared a policy of abstentionism. Its candidates would stand for election but would refrain from entering the illegitimate parliaments if elected. This strategy ultimately failed, and votes for Sinn Féin dwindled because most Irishmen accepted the Free State and rejected as nonsensical the idea of voting for a political party that refused to participate in a legitimate government.

Sinn Féin split again in 1926 when De Valera decided to participate in parliamentary politics and left in order to found Fianna Fail. Dedicated to advancing republicanism in Ireland through constitutional means, Fianna Fail formed a government by 1932 and used its power to reconcile many republicans to normal politics. By the end of World War II, De Valera's constitutional republicanism and wartime security measures had all but destroyed the IRA and Sinn Féin.

The IRA enjoyed a brief revival after 1945, training and arming for a campaign against British interests in Northern Ireland. The offensive, known as the Border Campaign, began in 1956, and in the next year's elections, Sinn Féin won its first seats in the Dáil since 1927. The Border Campaign faltered soon thereafter and ended with a whimper in 1962.

After 1962, new leftist leaders moved the IRA and Sinn Féin toward revolutionary Marxism and away from abstentionism and military action. In December 1969, however, the IRA divided over the proper response to the outbreak of sectarian violence in Northern Ireland during the previous summer. The Provisional IRA supported armed struggle. The Official IRA, on the other hand, decided on a long-term political strategy based on Marxist theories. In January 1970, Sinn Féin split along the same lines.

The Official IRA soon repudiated military action in Northern Ireland and elsewhere, dumping its arms in 1972 and essentially dissolving as a military organization. Official Sinn Féin devoted itself to left-wing politics. In 1977 it became Sinn Féin: The Workers Party, and in 1982 it dropped "Sinn Féin" from its title.

During the 1970s, Provisional Sinn Féin (as with the IRA, the modifier soon disappeared) maintained its refusal to engage in normal politics and mainly acted as a mouthpiece for the IRA. The widespread revulsion at the deaths of republican hunger strikers in 1981 prompted republican leaders to reconsider their traditional rejection of politics. In the early 1980s, the republicans adopted a bullet and ballot box strategy. Sinn Féin became a somewhat conventional leftist political organization, while the IRA continued its military operations. In 1986, Sinn Féin's president, Gerry Adams, declared that abstentionism no longer applied to Ireland's Dáil, prompting another republican split and the consequent creation of Continuity IRA and Republican Sinn Féin.

By the early 1990s, the IRA–Sinn Féin leadership acknowledged that a military victory was unattainable. Encouraged by Sinn Féin's successes as a democratic socialist party on both sides of the border, it announced the cessation of military operations by the IRA in 1994 and, except for five months in 1997, has held to this cease-fire. The terms of the 1998 Belfast Agreement ensured Sinn Féin a place in Northern Ireland's new Assembly, effectively ending its more than seven decades in Ireland's political wilderness.

Scott Belliveau

See also
Adams, Gerard, Jr.; De Valera, Eamon; Irish Republican Army; Ireland, Northern; Ireland, Republic of; Paisley, Ian; United Kingdom
References
Dangerfield, George. *The Damnable Question: A Study in Anglo-Irish Relations.* Boston: Little, Brown, 1976.
English, Richard. *Armed Struggle: The History of the IRA.* Oxford and New York: Oxford University Press, 2003.
Kee, Robert. *The Green Flag: The Turbulent History of the Irish National Movement.* New York: Delacorte, 1972.
Moloney, Ed. *A Secret History of the IRA.* New York: Norton, 2002.
O'Brien, Brendan. *The Long War: The IRA and Sinn Fein.* 2nd ed. Syracuse, NY: Syracuse University Press, 1999.

Sino-Indian Border Confrontations (1959–1988)

Protracted border dispute, culminating in a war in 1962 between the People's Republic of China (PRC) and India that compromised India's standing among nonaligned nations and has not yet been settled. While the dispute between the PRC and India, a nonaligned nation, became an issue in the context of the Cold War, the origins of the Sino-Indian conflict date back to the nineteenth century. Both the British, who ruled India until 1947, and the imperial Chinese government had made claims to regions on India's northeastern frontier. Neither side, however, committed troops or exerted significant political pressure to settle claims over the contested area.

By the 1950s, this situation changed dramatically because of a variety of factors. Greater mobility and instant communications made it easier for the now-independent Indians and Chinese to attempt to exert control over the border areas. In addition, the incorporation of Tibet into China in 1950 substantially lengthened the Sino-Indian border, thereby increasing the likelihood of a conflict. The possibilities for a border clash increased dramatically in 1956 when the Chinese began to construct a military highway in the disputed territory. This led to a series of diplomatic protests and exchanges, followed in 1959 by an Indian military buildup along the border. Although there were no major military operations in the area, frequent military patrol missions and occasional small-scale skirmishes did occur.

In the summer of 1962, however, the border conflict escalated, with heavier than usual clashes. Heavy fighting then occurred in October and November, ending with a cease-fire on 21 November 1962. At the conclusion of this brief war, the PRC had taken all the contested area over which it had made claims, although it stopped short of advancing into Indian territory proper.

With the cease-fire, the Chinese withdrew to the positions they had held before the beginning of the war. The following month, a conference opened in Colombo, Sri Lanka, with representatives of Egypt, Burma, Sri Lanka, Cambodia, Ghana, and Indonesia. These representatives, negotiating with the Indian and PRC governments, formulated what became known as the Colombo Proposals. The proposals called for PRC forces to withdraw 20 kilometers (12 miles) from their positions before the war and India not to advance its own troops. Although never formally ratified, the proposals were accepted by both sides.

Thus ended the actual conflict between India and the PRC, although for the next twenty-six years relations between the two major powers remained frigid. The movement of Chinese troops near the border in 1963, alleged Indian movements across the border, and the incorporation of northern areas as part of India all produced hostile rhetoric. PRC support of Pakistan during the latter's conflicts with India and Chinese opposition to the creation of Bangladesh, championed by India, were other manifestations of the poor relations between the two nations.

There were sporadic attempts on both sides to improve relations. Informal talks between Indian and Chinese diplomats occurred in the early 1970s, and in 1976, fourteen years after the conclusion of the war, full diplomatic relations were restored. In 1988, the two nations agreed to the establishment of a bipartite commission to resolve the border question. Not until 2005 did the leaders of both India and the PRC announce a settlement of the dispute, although details remained to be arranged.

The conflict had especially pronounced effects in India. Jawaharlal Nehru's final months as prime minister were clouded by both his miscalculations that had led to the war and the loss of standing that the war had brought India within the Non-Aligned Movement.

Robert N. Stacy

See also
China, People's Republic of; India; India-Pakistan Wars; Nehru, Jawaharlal; Non-Aligned Movement; Tibet
References
Hoffman, Steven A. *India and the China Crisis.* Berkeley: University of California Press, 1990.
Jetly, Nancy. *India-China Relations, 1947–1977: A Study of Parliament's Role in the Making of Foreign Policy.* Atlantic Highlands, NJ: Humanities Press, 1970.
Palit, D. K. *War in High Himalaya: The Indian Army in Crisis, 1962.* New York: St. Martin's, 1990.
Vertzberger, Yaacov. *Misperceptions in Foreign Policymaking: The Sino-Indian Conflict, 1959–1962.* Boulder, CO: Westview, 1984.

Sino-Soviet Border Incident (2 March– 11 September 1969)

A series of armed clashes during 2 March–11 September 1969 between the People's Republic of China (PRC) and the Soviet Union over the demarcation of the Sino-Soviet boundary. This clash marked the height of the Sino-Soviet split and pushed the two nations to the brink of a nuclear confrontation.

By a number of unequal nineteenth-century treaties, Russia and the Chinese government agreed on a 4,500 mile-long border, running from the east through the northern border of modern Mongolia to the west of the PRC's Xinjiang Province. In the east, the demarcation line was drawn along the Amur River, known to the Chinese as Heilongjiang (literally meaning "the Black Dragon River"), along Heilongjiang Province's northern border, and along the Ussuri River, an Amur tributary between the eastern border of Heilongjiang and Russian Siberia. This border remained as it was after the fall of the Chinese Qing Dynasty and the Russian regime in the late 1910s and was twice reiterated, first with the Republic of China (ROC) in 1945 and then with the PRC in 1951.

Owing to its heavy reliance on the Soviet Union and the need to maintain Sino-Soviet solidarity, the PRC had consistently refrained from raising the border issue despite its nationalistic effort to eliminate the unequal treaties and restore territorial integrity. As the PRC sought to establish its independence from Soviet influence and the Sino-Soviet split loomed, the border issue surfaced in 1960 when the PRC revoked the unequal treaties. Border negotiations began in February 1964 in Beijing but broke off in October 1964 when the Soviets insisted on maintaining the status quo. Tensions subsequently mounted along the Sino-Soviet border, with increased armed incidents. By 1969, there were 658,000 Soviet troops confronting 814,000 Chinese troops along the Amur River. The Soviet Union had also secured the permission of the Mongolian government to base Soviet ground and air forces in that nation.

On 2 March 1969, a Soviet border patrol was ambushed by Chinese troops on Damansky Island in the Ussuri River, resulting in 31 Soviet deaths. On 15 March 1969, the Soviet Union retaliated by firing on Chinese troops on Damansky Island, causing nearly 800 deaths. Cascades of diplomatic protests and counterprotests and more border clashes followed. The most serious border incident occurred on 13 August 1969 on the border between China's Xinjiang Province and the Soviet Republic of Kazakhstan, pushing the PRC and the Soviet Union to the brink of nuclear confrontation. In response to the PRC's successful explosion of its first atomic bomb in October 1964, the Soviet Union had increased its nuclear forces in Asia, including those in the Democratic People's Republic of Korea (DPRK, North Korea) and Mongolia. By 1969, the Soviet Union had installed an antiballistic missile system directed against the PRC. The Soviet action on the Xinjiang border seemed to confirm the PRC's suspicion that the Soviets were planning a preemptive strike against Chinese nuclear installations in Xinjiang.

A war was averted when, on 11 September 1969, Soviet Premier Alexei Kosygin visited Beijing, meeting with Premier Zhou Enlai to settle the border conflict. Both sides agreed on three principles: keeping the status quo of the Sino-Soviet border, not employing military forces, and preventing future military clashes. On 20 October 1969, the border talks suspended in 1964 resumed in Beijing, with concentration on the Amur-Ussuri demarcation line.

These negotiations made little progress, however. The Soviet Union continued its military buildup along the border throughout the 1970s. By the end of the decade, the Soviet Union had tied down 25 percent of its conventional forces along the border. Perceiving this massive deployment as a threat, the PRC decided to normalize its relationship with the United States, culminating in the formal establishment of the Sino-U.S. diplomatic relationship in 1979.

Tensions along the Sino-Soviet border began to ease in July 1986, when Soviet leader Mikhail Gorbachev expressed his desire to restore Sino-Soviet harmony and settle the border disputes. In 1990, Soviet border forces were drastically reduced. Significant progress in the border talks was only achieved after the Cold War ended and the Soviet Union was dissolved. As a first step, Russia returned Zhenbao Island to the PRC on 19 May 1991. Finally, on 14 October 2004, both sides proclaimed the demarcation of the 4,500-mile Sino-Soviet boundary as complete and uncontested.

Law Yuk-fun

See also

China, People's Republic of; Sino-Soviet Split; Soviet Union

References

Ginsburgs, George. *The Damansky/Chenpao Island Incidents: A Case Study of Syntactic Patterns in Crisis Diplomacy*. Edwardsville: Southern Illinois University Press, 1973.

Lowell, Dittmer. *Sino-Soviet Normalization and Its International Implications, 1945–1990*. Seattle: University of Washington Press, 1992.

Wishnick, Elizabeth. *Mending Fences: The Evolution of Moscow's China Policy, from Brezhnev to Yeltsin*. Seattle: University of Washington Press, 2001.

Sino-Soviet Split (1956–1966)

The collapse of the Sino-Soviet alliance marked the transformation of the Cold War world from bipolarity to multipolarity. Superficially an ideological partnership between the world's two largest communist countries, the Sino-Soviet alliance began on 14 February 1950 with the conclusion of the Sino-Soviet Treaty. From its inception, the seemingly monolithic union was fraught with constantly shifting expectations about its precise place in the socialist world, subjected to American attempts to split it, and afflicted by the progressively ideological radicalism of People's Republic of China (PRC) Chairman Mao Zedong. Although Sino-Soviet disagreements over Soviet leader Nikita Khrushchev's 1956 de-Stalinization campaign remained hidden for a time, the advanced state of the alliance's disintegration became known to the outside world by the early 1960s. Because Mao exploited ideological conflict for domestic purposes, the final breakdown of the Sino-Soviet partnership in mid-1966 coincided with the beginning of the Cultural Revolution (1966–1976), launched both to purge the Chinese Communist Party (CCP) of alleged ideological revisionists and to create a communist utopia.

Viewing any alliance with a great power solely as a temporary means to help restore past Chinese glory and power, the Chinese Communists by the late 1940s had decided to lean toward the Soviet Union. Surprised by Mao's request in late 1949 for an economic and military alliance, Soviet leader Josef Stalin first hesitated but then agreed for utilitarian reasons to conclude a Friendship and Alliance Treaty that provided the Soviet Union access to railroads, warm-water ports, and important raw materials deposits in Manchuria and Xinjiang in exchange for Soviet military and economic aid. Stalin's limited support of the PRC during the Korean War (1950–1953), however, revealed the limits of the military aspects of the alliance. After the dictator's 1953 death, the end of the Korean War, and Khrushchev's ascendancy to power, the focus of the Sino-Soviet relationship gradually shifted toward assistance in economic development and improved party relations.

Khrushchev's "secret speech" of 25 February 1956, charging Stalin with arbitrary and criminal rule, undermined Mao's growing personality cult in China but strengthened his hand

People's Republic of China (PRC) leader Mao Zedong confers with leader of the Soviet Union Nikita Khrushchev during the latter's 1958 visit to Beijing. (Library of Congress)

in his relations with the Soviet leaders. After increasing his influence in the socialist world through diplomatic mediation during the 1956 Hungarian Revolution, Mao concluded that although he considered Khrushchev's criticism of Stalin unfair and imbalanced, it had nevertheless revealed the need to preempt internal dissent in China in order to prevent a crisis similar to the Hungarian Revolution. The PRC's Hundred Flowers campaign in the spring of 1957 was designed to allow party members and intellectuals to vent their pent-up frustrations in a highly controlled framework but threatened within only a few weeks to undermine the Chinese communist regime. While Beijing launched the Anti-Rightist campaign in the summer of 1957 to stamp out internal dissent, Khrushchev survived the so-called Anti-Party Incident, which the remaining Stalinists in the party leadership staged with the goal of reversing de-Stalinization. Both events proved to be crucial for the further development of the Sino-Soviet relationship, since they put the PRC and the Soviet Union on two conflicting political, ideological, and economic paths.

As modest liberalization continued in the Soviet Union in 1958, Mao, following the Anti-Rightist campaign, radicalized the domestic political discourse in the run-up to the Great Leap Forward, which was supposed to propel the PRC into full-fledged communism. These internal changes led to a more aggressive and anti-American foreign policy before and during the Second Taiwan Strait Crisis (August–September 1958). Mao's willingness, stated to Soviet Foreign Minister Andrey Gromyko in early September, to trigger a nuclear war over a series of small, disputed islands in the Taiwan Strait placed the first significant strains on the Sino-Soviet relationship.

Faced with widespread famine as a result of the misguided economic policies of the Great Leap Forward, the CCP leadership undertook internal discussions in mid-1959 about economic reforms aimed at averting further disaster. Fearing challenges to his leadership, Mao was able both to purge his opponents within the party and to relaunch an unreformed Great Leap Forward in late 1959 in order to save his vision of a communist utopia. The economic catastrophes resulting from the Great Leap Forward, however, shocked the Soviet Union. Furthermore, Mao's radical anti-American stance also clashed with Khrushchev's rapprochement policies.

The unexpected April 1960 Chinese publication of the so-called Lenin Polemics—three articles released on the occasion of Vladimir I. Lenin's ninetieth birthday that promoted ideologically radical positions diametrically opposed to Soviet viewpoints—revealed the brewing Sino-Soviet tensions to the world. After ideological clashes between the Soviet and CCP delegations during the Third Romanian Party Congress in late June 1960, the Soviet Union decided to punish the PRC by withdrawing all of its advisors from the PRC in July 1960.

Although the Great Leap Forward had caused the complete collapse of China's economy and had brought Sino-Soviet trade to a virtual standstill, Beijing used the withdrawal to blame Moscow for its economic problems. Until the mid-1960s, the PRC shifted much of its foreign trade away from the Soviet Union toward Japan and Western Europe. Because of China's pressing economic problems and the failure of Khrushchev's rapprochement with U.S. President Dwight D. Eisenhower after the May 1960 U-2 Crisis, however, both sides realized the necessity of an ideological truce, which they formally reached at the Moscow Conference of the world's communist parties in late 1960.

Shunted aside from domestic decision making because of his close association with the failed Great Leap Forward, Mao used the 1961 Soviet-Albanian conflict as a tool to rebuild his political fortunes at home. Subsequent anti-Soviet propaganda in the PRC triggered conflicts between Soviet citizens and ethnic Central Asians living in Xinjiang on the one side and the local Chinese administration on the other. The mass flight of 67,000 people to Soviet Kyrgyzstan in the late spring of 1962 caused Beijing to abrogate its consular treaty with Moscow on the basis of alleged Soviet subversive activities in western China. Mao used these developments to restore his standing in the CCP leadership and to push for more anti-Soviet policies in the second half of 1962. Khrushchev's nuclear provocation and sudden retreat under U.S. pressure during the 1962 Cuban Missile Crisis provided Mao with an unexpected opportunity to attack the Soviet leadership publicly for ideological inconsistency and political unreliability.

The United States had been intent on splitting the Sino-Soviet alliance since 1950, but only in the aftermath of the Cuban Missile Crisis was it able to use the Soviet-British-American negotiations on the Partial Test Ban Treaty (PTBT) to deepen the Sino-Soviet rift. Aware of the problems between Beijing and Moscow, Washington played on Soviet fears about China's nuclear weapons program and Khrushchev's dissatisfaction with Mao's ideological warfare. Despite the fact that the PTBT (initialed on 25 July 1963) did not infringe on China's nuclear program, the signing of the treaty by almost all countries of the world within five months isolated the PRC internationally.

The period from mid-1963 to mid-1966 witnessed the final collapse of Sino-Soviet party and military relations. Convinced that the Sino-Soviet pact had fulfilled its usefulness, Mao fanned and exploited ideological conflict and territorial disputes with his Soviet comrades for domestic purposes.

Because the launching of the Cultural Revolution required a prior break with what Mao termed Soviet "revisionists, traitors of Marxism-Leninism, and fascists," he eventually broke party relations in early 1966 by his refusal to send a delegation to the Twenty-Third Soviet Party Congress. Simultaneously, his radical ideological stances precluded the invocation of Sino-Soviet Treaty obligations in support of the Democratic Republic of Vietnam (DRV, North Vietnam) during the Vietnam War (1964–1973). By the mid-1960s, the military alliance between Beijing and Moscow factually ceased to exist, although the treaty did not officially expire until 14 February 1980. Until the rapprochement initiated by Soviet President Mikhail Gorbachev in the late 1980s, for nearly twenty-five years Sino-Soviet relations consisted only of low-level cultural relations and limited trade links.

Lorenz M. Lüthi

See also
China, People's Republic of; Cultural Revolution; Hungarian Revolution; Khrushchev, Nikita; Mao Zedong; Sino-Soviet Treaty; Stalin, Josef; Taiwan Strait Crisis, Second

References
Dittmer, Lowell. *Sino-Soviet Normalization and Its International Implications, 1945–1990.* Seattle: Washington University Press, 1992.
Hunt, Michael H. *The Genesis of Chinest Communist Foreign Policy.* New York: Columbia University Press, 1996.
Lüthi, Lorenz M. "The Sino-Soviet Split, 1956–1966." Unpublished doctoral diss., Yale University, 2003.
Robinson, Thomas W., and David Shambaugh, eds. *Chinese Foreign Policy: Theory and Practice.* Oxford, UK: Clarendon, 1998.
Westad, Odd Arne, ed. *Brothers in Arms: The Rise and the Fall of the Sino-Soviet Alliance, 1945–1953.* Washington, DC: Woodrow Wilson Center Press, 1998.

Sino-Soviet Treaty (14 February 1950)

Treaty signed between the Soviet Union and the People's Republic of China (PRC) on 14 February 1950. The Sino-Soviet Treaty of Friendship and Alliance marked the culmination of PRC Chairman Mao Zedong's two-month state visit to the Soviet Union (16 December 1949–14 February 1950). Negotiating a treaty was not the sole purpose of Mao's visit to Soviet leader Josef Stalin, for he was also in desperate need of economic aid and diplomatic support. Yet for Mao, the treaty had a substantial symbolic value, as it would replace an existing Sino-Soviet Treaty, signed in August 1945 between Stalin and Guomindang (GMD, Nationalist) leader Jiang Jieshi, Mao's enemy in the civil war that had consumed China on and off during 1927–1949.

To Mao's perplexity, Stalin initially proved reluctant to sign a treaty. Stalin prevaricated, vaguely insinuating that a new treaty would upset agreements reached with the West at the

February 1945 Yalta Conference. Only in January, when Mao had begun to complain about the lack of progress, did the Soviet leader change his mind. On 22 January 1950, Stalin told Mao that he was no longer concerned with how the Western powers might react to a new treaty, declaring "to hell with Yalta."

Chinese Foreign Minister Zhou Enlai was then summoned to Moscow to undertake the detailed negotiations. The treaty, to be in force for thirty years, committed each party to aid the other in the event of an attack by Japan "or states allied with it." Additional agreements modified rights that the Soviet Union had obtained under the 1945 treaty. The Chinese Changchun Railway was to be returned to the PRC no later than 1952, the Soviets would have no rights to Port Arthur after 1952, and the administration of Dalny was to be immediately returned to the PRC.

But Stalin made additional demands, encapsulated in secret protocols. Mao had to acknowledge the formal independence of Soviet-dominated Outer Mongolia, the Chinese were to grant rights of passage across their territory in time of war, and under another protocol, no third party would be granted economic rights in the Chinese regions of Manchuria or Xinjiang. Stalin further sought to set up joint companies with the Chinese to explore and exploit mineral deposits as well as to pressure the Chinese to deliver scarce raw metals to Russia. Mao later complained of these clauses as being semicolonial, but at the time he had little option other than to accept them. The Soviets did, however, grant $300 million in credits to the PRC and agreed to send technical experts to China to assist in economic development. Although Mao made many concessions, the treaty was undoubtedly an achievement for him, and the Soviet aid was most welcome.

Paul Wingrove

See also

China, People's Republic of; Mao Zedong; Soviet Union; Stalin, Josef; Zhou Enlai

References

Goncharev, Sergei, John Lewis, and Xue Litai. *Uncertain Partners: Stalin, Mao, and the Korean War.* Stanford, CA: Stanford University Press, 1993.

Heinzig, Dieter. *The Soviet Union and Communist China, 1945–50.* Armonk, NY: Sharpe, 2003.

Westad, Odd Arne, ed. *Brothers in Arms: The Rise and the Fall of the Sino-Soviet Alliance, 1945–1953.* Washington, DC: Woodrow Wilson Center Press, 1998.

———. *Decisive Encounters: The Chinese Civil War, 1946–1950.* Stanford, CA: Stanford University Press, 2003.

Sino-Vietnamese War (17 February–5 March 1979)

Short war between the People's Republic of China (PRC) and the Socialist Republic of Vietnam (SRV). Known to the Chinese as the Punitive War, its principal cause was the December 1978 Vietnamese invasion of Cambodia (Kampuchea). Although the Vietnamese-backed Cambodian government of Heng Samrin soon controlled the cities and received official recognition from the SRV, the Soviet Union, Laos, and most other communist states, Pol Pot's ousted Khmer Rouge conducted guerrilla warfare. The Khmer Rouge received assistance from China, which saw Cambodia as being in its sphere of influence. The United States also aided the Khmer Rouge, despite the latter's genocidal activities.

When Vietnam refused to withdraw its forces from Cambodia, the PRC threatened military force. In early January 1979, Deng Xiaoping, Chinese deputy premier and chief of staff of the People's Liberation Army (PLA), announced that China might be forced to take measures contrary to its desire for peace. The PRC leadership considered the Vietnamese invasion as part of a greater Soviet expansionist design aimed at China.

There had also been numerous border disputes between the PRC and the SRV over their common 797-mile-long border, which had been delineated by the French. Although the territory under dispute was small, border incidents had multiplied. The two states also had conflicting claims over the Paracel and Spratly Islands in the South China Sea and waters in the Gulf of Tonkin, spurred by the possibility of oil deposits there.

Another major catalyst of the war was Vietnam's treatment of its Chinese Hoa minority. Some 1.5 million Hoa lived in Vietnam, most of them in Ho Chi Minh City (Saigon). They were an important economic force, but many refused to become Vietnamese citizens. In March 1978 the SRV abolished private trading, confiscating at least 50,000 Chinese firms and forcing some 320,000 Chinese into the countryside for agricultural work as part of a plan to reduce the population of Ho Chi Minh City.

Many Chinese fled overland into China, and by early July more than 150,000 had crossed the border. Many more attempted to escape by sea. This exodus of boat people was prompted by provocateurs working for the government and by gangsters motivated by greed. Many refugees perished at sea or were preyed upon by pirates. China expressed outrage over what it considered a deliberate SRV policy, recalling its ambassador and suspending aid to the SRV. The Chinese exodus slackened off after July 1979, but it remained a serious cause of friction.

Some historians have also suggested that the war may have been in part motivated by Deng's desire to highlight the technological deficiencies of the Chinese Army in order to make a case for its modernization or that Deng sought to keep the army occupied while he consolidated power.

Militarily, the PRC appeared to enjoy tremendous advantages. Its PLA numbered 3.6 million men in 175 divisions, but

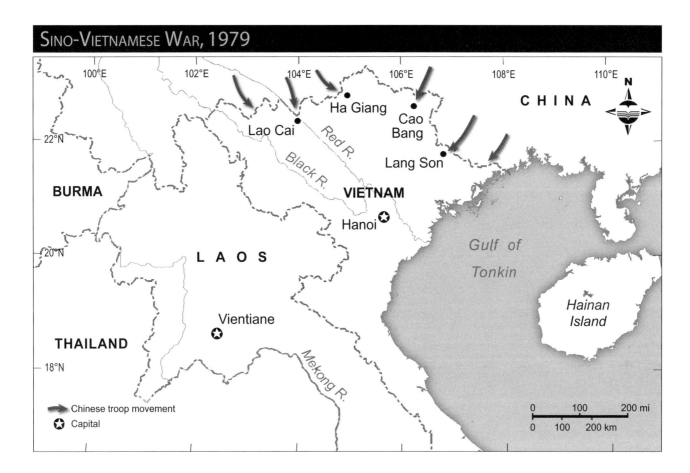

SINO-VIETNAMESE WAR, 1979

it was basically an inadequately equipped infantry force. With the exception of a brief clash with India in 1962, the PLA had not fought a major war since the Korean conflict. The navy numbered 280,000–300,000 men and 1,050 vessels, and the air force had about 400,000 men and 5,000 mostly obsolete combat aircraft. In preparation for war, Beijing evacuated its side of the border. The government also placed on maximum alert its forces on the Soviet border. Deng assumed overall command, assembling thirty-one divisions and 1,200 tanks in the Vietnam border area.

The SRV's entire military establishment numbered only about 615,000 men, centered on twenty-five infantry divisions. Its military, the People's Army of Vietnam (PAVN), was a modern, relatively well-equipped, well-disciplined force hardened by war. But six of the divisions were in Laos, and fourteen were in Cambodia. That left only five in Vietnam, four of which protected Hanoi. Some 70,000 Border Security Forces guarded the border with China, with another 50,000 lightly armed militia also available. Vietnam possessed up to 485 combat aircraft. The Vietnamese prepared for war by placing obstacles and laying minefields along the border and covering possible invasion approaches with artillery.

On 17 February 1979, 100,000 Chinese troops commanded by General Xu Shiyou attacked simultaneously at forty-three different points along the border, seeking to spread the de-

fenders and probe for weak spots. The main Chinese attacks came along the half dozen traditional invasion routes to Hanoi, with the PLA intent on securing the key mountain passes. Everywhere the Chinese encountered tenacious Vietnamese resistance.

Advancing into the SRV an average of 10 miles, the Chinese then halted for two days to regroup. Soon there were some 200,000 Chinese troops engaged. On 22 February the Chinese captured the important border cities of Lao Cai and Cao Bang. SRV Defense Minister Vo Nguyen Giap worked closely with army commander Senior General Van Tien Dung. The two men chose to wait to see where the major Chinese thrust would develop. Finally, on 3 March, Hanoi committed one division to the battle for Lang Son, which soon fell to the PLA. A second PAVN division was sent north along the coast, and Hanoi also withdrew a division from Cambodia, although it did not arrive in time to take part in the fighting. Had the war lasted longer, Hanoi would certainly have been forced to recall additional forces. Neither side employed its air force in the war.

The Chinese advanced up to 40 miles into Vietnam, but on 5 March Beijing abruptly announced that it had accomplished its goals and was withdrawing. As it departed, the PLA carried out a scorched-earth policy. The Vietnamese simply watched the Chinese depart, the withdrawal completed by 16 March.

Chinese tank crewman taken prisoner by the Vietnamese during the 1979 Sino-Vietnamese War. (Bettmann/Corbis)

Likely casualty totals in the war were 26,000 Chinese killed and 37,000 wounded, with Vietnamese casualties of 30,000 killed and 32,000 wounded. After the war, the Chinese exchanged 1,636 Vietnamese prisoners for 260 Chinese.

China obtained only a portion of its objectives. It had not destroyed any SRV regular divisions, had not forced Vietnam to withdraw from Cambodia, and had not altered Hanoi's policies toward its Chinese minority. The war also exposed glaring Chinese weaknesses, in communications especially but also in transport and weaponry.

During the war, the Soviet Union had airlifted supplies to Vietnam. Over the next year, the Soviet Union doubled its military advisors in Vietnam and its naval units in Vietnamese waters. Despite these moves, the war had exposed shortcomings in Soviet-Vietnam ties, which may have been another Chinese goal of the war.

Spencer C. Tucker

See also

Cambodia; Cambodia, Vietnamese Occupation of; China, People's Republic of; Deng Xiaoping; Pol Pot; Vietnam; Vo Nguyen Giap

References

Chen, King C. *China's War with Vietnam: Issues, Decisions, and Implications, 1979.* Stanford, CA: Hoover Institution Press, Stanford University, 1987.

Morris, Stephen J. *Why Vietnam Invaded Cambodia: Political Culture and the Causes of Wars.* Stanford, CA: Stanford University Press, 1999.

O'Ballance, Edgar. *The Wars in Vietnam, 1954–1980.* New York: Hippocrene, 1981.

Skybolt Affair and Nassau Conference

Defense procurement issue that shook relations between Great Britain and the United States. Toward the end of 1962, Great Britain faced the prospect of having no means of delivering its atomic weapons apart from its aging V-bombers. A British missile project, Blue Streak, had been recently abandoned because of technical problems. British Prime Minister Harold Macmillan thus turned to the American Skybolt missile, which

President Dwight D. Eisenhower's administration had promised to sell to Britain in March 1960. But in 1962, hearing rumors that the Americans might scrap Skybolt, Macmillan asserted that the United States was not fully supportive of other Western states possessing independent nuclear capability, preferring instead to rely on a vaguely multilateral arrangement defined by the North Atlantic Treaty Organization (NATO). The Skybolt Affair caused a great rift in Anglo-American relations, possibly the worst one in several generations.

In his memoirs published in 1973, Macmillan wrote that "it was difficult to suppress the suspicion that the failure of Skybolt might be welcomed in some American quarters as a means of forcing Britain out of the nuclear club." For the prime minister, this was a fundamental issue, as the United Kingdom's independent deterrent showed that "we were not just satellites or clients of America." More to the point, a British bomb was a hedge against the possibility that the United States might not always be relied upon to use its weapons in defense of Europe.

Against this background, Macmillan and President John F. Kennedy agreed to meet in Nassau, Bahamas, in December 1962, but in deference to French President Charles de Gaulle's sensitivities about Anglo-American collusion, Macmillan met with de Gaulle first in Rambouillet, France. In generally even-tempered talks, de Gaulle hinted that he might veto Britain's application to join the Common Market, at that time still in negotiation. He also stated that the French, like the British, sought an independent nuclear deterrent and that he too was unclear about the implications of a multilateral nuclear force.

When Kennedy and Macmillan met on 19 December 1962, the prime minister immediately established Britain's credentials by enlarging on the crucial British scientific contribution in developing nuclear weapons and subsequent Anglo-American cooperation. President Eisenhower, he claimed, had promised him Skybolt as well as the submarine-launched Polaris missile "if necessary." Thus, Macmillan made it clear that if the Skybolt missile were now unavailable, he wanted the Polaris. Kennedy confirmed that Skybolt was indeed to be abandoned but suggested the sharing of development costs of a new missile, a quixotic offer that Macmillan declined. But Kennedy resisted offering Polaris to the British, unconvincingly arguing that to do so would alienate de Gaulle.

Macmillan was distressed by Kennedy's seeming disingenuousness and the importance that the Americans attached to their plan for the NATO-led multilateral control of nuclear weapons. He fought fiercely for Polaris but, in the process, had to concede something to the American demand for multilateralism, offering to make British nuclear forces available to NATO except where supreme national interests were involved. With that concession, Kennedy agreed at the Nassau Conference to provide the Polaris missile.

Paul Wingrove

See also
Kennedy, John Fitzgerald; Macmillan, Maurice Harold; Missiles, Polaris; North Atlantic Treaty Organization, Origins and Formation of
References
Ashton, Nigel J. *Kennedy, Macmillan and the Cold War: The Irony of Interdependence.* New York: Palgrave Macmillan, 2002.
Horne, Alistair. *Macmillan, 1957–1986.* London: Macmillan, 1989.
Macmillan, Harold. *At the End of the Day, 1961–1963.* London: Macmillan, 1973.
Neustadt, Richard E. *Report to JFK: The Skybolt Crisis in Perspective.* Ithaca, NY: Cornell University Press, 1999.

Slánský, Rudolf Salzmann (1901–1952)

Czechoslovak communist politician, general-secretary of the Communist Party of Czechoslovakia (CPCz) during 1946–1951, and deputy prime minister during 1948–1951. Rudolf Slánský was born into a Jewish family in Nezvěstice, Bohemia, on 31 July 1901. He was a founding member of the CPCz in 1921, becoming editor of its daily newspaper *Rudé právo* in 1924. Later, he became the Ostrava regional party secretary and joined the Central Committee of the CPCz. He was elected to the National Assembly in 1935.

Following the 1938 Munich Agreement, Slánský moved to the Soviet Union, where he worked with the exiled CPCz in Moscow, becoming a close friend of Czechoslovak leader Klement Gottwald. Slánský returned to occupied Czechoslovakia in 1944 and took part as a partisan in that year's unsuccessful Slovak National Uprising.

After the war, Slánský returned to his seat in the Czechoslovak National Assembly and became the CPCz general secretary in 1946. He played an instrumental role in the CPCz's February 1948 coup, after which he became deputy prime minister. He then helped introduce Stalinism in Czechoslovakia.

In 1951 the Czechoslovak government began a search for scapegoat communist leaders in order to stage Stalinist-style purges and show trials, and Slánský was targeted because of his Jewish background. In September 1951 he was removed as CPCz general secretary and stripped of the deputy premiership. Two months later he was arrested on charges of being a Zionist, spying for the West, and conspiring to assassinate President Gottwald.

After enduring psychological and physical torture, Slánský was placed on trial. His show trial, along with those of thirteen other former high-ranking CPCz members, took place in November 1952. Eleven of the defendants were found guilty and sentenced to death. Slánský was hanged in Prague on 3 December 1952. He received posthumous rehabilitation in 1963, and his party membership was restored in 1968.

Gregory C. Ference

See also
Czechoslovakia; Gottwald, Klement; Slánský Trial
References
Kaplan, Karel. *Report on the Murder of the General Secretary.*
    Translated by Karel Kovanda. Columbus: Ohio State University
    Press, 1990.
London, Artur. *On Trial.* Translated by Alastair Hamilton. London:
    Macdonald, 1970.
Slánská, Josefa. *Report on My Husband.* Translated by Edith
    Pargeter. New York: Atheneum, 1969.

Slánský Trial (1952)

Infamous 1952 Czech show trial. On 6 September 1951, Rudolf Slánský was dismissed from his post as general secretary of the Communist Party of Czechoslovakia (CPCz). At the time of his dismissal, he was second only to President Klement Gottwald and had introduced Stalinist policies to postwar Czechoslovakia. On 24 November, agents of the Státni Tajna Bezpecnostni (STB), Czechoslovak secret police, arrested Slánský. Despite the fact that he had been a lifelong communist and an ardent follower of the orthodox party line, he was charged with high treason, espionage, conspiring to kill Gottwald, and Zionism.

Slánský was apparently targeted because of an intercepted communication from OKAPI, the code name for an intelligence organization of Czechoslovak émigrés established in 1948 by the United States in Bensheim, Germany. One of its analysts noticed that Moscow had failed to mark Slánský's fiftieth birthday with the obligatory congratulatory telegram. This led operatives at OKAPI to conclude that Slánský could be persuaded to defect. On 8 November 1951, an OKAPI letter to Slánský offering him political asylum in the United States was intercepted by the STB and sent to Moscow.

Soviet leader Josef Stalin had expressed doubts about Slánský since July 1951. Now Stalin had "evidence" that the former general secretary was in communication with U.S. intelligence. With the OKAPI letter in hand, Stalin demanded Slánský's arrest.

By January 1952, physical torture and psychological duress led Slánský to admit his guilt to all the trumped-up charges against him. In his November 1952 show trial, the prosecutor depicted him as the head of an antistate conspiracy. Slánský and his thirteen codefendants followed the script prepared by the STB and its Soviet advisors and confessed to crimes they had never committed. All were found guilty. Slánský and ten others were summarily sentenced to death on 27 November 1953 and were executed in Prague on 3 December 1952. When the noose was placed around his neck, Slánský is reported to have said, "Thank you. I'm getting what I deserve."

The show trial in Prague helped to advance Stalin's geopolitical aims in two ways. First, all but three of the defendants were Jewish and were ostentatiously identified by the prosecution as Zionists. Their trial enabled Stalin to signal a reorientation of Soviet Middle Eastern policy in favor of Israel's Arab rivals. Second, the trial took place in the midst of the Soviet-Yugoslav split. The message to Central and East European governments was that if Slánský, a loyal Stalinist, was not safe, then no one was. Stalin would accept only strict obedience. The practice of modifying Soviet policies to take into account specific conditions in each satellite country would not be tolerated.

The Slánský trial seriously damaged the cause of communist ideology. Before it, many European intellectuals associated communism with optimism and hope. Slánský's bizarre confession, delivered in the monotonous and tired voice of a tortured man, showed communism's real face.

Igor Lukes

See also
Czechoslovakia; Gottwald, Klement; Slánský, Rudolf Salzmann;
    Soviet-Yugoslav Split
References
Kaplan, Karel. *Report on the Murder of the General Secretary.*
    Translated by Karel Kovanda. Columbus: Ohio State University
    Press, 1990.
Loebl, Arthur. *Sentenced and Tried: The Stalinist Purges in
    Czechoslovakia.* London: Elek Books, 1969.
Lukes, Igor. "The Rudolf Slánský Affair: New Evidence." *Slavic
    Review* 58(1) (1999): 160–187.

Slessor, Sir John Cotesworth (1897–1979)

Marshal of the British Royal Air Force (RAF) and noted military theorist. Born in Rahniket, India, on 3 June 1897, John Slessor joined the Royal Flying Corps in 1915 during World War I and saw action in the defense of London and in France, Egypt, and Sudan. Between the wars he served in a range of posts, including instructor, duty, and staff positions in the Air Ministry. He spoke and wrote about airpower extensively, authoring a book titled *Air Power and Armies* in 1936. He was a key RAF planner just before and during the early years of World War II. He was assigned to a series of senior command positions in Bomber Command, Coastal Command, and the Mediterranean and Middle East forces, with promotions to air commodore in September 1939, air vice marshal in January 1941, and air marshal in February 1943. He was the lead planner for the postwar RAF force structure, earning promotion to air chief marshal in 1946.

Slessor served as chief of the Air Staff from January 1950 to January 1953, when he retired from active duty. He was promoted to marshal of the RAF in June 1950. He ardently advocated a nuclear-armed, long-range bomber force. After retirement in 1953, he became a commentator on strategic issues and published two books on defense policy, *Strategy for the West* and *The Great Deterrent,* as well as an autobiography. He advocated a force structure that included adequate conventional forces but relied on thermonuclear weapons for strategic deterrence against the Soviet Union and tactical nuclear weapons for enhanced firepower in smaller conflicts and theater operations. His concepts were similar to the New Look defense posture of President Dwight D. Eisenhower. Slessor died in Wroughton, England, on 12 July 1979.

Jerome V. Martin

See also

New Look Defense Policy; Royal Air Force

References

Probert, Henry. *High Commanders of the Royal Air Force.* London: HMSO, 1991.

Slessor, Sir John Cotesworth. *Central Blue: The Autobiography of Sir John Slessor, Marshal of the RAF.* New York: Praeger, 1957.

———. *The Great Deterrent.* New York: Praeger, 1957.

———. *Strategy for the West.* New York: William Morrow, 1954.

Small Arms

The term "small arms" generally refers to those types of handheld firearms that an individual can carry and operate by oneself. The introduction of assault rifles—independently developed in both the Eastern and the Western blocs—came to symbolize the history of military firearms in the Cold War era. Assault rifles, pioneered by the German Kurz MP 44 (Sturmgewehr 44) during World War II, are lightweight, short-barreled military rifles that fire smaller-sized rifle cartridges at either a fully automatic or semiautomatic setting.

The Soviets were the first to successfully develop assault rifles for practical use. Emphasizing mass production and durability, Mikhail Kalashnikov designed what would become the most common rifle in military history, the AK-47 (Avtomat Kalashnikova of 1947.) Through the 1950s and 1960s, the Soviet Union and its satellite countries mass-produced the AK-47 and its derivatives. As the legacy of their military cooperation during the Cold War and as the result of the tremendous trade of Soviet weapons after the collapse of European communism in the late 1980s, today the AK-47 type assault rifle remains in common use throughout Africa and the Middle East.

Pressured by Moscow during the Cold War, most Eastern bloc armed forces had to adopt the standard weapons of the Soviet Union. This allowed the Warsaw Pact countries to enjoy among themselves the benefits of standardized and interchangeable weapons, military equipment, and training. The Warsaw Pact forces uniformly used the 7.62mm × 39 intermediate-powered round (M 43) developed by the Soviet Union along with the AK-47. The Eastern bloc countries also manufactured variations of the AK-47 rifle.

To produce a lighter rifle and to increase productivity, the Soviets developed the AKM rifle in 1957, an improved version of the AK-47. Warsaw Pact nations such as the German Democratic Republic (GDR, East Germany), Hungary, and Romania soon adopted the new version. However, the People's Republic of China (PRC), a large-scale manufacturer of the AK-47 rifle, did not switch to the new Soviet weapon, perhaps an early sign of the coming Sino-Soviet split.

Meanwhile, the Western bloc countries under the North Atlantic Treaty Organization (NATO) also standardized their assault rifles to use the 7.62mm × 51 NATO cartridge in 1954. Later, some fifty noncommunist countries outside NATO adopted the 7.62mm NATO cartridge as well. Unlike the Eastern bloc countries, however, each Western bloc country designed its own assault rifles using the 7.62mm NATO cartridge. Among them, the U.S. M-14 rifle, the Belgian Fusil Automatique Léger (FAL), the Spanish CETME, and the West German Gewehr 3 A3 are well known.

Wishing to increase accuracy at full-automatic mode, in 1955 the United States began designing an improved version of the M-14. This new assault rifle, the AR-15 (Armalite) fired the .223 Remington 5.56mm × 45 cartridge, a smaller caliber than the 7.62mm NATO round. The AR-15 became a standard weapon for U.S. armed forces as the M-16 rifle.

During the Vietnam War the M-16 did not function well, especially in jungle environments. In response, the Americans introduced the revised M-16A1 rifle. A newer version, the M-16A2 rifle, debuted in the 1980s and remains the standard U.S. weapon. With the successive conversions to newer versions, the United States periodically sold its old M-16 rifles to other countries in the Middle East, Africa, Latin America, and Asia. Consequently, the M-16 rifle, as with the AK-47, became ubiquitous in various armed conflicts around the world. Indeed, the AK-47 and the M-16 epitomized the split between East and West that divided the world during the Cold War.

During the 1960s and 1970s, many Western bloc countries adhered to the 7.62mm NATO cartridge and produced high-quality military rifles for the cartridge. It took time for them to recognize the superiority of smaller-caliber assault rifles such as the M-16A1, which can be loaded with more ammunition. In 1980, NATO adopted the .223 Remington cartridge as the 5.56mm NATO. Some Western bloc countries began experimenting on designs of smaller-caliber military rifles in the mid-1970s. Among those, the bull-pup type rifles such as the British Lee Enfield L-70 automatic rifle, the Austrian Steyr AUG, and the French MAS 5.56 automatic rifle featured

A U.S. Air Force master sergeant fires his M-16 rifle during a training exercise at Hickam Air Force Base, Hawaii, in October 1980. (U.S. Department of Defense)

a shorter body without shortening the barrel by fitting the magazine behind the trigger.

The Eastern bloc also studied smaller-caliber assault rifles. The Soviet Union developed the AK-74 rifle that can fire the 5.54mm × 39 cartridge. After officially adopting the AK-74 in the 1970s, the Soviet Union displayed the power of the new assault rifles in its invasion of Afghanistan (1979–1989).

As for the development of military pistols during the Cold War, both the Eastern and Western blocs adopted automatic pistols. The Western bloc possessed the .45 ACP (Automatic Colt Pistol) represented by the U.S. M1911A1 (Colt Government Model Automatic Pistol) and various types of the 9mm Parabellum among West European countries. Among Eastern bloc countries, the Soviet TT33 (Tokarev) with the 7.62mm caliber cartridge and the PM (Makarov) with the 9mm caliber cartridge became the principal military pistols. Most communist nations imported these pistols from the Soviet Union or manufactured them under a Soviet licensing system.

Asakaw Michio

See also
Machine Guns
References
Diagram Groups, The. *Weapons.* New York: St. Martin's, 1990.

Hogg, Ian V., and John Walker. *Small Arms: Pistols and Rifles.* Greenhill, PA: Stackpole, 2003.
Huon, Jean. *Military Rifle and Machine Gun Cartridges.* Alexandria, VA: Ironside International, 1986.
Kinard, Jeff. *Pistols: An Illustrated History of the Impact.* Weapons and Warfare Series. Edited by Spencer C. Tucker. Santa Barbara, CA: ABC-CLIO, 2003.
Westwood, David. *Rifles: An Illustrated History of the Impact.* Weapons and Warfare Series. Edited by Spencer C. Tucker. Santa Barbara, CA: ABC-CLIO, 2003.

Smith, Ian Douglas (1919–)

Premier of the British colony of Southern Rhodesia during April 1964–November 1965 and prime minister of Rhodesia (present-day Zimbabwe) during 1965–1979. Born on 8 April 1919 in Selukwe (now Shurugwi), Ian Smith was educated in Gwelo before study at South Africa's Rhodes University.

Smith interrupted his studies to serve with the Royal Air Force (RAF) in World War II. He returned home to complete his degree in 1947 and farm in Selukwe. He became active in politics, first in the Liberal Party, then in the United Federal Party. In 1962, he cofounded the prosettler Rhodesian Front

(RF) that won a slim parliamentary majority that same year. Two years later, in April 1964, Smith was appointed leader of the RF, replacing Winston Field as premier of Southern Rhodesia. When the white settler colony declared independence from Britain on 11 November 1965, Smith became prime minister of Rhodesia.

Smith adamantly opposed the transfer of political control to Rhodesia's black majority. Opponents of minority rule were labeled as communists and, after the outbreak of civil war in 1966, were considered terrorists. Rhodesia was subjected to international condemnation and sanctions, although neighboring South Africa did not support such actions.

In 1974, after spirited discussions with U.S. Secretary of State Henry Kissinger and under pressure from South African Prime Minister John Vorster, Smith reluctantly accepted that the end of minority rule was inevitable. In 1979, under an internal agreement, multiracial elections were held, which brought Bishop Abel Muzorewa to power as the state's first black prime minister. Smith remained in the new multiracial cabinet.

Nevertheless, the civil war in the country continued, during which Rhodesian forces, with the assistance of dissident Mozambicans, breached the country's border. This precipitated great internal destabilization. Intervention by the British government, under the leadership of Foreign Secretary Lord Peter Carrington, led to the Lancaster House Conference, which finally ended the Rhodesian impasse in December 1979.

New elections in 1980 brought Rhodesia full independence, ending its long international isolation. Robert Mugabe was elected the country's first president, and Smith became leader of the opposition, although his political base had been badly eroded. In 1982, Smith retired to his farm in Shurugwi, ending a political career of almost thirty years. In his retirement, he remained an outspoken critic of Zimbabwe's government.

Peter Vale

See also
Africa; Frontline States; Kaunda, Kenneth David; Lusaka Agreement (1994); Lusaka Agreement (1999); Mozambique; Mozambique Civil War; Mugabe, Robert Gabriel; Namibia; Nkomo, Joshua; South Africa; United Kingdom; Verwoerd, Hendrik Frensch; Vorster, Balthazar Johannes; Zimbabwe

References
Berlyn, Phillippa. *The Quiet Man: A Biography of Ian Douglas Smith, I.D. Prime Minister of Rhodesia.* Salisbury, Rhodesia: M. O. Collins, 1978.
Carrington, Peter. *Reflect on Things Past: The Memoirs of Lord Carrington.* London: Collins, 1988.
Mungazi, Dickson A. *The Last Defenders of the Laager: Ian D. Smith and F. W. De Klerk.* Westport, CT: Praeger, 1998.
Smith, Ian. *Bitter Harvest.* London: Blake, 2001.
———. *The Great Betrayal: The Memoirs of Ian Douglas Smith.* London: Blake, 1997.

Smith, Walter Bedell (1895–1961)

U.S. Army general, director of the Central Intelligence Agency (CIA) during 1950–1953, and undersecretary of state during 1953–1954. Born in Indianapolis, Indiana, on 5 October 1895, Walter Bedell Smith was educated at Manual Training High School in Indianapolis and briefly attended Butler University. He decided on a military career and in 1910 enlisted as a private in the Indiana National Guard. In the interwar years Smith, who had risen to the rank of major in 1939, acquired the organizational, administrative, and planning skills essential to managing modern warfare. He served with the Bureau of Military Intelligence, the Bureau of the Budget, and the Federal Liquidation Board and had several assignments either studying or instructing at the Infantry School at Fort Benning, Georgia; the Command and General Staff School at Fort Leavenworth, Kansas; and the Army War College.

General George C. Marshall, appointed U.S. Army chief of staff in 1939, noted Smith's abilities and in October 1939 summoned him to Washington to assist in swiftly building up the military from its existing weakness to full wartime strength and capability. In September 1942 Smith was assigned to Dwight D. Eisenhower, commander of the European theater of war, as chief of staff, where he remained until the end of 1945, winning a stellar reputation as one of the finest army chiefs of staff.

Smith returned to Washington in January 1946 as chief of the Operations and Planning Division of the Joint Chiefs of Staff (JCS), but two months later President Harry S. Truman appointed him ambassador to the Soviet Union, where he remained until 1949. Smith's experiences in this post, as the Cold War steadily and rapidly intensified, convinced him that the United States must take a firm line to contain Soviet expansion but also that the Soviets did not deliberately seek war and would back down when confronted by American strength.

In late June 1950 Truman named Smith, then commanding the First Army, director of the CIA. He was advanced to full general in July 1951. The president hoped that Smith would improve leadership and organization within the agency, then attracting heavy criticism for its failure to predict the Democratic People's Republic of Korea (DPRK, North Korea) invasion of the Republic of Korea (ROK, South Korea). Smith's reputation as an outstanding bureaucrat and a staunch anticommunist helped to deflect further criticism from the CIA, which he centralized and coordinated, persuading Douglas MacArthur not only to allow the agency to operate in Korea but to utilize its intelligence. Under Smith, the CIA nonetheless wrongly predicted that China would not intervene in the Korean conflict and also failed to anticipate assorted coups

U.S. Army General Walter B. Smith performed important service as a staff officer during World War II. During the postwar period, he served capably as ambassador to the Soviet Union, the second director of the Central Intelligence Agency (CIA), and undersecretary of state. (Library of Congress)

in Latin America. Smith tightened the flow of intelligence, restricting the overall picture to a few high-ranking officers, and instituted a training program to develop a group of career intelligence officers.

As undersecretary of state during 1953–1954 in the Eisenhower administration, Smith provided a degree of continuity. After his retirement in 1954 an embittered Smith, who never received either the fifth star or appointment as chief of staff of the army that he believed he deserved, turned to business, amassing an estate valued at almost $2.5 million. In 1958 John Foster Dulles appointed Smith, a staunch and vocal supporter of nuclear expansion, as his special advisor on disarmament. Smith died in Washington, D.C., on 9 August 1961.

Priscilla Roberts

See also
Central Intelligence Agency; Containment Policy; Dulles, John Foster; Eisenhower, Dwight David; Korean War; MacArthur, Douglas; Marshall, George Catlett; Truman, Harry S.; United States Army

References
Crosswell, D. K. R. *The Chief of Staff: The Military Career of General Walter Bedell Smith.* New York: Greenwood, 1991.
Mayers, David. *The Ambassadors and America's Soviet Policy.* New York: Oxford University Press, 1995.
Montague, Ludwell Lee. *General Walter Bedell Smith As Director of Central Intelligence, October 1950–February 1953.* University Park: Pennsylvania State University Press, 1992.
Smith, Walter Bedell. *My Three Years in Moscow.* Philadelphia: Lippincott, 1949.

Smuts, Jan Christian (1870–1950)

South African military leader, international statesman, and prime minister (1919–1924, 1939–1948). Born in Bovenplaats, Cape Colony (now South Africa), on 24 May 1870, Jan Smuts was educated at Christ's College, Cambridge University, where he read law. He earned his degree in 1895 and then built a successful law practice in Johannesburg. Although born a British subject, he was extremely proud of his Boer ancestry and was an effective guerrilla leader in the Boer War (1899–1902). In 1910, he and his close friend Louis Botha worked together to create the Union of South Africa. Smuts then entered politics in Botha's cabinet, serving in several ministerial positions.

At the beginning of World War I, Smuts was serving as defense minister under Prime Minister Botha. Smuts commanded the offensive that took control of German Southwest Africa (the future Namibia) from the Germans. Made a British Army general, Smuts then took charge of British operations in East Africa. Before the end of the war, he joined the British Imperial War Cabinet as minister of air and helped to organize the Royal Air Force, the world's first independent air force. Smuts represented South Africa during the 1919 Paris Peace Conference, where he supported the League of Nations and helped develop the mandate system.

During 1919–1924 and again in 1939–1948, Smuts served as South Africa's prime minister. He returned to power in September 1939 as an advocate of war with Germany. He was also minister of defense, and from June 1940 he commanded South African armed forces in the war. Made an honorary field marshal in the British Army in 1941, he was throughout the war one of British Prime Minister Winston Churchill's closest advisors.

Smuts believed that cooperation was the key to international stability and peace. After World War II, he took a leading role in the creation of the United Nations (UN) and was a strong supporter of South African cooperation with the British. Unfortunately, Smuts's visions of cooperation were never fully realized. At the time of his death in 1950, the Cold War was well established, and the world was no closer to genuine peace. Smuts died in Irene (near Pretoria), South Africa, on 11 September 1950.

Maurice Williams and Takaia Larsen

See also
Paris Peace Conference and Treaties; South Africa; United Nations
References
Hancock, W. K. *Smuts*. 2 vols. Cambridge: Cambridge University Press, 1962, 1968.
Ingham, Kenneth. *Jan Christian Smuts: The Conscience of a South African*. New York: St. Martin's, 1986.
Smuts, J. C. *Jan Christian Smuts*. London: Cassell, 1952.
Williams, Basil A. F. *Botha, Smuts and South Africa*. New York: Collier, 1962.

Snow, Edgar Parks (1905–1972)

American journalist, author, and leading Western authority on the Chinese communist movement and the Chinese Civil War. Born in Kansas City, Missouri, on 19 July 1905, Edgar Snow graduated from the University of Missouri in 1926 and attended the Columbia School of Journalism for a year before joining the staff of the *Kansas City Star* in 1927. In 1928 he went to work for *The New York Sun* and eventually journeyed to China, where he reported until 1941 on politics and war in East Asia for various U.S. publications, including the widely read *Saturday Evening Post*.

In 1936, Snow crossed through Nationalist Chinese lines to enter Shaanxi (Shensi) Province, the communist base of operations. He spent several months there reporting on the activities and political plans of communist leaders Mao Zedong and Zhou Enlai. Snow sent out to the Western world the only reliable reports on the Chinese communist movement. Contrary to Guomindang (GMD, Nationalist) propaganda that characterized the communists as thugs and bandits, Snow portrayed Mao and his lieutenants as thoughtful, committed revolutionaries who championed wide-ranging political and social reforms. Snow's seminal work *Red Star over China* (1937) was the best account of the early communist struggle in China. In 1941, he left China to serve as a war correspondent in India and the Soviet Union.

Following the war, Snow returned to the United States. But with the October 1949 communist victory in China and the Red Scare that soon followed, Senator Joseph R. McCarthy and his allies condemned Snow for his sympathetic reporting of Mao's movement and accused him of being a communist agent. Blacklisted in many journalistic circles, Snow found it increasingly difficult to make a living in the United States.

In 1959 Snow and his family moved to Switzerland. His purge proved similar to that of numerous State Department China specialists, including John Paton Davies Jr. and John Stewart Service. Such men faced the wrath of the anti-

communist China Lobby in Congress and the media. According to Secretary of Defense Robert McNamara, the absence of these men's nuanced insights on China and East Asia handicapped U.S. intelligence assessments in the early years of the Vietnam War.

In 1960, Snow returned to China to analyze the changes wrought by more than a decade of communist rule. He interviewed Mao and Zhou and published *The Other Side of the River: Red China Today* in 1962. In 1970 Snow traveled to China for the final time as both a journalist and an unofficial diplomat for President Richard Nixon's administration, exploring the possibilities of a thaw in U.S.-China relations. Snow died on 15 February 1972 in Eysins, Switzerland.

Michael E. Donoghue

See also
Chinese Civil War; Mao Zedong; McCarthyism; Zhou Enlai
References
Farnsworth, Robert M. *From Vagabond to Journalist: Edgar Snow in Asia, 1928–1941*. Columbia: University of Missouri Press, 1996.
Hamilton, John Maxwell. *Edgar Snow: A Biography*. Bloomington: Indiana State University Press, 1988.
Thomas, S. Bernard. *Season of High Adventure: Edgar Snow in China*. Berkeley: University of California Press, 1996.

Soares, Mário (1924–)

Portuguese socialist politician, prime minister (1976–1978, 1983–1985), and president (1986–1996). Born on 12 July 1924 in Lisbon, Mário Alberto Nobre Lópes Soares graduated with a degree in history, philosophy, and law from the University of Lisbon in 1957. While there, he joined the Portuguese Communist Party. He was arrested multiple times during the era of the Estado Novo (New State), the conservative, clerical fascist regime under António de Oliveira Salazar, who ruled Portugal during 1932–1968. In 1951 Soares quit the Communist Party and went back to college to study law. By the 1960s he had aligned himself with the socialists and in April 1964, together with Francisco Ramos da Costa and Manuel Tito de Morais, created the Acção Socialista Portuguesa (Portuguese Socialist Action).

In March 1968, Soares was again arrested and banished for eight months to the island of São Tomé. He returned to Portugal but by 1970 had been banished again, this time to Italy, although he eventually settled in France. He returned to Portugal after the 25 April 1974 Carnation Revolution that ousted Marcelo Caetano.

In the aftermath of the coup, Soares was appointed minister for overseas negotiations and helped arrange the independence of Mozambique. However, the coalition government of the Movement of the Armed Forces (MFA), coupled with the growing strength of the Portuguese Communist Party, caused Soares to question the direction of the revolution. He was instrumental in the resignation of Premier Vasco dos Santos Gonçalves. Elections were held in April 1976, and the socialists won sufficient seats for Soares to become premier. In July 1976, Soares was sworn in as the first premier under the new Portuguese constitution.

Soares and the socialists were unable to form a strong majority on the Left because of a rift with the communists. In 1997 he applied for Portugal to join the European Economic Community (EEC). He resigned in late 1978. Reelected in 1983, he served until 1985, when he lost to the Social Democrats and Aníbal Cavaco Silva.

Soares subsequently ran for president in 1986, winning by a narrow margin, but he won reelection in 1991 with a clear majority. He did not seek reelection in 1996, but in 1999 he headed the socialist ticket in elections to the European Parliament, where he served until the 2004 elections.

David H. Richards

See also
Portugal
References
Janitschek, Hans. *Mario Soares: Portrait of a Hero.* New York: St. Martin's, 1986.
Soares, Mário. *Portugal's Struggle for Liberty.* London: Allen and Unwin, 1975.

Sokolovsky, Vasily Danilovich (1897–1968)

Soviet general and defense official. Born the son of peasants in the village of Kozliki, near Grodna (then Poland, now Belarus), on 9 July 1897, Vasily Sokolovsky in 1918 joined the Red Army. As a participant in the Russian Civil War, he commanded a company, a regiment, a brigade, and finally the 32nd Rifle Division. He graduated from the Red Army Staff Academy in 1921 and then served in Central Asia in the Operations Directorate of the General Staff. He was then chief of staff first of a division and then a corps. Later he was chief of staff of first the Urals and then the Volga Military Districts.

Promoted to major general in May 1938 and to lieutenant general in June 1940, Sokolovsky became deputy chief of the General Staff in February 1941. In midsummer he was chief of staff of the Western Front, with responsibility for the defense of Moscow. Promoted to colonel general in June 1942, he took command of the Western Front in early 1943. In August 1943 he was promoted to general of the army. From April 1944 he was chief of staff of the First Ukrainian Front. In the last months of the war he was deputy commander of the First Belorussian Front.

After the war, Sokolovsky became deputy commander of Soviet occupation forces in Germany and governor of the So-

viet zone of Berlin. During 1946–1949 he commanded Soviet occupation forces in Germany, a period that coincided with the Berlin Blockade of 1948–1949. Indeed, it was Sokolovsky who suggested that American, British, and French soldiers in the western sectors of Berlin were guests of the Soviets rather than fellow occupiers.

Returning to the Soviet Union in 1949, Sokolovsky continued to play a major role in the Soviet military. During 1949–1960 he was first deputy minister of defense and then chief of the General Staff (1952–1960). At the end of his military career, he served as inspector general for the Ministry of Defense and oversaw the writing of *Voennaia strategiia* (Military Strategy), a 1962 planning manual that shaped Soviet thinking for most of the remainder of the Cold War. Sokolovsky died in Moscow on 10 May 1968.

Roger Chapman and Spencer C. Tucker

See also
Berlin Blockade and Airlift; Soviet Union, Army; Soviet Union, Navy
References
Parrish, Thomas. *Berlin in the Balance.* Reading, MA: Perseus, 1998.
Richie, Alexandra. *Faust's Metropolis: A History of Berlin.* New York: Carroll and Graf, 1998.
Seaton, Albert, and Joan Seaton. *The Soviet Army: 1918 to the Present.* New York: New American Library, 1987.
Sokolovsky, Vasily. *Military Strategy: Soviet Doctrine and Concepts.* New York: Praeger, 1963.

Solidarity Movement

Polish independent labor union established in September 1980, credited with bringing democracy to Poland and helping to end the Cold War. On 1 July 1980, the Polish government, headed by Prime Minister Edward Babiuch and communist First Secretary Edward Gierek, announced across-the-board price increases. Immediately, factory workers throughout Poland staged protest strikes. These proliferated and soon reached the Baltic coast, affecting Poland's largest port cities of Gdańsk and Gdynia.

Workers at the Lenin Shipyards in Gdańsk went on strike at the beginning of August. The local strike committee, led by electrician Lech Wałęsa, was soon transformed into the Inter-Factory Strike Committee. It was unprecedented in both size and form, as it claimed to represent not just the shipyard workers but all Polish workers. The Strike Committee put forth a list of twenty-one demands to be met by the Polish Communist Party. These demands included the right to form independent labor unions, the right to strike, freedom of speech and press, the release of political prisoners, and other social and economic demands. On 31 August 1980, Wałęsa's committee signed an agreement in Gdańsk with Deputy Prime Minister Mieczysław Jagielski by which the government agreed

During a 1987 visit to Poland by Pope John Paul II, demonstrators march down a street carrying banners reading "Solidarność" (Solidarity), the name of the first Polish trade union, formed despite communist government opposition. (Peter Turnley/Corbis)

to the workers' demands, including the formation of independent trade unions. Similar agreements were signed in Szczecin and Jastrzębie. Several days later, Gierek resigned his post.

As soon as the agreements were signed, workers began to organize themselves into union groups. Inter-Factory Strike Committees became Inter-Factory Founding Committees. Until this point, Polish labor unions had been an extension of the Communist Party and had no true independence.

On 17 September 1980, the Founding Committees decided to organize one umbrella labor union known as Solidarność (Solidarity). By this time, union membership was close to 4 million people, and the decision to form one central union was deeply troubling to Polish authorities. On 10 November 1980, following a series of difficult negotiations, Solidarity was officially registered as a union.

Moscow and Warsaw eyed Solidarity with great trepidation. The movement was large, and Soviet leaders especially viewed its antisocialist elements as particularly troubling. They also feared that it would set a precedent that might be followed in other communist bloc nations. Over the next thirteen months, an uneasy relationship existed between the Communist Party and Solidarity. Solidarity was gradually realizing its demands through strikes or the threat of strikes.

These demands were in most cases limited to working conditions, wages, and workers' rights. By the end of 1981, nearly 10 million members, some 80 percent of the national workforce, had joined the movement.

Polish authorities never fully accepted the legitimacy of Solidarity. In fact, they had resorted to stalling tactics and harassment of union activists in the hope of weakening the movement. Meanwhile, the authorities were preparing plans to crush Solidarity, by military means if necessary. Tensions between Solidarity and the government peaked during the Solidarity Congress in September–October 1981. Solidarity's 8 September 1981 "Message to the Working People of Eastern Europe," which urged workers in other communist bloc nations to unite, brought applause among union members and near panic on the part of Polish and Soviet authorities. By then, it was clear that Solidarity had become a grave threat to communist rule. Moscow threatened Polish leaders with armed intervention unless Solidarity was shut down. For a time, the real threat of a Soviet military invasion loomed.

Then, on 13 December 1981, the Polish government, now headed by General Wojciech Jaruzelski, imposed martial law and declared Solidarity illegal. Almost 10,000 Solidarity members were detained. Wałęsa was among those arrested.

Pope John Paul II and the Catholic Church publicly supported the struggles of Solidarity and its imprisoned principals while clandestinely sending messages of encouragement to Wałęsa and others. Wałęsa credited the eventual triumph of Solidarity to the pope's intercession.

In April 1982, Solidarity activists who had avoided arrest formed the Solidarity Temporary Coordinating Committee to stage underground union activity. Four years later, in September 1986, Wałęsa initiated an open, albeit illegal, Solidarity Committee. The government refused to recognize this committee, and its members were closely watched by the secret police. Nevertheless, Wałęsa, who had won the 1983 Nobel Peace Prize, was now a prominent international figure. Silencing him was therefore exceedingly difficult for Polish authorities.

In August 1988, Polish authorities, together with the Catholic Church and the still-illegal Solidarity movement, commenced negotiations concerning the future of Poland. During February–April 1989, a roundtable brought together communists, opposition leaders, Solidarity members, and Catholic Church representatives. The talks brought an end to the government prohibition of Solidarity. In the elections that followed in June 1989, in which 35 percent of the seats were to be decided by election, Solidarity candidates won 161 of 161 seats in the Sejm and 99 of 100 in the Senate. In August 1989, Tadeusz Mazowiecki, one of Solidarity's founders, formed the first noncommunist post–World War II Polish government. After 1989, Solidarity became a traditional political labor party.

Jakub Basista

See also
Gierek, Edward; Jaruzelski, Wojciech; John Paul II, Pope; Poland; Wałęsa, Lech

References
Ash, Timothy Garton. *The Polish Revolution: Solidarity 1980–1982.* London: Jonathan Cape, 1983.
Biskupski, M. B. *The History of Poland.* Westport, CT: Greenwood, 2000.
Goodwyn, Lawrence. *Breaking the Barrier: The Rise of Solidarity in Poland.* New York: Oxford University Press, 1991.
Ost, David. *Solidarity and the Process of Anti-Politics: Opposition and Reform in Poland since 1968.* Philadelphia: Temple University Press, 1990.

Solzhenitsyn, Aleksandr (1918–)

Soviet-Russian dissident and writer. Born in Kislovodsk on 11 December 1918, the son of an artillery officer, Aleksandr Isaevich Solzhenitsyn studied mathematics and physics at the University of Rostov-on-Don. Graduating in 1941, he briefly worked as a physics teacher. Following the German invasion of the Soviet Union in June 1941, he was drafted and served as an artillery captain.

In February 1945, Solzhenitsyn was arrested in East Prussia for his criticism (in a private letter) of the policies of Soviet dictator Josef Stalin and sentenced to eight years of hard labor in a gulag. In 1953 Solzhenitsyn was exiled to a village in Kazakhstan. Following his release in 1956, he settled in Riazan in 1957, working as a high school math teacher, all the while writing furiously.

In 1962, the leading Soviet literary journal *New World* published Solzhenitsyn's novella *One Day in the Life of Ivan Denisovich.* A sensational success, it made the author famous. Never before had the conditions in a Soviet labor camp been described in such gritty detail and laconic poignancy. The support of Soviet leader Nikita Khrushchev then allowed Solzhenitsyn to pursue a career as a freelance writer and essayist.

Solzhenitsyn proved a brilliant strategist, preparing a profound assault on the moral legitimacy of the Soviet system by analyzing its labor camp system in his three-volume *The Gulag Archipelago* (1973–1975). In his cat-and-mouse games with the Komitet Gosudarstvennoi Bezopasnosti (KGB) and its literary minions that he later described in *The Oak and the Calf* (1975), he was always mindful of the international position in which the Soviet Union found itself during the Cold War. After the confiscation of manuscripts in 1965 and subsequent harassment by Soviet officials, Solzhenitsyn employed dissident tactics such as writing an open letter to the Fourth Congress of Soviet Writers in 1967, having manuscripts smuggled to the West, and publishing them illegally through samizdat (chain mail–style self-publishing).

In the late 1960s, Solzhenitsyn's life became increasingly dramatic and regularly made international headlines. In 1969 he was excluded from the Soviet Writers' Union, but the following year he won the Nobel Prize in Literature. Soviet officials viewed the latter as a provocation, despite the backing that Solzhenitsyn received from leftist intellectuals such as Heinrich Böll, who had nominated him for the prize.

The publication of the first volume of Solzhenitsyn's *The Gulag Archipelago* in 1973 caused a cultural and political uproar and left no doubt that the author was beyond reconciliation with the Soviet system. In 1974, Solzhenitsyn was charged with treason and forced to leave the Soviet Union. After living briefly in Zürich, in 1976 he settled in Cavendish, Vermont. During his years in the United States, he led a secluded existence, rarely granting interviews and concentrating on his multivolume chronicle *The Red Wheel,* which focused on World War I and the factors that led to revolution in Russia in 1917. His 1978 Harvard University commencement speech made it clear that he was not a liberal reformer but rather an archconservative who rejected communism because of his ethical, spiritual, and national outlooks.

Soviet leader Mikhail Gorbachev's perestroika and glasnost reforms permitted a gradual acceptance of Solzhenitsyn in the Soviet Union. In 1989 he was reinstated to the Soviet Writers' Union, and his citizenship was restored in 1990. Solzhenitsyn's book-length essay *How We Can Rebuild Russia* (1990) advocated grassroots democracy modeled after Switzerland and rejected a "consumerist civilization." Solzhenitsyn returned to Russia in 1994, visiting numerous cities on his triumphant sojourn to Moscow. Yet after several years, the writer's openly antimodern worldview turned him into an anachronism seemingly out of touch with postcommunist realities. He therefore rapidly lost his authority as a social visionary. Solzhenitsyn's nonfictional historical exploration *Two Hundred Years Together* (2001–2002) generated much controversy and led to accusations of anti-Semitism.

Peter Rollberg

See also

Glasnost; Gulags; Perestroika; Soviet Union

References

Ericson, Edward. *Solzhenitsyn: The Moral Vision.* Grand Rapids, MI: Eerdmans, 1980.

Klimoff, Alexis, ed. *One Day in the Life of Ivan Denisovich: A Critical Companion.* Evanston, IL: Northwestern University Press, 1997.

Scammel, Michael. *Solzhenitsyn: A Biography.* New York: Norton, 1984.

Somalia

East African nation covering 246,199 square miles with a 1945 population of approximately 1.7 million people. Somalia is slightly smaller than the U.S. state of Texas and is bordered by the Gulf of Aden to the north, the Indian Ocean to the east, Djibouti to the northwest, Ethiopia to the west, and Kenya to the southwest. Part of the strategically important Horn of Africa, Somalia served as a counterbalance to first the Soviet Union and then the United States for the other's presence in neighboring Ethiopia.

When Somalia achieved independence in 1960, the Soviet Union established relations with the new state, which became stronger when Major General Mohammed Siyad Barre seized power in 1969 and established a socialist state. During his failed attempt to seize the Ogaden region of Ethiopia during 1977–1978, he broke ties with the communist bloc and turned instead to the United States. As Somalia's internal problems worsened during the 1980s and clan rivalries intensified into civil war, however, the United States withdrew its support. Barre fled Somalia in 1991, but no new leader emerged, and civil war continues to plague the impoverished nation.

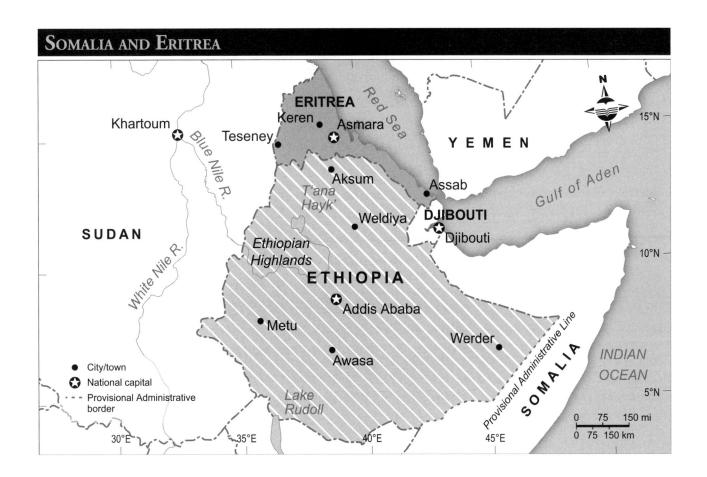

SOMALIA AND ERITREA

On 1 July 1960, the former colony of British Somaliland and the United Nations (UN) trusteeship of Italian Somaliland merged to form Somalia. Although the inhabitants shared a common ethnicity, clan loyalties divided the population and formed the basis of the political parties that continually vied for power. During 1960–1967, Aden Abdulla Osman served as president and was succeeded by Abdirashid Ali Shermarke (1967–1969).

In 1960, recognizing Somalia's potential as a counterbalance to the American presence in neighboring Ethiopia, Soviet leader Nikita Khrushchev established relations with Somalia and offered economic aid and expanded the port facilities at Berbera. In October 1969, following President Shermarke's assassination, Barre, commander in chief of the armed forces, seized power. He dismissed the elected government and proclaimed Somali socialism. Barre's attempts to improve conditions within Somalia included the adoption of an official script for the Somali language, improved education and health care facilities, and large-scale agricultural projects. He also granted the Soviets access to military facilities and received military aid sufficient to make Somalia one of the most heavily armed states in Africa. The Soviet-Somali Treaty of Friendship and Cooperation was signed in July 1974, the same year that Somalia joined the Arab League. In 1976, the Somali Revolutionary Socialist Party was founded.

Nationalism and irredentism—not communism—motivated Barre. He believed that the European scramble for Africa in the nineteenth century had destroyed his nation by dividing among the colonial powers the land inhabited by the Somali people. Barre wanted to reunite ethnic Somalis in neighboring Ethiopia, Kenya, and Djibouti with the rest of the Somali nation but was constrained by the 1964 Cairo Resolution that pledged African states to maintain existing borders. With diplomatic backing unlikely, Barre resorted to military conquest to implement his plans, whereby chances of victory would be improved by external support. Hence, he tightened relations with the Soviet Union.

Barre began his campaign in July 1977 when, supported by Soviet arms and advisors, he attempted to seize the Ogaden region of Ethiopia. However, his fears that the Soviets had developed relations with Somalia only because they could not control Ethiopia were soon realized. Although Ethiopia and Somalia had both received military aid from the Soviet Union since 1974, the onset of the Ogaden War forced the Soviet Union to choose sides. In October 1977, Moscow halted military aid to Somalia.

In November 1977, Barre broke ties with the communist bloc and turned instead to the United States, hoping that the Americans would appreciate Somalia's value as a Cold War counterbalance. However, newly elected President Jimmy Carter was attempting to focus foreign policy on such principles as human rights rather than the Cold War. Citing Barre's

deplorable human rights record and violation of international law by invading Ethiopia, Carter refused to help. With no external support and with the might of the communist bloc aiding Ethiopia, the war reached an inevitable conclusion. On 9 March 1978, Barre announced the withdrawal of all Somali forces from Ethiopia.

By 1980, however, the changing international environment, particularly the 1979 Soviet invasion of Afghanistan and the 1979 Iranian Revolution, compelled Carter to steer U.S. foreign policy toward a more traditional Cold War orientation. In August 1980, an agreement was reached that granted the Americans access to military facilities in Somalia in return for military aid, thus countering the Soviet presence in Ethiopia and facilitating American military operations in the Indian Ocean. Barre's reputation prevented a closer relationship, and in 1989 his continued human rights violations prompted the U.S. Congress to halt military assistance.

As conditions in Somalia deteriorated, the misgivings felt by the Americans were progressively shared by the Somali people. During the 1980s the economy declined steadily, and periodic droughts aggravated food shortages caused by poor agricultural policies and government price controls. Barre's

A member of the rebel Somali National Movement militia points his gun at a broken portrait of President Mohammed Siyad Barre in northern Somalia, 1989. Barre's regime was overthrown in January 1991. (AFP/Getty Images)

persistence in awarding key positions to members of his own Marehan clan and subclans of the Darod clan exacerbated clan rivalries and government corruption. Increasingly, dissent manifested itself through violence. The country entered a state of virtual civil war following an uprising that began in northern Somalia in May 1988 and then consolidated under the leadership of the Issaq-led Somali National Movement (SNM). Barre provided the Darod clan with arms with which to oppose the SNM, but Darod loyalty to Barre was diminishing. In April 1988 he lost support of the Ogadeeni subclan when Somalia and Ethiopia signed a peace treaty in which Barre renounced all claims to the Ogaden.

Opposition from the Hawiye clan led to the formation of the United Somali Congress (USC), which concentrated on efforts to take control of Mogadishu, prompting Barre to withdraw those troops still loyal to him to defend the capital. By December 1990, much of Mogadishu had been destroyed and thousands had been killed in the fighting. On 27 January 1991, Barre fled Mogadishu, and the USC took control of the city. With the common enemy gone, however, clan rivalries exploded once more and civil war resumed, which, despite attempts by the international community—including the UN—to quell, continues.

Donna R. Jackson

See also
Africa; Africa, Soviet Interventions in; Africa, U.S. Interventions in; Barre, Mohammed Siyad; Decolonization; Ethiopia; Human Rights; Ogaden War
References
Henze, Paul B. *The Horn of Africa: From War to Peace.* London: Macmillan, 1991.
Lefebvre, J. A. *Arms for the Horn: U.S. Security Policy in Ethiopia and Somalia, 1953–1991.* Pittsburgh, PA: University of Pittsburgh Press, 1991.
Patman, Robert. *The Soviet Union in the Horn of Africa.* Cambridge: Cambridge University Press, 1990.
Schraeder, Peter J. *United States Foreign Policy toward Africa: Incrementalism, Crisis and Change.* Cambridge: Cambridge University Press, 1994.

Somoza Debayle, Anastasio (1925–1980)

Nicaraguan dictator and president (1967–1972, 1974–1979). Born in León on 5 December 1925, Anastasio Somoza Debayle was the second son of Nicaraguan President Anastasio Somoza García (1936–1956). Often referred to as "Tachito," Somoza Debayle graduated from the United States Military Academy, West Point, in 1946 before heading Nicaragua's National Guard beginning in 1947. As commander of the National Guard, he helped his family maintain its hold on political power after his father's 1956 assassination. During his brother Luis Somoza Debayle's presidency (1956–1967),

Anastasio Somoza brutally suppressed protests, crushed potential rivals, and developed important political and business contacts.

The death of his brother in 1967 allowed Somoza to seize power. In contrast to his brother's reliance on political parties and rigged elections, Anastasio Somoza established a thoroughly authoritarian rule. Throughout the years, violent repression of opposition groups, rigid press censorship, and challenges to businesses that rivaled the growing interests of the Somoza dynasty mounted. At the same time, Somoza maintained close relations with the United States and was viewed as a bulwark against communist subversion in Central America.

In 1972, Somoza was constitutionally forbidden from serving another presidential term, although he continued to be the de facto head of state. In December 1972 a massive earthquake virtually leveled Managua, and Somoza used the ensuing chaos to declare martial law, making him—as head of the National Guard—the ruler of the state. The earthquake resulted in considerable international aid to Nicaragua, but revelations that Somoza had embezzled much of the aid led to his political isolation. Nevertheless, he was reelected president in 1974. Soon thereafter, the leftist National Liberation Front (FSLN, Sandinistas) launched a guerrilla war against the Somoza dictatorship. When the government lashed out at its enemies, popular support for the FSLN grew.

In response to the situation in Nicaragua, U.S. President Jimmy Carter sharply reduced financial and military aid to the Somoza regime. By 1978, the military situation in Nicaragua had turned against the dictatorship. In July 1979, facing condemnation at home and abroad, Somoza fled the country for Miami, Florida. He was assassinated in Asunción, Paraguay, on 17 September 1980.

Daniel Lewis

See also
Contras; Nicaragua; Sandinistas; Somoza García, Anastasio
References
Crawley, Eduardo. *Dictators Never Die: A Portrait of Nicaragua and the Somoza Dynasty.* New York: St. Martin's, 1979.
Lake, Anthony. *Somoza Falling.* Boston: Houghton Mifflin, 1989.
Millett, Richard. *Guardians of the Dynasty.* Maryknoll, NY: Orbis, 1977.

Somoza García, Anastasio (1896–1956)

Nicaraguan military leader and president (1937–1947, 1950–1956). Born in San Marcos on 1 February 1896, Anastasio Somoza García was the founder of the Somoza political dynasty (1939–1979). Somoza's close ties to the United States began when he attended but did not graduate from the Pierce School of Business Administration in Philadelphia. He returned to

Nicaragua in 1919 and pursued a military career. In 1933 he was named the first commander of the Nicaraguan National Guard, which the United States had helped create in 1927. Although the National Guard was designed as an apolitical force, Somoza nevertheless used it to seize political power. He ordered the assassination of political rivals, including Augusto César Sandino in 1934, and increased the National Guard's size and authority after seizing power in 1936 and installing himself as president in 1937.

Through World War II, Somoza maintained strong relations with the United States. He also launched a campaign against Nazi subversion in Nicaragua, an effort that allowed him to take control of German-owned assets throughout the country. These seized properties bolstered the family's sizable fortune and helped sustain the dynasty's political and economic ambitions for decades.

When the Franklin Roosevelt and Harry Truman administrations encouraged democratic trends in the Western Hemisphere after 1944, Nicaraguan opposition groups organized to push Somoza from power. Acting quickly, he promised reforms and scheduled elections to ensure a change of administrations in the near future, which stalled the opposition movement. He then reinforced his grip on power by invading Costa Rica in 1946. Declaring the invasion a necessary intervention against communist subversion, he transformed himself into a staunch Cold Warrior and secured strong support from the United States.

Having faced down one challenge, Somoza used a combination of rewards and repression to manage Nicaraguan politics. He orchestrated social and economic reforms that improved working conditions and fostered economic growth in urban centers. He also allowed for the formation and operation of token opposition parties and loosened press restrictions. In January 1947 he symbolically stepped down as president but one month later ousted his successor and installed a puppet president while he held de facto power until 1950, when he arranged for his reelection.

Somoza continued to cultivate support from the United States. When Guatemalan President Jacobo Arbenz Guzmán embarked on a series of significant economic reforms, most notably land reform, beginning in 1952, Somoza helped the U.S. Central Intelligence Agency (CIA) train mercenaries in Nicaragua, from which they launched an invasion that toppled the Arbenz regime in 1954.

Having survived two decades in power, Somoza was shot by an assassin in León on 21 September 1956 and died of his wounds on 29 September. His eldest son, Luis Somoza Debayle, inherited the presidency. A second son, Anastasio Somoza Debayle, already commander of the National Guard, maintained the family's control over the military and later gained the presidency.

Daniel Lewis

See also
Americas; Nicaragua; Somoza Debayle, Anastasio
References
Clark, Paul Coe, Jr. *The United States and Somoza, 1933–1956.* Westport, CT: Praeger, 1992.
Millett, Richard. *Guardians of the Dynasty.* Maryknoll, NY: Orbis, 1977.

Song Meiling (1897–2003)

Wife of Jiang Jieshi, Guomindang (GMD, Nationalist) leader and president of the Republic of China (ROC, Taiwan). Born in Shanghai, Jiangsu Province, on 5 March 1897, Song Meiling, daughter of a Methodist minister, was educated in the United States and graduated from Wellesley College in 1917. When she returned to Shanghai at year's end, she engaged in church affairs and social welfare outreach until 1927, when she married Jiang, the leader of the GMD and future president of the ROC.

Song served as Jiang's closest aide, personal secretary, and English interpreter. From 1930 to 1932, she also held a membership in the Legislative Yuan. In 1934, she headed the women's department of Jiang's New Life Movement, a reform program aimed at halting the spread of communism by stressing traditional Chinese values.

During the Xi'an Incident of December 1936, Song played a critical role in securing Jiang's release from the rebellious GMD military generals and facilitated the GMD's cooperation with the Chinese communists to fight the Japanese during 1937–1945. Besides continuing the New Life Movement and leading Chinese women to fight against China's enemies, Song's other contribution during both the Sino-Japanese War and the Chinese Civil War was to capture international attention and seek foreign assistance, especially from the United States. Throughout the 1940s she visited Washington frequently, lobbying for economic and military assistance to save the GMD government from collapse. This made her something of a celebrity in America, especially with the China Lobby.

In January 1950 Song went to Taiwan, joining Jiang, who had been defeated in the Chinese Civil War and forced to relocate the GMD headquarters on Taiwan. There Song continued her works in organizing women and seeking, largely in vain, U.S. assistance to defend the ROC. After Jiang's death in 1975, she moved to New York City and lived in semiseclusion. Song died on 23 October 2003 in New York City.

Law Yuk-fun

See also
China, Republic of; Chinese Civil War; Jiang Jieshi
References
Clarke, Elmer Talmage. *The Chiangs of China.* New York: Abingdon-Cokesbury, 1943.

Seagrave, Sterling. *The Soong Dynasty*. New York: Harper and Row, 1985.

See also
China, People's Republic of; China, Republic of; Chinese Civil War; Jiang Jieshi; Song Meiling
References
Seagrave, Sterling. *The Soong Dynasty*. New York: Harper and Row, 1985.
Zhang, Rong. *Mme. Sun Yat-sen: Soong Ching-ling*. Harmondsworth: Penguin, 1986.

Song Qingling (1892–1981)

Vice chairwoman of the People's Republic of China (PRC). Born in Shanghai, Jiangsu Province, on 27 January 1892, Song Qingling was educated in the United States and graduated from Wesleyan College in 1913. In 1914, on her way back to China, she stopped in Tokyo, where she met and immediately married Sun Yixian, founder of both the Republic of China (ROC) and the Guomindang (GMD, Nationalists). During her marriage to Sun, which ended with his death in 1925, she developed her own career in revolutionary politics.

As Sun's widow, Song assumed a greater role in politics. She was elected to serve on the GMD's Central Executive Committee until 1945. In 1927, she was also appointed a member of the State Council in the GMD government led by Jiang Jieshi, her brother-in-law as well as Sun's successor. Despite these familial connections, Song grew increasingly resentful of Jiang's hostility toward the Chinese communists, which she perceived as a betrayal of Sun's ideals of national unification. Embittered and frustrated, she left China and traveled to the Soviet Union and Europe in late 1927. She returned to China in 1931 and resisted taking part in politics, focusing instead on social welfare issues.

During the Sino-Japanese War, Song founded the China Defense League to promote the anti-Japanese war drive, an effort that included cooperation with the Chinese communists. Song's anti-Jiang and procommunist stance became even more obvious after the war, when she transformed the league into the China Welfare Fund, which supported communist-oriented organizations during the Chinese Civil War.

Upon the establishment of the PRC in 1949, the Chinese communists paid Song special treatment and great respect, primarily due to her symbolic value as a link between the PRC and Sun's revolutionary movement. Because of her past GMD connections, however, her PRC appointments were largely ceremonial in nature, carrying with them no real power or responsibility. She was, for a time, one of three noncommunist vice chairpersons in the new PRC government, a post she held until 1954, when Mao Zedong reorganized the government. She was also made the vice chairperson of the Sino-Soviet Friendship Association, owing to her earlier contacts with the Soviet Union. In 1959 she became one of the two vice chairpersons of the PRC, a post she retained until 1980. In early 1981, she was named honorary president of the PRC. Song died on 29 May 1981 in Beijing.

Law Yuk-fun

South Africa

Located on the southern tip of Africa, South Africa covers 471,008 square miles, making it roughly three times as large as the U.S. state of California. South Africa, which had a 1945 population of approximately 15 million people, is bordered by the Indian Ocean to the south and east, the Atlantic Ocean to the west, Namibia to the northwest, Zimbabwe and Botswana to the north, and Swaziland and Mozambique to the northeast.

South Africa's Cold War history is essentially the history of apartheid, or racial separation. The National Party (NP), which came to power in 1948 and would dominate South Africa until 1990, fully codified apartheid. The NP built a strong state, and consequently South Africa became the preponderant power in southern Africa. But its racial policies also rendered it a pariah in the international community. Still, South Africa, through its involvement in civil wars in Angola and to a lesser extent Mozambique and Zimbabwe, played an important role in Cold War geopolitics.

The apartheid era, which neatly coincides with the Cold War, can be divided into four periods: 1948–1958, including the administrations of D. F. Malan (1948–1954) and Johannes Strijdom (1954–1958); the premiership of Hendrik Verwoerd (1958–1966); the reign of Prime Minister John Vorster (1966–1978); and P. W. Botha's premiership beginning in 1978 and resignation as state president in 1989. The subsequent rise of F. W. de Klerk marked apartheid's denouement, hastened by the end of the Cold War.

During the late 1940s and 1950s, the NP's consolidation of state power was most clearly reflected by its policy of job reservation for whites. In the late 1950s, many businesses, most of which were run by English speakers, preferred to hire cheap black labor. The government responded by reserving fifteen different occupations for whites. This period also witnessed the inchoate institutionalization of apartheid by, for instance, the Prohibition of Mixed Marriages Act (1949), the Suppression of Communism Act (1950), the Population Registration Act (1951), and the Bantu Education Act (1955). Domestic resistance to apartheid was barely active during this period and came mainly from black political groups through civil protests.

Segregated stands in a sports arena in Bloemfontein, South Africa. (Corel)

Malan, and then Strijdom, advanced Afrikaner dominance while the colonial (white) dominance of the rest of Africa was in full retreat. Shielding South Africa from what they saw as the contagion of decolonization and the advancement of majority rule was their chief foreign policy priority. Malan outlined his Africa policy in a document titled *The African Charter* (1949), which was imbued with the notion of an African continent safe for "Western European Christian Civilization." Strijdom took a somewhat more pragmatic and prudent path. For instance, the growing importance of Africa to South Africa's foreign policy was reflected by the 1959 creation of South Africa's Africa Division in the Department of Foreign Affairs, its first geographic division. Throughout the 1950s, South Africa maintained a favored position in the West.

Civil unrest and the brutality at Sharpeville defined Verwoerd's premiership. In March 1960, the South African police fired on a group of demonstrators whom the Pan Africanist Congress (PAC) had called upon to protest the South African Pass Laws, enacted by the government to restrict the movement of nonwhites. (Except when required for domestic help or other certified jobs, blacks had to remain in their own designated areas.) In the confrontation, 67 Africans were killed and another 126 wounded. Without doubt, Sharpeville changed the nature of the antiapartheid resistance. In 1961, Umkhonto we Sizwe (MK, Spear of the Nation), made up of African National Congress (ANC) and South African Communist Party (SACP) cadres, was formed as the armed wing of the ANC. And Poqo ("pure" or "only") was formed as the armed wing of the PAC. The antiapartheid movement also began to reach beyond South Africa's borders as neighboring countries became rear guards for the antiapartheid struggle.

Nonetheless, while domestic and international opposition to apartheid intensified, Verwoerd advanced Afrikaner dominance at home and only further entrenched apartheid. The South African state successfully suppressed the antiapartheid struggle. Antiapartheid crusader Nelson Mandela was arrested in 1962, and seventeen of the MK's high command were arrested in Rivonia the following year. Because South Africa was in the middle of the Great Boom (1961–1970), the NP further consolidated its power, had greater economic resources to maintain the apartheid edifice at home, and was able to protect itself from black majority rule in the rest of Africa.

Vorster's premiership actually encompasses two distinct periods. He rode to office in 1966 on the tailwind of Verwoerd's strong state, South Africa's economic boom, and a mature apartheid. But he left office in 1978 with the apartheid system under siege and South Africa in an economic tailspin. The second phase of Vorster's tenure presented him with a new set of economic and political dynamics. By 1975, the economy was in serious decline, with the growth rate down 2.2 percent for the year. The Vorster government also faced the inchoate black union movement, symbolized by the Durban strikes of 1973, leading to the Bantu Labour Relations Regulation Amendment Act, which gave black Africans a limited right to strike. The impact of South Africa's economic downturn was felt mainly in the townships.

Soweto most certainly defined Vorster's latter period. On 16 June 1976, 15,000 school children gathered to protest the government's insistence that Afrikaans be the official language in black schools. A subsequent confrontation with police triggered a month-long revolt, causing 1,000 deaths. The government reacted to Soweto by becoming even more repressive, while businesses responded by calling for more reform, forming the Urban Foundation to lobby the government for change, especially concerning housing for blacks.

Vorster's Africa policy was known as the outward policy. It differed from South Africa's earlier Africa policies by accepting the irreversibility of the transfer of power from the European metropoles to the African centers, ending a long period of stubborn denial. South Africa could accept the reality of a steady transfer of power to African centers because in the first half of the 1970s its cordon sanitaire was still intact and its economy was booming.

After the oil crisis of 1973–1974, Pretoria argued that its store of key raw materials (platinum, manganese, chrome, and vanadium), vital sea-lanes, and strong anticommunism made it an ideal ally of the West. But there was also a growing movement in Africa to condemn South Africa's domestic and regional policies. In September 1969, the Organization of African Unity (OAU) adopted the Lusaka Manifesto, calling for an end to colonialism in Mozambique, Angola, Rhodesia (Zimbabwe), and South West Africa (Namibia). It also included South Africa within its anticolonialism mandate.

The matrix of threat and opportunity facing South Africa inalterably changed on 24 April 1974, when Portugal's President António Salazar was overthrown. The cordon sanitaire was broken. Northern Namibia was now open to attacks by the anti–South African guerrilla force, SWAPO, from southern Angola. Mozambique became a base for forces fighting the Ian Smith regime in Rhodesia, and South Africa was now directly vulnerable to ANC and PAC penetration from Mozambique. South Africa was pulled into the Angolan Civil War, with at least tacit support from the United States. In 1975, the U.S. Congress passed the Clark Amendment, however, ending covert Central Intelligence Agency (CIA) assistance to UNITA, the rebel group fighting the Soviet Union/Cuban–backed Angolan government.

Growing global hostility toward South Africa led to the promotion of secret ventures initiated by Dr. C. P. Mulder, minister of information, and Eschel Rhodie, secretary of the South African Department of Information, to shore up South Africa's international image. The exposure of these activities, which became known as Infogate, led ultimately to the fall of Vorster.

Botha came to power on 28 September 1978 promising to accelerate the reform process begun by Vorster. Instead, Botha instituted a near-totalitarian state. The 1980s were a period of stagnation and decline for the South African economy. South Africa's real economic growth rate since World War II had averaged more than 5 percent annually. By 1979, however, it declined in every five-year period thereafter. During 1975–1980, the real growth rate was 2.8 percent, whereas during 1980–1985 it was a mere 1.1 percent.

Botha did allow for the abrasion of the petty aspects of apartheid, but his most radical and important reform was the 1983 constitution. It was meant to placate international public opinion by replacing the white-only franchise with a multiracial franchise. However, the new franchise and its two new chambers included only Indians and coloreds (people of mixed race or Malaysians). The first election in 1984 under the new constitution witnessed only a 29.6 percent turnout by coloreds and a 20.2 percent turnout for Indians. But most importantly, the new constitution triggered new instability and political changes.

The 1984 disturbances were to the Botha administration what Soweto had been to Vorster and what Sharpeville had been to Verwoerd. And, just as Soweto was a greater threat to apartheid than was Sharpeville, the 1984–1986 disturbances were a qualitatively different phenomenon than their precursors. The trade unions, the United Democratic Front (UDF), and the ANC were better organized and had deeper support both within and outside the country. In addition, portions of the white population were becoming increasingly critical of the government. Rising emigration and a growing reluctance to serve in the armed forces reflected the weakening confidence in the state.

The new constitutional dispensation triggered the August 1983 formation of the UDF, which was not a political party but rather an umbrella organization encompassing many local groups that had accepted the ANC's 1955 Freedom Charter, which had advocated ideals of justice, equality, and economic development through state intervention in the best interest of the entire population. By March 1984, the UDF had more than 600 affiliated organizations with a combined membership of more than 2 million. Also, the new constitution led to a split in the NP. In 1982, Dr. Andries Treurnicht, NP leader for the Transvaal, and twenty-one other NP members refused to support Botha's reforms and were expelled from the party. Treurnicht subsequently formed the Conservative Party.

South Africa's foreign policy under Botha, which was run out of the State Security Council (SSC), was part of South Africa's total national strategy, a reaction to what was labeled as the total onslaught of communism. It held that the Soviet Union would cling to any territory over which it acquired control in Africa and would only surrender it if the center collapsed or if overall strategy favored such a move and that in black Africa, the Soviets had already selected and effectively controlled at least three states and were preparing the ground for three more: Zimbabwe, Namibia, and South Africa. To combat this perceived threat, Pretoria undertook a massive destabilization program, which included military forays as far north as Zambia and cost the region an estimated 1.5 million lives during 1980–1988 with a cumulative cost to the region of approximately $60.5 billion.

On 15 August 1985, Botha gave his much-anticipated "Rubicon Speech" at the Annual National Party's Province Congress in Durban. South Africa's foreign minister, Roelof Frederik Botha, had briefed Western leaders in advance, and the speech was in fact broadcast to the United States, Great Britain, and the Federal Republic of Germany (FRG, West Germany). However, what P. W. Botha delivered was not a radical departure from apartheid but rather a continuation of incremental reforms and the maintenance of apartheid. The international community was shocked. The South African rand, which had been falling since 1983, fell to a low of 0.35 to the American dollar in August 1985; the Johannesburg Stock Exchange was closed for the first time since Sharpeville; and Chase Manhattan Bank in New York decided not to roll

1176 South African Destabilization Campaign

over maturing short-term loans to South Africa. Other banks soon followed suit. South Africa had sunk to the depths of its pariah status.

In 1984, Pretoria reached an agreement with Mozambique, via the Nkomati Accord, which was to end South African support for the Resistencia Nacional Moçambicano (RENAMO), the rebel force fighting the Mozambique government, in return for an end to Mozambique's support for the ANC. The Nkomati Accord was as much a signal to the West as a sincere effort to improve regional relations. Botha followed this success with an eight-nation tour of Europe. In 1988, military stalemate in the southern Angolan town of Cuito Cuanavale precipitated the end of South Africa's Angola war, which had become Pretoria's Vietnam.

Ill health ended Botha's reign in 1989, and an internecine struggle within the NP ensued. The next president, de Klerk, would case South Africa into its transition away from apartheid, if not actually direct it, although the transition was certainly hastened by the end of the Cold War.

De Klerk released Mandela from Robben Island Prison on 11 February 1990. Mandela had been incarcerated for twenty-seven years. Nine days prior to his release, all opposition groups, including the ANC, were unbanned. Apartheid was in full retreat, and South Africa then entered a transition period that led, four years later, to full democratic freedoms.

James Hentz

See also

Africa; Botha, Pieter Willem; Botha, Roelof Frederik; Constructive Engagement; Decolonization; Malan, Daniel François; Mandela, Nelson; Mozambique; Mozambique Civil War; Namibia; Race Relations, United States; Smuts, Jan Christian; South African Destabilization Campaign; Strijdom, Johannes Gerhadus; Verwoerd, Hendrik Frensch; Vorster, Balthazar Johannes

References

Barber, James, and John Barratt, eds. *South Africa's Foreign Policy: The Search for Status and Security, 1945–1988.* Johannesburg: Southern Books, 1990.

Frankel, Philip. *Pretoria's Praetorians: Civil-Military Relations in South Africa.* Cambridge: Cambridge University Press, 1984.

Geldenhuys, Deon. *The Diplomacy of Isolation: South African Foreign Policy Making.* Pretoria: AIIA, 1984.

Grundy, Kenneth W. *Confrontation and Accommodation in Southern Africa: The Limits of Independence.* Berkeley: University of California Press, 1973.

Price, Robert. *The Apartheid State in Crisis: Political Transformation in South Africa.* New York: Oxford University Press, 1991.

South African Destabilization Campaign

South African government program of forward defense in southern Africa designed to quash nationalist movements in the region, thereby preventing them from spreading to South Africa. Beginning in the late 1970s, South Africa began a concerted effort to cripple independent African states in the region. There were two components: one military, the other economic.

First, South Africa routinely violated the sovereignty of the neighboring states of Mozambique, Lesotho, Swaziland, Botswana, and (less frequently) Zimbabwe. Rationalized as hot pursuit, the purpose was to flush out members of the outlawed African National Congress (ANC), especially its armed wing, Umkhonto we Sizwe (MK, Spear of the Nation). While methods differed in each military foray, four basic tactics were employed: commando raids, assassination of key leaders, aerial bombardment, and, in 1981, a coup attempt against the government of the Seychelles. These were complemented by a series of dirty wars similar to those used by the U.S.-backed Contras in Nicaragua, which the South Africans waged against Mozambique, Lesotho, and Angola.

The decision to destabilize Marxist-oriented Mozambique was taken by the Rhodesian regime that, in the mid-1970s, had founded and supported a dissident group known as National Resistance of Mozambique (RENAMO). After Zimbabwean independence in 1980, RENAMO was clandestinely adopted by the South African state and used by the South African Defence Force (SADF). Now backed with more firepower, RENAMO was active in all parts of the country. This campaign, along with increased economic pressure by South Africa on Mozambique, was highly effective and enabled the signing of the 1984 Nkomati Accord.

The SADF provided covert support to the Lesotho Liberation Army, which conducted a low-intensity war against the Lesotho government. This support, together with SADF raids on Lesotho and economic pressure, was also successful, culminating in the formal denial of refuge to the ANC by the Lesotho government. South Africa also occupied large parts of southern Angola, a tactic that began in 1974 when South Africa invaded that country ostensibly to fight communism. The occupation enabled the SADF to fight in the civil war in Angola on the side of the Uniao Nacional para a Independência Total de Angola (UNITA), a West-leaning liberation movement.

The economic component of the destabilization campaign was more subtle. South Africa's economy dwarfed those of its neighbors. Moreover, most regional transport routes passed through South Africa. In addition, many states in the region were dependent on employment offered in South Africa, especially in the mining sector. By manipulating one or more of these factors, South Africa created extensive economic dislocation in neighboring countries.

In response, the region sought support from the international community. The West offered sporadic aid, while the Soviet bloc provided some military assistance, including weapons and training. Solidarity for the affected states was strong among African states in the Organization of African

Unity (OAU), especially its Liberation Committee. In this forum, the idea of developing Frontline States took root, and, in these same councils, the Southern African Development Co-ordination Conference (SADCC) was conceived. The SADCC sought to mitigate South Africa's economic preponderance. The nonaligned states were also vociferous in their condemnation of South Africa's destabilization effort. The U.S. policy of constructive engagement was interpreted as being sympathetic to destabilization, and the Americans were initially reluctant to condemn South Africa. As circumstances deteriorated, however, individual acts of destabilization were condemned by President Ronald Reagan's administration.

A United Nations (UN) study estimated the costs of South Africa's destabilization campaign to be more than $60 billion during 1980–1988, while as many as 1.5 million people were thought to have perished due to war, terrorism, malnutrition, and epidemics.

Peter Vale

See also
Africa; Constructive Engagement; Dirty War; Frontline States; Mozambique; Mozambique Civil War; Namibia; Nkomati Accord; Non-Aligned Movement; South Africa; Southern African Development Co-ordination Conference; Tanzania; Zimbabwe
References
Davies, Robert, and Dan O'Meara. "Total Strategy in Southern Africa: An Analysis of South African Regional Policy since 1978." *Journal of Southern African Studies* 11(2) (1985): 183–211.
Hanlon, Joseph. *Beggar Your Neighbours: Apartheid Power in Southern Africa.* London: James Currey, 1986.
Klare, Michael T., and Peter Kornbluh, eds. *Low-Intensity Warfare: Counterinsurgency, Proinsurgency, and Antiterrorism in the Eighties.* New York: Pantheon, 1988.
Minter, William. *Apartheid's Contras: An Inquiry into the Roots of War in Angola and Mozambique.* London: Zed, 1994.
———. *King Solomon's Mines Revisited: Western Interests and the Burdened History of Southern Africa.* New York: Basic Books, 1986.

South Asia

World War II ended with the certain prospect for South Asia that British imperial power in the region, which had stood uncontested for more than a century, was about to come to an end. What was not clear was whether a single postimperial polity would emerge or whether South Asia would be divided into a number of successor states with competing interests and values. Also in question was whether one of the global superpowers would follow the British precedent and enforce its hegemonic suzerainty across the Indian Ocean. A half century later, it is still too soon to address these questions.

The Cold War history of South Asia is a story of incompleteness. Bitter grievances have been fought over with no decisive result, and enormous human and natural resources remain largely untapped. The Indian subcontinent did not prove to be as volcanic a juncture between the Eastern and Western blocs as, say, neighboring Southeast Asia, but the vacuum of power left by the retreating British attracted at various times the attentions of the United States, the People's Republic of China (PRC), and the Soviet Union, all of which vied unsuccessfully to secure a monopoly of influence.

The partition of the British Raj remains the starting point for any discussion of modern South Asia. Contrary to popular assumption, the British were never enthusiastic about the breakup of their Indian empire—divide and conquer played no part in British calculations in 1947. On the contrary, Prime Minister Clement Attlee's Labour government wanted a strong and united postcolonial India that (so it believed at the time) could still serve British interests through informal Commonwealth ties. But this preference for unity was less important than a bloodless exit from the theater. After it became clear that India's Islamic minority, led by Mohamed Ali Jinnah's Muslim League, would not accept a single-state solution without violence, British Viceroy Lord Louis Mountbatten resigned himself to partition.

In fact, Attlee's secretary of state for India, Frederick Pethick-Lawrence, had come close to brokering a one-India solution in 1946. His proposal for a three-tier federal state received tentative consent from Jinnah (whose cautious pragmatism is mostly forgotten today) and the Hindu-dominated Congress Party, but the plan was scotched when Congress's President Jawaharlal Nehru made a public statement appearing to renounce Pethick-Lawrence's constitutional assumptions. The result was a wave of sectarian bloodshed that left cross-party cooperation impossible. It must be said that even the most conciliatory behavior by Jinnah and Nehru would have still left unsolved the problem of India's large and restless Sikh population, which had separatist ambitions unaddressed by the Pethick-Lawrence plan. Partition may have been a historical inevitability, at least by the end of World War II.

The ethnic cleansing of the India-Pakistan frontier following independence in August 1947 was the legacy of this political failure, a South Asian trauma that had vast psychological as well as material consequences for the future of the region. At least 1 million Hindus, Sikhs, and Muslims died in what can only be described as spontaneous cross-border genocide. Between 10 million and 15 million more found themselves unwelcome foreigners in a state now hostile to their faith and were forced into permanent exile.

The inhumane exchange of population did not resolve the problem of religious minorities for either of the new nations, for 40 million Muslims still remained in India, and 10 million Hindus remained in Pakistan. Nor did it provide for a stable or mutually acknowledged border. The new Pakistani state was strung awkwardly across India's northern perimeter,

Oxen and camels drafted to carry the belongings of Muslims fleeing to Pakistan following the separation of India, 5 September 1947. (Bettmann/Corbis)

with roughly equal numbers to east and west. This arrangement would ultimately prove untenable. And a number of the historic princely states with populations of mixed confession were hard to incorporate into the partition. Among these, Kashmir proved so intractable a problem that it set off a series of informal Wars of the British Succession among India, Pakistan, and, to a lesser degree, China.

The postcolonial order proved unsatisfactory to a number of South Asian constituencies who believed that they were inadequately represented by the terms of 1947. India's untidy internal borders, a legacy of the ad hoc development of British imperial rule, were reorganized several times from the 1950s onward to try to appease the particularistic claims of language groups. Thus, the old province of Madras was broken up into Tamil and Telugu districts, and Bombay was partitioned between Marathi and Gujarati speakers. These reforms were, however, straightforward compared to the problem of postindependence Punjab and its Sikh minority. The traditional province of Punjab was carved up in the partition, and

its namesake successor within post-1947 India went through a number of contortions before an agreeable all-Punjabi speaking unit was demarcated in 1966. But this concession failed to assuage the passions of secessionist Sikh radicals of the Shiromani Akali Dal Party, who sought the establishment of a free Khalistan state and, from the early 1980s onward, demonstrated an increasing willingness to use terrorist methods of political persuasion. The violent occupation of the Golden Temple of Amritsar by Sikh zealots in 1984 and the equally ferocious counterresponse by the Indian Army not only led to the assassination of Prime Minister Indira Gandhi that same year but also brought a round of depressingly familiar retaliatory pogroms against Sikhs in Delhi.

Independent Ceylon (Sri Lanka after 1972) was dogged by internecine conflict on a similar model, making stable postcolonial rule just as difficult. The genteel paternalism of the country's first Westernized elite was rejected after 1956, when the Sri Lanka Freedom Party achieved parliamentary power, and its strident peasant-based Sinhalese nationalism became the characteristic motif of Ceylon's politics. Educational and religious laws brazenly favoring the Sinhalese language, culture, and Buddhist faith alienated the Tamil minority, leading to the vicious response of the Liberation Tigers of Tamil Eelam (LTTE) in the 1970s. The Tamil Tigers seized de facto control of much of the island's forested northern and eastern regions, but their success eventually triggered intervention by the Indian government, which with a large and politically turbulent Tamil community of its own had no desire to see Sri Lanka's civil war spill across the Laccadive Sea.

India's three-year military expedition to the war-torn LTTE homeland, beginning in 1987, was an attempt to enforce a shaky peace deal that ultimately failed. The price that India paid for its interference was the murder of Indira Gandhi's son Rajiv (prime minister during 1984–1989) by Tamil extremists, continuing the subcontinent's wretched tradition of political assassination.

Perhaps the best illustration of the irreducible nature of the problem is Bangladesh. The former East Pakistan emerged as a breakaway region seeking autonomy from its distant and imperious central government, but after independence in 1971, its own army engaged in sporadic campaigns across the southeastern Chittagong Hill Tracts, trying to suppress Buddhist tribes who themselves objected to Dhaka's overbearing style.

The subcontinent's internal disputes did not, of course, go unnoticed by the Cold War powers. The Soviet Union inherited from tsarist Russia a desire to break out of its landlocked Central Asian hinterland and expand its influence southward, a continuation of the Victorian era's Great Game. For its part, the United States had no desire to allow for a Soviet presence on the shores of the Indian Ocean, which would threaten Western lines of communication to the oil-rich Middle East. India, by far the largest and most populous state, was the key to regional hegemony, but neither side was able to secure its patronage for long, partly because successive Indian governments were able to play one side against another and partly because of the vague but cyclical appeal in New Delhi of the so-called Asian Resurgence, by which India, perhaps in partnership with the PRC, would reject the bipolarity of the Cold War and forge a third way.

Nehru, who acted as his own foreign minister during his premiership (1947–1964), brought the moral glamour of his long anticolonial career to the conference table and was something of a diplomatic celebrity during the first decade of India's independence. His commitment to self-determination and nonalignment policies had a fashionable cachet in the 1950s, encapsulated in the "Five Principles of Peaceful Coexistence" drawn up with the PRC in 1954 and later the foundation of the Bandung Conference and the Non-Aligned Movement. However, Nehru's high-mindedness was called into question when his government publicly supported the Soviet Union's invasion of Hungary in 1956, a decision that cynics not unreasonably connected to the contemporaneous expansion of Soviet development aid to India.

Pakistan, meanwhile, smarting from the disappointing result of the First Kashmir War, sought and received military and economic support from Great Britain and the United States. It confirmed this Western tilt with founding memberships in the Manila Pact (the Southeast Asia Treaty Organization, or SEATO) in 1954 and the Anglo-Iranian Middle East Treaty Organization (later the Central Treaty Organization, or CENTO) the following year.

The dream of Sino-Indian fraternal leadership in Asia was abruptly brought to an end in 1962 when Chinese leader Chairman Mao Zedong's People's Liberation Army (PLA) hammered Indian border positions in Arunachal Pradesh and Aksai Chin at the Himalayan extremes of their long and imperfectly mapped frontier. Tensions with China had been more or less inevitable since 1950, when the traditional buffer region of Tibet was swallowed up by the PRC, but India's military drubbing that year and its reliance on hastily deployed American and British armaments was a stark reminder that rhetorical disengagement from the Cold War and pious appeals to nonviolence could not guarantee national security. The Sino-Indian War brought about a regional shift in allegiances. The PRC made successful approaches to Pakistan (which still enjoyed Western support), while India took advantage of the split within the international communist movement to forge closer ties with the Soviet Union. The second round of major Indo-Pakistani fighting in 1965 underwrote this diplomatic realignment but bogged down in stalemate, with both sides having to rely on the bittersweet consolation that their opposition's war effort had been as badly managed as their own.

Until 1971 the balance of power in South Asia was still roughly divided between India and Pakistan, despite the large differences in size and population between the two. But the successful Bengali revolt that year and Pakistan's clear defeat by Indian forces in the field demonstrated the latter's resurgence under the virtuoso leadership of Nehru's daughter, Indira Gandhi. India's victory in 1971 was far more than military, for Pakistan's genocidal atrocities in Bangladesh had been so embarrassing to the West that Britain and France had broken ranks with President Richard Nixon's administration in supporting their habitual ally in the region. Gandhi meanwhile secured a twenty-year Treaty of Peace, Friendship, and Cooperation with Soviet leader Leonid Brezhnev's regime that provided conventional Warsaw Pact hardware as well as the technical support to launch an independent nuclear weapons program. The underground detonation of India's first atomic bomb in 1974 was the confirmation, if anyone still needed it, that India was now the preeminent power in the subcontinent. As the rapport between New Delhi and Moscow continued to improve throughout the 1970s and as Pakistan languished in despotic chaos, it looked as though the West had backed the wrong horse in South Asia.

The Soviet Union's temporary advantage was squandered, however, by its ill-advised invasion of Afghanistan in 1979, which uselessly soaked up prestige and resources. The war placed South Asia in the front line of the Cold War for the first time and proved particularly important for Pakistan, which the United States viewed as a vital logistical support base for anti-Soviet Afghani insurgents. The Afghan conflict proved at best a mixed blessing for the Islamabad regime, which was also under pressure from neighboring Iranian fundamentalists after the 1979 revolution. The United States poured arms and money into the country, but the influx of Afghan refugees and mujahideen guerrilla fighters in its northern provinces placed social and economic strains on an already fragile state. At the same time, Indira Gandhi's 1984 assassination and the political emergence of her much less Russophile son Rajiv opened the possibility of a rapprochement between the United States and India. The younger Gandhi was unenthused by India's traditional socialist practices and sought American ideas and capital to reinvigorate his country's economy in the computer age.

The weakening of India's entente with the Soviet Union also led to some improvement in its relationship with the PRC. While little concrete progress was made on the serious disputes over the Line of Actual Control along the Himalayan border or the ongoing occupation of Tibet (the Dalai Lama had operated a government-in-exile in Dharamsala since 1959), there was at least some symbolic economic and technological assistance, and the Chinese took a less emphatically pro-Pakistani line at the conference table. The creation of the South Asia Association for Regional Cooperation (SAARC) in 1985 was a welcome cross-border initiative that proposed cooperative efforts to tackle the region's social and environmental problems—overpopulation, poverty, rural and urban squalor, and illiteracy—but a dialogue could only begin by avoiding any mention of ongoing political differences. Indeed, the Cold War ended without any major breakthroughs in key South Asian diplomatic problems. Kashmir, for instance, remained as much an Indo-Pakistani flash point as it had been in 1947.

Britain's withdrawal after World War II left the Indian subcontinent's smaller states without their traditional patron. Nepal, one of the most isolated polities in the world, still lingered in a premodern atmosphere of court intrigue, its domestic affairs dominated by the rivalry between the Shah dynasty and a number of feuding noble houses. After the dominant Rana clan was deposed in 1950, the Crown reasserted its authority, and the country thereafter went through cycles of royal authoritarianism interspersed with failed experiments in constitutional government. The smaller Himalayan kingdoms of Bhutan and Sikkim were left in an even more exposed position after the British retreat, particularly once the invasion of Tibet raised the specter of frontier conflict with the PRC. Both accepted Indian client status as they emerged unsteadily into the modern world, with Sikkim ultimately proving untenable as an independent nation and choosing complete absorption into its giant southern neighbor in 1975. Aside from feudal microstates of this type, the end of the Raj also left South Asia with a scattering of colonial anachronisms. Most significant were the so-called princely states that had never been formally administered by British India, Kashmir being the most notorious of these. Most of the others voluntarily became Indian provinces at independence, but the large landlocked kingdom of Hyderabad refused to cooperate despite the hopelessness of its position, and a year-long standoff ensued that ended only when India sent in troops in 1948.

There were also lingering remnants of European colonization, notably the French Indian territories on the Coromandel Coast and Portugal's old factory concession at Goa. The former were painlessly integrated into India proper in 1954. The latter resisted decolonization until 1961, when Indian forces again moved in and unilaterally annexed the territory—another move difficult to reconcile with Nehru's much-touted renunciation of political force.

Alan Allport

See also

Bangladesh; Bhutto, Benazir; Bhutto, Zulfikar Ali; Gandhi, Indira; Gandhi, Mohandas Karamchand; Gandhi, Rajiv; India; India-Pakistan Wars; Jinnah, Mohamed Ali; Kashmir Dispute; Mountbatten, Louis, 1st Earl Mountbatten of Burma; Nehru, Jawaharlal; Nepal; Pakistan; Pandit, Vijaya Lakshmi; Sino-Indian Border Confrontations; Sri Lanka

References

Bose, Sugata, and Ayesha Jalal. *Modern South Asia: History, Culture, and Political Economy* London: Routledge, 1998.

Chaturvedi, Gyaneshwar. *India-China Relations: 1947 to Present Day.* Agra: M.G. Publishers, 1991.

Dixit, J. N. *India-Pakistan in War and Peace.* London: Routledge, 2002.

McMahon, Robert J. *The Cold War on the Periphery.* New York: Columbia University Press, 1996.

Naik, J. A. *Russia's Policy towards India: From Stalin to Yeltsin.* New Delhi: MD Publications, 1995.

Norton, James K. *Global Studies: India and South Asia.* Guilford, CT: Dushkin, 1993.

South Korea

See Korea, Republic of

South Vietnam
See Vietnam

Southeast Asia

World War II and the Cold War both had a dramatic impact on Southeast Asia. This region includes Myanmar (Burma), Thailand, Laos, Cambodia, Vietnam, Malaysia, Singapore, Indonesia, and the Philippines. While it was the scene of other conflicts, Southeast Asia also experienced two of the Cold War's most serious and prolonged armed conflicts: the Indochina War (1946–1954) and the Vietnam War (1959–1975).

The Cold War affected Southeast Asia in a strikingly different manner than it did Europe. For one thing, the effort by the colonial powers to reestablish their authority at the end of World War II gave stimulus to nationalist movements throughout a region that already contained significant communist elements. Also, unlike Europe, where the bipolar system remained static and rival alliances for the most part maintained their internal cohesion, Southeast Asia witnessed frequent shifts in alliances as national interests often trumped ideology. In its later stages, Machiavellian rather than ideological considerations marked the Cold War in Asia.

Vietnam saw the most intense and prolonged turmoil in the region during the Cold War. There in 1941, veteran communist Ho Chi Minh established an umbrella nationalist organization known as the Viet Minh to fight for Vietnamese independence from the French and Japanese. By the end of World War II, the Viet Minh had gained widespread popular support and had liberated much of Tonkin. Indeed, Ho formally declared the independence of the Democratic Republic of Vietnam (DRV, North Vietnam) in Hanoi in September 1945. When both the United States and the Soviet Union refused to assist North Vietnam, however, Ho was obliged to negotiate with the French authorities.

The determination of the French to reestablish their control over their richest colony in addition to mutual mistrust and the breakdown of talks in France led to open warfare between the French and Vietnamese nationalists in November 1946 and the beginning of what would be, in its French and U.S. phases, the longest shooting conflict of the Cold War. At the beginning of the Indochina War, the French easily established control over the population centers, but the Viet Minh controlled much of the countryside and increasing amounts of it as the war went on.

The establishment of the People's Republic of China (PRC) in 1949 spelled defeat in the war for the French, for it opened up the long Vietnam-China border for resupply to the forces fighting the French. The PRC also provided training camps on its territory for the Viet Minh. The United States was increasingly drawn into the conflict in support of the French, not only because of communist Chinese support for the Viet Minh but also because of the Chinese military intervention in Korea. The French claimed that the two fronts of Korea and Indochina were interrelated. By the end of the Indochina War in 1954, the United States was paying some 80 percent of the cost of the war. The French also refused to grant true independence to Vietnam. They continued to control, down to the end of the war, the institutions of the State of Vietnam, which they created in 1949.

The war had become immensely unpopular in France, and the French defeat in the 1954 Battle of Dien Bien Phu allowed politicians in Paris to shift the blame to the generals and extricate the nation from the conflict. Under the terms of the 1954 Geneva Accords, Laos, Cambodia, and Vietnam were all to be independent. Vietnam was temporarily divided at the 17th Parallel, with elections to reunify the country scheduled to occur in 1956.

President Dwight Eisenhower's administration firmly believed in the domino theory: if one Southeast Asian country became communist, the remainder would fall to communism. Determined to prevent further losses in Southeast Asia, U.S. policymakers decided to form a regional security alliance. On 8 September 1954, Australia, France, New Zealand, Pakistan, the Philippines, Thailand, the United States, and the United Kingdom signed the Manila Pact, establishing the Southeast Asia Treaty Organization (SEATO). The signatories extended the alliance's collective security guarantees to Cambodia, Laos, and the Republic of Vietnam (RVN, South Vietnam).

The government of South Vietnam, headed by President Ngo Dinh Diem, refused to hold the elections called for by the Geneva Accords. The United States supported Diem in his stand. Viewing Vietnam through the history of communist regimes elsewhere, President Eisenhower was convinced that the communists would not abide by the democratic process. The decision not to hold the elections in South Vietnam led to a renewal of fighting, begun by Viet Minh political cadres who had remained in South Vietnam to prepare for the elections. The North Vietnamese government undertook to support the insurgency and then took over the entire direction of the war.

With the communists gaining ground in South Vietnam, President John F. Kennedy had to make difficult choices. He sent significant economic and military aid, along with several thousand U.S. advisors, helicopter pilots, and support personnel, to the Diem regime. Diem proved inept at running the war, and South Vietnamese forces failed to make any headway against the communists. With the tacit approval of Washington, South Vietnamese generals overthrew Diem in

A Soviet BTR-40 armored personnel carrier shown on Route 7 in northern Laos, October 1961. (U.S. Department of Defense)

November 1963. In the short term, this brought more chaos and a revolving-door political leadership in South Vietnam.

Kennedy also had to deal with developments in Laos. A 1957 agreement had led to the creation of a coalition government there under neutralist Prime Minister Souvanna Phouma that included the communist Pathet Lao. The coalition collapsed in 1959, leading to a power struggle among the American-supported rightists, the neutralists, and the Pathet Lao supported by North Vietnam. Kennedy favored diplomacy rather than intervention by SEATO to resolve the problem.

A cease-fire in 1961, followed by another Geneva Conference in 1962, led to the establishment of a unified government and the neutralization of the country. This arrangement soon broke down, however, with Pathet Lao forces supported by North Vietnam battling the neutralist regime. Thailand became critical of tentative U.S. policies that failed to check the Pathet Lao. Washington mollified Bangkok through increased military and economic aid, a secret agreement to defend Thailand, and the stationing of American forces in Thailand.

Meanwhile, the Vietnam War steadily escalated. With South Vietnamese communist Viet Cong (VC) attacks on U.S. bases, in 1965 President Lyndon Johnson dispatched first the Marines and then substantial numbers of army ground forces. At the height of the war in early 1968, the United States had more than half a million troops in Vietnam. In an effort to halt infiltration into South Vietnam, the United States extensively bombed both North Vietnam and Laos.

Laos, in fact, became the most heavily bombed country in the history of air warfare as the United States sought, without success, to halt infiltration along the Ho Chi Minh Trail through eastern Laos into South Vietnam. Haunted by fears of a repeat of the Korean War, when the PRC had entered the war with the UN invasion of North Korea, the administrations of Johnson and Richard Nixon never did contemplate an invasion of North Vietnam, which meant handing the strategic initiative to the North Vietnamese.

With public pressure in the United States mounting for an end to U.S. participation, especially after the communist Tet

Offensive of January 1968 (ironically, a U.S.–South Vietnamese victory over the communists), President Nixon accelerated American troop withdrawals. To purchase more time for the program of turning over more of the war to the South Vietnamese (Vietnamization), Nixon expanded the war into Cambodia. The United States supported General Lon Nol's overthrow of the neutralist Norodom Sihanouk regime in Cambodia in March 1970 and conducted first secret bombing and then troop incursions by South Vietnamese and U.S. soldiers. These decisions helped to bring the communist Khmer Rouge to power in that country.

After finally reaching accord with Hanoi, in January 1973 the United States withdrew its forces from South Vietnam, leaving the South Vietnamese government largely to fend for itself. In April 1975, South Vietnam fell to a North Vietnamese military offensive. Vietnam was reunited under the communist government in Hanoi, and the long war was over.

During the remainder of the Cold War, the Vietnamese government picked up the pieces of the war and worked to integrate the capitalist South into the North's communist system, with varying success. Vietnam also invaded and occupied Cambodia (1978–1992), fought a brief war with the PRC in 1979, and worked to secure international recognition and trade with the noncommunist states of Asia. Relations with the United States remained difficult, and there were no formal diplomatic ties. Vietnam battled major problems, and economic success was obtained only with the decision by the leadership to allow limited private enterprise. Ironically, the South became the economic engine driving the remainder of the country. Vietnam did establish close ties with the Soviet Union, which took over former U.S. bases at Cam Ranh Bay and Da Nang. In 1975, the Pathet Lao took over full control of Laos, making it a satellite of Hanoi, and the communist Khmer Rouge came to power in Cambodia.

Elsewhere in Southeast Asia, decolonization proceeded relatively more peacefully. Indonesian rebels led by Sukarno proclaimed independence in the Dutch East Indies on 17 August 1945. When the Netherlands sent out military reinforcements and resorted to force to regain control over their colony, the Soviet Union sided with the Indonesians. American attitudes toward the struggle were at first ambivalent. Later fearful that Indonesia might move into the Soviet camp, Washington applied economic pressure on the Netherlands, and the Dutch finally capitulated. Indonesia became formally independent on 27 December 1949.

Indonesia's leaders embraced nonalignment, rejecting a 1950 proposal by the Philippines for an anticommunist Pacific Pact. A high point of Jakarta's diplomacy was the April 1955 Bandung Conference of Afro-Asian states. The PRC and Indonesia used the occasion to solidify Chinese-Indonesian relations. Despite the resumption of American economic aid to Indonesia in 1956 and a visit by Secretary of State John Foster

Dulles, U.S.-Indonesian relations sharply deteriorated when the United States supported the Dutch in the dispute over West Irian in 1957 and, rejecting Indonesian requests for American arms, supported secessionist Sumatran rebels. Although Washington soon abandoned its support of the rebels and agreed to sell small arms to Indonesia, Sukarno turned to the Soviet bloc for aircraft, destroyers, and submarines. Following a visit by Soviet leader Nikita Khrushchev to Indonesia in 1960, Jakarta became a leading recipient of Soviet-bloc economic and military aid.

Even before World War II, Washington had promised to grant the Philippines independence. Buoyed by this pledge, most Filipinos had remained loyal to the United States during the war, and the United States granted the archipelago its independence on 4 July 1946. The United States retained key military bases there, however, and the Philippines remained under the U.S. defense umbrella throughout the Cold War as a key component in Washington's offshore defensive line to contain the PRC. Subic Bay Naval Base and Clark Air Base on the islands, the largest U.S. military facilities outside U.S. territory, proved indispensable during the Vietnam War. Unfortunately, however, U.S. policy toward the Philippines encouraged political repression and economic stagnation. The Ferdinand Marcos regime was a prime example. In power continuously during 1965–1986, Marcos savagely repressed his political opponents, subverted the democratic process, and bilked the government of billions of dollars. Meanwhile, most Filipinos lived in abject poverty. The United States tolerated and supported Marcos because of Cold War imperatives. When his rule became truly intolerable by late 1985, Filipinos rose up and forced Marcos and his spendthrift wife Imelda to flee to the United States in February 1986.

Racked by civil war and under military rule throughout much of the Cold War, Burma's only direct involvement in the Cold War came soon after its independence in 1948. In late 1949, following the Guomindang (GMD, Nationalist) defeat in the Chinese Civil War, remnant GMD forces entered Burma. Using arms and supplies air-dropped by the U.S. Central Intelligence Agency (CIA), they sustained their futile and clandestine activities until 1961.

In 1948, an insurgency by members of the pre–World War II Communist Party, mainly of Chinese ethnicity, who had served as the only real active guerrilla opposition to the Japanese, began in the Federation of Malaya. The guerrillas sought to carry out a war of liberation along Maoist lines against the British. Calling themselves the Malaysian Races' Liberation Army (MRLA), the communists enlisted the support of other Chinese in the colony. The insurgency reached a high point in 1952 with the assassination of High Commissioner Sir Henry Gurney. Tough new British measures brought the insurgency under control by 1960.

In 1963 the Malay Federation, which had become independent in 1957, became the Federation of Malaysia with the addition of Sabah, Sarawak, and Singapore. Indonesia opposed its formation and initiated a low-intensity, undeclared war, known as the Konfrontasi, against Malaysia. The Western powers supported Malaysia. In 1968, Britain announced the impending closure of its bases in Malaysia and Singapore as part of its decision to withdraw its forces from east of the Suez.

U.S.-Indonesian relations improved temporarily after the Kennedy administration mediated a final settlement of the West Irian issue in 1962. In the Sino-Soviet schism, Indonesia sided with Beijing. After an abortive coup by some pro-Chinese military officers with ties to the Indonesian Communist Party, the Indonesian Army ousted Sukarno from power in 1966. A massacre of suspected communists followed. With the strongly anticommunist army dominating, Indonesia moved away from the PRC, suspending diplomatic relations with Beijing in 1967. Indonesia also ended its confrontation with Malaysia and moved closer to the U.S. camp while remaining technically nonaligned.

In Thailand, the sole Southeast Asian state not under prior colonial rule but nonetheless dominated by Japan during World War II, the army overthrew the elected government in November 1947, alleging antiroyalist plotting by procommunist elements. In April 1948, the army restored Thailand's wartime prime minister, Phibunsongkhram (Phibun). His anti-Chinese and anticommunist policies endeared him to the United States, despite his record of collaboration with Japan in World War II. Thailand became a staunch American ally in the Cold War and received extensive U.S. financial and military assistance. Thailand was in fact the first Asian nation to send troops to the Korean War.

Meanwhile, disillusioned with SEATO and unwilling to see themselves used as pawns in the superpower game, Indonesia, Malaysia, the Philippines, Singapore, and Thailand began in the early 1960s to explore the formation of a regional organization of their own. As such, they established the Association of Southeast Asian Nations (ASEAN) in August 1967. At its Kuala Lumpur summit in 1971, ASEAN proposed establishing a Zone of Peace, Freedom, and Neutrality (ZOPFAN) in the region.

The East-West stage of the Cold War in Southeast Asia ended with the domino theory only partly fulfilled. Vietnam, Laos, and Cambodia became communist, but no state outside of the former French Indochina fell to communism. Having defeated the United States, the victors began fighting among themselves. In Vietnam, the remainder of the Cold War saw the leadership of that state endeavoring to extricate the country from the consequences of its success against the United States.

In Cambodia, the Khmer Rouge entered the capital of Phnom Penh in April 1975 on the departure of Lon Nol and

With a skull on the muzzle of his M-16 rifle, a Khmer Rouge soldier waits with his comrades for the word to move out from Dei Kraham, some 12 miles south of Phnom Penh, during an operation along Highway 2 on 5 September 1973. (Bettmann/Corbis)

the Americans. Led by Pol Pot, the Khmer Rouge regime unleashed a savage policy to return Cambodia, renamed Kampuchea, back to the Middle Ages. The Khmer Rouge in effect waged genocide against its population. The massacre of ethnic Vietnamese in Cambodia and clashes with Vietnamese forces along the border between the two states brought the Vietnamese invasion and occupation of Kampuchea beginning in December 1978. Vietnam set up a puppet government and sought to wipe out the remnants of the Khmer Rouge, now actively supported by Thailand and the PRC and indirectly by the United States.

In 1982, a coalition of Cambodian resistance groups, including the Khmer Rouge, headed by Prince Sihanouk and supported by the PRC and Thailand, assumed Cambodia's UN seat with the backing of ASEAN and the West. The Vietnam-backed regime in Phnom Penh never gained international legitimacy, despite the fact that it had ended one of the most brutal regimes in modern times. In 1992, under heavy international pressure and with Hanoi having settled on other priorities, Vietnamese forces were withdrawn. Negotiations among the warring Cambodian factions proved long and difficult, however.

As the Cold War came to an end, ASEAN emerged as a vibrant community. The new realities of the post–Cold War era became further evident as countries such as Malaysia and Indonesia fretted that the complete Soviet withdrawal from the region would invite interference by the PRC. By the time the Cold War ended, forty-five years of interstate and intrastate wars in Southeast Asia had combined to create one of history's great human tragedies. The wars and immense loss of life had continuing effects, especially on the Indochinese states. Democracy became one of the casualties of the Cold War in Southeast Asia. While the Soviets and Chinese supported communist factions favoring their line wherever they existed, the West often sided with authoritarian regimes, overlooking their oppressive and corrupt domestic policies as long as they opposed communism. Communist treatment of political opponents was matched by anticommunist witchhunts in Thailand and Indonesia.

While the Cold War progressed, some of the Southeast Asian states made rapid economic strides. By the end of the Cold War, Indonesia, Malaysia, Thailand, and above all Singapore were leaders of the Asian economic miracle. Vietnam was actively seeking to join them. Burma, Laos, Cambodia, and the Philippines, however, were still plagued by stagnant economies and political instability. Nevertheless, Southeast Asia appeared set on emulating Europe, the Cold War's original theater, in progressing toward regional cooperation and prosperity rather than interstate rivalry and economic hardship.

Appu K. Soman and Spencer C. Tucker

See also
Association of Southeast Asian Nations; Burma; Cambodia; Cambodia, Vietnamese Occupation of; Dien Bien Phu, Battle of; Domino Theory; Geneva Conference (1954); Ho Chi Minh; Indochina War; Indonesia; Khmer Rouge; Laos; Malaysia; Ngo Dinh Diem; Philippines; Singapore; Sino-Vietnamese War; Southeast Asia Treaty Organization; Sukarno; Tet Offensive; Thailand; Vietnam; Vietnam War

References
Burszynski, Leszek. *Gorbachev and Southeast Asia.* London: Routledge, 1992.
Chandler, David, ed. *In Search of Southeast Asia: A Modern History.* Rev. ed. Honolulu: University of Hawaii Press, 1987.
Dommen, Arthur. *The Indochina Experience of the French and the Americans: Nationalism and Communism in Cambodia, Laos, and Vietnam.* Bloomington: Indiana University Press, 2001.
Gaiduk, Ilya. *The Soviet Union and the Vietnam War.* Chicago: Ivan R. Dee, 1996.
Herring, George C. *America's Longest War: The United States and Vietnam, 1950–1975.* 4th ed. New York: McGraw-Hill, 2001.
Kiernan, Ben. *The Pol Pot Regime: Race, Power, and Genocide in Cambodia under the Khmer Rouge, 1975–79.* New Haven, CT: Yale University Press, 1996.
Liefer, Michael. *Indonesia's Foreign Policy.* London: Allen and Unwin, 1983.
Tarling, Nicholas. *Southeast Asia: A Modern History.* Oxford: Oxford University Press, 2001.
Tucker, Shelby. *Burma: The Curse of Independence.* London: Pluto, 2001.
Tucker, Spencer C. *Vietnam.* Lexington: University Press of Kentucky, 1999.
Wyatt, David K. *A Short History of Thailand.* New Haven, CT: Yale University Press, 2003.

Southeast Asia Treaty Organization

Multilateral, regional political and mutual security alliance among eight nations: the United States, Great Britain, France, Australia, New Zealand, Thailand, the Philippines, and Pakistan. The Southeast Asia Treaty Organization (SEATO) was established by the Southeast Asia Collective Defense Treaty signed in Manila on 8 September 1954. A supplementary Pacific Charter, declaring the self-determination of Asian peoples, accompanied SEATO's formation. While the charter established principles of economic, social, and cultural cooperation among signatory nations, SEATO's main goal was collective security. Member states agreed to defend one another and other designated nations against aggression from external or internal threats.

Established only weeks after the end of the 1954 Geneva Conference, SEATO was created in the wake of the French withdrawal from Indochina. The organization was the brainchild of U.S. Secretary of State John Foster Dulles, who hoped that the alliance would fill the void left by France's retreat and prevent the spread of communism in Southeast Asia. SEATO also represented the first binding commitment by the United States to the defense of the region. Moreover, it came alongside expanded efforts by President Dwight Eisenhower's administration to build a viable regime in the southern half of Vietnam.

SEATO's structure and focus were problematic from the start. Unlike the North Atlantic Treaty Organization (NATO), SEATO had no standing military force, and its membership included only two Southeast Asian nations. Thus, the organization was not truly representative of the region as a whole. The exclusion of Indonesia, Burma, and Malaya—all facing significant communist insurgencies—was a glaring weakness. In addition, the inclusion of Pakistan stirred the anger of India, driving it farther away from the Western bloc. British and French participation was viewed as anachronistic by Asian members, an unwelcome remnant of European imperialism.

London and Paris viewed SEATO and its role quite differently than did Washington. The British did not fully share

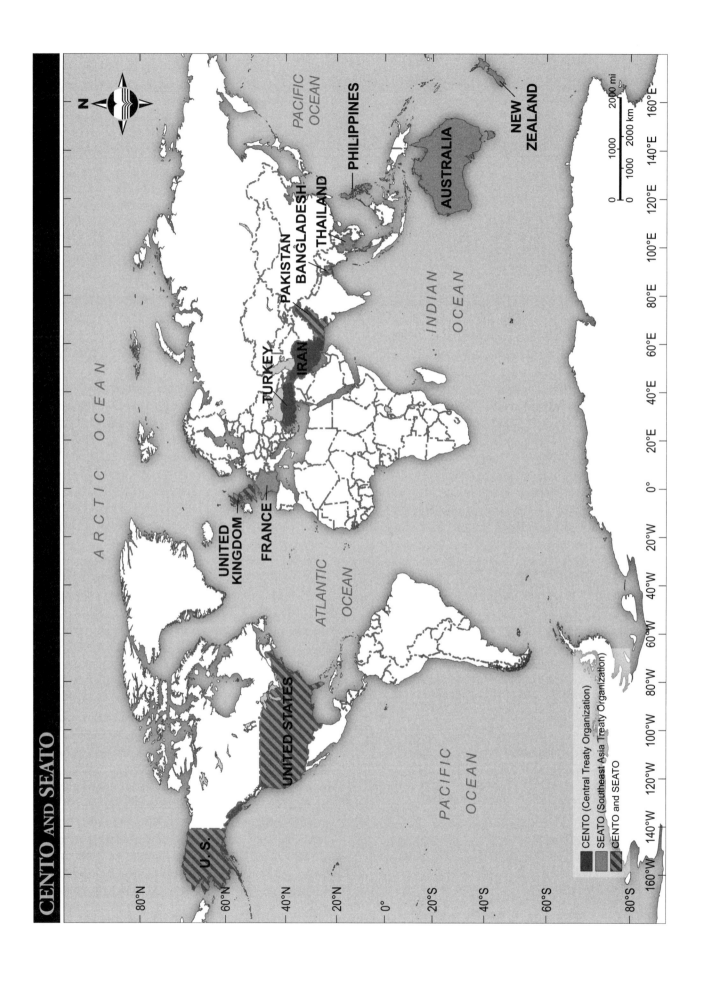

CENTO AND SEATO

N

ARCTIC OCEAN

PACIFIC OCEAN

UNITED KINGDOM
FRANCE
TURKEY
IRAN
PAKISTAN
BANGLADESH
THAILAND
PHILIPPINES

ATLANTIC OCEAN

INDIAN OCEAN

AUSTRALIA

NEW ZEALAND

UNITED STATES

U.S.

PACIFIC OCEAN

80°N
60°N
40°N
20°N
0°
20°S
40°S
60°S
80°S

160°W 140°W 120°W 100°W 80°W 60°W 40°W 20°W 0° 20°E 40°E 60°E 80°E 100°E 120°E 140°E 160°E

0   1000   2000 mi
0   1000   2000 km

CENTO (Central Treaty Organization)
SEATO (Southeast Asia Treaty Organization)
CENTO and SEATO

The national delegations of the Southeast Asia Treaty Organization (SEATO) meet at the Social Hall of Malacanang Park in Manila, the Philippines, on 8 September 1954. (Bettmann/Corbis)

American convictions about the threat posed by the People's Republic of China (PRC) in Southeast Asia. Nor did the British see the French defeat in Indochina as an absolute failure, as did U.S. officials. The British also hoped that SEATO would serve as the basis for a broader, regional nonaggression pact, perhaps eventually initiating détente with China. For their part, the French were never very interested in SEATO, especially given their humiliation in Indochina.

Equally troubling was Thailand's viewpoint. The Thais initially hoped that SEATO signaled a genuine commitment to fight communism on their doorstep, but they soon lost faith in it. Bangkok was chosen as SEATO headquarters, and in many ways Thailand, on the front lines of the communist advance, was the centerpiece of the organization. But against the backdrop of the worsening crisis in Laos, by the early 1960s Thai leaders saw SEATO as little more than a paper tiger.

The crux of the problem for Thailand, and often the United States, was the rule of unanimity incorporated into the SEATO voting structure. The Thais frequently proposed forceful SEATO action against communism in the region, including resolutions approving the deployment of military forces to Laos and Vietnam by member states. The French and British refused to endorse such actions, however. Despite their anticommunist rhetoric, Pakistan and the Philippines also eschewed such commitments. SEATO planning sessions, training exercises, and joint military maneuvers were held annually, but behind this façade of unity the organization was paralyzed by dissension.

Few American officials saw SEATO as anything more than a military alliance. Dulles and others hoped that SEATO provisions in the Geneva Agreements would circumvent the barring of aid to Indochina. With this in mind, the Americans insisted that SEATO declare the intention to maintain a "protective area" over the Republic of Vietnam (RVN, South Vietnam), Laos, and Cambodia. Problems soon arose with other members over how this should be fulfilled. For the United States, SEATO was the principal mechanism through which military support for South Vietnam could be justified.

By the early 1960s, U.S. policymakers had less ambitious plans for SEATO. Presidents Eisenhower and John F. Kennedy both hoped that SEATO would resolve its difficulties and represent a viable alternative to unilateral commitments in the region, but as its ineffectiveness became ever more apparent, the emphasis in Washington shifted to maintaining the alliance for symbolic purposes. It was believed that the organization would at least help combat defeatism among governments in the region.

SEATO was not, however, entirely ineffective. Under the auspices of its military planning and training exercises, the Americans developed a considerable array of covert and overt operations in Thailand for use in Indochina. Washington also later used the organization to solicit commitments from Australia and Thailand to send troops to Vietnam. Moreover, although member states knew SEATO to be generally ineffective, the specter of unified military intervention by SEATO signatories may have in fact prevented more significant PRC and Democratic Republic of Vietnam (DRV, North Vietnam) support for communist insurgencies in the region.

In Indochina, however, by the mid-1960s SEATO was obviously toothless. As U.S. troops began pouring into Vietnam after 1965, France and Pakistan refused to sanction American policy, openly signaling SEATO's grave limitations. As the war intensified and expanded, even the pretensions of SEATO cohesion evaporated. American commitments to Asian member states, and those in the so-called protective area, were governed almost exclusively by bilateral agreements rather than by SEATO itself.

As U.S. forces began their withdrawal from Southeast Asia in the early 1970s, SEATO fell apart. Embroiled in its continuing conflict with India, Pakistan formally withdrew in November 1973. France followed in June 1974. Following the communist victories in Indochina in early 1975, the remaining members decided to disband the organization in September 1975. SEATO was finally dissolved in February 1977.

Arne Kislenko

See also

Domino Theory; Dulles, John Foster; Geneva Conference (1954); Indochina War; Vietnam War

References

Anderson, David L. *Trapped by Success: The Eisenhower Administration and Vietnam, 1953–61.* New York: Columbia University Press, 1991.

Busczynski, Leszek. *SEATO: The Failure of an Alliance Strategy.* Singapore: Singapore University Press, 1983.

Daum, Andreas W., Lloyd C. Gardner, and Wilfried Mausbach, eds. *America, the Vietnam War, and the World: Comparative and International Perspectives.* Cambridge: Cambridge University Press, 2003.

McMahon, Robert J. *The Limits of Empire: The United States and Southeast Asia since World War II.* New York: Columbia University Press, 1999.

Schoenl, William, ed. *New Perspectives on the Vietnam War: Our Allies' Views.* Lanham, MD: University Press of America, 2002.

Southern African Development Co-ordination Conference

Southern African regional organization designed initially to foster political stability and security, later expanded to encourage economic development. In 1980 nine states in southern Africa sought to lessen their dependency on the apartheid regime in South Africa. The Lusaka Declaration of 7 August 1979 brought the Southern African Development Co-ordination Conference (SADCC) into being to enhance political stability and national security. In 1992 it changed its name to the Southern African Development Community (SADC) and under the Treaty of Windhoek of 17 August 1992 shifted from political ends to economic ones. After 1996, SADC was based on free trade principles.

South Africa abandoned apartheid in 1991 and joined SADC in 1994. Mauritius joined in 1995, followed by the Democratic Republic of the Congo and the Seychelles in September 1997. The fourteen SADC countries as of 2006 were Angola, Botswana, the Democratic Republic of the Congo, Lesotho, Malawi, Mauritius, Mozambique, Namibia, Seychelles, South Africa, Swaziland, Tanzania, Zambia, and Zimbabwe.

Economic growth created disunity as each new member sought its own direction, and the SADC was unable to forge unanimity. SADC economies depend largely on raw materials production and as such have little to trade with each other. Indigenous industries are highly vulnerable to outside competition, which the organization has been powerless to control. Each SADC member has its own needs, commitment, and capacity, although all members share a general economic weakness. Many member nations have ties to larger groups such as the Common Market for Eastern and Southern Africa (COMESA), a customs union, and the European Union (EU). The SADC remains a weak organization unable to overcome the legacies of historical conflict, colonialism, and chronic underdevelopment.

John H. Barnhill

See also

Africa; Decolonization

References

Abegunrin, Olayinols. *Economic Dependence and Regional Cooperation in Southern Africa: SADCC and South Africa in Confrontation.* Lewiston, NY: Edwin Mellen, 1990.

Amin, Samir, Derrick Chitala, and Ibbo Mandaza, eds. *SADCC: Prospects for Disengagement and Development in Southern Africa.* London: Zed, 1987.

Bureau of Public Affairs, U.S. Department of State. *Southern African Development Coordination Conference.* Washington, DC: U.S. Government Printing Office, 1987.

Lee, Margaret C. *SADCC: The Political Economy of Development in Southern Africa.* Nashville, TN: Winston-Derek, 1990.

Tostensen, Arne. *Dependence and Collective Self-Reliance in Southern Africa.* Uppsala, Sweden: Scandinavian Institute of African Studies, 1982.

Souvanna Phouma, Prince (1901–1984)

Lao prince and premier of Laos (1951–1954, 1956–1958, 1960, 1962–1975). Born in Luang Prabang on 7 October 1901, the son of Prince Bounkhong, viceroy of the Kingdom of Luang Prabang, and Princess Thongsi, Souvanna Phouma received his secondary education in Hanoi. He then studied in France, earning degrees in architectural engineering from the University of Paris and in electrical engineering from the University of Grenoble.

Returning to Laos, Souvanna Phouma entered the Public Works Service in 1931 at Vientiane and by 1945 headed that body. In 1945, following the Japanese surrender, when his half brother, Prince Phetsarath, formed an independent government, Souvanna Phouma joined it as a minister, along with another half brother, Prince Souvannaphong. Upon the return of the French, the three men and other nationalist ministers fled to Thailand.

When the French granted greater liberties to Laos, Souvanna Phouma returned. He favored gradual Lao independence, unlike Princes Souvannaphong and Phetsarath who advocated radical change. Souvannaphong subsequently joined the Pathet Lao (Country of Lao), which supported a communist revolution. In November 1951, Souvanna Phouma became premier, his party having won sixteen of thirty-five seats in the Lao national election. He remained in power through the end of the Indochina War, until October 1954. He became premier again in March 1956, pledging to integrate the Pathet Lao into the government, a policy strongly opposed by the United States.

Negotiations with the Pathet Lao yielded an agreement at the end of 1957, but following victory by the Pathet Lao's political party, the Neo Lao Hak Set, in the national elections of 1958, Souvanna Phouma resigned in July and became ambassador to France.

Souvanna Phouma returned to Laos in 1960 and was briefly premier that August following a coup by Royal Lao Army Captain Kong Le. The government then fell into the hands of rightists backed by the United States. That December, Souvanna Phouma fled to Phnom Penh, claiming to be the legitimate premier. He subsequently set up headquarters at Khang Khay on the Plain of Jars in northern Laos.

Following sporadic fighting between the Lao factions, a cease-fire was negotiated in May 1961, followed by a fourteen-nation conference in Geneva in June. Agreement there led to Souvanna Phouma being named premier of the coalition government.

But both sides violated the spirit of the Geneva Accords. Rightists and their American backers considered Souvanna Phouma a communist sympathizer, or at best terribly naive. They eventually accepted his leadership but, fearing communist influence, successive U.S. administrations pursued covert operations against the Pathet Lao alongside diplomacy. This secret war in Laos paralleled the Vietnam War. The People's Republic of China (PRC) and the Democratic Republic of Vietnam (DRV, North Vietnam) also fought a secret war by supporting the Pathet Lao and using Lao territory to supply insurgents in the Republic of Vietnam (RVN, South Vietnam) down the Ho Chi Minh Trail. The coalition eventually collapsed, but Souvanna Phouma remained as premier and eventually received U.S. support. The People's Army of Vietnam (PAVN, North Vietnamese Army) and the Pathet Lao, meanwhile, fought U.S.-supported Hmong irregulars under General Vang Pao.

The Lao government collapsed altogether in December 1975. Souvanna Phouma, who was in poor health (he had suffered a heart attack in July 1974), resigned and was named to the honorific post of advisor to the government of the Lao People's Democratic Republic. He died in Vientiane on 11 January 1984.

Arne Kislenko and Spencer C. Tucker

See also

Indochina War; Laos; Southeast Asia; Souvannaphong, Prince; Viet Minh; Vietnam War

References

Dommen, Arthur J. *Conflict in Laos: The Politics of Neutralization.* New York: Praeger, 1971.

Evans, Grant. *A Short History of Laos: The Land in Between.* Crows Nest, Australia: Allen and Unwin, 2002.

Gunn, Geoffrey C. *Political Struggles in Laos, 1930–54.* Bangkok: Editions Duang Kamol, 1988.

Stuart-Fox, Martin. *A History of Laos.* Cambridge: Cambridge University Press, 1997.

Souvannaphong, Prince (1909–1995)

Minister of planning (1956–1958), deputy prime minister and economic minister (1962–1963), first president of the Lao People's Democratic Republic (1975–1986), and one of the three princes who, along with Souvanna Phouma and Bounoum, dominated politics in Laos during the Cold War.

Prince Souvannaphong, first president of the Lao People's Democratic Republic, shown here in December 1975. (Bettmann/Corbis)

Born in Luang Prabang on 13 July 1909, Prince Souvannaphong (Souphanouvong) was highly intelligent. He spoke eight languages, studied engineering in Hanoi and in Paris, and was a certified civil engineer. Unlike those of his half brothers Souvanna Phouma and Phetsarath, Souvannaphong's mother was a commoner. Some believe that this turned him against royalty, although a more likely explanation was the influence of communist revolutions in China and Vietnam.

At the time of the Japanese surrender in August 1945, Souvannaphong was at Vinh in Vietnam. He then traveled to Hanoi, where he met Ho Chi Minh. Ho sent Souvannaphong to Savannakhet in Laos to rally anti-French forces there. Serving with the nationalist Lao Issara (Free Lao) movement, Souvannaphong was wounded fighting the French in 1946. In 1949 he presided over the formation of the communist-dominated Lao resistance movement, the Pathet Lao (Country of Lao), fighting the French. He also secretly joined the Indochinese Communist Party in 1954, although he was always careful to declare himself a neutralist.

For more than twenty years, Souvannaphong was the public face of the Pathet Lao, supporting its claim as a nationalist movement. During 1956–1958 he served as minister of planning in a coalition government led by Souvanna Phouma.

When rightists seized power in 1960, Souvannaphong was imprisoned, although his dramatic escape that May helped win popular support for the Pathet Lao.

The 1962 Geneva Accords provided for another coalition government under Souvanna Phouma, and Souvannaphong served as deputy prime minister and minister of the economy. However, continuing power struggles forced his resignation in April 1963.

Souvannaphong remained politically important as the crucial link between communists and the royal family, with whom the Pathet Lao never openly broke. In September 1973 he joined the new Consultative Council in a coalition government under Souvanna Phouma but dominated by communists. When the Pathet Lao finally seized power in 1975, Souvannaphong secured the abdication of the Lao King Savang Vatthana. That December, Souvannaphong was named president of the new Lao republic, although real power rested with the Communist Party. He held the ceremonial post until his resignation in 1986. Souvannaphong died at Vientiane, Laos, on 9 January 1995.

Arne Kislenko

See also
Ho Chi Minh; Laos; Southeast Asia; Souvanna Phouma, Prince; Viet Minh

References
Evans, Grant. *A Short History of Laos: The Land in Between.* Crows Nest, Australia: Allen and Unwin, 2002.
Gunn, Geoffrey C. *Political Struggles in Laos, 1930–54.* Bangkok, Thailand: Editions Duang Kamol, 1988.
Stuart-Fox, Martin. *A History of Laos.* Cambridge: Cambridge University Press, 1997.

Soviet Union

A large, ethnically diverse Eurasian nation slightly less than 2.5 times the size of the United States, the Union of Soviet Socialist Republics (USSR, Soviet Union) was formed in 1922 and dissolved in 1991. Since 1940, it was divided into fifteen constituent or union republics (Armenia, Azerbaijan, Belorussia, Estonia, Georgia, Kazakhstan, Kirghizia, Latvia, Lithuania, Moldavia, Russia, Tadzhikstan, Turkmenistan, Ukraine, and Uzbekistan). The Soviet Union abutted twelve nations, six in Asia and six in Europe. To the south, its Asian neighbors were the Democratic People's Republic of Korea (DPRK, North Korea), the People's Republic of China (PRC), Mongolia, Afghanistan, Iran, and Turkey. To the west, Soviet European neighbors included Romania, Hungary, Czechoslovakia, Poland, Norway, and Finland. To the north the Soviet Union bordered on the Arctic Ocean, and to the east it bordered on the North Pacific Ocean. Its population in 1945 was 145–150 million people.

As the world's leading communist power during the Cold War, the Soviet Union was the principal antagonist and opponent of the United States. Tensions between the two powers dated back to the revolution and civil war that led to the creation of the Soviet Union. It was not until 1933 that the U.S. government extended diplomatic recognition, and relations remained chilly until 1941, when the two powers found themselves on the same side of the war against Germany. As World War II drew to a close, however, lingering mistrust between the two reappeared and, combined with fundamental ideological differences, led to the Cold War.

The principal postwar goal of the Soviet Union under the leadership of Josef Stalin was national security. Stalin sought to acquire territorial buffer zones that would provide physical defense against first Germany and then any possible Western attack. Soviet leaders believed that this, along with reparations to restore the shattered economy and society of the Soviet Union, was the least they deserved for their role in defeating Germany. At the same time, they hoped to secure and expand the future of communist ideology by surrounding the Soviet Union with like-minded regimes. Although his policies appear to have been fundamentally motivated by practical concerns of national security, Stalin was also a con-

vinced socialist who saw the future in Marxian terms as a struggle between capitalism and communism.

In domestic politics, immediately after the war Stalin attempted to restore the party line. Prisoners of war returning from the West who might have been infected with dangerous ideologies were sent to the gulags. The leniency shown in Soviet culture during the war, when nationalism and orthodoxy were allowed to flourish in order to rally the populace, quickly disappeared. In 1946, Soviet authorities launched the Zhdanovschina, a campaign named for Leningrad party boss Andrei Zhdanov intended to force artists, writers, and other cultural figures to follow strict Stalinist ideals in their works. Three years later, Stalin used the excuse of Zhdanov's death to launch a purge of the Leningrad party apparatus. Yet another major purge was being prepared in 1953, indicating that Stalin remained intent on bending the nation and the party to his will.

In the international arena though, it is clear now that the Soviets knew they were not dealing from strength at the outset of the Cold War. In addition to vast property destruction, the Soviet Union had lost 25–27 million people dead in World War II, and it faced a United States that possessed nuclear weapons. As a counter, the Red Army was in physical

Columns of Moscow workers entering Red Square in 1948 during a mass demonstration in honor of the thirty-first anniversary of the Communist Revolution of November 1917. (Library of Congress)

SUCCESSOR STATES TO THE SOVIET UNION

possession of much of Central and Eastern Europe, and the Allies had allowed the Soviet Union to annex eastern Poland. To secure Soviet participation in the war against Japan, the British and U.S. governments also agreed to allow the Soviet Union to annex the Kurile Islands (which had never been Russian territory) and southern Sakhalin Island and to receive concessions in the Liaodong Peninsula of China (which included Darien and Port Arthur).

Stalin's initial pragmatic approach led him to withdraw Soviet forces from northern Iran in 1946, to disassociate himself from the communist rebellion in Greece, and to try to rein in the Chinese communists. The Soviets' inability to reach an acceptable agreement regarding the future of Germany, however, gradually drove Stalin to take a harder ideological line. Recent archival revelations indicate that Stalin desired a unified Germany that would be friendly toward, if not completely within, the Soviet sphere of influence.

Already in control of Poland and the remainder of Eastern Europe, after 1945 the Soviets exerted their influence within their zone of occupation in Germany. Harsh actions by the occupying Red Army had alienated most Germans. Soviet occupation authorities also shipped off to the Soviet Union anything of value, including entire factories. German prisoners of war also remained in the Soviet Union as slave

laborers, some of them until 1955, while thousands of other Germans were also sent to the Soviet Union to serve in the same capacity.

Stalin avoided any blatant displays of disagreement over Germany until the spring of 1947, when the announcement of the Marshall Plan apparently convinced him that the United States was trying to build an industrial base in Western Europe for future attacks against communism. The Soviet response was to blockade Berlin, which lay deep within the Soviet zone. The Soviets hoped to win support by providing food and energy to the population and to force the Allies from the city, which they could then use as a bargaining chip. British and American resolve, manifested in the Berlin Airlift and a counterblockade of the Soviet zone, forced Stalin to admit defeat in May 1949.

Even before that, however, the Soviets had subtly abandoned their policy of accommodation. In September 1947, Stalin orchestrated the creation of the Communist Informational Bureau (Cominform), a renewal of the Communist International that had been abandoned during World War II as a gesture of goodwill. During 1948–1949, the carefully balanced and "democratic" governments of states within the Soviet sphere were purged of any potential opposition to Soviet control, even by native communists. The new loyal regimes assented to the formation of the Council for Mutual Economic Assistance (Comecon), the Soviet substitute for the Marshall Plan, in January 1949.

The Soviet zone of occupation in Germany quickly evolved into a separate state, the German Democratic Republic (GDR, East Germany), which the Soviet Union recognized in October 1949. Meanwhile, bloody purges occurred in the governments of Eastern Europe as Stalin tightened Soviet control of the region.

Even as the Iron Curtain rang down in Europe, the Soviet Union faced a new challenge in Asia. In 1949 the Chinese communists led by Mao Zedong emerged triumphant in the long struggle for power in China, establishing the People's Republic of China (PRC) in October 1949. Although the Soviet Union publicly welcomed the arrival of a second communist power and championed Mao's regime in the United Nations (UN), Stalin was less than delighted. Not only had he failed in his attempt to subjugate the Chinese communist movement, but Mao's ideology challenged the hegemony of Soviet communism in the international arena. When Mao visited Moscow in the winter of 1949–1950, Stalin initially refused to treat with him. The fear that China might emerge as the leader of Asian communism not only led Stalin to relent in January 1950 but also influenced his decision to support the national ambitions of Kim Il Sung, the communist leader of North Korea. Meanwhile, in August 1949 the Soviet Union exploded its first atomic bomb.

With substantial Soviet military assistance and the support of the PRC, in June 1950 North Korean forces invaded the Republic of Korea (ROK, South Korea). The Soviets' absence from the UN General Assembly (in protest over the refusal to allow Mao's regime to assume the Chinese seat) allowed the United States to marshal international support in what was the UN's first war. In October, the PRC entered the war. The Soviet Union provided air defense for China proper, but Mao was angry that this did not include air support for Chinese forces within Korea, which he believed he had been promised.

While Stalin's maneuvers preserved at least the appearance of Soviet ideological leadership and communist solidarity, the costs were significant. Fearing monolithic communist power bent on world domination, the Western Allies rallied together. They opened negotiations to rearm the Federal Republic of Germany (FRG, West Germany) and bring it into the North Atlantic Treaty Organization (NATO) to defend against any communist aggression in Europe. The United States also signed a separate peace treaty with Japan, pairing it with a defense treaty that not only denied the Soviet Union de jure recognition of its territorial acquisitions in Asia but also provided military bases to support the American strategy of containment. Although Stalin attempted to regain the initiative by proposing a united, neutral Germany in March 1952, there

was little hope of this being accepted. When the Soviet dictator died in March 1953 the Cold War was at its peak, with a proxy war going on in Korea and both sides racing to build up their armaments in case a hot war should break out.

In the uncertainty that followed, Stalin's successors moved quickly to lessen tensions both domestically and internationally. Although both Vyacheslav Molotov, Stalin's notoriously hard-line foreign minister, and Lavrenty Beria, the infamous head of the Soviet secret police, were in the initial group that succeeded the dictator, it was Georgy Malenkov and Nikita Khrushchev who really directed policy. Both men favored pragmatic politics and better relations with the West. They lowered food prices and shifted somewhat the focus of the Soviet economy from industrial goods to consumer products. The purge already in progress, the so-called Doctors' Plot, was curtailed, and the accused were released. Thousands of other inmates from Stalin's camps also received their freedom. Beria himself, however, was arrested, tried in secret, and executed.

The thaw in the ideological battle also extended to foreign affairs. In July 1953 an armistice was concluded in Korea, and a year later, Soviet concessions led to the conclusion of the Austrian State Treaty, breaking a decade-long deadlock over the future of that state. Khrushchev, who had emerged as the dominant figure in the new Soviet leadership, reconciled with Josip Broz Tito and visited Belgrade. In 1955 the nations of Eastern Europe signed the Warsaw Pact, pledging mutual defense. That July, Khrushchev met with Western leaders in Geneva in an attempt to mitigate tensions. Then, in February 1956 Khrushchev denounced Stalin's policies and methods in his famed "secret speech" to the Twentieth Congress of the Communist Party of the Soviet Union.

Similar criticisms of Stalinist policy immediately after the dictator's death had led to an uprising in East Germany on 16–17 June 1953. The new accusations caused rebellions first in Poland and then in Hungary. Popular protests against the Soviet occupation forced the Red Army to withdraw from Budapest. When protracted negotiations failed to produce a solution and Imre Nagy announced that Hungary would withdraw from the Warsaw Pact, however, in November 1956 Khrushchev ordered in the Soviet Army, which suppressed the rebellion in bloody street fighting. This Soviet action and the inaction of the Western powers, who were distracted by the concurrent Suez Crisis, made it clear that the spheres of influence delineated after the war would not be challenged.

The rest of the world, however, was under contention. Khrushchev's adopted philosophy of peaceful coexistence held that war between the superpowers was neither inevitable nor desirable but that competition was allowed. He and other members of the Soviet leadership accordingly traveled extensively, offering friendship and Soviet aid. In 1955, Khrushchev and

President Nikolai Bulganin had visited India, Burma, and Afghanistan. When Fidel Castro's revolutionary movement gained power in Cuba in 1959, Khrushchev was quick to recognize the regime as an ally and proffer assistance. A new Sino-Soviet Friendship Pact extended large-scale technical and financial aid to China in 1959 as well. Khrushchev's largest and best-known venture in this regard, however, was to subsidize construction of the Aswan High Dam in Egypt, extending Soviet influence into the Middle East.

Khrushchev sincerely believed that the Soviet economy could overtake the United States, prove the superiority of communist doctrine, and provide an attractive model for third world nations to emulate. He initiated a series of reforms with this aim in mind, beginning in 1957 with the reorganization of the central economic ministries of the Soviet Union. The following year saw an adjustment in state investment priorities, and in 1959 the Soviet Union adopted a new, aggressive Seven-Year Plan designed to increase agricultural output and production of consumer goods. The Soviet leader was so confident of success that he allowed an exhibit of the American way of life in Moscow in 1959, where he engaged U.S. Vice President Richard Nixon in the famed Kitchen Debate on the merits of the two economic systems. In September of that year, Khrushchev became the first Soviet leader to visit the United States.

Although Khrushchev had his successes, most notably in space (which he had aggressively promoted) with the launch of *Sputnik I* in 1957 and Yuri Gagarin's orbiting of Earth in 1960, the Soviet Union made little progress economically. Khrushchev's highly touted Virgin Lands program to vastly expand the cultivated areas of Soviet Central Asia was a failure. His rapprochement with the United States angered the Chinese, who accused the Soviets of revisionism. Mao argued in 1960 that even nuclear war would be preferable to peaceful dealings with the United States.

U.S.-Soviet relations remained tense throughout the period, though, thanks largely to Khrushchev's habit of fomenting crisis as a matter of policy. The Soviets produced their own hydrogen bomb in August 1953, and four years later they successfully tested an intercontinental ballistic missile (ICBM) capable of delivering such weapons to the U.S. mainland. Khrushchev used the missile threat liberally, convincing many Western analysts that the Soviet Union had in fact surpassed the United States in that area. He also revisited the issue of Berlin in November 1958, threatening to sign a separate peace treaty with East Germany if the Allies did not sign a treaty recognizing the existence of two Germanies and "the free city of West Berlin." The Soviet leader intended to use the city as a lever to open talks with the United States that he believed would lead to a European settlement and perhaps even the end of the Cold War. Although no progress was made even on smaller issues, a 1959 meeting with President Dwight D.

Corn-growing brigade leader A. G. Nee at Sverdlov Collective Farm in Tashkent Oblast, Uzbek Soviet Socialist Republic, July 1960. (Library of Congress)

Eisenhower was cordial enough and seemed to bode well for the future.

It did not help Khrushchev's cause, however, when the Soviets shot down a U.S. U-2 spy plane on 1 May 1960. The event scuttled a second summit with Eisenhower, and when Khrushchev did meet with President John F. Kennedy in June 1961, progress was limited by the Soviet leader's condescending attitude. The construction of the Berlin Wall in August 1961, in combination with renewed Soviet nuclear testing, also helped curtail any realistic chance for an understanding with the United States.

The final blow to Khrushchev's aspirations, however, came with the Cuban Missile Crisis of October 1962. Hoping to steal a march on the Americans and force them to recognize the Soviet Union as an equal in the game of global power politics, Khrushchev had arranged for the placement of Soviet missiles on Cuba, only 120 miles from the coast of Florida. American intelligence discovered the installations before the missiles could be deployed, and in early October 1962 Kennedy ordered a naval blockade of Cuba to prevent the arrival of additional weaponry. After a period where the world held its breath while Soviet cargo ships approached the Caribbean and nuclear war seemed imminent, Khrushchev backed down. The Soviet ships bearing the weapons and their support systems returned to the Soviet Union. This humiliation, combined with the failure of several domestic economic reforms in the early 1960s, finally convinced the other members of the Soviet Presidium that Khrushchev had to go, and he was duly removed in October 1964.

As in 1953–1954, the change in leadership brought uncertainty and change to Soviet foreign policy. The Soviet grip on Eastern Europe, in particular, loosened once again as pressure for reform mounted in Moscow. In Hungary, East Germany, and Czechoslovakia, new economic systems emphasizing market mechanisms instead of centralized control came into effect by 1968. Alexander Dubček, who became leader of the Communist Party of Czechoslovakia (CPCz) in January 1968, boldly permitted political reforms as well.

By allowing independent pressure groups and relative freedom of the press, Dubček hoped to create "socialism with a human face," an aim not far off Khrushchev's desire for communism led by economic success. Like Khrushchev, Dubček miscalculated the effect of his policy. The new Soviet leadership headed by Leonid Brezhnev was not prepared to tolerate such developments. Soviet tanks rolled into Prague on the night of 20–21 August 1968, bringing an end to the so-called Prague Spring and to most hopes of reform in Central and Eastern Europe. Although the Soviet Union allowed Poland to raise loans in the West to facilitate economic expansion in 1970, the Brezhnev Doctrine of 1968 emphatically restated the principle of 1956 that Soviet influence remained supreme in that sphere.

Although that statement of policy went unchallenged by the West, it stirred dissent among other communist states. Albania, Romania, and Yugoslavia all condemned the Soviet action. Only sixty-one of seventy-five nations attending a June 1969 meeting in Moscow agreed to sign the main protocol. China denounced the Soviet Union in strident terms, and skirmishes along the Siberian border between the two powers raised the possibility of open warfare between the two communist giants.

On all other fronts, however, Brezhnev and his cronies were more successful in pursuing Khrushchev's foreign policy than Khrushchev himself had been. Soviet friendship with Cuba remained warm, and the Soviet Union pursued close ties with India and, to a lesser extent, Pakistan. Relations with West Germany also improved, and a treaty recognizing both German states was signed in 1970. While Soviet-supported Democratic Republic of Vietnam (DRV, North Vietnam) forces wore

down U.S. and Republic of Vietnam (RVN, South Vietnam) forces in South Vietnam, Brezhnev repeatedly trumpeted the Soviet Union's support for national liberation movements everywhere. The Soviet Union joined Cuba in sending aid to liberation movements in Angola and Mozambique.

Despite these Soviet adventures, relations with the United States were cordial enough to merit an upgrade from peaceful coexistence to détente. The United States and the Soviet Union signed the Nuclear Non-Proliferation Treaty (NPT) and began the Strategic Arms Limitations Talks (SALT) in 1969. The resulting Anti-Ballistic Missile (ABM) Treaty was signed in 1972. Visits between American and Soviet leaders became a fairly regular occurrence, with President Nixon visiting Moscow in 1972 and 1974, while Brezhnev came to New York in 1973. In 1975, both states signed the Helsinki Final Act, culminating several years of negotiations on questions of European boundaries and human rights.

Tensions did not, of course, disappear completely. In 1977 the Soviet Union stationed new SS-20 missiles in Eastern Europe. The United States retaliated by introducing cruise missiles to bases in West Germany and the United Kingdom and sent new Pershing missiles to West Germany as well. A second round of SALT prevented crisis and also reaffirmed the policy of détente by reaching a tentative agreement on missile placement in Europe in 1979.

Whatever goodwill existed between the two states in the 1970s, however, dissipated in the wake of the Soviet decision to send troops into Afghanistan in December 1979. U.S. President Jimmy Carter ordered an immediate increase in defense spending, and détente collapsed. The ideological divide between the two superpowers deepened when Ronald Reagan won the presidency in November 1980 and again when the Soviet Union approved the imposition of martial law in Poland in December 1981. Even Brezhnev's death in November 1982 and another transition period failed to halt the Cold War.

As it had in 1953 and in 1964, Soviet policy moved toward reform and compromise during the period of transitional leadership. Brezhnev's successor, Yuri Andropov, strove to revitalize the Soviet system by introducing new discipline. He implemented anticorruption and antidrinking programs, introduced new measures to ensure punctuality in the workplace, and commissioned studies for sweeping economic restructuring. To gain the requisite fiscal breathing space, he also attempted to resuscitate détente. He called for a summit with Reagan, proposed further reductions in nuclear arms, suggested a nuclear test ban, and, most startlingly, in January 1983 offered the possibility of a treaty forswearing attack.

Reagan responded by announcing the funding of research on a Strategic Defense Initiative (SDI), the so-called Star Wars system for space defenses against any missile attack, in March 1983. Andropov refused to believe that any such system would be purely defensive, and suspicions mounted on both sides. It appeared that relations might reach crisis proportions when the Soviets shot down a South Korean airliner, flight KAL Flight 007, that strayed into Soviet airspace on 1 September 1983. Diplomats on both sides acted quickly to defuse the situation but were unable to renew the thaw of the 1970s. Any chances of further progress were forestalled by Andropov's declining health and death in February 1984 and then by the illness and incompetence of his successor, Konstantin Chernenko, an octogenarian who suffered from emphysema and lived only until March 1985.

The man who succeeded Chernenko, however, moved with speed great enough to make up for both his predecessors. A protégé of Andropov, Mikhail Gorbachev was known as a reformer, a practical intellectual, and an ambitious man of action. He had traveled in Western Europe, and both he and his wife Raisa appeared at ease in Western society, a marked difference from all Soviet leaders since Lenin. Gorbachev was, however, a committed socialist. He believed that vigorous reforms would prove the viability of the system and that Soviet communism and capitalism could coexist peacefully even as they competed economically.

Gorbachev's initial moves thus came in domestic policy with attempts to revitalize Soviet agriculture and manufacturing through a program of acceleration (uskorenie) and openness (glasnost). These soon gave way to a general restructuring (perestroika) that included foreign affairs and especially Eastern Europe. As Andropov had, Gorbachev sought on the one hand a respite from the arms race and from international distractions. On the other hand, he also believed that a reformed and reenergized Soviet socialist economy could deal with the challenges of the United States and world capitalism. If the United States would not negotiate, he would act unilaterally.

Gorbachev stated his intention to reverse the long-standing Soviet policy of controlling internal developments in the states of Central and Eastern Europe at a meeting of Warsaw Pact leaders in March 1985 and initiated plans to extricate the Soviet Union from Afghanistan in October. He had cordial meetings with President Reagan in Geneva in November 1985 and in Reykjavík, Iceland, in October 1986. At the second meeting, he briefly won Reagan's agreement that all nuclear weapons on both sides should be destroyed within a decade before U.S. advisors effectively vetoed the accord. Negotiations continued, however, and the Intermediate-Range Nuclear Forces (INF) Treaty stipulating the destruction of all ground-based nuclear weapons of a particular range was signed in December 1987. In April 1988, the Soviet Union pledged to withdraw all its troops from Afghanistan by the end of the year, and Gorbachev later announced a 10 percent reduction in the size of the Soviet Army that would coincide with the recall of six Soviet divisions from Eastern Europe.

A woman holding a sign above the crowd at a Ukrainian proindependence rally in 1991. (Peter Turnley/Corbis)

These measures led to the end of the Cold War, but not in the way that Gorbachev imagined. The leaders of the Soviet satellites in Eastern Europe felt betrayed by Gorbachev's initiatives, while nationalists and dissidents within the Soviet Union used their new freedom to explore various means of escaping Russian domination. The Baltic states, citing the secret clauses of the Molotov-Ribbentrop Pact of August 1939 that Gorbachev had made public, clamored for independence. Large public demonstrations for independence also occurred in Georgia, Armenia, Azerbaijan, Moldova, Uzbekistan, and Ukraine.

By the middle of 1989, the movement for independence and democracy had spread to Eastern Europe. Poland held free, if limited, elections in June 1989 that the opposition won handily. In September, the Hungarian government dismantled its fortified frontier with Austria and permitted free movement across the border. Thousands of East Germans exploited this loophole to escape to the West, while thousands of others demonstrated in the streets of Leipzig and other East

German cities. Erich Honecker resigned as chairman of the East German Council of State in October 1989. The Berlin Wall, long a symbol of the divided world of the Cold War, came down the next month. The communist leaders of Bulgaria and Czechoslovakia stepped down, and Romania's Nicolae Ceaușescu was overthrown and executed.

The Soviet Union did nothing. Within eighteen months, it too would cease to exist, unable to either reform or sustain the communist system that had existed since 1918. And with that, the Cold War, the ideological divide that had held the world in thrall for nearly fifty years, came to a close.

Timothy C. Dowling

See also

Acheson, Dean Gooderham; Afghanistan; Andropov, Yuri; Anti-Ballistic Missile Treaty; Austrian State Treaty; Beria, Lavrenty Pavlovich; Berlin Blockade and Airlift; Berlin Crises; Berlin Wall; Brezhnev, Leonid; Castro, Fidel; Ceaușescu, Nicolae; Chernenko, Konstantin Ustinovich; China, People's Republic of; Comecon; Cominform; Containment Policy; Cuban Missile Crisis; Détente; East Berlin Uprising; Ehrenburg, Ilya; Gagarin, Yuri; German Democratic Republic; Germany, Federal Republic of; Glasnost; Gorbachev, Mikhail; Hungarian Revolution; Intermediate-Range Nuclear Forces Treaty; KAL Flight 007; Kennedy, John Fitzgerald; Khrushchev, Nikita; Kim Il Sung; Korea, Democratic People's Republic of; Malenkov, Georgy Maksimilianovich; Mao Zedong; Marshall Plan; Molotov, Vyacheslav Mikhaylovich; Nixon, Richard Milhous; North Atlantic Treaty Organization, Origins and Formation of; Pasternak, Boris Leonidovich; Peaceful Coexistence; Perestroika; Prague Spring; Reagan, Ronald Wilson; Solzhenitsyn, Aleksandr; *Sputnik;* Stalin, Josef; Strategic Arms Limitation Talks and Treaties; Suez Crisis; Tito, Josip Broz; Truman, Harry S.; Truman Doctrine; Ulbricht, Walter; United Nations; United States; Warsaw Pact; Zhdanov, Andrei Aleksandrovich

References

Dobrynin, Anatoly. *In Confidence: Moscow's Ambassador to America's Six Cold War Presidents, 1962–1986.* New York: Times Books, 1995.

Donaldson, Robert, ed. *The Soviet Union and the Third World: Successes and Failures.* Boulder, CO: Westview, 1980.

Gaddis, John Lewis. *We Now Know: Rethinking Cold War History.* New York: Oxford University Press, 1997.

Gorodetsky, Gabriel, ed. *Soviet Foreign Policy, 1917–1991: A Retrospective.* London: Frank Cass, 1994.

Gromyko, Andrei A., and Boris Ponomarev, eds. *Soviet Foreign Policy, 1917–1980.* 2 vols. Moscow: Progress Publishers, 1981.

Kennan, George. *The Nuclear Delusion: Soviet-American Relations in the Atomic Age.* New York: Pantheon, 1982.

Lowe, Norman. *Mastering Twentieth-Century Russian History.* Houndsmill, UK: Palgrave, 2002.

MacKenzie, David. *From Messianism to Collapse: Soviet Foreign Policy, 1917–1991.* Ft. Worth, TX: Harcourt Brace, 1994.

Malia, Martin. *The Soviet Tragedy: A History of Socialism in Russia, 1917–1991.* New York: Free Press, 1994.

Mastny, Vojtech. *The Cold War and Soviet Insecurity: The Stalin Years.* Oxford: Oxford University Press, 1996.

Menon, Rajnan. *Soviet Power in the Third World.* New Haven, CT: Yale University Press, 1986.

Suny, Ronald Grigor. *The Soviet Experiment: Russia, the USSR, and the Successor States.* Oxford and New York: Oxford University Press, 1998.

Zubok, Vladislav, and Constantine Pieshakov. *Inside the Kremlin's Cold War: From Stalin to Khrushchev.* Cambridge: Harvard University Press, 1996.

Soviet Union, Army

The Cold War Soviet Army was both the Soviet Union's most important military tool and the Communist Party's main guarantor of power. The Red Army emerged from World War II as the most powerful land force in the world. The Soviets' navy and air force, however, paled in comparison to those of their Western counterparts. The Soviet Red Army occupied the majority of Eastern Europe in 1945, making Poland, East Germany, Czechoslovakia, Hungary, Romania, and Bulgaria unwilling satellites of the Soviet Union. Throughout the Cold War, the Red Army was the key factor in guaranteeing control of local communist governments there. From 1948 to 1949, the Red Army subsequently cut off Berlin from the West, precipitating the Berlin Airlift. After Soviet leader Josef Stalin's death, Nikita Khrushchev, his successor, shifted Soviet military emphasis from land forces to nuclear weaponry. Khrushchev also began training and supporting proxy forces against the West. Meanwhile, the Soviet Army ensured continued communist rule over Hungary in 1956, helped build the Berlin Wall in 1961, crushed the infant Czechoslovakian revolution in 1968, and clashed with the People's Republic of China (PRC) along the Soviet-PRC border in 1969. By the early 1970s, the Soviet nuclear arsenal also reached rough parity with the West. The Soviet Army, however, faced its greatest challenge in fighting the Afghanistan War (1979–1989).

At the end of World War II, the Soviet Red Army, immense and battle-hardened, was the most powerful land military force in the world. The force that took Berlin alone consisted of 110 infantry divisions, 11 tank and mechanized corps, and 11 artillery divisions, making it larger than all the World War II American land forces in Europe and Asia combined. The Red Army had also learned valuable lessons in fighting the German Army from 1941 to 1945. This experience paid off in the form of great operational skill, experienced leaders, and a cadre of elite, battle-tested units.

In 1946 Stalin renamed the Red Army the Soviet Army and supervised its continued mechanization. He envisioned an army capable of conducting deep penetrations with ground support aircraft, mimicking the Germans' strategy during the early part of World War II. Stalin planned to use his army as a counterbalance to the Americans' atomic monopoly. He believed that the threat of this massive force invading Western

Soviet motorized infantry troops on a tactical exercise in May 1984. (Department of Defense)

Europe would prevent American atomic blackmail. This approach remained in place until Stalin's death in 1953.

The Soviet Army played a more active role in Soviet politics after Stalin's death. For example, Khrushchev enlisted the help of World War II Red Army hero Marshal Georgi Zhukov, whom Stalin had pushed out of the spotlight, to ensure his ascension as premier. Khrushchev made Zhukov minister of defense as a reward for his help. Khrushchev, like Stalin, grew to fear Zhukov's power, popularity, and ambition and in 1957 removed the old marshal from power.

When Khrushchev became premier, he set out to make the Soviet Army more effective by curbing the worst excesses of the Stalinist system. He reduced the army from 5.3 million men to 3.6 million men as a way to cut expenses and invested more resources in nuclear weapons. These changes, however, unwittingly led to independence and autonomy movements in Soviet satellite states. Soviet leaders subsequently called upon the army to force Eastern bloc governments to toe the line. For example, the Soviet Army brutally suppressed the Hungarian Revolution in 1956 by using 30,000 men supported by armor to fight for ten days, mostly in Budapest.

Efforts to bolster the Soviet Army came to fruition in the late 1950s as it developed into a fully armored and motorized force. New tanks replaced World War II–era tanks, and Soviet industry supplied the army with huge numbers of armored

personnel carriers (APCs). While its equipment and numbers were impressive, however, the Soviet Army still relied on the same basic structure and strategy of Stalin's Blitzkrieg-style vision of warfare. This doctrine may have served the Soviet Army well in a general—and conventional—war, but it would prove to be woefully inadequate in future conflicts, such as the war in Afghanistan. Moreover, the officer corps retained older leaders wedded to old doctrine. This problem was so endemic that many Soviet generals in the 1980s and 1990s had been serving since before the German invasion, calcifying Soviet military strategy and doctrine.

The Strategic Rocket Force (SRF) grew to be an integral part of the defense of the Soviet Union in the 1950s. The SRF became an independent military branch in 1959, charged with command and control over the Soviet Union's burgeoning fleet of intercontinental ballistic missiles (ICBMs). The SRF, as it turned out, proved to be too small and inaccurate to deter the Americans during the 1962 Cuban Missile Crisis.

After the humiliating Cuban Missile Crisis, Alexei Kosygin and Leonid Brezhnev replaced Khrushchev in 1964. Brezhnev decided to build up both nuclear and conventional military forces. The consequent buildup of the SRF led to the introduction of the SS-11 missile system in 1966, followed by the SS-9 in 1967 and the SS-13 in 1969. By 1970, the Soviet Union outnumbered the United States in ICBMs 1,299 to 1,054. Subsequently, the Soviets developed a more powerful family of the SS-17, SS-18, and SS-19 ICBMS, now armed with multiple independently targeted reentry vehicles (MIRVs). Thus, the Soviets had reached nuclear parity, if not superiority, with the United States.

While the SRF increased in size and capability, the Soviet Army remained active. It invaded Czechoslovakia in 1968 to quell an uprising, which lasted less than one full day. The Soviet Army also supported other communist regimes and proxy insurgencies, including those in the Democratic People's Republic of Korea (DPRK, North Korea), the Democratic Republic of Vietnam (DRV, North Vietnam), and Cuba.

Despite the West's view of monolithic communism, the Sino-Soviet split in the 1950s led to a border clash in 1969. This schism was ostensibly due to ideological differences, but other issues were also involved. PRC leader Mao Zedong believed that he should have become the international leader of communism after Stalin's death. Khrushchev, however, had no intention of according Mao such status.

The Soviet war in Afghanistan, which lasted from 1979 to 1989, had many correlations to the American experience in Vietnam. After a Marxist party overthrew the Afghan government in 1978, the Soviet Army moved in to support the failing communist regime in December 1979 with one airborne and four motorized rifle divisions. Thus, Soviet mechanized forces secured the People's Democratic Party of Afghanistan. The Soviet-backed Afghan government controlled only the country's urban areas, however. The Afghan guerrillas, or mujahideen, put up a fierce fight that Soviet politicians and military planners had failed to foresee. Opposition increased during the first four years of the war as the Soviet Army attacked the mujahideen in remote and rugged mountainous areas. Analogous to the Viet Cong's use of Cambodia and Laos, the mujahideen used sanctuaries in Pakistan and Iran as safe havens, while the Soviet Army tried valiantly to combat this unconventional style of warfare.

Soviet forces began to use massive airborne operations for rapid movement and attack as well as scorched-earth tactics to starve and terrorize guerrillas. These tactics, however, only served to strengthen the resolve of the mujahideen. When Konstantin Chernenko became Soviet premier in 1984, he decided to change tactics in Afghanistan by attacking the support network and infrastructure of the Afghan resistance, including supply lines and safe havens. Although for a time these tactics appeared to be somewhat effective, the mujahideen's will to resist remained intact.

In 1986, the United States decided to send the Afghan guerrillas Stinger antiaircraft missiles and other high-tech weapons. With their new American weapons, the mujahideen began to shoot down roughly one Soviet aircraft per day. The Soviet Army could not sustain such losses, nor could it continue to effectively attack the guerrillas without helicop-

ters. This led to the Soviet Army's use of mechanized ground forces to attack the guerrillas, but the army lacked the mobility to combat the elusive mujahideen. As with Vietnamization, the Soviets began to turn the battle over to the Afghan communists. The last Soviet troops left the country on 15 February 1989.

When Mikhail Gorbachev succeeded Chernenko in 1985, he ushered in a completely new era. In 1987 Gorbachev agreed with President Ronald Reagan to destroy all intermediate-range nuclear missiles. In July 1991, Gorbachev and President George H. W. Bush signed the Strategic Arms Reduction Treaty (START I), drastically reducing the superpowers' strategic nuclear warheads.

Jonathan P. Klug

See also

Afghanistan War; Berlin Blockade and Airlift; Berlin Crises; Berlin Wall; Brezhnev, Leonid; Chernenko, Konstantin Ustinovich; Cuban Missile Crisis; Gorbachev, Mikhail; Hungarian Revolution; Khrushchev, Nikita; Prague Spring; Sino-Soviet Border Incident; Sino-Soviet Split; Soviet Union; Stalin, Josef

References

Jones, Ellen. *Red Army and Society: A Sociology of the Soviet Military.* Boston: Allen and Unwin, 1985.

Reese, Roger R. *The Soviet Military Experience: A History of the Soviet Army, 1917–1991.* New York: Routledge, 2000.

Schofield, Carey. *Inside the Soviet Military.* New York: Abbeville, 1991.

Seaton, Albert, and Joan Seaton. *The Soviet Army: 1918 to the Present.* New York: New American Library, 1987.

Suvorov, Viktor. *Inside the Soviet Army.* New York: Macmillan, 1982.

Soviet Union, Army Air Force

The Red Army Air Force played an important role in World War II. During the war, Soviet pilots reportedly flew 3.125 million sorties. By 1943, Soviet aircraft production surpassed that of Germany. With more than 36,000 built, the Soviet Ilyushin Il-2 ground support aircraft was the most-produced plane of the war by any nation. The effectiveness of Soviet aviation was enhanced by the country's receipt of some 20,000 U.S. and British aircraft. Nonetheless, the Soviet air arm operated primarily in a ground support role. The Soviets had nothing that approached U.S. or British strategic bombing capability.

The Voyenno-Vozdushnyye Sily (VVS, Soviet Air Force) became an entirely independent military service in 1946. Soviet concerns over U.S. strategic bombing and nuclear weapons also led to the establishment of a separate Soviet Air Defense Service as an independent branch with its own interceptor air arm in 1954. In addition, the navy retained its own air arm, and the rise of nuclear weapons led to the creation of a separate strategic striking force to control long-range strategic nuclear missiles. Nonetheless, their World War II experience caused the VVS to place primary emphasis on support of ground forces.

The VVS was composed of three major operational branches, the most important being the theater support arm, Frontovaya Aviatsiya (FA, Frontal Aviation). The other two components were Voenno-Transportnaya Aviatsiya (VTA, Military Transport Aviation) and Dal'naya Aviatsiya (DA, Long Range Aviation), both of which supported theater operations but also served as strategic national resources under the Soviet General Staff.

FA units provided tactical air support for Soviet theater operations, with responsibility for defensive and offensive counter-air operations, deep attacks on critical theater targets, fire support for ground units, reconnaissance, and electronic combat operations. During the 1950s, the FA component numbered as many as 12,000 aircraft.

Compared to Western systems, Soviet aircraft designs tended to be less technologically advanced. Building on German jet engine design, in 1946 the Soviets placed into production their first jet fighters, the Mikoyan-Gurevich MiG-9 and Yakovlev Yak-15. For their strategic bomber, on Soviet leader Josef Stalin's order the Soviets produced a carbon copy of the U.S. Boeing B-29, some of which had been forced to land on Soviet territory during the war. The result, produced by reverse engineering, was the Tupolev Tu-4. The first Soviet

jet bomber, the handsome and versatile twin-engine Il-28, entered service in 1950.

During the Korean War (1950–1953), the Soviets sent substantial air units to southern Manchuria to fight on the side of the Democratic People's Republic of Korea (DPRK, North Korea) and the People's Republic of China (PRC). Soviet pilots dueled with United Nations Command (UNC) aircraft in far North Korea. They also trained units of the Chinese air arm and then turned over their aircraft to them, creating the Chinese Air Force.

Soviet fighter attacks did force the UNC to end daytime raids by B-29 bombers, but the Soviets refused to supply air support to communist ground units in Korea. Reportedly, the Soviets lost 120 pilots and 335 aircraft in the war. Their MiG-15 aircraft was one of the most successful of Soviet jet fighters and a close match for the North American F-86, which was hastily rushed to the Korean theater to meet the Soviet MiG-15. In dogfights with the MiG-15, the F-86 generally prevailed, thanks largely to superior American pilot training.

In aircraft design, the Soviets continued to emphasize maneuverability and interception capability in their fighter aircraft. Their MiG-19, entering service in 1955, was the first Soviet supersonic fighter aircraft. That same year, the turboprop Tu-95 entered service. It was the world's fastest propeller-driven aircraft and the first true Soviet intercontinental

A Soviet naval air force Tu-95 Bear D aircraft, July 1991. (Department of Defense)

bomber. Already in 1950 the Soviets had in service their first military helicopters.

The progress of the Cold War and the threat posed by nuclear and thermonuclear war as well as the development of missile technology led to major changes in the VVS. Beginning in the 1960s, the Soviets modernized their fleet of strategic bombers. In 1961, the Tu-22 entered service as the Soviets' first supersonic strategic bomber. This process reached its culmination with the 1987 appearance of the Tu-160. With a gross weight of some 590,000 pounds, the Tu-160 is the heaviest warplane ever built. Capable of carrying a payload of 36,000 pounds, the Tu-160 carries a bigger payload and is faster than its rival North American/Rockwell B-1B. Although only fourteen Tu-160s were delivered by 1991, when combined with the extensive development of cruise missiles it gave the Soviets the capability to carry out deep strikes around the world.

Strategic bombers nonetheless played a less-significant role than land-based and submarine-launched ballistic missiles (SLBMs), especially compared to the American triad structure. The Soviet bomber program was relatively small compared to that of the U.S. Air Force, reaching a high point of more than 800 aircraft and an average inventory in the 600s, with fewer than 200 truly intercontinental-ranged bombers.

At the same time, the Soviets continued to develop their fighter and interceptor capability, bringing on-line a wide range of fighter aircraft with the MiG-21, MiG-23/27, MiG-25, MiG-29, and MiG-31 as well as the Sukhoi Su-9, Su-11, Su-15, and Su-27. Ground attack aircraft appeared in the form of the MiG-27, Su-7, Su-17, Su-24, and Su-25. With the increasing importance of helicopters, in 1973 the Soviets introduced the superb Mikhail Mil–designed Mi-24 attack helicopter, prompted by U.S. development of the Bell AH-1 Cobra. The heavily armored Mi-24 saw wide service in Afghanistan.

The VTA component of the VVS performed long-range air transportation functions. The VTA controlled tactical—parachute and airfield assault landing and resupply—and international or strategic airlift. With a peak strength of 1,500 aircraft, the VTA was also charged with the delivery of Soviet airborne forces, which were also controlled as a strategic national asset. Transport aircraft extended their range and capabilities in the Antonov An-22, An-24, and An-26 and the Il-76. Entering service in 1987, the An-124 Ruslan, with a gross weight of nearly 893,000 pounds, surpassed the U.S. Lockheed C-5A as the world's largest aircraft to achieve production status. In 1988 it was edged out by a stretched version, the An-225. Although only two of the latter have been built, they are the largest aircraft in world history.

Unlike the U.S. structure of assigning intercontinental ballistic missiles (ICBMs) along with the bombers to the Strategic Air Command (SAC) of the U.S. Air Force, the Soviets' land-based missile forces were not assigned to the VVS but rather to the separate service of the Raketnye Voyska Strate-

gicheskogo Naznacheniya (RVSN, Strategic Rocket Forces). The RVSN was created in 1959 to control the newly developed ICBM capability as well as intermediate-range ballistic missiles (IRBMs) and medium-range ballistic missiles (MRBMs). The Soviet military considered the RVSN to be the elite service of their force structure, with responsibility for ensuring Soviet security through the capability to conduct effective nuclear strikes at the beginning of any conflict, setting the stage for victory.

The nuclear capabilities of the DA and RVSN were further supported by the SLBM component of the Soviet Navy. The navy maintained a sizable long-range aircraft capability that provided maritime reconnaissance, antiship, and antisubmarine capabilities as well as air-to-surface missile strikes against land targets. Aircraft included the VTOL (vertical takeoff and landing) Yak-36, which entered service in 1976 on the first Soviet aircraft carriers. The Soviets also introduced the Kamov Ka-25 helicopter with an antisubmarine warfare capability.

The final component of the Soviet airpower force structure was the Voyska Protivovozdushnoy Oborony Strany (PVO Strany, Troops of National Air Defense). The Soviet leadership created the independent PVO Strany in 1948, giving it responsibility for the integrated air defense system of the homeland. The PVO Strany organization controlled the substantial air defense system through early warning radars, weapons control systems, and a communications network. The technical systems were operated by the Radiotekhnicheskiye Voyska (RTV, Radio-Technical Troops). The extensive interceptor force assigned to PVO Strany was organized as the Istrebitel'naya Aviatsyiya PVO (IA PVO, Fighter Aviation of Air Defense). The interceptors were tightly controlled by the overarching command and control structure, which also integrated fighters that could be assigned to the national air defense role in an emergency. The Soviet interceptor inventory peaked at more than 5,000 aircraft in the late 1950s. PVO Strany also integrated the interceptor activities with the thousands of surface-to-air missiles (SAMs) that it controlled through the Zenitnyye Raketnye Voyska (ZRV, Zenith Rocket Troops) organization. These strategic SAMs could also be supported by the numerous tactical SAM systems that were deployed in the military districts across the Soviet Union as part of the Voyska Protinvovozdushnoy Oborony Sukhoputnykh Voysk (PVO SV, Troops of Air Defense of the Ground Forces). When ICBMs became a significant component of the U.S. force structure in the early 1960s, the Soviets reacted by expanding the PVO Strany organization to include an antimissile defense component (designated PRO). Active antimissile sites were deployed around Moscow. Likewise, as space systems were developed by the United States and the Soviet Union in the early 1960s, the Soviet military added an antisatellite component (designated PKO) to PVO Strany.

During the 1980s, the Soviet military developed the air operation concept, an aggressive offensive use of airpower at the start of a theater campaign, designed to seize the initiative and create conditions for a rapid ground victory. The air offensive was intended to reduce an enemy's offensive striking power—especially nuclear delivery systems and air, missile, and heavy artillery firepower—and establish at least localized air superiority over the main axes of attack. Additionally, the air attacks would help soften enemy defenses at and behind the points of attack and would limit enemy maneuvering capability in response to Soviet advances. Soviet theater operations would also include parachute and helicopter assaults to seize key enemy targets and support the rapid advance of the main ground assault. Reflecting their support role, FA units were assigned to the theater or front commander (in peacetime to the Military District commander in the USSR or to the Soviet Group of Forces outside the USSR).

By the mid-1980s, the VVS deployed some 6,000 tactical fighters, ground support, and reconnaissance aircraft as well as 670 strategic bombers. The Soviets also fielded 1,300 fighter interceptors. The VVS possessed some 3,500 helicopters and 650 transport aircraft. Soviet naval aviation added another 1,100 airplanes and helicopters.

Soviet air forces were an important component of Soviet theater war capabilities and operational concepts during the Cold War era. VVS units served during the Cold War not only in the Soviet Union but also in Central and Eastern Europe, Mongolia, and Afghanistan. Noteworthy Cold War service came during the Korean War, the 1962 Cuban Missile Crisis, and especially the Soviet invasion and occupation of Afghanistan (1979–1989). Soviet instructors and pilots saw air combat in the Korean War and the Vietnam War. They also served with the Egyptian Air Force during the War of Attrition (1969–1970), in Angola (1975–1990), and in Ethiopia (1977–1979). Such service demonstrated the wide reach of the VVS and provided much useful training, but it also revealed serious shortcomings in equipment, logistics, and organization and could not conceal that the Soviets placed reliance on numbers and tight control rather than on more flexible training and innovation.

Jerome V. Martin and Spencer C. Tucker

See also

Aircraft; Bombers, Strategic; Missiles, Intercontinental Ballistic; Missiles, Intermediate-Range Ballistic; Missiles, Submarine-Launched Ballistic; Nuclear Arms Race; Soviet Union, Navy; Strategic Air Command; Triad; United States Air Force

References

Epstein, Joshua M. *Measuring Military Power: The Soviet Air Threat to Europe.* Princeton, NJ: Princeton University Press, 1984.

Higham, Robin, and Jacob W. Kipp. *Soviet Aviation and Air Power: A Historical View.* Boulder, CO: Westview, 1977.

Mason, R. A., and John W. R. Taylor. *Aircraft, Strategy and Operations of the Soviet Air Force.* New York: Jane's Publishing, 1986.

Murphy, Paul J., ed. *The Soviet Air Forces.* Jefferson, NC: McFarland, 1984.

Scott, Harriet Fast, and William F. Scott. *The Armed Forces of the U.S.S.R.* 4th ed. Boulder, CO: Westview, 2002.

Whiting, Kenneth. *Soviet Air Power.* Boulder, CO: Westview, 1986.

Soviet Union, Navy

During the Cold War, the Soviet Navy evolved from little more than a coastal protection force to a robust rival to the West's powerful maritime forces. The Red Navy at the end of World War II was small and technologically obsolete. Consequently, the Soviet government built a stronger naval arm to challenge the West's dominance of the seas. When Nikita Khrushchev became the Soviet premier and Admiral Sergey Gorshkov became admiral of the fleet, the Soviet Union laid plans for a powerful Red Navy. The Soviets' inability to challenge the U.S. Navy during the 1962 Cuban Missile Crisis marked a crucial turning point for the Soviet Navy. Because it lacked the capability to challenge the U.S. Navy around Cuba, the Soviets set upon building a navy to vie for control of the seas. By the 1980s, the Soviet Navy was numerically larger than the U.S. Navy but still lagged behind in terms of technology. However, the Soviet Navy—a victim of Gorshkov's 1985 retirement and of economic strain—was one of the first Soviet institutions to foreshadow the collapse of the Soviet Union.

The Soviet Navy was primarily a coastal defense force at the end of World War II. But Soviet leader Josef Stalin feared a large-scale amphibious invasion by the West and wanted the Soviet Red Navy to deter such a threat. Stalin also wanted a large blue-water navy as yet another tool in the Soviet military and diplomatic arsenals. Economic constraints, however, prevented him from building such a fleet. The Soviet naval program was put on hold until the economy recovered sufficiently from World War II.

Shortly after Stalin's death in 1953, the Soviet government created a separate Naval Ministry. When Khrushchev assumed control, he reviewed all Soviet military capabilities with respect to the West. In the process, he emphasized nuclear weapons above other military capabilities and, in January 1956, appointed Admiral Gorshkov as head of the navy. Gorshkov's goal was to create an oceangoing nuclear fleet. Thus, the navy introduced both nuclear reactors and nuclear weapons into its forces, representing a marked change in the Soviet Navy's mission. Gorshkov not only had to pioneer a new Soviet maritime strategy but also had to deal with ice, choke points, and long distances. To these ends, he oversaw the building of a huge icebreaker fleet, the resupply of ships, and the establishment of overseas ports.

A key to the Soviet Navy's future was the submarine-launched ballistic missile (SLBM). Its operational history

A Soviet Victor III–class nuclear-powered fleet ballistic missile submarine (SSN) underway, 26 October 1983. (Department of Defense)

began in 1955 when the Soviets launched their first ballistic missile from a submarine. Then, in 1957, the Soviets constructed their first nuclear-powered submarine. This combination of SLBMs and nuclear-powered submarines provided a linchpin of Soviet defense.

In October 1962 one of the seminal events of the Cold War, the Cuban Missile Crisis, showcased the Soviet Navy's vulnerabilities, as it was unable to challenge the U.S. Navy's quarantine of Cuba. Moscow deployed several attack submarines to the area but was unable to seriously confront the American naval quarantine. The showdown embarrassed the Soviet Union in many ways, but the impotence of the Soviet Navy proved especially humiliating. Khrushchev vowed to make improvements to remedy Soviet naval deficiencies and to transform the Soviet Navy into the world's most powerful oceangoing force. Gorshkov received the support he needed in the form of a massive Soviet naval-building program.

Soviet SLBMs, like those of the Americans, came to the fore during the 1960s. Soviet SLBM submarines could survive an enemy first strike and thus posed a credible and effective deterrent. This force grew considerably and was a key component of Soviet defenses until the collapse of the Soviet Union in 1991. The Soviet submarine fleet grew from two submarines in 1967 to sixty-one in 1986, compared to the U.S. Navy's thirty-eight. However, the United States retained superiority in the overall number of SLBM warheads because its missiles carried more warheads than those of the Soviets. The Soviets also employed nuclear-powered submarines armed with antiship cruise missiles. These cruise missile subs, coupled with the Soviet Navy's surface vessels and numerous fixed-wing aircraft, provided a deadly threat to the navies of the West, especially near the Soviet mainland.

The expansion of the Soviet Navy extended beyond submarines. Numerically, the navy grew to be the largest in the world, although its vessels were smaller and less advanced than those of its major foes. At its peak, the Soviet Navy had the capability to operate on and under every ocean during a modern war. The navy also expanded its land-based aircraft

Sailors man the rails of the destroyer *Admiral Vinogradov,* 31 July 1990. (Department of Defense)

fleet's size and capabilities. As the Soviet buildup continued, the two superpowers' navies played a stressful and dangerous game of cat-and-mouse on the high seas. These confrontations included the ubiquitous presence of Soviet fishing trawlers, which were conducting electronic intelligence operations against the technologically superior U.S. Navy.

In 1972 the Soviets began a long-term program to build large nuclear-powered cruisers. These included hybrid aviation cruisers of various types as well as battle cruisers. The aviation cruisers consisted of the two-ship Moskva class that had a cruiser bow and carrier stern and the four-ship Kiev class with a cruiserlike bow and a full angled flight deck. Both classes were capably armed with their own array of surface weapons systems as well as supporting helicopters and VTOL jet aircraft. The battle cruisers, three of which were commissioned before 1991, consisted of the more modern nuclear-powered Kirov class, which had great staying power and long range. The Soviet Union's first true aircraft carrier, the *Admiral Kuznetsov* (ex-*Tbilisi*) joined the fleet in January 1991.

After Gorshkov's retirement in 1985, the Soviet Navy began to steadily decline. Its vessels spent more and more time in port between patrols, and they also required more unscheduled maintenance because of lax general maintenance due to poor operational funding. These problems grew increasingly worse until the collapse of the Soviet Union, by which time the Soviet Navy had become a mere shadow of its former self.

Jonathan P. Klug

See also

Aircraft Carriers; Cuban Missile Crisis; Gorshkov, Sergey Georgyevich; *K-19;* Khrushchev, Nikita; Missiles, Submarine-Launched Ballistic; Soviet Union; Stalin, Josef; Submarines; United States Navy; Warships, Surface

References

Jordan, John. *Soviet Warships: 1945 to the Present.* New York: Arms and Armour, 1992.

Morris, Eric. *The Russian Navy: Myth and Reality.* New York: Stein and Day, 1977.

Polmar, Norman. *Guide to the Soviet Navy.* Annapolis, MD: Naval Institute Press, 1986.

Raft, Bryan, and Geoffrey Till. *The Sea in Soviet Strategy.* Annapolis, MD: Naval Institute Press, 1989.

Soviet-Yugoslav Split (1948)

The conflict between the leadership of the Communist Party of the Soviet Union (CPSU) and the Communist Party of

Yugoslavia (CPY) that erupted in 1948 and led to the first public schism in the international communist movement. The reasons for the Soviet-Yugoslav split were the unwillingness of the Soviet leadership to tolerate insubordination, the ultraleftist orientations of Yugoslav leaders, and the Yugoslavs' aspirations to regional hegemony. The split ultimately paved the way for an independent form of socialism in Yugoslavia as well as for a neutral and later nonaligned foreign policy, strengthened movements of national communism in Eastern Europe, and broke up the seemingly fixed bipolar structure in Southeastern Europe.

In the immediate postwar period, the CPY was generally considered the most Stalinist communist party in Central and Eastern Europe and the closest ally of the Soviet Union. This was confirmed by the prominent role played by Yugoslav representatives at the founding session of the Cominform in September 1947. At the beginning of 1948, however, serious differences emerged, the immediate reasons being Yugoslavia's ambitions toward Albania and its continuing aid to the communist side in the Greek Civil War. Soviet leader Josef Stalin accused Yugoslav leaders of pursuing expansionist policies in the Balkans. Yet the Soviets' complaints, albeit containing some truth, were primarily motivated by the hegemonic aspirations of the Soviet leadership itself. It did not want to loosen its grip on Albania, to endanger the October 1944 Stalin-Churchill percentage agreements regarding influence in the states of Southeastern Europe that had placed Greece in the Anglo-American sphere, or to tolerate independent moves by Yugoslavia and Bulgaria. The essential aim was thus to strengthen Soviet supremacy over Yugoslavia and Eastern Europe.

Under the leadership of Josip Broz Tito, however, the overwhelming majority of the CPY leadership dismissed the Soviet criticism. In fact, it resisted Soviet tutelage and Moscow's attempts to interfere in internal affairs. In order to increase the pressure on the Yugoslav leadership, the Soviets recalled their military advisors, instructors, and civil experts from Yugoslavia in March 1948. They also initiated, with the first of three letters signed by Stalin and Foreign Minister Vyacheslav Molotov, a public attack on top Yugoslav leaders. The letters accused the Yugoslavs of opposing prescribed socialist principles.

The Yugoslav leadership repudiated the accusations and refused to take part in the hastily convoked June 1948 Cominform session, which turned out to be a tribunal, of sorts, against the rogue CPY. The Cominform's resolution, published on 28 June 1948, called upon the "healthy elements" of the CPY to force a policy change or, if necessary, to overthrow its leadership and replace it with a "new internationalist" one.

Belgrade tried to convince Moscow of its lasting loyalty to socialism, the Soviet Union, and Stalin, claiming that the accusations were simply not justified. At the same time, the

Yugoslav leadership did not hesitate to fight Soviet Stalinism with Stalinist methods, purging the CPY of pro-Soviet members, called "Cominformists," of whom more than 55,000 were prosecuted and more than 15,000 were sent to the notorious labor camp at Goli Otok (Naked Island). In the years that followed, Soviet-Yugoslav relations deteriorated further, with Moscow engaging in strident propaganda, labeling the CPY leadership a "gang of spies and murderers," and accusing it of having turned the CPY into a "fascist party." During the most spectacular show trials of former East European leaders—Traicho Kostov in Bulgaria in 1948, László Rajk in Hungary in 1949, and Rudolf Slánský in Czechoslovakia in 1952—one of the most serious charges leveled was that all were "Titoist agents."

The Yugoslavs steadfastly resisted Soviet pressure tactics and gradually changed their policies in the early 1950s. Although Yugoslavia remained a dictatorship, it liberalized its economic policy, developing a new system of self-management socialism. In its foreign policy, Yugoslavia improved its relations with the West but remained independent and later became one of the leading members of the Non-Aligned Movement. After Stalin's death in 1953, the new Soviet leadership began to reassess its position vis-à-vis Yugoslavia. Finally, Nikita Khrushchev, who emerged as Stalin's successor, sought to normalize relations with the Yugoslavs, visiting Belgrade in June 1955. Nevertheless, until the dissolution of both states in 1991, Yugoslavia always kept some distance from the Soviets, and its relationship with the superpower to the east remained an ambiguous one.

Magarditsch Hatschikjan

See also
Cominform; Khrushchev, Nikita; Non-Aligned Movement; Rajk, László; Slánský, Rudolf Salzmann; Slánský Trial; Soviet Union; Stalin, Josef; Tito, Josip Broz; Yugoslavia

References
Banac, Ivo. *With Stalin against Tito: Cominformist Splits in Yugoslav Communism.* Ithaca, NY: Cornell University Press, 1988.
Bass, Robert H., and Elizabeth Marbury, eds. *The Soviet-Yugoslav Controversy: A Documentary Record.* New York: Prospect Books, 1959.
Vucinich, Wayne S., ed. *At the Brink of War and Peace: The Tito-Stalin Split in a Historic Perspective.* New York: Columbia University Press, 1982.

Spaak, Paul-Henri (1899–1972)

Belgian socialist politician, international statesman, foreign minister (1936–1939, 1947–1949, 1954–1957, 1961–1966), and premier (1938–1939, 1946, 1947–1949). Born in Schaerbeek, Belgium, on 25 January 1899, Paul-Henri Spaak earned a degree in jurisprudence from Brussels University in 1921. He began his political career as a socialist member of the

Chamber of Deputies in 1932. His efforts to keep Belgium out of World War II were in vain, and after the Belgian capitulation to Germany in May 1940, he went into exile first in Paris and then in London.

After the war, Spaak became a staunch supporter of international cooperation and collective security. He helped draft the United Nations (UN) Charter and served as the UN General Assembly's first chairman in 1946. On 28 September 1948 he delivered his famous "Speech of Fear" to the UN, denouncing Moscow's early Cold War policies and enunciating the reasons that Western countries feared the Soviet Union.

A brilliant speaker and an advocate of European integration, Spaak promoted the creation of the Benelux Customs Union (among Belgium, the Netherlands, and Luxembourg) in 1948. In August 1949 he became president of the Council of Europe, an office from which he resigned in protest in 1951 over the lack of support from member governments. He played a leading role in the creation of the European Coal and Steel Community (ECSC) and presided over its General Assembly during 1952–1954. He was also committed to the formation of the European Defense Community (EDC), which was eventually defeated by the French National Assembly in August 1954. In 1955, the Messina Conference of European leaders appointed him to chair a committee charged with the preparation of a report on the creation of a common European market. The "Spaak Report" led to the March 1957 Treaty of Rome, establishing the European Economic Community (EEC) and the European Atomic Energy Community (EURATOM).

In December 1956, when Spaak was chosen as second secretary-general of the North Atlantic Treaty Organization (NATO), the organization was deeply split because of the autumn 1956 Suez Crisis. Spaak was a resolute advocate of the transformation of NATO from a military defense organization into an effective political instrument. As such, in 1957 NATO began to play an important role as a Western clearinghouse on East-West relations. When General Charles de Gaulle returned to power in France in June 1958, however, French nationalist policies reduced NATO's effectiveness and increasingly frustrated Spaak. De Gaulle's obstructionism within NATO contributed to Spaak's decision to relinquish his post in January 1961.

During 1961–1965 Spaak served as Belgium's deputy prime minister, minister for African Affairs, and foreign minister. The Congo crisis demanded most of his attention. He also launched several new plans for a European political community. During July 1965–February 1966 he was foreign minister in the cabinet of Pierre Harmel. After a quarrel with his Socialist Party members over the relocation of NATO headquarters from Paris to Brussels following de Gaulle's withdrawal from the alliance's military command in February 1966, Spaak resigned from politics in March 1966.

Spaak remained closely associated with NATO, however, serving as chair of a NATO special group tasked with establishing closer relations among NATO members during 1967–1972. In 1969, he published his memoirs, *Combats inachevés* (Unfinished Battles). Spaak died on 31 July 1972 in Brussels.

Christian Nuenlist

See also

Belgium; European Atomic Energy Community; European Coal and Steel Community; European Defense Community; European Economic Community; European Integration Movement; Europe, Western; North Atlantic Treaty Organization, Origins and Formation of

References

Dumoulin, Michel. *Spaak.* Brussels: Racine, 1999.

Jordan, Robert S., with Michael W. Bloome. *Political Leadership in NATO: A Study in Multinational Diplomacy,* Boulder, CO: Westview, 1979.

Spaak, Paul-Henri. *The Continuing Battle: Memoirs of a European, 1936–1966.* Translated by Henry Fox. Boston: Little, Brown, 1971.

Space Race

The competition between the United States and the Soviet Union to explore outer space, most often defined by the race to place a human on the moon. The space race was an integral part of the Cold War. Each side used the competition to demonstrate its technological prowess in the areas of science, education, engineering, and management. Both nations also used rocket and missile development gleaned from the space race to strengthen their military establishments. The two superpowers had been working on missile development for some time in hopes of developing intercontinental ballistic missiles (ICBMs) to deliver nuclear warheads. Both sides thus hoped that these programs would help develop a rocket capable of placing a satellite into orbit.

The space race officially began on 4 October 1957 with the successful Soviet launch of the *Sputnik I* satellite. The orbiting *Sputnik I* not only established an early Soviet lead in the space race but was a major blow to American prestige, since U.S. leaders believed that the Soviets were incapable of such a breakthrough. The Soviet program, led by chief designer Sergei Korolev, who was largely unknown in the West, continued to reveal the American rocket program as unequal to the task. The Soviets' advantage was confirmed in their launching of the much-heavier payload *Sputnik II* on 3 November 1957.

Americans were surprised to learn that the United States lagged badly behind Soviet rocket and missile technology. Politicians were outraged and proclaimed the existence of an alleged missile gap, which Senator John F. Kennedy exploited during his 1960 presidential campaign. Other Americans used

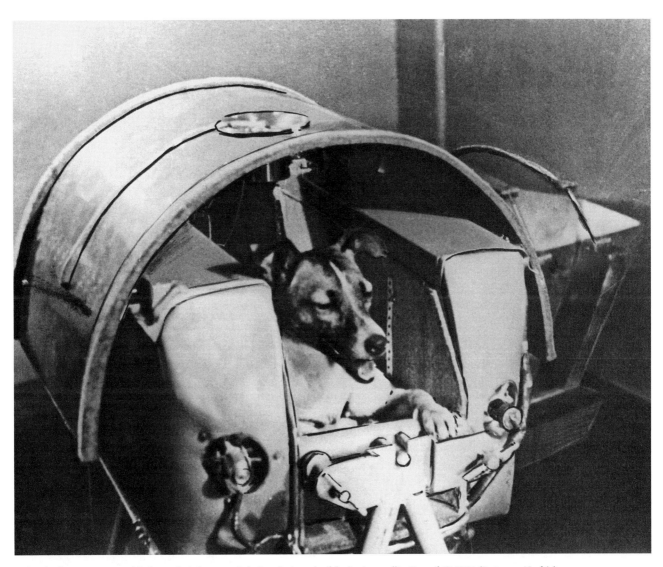

Laika, the first creature to orbit the earth, in her capsule before the launch of the Soviet satellite *Sputnik II,* 1957. (Bettmann/Corbis)

the Soviet space lead to suggest a lack of rigor in American secondary schools in the fields of science and mathematics. While President Dwight D. Eisenhower rejected the notion of American weakness, the public was shocked when on 6 December 1957 Project Vanguard was unable to place an American satellite in orbit.

Another American program, the Explorer project under the direction of the U.S. Army and headed by former German rocket scientist Wernher von Braun, served notice that the Americans had not yet yielded the space field to the Soviets. On 31 January 1958 the United States successfully launched *Explorer I,* a light satellite that proved more scientific than symbolic when it discovered the Van Allen Radiation Belts. Also, to provide overall direction to the American civilian space effort and to match Soviet successes, Congress created a new government agency, the National Aeronautics and Space Administration (NASA). It began operations on 1 October 1958.

The Soviets continued to produce other impressive space firsts that the United States seemed unable to duplicate. The Soviet *Luna 1* was the first satellite to escape Earth's gravity when it entered solar orbit on 2 January 1959, although it missed its target of the moon. *Luna 2,* launched on 12 September 1959, sent back clear images of the moon's surface, while *Luna 3* on 7 October 1959 photographed the far side of the moon.

As successful satellite launches became routine, both sides sought to be the first to place a man in orbit. The Soviets won this competition with the launch of cosmonaut Yuri Gagarin into a one-orbit voyage around Earth on 12 April 1961. The United States successfully put astronaut Alan Shepard into a suborbital low-level space flight on 5 May 1961. On 25 May 1961 President Kennedy classified the space race as an integral part of the battle between freedom and tyranny and raised the stakes when he announced the American goal of placing a man on the surface of the moon by the end of the decade.

On 20 February 1962 the Americans finally matched the Gagarin flight by putting a man into Earth's orbit with the three-orbit trip of astronaut John Glenn.

Following Gagarin's mission, the Soviet Union's other firsts in manned flight included the first day-long space flight of Gherman Titov on 6 August 1961; the first female in space, Valentina Tereshkova, on 16 June 1963; and the first space walk, by Alexei Leonov, on 18 March 1965. Unmanned Soviet moon flight firsts included the *Luna 9* soft landing on the moon with the first photos from the lunar surface on 3 February 1966 and *Luna 10,* the first to be in moon orbit, on 3 April 1966. The Soviets made an impressive unpiloted flight to the moon with a return to Earth with *Zond 5* on 14 September 1968, which seemed to suggest that they were on the verge of sending the first man to the moon.

Although it appeared to many that the Soviets remained ahead in the space race, the United States worked feverishly to meet Kennedy's challenge and budgeted funds for it that the Soviet Union could not match. The Americans gradually eliminated the early Soviet race lead by securing qualitative advances, which translated into successes such as the rendezvous and docking of two manned spacecraft and the development and flight testing of the *Lunar Module,* both of which were essential to placing a man on the moon's surface. The United States also matched other Soviet achievements when it conducted several space walks and long-duration flights, and it achieved a soft landing on the moon with *Surveyor I* (2 June 1966). The United States achieved a major breakthrough with the year-long *Lunar Orbiter* low-level photomapping of the moon's surface beginning in August 1966, undertaken in preparation for a manned landing.

Both sides suffered human losses and engineering failures during the race. The most notable American loss occurred during the *Apollo 1* fire, which began during a routine launch

Astronaut Buzz Aldrin stands beside a U.S. flag on the moon on 20 July 1969 during the *Apollo 11* space mission. (National Aeronautics and Space Administration)

pad test on 27 January 1967 and killed American astronauts Gus Grissom, Edward White, and Roger Chaffee. The results of the subsequent investigation appeared to doom the effort to meet President Kennedy's deadline. The Soviets suffered the first loss of a man during actual space flight when they announced the death of cosmonaut Vladimir Komarov on 24 April 1967 during the crash landing of *Soyuz 1*. Other Soviet failures were masked by the secrecy and closed society of the Soviet Union, which also concealed its inability to keep pace with American successes.

While the Soviets were secretive, the United States won the publicity war. It announced its space mission schedule and proudly showed off its astronauts as men with "the right stuff." This effort earned positive media coverage and the support of the viewing public. The Soviet Union's propaganda machine also played up the country's own progress, but most Soviet space missions were announced only after success was certain. Only after the collapse of the Soviet Union and the end of the Cold War did the world learn of the major flight limitations of the Soviet successes, their space failures, and the many near disasters that the cosmonauts endured.

The United States recovered relatively quickly from the *Apollo 1* disaster of January 1967. On 21 December 1968, American astronauts Frank Borman, James Lovell, and William Anders were launched into space in *Apollo 8* and three days later orbited the moon. By then, the United States had a clear lead in the space race that the Soviets seemed incapable of closing.

When *Apollo 11* (Neil Armstrong, Edward "Buzz" Aldrin, and Michael Collins) landed on the moon on 20 July 1969, the Americans stood victorious in the space race. Five more successful landings on the moon went unchallenged by the Soviets. In September 1970 the Soviet Union succeeded in landing on the moon the *Luna 16* probe, which returned lunar samples to Earth. The Soviets were the first to establish a space station in orbit with *Salyut 1* on 19 April 1971. But in reality, once *Apollo 11* landed in the Sea of Tranquillity and returned safely home, the space race had ended.

Although the sense of a race was largely abandoned by both sides, further space exploration by both countries continued but without the Cold War fervor over which society was the most technologically advanced. In light of budget pressures and many unsolved domestic problems, leaders in both countries began to question the costs of space exploration. The spirit of political détente between the two superpowers began to reach into the field of space exploration. On 15 July 1975 both nations took a giant first step in long-term outer space cooperation with the launch and rendezvous of the *Apollo-Soyuz* mission. Cooperation between the two former adversaries continued in 1993 when the Soviets were invited to participate in the International Space Station.

The space race proved an energetic stimulus to both nations. The United States committed the funding necessary to win the race and, amid the unhappiness of the Vietnam War era, gave the nation a badly needed lift. While the Soviets could never match the United States in funding, they still achieved a stunning number of space firsts. These, however, came at the expense of those mission essentials required to send a man to the moon.

Thomas D. Veve

See also
Explorer I; Gagarin, Yuri; Missile Gap; Outer Space Treaty; *Sputnik*
References
Aldrin, Buzz, and Malcolm McConnell. *Men from Earth.* New York: Bantam, 1989.
Breuer, William B. *Race to the Moon: America's Duel with the Soviets.* Westport, CT: Praeger, 1993.
Launius, Roger D. *Frontiers of Space Exploration.* Westport, CT: Greenwood, 1998.
Schefter, James L. *The Race.* New York: Doubleday, 1999.

Spain

Southwestern European state. The Kingdom of Spain occupies some 85 percent of the Iberian Peninsula, which it shares with Portugal. Spain covers 194,968 square miles and had a 1945 population of some 27.5 million people. It is bordered by the Bay of Biscay and France to the north, Portugal to the west, the Mediterranean Sea to the south, and the Atlantic Ocean to the southwest.

Spain was united into a kingdom in 1492 and during the sixteenth century was among the most powerful states in Europe. Sapped by wars and not unrelated economic reverses, the country began a period of decline at the end of the sixteenth century and lost most of its vast overseas empire in the course of the nineteenth century. Spain lagged behind the rest of Western Europe in social and political reforms, leading to the expression "Europe stops at the Pyrenees."

Considerable political turmoil developed in Spain as the nation industrialized, leading to the terrible bloodletting of the Spanish Civil War (1936–1939). The fighting pitted forces seeking modernization (the Republicans) against those favoring traditional Spanish values (the Nationalists). Perhaps half a million people died in the fighting and reprisals following the Nationalist victory. General Francisco Franco held power. One party alone, the Falange Española Tradicionalista, was permitted. The Falange's doctrines were a blend of nationalism, traditionalism, and belief in a hierarchical order.

Spain was not officially a belligerent in World War II, although Franco was sympathetic to the fascist side and sent a division of troops (ostensibly volunteers) to the Eastern Front. Franco also opened Spanish ports to German submarines, and he annexed the international zone of Tangier, only to evacuate it in 1945. He made no move, however, against the principal British base at Gibraltar. Following the November 1942 American and British landings in North Africa, the Franco regime reverted to a more strict neutrality.

After the war, Spain was very much a pariah, especially as leftist parties controlled or influenced so many European governments. The United Nations (UN) voted overwhelmingly to deny Spain membership and, in December 1946, called for diplomatic sanctions against Madrid. Spain was also excluded from Marshall Plan aid.

This quarantine changed with the Cold War. In 1953 the United States and Spain signed a mutual aid agreement that provided U.S. military and economic assistance in return for air and naval bases. In 1955, the United States and Latin American states secured Spain's admission to the UN.

The United States played a leading role in keeping the Spanish economy afloat. Between 1953 and 1975, Washington extended some $3 billion in economic and military assistance. As Spanish liberals were quick to point out, this aid helped maintain Franco in power.

The Spanish Cortes (parliament) had begun to function again in 1942, but it was not representative of the people. The 1947 Law of Succession declared Franco chief of state for life and established a Council of the Kingdom to deal with the question of succession. Franco distrusted Don Juan, the son of King Alfonso XIII and heir to the throne, and in 1969 officially designated Don Juan's son, Juan Carlos, as his successor. Franco also arranged a concordat with the Catholic Church in 1953. Roman Catholicism was declared the official religion of Spain, and the Church received guarantees of special privileges and financial assistance.

Most of Spain's small overseas colonies vanished after the war. Spanish Morocco became part of the Kingdom of Morocco, but the almost purely Spanish cities of Cueta and Melilla across the Straits of Gibraltar in North Africa remained Spanish. Moroccan nationalists continued to demand the return of these as well as Ifni and the phosphate-rich Spanish Sahara, and the latter was indeed given up in 1975. Spanish Equatorial Africa also received independence in 1968. Spain retained the Balearic (Minorca and Mallorca) and Canary Islands.

The Spanish attempted to turn nationalism to their own advantage by mounting an intense and unsuccessful campaign against the British to return Gibraltar, which had been lost in 1704. This included banning British flights over Spain and closing the border with Gibraltar from the land side (1969–1985).

Franco died in November 1975 and was succeeded as head of state by thirty-seven-year-old King Juan Carlos I. To this energetic and charismatic ruler goes considerable credit for both the restoration and survival of democracy in Spain. The new king inherited serious problems. Inflation was running at 20 percent, and there was high unemployment and a growing trade deficit. Politically, there were threats from the Right, especially from among the military. Terrorism by Basque separatists had also increased. The king was, however, committed to democracy and change.

Juan Carlos initially continued Franco's premier, Carlos Navarro, in office. Six months later, however, Juan Carlos named Adolfo Suárez to the post. Suárez organized his own party, the Union de Centre Democratico (UCD, Union of the Democratic Center). He also legalized forty-eight political parties, including the Communist Party, and in 1977 he led the nation into its first free elections—which he won—since 1936. Suárez also began loosening the censorship laws of the Franco era.

A new constitution declared Spain a parliamentary monarchy with seats in the Cortes allotted on the basis of the parties' total votes. The constitution separated church and state, guaranteed human rights, abolished the death penalty, legalized divorce, recognized separate nationalities within Spain, and extended the vote to eighteen-year-olds.

Suárez also moved to give the Basques and Catalonia their own autonomous parliaments under overall Spanish administration. These two were the only regional groups that had been autonomous before Franco revoked such rights after the Civil War, and they were the first two to receive home rule. The Right protested these moves, fearful that they would lead to the breakup of Spain. Terrorism continued in the Basque country, but over time support for the terrorists diminished.

In February 1981, the militant Right attempted to seize power. Lieutenant Colonel Antonio Molina led some 200 armed Civil Guards in bursting into the Cortes when it was in session. They ordered deputies to the floor and fired shots into the ceiling. The whole episode was carried live on Spanish radio and television. Molina demanded military rule, and ultimately four of Spain's nine top generals declared for the putschists. Juan Carlos, clad in military uniform, made a dramatic television appearance and told Spaniards that he would never agree to an attempt by force "to interrupt the democratic process." This step probably saved democracy in Spain. The rebellion quickly collapsed, and the siege of parliament lasted only eighteen hours. Millions of Spaniards marched through the streets throughout the country to demonstrate their support for democracy. In both 1982 and 1985 the government discovered and foiled other plots.

Although the ruling UCD continued in power, Leopoldo Sotelo replaced Suárez as premier. Meanwhile, Suárez formed a new party, the Democratic and Social Center, looking to cooperate with the socialists. In 1982 Spain joined the North Atlantic Treaty Organization (NATO). Its modernizing military had 370,000 troops, more than 190 aircraft, 29 warships, and 8 submarines. More important was Spain's strategic

A Civil Guardsman who was inside the Spanish Congress of Deputies leaves through a window and surrenders, 24 February 1981. The failed coup d'état saw 200 armed Guardia Civil hold members of the Congress hostage for eighteen hours. King Juan Carlos I played a key role in quelling the coup attempt. (EFE/Corbis)

geographical position controlling the western mouth of the Mediterranean.

In October 1982, the Spanish Socialist Workers' Party (PSOE) won a solid majority in the parliamentary elections, which turned on economic issues. Márquez Felipe González became the first socialist premier in Spain since the Spanish Civil War. This also marked the first time in Spanish history that the socialists held an absolute majority in the parliament. The charismatic González turned the party away from Marxism. The socialists promised the creation of new jobs as well as continuation of the democratizing process.

A high point of González's first term was Spain's entry into the European Common Market in January 1986 (full membership came in 1992). The PSOE had come to power insisting on a referendum on membership in NATO. Once in power, the PSOE supported continued membership but had to proceed with the referendum, which passed. The PSOE did insist on a continued ban of nuclear weapons in Spain (a U.S. bomber had accidentally released an atomic bomb off the coast of Spain), maintenance of the Spanish military outside the NATO command structure, and a cutback in U.S. troops in Spain.

In the January 1986 parliamentary elections, the PSOE again won a majority, and González returned to the premiership. After a year of sometimes acrimonious talks, a base agreement was worked out with the United States. Some 12,500 U.S. military personnel were stationed at three air bases (Zaragoza, Torrejon, and Moron) and a naval base (Rota) that provided support for the U.S. Sixth Fleet in the Mediterranean. There was considerable resentment on the part of the Left over U.S. support for Franco and what was seen as U.S. heavy-handedness in foreign policy, particularly toward the Middle East. Many Spaniards also opposed U.S. Latin American policies, and there was no sense of a threat to Spain from the Soviet Union.

In October 1989, González and his governing PSOE won a narrow national election victory and a margin of one seat in the Cortes. The New Right in Spain actively supported the socialists, who were completely committed to a market-driven economy. By the end of the Cold War, Spain had come far indeed. Democracy appeared solidly rooted, and Spain was the world's twelfth-largest industrial power.

Melissa Jordine and Spencer C. Tucker

See also
Basque Separatism; Franco, Francisco; González Márquez, Felipe; Juan Carlos I, King of Spain

References
Carr, Raymond, and Juan Pablo Fusi. *Spain, Dictatorship to Democracy.* London: Allen and Unwin, 1981.
Gillespie, Richard, Fernando Rodrigo, and Jonathan Story, eds. *Democratic Spain: Reshaping External Relations in a Changing World.* New York: Routledge, 1995.
Payne, Stanley. *The Franco Regime, 1936–1975.* Madison: University of Wisconsin Press, 1987.
Pollack, Benny, and Graham Hunter. *The Paradox of Spanish Foreign Policy.* New York: Palgrave Macmillan, 1987.
Preston, Paul. *Franco: A Biography.* New York: Basic Books, 1994.
———. *The Triumph of Democracy in Spain.* New York and London: Methuen, 1986.

Spiegel Affair (1962)

Political scandal involving top-level political leaders in the Federal Republic of Germany (FRG, West Germany). The 1962 *Spiegel* Affair initially involved West German Minister of Defense Franz Josef Strauss. Ultimately, however, it led to the forced retirement of Konrad Adenauer, West Germany's first chancellor, in 1963.

In the 8 October 1962 issue of *Der Spiegel,* West Germany's leading weekly news magazine, an article appeared that was highly critical of the German Army (Bundeswehr) during joint

North Atlantic Treaty Organization (NATO) military maneuvers (FALLEX 62). The article, one in a series of articles aimed at discrediting Strauss by accusing him of misconduct and corruption, revealed the inadequacy of the West German military. In retaliation, Strauss ordered a raid on the offices of *Spiegel*. Eleven staff members were arrested and subsequently charged with leaking state secrets.

The article itself quickly became less important than the issue of freedom of the press in a democratic society. Strauss, an influential politician because of his high-profile role in the Christian Social Union (CSU), the sister party in Bavaria of the Christian Democratic Union (CDU), compounded the damage by lying about his role in the arrest of a *Spiegel* staffer in Spain. It soon became apparent that both Strauss and Adenauer had misled members of the Bundestag (parliament) when they had been questioned by the legislative body concerning their roles in the affair. Some of the tactics used in the affair, moreover, reminded Germans of Nazi measures in the 1930s. Adenauer eventually agreed to accept Strauss's resignation and confirmed that he would retire as chancellor in 1963.

When the *Spiegel* Affair broke, Adenauer failed to recognize the gravity of the situation and tried to use his considerable influence to preserve Strauss's position. For more than a decade, Adenauer had practiced what some observers termed "chancellor democracy," an approach to representative government that emphasized the importance of a powerful chancellor, and he had become accustomed to getting his way. The *Spiegel* Affair was a great test of West Germany's democratic institutions. In the end, democracy and the rule of law prevailed. Adenauer's exit also opened the way toward more representative democracy.

Michael D. Richards

See also
Adenauer, Konrad; Germany, Federal Republic of; Germany, Federal Republic of, Armed Forces; Strauss, Franz Josef
References
Bark, Dennis L., and David R. Gress. *A History of West Germany.* Oxford, UK: Blackwell, 1989.
Fulbrook, Mary. *The Divided Nation: A History of Germany, 1918–1990.* New York and Oxford: Oxford University Press, 1992.
Turner, Henry Ashby. *Germany from Partition to Reunification.* New Haven, CT: Yale University Press, 1992.

Spinola, António de (1910–1996)

Portuguese military officer and first president of Portugal's Provisional Government (April–September 1974) following the April 1974 revolution. António de Spinola was born in Estremoz, Portugal, on 11 April 1910. He entered the army after graduating from the Colégio Militar (Military College)

in 1928. He served in the Portuguese intervention forces in the Spanish Civil War (1936–1939) and accompanied the German Army as an observer on the Eastern Front during World War II.

During 1961–1963 Spinola served in the beginning stages of the Angolan nationalist insurgency. By 1968 he was named commanding general and high commissioner of Guinea-Bissau, where the Party for the Independence of Guinea and Cape Verde was gaining strength, thanks in part to Soviet support. Despite the innovative counterinsurgency tactics that he employed in Guinea with moderate success, he became convinced of the ultimate futility of Portugal's African wars, which were consuming the lion's share of Portugal's resources. Furthermore, he was disillusioned by dictator Marcelo Caetano's refusal to allow any negotiations with the insurgents. It was during his time in Guinea that Spinola's charisma and outspokenness made an impression on the younger generation of officers who later would topple Caetano.

Upon his return from Africa in 1973, Spinola was named chief of staff of the armed forces. In February 1974, without government approval, he published his influential book *Portugal and the Future*. It called for liberalization and democratization at home and an immediate political solution to end the anticolonial wars in Africa. The book became a best-seller and heralded the end of Caetano's Estado Novo (New State). In April 1974 a group of young officers known as the Armed Forces Movement (MFA), many of whom had served under Spinola, toppled Caetano in a nearly bloodless coup and established the Second Republic. They first named Spinola head of the Junta of National Salvation and then provisional president of Portugal.

Spinola and the officers of the MFA disagreed, however, about the extent to which the coup should entail substantial social change and especially about how quickly and thoroughly Portugal should divest itself of its colonies. Spinola envisioned a gradual withdrawal and possibly a Portuguese federation to replace the empire. The more radical leaders of the MFA wanted unequivocal and immediate withdrawal of all troops. Spinola resigned in September 1974, and the next year he conspired with conservatives to overthrow the government but was forced into temporary exile. Following his departure, the establishment of the republic, and decolonization, some of Portugal's former colonies—especially Angola—attracted increased Soviet, Cuban, and American involvement. Spinola died in Lisbon on 13 August 1996.

Eric W. Frith

See also
Decolonization; Eanes, António; Mozambique Civil War; Namibia; Portugal
References
Graham, Lawrence, and Harry M. Mlaker, eds. *Contemporary Portugal: The Revolution and Its Antecedents.* Austin: University of Texas Press, 1979.

Maxwell, Kenneth. *The Making of Portuguese Democracy.* Cambridge and New York: Cambridge University Press, 1995.

Spinola, Antonio de. *Portugal and the Future.* Johannesburg: Perskor, 1974.

Spirit of Camp David
See Camp David, Spirit of

Sputnik (4 October 1957)

First man-made, Earth-orbiting satellite, launched by the Soviet Union on 4 October 1957. Although commonly used to describe the first satellite, *Sputnik,* meaning "fellow traveler," actually designates a series of satellites that were numbered sequentially. *Sputnik I* weighed 184 pounds, excluding the propulsion vehicle, and was placed into space as part of the 1957–1958 International Geophysical Year (IGY), which included the objective of launching artificial satellites for scientific research. *Sputnik I* was followed by the 3 November 1957 launch of *Sputnik II,* a 1,118-pound capsule with a dog named Laika as a passenger. These two stunning Soviet successes occurred before the failed launch attempt of *Vanguard,* the American contribution to the IGY scientific effort, on 6 December 1957.

The *Sputnik* launches, especially when contrasted with the American failure, were important symbols of Soviet technological prowess, which marked the beginning of the intense space competition with the United States that became known as the space race. The launch provided the Soviet Union with an important propaganda tool that was used to publicize the alleged advanced nature of Soviet society and the progress that was possible in a modern communist society.

The American public was shocked by the *Sputnik* success, and American domestic politics were soon dominated by discussions of the Soviets' technological superiority and of the implied threat to the United States. American political leaders quickly pushed for changes that would restore public confidence and retain technological superiority over the Soviets. The U.S. government responded to the challenge by passing the 1958 National Defense Education Act, which provided incentives to promote the study of science, mathematics, engineering, technical education, and other fields deemed necessary to national security. Additionally, the National Aeronautics and Space Act of 1958 created the National Aeronautics and Space Administration (NASA) to help centrally organize and coordinate American space efforts. However, military-oriented space programs, such as recon-naissance satellites, remained outside NASA and were cloaked in secrecy.

Militarily speaking, the launch of a Soviet R-7 rocket, which propelled *Sputnik* into orbit, confirmed the Soviets' capability to field nuclear-armed intercontinental ballistic missiles (ICBMs). This created an impression of vulnerability in the United States and led to intensified American efforts to enhance early warning and defensive systems, expand the national civil defense program, and strengthen strategic nuclear forces. *Sputnik* directly contributed to the erroneous idea that a missile gap had developed between the Americans and Soviets, placing the United States at a comparative disadvantage. President Dwight D. Eisenhower knew that no such gap existed but was bound to maintain silence on the issue, as the information was highly classified. Ultimately, the missile gap became a hot-button issue in the 1960 presidential campaign.

For the Eisenhower administration, there was a beneficial side to *Sputnik,* however, as it removed concerns that the Soviet Union would raise national sovereignty issues in response to an orbital overflight by an American satellite. *Sputnik* established a precedent for satellites operating over sovereign territories and opened the legal window for reconnaissance satellite operations that were already being planned by the U.S. government. *Sputnik I* was an important scientific first, a clear public relations victory in the Cold War, and an important event that shaped the continuing international struggle between the United States and the Soviet Union.

Jerome V. Martin

See also
CORONA Program; Eisenhower, Dwight David; *Explorer I;* Gaither Report; Missile Gap; Missiles, Intercontinental Ballistic; Open Skies Proposal; Space Race

References
Divine, Robert A. *The Sputnik Challenge.* New York: Oxford University Press, 1993.

Harford, James. *Korolev: How One Man Masterminded the Soviet Drive to Beat America to the Moon.* New York: Wiley, 1997.

Levine, Alan J. *The Missile and the Space Race.* Westport, CT: Praeger, 1994.

McDougall, Walter A. *The Heavens and the Earth: A Political History of the Space Age.* Baltimore: Johns Hopkins University Press, 1997.

Sri Lanka

Island nation in southern Asia. Known as Ceylon until 1972, Sri Lanka lies just 20 miles off the southern tip of India, in the Indian Ocean. Sri Lanka encompasses 25,332 square miles, slightly larger than the U.S. state of West Virginia, and had a 1945 population of approximately 7.2 million people. Largely shaped by India, Sri Lanka's political and cultural development was nonetheless unique. Moreover, unlike India, Sri Lanka never commanded the full attention of the superpowers during the Cold War. Rather, its modern history has been dominated by internal conflict between two principal cultures—the Buddhist Sinhalese and the Hindu Tamils—that still exists today.

As an important source of tea, coffee, spices, and rubber, Ceylon witnessed nearly 450 years of colonialism under Indian kingdoms as well as the Portuguese, Dutch, and British. In the nineteenth century, the British imported Tamil laborers from southern India to work Ceylonese plantations. This changed the balance between ethnicities but still left the Sinhalese comprising 75 percent of the population compared to a Tamil minority in northern and eastern Ceylon at just 20 percent.

Despite this divide, the process of decolonization came relatively peacefully for Ceylon. Strategically located, it was headquarters for the Anglo-American Southeast Asia Command during World War II. Nonetheless, in 1946 the British pulled out. Whereas in India the British faced tremendous pressure from nationalists, in Ceylon there was little activity by either Sinhalese or Tamils. Independence was more the result of British disengagement than any internal impulse. Indeed, many Ceylonese wished to remain part of the British Empire.

With British encouragement, however, Sinhalese leaders passed a constitution in 1946 and a bill of independence in 1947. On 4 February 1948, Ceylon became a self-governing dominion within the British Commonwealth but remained highly dependent on Britain for trade and aid during the first decade of independence. In 1950, Ceylon's capital hosted Commonwealth and Western nations in the so-called Colombo Plan for economic development in Asia. Anxious about possible Indian designs, Ceylon also relied on the British for defense, allowing them to maintain their Indian Ocean naval base at Trincomalee. Accordingly, Ceylon pursued a predominantly pro-Western foreign policy. At the same time, however, relations with the communist world were amicable. Ceylon recognized the People's Republic of China (PRC) in 1950 and concluded trade pacts with Beijing in 1952. In 1955, Ceylon gained admission to the United Nations (UN) after the Soviet Union dropped its opposition. Two years later, the two nations exchanged diplomatic representation and signed trade accords.

Ceylon's foreign policy during the Cold War was shaped most by Solomon Bandaranaike, prime minister during 1956–1959. He nationalized major industries, abrogated the defense agreement with Britain in 1959, and pursued a self-professed neutral foreign policy by joining the Non-Aligned Movement. In reality, Bandaranaike's foreign policy was more opportunistic, playing the great powers against each other. He strengthened ties with communist countries, concluding agreements with the PRC that brought Ceylon $41 million in aid during 1957–1967. At the same time, he maintained relatively good relations with the United States. Washington cut aid to Ceylon in 1963 following the nationalization of petroleum industries but resumed the flow in 1966 after American companies were compensated. By 1991, the United States had granted more than $1 billion in aid. Throughout the Cold War, the Voice of America operated in Ceylon, and U.S. naval vessels made regular calls there. This balancing act remained the consistent focus of Ceylon's foreign policy until the 1990s.

Bandaranaike's domestic policies were equally important. He ignited conflict between the Sinhalese and Tamils by making Sinhalese the only official language and by implementing other policies that exacerbated communal politics. The Tamils began a civil disobedience movement, and occasional violence erupted. In 1959 Bandaranaike was assassinated, not by Tamils but by a Buddhist radical who wanted the prime minister to do even more to establish Sinhalese dominance.

The April 1960 elections were won by Bandaranaike's widow, Sirimavo Bandaranaike, the world's first female prime minister. She expanded her husband's foreign and domestic policies during two terms in office (1960–1965, 1970–1977). In 1962 she hosted a conference of neutrals to mediate the Sino-Indian War. In 1972 she changed the country's name to Sri Lanka (Sinhalese for "resplendent land") and declared it a republic. She then promulgated a new constitution and made Buddhism a state religion, further alienating the Tamils. Bandaranaike also faced insurrection from the Maoist People's Liberation Front (MPLF) that prompted a state of emergency lasting six years (1971–1977).

In 1977 Bandaranaike was ousted by J. R. Jayawardene, who served as prime minister and president during 1977–1988. Later that year the National Assembly adopted a presidential system of government, appointing Jayawardene to the office. Criticized by some as corrupt and authoritarian, he liberalized the economy and tilted to the West. He was elected president again in 1982 but had to contend with an increasingly divided nation. In May 1983, thirteen Sri Lankan soldiers were killed by the Liberation Tigers of Tamil Eelam (LTTE, or Tamil Tigers), militants who demanded an independent homeland. Ethnic violence then rocked the country, prompting the government to declare a state of emergency. Attempts to crush the insurgents failed. Aided secretly by supporters in the southern Indian state of Tamil Nadu, the guerrillas were effectively organized and well armed.

Agreements in 1987 brought Indian troops, ostensibly as peacekeepers, to diffuse the situation. They remained until 1990 but failed to stop the violence. In fact, the unrest grew worse. Supporting the Tamils, the MPLF renewed attacks on the government in 1989. In 1990 Tamil guerrillas turned against Muslims who supported the Sinhalese. In 1991 the Indian government took over direct rule of Tamil Nadu,

Krishna, Sankaran. *Postcolonial Insecurities: India, Sri Lanka, and the Question of Nationhood.* New York: Oxford University Press, 2000.
Nubin, Walter. *Sri Lanka: Current Issues and Historical Background.* Bloomington: Indiana University Press, 2004.

Tamil guerrilla on patrol in Sri Lanka, February 1986. (Michel Philippot/Sygma/Corbis)

provoking the LTTE suicide bomb attack that killed former Indian Prime Minister Rajiv Gandhi that May. By 1992 nearly 20,000 people had been killed in the insurgency, including many senior military and government officials. Then, in May 1993, the LTTE assassinated President Ranasinghe Premadasa, causing even more bloodshed.

In August 1994, Chandrika Kumaratunga became prime minister of a coalition government that bridged both Buddhist extremists and Marxist revolutionaries. In November 1994 she became the first woman elected president in Sri Lanka. Her government thereafter veered between military campaigns and peace negotiations, the most recent of which started through Norwegian intermediaries in 2001.

Arne Kislenko

See also
Bandaranaike, Sirimavo; Colombo Plan; Non-Aligned Movement; South Asia
References
Bullion, Alan J. *India, Sri Lanka and the Tamil Crisis, 1976–1994: An International Perspective.* London: Pinter, 1995.
De Silva, Chandra Richard. *Sri Lanka: A History.* 2nd ed. New Delhi: Vikas, 1997.

Staatssicherheitsdienst der Deutschen Demokratischen Republik
See Stasi

Stalin, Josef (1879–1953)
Russian revolutionary and dictator of the Soviet Union (1929–1953). More absolute a ruler than any Russian tsar, Josef Stalin (born Iosif Vissarionovich Dzhugashvili) was one of the most powerful and influential figures in history and certainly one of its most horrific. As many as 20 million people may have died as a direct result of his policies.

Much of Stalin's early life remains obscure, in part because he took pains to rewrite it. Born in the town of Gori, Georgia, in the Caucasus on 21 December 1879, he was the only child of his parents to survive infancy. His father was a cobbler and his mother a washerwoman and domestic. His father (who died in a barroom brawl) was an alcoholic and beat young Josef regularly.

Stalin's mother wanted Dzhugashvili to become a priest, and he graduated from the four-year elementary ecclesiastical school in Gori in 1894 and then entered a theological seminary in Tiflis (Tblisi) on a scholarship. He grew up to be a small man, barely five feet in height, with a pockmarked face and a withered arm (or at least one of sufficient infirmity to keep him out of the Russian Army). He either quit the seminary or was expelled. In any case, he said it was there that he was introduced to Russian Marxism.

In 1901 Dzhugashvili joined the Russian Social Democratic Labor Party. His activities to secure funds included robberies and counterfeiting operations. He was subsequently arrested, tried, and convicted. Exiled to Siberia in 1903, he escaped a year later. His enemies would later charge that he was also in the pay of the tsarist secret police.

One of Dzhugashvili's aliases, the one by which he became best known, was that of Stalin (Man of Steel), given to him by his fellow revolutionaries for his strength and ruthlessness. Coarse and ill-mannered, Stalin was six times arrested and exiled and escaped five times. Freed during the March 1917 Revolution, he returned to Petrograd and became editor of the party newspaper, *Pravda* (Truth). His role in the Bolshevik

Josef Stalin, dictator of the Soviet Union during 1929–1953. (Library of Congress)

seizure of power that November is unclear, but he clearly did not take a leading part. Leon Trotsky, a rival for power later, remembered Stalin's role as "a gray blur."

Stalin was active in the Russian Civil War (1918–1921) and the Russo-Polish War (1920–1921), and from 1920 to 1923 he was commissar of nationalities. In 1923 he assumed the post of secretary-general of the Communist Party of the Soviet Union (CPSU), a position he used as a springboard to power. His political rise has been ascribed to his skill at infighting and playing one faction against another as well as his absolute ruthlessness, but he also put in long hours at his job and deserves considerable credit for his achievement.

By the late 1920s, Stalin had triumphed over his rivals, chief among them Trotsky, to wield absolute power in the Soviet Union. Stalin created the bureaucratic system and refined both the secret police and slave labor camps begun under his predecessor, Vladimir Lenin. Stalin abandoned Lenin's New Economic Policy (NEP) that permitted a degree of capitalism in Russia and initiated a series of five-year plans to modernize the economy, concentrating on heavy industry. Stalin's economic policies included the forced collectivization of agriculture that claimed an estimated 10–15 million lives.

Stalin was personally responsible for the Great Purge trials of the 1930s that consumed virtually all of the top party leadership. Also falling victim to the Great Purge were military leaders, including 60 percent of Red Army officers above the rank of major. In the so-called Deep Comb-Out that accompanied the show trials, hundreds of thousands of Soviet citizens simply vanished without benefit of judicial procedure.

Much of the blame for the dismal showing of the Red Army in the 1939–1940 war with Finland and at the outset of the German invasion of the Soviet Union in June 1941 must be attributed to Stalin's policies. He had also labeled repeated warnings of an impending German attack as "Western disinformation." He grew in stature as a military commander and strategist during the war, however. Learning the art of war and absorbing specialist military information, he made all important strategic decisions for the Red Army as well as taking many decisions on the tactical level.

In foreign affairs, Stalin seized opportunities that presented themselves in Eastern Europe and the Balkans. Knowing exactly what he wanted, he met with Western leaders in Moscow and at the Tehran, Yalta, and Potsdam conferences. In 1919, following World War I, the West had quarantined the new communist Russia with a series of new successor states, endeavoring to contain communism with a cordon sanitaire. Now, following World War II, Stalin sought the reverse, insisting at the very least on governments friendly to the Soviet Union in order to provide security for a badly wounded Soviet empire. Throughout his long reign, Stalin was intensely suspicious of foreigners and foreign, above all Western, influences. Thus, Soviets who had been in the West, including Red Army personnel captured during the war, were immediately suspect and treated as enemies. A great many people who had been in the West, voluntarily or involuntarily, were shipped off to the gulags. Many Soviet citizens had openly cooperated with the Germans during the war. Although Ukrainians were far too numerous to be uprooted, Stalin did make an example of the Crimean Tartars. He ordered some 300,000 of them sent to Uzbekistan in Central Asia.

Although there were fears in the West that Stalin's plans included the communization of Western Europe, the dictator's immediate motivation was simply that of securing the Soviet empire. Because of the Red Army presence on the ground, there was little that Western leaders could do to prevent this short of war with the Soviet Union, which despite the U.S. nuclear monopoly was unimaginable to Washington in 1945. Stalin's regime emerged from the war with all of Eastern Europe and much of Central Europe under its control.

The Soviet Union had suffered grievously during the war, with perhaps 27 million people dead and widespread physical destruction. Stalin put the population to work rebuilding, although his people paid for this in retention of the forty-eight-hour workweek and living standards well below those of 1940. In a new five-year plan, he continued his emphasis on building heavy industry, although some attention was paid to pressing housing needs.

To unite the Soviet people under his leadership, Stalin proclaimed the belief of a communist world threatened by encircling enemies. Everything was done to maintain the intense nationalist sentiments aroused by the ordeal of the long struggle against the Germans in World War II. Andrei Zhdanov, political boss of Leningrad, became the guiding spirit of this ideology, known as Zhdanovshchina. It championed Russian nationalism and attacked Western influence (now known as bourgeois cosmopolitanism), glorified communism, and above all trumpeted the accomplishments and inspiration of the Great Leader, Stalin, attributing to him all Soviet successes.

Once Stalin rejected a closer relationship with the West, the Cold War was launched in earnest. Stalin refused to allow the East European Soviet satellites to participate in the European Recovery Program (Marshall Plan), and following an impasse over German reunification on Soviet terms and impending Western currency reform in the Allies' zones of Germany, in the summer of 1948 Soviet troops cut off Western land access to the city of Berlin. This sparked a major East-West confrontation and led to the Berlin Airlift. Stalin's tactics and saber rattling resulted in the 1949 formation of the North Atlantic Treaty Organization (NATO) and prompted the movement toward West European unity.

Stalin pushed hard to develop an atomic bomb, a process greatly accelerated by Soviet espionage. Following the explosion of the Soviet Union's first nuclear device in late 1949, he adopted a less militant foreign policy, jettisoning the militant expansionism of the immediate postwar years in favor of one that was comparatively defensive in nature. While maintaining the traditionally truculent Soviet tone, he abandoned the further extension of his European empire. This move was accompanied by a massive propaganda effort, the great Stalinist Peace Campaign. Agitation against colonialism was increasingly used to weaken the Western hold on global military bases, while Soviet foreign policy also sought to sow discord between the United States and its allies.

Early in 1950, Stalin gave his blessing to plans by Democratic People's Republic of Korea (DPRK, North Korea) leader Kim Il Sung to invade the Republic of Korea (ROK, South Korea) and reunify the peninsula under communist rule. Stalin evidently believed Kim's contention that the United States would either do nothing or would not react in time to save South Korea. Later, when the war went badly for Kim and North Korea, Stalin sanctioned military intervention by the People's Republic of China (PRC).

The last act in the Stalinist drama was the so-called Doctors' Plot. Fed by Stalin's continuing paranoia, nine doctors, six of them Jewish, were accused of employing their medical skills to assassinate prominent individuals, among them Zhdanov, Stalin's heir apparent. Many in the Soviet Union believed that this heralded a return to the purges of the 1930s. But it may only have been a maneuver to strike out against the growing ascendancy of a leadership group headed by Georgy Malenkov and Lavrenty Beria or perhaps an effort to imbue the bureaucracy with renewed revolutionary zeal, much the way that Mao Zedong would do in the Cultural Revolution in China. Whatever the reasons, Stalin's death in Moscow on 5 March 1953, following a paralytic stroke, came as a relief to many in highly vulnerable Soviet leadership positions. His eventual successor, Nikita Khrushchev, began the slow process of de-Stalinization and denounced the many excesses of the Red Tsar.

Spencer C. Tucker

See also
Beria, Lavrenty Pavlovich; Berlin Blockade and Airlift; European Integration Movement; Khrushchev, Nikita; Korean War; Lend-Lease; Malenkov, Georgy Maksimilianovich; Mao Zedong; North Atlantic Treaty Organization, Origins and Formation of; Soviet Union; World War II, Allied Conferences; Zhdanov, Andrei Aleksandrovich

References
Bullock, Alan. *Hitler and Stalin: Parallel Lives.* New York: Knopf, 1992.
Conquest, Robert. *Stalin: Breaker of Nations.* London: Weidenfeld and Nicolson, 2000.
Deutscher, Isaac. *Stalin: A Political Biography.* New York: Oxford University Press, 1969.
McNeal, Robert H. *Stalin: Man and Ruler.* New York: New York University Press, 1988.
Todd, Allen. *The European Dictatorships: Hitler, Stalin, Mussolini.* Cambridge: Cambridge University Press, 2002.
Tucker, Robert C. *Stalin As Revolutionary, 1879–1929.* New York: Norton, 1973.
———. *Stalin in Power: The Revolution from Above, 1928–1941.* New York: Norton, 1990.
Ulam, Adam B. *Stalin: The Man and His Era.* Expanded ed. Boston: Beacon, 1989.
Volkogonov, Dimitrii. *Stalin: Triumph and Tragedy.* Translated and edited by Harold Shukman. New York: Grove Weidenfeld, 1991.

Stalin, Svetlana Iosifovna (1926–)

Only daughter of Soviet dictator Josef Stalin. Born in Moscow on 28 February 1926, Svetlana Iosifovna Stalina (who upon her decision to defect in the 1960s began employing the surname of her mother, Nadezhda Sergeyevna Alliluyeva, who died in

1932) married Grigorii Morozov when she was eighteen. They had a son before divorcing in 1947. In 1949, she married Yari Zhdanov, son of Andrei Zhdanov, one of her father's top advisors. The couple had a daughter, but the marriage lasted less than two years.

In 1963, Alliluyeva began a romance with Indian communist Brajesh Singh, whom she met when he visited Moscow. In 1965 Singh moved to Moscow to work as a translator, but the couple was forbidden to marry. When he died in 1966, Alliluyeva insisted on returning Singh's ashes to India. She stayed in New Delhi for several months before deciding to defect, leaving her two children behind. On 6 March 1967, she went to the U.S. embassy and announced her intention to seek political asylum, an event that stunned the world and provided a propaganda bonanza for the West.

Although Westerners anticipated that Alliluyeva would provide insights into the workings of the Kremlin hierarchy, she insisted that her father had kept her shut off from his political life. In her initial meetings with Western reporters, she did strongly denounce her father's cruelties. Alliluyeva then went to the United States, where she secured citizenship. In 1970 she married architect William Wesley Peters. Taking the name Lana Peters, she gave birth to a daughter, Olga, but this marriage also ended in divorce in 1971. Alliluyeva then lived a relatively sheltered life until she moved, with her American-born daughter, to Cambridge, England, in 1982. As with fellow dissident Aleksandr Solzhenitsyn, Alliluyeva was first warmly received in the West but was viewed differently when she became critical of Western society.

In 1984, Alliluyeva returned to the Soviet Union, was granted citizenship, and settled in Tbilisi, Georgia. In 1986 she returned to the United States. Alliluyeva spent time in Britain in the 1990s and now lives in retirement in Wisconsin.

Michael J. Polley

See also
Defections; Solzhenitsyn, Aleksandr; Stalin, Josef
References
Alliluyeva, Svetlana. *Only One Year.* New York: Harper and Row, 1969.
———. *Twenty Letters to a Friend.* New York: HarperCollins, 1967.
Ebon, Martin. *Svetlana: The Story of Stalin's Daughter.* New York: New American Library, 1967.
Schad, Martha. *Stalins Tochter: Das Leben der Svetlana Allilujewa.* Bergisch Gladbach, Germany: G. Lübbe, 2004.

Star Wars
See Strategic Defense Initiative

Starry, Donn Albert (1925–)

U.S. Army general and one of the most significant reformers of the army following Vietnam. Born on 31 May 1925 in New York City, Donn Starry served as an enlisted soldier during World War II and entered the U.S. Military Academy, West Point, from the ranks. He graduated in 1948 and was commissioned in armor. Reporting to Germany for his first assignment as a platoon leader, his battalion commander was Creighton Abrams, a highly successful tank battalion commander in World War II. An innovative and dynamic military thinker himself, Abrams was a significant influence on Starry.

Starry served two tours in Vietnam during that war. During his second tour he commanded the 11th Armored Cavalry Regiment as a colonel, leading it during the 1970 Cambodia incursion, Operation TOAN THANG 43. Following Vietnam, he commanded the Armor School at Fort Knox, Kentucky, as a major general. There he wrote the influential monograph *Mounted Combat in Vietnam,* part of a series of official U.S. Army studies. He then commanded V Corps in Germany as a lieutenant general. In 1977 he was promoted to full general and succeeded General William E. DePuy as the second commanding general of the Training and Doctrine Command (TRADOC). With the possible exception of DePuy, Starry was the most influential commander of TRADOC. Seizing upon the deep internal debate and controversy surrounding the 1976 edition of *FM 100–5 Operation* and DePuy's concept of Active Defense, Starry presided over and personally directed the development of AirLand Battle doctrine and the long overdue recognition by the U.S. military of the Operational Level of War. Based heavily on classic German concepts of rapidly moving war-fighting, AirLand Battle became the doctrine with which the U.S. Army fought both Gulf Wars. While he was TRADOC commander, Starry also introduced the concept of sergeants' business, which became a critical tool in rebuilding the noncommissioned officer (NCO) corps that had been decimated by Vietnam.

Starry retired from the army in 1983. His last assignment was commanding general of the U.S. Army Readiness Command. He is one of a handful of key officers who rebuilt the U.S. Army in the decade following the Vietnam War into a genuine threat to the Soviet Army and the Warsaw Pact.

David T. Zabecki

See also
AirLand Battle; DePuy, William Eugene; War, Operational Art of
References
Herbert, Paul H. *Deciding What Has to Be Done: General William E. DePuy and the 1976 Edition of FM 100–5.* Leavenworth Papers,

Number 16. Leavenworth, KS: U.S. Army Combat Studies Institute, 1988.

Romjue, John L. *From Active Defense to AirLand Battle: The Development of Army Doctrine, 1973–1982.* Fort Monroe, VA: U.S. Army Training and Doctrine Command Historical Office, 1984.

Starry, Donn A. *Mounted Combat in Vietnam.* Washington, DC: Department of the Army, 1978.

Starry, Donn A., and George F. Hofmann, eds. *From Camp Colt to Desert Storm: The History of the U.S. Armored Forces.* Lexington: University Press of Kentucky, 1999.

Stasi

Secret police of the German Democratic Republic (GDR, East Germany). The Staatssicherheitsdienst der Deutschen Demokratischen Republik, known simply as the Stasi, was one of the central pillars of the highly repressive East German regime. The Stasi functioned as a secret intelligence service, a political secret police force, and a judicial inquiry organization. In Bautzen, the Stasi even maintained a prison for political dissidents. Allegedly, the Stasi was supervised by the Council of Ministers, but its real purpose was securing the Socialist Unity Party's (SED) hold on power.

The Stasi identified itself as a revolutionary organ, with a tradition that dated back to the 1917 foundation of the Bolshevik security service, the Cheka. Many Stasi officers were members of the Communist Party of Germany (KPD), and some had even worked for the Soviet Komitet Gosudarstvennoi Bezopasnosti (KGB). In correspondence with these and other secret police ministries, the Stasi saw itself as the shield and sword of the single Communist Party. This was clear from the beginning. The Soviet Military Administration in Germany (SMAD), after having defeated Adolf Hitler's forces, took full control in the Soviet Occupation Zone (SBZ). Together with German communists, they began to build a secret police organization as early as the spring of 1945. This department (K-5) of the Kriminalpolizei was headed by Erich Mielke, a confirmed party soldier. But not until the founding of East Germany in October 1949 was a ministry of secret service instituted. On 8 February 1950 a proclamation was made creating the Ministry of State Security, headed by Wilhelm Zaisser (and later Ernst Wollweber). Nevertheless, throughout the 1950s, KGB officers and instructors dominated the Stasi.

Because the Stasi employed its personnel based on their political beliefs and socialist zeal rather than their education and skills, its performance was seriously flawed during its first two decades. The East Berlin Uprising of 17 June 1953 caught the Stasi by surprise. It reacted with singular brutality, kidnapping Germans from the Federal Republic of Germany (FRG, West Germany) and West Berlin, torturing detainees, and worse. Only in the 1960s did the Stasi develop more sophisticated and subtle methods. When Erich Mielke took over the organization in 1957, the Ministry of State Security employed 14,000 official workers. Ten years later their number had grown to 33,000. By 1977 Stasi personnel reached 66,000, and at its peak in 1987, some 90,000 people worked for the Stasi.

The number of unofficial employees (agents, or *Inoffizielle Mitarbeiter*) was even higher, at 173,000 during the late 1980s. These unofficial collaborators were counted as the Stasi's most effective weapon in the battle against the enemy, that is, anyone who endangered the socialist order. These elements included foreign enemies, reactionaries in West Germany, or domestic oppositionists. To combat these divisive elements, the foreign intelligence service (HVA), headed by the charismatic Markus Wolf during 1952–1986, and the secret police department (the Hauptabteilung XX) cooperated closely.

Beginning in the 1970s, the ministry developed into a central institute for security, repression, and party power. The Stasi, under the reign of Mielke, was wholly dedicated to the single Communist Party and deeply intertwined with it. It was not subject to parliamentary control and took orders directly from party officials. However, during the autumn of 1989, when the East German regime collapsed, the Stasi quickly disintegrated. Dissidents occupied Stasi headquarters in Berlin. The ministry was dissolved in early 1990, and its files can now only be accessed by the public under certain conditions.

Beatrice de Graaf

See also

East Berlin Uprising; German Democratic Republic; Honecker, Erich; Komitet Gosudarstvennoi Bezopasnosti; Mielke, Erich; Wolf, Markus

References

Dennis, Mike. *The Stasi: Myth and Reality.* London: Pearson-Longman, 2003.

Gieseke, Jens. *Die hauptamtliche Mitarbeiter der Staatssicherheit: Personalstruktur und Lebenswelt, 1950–1989/90* [The Main Official Collaborators of the State Security Agency: Personnel Structure and Milieu, 1950–1989/90]. Berlin: Chr. Links Verlag, 2000.

Naimark, Norman. *The Russians in Germany: A History of the Soviet Zone of Occupation, 1945–1949.* Cambridge: Belknap Press of Harvard University, 1995.

Stepinac, Aloysius, Archbishop (1898–1960)

Roman Catholic archbishop, cardinal, and Croatian patriot. Born in Brezarić on 8 May 1898, the eighth of twelve children of a peasant family, Aloysius Stepinac joined the Austro-

Hungarian Army in 1916 as a second lieutenant and was taken prisoner in the war against Italy. Upon his release in 1919, he began undergraduate studies in agriculture at Zagreb University.

Stepinac decided to become a priest and went to Rome in 1924. During 1924–1929 he obtained two doctorates (one in theology, the other in philosophy) and returned home in October 1930. He was then appointed secretary to the archbishop of Zagreb and in June 1934 was nominated to be coadjutor of the archbishop. When the archbishop died in December 1937, Stepinac became archbishop of Zagreb.

Stepinac's behavior during World War II is controversial. Some sources accuse him of direct involvement with the fascist Ustashi regime, while others maintain that he acted with diffidence toward the government. In any case, with the end of the war, Yugoslav communist leader Josip Broz Tito proposed that Stepinac establish an autonomous Catholic Church independent of the Vatican. He refused and on 18 September 1946 was arrested and charged with cooperating with the Ustashi regime. In October 1946 Stepinac was sentenced to sixteen years imprisonment. He remained in prison until 1951, when Tito's government commuted his sentence to house arrest in Krašić.

In an investiture ceremony in Rome on 12 January 1953, Pope Pius XII made Stepinac a cardinal, a gesture that led to the breaking of diplomatic relations between Yugoslavia and the Holy See. Stepinac died on 10 February 1960 at Krašić and was buried behind the main altar in the cathedral in Zagreb. He was subsequently rehabilitated and beatified by Pope John Paul II on 3 October 1998.

Lucian N. Leustean

See also
Roman Catholic Church; Tito, Josip Broz; Yugoslavia
References
Bulajic, Milan. *The Role of the Vatican in the Break-up of the Yugoslav State: The Mission of the Vatican in the Independent State of Croatia; Ustashi Crimes of Genocide.* Belgrade: Ministry of Information of the Republic of Serbia, 2003.
Stella, Alexander. *The Triple Myth: A Life of Archbishop Alojzije Stepinac.* Boulder, CO: East European Monographs, 1987.

Stettinius, Edward Reilly, Jr. (1900–1949)

U.S. Lend-Lease administrator during 1942–1943, undersecretary of state during 1943–1944, secretary of state during 1944–1945, and ambassador to the United Nations (UN) during 1945–1946. Born on 22 October 1900 in Chicago, Illinois, Edward Stettinius was the son of a prominent industrialist who moved to New York in 1914 to direct Allied purchasing for the private banking house J. P. Morgan and Company during World War I. After attending the University of Virginia,

U.S. Secretary of State Edward Stettinius Jr. (Library of Congress)

where he spent much time on extracurricular social work, he joined General Motors and implemented innovative employee benefit programs. Moving to United States Steel in 1934, four years later he became chairman of the board.

In 1940 Stettinius's earlier business-government liaison work on New Deal industrial recovery programs brought him the position of chairman of the War Resources Board. The following year he became director of priorities in the Office of Production Management, where he encouraged the development of synthetic rubber. In 1942 President Franklin D. Roosevelt appointed Stettinius administrator of the Lend-Lease Administration, whose organization he streamlined and rationalized while successfully winning congressional support for its sometimes controversial aid programs to the Allies.

In September 1943 Stettinius became undersecretary of state, working under Secretary Cordell Hull with a commission to improve and coordinate the State Department's notoriously inefficient structural organization and improve its lackluster public image. Stettinius's other major responsibility was the creation of an international security organization, the UN. After laying the groundwork for this in discussions with British Foreign Office counterparts in the spring of 1944, Stettinius attended the August 1944 Dumbarton Oaks conference, where he played a major role in drafting the UN Charter.

When poor health caused Hull's resignation in November 1944, Stettinius succeeded him. The new secretary instituted public relations policies that greatly enhanced his department's popularity. He attended the controversial February 1945 Yalta Conference of Allied leaders, helping to draft American proposals for a Declaration on Liberated Europe and further clarifications of the UN Charter. Stettinius's greatest diplomatic contributions occurred from April to June 1945 at the San Francisco Conference of Allied Nations, which drafted the final UN Charter. His diplomatic skills were instrumental in persuading the numerous delegates to reach consensus on a charter that all could support.

Many officials considered Stettinius a lightweight. During the San Francisco Conference, President Harry S. Truman, who succeeded Roosevelt in April 1945, decided to replace Stettinius with South Carolina Democrat James F. Byrnes. On 27 June 1945, one day after the conference ended, Stettinius resigned to become the first U.S. representative to the new UN.

Disillusioned with the Truman administration's failure to use UN mechanisms to resolve the developing Cold War, in June 1946 Stettinius left the organization and became rector of the University of Virginia. In 1949 he published a carefully documented account of the Yalta Conference, defending Roosevelt's decisions there. Stettinius died of a heart attack in Greenwich, Connecticut, on 31 October 1949.

Priscilla Roberts

See also

Hull, Cordell; Roosevelt, Franklin Delano; Truman, Harry S.; United Nations

References

Campbell, Thomas M., and George C. Herring, eds. *The Diaries of Edward R. Stettinius, Jr., 1943–1946.* New York: New Viewpoints, 1975.

Schlesinger, Stephen C. *Act of Creation: The Founding of the United Nations; A Story of Superpowers, Secret Agents, Wartime Allies and Enemies, and Their Quest for a Peaceful World.* Boulder, CO: Westview, 2003.

Stettinius, Edward R. *Lend-lease, Weapon for Victory.* New York: Macmillan, 1944.

———. *Roosevelt and the Russians: The Yalta Conference.* Edited by Walter Johnson. Garden City, NY: Doubleday, 1949.

Walker, Richard, and George Curry. *The American Secretaries of State and Their Diplomacy,* Vol. 14, *E. R. Stettinius, Jr., and James F. Byrnes.* New York: Cooper Square, 1965.

Stevenson, Adlai Ewing, II (1900–1965)

U.S. politician, Democratic Party presidential candidate, and ambassador to the United Nations (UN). Born in Los Angeles, California, on 5 February 1900, Adlai Stevenson attended the elite Choate School and Princeton University and then earned a law degree from Northwestern University Law School. Joining the leading Chicago law firm of Cutting, Moore and Sidley, he rapidly won social prominence and a wide circle of intellectual friends, serving on many public service organizations, most notably the Chicago Council on Foreign Relations. Elected its president in 1935, he worked energetically on its behalf, winning a reputation as a stellar public speaker.

A firm supporter of American intervention in World War II, in 1940 Stevenson headed the Chicago chapter of the Committee to Defend America by Aiding the Allies. In 1941 he joined the Navy Department, remaining there until 1944. Shortly afterward, he joined the State Department as a special assistant to the secretary of state, where he stayed until 1947, serving on the American team at the 1945 San Francisco conference that created the UN and attending several UN General Assemblies.

Returning to Illinois, in 1948 Stevenson was elected governor on the Democratic ticket. As governor, he launched an activist and progressive social reform program and attempted to eradicate corruption. An outspoken opponent of McCarthyism, Stevenson quickly won national recognition as a remarkably eloquent rising political star. He was drafted on the third ballot at the Democratic National Convention in 1952, an open contest since the incumbent president, Harry S. Truman, damaged by McCarthyism and the Korean War, had chosen not to run again. Despite unstinting liberal enthusiasm for Stevenson, he faced an uphill battle against Dwight D. Eisenhower, the popular Republican candidate. Little divided them on foreign policy. Both were staunch Cold Warriors who implicitly endorsed the Truman administration's containment policy. In practice, Stevenson's position on Korea closely resembled that of Eisenhower, yet Stevenson offered no new initiatives but rather an indefinite continuation of the existing Korean stalemate. In 1952 and again in 1956, Eisenhower defeated Stevenson by wide margins.

In 1961, Stevenson hoped that the new Democratic president, John F. Kennedy, would name him secretary of state, but he instead became ambassador to the UN, a position he held for the rest of his life. Both John and Robert Kennedy regarded Stevenson as overly liberal, weak, and indecisive, so they treated him rather contemptuously. For fear of provoking congressional conservatives and the China Lobby, Stevenson was forbidden to express his personal preference for U.S. recognition of the communist People's Republic of China (PRC). Left ignorant of planning for the April 1961 Bay of Pigs invasion of Cuba, Stevenson at first erroneously informed the UN that his country had played no part in it.

Stevenson's finest hour came during the Cuban Missile Crisis, when he aggressively demanded that the Soviet UN representative confirm whether or not his country had deployed nuclear missiles in Cuba and advised the president to take a relatively moderate line during the crisis. Stevenson died in London on 14 July 1965.

Priscilla Roberts

See also
Bay of Pigs; China, People's Republic of; Containment Policy; Cuba; Cuban Missile Crisis; Eisenhower, Dwight David; Kennedy, John Fitzgerald; Kennedy, Robert Francis; Korean War; McCarthyism; Truman, Harry S.; United Nations

References
Broadwater, Jeff. *Adlai Stevenson and American Politics: The Odyssey of a Cold War Liberal.* New York: Twayne, 1994.

Johnson, Walter, ed. *The Papers of Adlai E. Stevenson.* 8 vols. Boston: Little, Brown, 1972–1979.

Martin, John Bartlow. *Adlai Stevenson and the World: The Life of Adlai E. Stevenson.* Garden City, NY: Doubleday, 1977.

McKeever, Porter. *Adlai Stevenson: His Life and Legacy.* New York: William Morrow, 1989.

Stimson, Henry Lewis (1867–1950)

U.S. secretary of war (1911–1913, 1940–1945) and secretary of state (1929–1933). Born in New York City on 21 September 1867, Henry Stimson was educated at Phillips Andover Academy, Yale University, and Harvard Law School. In 1891 he entered the law firm of Root and Clark. Its leading partner, Elihu Root, a future secretary of war and secretary of state, became one of two role models, the other being future president Theodore Roosevelt, whom Stimson would try to emulate throughout his career.

Like Roosevelt, Stimson found public service more satisfying than a career in law and soon became active in New York Republican politics. Appointed secretary of war in 1911, he followed in Root's footsteps in attempting to modernize the U.S. Army, improving troop training and the efficiency of the General Staff, although congressional opposition blocked his contemplated consolidation and rationalization of army posts around the country.

When World War I began in Europe in 1914, the staunchly interventionist and pro-Allied Stimson campaigned ardently for preparedness, massive increases in American military budgets in anticipation of war with Germany, and universal military training. After American intervention, he volunteered and served in France as a lieutenant colonel of artillery. Returning from the war, he was convinced that the United States must assume a far greater international role.

Appointed by President Herbert Hoover as secretary of state in 1929, Stimson protested firmly against Japan's 1931 establishment of the puppet state of Manzhuguo, instituting the policy of American nonrecognition of its government. In the later 1930s, he was among the strongest advocates of firm American opposition to fascist states' demands. When World War II began in Europe in 1939, Stimson, a firm believer in

In the course of his distinguished public service career, Henry L. Stimson served in the cabinets of four presidents. As secretary of state in 1932, he established a policy, later called the Stimson Doctrine, following the Japanese invasion of Manchuria not to recognize changes in violation of existing international nonaggression pacts. As secretary of war from 1940 to 1945, he recommended employing the atomic bomb against Japan. (Library of Congress)

an Anglo-American alliance, outspokenly demanded massive American assistance to the Allies.

Although or perhaps because he was a prominent Republican, in summer 1940 Democratic President Franklin D. Roosevelt made him secretary of war, a position Stimson held until the war ended. He attracted an able group of younger lawyers and businessmen such a Robert A. Lovett, Robert P. Patterson, and John J. McCloy who not only oversaw the massive recruitment and industrial mobilization programs that the war effort demanded but also accepted and wished to carry forward the forceful internationalist tradition that their revered chief embodied.

In the spring of 1945, Stimson was the first official to inform President Harry S. Truman that his country and Britain had developed an atomic weapon. Stimson approved its use against Japan but was largely responsible for the July 1945 Potsdam Declaration, whereby the Allies first invited Japan to surrender or face attack by unspecified but highly destructive new weapons. He later published an article justifying his own and other American officials' decision to use atomic weapons against Japan on the grounds that ultimately this saved more lives than it cost. He also initially suggested that in order to disarm Soviet suspicions, the Allies should share the secrets of nuclear power with the Soviet Union, plans that ultimately proved fruitless.

After retiring in 1945, Stimson endorsed a greatly enhanced American international role, publicly supporting the Marshall Plan and the creation of the North Atlantic Treaty Organization (NATO). He published an influential volume of memoirs, setting forth his views on his country's international position. Stimson died on 20 October 1950 at Huntington, New York.

Priscilla Roberts

See also
Atomic Bomb; Lovett, Robert Abercrombie; Marshall Plan; McCloy, John Jay; Military-Industrial Complex; North Atlantic Treaty Organization, Origins and Formation of; Roosevelt, Franklin Delano; Truman, Harry S.

References
Hodgson, Godfrey. *The Colonel: The Life and Wars of Henry Stimson, 1867–1950.* New York: Knopf, 1990.
Isaacson, Walter, and Evan Thomas. *The Wise Men: Six Friends and the World They Made; Acheson, Bohlen, Harriman, Kennan, Lovett, McCloy.* New York: Simon and Schuster, 1986.
Schmitz, David F. *Henry L. Stimson: The First Wise Man.* Wilmington, DE: Scholarly Resources, 2000.
Stimson, Henry L., and McGeorge Bundy. *On Active Service in Peace and War.* New York: Harper, 1948.

Stockholm Document (1986)

Final document of the Stockholm Conference on Confidence- and Security-Building Measures (CSBMs) in Europe. The 1975 Helsinki Final Act of the Conference on Security and Cooperation in Europe (CSCE) included a modest set of measures to improve cooperation in a range of areas. The key component dealt with security issues and proposed a series of confidence-building measures (CBMs) designed to lessen tensions between the North Atlantic Treaty Organization (NATO) and the Warsaw Pact. The Helsinki CBMs focused on advanced notice and exchanges of information concerning military maneuvers.

The Helsinki Final Act also called for follow-up meetings to assess progress and develop further CBMs. Little was accomplished at the first of these in Belgrade (1977–1978) and Madrid (1980–1983), largely because of the deterioration in East-West relations at the time. However, the Madrid meeting did agree to a call for a new conference on Confidence and Security-Building Measures, to be held in Stockholm, with a mandate to develop a more comprehensive and verifi-

able set of CBMs, now termed CSBMs. All CSCE members would participate. The Stockholm Conference, as it was better known, began on 17 January 1984 and concluded on 21 September 1986 with the adoption of the Document of the Stockholm Conference, which became effective on 1 January 1987.

The Stockholm Document included agreed provisions for CSBMs in several areas related to the activities of ground and air forces and covered a geographic region from the Atlantic to the Urals. All parties to the agreement pledged to refrain from the threat or use of force and also agreed to give all other parties forty-two days' advanced notice of any military activity involving the movement of more than 13,000 troops or 300 tanks. Notice was also required if more than 200 aircraft sorties would be associated with a notifiable troop movement, if any parachute or amphibious exercise involved more than 3,000 troops, and for the movement of any division-strength force into the covered area. All parties were permitted two observers at any exercise or transfer involving more than 17,000 troops or any parachute or amphibious exercise of more than 5,000 troops. All parties would also submit to all other parties an annual calendar listing notifiable activities at least one year in advance and for any involving more than 40,000 troops two years in advance. Movements of more than 75,000 troops were banned without a two-year notification, while those between 40,000 and 75,000 were banned without a one-year notification. Finally, all parties were granted the right to conduct on-site inspections by air and ground with four inspectors within thirty-six hours of a request, although no state had to accept more than three such inspections per year. This marked the first time that the Soviet Union accepted guaranteed on-site inspections.

The Stockholm Document marked considerable success in the process of developing meaningful CSBMs, which helped provide stability during the turmoil associated with the collapse of communism in Eastern Europe, but it was not the end of the process. A new round of negotiations beginning in 1989 would produce enhanced CSBMs in the Vienna Document (1990).

Steven W. Guerrier

See also
Helsinki Final Act; North Atlantic Treaty Organization, Origins and Formation of; Security and Cooperation in Europe, Conference on; Vienna Document; Warsaw Pact

References
Blackwell, Robert D., and F. Stephen Larrabee, eds. *Conventional Arms Control and East-West Security.* Durham, NC: Duke University Press, 1989.
Goodby, James E. "The Stockholm Conference: Negotiating a Cooperative Security System for Europe." Pp. 144–172 in *US-Soviet Security Cooperation: Achievement, Failures, Lessons,* edited by Alexander L. George, Philip J. Farley, and Alexander Dallin. New York: Oxford University Press, 1988.

Strategic Air Command

Primary U.S. air command for nuclear deterrence during the Cold War. The Strategic Air Command (SAC), a combat command of the U.S. Air Force, was responsible for long-range bombers and intercontinental ballistic missiles (ICBMs), two-thirds of the nation's strategic nuclear triad. SAC's main goal was to maintain a strong, credible strategic nuclear force that could swing into action within minutes, either to prevent a nuclear strike or to inflict one on an enemy nation.

SAC was formed in 1946, a year before the U.S. Air Force became a separate military service. Originally, SAC consisted of World War II B-17 and B-29 bombers. Its first commander was General George Kenney. On 19 October 1948, Lieutenant General Curtis LeMay took command and oversaw the move of SAC headquarters from Andrews Air Force Base in Maryland to Offutt Air Force Base outside Omaha, Nebraska. He quickly established stringent standards of performance, strict evaluation procedures, and incentive and retention programs. He also changed the way that personnel viewed the command.

During LeMay's tenure, SAC added B-50 and B-36 bombers. In its early years, the command had its own jet fighters for bomber protection and its own airlift. B-29 bombers were modified to be used as aerial tankers, with aerial refueling becoming an integral part of SAC and the nuclear war plan. In 1951, SAC began taking delivery of the all-jet B-47 bomber and the KC-97 tanker. These two aircraft were the mainstays of SAC forces into the early 1960s. In 1955, SAC received its first B-52 Stratofortress eight-engine bomber. SAC entered the missile age with the Snark subsonic intercontinental cruise missile and the Rascal, designed to be launched against ground targets from the B-47. The following year, the KC-135 Stratotanker, a four-engine jet air refueling aircraft, entered service.

At least one-third of all aircraft and almost all missiles were on alert at SAC bases twenty-four hours a day, seven days a week. During the 1960s, B-52 bombers armed with nuclear weapons were on airborne alert, ready to strike targets from orbits outside the Soviet Union. The airborne alerts were terminated in late 1968.

In 1959, SAC employed 262,600 personnel, 3,207 aircraft, and 25 missiles, including the Snark, the first Atlas ICBMs, Thor intermediate-range ballistic missiles (IRBMs), and the Hound Dog, an air-launched cruise missile (ALCM) carried by the B-52. By 1959, SAC's bomber force was an all-jet force. In 1960, the Joint Strategic Target Planning Staff (JSTPS) was formed with SAC's commander as director and a vice admiral as deputy director. The JSTPS was established to provide centralized planning for the entire U.S. nuclear triad, SAC bombers and missiles as well as submarine-launched ballistic missiles (SLBMs), nuclear-armed tactical aircraft, and IRBMs.

In the early 1960s, the Snark and Thor missiles were deactivated to make room for the new Atlas and Titan I ICBMs. B-47s and KC-97s were phased out, and the supersonic B-58 bomber was put into service. By 1962, the new Titan II and Minuteman I ICBMs came on-line. SAC reconnaissance aircraft included the U-2 and the SR-71, which was commissioned in the late 1960s. At its peak strength peak in 1962, SAC employed more than 282,000 personnel.

During the next thirty years, SAC's mission remained unchanged. Missile forces stabilized with a mix of 1,000 Minuteman II and III ICBMs (with 50 Peacekeeper ICBMs replacing 50 Minuteman IIIs in the late 1980s) and 54 Titan II ICBMs (phased out in the mid-1980s). SAC aircraft included, at various times, a mix of B-1, B-52, and FB-111 bombers armed with gravity weapons, short-range attack missiles, and ALCMs; a tanker force of KC-135s and KC-10s; and U-2 and SR-71 reconnaissance aircraft.

SAC B-52 bombers played a major role in the Vietnam War. The SAC airborne command post, dubbed "Looking Glass," with an airborne battle staff commanded by a general officer, was on alert with at least one EC-135 aircraft airborne at all times during 1961–1992. The number of people in the command remained near 200,000 until reductions in the bomber force caused a slow exodus. SAC had about 110,000 personnel when it was deactivated on 1 June 1992.

After the dissolution of the Soviet Union in 1991, the U.S. Air Force underwent a fundamental reorientation in structure and doctrine. Air force leadership acknowledged that SAC had accomplished its mission. It had maintained nuclear superiority—and peace—for forty-six years. After it was deactivated, SAC's aircraft became part of new U.S. Air Force operational commands.

Charles G. Simpson

See also
Aircraft; Bombers, Strategic; Missiles, Cruise; Missiles, Intercontinental Ballistic; Missiles, Intermediate-Range Ballistic; Missiles, Pershing II; Missiles, Polaris; Missiles, Poseidon; Mutual Assured Destruction; Nuclear Arms Race; United States Air Force

References
Anderton, David A. *Strategic Air Command: Two-Thirds of the Triad.* New York: Scribner, 1967.
Coard, Edna A. *U.S. Air Power: Key to Deterrence.* Maxwell Air Force Base, AL: Air University Press, 1976.
Freedman, Lawrence. *The Evolution of Nuclear Strategy.* 3rd ed. Houndmills, UK: Palgrave Macmillan, 2003.

Strategic Arms Limitation Talks and Treaties

Series of negotiations and agreements between the United States and the Soviet Union that attempted to control the nuclear arms race. Following the 1962 Cuban Missile Crisis, the United States and the Soviet Union began to move away from the abyss of nuclear war and toward the reduction of nuclear armaments. The two superpowers also sought cooperation on this issue because of the immense cost of the nuclear arms race. Continued production of nuclear weapons was becoming superfluous, as each side had more than enough capability to cripple the other even if only a small percentage of the weapons, should they be launched, actually struck their targets. The leadership of both nations was sufficiently motivated to seek an agreement on nuclear arms reduction. Adding to American motives were concerns that the Soviets might soon undermine U.S. superiority in nuclear arms and that the People's Republic of China (PRC) had acquired nuclear weapons beginning in 1964. Although the United States first approached the Soviet Union concerning strategic arms reduction talks in 1964, efforts to begin a dialogue failed repeatedly until the end of the decade.

Anti-Ballistic Missile Treaty. Arms reduction talks between the two nations began in November 1969 and, after two and a half years of detailed negotiations, a two-part agreement was reached. The first major agreement to come out of the talks was the Anti-Ballistic Missile (ABM) Treaty, signed in Moscow on 26 May 1972. This treaty reflected a belief on the part of both nations that they should seek to limit the deployment of antiballistic missile systems.

ABMs were designed to destroy enemy missiles before they could strike their targets. The United States had sought an agreement with the Soviets since the late 1960s on ABMs, which the Soviets had begun to deploy, arguing that their continued deployment would lead the United States to develop larger nuclear weapons to defeat these defenses. Therefore, rather than slowing the arms race, the development and deployment of ABMs would only intensify the arms race. The Soviets finally accepted this line of reasoning. The preamble to the treaty reflected this understanding: "Effective measures to limit anti-ballistic missile systems would be a substantial factor in curbing the race in strategic offensive arms and would lead to a decrease in the risk of outbreak of war involving nuclear weapons."

The treaty had unlimited duration, with five-year reviews. The two sides created the Standing Consultative Commission to serve as the forum for discussing compliance issues or other problems with the treaty. The commission met in Geneva, Switzerland.

The ABM Treaty prohibited deployment of an ABM system for "the defense of the territory" or the provision of "a base for such defense." This effectively restricted the creation of a nationwide defensive system while permitting the Soviets and Americans to maintain two ABM sites, comprising no more than one hundred interceptor missiles at each location. Each country could position one ABM site to defend its

capital, and the other could shield one group of land-based intercontinental ballistic missiles (ICBMs). The agreement also prohibited transferring ABM sites to other nations.

Each side would verify compliance with the treaty through the use of national technical means. A 1974 Protocol to the treaty further limited each side to one ABM deployment site. The United States chose to place its system near the ICBM missile fields of Grand Forks, North Dakota, and the Soviet Union chose to defend Moscow.

The United States and Russia signed a series of agreements on 27 September 1997 that allowed Belarus, Kazakhstan, Russia, and Ukraine to succeed the Soviet Union as state parties to the treaty. These agreements also attempted to establish the demarcation between theater and national ballistic missile defense systems.

Ultimately, both sides realized that ABM systems lacked any real military value and were prohibitively expensive. The United States closed its sole ABM site in 1975. Russia's Galosh system surrounding Moscow is still operational. Citing national security concerns and a need to deploy a limited national missile defense system, the United States withdrew from the treaty on 13 June 2002.

Interim Agreement on Strategic Offensive Arms: SALT I. Of greater importance was the wider-ranging arms control agreement that emerged from the Strategic Arms Limitation Talks (SALT). The Interim Agreement between the United States of America and the Union of Soviet Socialist Republics on Certain Measures with Respect to the Limitation of Strategic Offensive Arms, which came to be known as SALT I, was signed in Moscow by President Richard M. Nixon and Soviet Premier Leonid Brezhnev on 26 May 1972, along with the ABM treaty. The SALT I accord, which was scheduled to last for five years, required the two superpowers to maintain nuclear arsenals that were roughly equivalent to one another in terms of offensive land- and sea-launching platforms. The agreement froze the number of Soviet offensive ICBMs to 1,618 land-based missiles and 950 submarine-launched ballistic missiles (SLBMs). The American arsenal was restricted to 1,054 land-based missiles and 710 SLBMs. Mobile missile systems were not addressed. While the Soviets seemed to have a numerical advantage in missile-launching capabilities, the United States continued to enjoy a substantial advantage in bombers (about 450 to the 260 for the Soviets) and could also rely on the nuclear deterrents belonging to their European allies. The Americans also took advantage of their technological superiority to develop multiple independently targeted reentry vehicles (MIRVs). The Nixon administration refused to negotiate any limits in regard to this technological advance, and the Soviets would later take advantage of this.

In order to verify compliance with the terms of the treaty, both countries agreed to satellite photo reconnaissance of each other's territory. Even so, there were flaws in the agreement. The biggest problems were that the agreement failed to sufficiently regulate the upgrading of current missile systems. And it said nothing about the replacement of existing systems with new ones.

Each side took advantage of the loopholes in the treaty. The Soviets began to deploy a new missile system, the SS-19, that carried a warhead with six MIRVed warheads. This missile carried twice as many nuclear warheads as the mainstay of the U.S. intercontinental missile arsenal, the Minuteman. Eventually, the Soviet Union would develop the ability to launch missiles carrying ten MIRVs. On the other hand, the United States began to work on the development of the cruise missile, arguing that such a system was not covered under the SALT I agreement. Further compromising the spirit of the treaty were the new Soviet Backfire bomber, capable of reaching targets in the United States, and American plans to build the North American/Rockwell B-1 bomber and the Trident submarine. Another flaw in the treaty was that it permitted the replacement of so-called light missiles with heavy missiles, without adequately defining the term "heavy."

SALT I was designed to be an interim agreement, and the treaty contained a provision calling for continued talks aimed at creating a more detailed and comprehensive plan to regulate nuclear arms. Reaching agreement on what would become SALT II proved difficult, however. Progress was stalled by numerous factors, including President Nixon's resignation over the Watergate scandal in August 1974, American concerns with human rights violations in the Soviet Union, and a general deterioration in U.S.-Soviet relations during the 1970s. The broad numerical outlines of the eventual SALT II agreement were laid out in a summit meeting between Brezhnev and President Gerald Ford in Vladivostok in November 1974, but this did not lead to forward progress for many years.

SALT II. Arms control talks continued between the two superpowers despite these obstacles. By 1979, both sides desired a new SALT agreement. Anxious to overcome numerous foreign policy setbacks, President Jimmy Carter's administration sought an arms deal to improve his chances for reelection in 1980. The Soviets sought an agreement chiefly for economic reasons, as the nation's rate of economic growth was quickly stagnating.

Concerned that the Soviets had an advantage in throw weight, or the size of the warhead that a missile could carry into space, Carter offered to cancel development of an experimental mobile ICBM that could carry ten warheads (the MX

U.S. President Jimmy Carter and Soviet General Secretary Leonid Brezhnev signing the second Strategic Arms Limitation Treaty (SALT II) on 18 June 1979 in Vienna. The treaty was the culmination of a second round of talks seeking to curtail further development of nuclear arms. (Jimmy Carter Library)

missile) if the Soviets would cut their heavy ICBM force in half. The Soviets refused to consider an offer to prevent deployment of what was still an experimental system. Carter then backed away from this position, and the negotiations began to move toward an eventual agreement. As a result, Carter and Brezhnev affixed their signatures to the SALT II Treaty at the Vienna summit meeting on 18 June 1979.

By the terms of the treaty, both sides agreed to a limitation on the number of warheads that would be allowed on an ICBM and the total number of allowable strategic launchers. Strategic nuclear launch vehicles were limited to 2,250 on each side, and no more than 1,320 of these missiles could be outfitted with MIRVs. Within that total, a further subcategory limited MIRVed ballistic missiles to 1,200, of which only 820 could be ICBMs. New ICBMs were limited to carry no more than ten warheads, and new SLBMs were limited to fourteen warheads each. The treaty also prohibited space-based nuclear weapons, fractional orbital missiles, and rapid-reload missile launchers.

A protocol to the treaty was signed at the same time and remained in effect until 31 December 1981. The Soviets agreed not to utilize their Tupolev Tu-22M Backfire bomber, which had the ability to reach targets throughout most of the United States, as an intercontinental weapon, while the Americans consented to delay deployment of ground- and sea-launched cruise missiles for three years. In addition, MIRVed ground-launched cruise missiles (GLCMs) and submarine-launched cruise missiles (SLCMs) with a range of more than 600 kilometers could not be tested.

The SALT II treaty ran into considerable opposition in the United States, as some liberals expressed disappointment that the treaty had failed to halt the arms race, and conservatives complained that the Soviets had retained a significant edge in throw weight.

Soviet actions in 1979 added immeasurably to the problem of ratifying the treaty. Their support of the Vietnamese invasion of Cambodia, the Sandinista uprising in Nicaragua, and the Soviet invasion of Afghanistan in December 1979 all but torpedoed any prospects that SALT II would be ratified by the U.S. Senate. Knowing that the Senate would not ratify the SALT II treaty under such circumstances, Carter withdrew the treaty from Senate consideration on 3 January 1980. Although the treaty was never ratified by the United States, both sides nonetheless honored the agreement until May 1986, when President Ronald Reagan, citing Soviet violations, declared that the United States would no longer be bound by the limits of the SALT agreements.

Jeffrey A. Larsen and A. Gregory Moore

See also
Anti-Ballistic Missile Treaty; Bombers, Strategic; Missiles, Cruise; Missiles, Intercontinental Ballistic; Moscow Meeting, Brezhnev and Nixon; Moscow Meeting, Gorbachev and Reagan; Moscow and Yalta Meeting, Brezhnev and Nixon; Nitze, Paul Henry; Nuclear Arms Race; Present Danger, Committee on the; Reykjavík Meeting; Vienna Meeting

References
Carnesdale, Albert, and Richard N. Haass, eds. *Superpower Arms Control: Setting the Record Straight.* Cambridge, MA: Ballinger, 1987.
Donley, Michael B. *The SALT Handbook.* Washington, DC: Heritage Foundation, 1979.
Garthoff, Raymond L. *Détente and Confrontation: American-Soviet Relations from Nixon to Reagan.* Rev. ed. Washington, DC: Brookings Institution Press, 1994.
Morris, Charles R. *Iron Destinies, Lost Opportunities: The Arms Race between the U.S. and USSR, 1945–1987.* New York: Harper and Row, 1988.
Newhouse, John. *Cold Dawn: The Story of SALT.* New York: Holt, Rinehart and Winston, 1973.
Nixon, Richard. *RN: The Memoirs of Richard Nixon.* New York: Grosset and Dunlap, 1978.
Smith, Gerard. *Doubletalk: The Story of SALT I by the Chief American Negotiator.* New York: Doubleday, 1980.
Talbott, Strobe. *Endgame: The Inside Story of Salt II.* New York: HarperCollins, 1979.
Wolfe, Thomas W. *The SALT Experience.* Cambridge, MA: Ballinger, 1979.

Strategic Arms Reduction Talks and Treaties

A series of bilateral arms control negotiations and treaties between the United States and the Soviet Union (later Russia) during the late 1980s and early 1990s that led to two treaties. The Strategic Arms Reduction Talks (START) resulted in the START I and START II treaties, which, unlike earlier arms control agreements that slowed or froze the rate of growth of strategic systems, were the first treaties to actually reduce the number of warheads and delivery systems on both sides.

Under President Ronald Reagan (1981–1989), in the early 1980s the United States launched an arms buildup that was part of an overall strategy to confront the Soviet Union. Reagan hoped to improve the American bargaining position vis-à-vis the Soviets by increasing the nation's military strength. He also hoped to force the Soviets to allocate more of their resources to the military in order to keep up. The most notable aspect of this renewed arms race was Reagan's Strategic Defense Initiative (SDI), which was an attempt to create a space-based missile shield that would render offensive nuclear weapons impotent and obsolete. Critics viewed the SDI proposal as an expensive, unworkable, and possibly offensive weapons system that violated the 1972 Anti-Ballistic Missile (ABM) Treaty.

The North Atlantic Treaty Organization (NATO) began installing Pershing II and ground-launched cruise missiles in Europe in 1983 in response to the Soviets' refusal to downsize their arsenal of forward-deployed SS-20 theater-range missiles. This move caused the Soviets to walk out of arms control talks that had been ongoing in Geneva since 1982. Negotiations did not resume until March 1985.

In October 1986, Reagan abruptly reversed himself. During his first summit meeting with new Soviet leader Mikhail Gorbachev in Reykjavík, Iceland, the American president expressed his willingness to remove intermediate-range nuclear force (INF) weapons from Europe and to eliminate all strategic nuclear weapons. The initiative failed because Reagan was unwilling to include SDI in the proposal, and Gorbachev was unwilling to proceed unless SDI was part of the package.

Some two months later, the Soviets declared that they would negotiate according to the agenda laid out by the Americans, although initially focusing on the INF issue. The Soviets accepted the American proposal in February 1987, which called for the complete elimination of medium-range nuclear weapons from Europe. At the Washington Summit in December 1987, Gorbachev and Reagan signed the INF Treaty. This treaty established a double-zero solution, calling for the removal of two classes of intermediate-range missiles—those with a range of roughly 600–3,500 miles and those with a range of 300–600 miles. An extensive on-site verification process was established as well. By the end of 1988, the removal of the missiles was complete.

START I. The START negotiations that had resumed in Geneva in 1985 bore fruit in 1991 with the signing of the Treaty between the United States and the Union of Soviet Socialist Republics on the Reduction and Limitation of Strategic Offensive Arms, also known as the START I treaty. Under Presidents George H. W. Bush and Gorbachev, the two nations concluded the treaty on 31 July 1991, just months before the collapse of the Soviet Union. The complex document served to reduce strategic nuclear delivery systems to 1,600 on each side, with attributed nuclear warheads (a somewhat arbitrary but agreed-upon number associated with certain delivery systems) restricted to 6,000 each.

There were additional sublimits for attributed warheads: 4,900 on deployed ballistic missiles, of which no more than 1,100 could be on mobile launchers. The Soviet Union was also limited to 154 heavy ICBMs, each carrying ten warheads. The treaty placed a limit on total nuclear throw weight, provided for verification processes, and also placed limitations on the types of vehicles that could carry nuclear warheads (includ-

U.S. President George H. W. Bush and Soviet leader Mikhail Gorbachev sign the first Strategic Arms Reduction Treaty (START I) in Moscow in July 1991. Aimed at reducing the nuclear arsenal of the United States and the Soviet Union, the START negotiations succeeded the Strategic Arms Limitation Talks of the 1970s. (George Bush Library)

ing limits on the numbers of U.S. nuclear armed cruise missiles and Russian Backfire bombers).

On 23 May 1992 the Lisbon Protocol was signed, making START I a multilateral agreement among the United States, Russia, Belarus, Kazakhstan, and Ukraine. The treaty entered into force on 5 December 1994. The three new member states returned their residual Soviet-era nuclear arsenals to Russia prior to the implementation of the treaty and also joined the Nuclear Non-Proliferation Treaty (NPT) as nonnuclear weapons states.

The START I treaty had a duration of fifteen years, with the option to extend it at five-year intervals. All parties officially reached their treaty limits on 5 December 2001. The parties created a Joint Compliance and Inspection Commission tasked with monitoring compliance with the treaty. The commission began meeting in Geneva, Switzerland, in 1991. The treaty is scheduled to expire in 2009.

START II. START I was followed by the signing of the Treaty between the United States and the Russian Federation on Further Reduction and Limitation of Strategic Offensive Arms, also known as START II, by Bush and Boris Yeltsin at the Moscow summit on 3 January 1993. START II relied heavily on START I for its definitions, procedures, and verification. The U.S. Senate ratified START II on 26 January 1996, and the Russian Duma ratified in on 14 April 2000.

This agreement called for a two-phase series of reductions. Phase one called for each side to reduce its deployed strategic forces to 3,800–4,250 attributed warheads within seven years of entry into force. There were sublimits for several categories within that total. Phase two, which was originally supposed to be completed by the year 2003, required each side to further reduce their deployed strategic forces to 3,000–3,500 attributed warheads. The following sublimits applied to phase two: 1,700–1,750 warheads on nuclear submarines, the elimination of multiple independently targeted reentry vehicles (MIRVs) on ballistic missiles, and the elimination of heavy ICBMs. America's B-2 bomber was left out of the START I treaty process since it was not scheduled to carry air-launched cruise missiles (ALCMs). In START II, however, the two parties agreed to include the B-2 as a strategic weapons delivery vehicle with a U.S. commitment not to hang ALCMs on its wings. This meant that it was accountable under the warhead limits and inspectable under the treaty's verification and compliance rules. The B-1 bomber was declared to have only a conventional mission. START II also significantly increased the level of on-site inspections necessary for implementation and compliance verification.

In March 1997, Yeltsin and President Bill Clinton met in Helsinki and agreed to extend the time period for START II implementation to 31 December 2007, as long as warheads were removed from the applicable systems by December 2003. Because of the delayed entry into force, phases one and two were to be completed simultaneously. The treaty parties created the Bilateral Implementation Commission, meeting in Geneva, Switzerland, to monitor the compliance regime.

Although eventually ratified by both sides, START II lost its relevance over the years, as the United States became more concerned with obtaining a modification to the ABM Treaty in order to deploy a ballistic missile defense system, to which the Russians remained opposed. START II was supplanted by the 2002 Strategic Offensive Reductions Treaty (the Moscow Treaty), signed by Presidents Vladimir Putin and George W. Bush in May 2002. That agreement further reduces the number of nuclear warheads that can be deployed by each nation to 1,700–2,200 by the year 2012. Neither country any longer feels obliged to abide by the provisions of the START II treaty, but both are complying with START I.

Jeffrey A. Larsen and A. Gregory Moore

See also

Anti-Ballistic Missile Treaty; Bombers, Strategic; Missiles, Cruise; Missiles, Intercontinental Ballistic; Moscow Meeting, Brezhnev and Nixon; Moscow Meeting, Gorbachev and Reagan; Moscow and Yalta Meeting, Brezhnev and Nixon; Nitze, Paul Henry; Nuclear Arms Race; Present Danger, Committee on the; Reykjavík Meeting; Vienna Meeting

References

Bunn, George. *Arms Control by Committee: Managing Negotiations with the Russians.* Stanford, CA: Stanford University Press, 1992.

Cimbala, Stephen J., ed. *Strategic Arms Control after SALT.* Wilmington, DE: Scholarly Resources, 1989.

Fitzgerald, Frances. *Way Out There in the Blue: Reagan, Star Wars, and the End of the Cold War.* New York: Simon and Schuster, 2000.

Graham, Thomas, Jr., and Damien J. LaVera. *Cornerstones of Security: Arms Control Treaties in the Nuclear Era.* Seattle: University of Washington Press, 2003.

Krepon, Michael. *Arms Control in the Reagan Administration.* Lanham, MD: University Press of America, 1989.

Mazarr, Michael J. *START and the Future of Deterrence.* London: Macmillan, 1990.

Talbott, Strobe. *Deadly Gambits: The Reagan Administration and the Stalemate in Nuclear Arms Control.* New York: Knopf, 1984.

———. *The Master of the Game: Paul Nitze and the Nuclear Peace.* New York: Knopf, 1988.

Strategic Defense Initiative

Space-based, antiballistic missile (ABM) system endorsed by U.S. President Ronald Reagan in 1983 as a way to neutralize the Soviet nuclear threat. Nicknamed "Star Wars" by its critics and the media, the Strategic Defense Initiative (SDI) foresaw the use of satellites, mirrors, and lasers that would detect, track, and destroy incoming nuclear missiles. Reagan believed that the SDI might force the Soviets to engage in nuclear arms reduction talks and serve as a partial solution to the threat posed by the nuclear arms race.

To counter the Soviet threat in the 1950s, the United States began work on an ABM system. Various incarnations emerged during the 1960s and early 1970s, until the United States and the Soviet Union signed the 1972 Anti-Ballistic Missile Treaty. This treaty limited the deployment of ABM systems to only two operational areas and stipulated that such a system could not protect the entire nation. Nevertheless, work continued in both nations to develop an effective means of nullifying an enemy nuclear attack.

Reagan had many motivations for pursuing the SDI. In principle, he disagreed with the concept of mutual assured destruction (MAD). MAD held that because of the catastrophic nature of thermonuclear war, any nation that initiated a nuclear exchange was guaranteed to suffer complete destruction in a counterstrike. Reagan believed that MAD was immoral and unacceptable. He was further motivated by the upcoming 1984 election and his desire not to be seen as a warmonger. Deploying a defensive system would demonstrate his desire to end the arms race.

Among those who supported the SDI were military contractors who stood to make money developing and deploying such a system. Other supporters included Robert McFarlane, Reagan's national security advisor during 1983–1985, who believed that the SDI could be used as a bargaining chip to motivate the Soviets to scale back their missile production. Opponents of the SDI, including some Reagan administration officials, mockingly nicknamed the plan "Star Wars" after the popular science fiction film series.

In a televised address on 23 March 1983, Reagan publicly announced his desire to pursue the SDI. The scientific task was difficult, he admitted, but the rewards would be worth it: a United States whose citizens did not have to live in fear of nuclear destruction. The SDI would be costly, perhaps in the trillions of dollars. Reagan lobbied his friend and ally British Prime Minister Margaret Thatcher, who initially opposed the SDI but eventually came to see it as a good idea.

Unlike previous ABM systems, the SDI would provide missile defense from space. In fact, to intercept missiles in flight, space-based weapons were the best option, because land-based weapons could not overcome the problems presented by the curvature of Earth. Because Soviet long-range missiles took only thirty minutes to reach their targets, there was just enough time to detect, track, and intercept the warheads before they reentered the atmosphere. As Reagan described it and as scientists conceived it, the SDI would employ a number of satellites and space-based radars to detect and track incoming missiles and land- or satellite-based lasers reflected off orbital mirrors to destroy a warhead in flight. Scientists planned lasers that would employ X-ray, infrared, ultraviolet, or microwave radiation. They also conceived of particle-beam weapons in which streams of charged atomic matter would be directed at incoming warheads.

From the perspective of some, particularly new Soviet leader Mikhail Gorbachev, the SDI was a great threat. When Reagan and Gorbachev first met in Geneva in 1985, the SDI proved the sticking point on any arms control agreements. Gorbachev fiercely objected to the SDI, arguing that such a system only made sense if the United States planned to launch a nuclear first-strike against the Soviet Union. Gorbachev also well understood that the Soviet Union lagged behind the United States in computer technology, an area crucial to such an advanced weapons system. For the Soviet Union to allow the SDI to move forward would be to admit defeat. Gorbachev therefore insisted that Reagan give up the SDI before agreements on limiting offensive weapons could be reached. Reagan refused, but he also told Gorbachev that the SDI was necessary and that when it was finally completed, he would share the technology with the Soviets. Gorbachev did not believe Reagan, and Reagan could see no logical argument against the SDI. Because of the SDI, the two men departed Geneva without a deal on arms control.

The Reagan administration ultimately failed to develop and deploy the SDI. The technology proved too daunting, and the costs were too high. Still, the mere threat of the SDI put tremendous pressure on the Soviets. Some scholars attribute the Soviet Union's 1991 collapse to Reagan's vigorous pursuit of the SDI. Others, however, regard the SDI as a costly boondoggle that only escalated Cold War tensions and contributed to swollen defense allocations and mammoth budget deficits.

Brian Madison Jones

See also

Anti-Ballistic Missile Treaty; Geneva Meeting, Gorbachev and Reagan; Gorbachev, Mikhail; Missiles, Antiballistic; Mutual Assured Destruction; Nuclear Arms Race; Reagan, Ronald Wilson

References

Duric, Mira. *The Strategic Defense Initiative: U.S. Policy and the Soviet Union.* Burlington, VT: Ashgate, 2003.

Fitzgerald, Frances. *Way Out There in the Blue: Reagan, Star Wars, and the End of the Cold War.* New York: Simon and Schuster, 2000.

Waller, Douglas C. *The Strategic Defense Initiative, Progress and Challenges: A Guide to Issues and References.* Claremont, CA: Regina Books, 1987.

Stratemeyer, George Edward (1890–1969)

U.S. Air Force general and commander of the Far East Air Force (FEAF) during the Korean War. Born in Cincinnati, Ohio, on 24 November 1890, George Stratemeyer graduated from the U.S. Military Academy at West Point in 1915 and served briefly in the infantry before beginning flight training. During and after World War I, he held various instructional and training positions, gaining a reputation as an effective administrator. During World War II, he served in the China-Burma-India theater as air advisor to Lieutenant General Joseph W. Stilwell and then commanded the Eastern Air Command. He became a major general in 1942. Promoted to lieutenant general in 1945, Stratemeyer took command of the U.S. Army Air Forces in China before returning to the United States in February 1946 to head the new Air Defense Command, later the Continental Air Command.

In April 1949 Stratemeyer assumed command of the FEAF, comprising the Fifth Air Force in Japan, the Thirteenth Air Force in the Philippines, and the Twentieth Air Force on Okinawa. By 1950, 75 percent of the men under his command were products of the Air Force Reserve training program he had organized. Known for his ability to get the most from his subordinates, Stratemeyer displayed effective leadership following the invasion of the Republic of Korea (ROK, South Korea) by the Democratic People's Republic of Korea (DPRK, North Korea) on 25 June 1950. When President Harry S. Truman ordered U.S. forces into action, Stratemeyer directed FEAF aircraft in the critical early days of the war, ordering attacks on the North Korean forces and providing air cover for the evacuation of Seoul. He then directed strategic bombing of North Korea to include the destruction of lines of communications, installations, and factories.

Following the Chinese military intervention in Korea, Stratemeyer opposed General Douglas MacArthur's flouting of directives. In late November 1950, after MacArthur unilaterally ordered the bombing of the Yalu River bridges, Stratemeyer informed his superiors in Washington, and the Joint Chiefs of Staff (JCS) then restricted air raids to the southern side of the river. Stratemeyer believed, however, that his air forces should be permitted to conduct operations against Mainland China.

In May 1951 Stratemeyer suffered a heart attack, and he retired from active duty in January 1952. Thereafter, he became a public advocate for unlimited military operations against the People's Republic of China (PRC), complaining in an interview that Washington had "handcuffed" MacArthur. "We were required to lose the war," Stratemeyer told a Senate subcommittee. He also lobbied for expanding U.S. airpower as the most economical way to win wars and maintain a strong defense, and in 1954 he tried to dissuade the U.S. Senate from censuring Senator Joseph McCarthy for his reckless anticommunist witch-hunt. Stratemeyer died in Orlando, Florida, on 9 August 1969.

James I. Matray

See also
Korean War; MacArthur, Douglas; McCarthy, Joseph Raymond; United States Air Force; Vandenberg, Hoyt Sanford
References
Blair, Clay. *The Forgotten War: America in Korea, 1950–1953.* New York: Times Books, 1987.

Futrell, Robert F. *The United States Air Force in Korea, 1950–1953.* Rev ed. Washington, DC: Office of the Chief of Air Force History, 1983.
Stratemeyer, George. *The Three Wars of Lt. Gen. George E. Stratemeyer: His Korean War Diary.* Edited by William T. Y'Blood. Washington, DC: Air Force History and Museums Program.

Strauss, Franz Josef (1915–1988)

Federal Republic of Germany (FRG, West Germany) minister for nuclear power (1955–1956), minister of defense (1956–1962), minister of finance (1966–1969), and minister-president of Bavaria (1978–1988). Born on 6 September 1915 in Munich, Franz Strauss studied to become a high school teacher at the University of Munich during 1935–1939 and then served in the German Army during World War II.

Following Strauss's brief internment in spring 1945, the American military occupation government appointed him deputy district president at Schöngau. In 1946 he cofounded the Christian Democratic Union (CSU), the sister party of the Christian Democratic Union (CDU) in Bavaria. In June 1947, he became the youngest member of the Economic Council of the U.S.-British Bizonia. He also served in the Bundestag during 1949–1978 and again in 1987. During 1950–1953 and again during 1963–1966, he was deputy chairman of the CDU/CSU and during 1971–1978 served as economic speaker for the CDU/CSU parliamentary group.

Strauss was appointed minister without portfolio in Chancellor Konrad Adenauer's cabinet in October 1953 and was subsequently appointed minister for nuclear power in October 1955. Strauss served as minister of defense beginning in October 1956, a post he held until 1962. In this post, he pushed forward a number of structural reforms within the German armed forces, including universal conscription, introduced in April 1957. Forced to resign from office in November 1962 following the *Spiegel* Affair, during 1966–1969 he served Kurt-Georg Kiesinger's government as finance minister. When the Social Democratic Party (SPD) and the Free Democratic Party (FDP) formed a coalition in 1969 and launched Ostpolitik, Strauss became a hawkish opponent of Chancellor Willy Brandt's foreign policies.

Strauss's conservative position brought him into bitter conflict with Rainer Barzel, chairman of the CDU/CSU parliamentary group, who showed more willingness to accept the new approach in foreign policy. Because of this controversy, Strauss demanded more independence for the CSU and was eager to establish his party nationwide, especially after Helmut Kohl, who was regarded as a moderate, became CDU chairman in 1973. When Strauss's plans failed in 1976, he committed himself to regional politics and became minister-president of Bavaria in 1978, an office he held until his death.

Franz Josef Strauss, minister of defense of the Federal Republic of Germany (FRG, West Germany), shown here in March 1958. (Bettmann/Corbis)

In his last years, to the surprise of many, Strauss developed a personal relationship with German Democratic Republic (GDR, East Germany) leader Erich Honecker, whom he met twice in 1983 and again in 1987. After their first meeting, Strauss negotiated a major bank credit for the East Berlin government. Strauss died on 3 October 1988 in Regensburg, Germany.

Bert Becker

See also
Adenauer, Konrad; Brandt, Willy; German Democratic Republic; Germany, Federal Republic of; Honecker, Erich; Kohl, Helmut; Ostpolitik; Scheel, Walter; Schmidt, Helmut; *Spiegel* Affair

References
Banchoff, Thomas. *The German Problem Transformed: Institutions, Politics, and Foreign Policy, 1945–1995*. Ann Arbor: University of Michigan Press, 1999.
Behrend, Manfred. *Franz Josef Strauss: Eine politische Biographie*. Köln, Germany: ISP, 1995.
Nicholls, Anthony James. *The Bonn Republic: West German Democracy, 1945–1990*. London and New York: Longman, 1997.
Strauss, Franz Josef. *Die Erinnerungen*. Berlin: Siedler, 1989.
Webb, Adrian. *Germany since 1945*. London and New York: Longman, 1998.

Strijdom, Johannes Gerhadus (1893–1958)

South African apartheid leader and prime minister of South Africa (1954–1958). Born in Klipfontein, South Africa, on 14

July 1893, Johannes Strijdom studied law at Victoria College, graduating in 1914. He then moved to Pretoria and entered the civil service. In 1929 he was elected to parliament for Waterberg Province. He became a leader in the all-white National Party, and on 30 November 1954 he was elected prime minister.

As prime minister of South Africa, Strijdom organized the infamous Treason Trials of South African activists who were seeking greater freedoms and rights for the black majority population. Among the 156 activists tried was antiapartheid crusader and future South African president Nelson Mandela. Strijdom built upon the policies of Daniel F. Malan (prime minister during 1948–1954) by strengthening apartheid segregation laws, banning blacks from voting, and fixing the Supreme Court so that it would rubber-stamp his policies. Strijdom also used the pretext of communist subversion and the 1950 Suppression of Communism Act to rein in leftist political parties and other antigovernment organizations.

Strijdom cut diplomatic ties with Moscow and suppressed trade unionism, which often had communist ties. His government also helped to formulate the Population Register for South Africa, which fixed each citizen's race as black, colored, or white. Strijdom died in office in Cape Town on 24 August 1958.

David H. Richards

See also
African National Congress; Malan, Daniel François; Mandela, Nelson; South Africa

References
Basson, J. L. *J. G. Strijdom: Sy politieke loopbaan van 1929 tot 1948* [J. G. Strijdom: His Political Career from 1929 to 1948]. Sinobille, Pretoria: Wonderboom, 1980.
Davenport, T. R. H. *South Africa: A Modern History*. Toronto: University of Toronto Press, 2000.
Thomson, Leonard. *A History of South Africa*. New Haven, CT: Yale University Press, 1990.

Students for a Democratic Society

Radical American political organization founded in 1959, considered the vanguard movement of the wave of Cold War progressive radicalism known as the New Left. The origins of Students for a Democratic Society (SDS) can be traced to the Student League for Industrial Democracy (SLID), the youth branch of the venerable Old Left society that campaigned on time-honored socialist issues of trade unionism and industrial rights during the 1930s.

The SDS's first official meeting was at Ann Arbor, Michigan, in 1960, but the movement's intellectual ideological platform did not come until the publication of the Port Huron (Michigan) Statement, written and adopted as the group's manifesto in 1962. Its author, Tom Hayden, who also became SDS president that year, spoke of the need for a "participatory democracy" to replace the bellicose and corrupt complacency that, according to him, characterized American political life at the time. In particular, Hayden implored America's college-age youth—the affluent products of the long postwar boom—to openly challenge the unjust conventions of their parents' generation through grassroots educational initiatives, nonviolent protest, and civil disobedience. Hayden's call to arms struck a ringing chord within a young left-wing community, the "red-diaper babies," that was dissatisfied with the narrowly defined interests of traditional American socialism and was becoming increasingly interested in the social critiques of the European existentialists and the Frankfurt School. This marriage of concrete political grievances with more diffuse complaints about the nature of Western industrial civilization became a distinctive feature of the 1960s' Counterculture Movement.

The early years of SDS were occupied in support of the civil rights protests against Jim Crow racial segregation in the South as well as initiatives in poor urban districts to encourage small-scale civic dissent. SDS members took a natural interest in campus politics, particularly the attempts by conservative regents to continue some of the more straight-laced curriculum of earlier college days. The turning point in the history of SDS, however, came with the escalation of America's military involvement in the Vietnam conflict beginning in 1965. From its founding, the group was harshly critical of what it saw as unnecessary international belligerence by the United States and the deleterious effect that the "warfare state" had on economic and social priorities at home.

The August 1964 Tonkin Gulf Resolution gave these concerns a particular intensity, and President Lyndon Johnson's decision in 1966 to limit draft deferments for college students gave the core SDS constituency a personal stake in the politics of Vietnam. The national group organized mass protest marches in Washington, D.C., and New York City, while local campus chapters sponsored draft card burnings, sit-ins, and disruption of military recruitment visits and ROTC events. The SDS slogan "Make Love Not War" became one of the signature phrases of the era and the motto of antiwar activists around the globe.

By 1968, the SDS boasted more than 100,000 members on 400 college campuses. But while the passions of the Vietnam protests had given a powerful boost to enrollment, they also created tensions within the movement between those who believed in the original nonviolent principles of the Port Huron Statement and others who believed that state violence had to be met with counterviolence. Confrontations between student agitators and the authorities became uglier as the Vietnam struggle took on the character of a generational culture conflict. In 1968, a series of raucous building occupations at

New York's Columbia University was met by a brutal police response that triggered a campuswide strike and the effective collapse of the college's academic program that year. In Chicago, student protestors outside the Democratic National Convention were among the thousands engaged in street battles against Mayor Richard Daley's notorious city troopers. The escalation of violence reached its peak in 1970 when six students were killed in separate incidents at Kent State University in Ohio and Jackson State College in Mississippi. The internal politics of the SDS themselves spun into turmoil as hard-line followers of PRC leader Chairman Mao Zedong began taking over chapters and a number of extremist splinter organizations emerged, most famously the terrorist Weather Underground, or Weathermen, that in turn gave J. Edgar Hoover's Federal Bureau of Investigation (FBI) the excuse to harass the mainstream organization.

Student protests ebbed with the American disengagement from Vietnam in the early 1970s, but by that point the SDS was already finished as a significant force for change. Some of its prominent members, such as Hayden, continued in mainstream politics and enjoyed successful independent careers. Aside from its achievements in specific policy areas, perhaps the organization's most important legacy was the model it provided for later grassroots activism, much of which was ironically conservative in character, such as the pro-life, antiabortion lobby.

Alan Allport

See also
Peace Movements; Vietnam War Protests; Weathermen
References
Breines, Wini. *Community and Organization in the New Left, 1962–1968: The Great Refusal.* New York: Praeger, 1982.
Heath, G. Louis. *Vandals in the Bomb Factory: The History and Literature of the Students for a Democratic Society.* Metuchen, NJ: Scarecrow, 1976.
Miller, Jim. *Democracy Is in the Streets: From Port Huron to the Siege of Chicago.* New York: Simon and Schuster, 1987.

Study Centers, Cold War
See Cold War Study Centers, Non-U.S.; Cold War Study Centers, U.S.

Suárez González, Adolfo (1932–)
Spanish interim president (1976–1977) and prime minister (1977–1981). Born on 25 September 1932 in Cebreros, Spain, Adolfo Suárez studied law at the Complutense University in Madrid and graduated in 1967. He then held several government posts during the Francisco Franco regime, including

head of the radio and television ministries. Suárez eventually was appointed secretary-general of the Movimiento Nacional (National Movement) party.

For most of the Franco regime, the National Movement was the only political party allowed to operate legally. Suárez was appointed interim president by King Juan Carlos I following Franco's 1975 death. Leftist and centrist politicians opposed Suárez's appointment, based on his close ties to the Franco regime. Nevertheless, Suárez proved to be a true reformer, spearheading political changes in 1976. He was also able to reform the military and return it to civilian control. These actions helped him form a more centrist party for the upcoming 1977 elections.

In 1977, during the first elections held after Franco's death, Suárez led the Unión de Centro Democrático (UCD, Democratic Center Union) to a majority in the parliament and was appointed premier. His government continued to institute democratic reforms, relying on a coalition of centrist politicians. One of the biggest reforms was the implementation of a new constitution in 1979. In the 1979 elections, Suárez and the UCD were again victorious. Government became increasingly problematic, however, with an economic downturn and an increase in regionalist agitation. Suárez resigned in 1981 and subsequently dropped out of the UCD. In 1982 he formed the Centro Democrático y Social (CDS, Democratic and Social Center), which enjoyed only moderate success. In 1991 Suárez announced his retirement from public life. In May 2005 his son announced that his father was suffering from advanced Alzheimer's disease and that he recalled little of his time in government.

David H. Richards

See also
Spain
References
Abad, José García. *Adolfo Suárez: Una tragedia griega.* Madrid, Spain: Esfera de los Libros, 2005.
Abella, Carlos. *Adolfo Suárez.* Madrid, Spain: Espasa, 1997.
Salvad, Francisco J. Romero. *Twentieth-Century Spain: Politics and Society in Spain, 1898–1998.* New York: St. Martin's, 1999.
Threlfall, Monica, ed. *Consensus Politics in Spain: Insider Perspectives.* London: Intellect, 2000.

Submarine-Launched Ballistic Missiles
See Missiles, Submarine-Launched Ballistic

Submarines

Submarines operate both submerged and on the surface. They were developed to scout for the main battle fleet and destroy enemy warships. In World War I, they were also employed effectively as commerce destroyers, and in World War II that and hunting enemy surface warships were their principal roles. The Cold War added the missions of hunting enemy submarines and serving as a launch platform for ballistic missiles.

At the beginning of the Cold War, all operational submarines used the diesel-electric drive. This required submarines to either surface frequently to recharge their batteries or be equipped with a snorkel breathing device for submerged diesel operation. Serious research into nuclear power for submarines, which promised essentially unlimited high-speed submerged operation, began immediately after World War II. The *Nautilus,* the first submarine with a nuclear power plant, was commissioned on 30 September 1954, although it was first under way under nuclear power on 17 January 1955. The *Nautilus,* 98.7 meters long with a beam of 8.43 meters, displaced 3,180 tons on the surface and 3,500 submerged. It could attain 22 knots on the surface and 23.3 knots submerged and was armed with six bow torpedo tubes with twenty-two torpedoes.

It was three years before the Soviets launched *K-3,* the first of a class of thirteen nuclear-powered submarines, on 9 August 1957. The *K-3* was commissioned on 7 January 1958. This Project 627–class (NATO-designated November-class) submarine was 107.4 meters long with a beam of 8.0 meters. It displaced 3,087 tons on the surface and 3,986 submerged. Its two-reactor power plant gave it a speed of 15.5 knots on the surface and 30.5 knots submerged. It had eight bow torpedo tubes and carried twenty torpedoes.

Nuclear power provided great cruising range. In 1960 the *Triton* sailed around the world while completely submerged, a trip of 41,519 miles. The *Triton* displaced 5,662 tons on the surface and 7,781 submerged, was 136.4 meters long and 11.26 meters in beam, had a speed of 27 knots both surfaced and submerged, and was armed with four bow and two stern torpedo tubes with fifteen torpedoes. Because submarines could now remain submerged for their entire duration at sea, they became much more difficult to track. However, nuclear power did not completely eclipse diesel submarines. Indeed, diesel submarines continue to be quieter and are considerably less expensive than those with nuclear power.

With the advent of nuclear weapons, including ballistic missiles, both the United States and the Soviet Union sought to protect their missiles from a first strike by the other power. One of the solutions seized upon was to launch ballistic missiles from submarines. The Soviet diesel-electric Project 611 A (NATO-designated Zulu-IV) submarine *B-62,* with a single launch tube, was the first to fire a ballistic missile, on 16 September 1955. The succeeding Project 611 AB-class (NATO-designated Zulu-V) submarines were the first operational ballistic missile boat, the first (*B-67*) being commissioned on 30 June 1956. With a length of 90.5 meters and a beam of 7.5 meters, these submarines displaced 1,890 tons on the surface and 2,450 submerged. They attained 16.5 knots on the surface and 12.5 knots submerged. They could launch 2 R-11FM missiles (NATO-designated Scud) from vertical tubes in the sail, and they mounted six bow and four stern torpedo tubes with twenty-two torpedoes. Initially, Soviet ballistic missile submarines were very vulnerable during launch because they had to surface to fire their missiles.

In 1955, the United States also began work on a submarine-launched ballistic missile (SLBM), which would ultimately become the Polaris. The first U.S. ballistic missile submarines used a design derived from that of the Skipjack-class attack boats, and their construction was expedited by redirecting materials, machinery, and equipment originally ordered for attack submarines. The first, the *George Washington,* was commissioned on 30 December 1959. These nuclear-powered

boats displaced 5,900 tons on the surface and 6,700 submerged, were 116.36 meters long and 10.06 meters in beam, attained 16.5 knots on the surface and 22 knots submerged, carried sixteen Polaris missiles in vertical launchers, and had six bow torpedo tubes with twelve torpedoes. The *George Washington* test-fired two Polaris missiles while submerged on 20 July 1960 in the Atlantic and departed on its first patrol on 15 November 1960.

On 10 September 1960, the Soviet submarine *B-62* also successfully fired a ballistic missile while submerged. The new D-4 launch system replaced the earlier D-2 system originally fitted in the first nuclear-powered Soviet Project 658–class (NATO-designated Hotel-I) ballistic missile submarines, first commissioned in December 1960. The upgraded Project 658M (NATO-designated Hotel-II) boats displaced 4,080 tons surfaced and 5,240 submerged and were 114.1 meters long and 9.2 meters in beam. Their two-reactor power plants

United States Navy ballistic submarine *George Washington,* the first nuclear-powered submarine designed to launch Polaris ballistic missiles while submerged, on its launching at Groton, Connecticut, 9 June 1959. The *George Washington* was built quickly by cutting an attack submarine in half and adding a missile compartment. (United States Naval Institute)

provided a maximum speed of 18 knots surfaced and 26 knots submerged. They carried three R-21 (NATO-designated Sark) missiles in vertical tubes plus four bow and four stern torpedo tubes. Recommissioning began in June 1964. On 24 February 1972 while on patrol some 800 miles northeast of Newfoundland, the *K-19,* the first of the class, suffered a catastrophic failure in its cooling system, resulting in the deaths of twenty-eight of its crew.

The Polaris missile was upgraded over time, its range increasing with each iteration. The fourth upgrade produced a new missile, the Poseidon, that featured multiple independently targeted reentry vehicles (MIRVs). Each missile could carry ten to fourteen independently targeted nuclear warheads. The Poseidon first departed aboard a submarine on patrol on 30 March 1971.

Both the United States and the Soviet Union continued to work toward the construction of larger ballistic missile submarines to accommodate bigger missiles. For the United States, this led to the Ohio-class submarines, the largest in the world at that time, embarking the Trident missile. The first of these, the *Ohio,* was commissioned on 11 November 1981. Ohio-class submarines displace 16,764 tons surfaced and 18,750 submerged, are 170.7 meters long with a beam of 12.8 meters, attain 18 knots surfaced and approximately 25 knots submerged, and carry 24 Trident ballistic missiles in vertical tubes and 24 torpedoes fired from 4 bow tubes. The eighteen Ohio-class Trident submarines remain in service, although four are being converted to launch up to 154 cruise missiles via twenty-two vertical tubes rather than ballistic missiles.

The Soviet Union countered with its Project 941–class ballistic missile submarines (NATO-designated Typhoon), the first, *TK-208,* commissioning on 12 December 1981. They are even larger than the Ohio-class boats and thus are the world's largest submarines, although they carried only twenty ballistic missiles apiece. They displace 23,200 tons surfaced and 33,800 submerged, are 172.0 meters long with a beam of 23.3 meters, attain 16 knots on the surface and 27 knots submerged, and have six bow torpedo tubes with twenty-two torpedoes, along with 20 R-39 ballistic missiles (NATO-designated Sturgeon) in vertical tubes.

Besides ballistic missile submarines, the other major categories of submarines are attack and cruise missile submarines. Such submarines are used to hunt other submarines, especially ballistic submarines, as well as enemy surface vessels. Along with the first generation of attack and cruise missile submarines, the Soviets developed submarines equipped with cruise missiles as a means of attacking U.S. aircraft carriers. As with ballistic missiles, cruise missiles initially had to be launched from the surface. It was not until the Project 670–class (NATO-designated Charlie-I) nuclear-powered cruise missile submarines that the Soviets developed the capability to launch cruise missiles while submerged. These

submarines displaced 3,580 tons on the surface and 4,550 submerged, were 94.0 meters long with a beam of 10.0 meters, attained 16 knots surfaced and 23 knots submerged, and were armed with eight cruise missiles on individual launchers and twelve torpedoes or antisubmarine missiles fired through six bow tubes. The United States first tested a cruise missile, the Regulus, from the USS *Tunny* on 15 July 1953. It saw limited service aboard five submarines (one nuclear-powered) but was retired in July 1964. Generally speaking, the U.S. Navy chose to rely on aircraft flown from aircraft carriers for antiship warfare purposes.

With the introduction of the second generation of attack and cruise missile submarines, missions included hunting other submarines. This mission was especially important for the Soviets, who built the Project 671–class (NATO-designated Victor) attack submarines specifically to hunt U.S. ballistic missile submarines. The most capable U.S. design in this category were the Thresher-class submarines. They displaced 3,750 tons surfaced and 4,310 submerged, were 84.9 meters long and 9.65 meters in beam, reached 15 knots surfaced and 28 knots submerged, and carried four torpedo tubes and twenty-three torpedoes or submarine rocket (SUBROC) antisubmarine missiles. This generation of submarines represented the bulk of American and Soviet submarine forces from 1961 until the end of the Cold War but is no longer in service.

The third generation of attack and cruise missile submarines are the American Los Angeles–class and the Soviet Project 971 boats (NATO-designated Akula). Production of this third generation of attack submarines was cut short by the end of the Cold War, but they remain in service today. The Los Angeles–class boats displace 6,080 tons surfaced and 6,927 submerged, are 110.3 meters long with a beam of 9.75 meters, and attain more than 30 knots submerged and possibly 20 knots on the surface. They have four torpedo tubes and carry twenty-six torpedoes (and also Tomahawk cruise missiles fired from vertical tubes in later boats). Their Soviet counterparts displace 6,300 tons surfaced and 8,300 submerged, are 108 meters long with a beam of 13.5 meters, travel at up to 20 knots on the surface and 35 knots submerged, and carry forty missiles (a mixture of torpedoes, antiship missiles, and up to twelve cruise missiles) fired through eight torpedo tubes (ten in later boats).

Two characteristics dominate the designs of the third-generation attack submarine classes: high underwater speed and greatly reduced noise emission. The much greater cost of nuclear submarines undoubtedly deterred many navies from adding them to their fleets, but the quest for low noise emission also encouraged development of advanced diesel-electric submarines.

From 1967, the German Type 209 epitomized these advanced conventionally powered boats. Early boats, of Type

209/1100, displaced 1,106 tons surfaced and 1,207 submerged, were 54.4 meters long with a beam of 6.2 meters, and could attain 11 knots surfaced or 21.5 knots submerged. The latest Type 209/1500 boats displace 1,660 tons surfaced and 1,850 submerged, are 62 meters long, and can reach 15 knots surfaced or 22 knots submerged. They are armed with fourteen torpedoes fired through eight tubes. More than forty boats have served with more than a dozen navies, and most are still operational. The new Type 212 that was developed from the Type 209 can be expected to achieve similar success.

The Soviets also continued to build diesel-electric attack submarines. The Project 877 boats (NATO-designated Kilo) displaced 2,350 tons surfaced and 3,126 submerged, were 72.6 meters long and 9.9 meters in beam, reached 12 knots surfaced and 25 knots submerged, and were armed with eighteen torpedoes fired through eight tubes. Although largely withdrawn from service in 2000, an export version of this exceptionally quiet design has proven very successful, with at least twenty sold to six navies since 1986.

Many other nations operated submarines. Among the principal Cold War navies with submarines were Great Britain and France. Britain launched its first nuclear-powered submarine, the attack-type *Dreadnought,* on 21 October 1960. The *Dreadnought* displaced 3,500 tons on the surface and 4,000 submerged, was 81 meters long and 9.8 meters in beam, attained 25 knots surfaced and 30 knots submerged, and was

armed with twenty-four torpedoes fired through six tubes. The *Dreadnought* had an American nuclear power plant, enabling the British to save both considerable time and money. The British took a similar path when building their first ballistic missile submarines, the four-boat Resolution-class, by purchasing Polaris missiles. These submarines displaced 7,500 tons on the surface and 8,500 submerged, were 129.54 meters long and 10.06 meters in beam, reached 20 knots on the surface and 25 knots submerged, and could launch sixteen Polaris missiles via vertical tubes and also carried twelve torpedoes fired through six tubes. These submarines provided the British with their own nuclear underwater deterrent force.

Under President Charles de Gaulle, the French also developed an independent submarine nuclear deterrent force. They took a different path than the Americans, British, and Soviets in that they built nuclear-powered ballistic missile submarines before their first nuclear-powered attack submarines. Altogether, the French built six Redoutable-class ballistic submarines, the first commissioning in 1971. They displaced 8,050 tons surfaced and 8,940 submerged, were 128.7 meters long and 10.6 meters in beam, attained 20 knots on the surface and 25 knots submerged, and carried sixteen ballistic missiles launched from vertical tubes plus eighteen torpedoes fired via four tubes. Five boats were decommissioned by 2003, but the four later Triomphant-class ballistic

The *Dreadnought* (1960), the United Kingdom's first nuclear-powered submarine. (Art-Tech)

missile submarines remain operational. France built a series of sophisticated conventionally powered attack submarines between 1961 and 1978 that also were successful export types. The first of France's six nuclear attack submarines, *Le Rubis*, was launched in 1976 and entered service in 1983. It displaces 2,410 tons surfaced and 2,680 submerged, is 75 meters long with a beam of 7.6 meters, attains 18 knots on the surface and 25 knots submerged, and is fitted with four torpedo tubes that can discharge a mix of fourteen torpedoes or Exocet missiles.

Dallace W. Unger Jr. and Paul Fontenoy

See also

Aircraft Carriers; France, Navy; *K-19;* Missiles, Cruise; Missiles, Polaris; Missiles, Poseidon; Missiles, Submarine-Launched Ballistic; Royal Navy; Soviet Union, Navy; United States Navy; Warships, Surface

References

Isenberg, Michael T. *Shield of the Republic: The United States Navy in an Era of Cold War and Violent Peace,* Vol. 1, *1945–1962.* New York: St. Martin's, 1993.

Pavlov, A. S. *Warships of the USSR and Russia, 1945–1995.* Translated from the Russian by Gregory Tokar. Annapolis, MD: Naval Institute Press, 1997.

Polmar, Norman, et al. *Chronology of the Cold War at Sea, 1945–1991.* Annapolis, MD: Naval Institute Press, 1997.

Polmar, Norman, and Kenneth J. Moore. *Cold War Submarines: The Design and Construction of U.S. and Soviet Submarines.* Washington, DC: Brassey's, 2004.

Preston, Antony. *The Royal Navy Submarine Service: A Centennial History.* London: Conway Maritime Press, 2001.

Sondhaus, Lawrence. *Navies of Europe, 1815–2002.* London: Pearson Education Limited, 2002.

Watson, Bruce W., and Susan M. Watson, eds. *The Soviet Navy: Strengths and Liabilities.* Boulder, CO: Westview, 1986.

Sudan

Northeast African nation. The largest country on the continent, Sudan covers 967,493 square miles, about one-fourth the size of the United States. It is bordered by Chad and the Central African Republic to the west, Libya and Egypt to the north, Ethiopia and Eritrea to the east, and Kenya, Uganda, and the Democratic Republic of the Congo to the south. It also has a 500-mile coast on the Red Sea and is divided from north to south by the Nile River. Sudan's 1945 population was just under 9 million people.

Sudan was under Anglo-Egyptian rule during 1898–1956. It declared its independence in 1956, but a succession of coups from 1958 on, together with a wide economic and cultural gap dividing northern and southern Sudan, fomented instability in the country, which led to an ongoing civil war. Throughout much of the Cold War, Sudan's foreign policy vacillated between alliance with the West and East, depending on which faction was in control at any given time. Beginning with the so-called Condominium Agreements of 1899, Sudan was jointly administrated by Britain and Egypt. But a 1924 mutiny in the Egyptian Army compelled the British to evacuate Egyptian personnel from Sudan.

The Sudanese nationalist movement was somewhat fragmented and was associated with two rival religious sects: the Ashigga Party, later the National Unionist Party (NUP), allied with the Khatmiyya sect; and the Umma Party, or Independence Front (IF), connected with the Mahdiyya sect. The former called for unity with Egypt, whereas the latter called for complete independence. Two other independence movements, secular in nature, were the Sudanese Communist Party (SCP) and Sudan's Labor Union.

In 1953, Great Britain and Egypt granted Sudan self-rule, phased in over a three-year period. Parliamentary elections resulted in a victory for the NUP, and its leader, Ismail al-Azhari, became the first Sudanese prime minister in January 1954. The NUP soon reversed its policy, however, and strove for independence, which was decided on 19 December 1955 by a unanimous parliamentary vote. Independence went into effect on 1 January 1956.

The issue of north-south relations in Sudan, with the Muslim north more developed and the non-Muslim south ruled as a separate entity, soon became a sticking point after independence. Anxieties about the prospects of Muslim domination and demands for a federal system resulted in riots in southern Sudan. In August 1955, the Equatorial Corps composed of southerners mutinied in Torit, killing several hundred northern traders and government officials.

Although the southern revolt was repressed, civil war soon erupted, lasting from 1955 to 1972. The deteriorating internal situation urged Prime Minister Abdallah Khalil to invite General Ibrahim Abboud, the commander of the army, to take control of the government in November 1958. The resultant military junta ended parliamentary rule and granted power to the Supreme Council of the Armed Forces. Political parties were dissolved, the constitution was suspended, trade unions were abolished, and strikes were outlawed. But in October 1964, following a series of popular uprisings, a transitional government comprised of representatives from all parties including the SCP and the Muslim Brotherhood replaced the Abboud regime.

The spring 1965 elections brought to power a coalition of the UP and NUP with Muhammed Ahmed Mahgoub as prime minister and Ismail al-Azhari as president of the Supreme Council of State. After Mahgoub's resignation in 1966, Sadiq al-Mahdi was elected prime minister.

The al-Mahdi government was overthrown in a bloodless coup led by Colonel Gaafar Muhammad Nimeri in May 1969, leading to the adoption of socialist policies, one-party rule by the Sudanese Socialist Union (SSU), closer relations with the Eastern bloc, and support for the Palestinian cause.

The Tripoli Charter of 27 December 1969, concluded by Nimeri, Muammar Qadhafi, and Anwar Sadat, established a union among Sudan, Libya, and Egypt. Announcement of this in the Sudan led to a coup against Nimeri that ousted him from power. Three days later, with widespread popular support, he returned to power and won the 1971 elections.

In 1972, Nimeri signed the Addis Ababa Agreement with southern rebels that granted regional autonomy for southern Sudan. The Addis Ababa peace agreement also signaled a rapprochement between Sudan and Ethiopia that would not survive Ethiopian Emperor Haile Selassie's fall in 1974, as Sudan was soon pressured by various Arab states to renew its support for the Eritreans in the ongoing Ethiopian-Eritrean conflict.

Leaders of the traditional Sudanese parties, excluded from involvement in politics, in 1974 organized a National Front (NF) to oppose the regime. On several occasions the NF staged abortive efforts to overthrow Nimeri. He continued to receive support from Libya, Ethiopia, Iraq, and Saudi Arabia. Meanwhile, as early as 1971, those opposed to Nimeri had also organized the Southern Sudan People's Liberation Movement (SPLM), later the Sudan People's Liberation Movement. In October 1982, Egypt and Sudan signed a charter of political and economic integration. However, Sudan's deep and seemingly intractable economic problems did not improve.

Nimeri's failure to respect the Addis Ababa Agreement and the introduction of traditional Islamic law, the Sharia, and martial law in 1983 led to the resumption of the civil war led by the Sudan People's Liberation Army (SPLA), the military arm of the SPLM. The disastrous economic situation increased dependence on the West, especially the United States, and brought the bloodless coup in April 1985 in which Lieutenant General Abd al-Rahman Mohammed Swar al-Dahab took control of Sudan through a Transnational Military Council (TMC). He also sought to improve relations with the Soviet Union, Ethiopia, and Libya. In response to the coup, the SPLA declared a cease-fire while at the same time demanding aid for the southern regions and the abolition of the Sharia.

In accordance with General Swar's promise, general elections occurred in April 1986, and parliamentary democracy was restored. A coalition government, headed by al-Sadiq al-Mahdi of the Umma party, ruled the country for the next three years. Although a 1988 agreement ending the civil war was supposed to stabilize Sudan, on 30 June 1989 General 'Umar Hasan Ahmed al-Bashir, supported by the National Islamic Front (NIF), led a bloodless coup and formed a fifteen-member Revolutionary Command Council for National Salvation (RCC). His primary aim was to end the southern rebellion by force. However, the ongoing civil war that claimed nearly 1.5 million people during 1983–1997 showed just how difficult this task would be.

Abel Polese

See also

Africa; Decolonization; Egypt; Eritrea; Ethiopia; Haile Selassie, Emperor of Ethiopia

References

Holt, P. M. *A Modern History of the Sudan.* 2nd ed. London: Weidenfeld and Nicolson, 1974.

Johnson, Douglas H. *The Root Causes of Sudan's Civil Wars.* Oxford, UK: International African Institute, 2003.

Petterson, D. *Inside Sudan.* Boulder, CO: Westview, 2003.

Voll, John O., ed. *Sudan: State and Society in Crisis.* Bloomington: Indiana University Press, 1991.

Suez Crisis (1956)

The Suez Crisis was one of the major events of the Cold War. It ended Britain's pretensions to be a world superpower, fatally weakened its hold on what remained of its empire, placed a dangerous strain on U.S.-Soviet relations, strengthened the position of Egyptian leader Gamal Abdel Nasser, and distracted world attention from the concurrent Soviet military intervention in Hungary.

The Suez Crisis had its origins in the development plans of Nasser. The Egyptian president hoped to enhance his prestige and improve the quality of life for his nation's growing population by carrying out long-discussed plans to construct a high dam on the upper Nile River at Aswan to provide electric power. To finance the project, he sought assistance from the Western powers. But he had also been endeavoring to build up and modernize the Egyptian military. Toward that end, he had sought to acquire modern weapons from the United States and other Western nations. When the U.S. government refused to supply the advanced arms, which it believed might be used against Israel, in 1955 Nasser turned to the communist bloc. This step incurred the displeasure of President Dwight D. Eisenhower, as did Nasser's recognition of the People's Republic of China (PRC) and his frequent denunciations of the U.S.-supported Baghdad Pact.

Resentment over Nasser's efforts to play East against West and especially his decision to turn to the communist bloc for arms led the Eisenhower administration to block financing of the Aswan Dam project through the World Bank. U.S. Secretary of State John Foster Dulles had earlier assured Nasser of U.S. support, but on 19 June 1956, Dulles announced that U.S. assistance for the Aswan Dam project would not be forthcoming. The British government immediately followed suit.

Nasser's response to this humiliating rebuff came a week later, on 26 July, when he nationalized the Suez Canal. He had contemplated such a move for some time, but the U.S. decision prompted its timing. Seizure of the canal would not only provide additional funding for the Aswan project but would also make Nasser a hero in the eyes of many Arab nationalists.

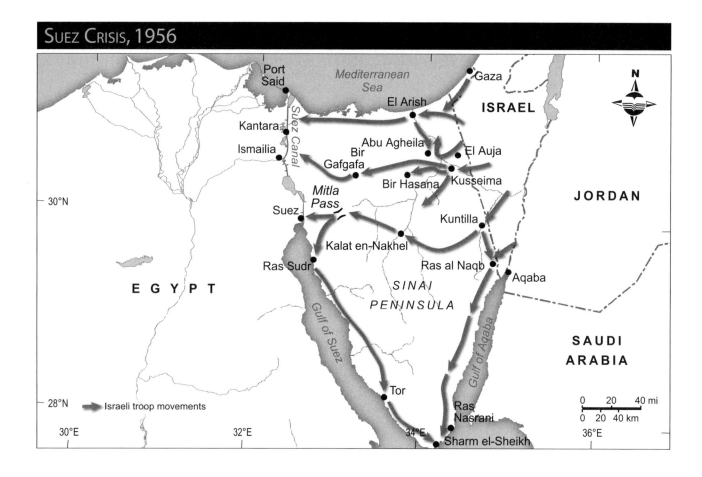

SUEZ CRISIS, 1956

The British government regarded the sea-level Suez Canal, which connected the eastern Mediterranean with the Red Sea across Egyptian territory, as its lifeline to Middle Eastern oil and the Far East. The canal, built by a private company headed by Frenchman Ferdinand de Lesseps, had opened to much fanfare in 1869. It quickly altered the trade routes of the world, and two-thirds of the tonnage passing through the canal was British. Khedive Ismail Pasha, who owned 44 percent of the company shares, found himself in dire financial straits, and in 1875 the British government stepped in and purchased his shares. In 1878 Britain acquired the island of Cyprus north of Egypt from the Ottoman Empire, further strengthening its position in the eastern Mediterranean north of Egypt. The British also increased their role in Egyptian financial affairs, and in 1882 they intervened militarily in Egypt, promising to depart once order had been restored. Britain remained in Egypt and in effect controlled its affairs through World War II.

In 1952, a nationalist coup d'état took place in Egypt that ultimately brought Nasser to power. He was a staunch Arab nationalist, determined to end British influence in Egypt. In 1954 he succeeded in renegotiating the 1936 treaty with the British to force the withdrawal of British troops from the Suez Canal Zone. The last British forces departed the Canal Zone only a month before Nasser nationalized the canal.

The British government now took the lead in opposing Nasser. London believed that Nasser's growing popularity in the Arab world was encouraging Arab nationalism and threatening to undermine British influence throughout the Middle East. British Prime Minister Anthony Eden (1955–1956) developed a deep and abiding hatred of the Egyptian leader. For Eden, ousting Nasser from power became nothing short of an obsession. In the immediate aftermath of Nasser's nationalization of the canal, the British government called up 200,000 military reservists and dispatched military resources to the eastern Mediterranean.

The French government also had good reason to seek Nasser's removal. Paris sought to protect its own long-standing interests in the Middle East, but more to the point, the French were now engaged in fighting the National Liberation Front (NLF) in Algeria. The Algerian War, which began in November 1954, had greatly expanded and had become an imbroglio for the government, now led by socialist Premier Guy Mollet (1956–1957). Nasser was a strong and vocal supporter of the NLF, and there were many in the French government and military who believed that overthrowing him would greatly enhance French chances of winning the Algerian War.

Israel formed the third leg in the triad of powers arrayed against Nasser. Egypt had instituted a blockade of Israeli ships at the Gulf of Aqaba, Israel's outlet to the Indian Ocean.

Also, Egypt had never recognized the Jewish state and indeed remained at war with it following the Israeli War of Independence during 1948–1949. In 1955, Israel mounted a half dozen cross-border raids, while Egypt carried out its own raids into Israeli territory by fedayeen, or guerrilla fighters.

During the months that followed Egyptian nationalization of the Suez Canal, the community of interest among British, French, and Israeli leaders developed into secret planning for a joint military operation to topple Nasser. The U.S. government was not consulted and indeed opposed the use of force. The British and French governments either did not understand the American attitude or, if they did, believed that Washington would give approval after the fact to policies undertaken by its major allies, which the latter believed to be absolutely necessary.

The British government first tried diplomacy. Two conferences in London attended by the representatives of twenty-four nations using the canal failed to produce agreement on a course of action, and Egypt refused to participate. A proposal by U.S. Secretary of State John Foster Dulles for a canal "users' club" of nations failed, as did an appeal to the United Nations (UN) Security Council. On 1 October, Dulles announced that the United States was disassociating itself from British and French actions in the Middle East and asserted that the United States intended to play a more independent role.

Meanwhile, secret talks were going forward, first between the British and French for joint military action against Egypt. Military representatives of the two governments met in London on 10 August and hammered out the details of a joint military plan known as MUSKETEER that would involve occupation of both Alexandria and Port Said. The French then brought the Israeli government in on the plan, and General Maurice Challe, deputy chief of staff of the French Air Force, undertook a secret trip to the Middle East to meet with Israeli government and military leaders. The Israelis were at first skeptical about British and French support. They also had no intention of moving as far as the canal itself. The Israelis stated that their plan was merely to send light detachments to link up with British and French forces. They also insisted that British and French military intervention occur simultaneously with their own attack.

General André Beaufre, the designated French military commander for the operation, then came up with a new plan. Under it, the Israelis would initiate hostilities against Egypt in order to provide the pretext for military intervention by French and British forces to protect the canal. This action would technically be in accord with the terms of the 1954 treaty between Egypt and Britain that had given Britain the right to send forces to occupy the Suez Canal Zone in the event of an attack against Egypt by a third power.

All parties agreed to this new plan. Meanwhile, unrest began in Hungary on 23 October, and the next day Soviet tanks entered Budapest to put down what had become the Hungarian Revolution. French and British planners were delighted at the news of an international distraction that seemed to provide them a degree of freedom of action.

On 29 October, Israeli forces began an invasion of the Sinai Peninsula with the announced aim of eradicating the fedayeen bases. A day later, on 30 October, the British and French governments issued an ultimatum, nominally to both the Egyptian and Israeli governments but in reality only to Egypt, expressing the need to separate the combatants and demanding the right to provide for the security of the Suez Canal. The ultimatum called on both sides to withdraw their forces 10 miles from the canal and gave them twelve hours to reply. The Israelis, of course, immediately accepted the ultimatum, while the Egyptians just as promptly rejected it.

On 31 October, the British began bombing Egyptian airfields and military installations from bases on Cyprus. British aircraft attacked four Egyptian bases that day and nine the next. When Eden reported to the House of Commons on events, he encountered a surprisingly strong negative reaction from the opposition Labour Party.

Following the British military action, the Egyptians immediately sank a number of ships in the canal to make it unusable. The Israelis, meanwhile, broke into the Sinai and swept across it in only four days against ineffective Egyptian forces. Finally, on 5 November, British and French paratroopers began an invasion of Port Said, Egypt, at the Mediterranean terminus of the canal.

The Eisenhower administration had already entered the picture. On 31 October, President Eisenhower described the British attack as "taken in error." He was personally furious at Eden over events and is supposed to have asked when he first telephoned the British leader, "Anthony, have you gone out of your mind?" The United States applied immediate and heavy financial threats, both on a bilateral basis and through the International Monetary Fund (IMF), to bring the British government to heel. Eisenhower also refused any further dealings with Eden personally.

A threat by the Soviet government against Britain on 5 November to send "volunteers" to Egypt proved a further embarrassment for the British government, but it was U.S. pressure that was decisive. Nonetheless, the world beheld the strange spectacle of the United States cooperating with the Soviet Union to condemn Britain and France in the UN Security Council and call for an end to the use of force. Although Britain and France vetoed the Security Council resolution, the matter was referred to the UN General Assembly, which demanded a cease-fire and withdrawal.

Israel and Egypt had agreed to a cease-fire on 4 November. At midnight on 6 November, the day of the U.S. presidential election, the British and French governments were also obliged to accept a cease-fire, the French only with the

Israeli soldiers shown with a British-made Archer self-propelled gun captured from the Egyptians, 3 November 1956. (Israel Government Press Office)

greatest reluctance. A 4,000-man UN Emergency Force (UNEF)—authorized on 4 November and made up of contingents from Brazil, Colombia, India, Indonesia, and the Scandinavian countries—arrived in Egypt to take up positions to keep Israeli and Egyptian forces separated. At the end of November, the British and French governments both agreed to withdraw their forces from Egypt by 22 December, and on 1 December Eisenhower announced that he had instructed U.S. oil companies to begin shipping supplies to both Britain and France.

Nasser and Arab self-confidence were the chief beneficiaries of the crisis. The abysmal performance of Egyptian military forces in the crisis was forgotten in Nasser's ultimate triumph. He found his prestige dramatically increased throughout the Arab world. Israel also benefited. The presence of the UN force guaranteed an end to the fedayeen raids, and Israel had also broken the Egyptian blockade of the Gulf of Aqaba, although its ships could still not transit the Suez Canal. The crisis also enhanced Soviet prestige in the Middle East, and the UN emerged from the crisis with enhanced prestige, helping to boost world confidence in that organization.

The Suez Crisis ended Eden's political career. Ill and under tremendous criticism in Parliament from the Labour Party, he resigned from office in January 1957. Events also placed a

serious, albeit temporary, strain on U.S.-British relations. More importantly, they revealed the serious limitations in British military strength. Indeed, observers are unanimous in declaring 1956 a seminal date in British imperial history that marked the effective end of Britain's tenure as a great power. The events had less impact in France. Mollet left office in May 1957 but not as a result of the Suez intervention. The crisis was costly to both Britain and France in economic terms, for Saudi Arabia had halted oil shipments to both countries.

Finally, the Suez Crisis could not have come at a worst time for the West, because the crisis diverted world attention from the concurrent brutal Soviet military intervention in Hungary. Eisenhower believed, rightly or wrongly, that without the Suez diversion there would have been far stronger Western reaction to the Soviet invasion of its satellite.

Spencer C. Tucker

See also

Anticolonialism; Arab-Israeli Wars; Ben-Gurion, David; Dulles, John Foster; Eden, Sir Anthony, 1st Earl of Avon; Egypt; Eisenhower, Dwight David; France; Israel; Lloyd, Selwyn; Macmillan, Maurice Harold; Middle East; Mollet, Guy; Nasser, Gamal Abdel; United Kingdom

References

Beaufre, André. *The Suez Expedition, 1956.* Translated by Richard Barry. New York: Praeger, 1969.

Cooper, Chester L. *The Lion's Last Roar: Suez, 1956.* New York: Harper and Row, 1978.

Eden, Anthony. *The Suez Crisis of 1956.* Boston: Beacon, 1968.

Freiberger, Steven Z. *Dawn over Suez: The Rise of American Power in the Middle East, 1953–1957.* Chicago: Ivan R. Dee, 1992.

Gorst, Anthony, and Lewis Johnman. *The Suez Crisis.* London: Routledge, 1997.

Hahn, Peter L. *The United States, Great Britain, and Egypt, 1945–1956: Strategy and Diplomacy in the Early Cold War.* Chapel Hill: University of North Carolina Press, 1991.

Kelly, Saul, and Anthony Gorst, eds. *Whitehall and the Suez Crisis.* London: Frank Cass, 2000.

Kingseed, Cole C. *Eisenhower and the Suez Crisis of 1956.* Baton Rouge: Louisiana State University Press, 1995.

Kyle, Keith. *Suez.* New York: St. Martin's, 1991.

Louis, William R., and Roger Owen, eds. *Suez, 1956: The Crisis and Its Consequences.* New York: Oxford University Press, 1989.

Lucas, W. Scott. *Divided We Stand: Britain, the United States and the Suez Crisis.* Rev. ed. London: Spectre, 1996.

Suharto (1921–)

Indonesian Army officer and second president of Indonesia (1967–1998). Born Mohammed Suharto in the hamlet of Kemusuk in Central Java on 8 June 1921, Suharto in the Javanese tradition used only his one name. He completed secondary school and then worked briefly as a bank clerk before joining the Royal Netherland's Indies Army (KNIL) in 1940. In 1943 during the Japanese occupation in World War II, he joined the Japanese-trained self-defense force Peta. He then joined the Army of the Republic of Indonesia in October 1945 and participated in the independence war against the Dutch. He was a lieutenant colonel at the time of Indonesian independence in 1949.

During 1957–1959, Suharto commanded the Diponegoro Division in Central Java. In 1962 he went on to command the Mandala Campaign during the liberation of West Irian from the Dutch. By 1965, the army was split into two factions, the leftists, who were loyal to President Sukarno, and the rightists, who included Suharto. On 1 October 1965, Sukarno's guards murdered six right-wing generals during an alleged coup attempt by communist civilians. This galvanized the rightists, who purged the Sukarno faction from the army and began to take steps to oust the president. In the meantime, Suharto had begun to set his sights on seizing control of the government himself.

In keeping with Javanese propriety, Suharto moved cautiously in deposing Sukarno, first obtaining the Supersemar (Letter of Authority) transferring power to him on 11 March 1966 and then installing himself as provisional president one year later. On 21 March 1967, he arranged for his election as president by the People's Consultative Assembly. As Suharto consolidated his power, some half million suspected communists were killed, and Indonesia's Chinese minority was subjected to severe repression. Once his rule had been "legitimized" by the obviously rigged election, Suharto consolidated his power by manipulating the political system. He was re-elected five consecutive times (1973, 1978, 1983, 1988, and 1993). Although he would provide unparalleled political stability and economic growth, the costs were steep.

Under Suharto's so-called New Order, parliament was purged of communists, labor organizations were liquidated, and freedom of the press was all but curtailed. Suharto strictly limited the number of political parties, and his Golkar Party established de facto one-party rule.

Suharto revamped Sukarno's state-oriented economic policies with the help of American-trained economists at the University of Indonesia. Suharto encouraged exports and foreign investments, received economic aid from the World Bank and the International Monetary Fund (IMF), stabilized the currency, and kept a tight lid on inflation. By the end of the 1960s, the economy was flourishing, and generally high growth rates were maintained until the 1997 Asian financial crisis, which decimated the Indonesian economic landscape.

Suharto's anticommunism was reflected in Indonesia's initially troubled relations with the Soviet Union and his severing of relations with the People's Republic of China (PRC). At the same time, he restored relations with Malaysia and encouraged regional cooperation that manifested itself in the formation of the Association of Southeast Asian Nations (ASEAN) in August 1967. During the 1970s, he turned increasingly to the West—especially the United States—for military and economic aid.

In 1975 Suharto ordered the invasion of East Timor, and in July 1976 Indonesia formally annexed that former Portuguese colony. In establishing control, Indonesian forces killed perhaps one-third of East Timor's population. As time went on, Suharto's human rights abuses became ever more appalling, and in 1997, during the Asian financial crisis, the World Bank accused Suharto of having embezzled as much as 30 percent of Indonesia's development funds over the years. The financial crisis ultimately brought Suharto down, as the economy spiraled downward and antigovernment protests increased. On 21 March 1998, he was forced from office. A year later, when his economic malfeasance became widely known, he was placed under house arrest. Some estimate that when he left office, he had enriched his family to the tune of $15 billion through embezzlement and a variety of state-run monopolies over which he exercised de facto control.

Paul G. Pierpaoli Jr.

See also

Association of Southeast Asian Nations; Indonesia; Non-Aligned Movement; Sukarno

References

Elson, R. E. *Suharto: A Political Biography.* Cambridge: Cambridge University Press, 2001.

Vatikiotis, Michael R. J. *Indonesian Politics under Suharto.* London: Routledge, 1993.

Sukarno (1901–1970)

Indonesian nationalist leader and first president of the Republic of Indonesia (1945–1967). Born Ahmed Sukarno in Surabaya, East Java, on 6 June 1901, like many Javanese Sukarno used only his last name. He studied in modern Dutch colonial schools and received a college degree in architecture from the Bandung Institute of Technology in 1926. Pursuing his passion for politics, he cofounded the Partai Nasional Indonesia (PNI, Indonesian Nationalist Party) in 1927 and became a leader of the independence movement.

Arrested by Dutch colonial officials for subversive activities, Sukarno utilized his trial to highlight the nature of imperialism and the importance of the PNI. Found guilty, he was imprisoned during 1929–1931. In July 1932, he was elected chairman of the Partai Indonesia, successor to the PNI. Arrested again on 1 August 1933 and exiled to Flores and then Bengkulu (in southern Sumatra), Sukarno's exile ended with the Japanese of invasion of Indonesia in 1942.

Sukarno embarked on active collaboration with the Japanese as a means to win Indonesian independence and used his considerable oratory skills to unify the people through radio broadcasts and personal appearances. He also secured significant concessions from the Japanese, such as administrative positions for Indonesians and permission to organize Indonesian political parties and military forces.

On 17 August 1945, only days after the Japanese surrender, Sukarno and fellow nationalist Mohammad Hatta declared Indonesian independence. A day later, the provisional parliament adopted a constitution that had already been drafted. It also elected Sukarno president. The 1945 constitution, based heavily upon Sukarno's political philosophy, encompassed the Pancasilla (Five Pillars): national unity, internationalism, representative democracy, Marxist-style social justice, and belief in God. Sukarno's sterling negotiating skills and reputation ultimately steered Indonesia through the

In the hopes of securing independence for his nation, Indonesian nationalist leader Sukarno actively collaborated with the Japanese during World War II. After the conflict, he was the first president of Indonesia during 1945–1967. (Library of Congress)

Battle of Surabaya, the Madiun Rebellion, and Dutch attempts to regain control over their colony.

Taken prisoner by Dutch forces in December 1948, Sukarno was released on 26 December 1949. The formal transfer of sovereignty from the Netherlands occurred on 27 December 1949. Indonesia's anticolonial battle was over.

Sukarno's powers as president were somewhat circumscribed by the 1950 provisional constitution that provided for a parliamentary system. However, the new constitution proved just as ineffectual as the first. The parliament gridlocked, while social, political, religious, and ethnic tensions grew in scope and severity. Political instability ultimately prompted Sukarno in 1959 to introduce what he termed "guided democracy" by dissolving parliament, exiling political rivals, and reinstating the 1945 constitution that conferred upon him vast executive powers. As he became more autocratic, his reliance on the army and the Communist Party of Indonesia increased dramatically.

Sukarno also moved boldly in foreign policy. He hosted the Pan-Asian-African Bandung Conference in April 1955, established formal ties with the People's Republic of China (PRC), and requested financial and military aid from the Soviet Union. His pursuit of the West Irian claim against the Dutch ended successfully in 1963, although his confrontation with Malaysia culminated in Indonesia's withdrawal from the United Nations (UN) in 1964.

After several attempts on his life in the late 1950s, Sukarno tightened control by establishing strict publishing laws, bringing more communists into the government, and increasing state-sponsored discrimination toward the Chinese minority. In July 1961, he was made president for life. On 30 September 1965, when an abortive coup led by communists and junior army officers resulted in the brutal killing of six senior right-wing generals, Sukarno reacted hesitantly. General Suharto, commander of the Kostrad (Strategic Reserve), took the initiative and gradually pushed Sukarno from power. On 21 March 1967, Sukarno was forced to cede control to Suharto, who then ordered Sukarno held under house arrest. Sukarno died on 21 June 1970 in Jakarta.

Paul G. Pierpaoli Jr.

See also

Anticolonialism; Bandung Conference; Decolonization; Indonesia; Malaysia; Southeast Asia; Suharto

References

Dahm, Bernhard. *Sukarno and the Struggle for Indonesian Independence.* Translated by Mary F. Somera Heidhues. London: Cornell University Press, 1969.

Hering, B. B. *Soekarno: Founding Father of Indonesia, 1901–1945.* Leiden, Netherlands: KITLV Press, 2002.

Legge, J. D. *Sukarno: A Political Biography.* 3rd ed. Singapore: Archipelago Press, 2003.

Sukarno. *Sukarno: An Autobiography.* New York: Bobbs Merrill, 1965.

Supreme Allied Commander Europe

U.S. military officer in charge of the integrated military command of the North Atlantic Treaty Organization (NATO). When NATO was founded on 4 April 1949, collective defense against communist aggression was the primary concern. Consequently, NATO created a military apparatus to make collective defense a reality. To this end, President Harry S. Truman named General of the Army Dwight D. Eisenhower to be NATO's first Supreme Allied Commander Europe (SACEUR). Eisenhower assumed his post on 19 December 1950. He subsequently established the Supreme Headquarters Allied Powers Europe (SHAPE) on 2 April 1951. Eisenhower and SHAPE laid the foundation for NATO's military operations.

U.S. Army General Matthew B. Ridgway followed Eisenhower as SACEUR on 30 May 1952 and helped to push NATO away from costly conventional forces to a reliance on nuclear weapons. Ridgway's successor, U.S. Army General Alfred M. Gruenther, became SACEUR 11 July 1953. General Lauris B. Norstad became the first U.S. Air Force SACEUR on 20 November 1956. He ushered in massive retaliation as NATO's new strategy in 1957 and steered NATO's military during the 1958 Berlin Crisis. He also commanded during the August 1961 erection of the Berlin Wall. After U.S. President John F. Kennedy took office, Norstad reluctantly supervised the change from massive retaliation to a flexible response defense posture.

U.S. Army General Lyman L. Lemnitzer became the next SACEUR on 1 January 1963. He oversaw the full implementation of the flexible response strategy and commanded during France's military withdrawal from NATO-integrated command in 1966. During Lemnitzer's tenure, NATO closely monitored the 1968 Soviet invasion of Czechoslovakia.

On 1 July 1969, NATO appointed its sixth commander, U.S. Army General Andrew J. Goodpaster. Most critically, the Soviet bloc surpassed the West in strategic nuclear weapons during his tenure. Goodpaster commanded NATO's military forces during several crises, including the Yom Kippur War, the 1973–1974 oil crisis, and the 1974 Cyprus Crisis.

NATO named U.S. Army General Alexander M. Haig to replace General Goodpaster on 15 December 1974. Haig's watchwords of readiness, rationalization, and reinforcement permeated NATO. He hoped that his policy would counter the growing power of the Soviet bloc. In 1975, he introduced the training exercises commonly referred to as REFORGER (Return of Forces to Germany).

U.S. Army General Bernard B. Rogers became the eighth SACEUR on 1 July 1979. Rogers believed that NATO's conventional forces were inadequate to withstand a Warsaw Pact conventional attack. He advocated the follow-on forces attack concept in order to attack the second and third echelon of the Warsaw Pact's conventional forces. Rogers's strong opposition to President Ronald Reagan's and Soviet Premier Mikhail Gorbachev's proposal to eliminate intermediate-range nuclear missiles played a major role in his 1987 retirement.

On 26 June 1987, U.S. Army General John R. Galvin assumed command as the ninth SACEUR. His tenure ended on 23 June 1992. Thus, he oversaw NATO's forces during the collapse of the Soviet Union, the fall of the Berlin Wall, and the unification of Germany. He also began the process of redefining NATO's military mission for the post–Cold War era.

Jonathan P. Klug

See also

Eisenhower, Dwight David; Flexible Response; Goodpaster, Andrew Jackson; Haig, Alexander Meigs, Jr.; Norstad, Lauris; North Atlantic Treaty Organization, Origins and Formation of; Ridgway, Matthew Bunker; Supreme Headquarters Allied Powers Europe; Western European Union

References

Kaplan, Lawrence S. *NATO and the United States: The Enduring Alliance.* New York: Twayne, 1994.

Kay, Sean, Victor Papacosma, and Mark R. Rubin, eds. *NATO: After Fifty Years.* Wilmington, DE: Scholarly Resources, 2001.

Schmidt, Gustave, ed. *A History of NATO: The First Fifty Years.* 3 vols. New York: Palgrave Macmillan, 2001.

Supreme Headquarters Allied Powers Europe

Administrative military headquarters for the North Atlantic Treaty Organization (NATO). NATO established the Supreme Headquarters Allied Powers Europe (SHAPE) on 2 April 1951, just four months after U.S. President Harry S. Truman named General Dwight D. Eisenhower as NATO's first Supreme Allied Commander Europe (SACEUR). SHAPE became the nerve center of NATO's integrated military forces. Originally located in Rocquencourt, France, SHAPE moved to Casteau, Belgium, in 1967 when French President Charles de Gaulle withdrew France from the NATO military command. Thus, the French military was autonomous from NATO, but France remained a member of NATO. Because Eisenhower wanted NATO to transcend individual nationalities, he fashioned SHAPE into a fully integrated command with officers from NATO nations acting as its staff officers. SHAPE served NATO well throughout the Cold War and continues to function to this day.

The origins of SHAPE date back to the Supreme Headquarters Allied Expeditionary Force (SHAEF), which was organized by Eisenhower and began as a combined staff between the United States and Britain during the Allied liberation of Europe (1944–1945). Two keys issues, however, pointed toward a smaller, integrated headquarters that would be the genesis of SHAPE. SHAEF's American and British planners had often worked on divergent paths and were not always efficient. Second, Americans lacked understanding of the British conference system. Consequently, American officers often did not fully comprehend the ramifications of these meetings and wasted time and effort attempting to rectify misperceptions. Those studying these problems concluded that a supreme allied headquarters should employ one integrated staff cognizant of the need to avoid affronts to national pride.

The March 1948 Brussels Pact was crucial to the formation of SHAPE. This pact included a common defense arrangement among Belgium, Luxembourg, the Netherlands, France, and Great Britain. The Western European Union was the mechanism for planning its military operations. Following the creation of NATO on 4 April 1949, the Western European Union headquarters, or the military headquarters of those European nations that would become part of NATO and were already allied, became the basis for SHAPE.

The integrated, multinational nature of SHAPE is evident in its first senior leaders: Eisenhower as SACEUR, British Field Marshal Bernard Montgomery as deputy SACEUR, and British Air Chief Marshal Hugh Saunders as the air deputy to SACEUR.

SHAPE presided over NATO's Cold War collective defense against the Warsaw Pact and had to be ready to produce the strategies that would act as a deterrent and defend NATO's constituent nations. Following the collapse of the Soviet Union in December 1991, SHAPE continued its service by controlling such NATO operations as those in Bosnia (1995–present) and in Kosovo (1999–present). Thus, SHAPE's mission has changed from collective defense to cooperative security.

Jonathan P. Klug

See also

Eisenhower, Dwight David; North Atlantic Treaty Organization, Origins and Formation of; Supreme Allied Commander Europe

References

Eisenhower, Dwight D. *Crusade in Europe.* New York: Doubleday, 1948.

Kay, Sean, Victor Papacosma, and Mark R. Rubin, eds. *NATO: After Fifty Years.* Wilmington, DE: Scholarly Resources, 2001.

Knowlton, William A. "Early Stages in the Organization of 'SHAPE.'" *International Organization,* 13(1) (Winter 1959): 1–18.

Wood, Robert J. "The First Year of SHAPE." *International Organization* 6(2) (May 1952): 175–191.

Suslov, Mikhail Andreyevich (1902–1982)

Soviet political leader. Born on 8 November 1902 in Shakhovskoye in western Russia, Mikhail Suslov served in local Kom-

Mikhail A. Suslov, member of the Presidium of the Soviet Union and hard-liner in matters of communist ideology and foreign policy, shown here in March 1956. (Bettmann/Corbis)

somol (Young Communist League) posts from 1918 to 1921 and then joined the Communist Party of the Soviet Union (CPSU). He graduated from the Prechistenskaia Workers' Faculty in Moscow in 1924 and from the Plekhanov Institute of the National Economy in 1928. He did graduate work at the Institute of Economics of the Communist Academy during 1929–1931 while teaching at Moscow University. During 1931–1935 he served in administrative posts in the party apparatus before attending the Moscow Economic Institute. Graduating in 1937, he was elected to the CPSU Central Committee in 1941 and worked in party administrative posts in Rostov and Stavropol until 1944. During World War II, he was also a member of the Military Council of the North Caucasus Front and served as chief of staff for regional partisan forces.

Beginning in 1944, Suslov held a succession of Central Committee posts. Named a Central Committee secretary in 1947, he had responsibility for enforcing party ideology. Following the purge of Andrei Zhdanov in 1948, Suslov also assumed responsibility for relations with foreign communist parties and served briefly as editor of *Pravda*. In 1952 he was elected to the expanded Presidium (Politburo), although he lost his seat when the body was reduced from twenty-five to

ten members in 1953. Shortly afterward, he became second secretary of the Central Committee. He returned to the Presidium in 1955 and served until his death, wielding considerable influence in matters of ideology and foreign affairs.

A party conservative, Suslov opposed Nikita Khrushchev's extensive attempts to implement a de-Stalinization campaign beginning in 1956. Suslov became the principal advocate of intervention in Hungary during the 1956 uprising and was in Budapest to help oversee its implementation. He was also responsible for the banning of the Boris Pasternak's novel *Dr. Zhivago*. While Suslov supported Khrushchev in the Politburo power struggles of 1956–1957, differences between the two men grew over a number of issues, including economic reform, foreign policy, and the publication of Aleksandr Solzhenitsyn's *One Day in the Life of Ivan Denisovich*, which Khrushchev permitted.

In October 1964, Suslov was a key figure in the ouster of Khrushchev. Suslov's conservative influence grew under Khrushchev's successor Leonid Brezhnev, especially in cultural affairs, in part because Suslov did not seek higher office himself. In foreign policy, he generally opposed détente, advocated intervention in Afghanistan in 1979, and urged similar action in Poland the following year. Suslov died in Moscow on 25 January 1982.

Steven W. Guerrier

See also
Afghanistan War; Brezhnev, Leonid; Cominform; Détente; Hungarian Revolution; Khrushchev, Nikita; Literature; Solzhenitsyn, Aleksandr; Soviet Union; Zhdanov, Andrei Aleksandrovich

References
Breslaur, George W. *Khrushchev and Brezhnev As Leaders: Building Authority in Soviet Politics*. London: Allen and Unwin, 1982.
Gelman, Harry. *The Brezhnev Politburo and the Decline of Détente*. Ithaca, NY: Cornell University Press, 1984.
Taubman, William C. *Khrushchev: The Man and His Era*. New York: Norton, 2003.

Suzuki Zenkō (1911–2004)

Japanese politician and prime minister (1980–1982). Born in Iwate Prefecture on 11 January 1911, Suzuki Zenkō graduated from the Fisheries Training School at the Ministry of Agriculture and Forestry in 1935. He then became active in labor union affairs. In 1947 he was elected to the Diet on the Socialist Party ticket, but by the 1949 election he had become a member of the Democratic Liberal Party and was reelected on that party's ticket. In 1960 he joined the first Ikeda Hayato cabinet as minister of posts and telecommunications and, after having served in several different cabinet positions, including a stint as chief cabinet secretary, became prime minister in July 1980.

As prime minister, Suzuki adopted what he called the politics of harmony, which emphasized increased political dialogue. At the same time, he advocated comprehensive security abroad by distancing his government from President Ronald Reagan's hard-line strategy toward the Soviet Union. During a visit to the United States in 1981, Suzuki's interpretation of the U.S.-Japanese alliance, which he said "does not imply a military connotation," angered the White House and strained U.S.-Japanese relations. Suzuki was in fact a dovish politician who concerned himself with limiting defense expenditures despite the effort of the Reagan administration's strong pressure to increase them.

In 1982 Suzuki declared that he would not run for election as party president. He dissolved his cabinet that November and retired from politics in 1990. Suzuki died in Tokyo on 19 July 2004.

Tomoyuki Takemoto

See also
Ikeda Hayato; Japan; Ōhira Masayoshi
References
Buckley, Roger. *US-Japan Alliance Diplomacy, 1945–1990.* New York: Cambridge University Press, 1992.
Ohtake Hideo. *Nippon No Boei To Kokunai Seiji* [Japan's Defense and Domestic Politics]. Tokyo: San-Ichi Shobo, 1983.
Schaller, Michael. *Altered States: The United States and Japan since the Occupation.* Oxford: Oxford University Press, 1997.
Uji Toshihiko. *Suzuki Seiken Happyaku-Rokuju-San Nichi* [The 863 days of the Suzuki Administration]. Tokyo: Gyosei Mondai Kenkyusho, 1983.

Svalbard

Island archipelago located north of Norway, well above the Arctic Circle and adjacent to strategic North Atlantic sea-lanes. The Svalbard islands, including Bear Island, extend over an area of 38,470 square miles. The strategic importance of the Svalbard archipelago, a dependency of Norway, became readily apparent with the German attack on the Soviet Union in 1941. The Allies conducted military operations on the islands, despite a provision in the 1925 Svalbard Treaty, signed by Norway, Denmark, Sweden, France, Italy, Japan, the Netherlands, Great Britain, Ireland, and the United States. But Allied plans to build military installations there were soon scrapped for lack of adequate sites. Instead, the British evacuated the Soviet and Norwegian inhabitants there in 1941 and later destroyed the settlements.

Economic interests (chiefly coal) and national prestige contributed to Moscow's demands in 1944 for the nullification of the Svalbard Treaty that gave Norway sovereignty over the archipelago. But the archipelago's position adjacent to the passages leading to the North Atlantic from the Soviet ports of Murmansk and Archangel was undoubtedly the most important consideration for Moscow in these demands. From the Soviet point of view, this issue had a clear parallel to maintaining secure passages through the Turkish and Danish straits from the Black and Baltic Seas.

Despite growing skepticism over the Soviet position on the Svalbard matter, the Norwegian government-in-exile in London during World War II initially did not flatly reject the Soviet demands. At the time, appeasing Moscow seemed an imperative, with Soviet troops fighting the Germans in northern Norway. On the other hand, accepting Soviet control—or even joint control—of the islands might tie Norway to the Soviet Union and damage its relations with the United States and Great Britain. The Norwegians initiated talks with the Soviets on the subject after the war in hopes of reaching a favorable outcome.

In 1947, Norway finally rejected the Soviets' repeated requests for joint control of the islands, arguing that discussing the defense of Norwegian territory with another state would be a breach of accepted policy. The expected Soviet protests never came, and the issue faded away. In the 1950s, the Norwegian government also rebuffed proposals from its own military for the construction of military installations on the Svalbards.

Despite its strategic position, the Svalbard archipelago never became a significant battleground between the United States and the Soviet Union. Not wanting to risk a dispute over its own bases and radar surveillance systems on Greenland and Iceland, the United States did not push the Svalbard matter, and Norway managed to preserve its sovereignty over the archipelago without outside help.

Frode Lindgjerdet

See also
Norway; Scandinavia
References
Holsmark, Svein G. *A Soviet Grab for the High North: USSR, Svalboard and Northern Norway, 1920–1953.* Oslo: Norwegian Institute for Defence Studies, 1993.
Lundestad, Geir. *America, Scandinavia and the Cold War.* Oslo: Universitetsforlaget, 1982.

Svoboda, Ludvík (1895–1979)

Czechoslovak general and president (1968–1975). Born on 25 November 1895 in Hroznatín, Moravia, to a peasant family, Ludvík Svoboda was drafted into the Austro-Hungarian Army during World War I. He deserted and joined the Czech Legion in Russia, attaining the rank of captain. At war's end, he returned to the new state of Czechoslovakia and joined its army. Following the German occupation of all Czechoslovakia in March 1939, he fled to Poland, where he organized a Czechoslovak military unit.

Following the German conquest of Poland in September 1939, Svoboda and his men went to the Soviet Union, where he led a Czechoslovak army corps against the Axis powers, becoming a brigadier general in 1943. Sympathetic to the communists, he secretly joined the Communist Party of Czechoslovakia (CPCz) during the war. In April 1945, President Edvard Beneš appointed Svoboda minister of defense, and Svoboda was promoted to full general in August 1945.

Svoboda officially and publicly joined the CPCz in October 1948, but the party hierarchy did not trust him and made certain that he had little power. During the Stalinist purges, he lost his positions in 1950 and was briefly imprisoned in 1951, after which he returned to his home village.

During his 1954 visit to Prague, Soviet leader Nikita Khrushchev personally interceded and demanded that Svoboda be politically rehabilitated. Svoboda then became the director of the Klement Gottwald Military Academy, retiring in 1959. A popular war hero, Svoboda was elected president of Czechoslovakia on 30 March 1968 during the Prague Spring.

After the August Warsaw Pact invasion, Svoboda refused to accept a Soviet puppet government or negotiate with the Soviets until he was assured that the leaders of the Prague Spring would not be harmed. So assured, he then agreed to Soviet demands that the Prague Spring reforms be reversed and accepted the normalization of Czechoslovakia, thereby losing much of his credibility. Illness forced his removal from office on 29 May 1975. Svoboda died in Prague on 20 September 1979.

Gregory C. Ference

See also
Czechoslovakia; Prague Spring

References
Dubček, Alexander, and Jiri Hochman. *Hope Dies Last: The Autobiography of Alexander Dubček.* New York: Kodansha America, 1993.
Fis, Teodor. *Mein Kommandeur, General Svoboda: Von Ural zum Hradschin.* Vienna, Austria: Europa Verlag, 1969.
Svoboda, Ludvík. *Cestami ñivota* [The Journeys of My Life]. 2 vols. Prague: Naše Voksko, 1992.

Sweden

Scandinavian nation. Sweden covers 173,731 square miles, slightly larger than the U.S. state of California, and had a 1945 population of approximately 6.8 million people. Sweden is bordered by Norway to the west, Finland to the north, the Gulf of Bothnia and the Baltic Sea to the east, and the North Sea to the south-southwest. Once a great power, Sweden was reduced to a regional power following the Napoleonic Wars. During both world wars, Sweden managed to maintain its neutrality. Thus, its wartime experiences were quite the opposite of many other Western democracies. Not having had to regret appeasement at Munich in 1938 or experience a Pearl Harbor, Swedish postwar foreign policy therefore became a continuation of its prior neutrality. Swedes adopted nonalignment in peace and neutrality in case of war. However, unlike Switzerland—another perennial neutral—Sweden did join the United Nations (UN) in 1946.

Following World War II, Sweden attempted to mollify the Soviets by forcing Baltic refugees to repatriate and granting Moscow substantial financial credits. The Soviets, however, did not show much gratitude. After Swedish diplomat Count Raoul Wallenberg negotiated the release of Hungarian Jews, he was apprehended by Soviet agents and disappeared. This aroused great anti-Soviet sentiments in Sweden. Other early Cold War Soviet provocations included the presumed Soviet downing of a Swedish surveillance aircraft in 1951 and Soviet efforts to disrupt the subsequent search and rescue mission.

In the immediate postwar years, Sweden failed in its attempt to create a nonaligned Nordic bloc to keep all of Scandinavia out of the Cold War. Finland signed a mutual aid, cooperation, and friendship treaty with the Soviet Union in 1948, while Denmark and Norway joined the North Atlantic Treaty Organization (NATO) in 1949. This constellation of Norwegian and Danish NATO membership, Swedish nonalignment, and Finland's ties to the Soviet Union has frequently been termed "the Nordic balance." During the early Cold War, Sweden's Social Democrats and center-rightist political parties differed little on the practical aspects of nonalignment. Nevertheless, Sweden conducted security-related consultations with the United States and NATO in both the political and military spheres. On occasion, the center-rightists did advocate a tougher line with the Soviets in regard to Eastern Europe.

Although Swedes experienced some economic dislocation in the immediate post–World War II years, having escaped wartime destruction meant that their economic, political, and social institutions were still intact in 1945. In the elections of that year, the Social Democrats formed a majority government under Prime Minister Per Albin Hansson. When he died the following year, Tage Erlander replaced him and held the premiership until 1969. During 1951–1957, the Social Democrats had to share power with the Peasant Party, as it had done during the interwar years.

Swedish society was thoroughly democratic and civic-minded in its social and political structures. Swedes enjoyed a well-functioning social welfare state, a high level of social and corporate organization, and a strong public sector. Much of this was made possible by a thriving industrial base, funded by domestic financing. Swedish exports included high-value industrial products such as automobiles, machine tools, and ball bearings. But the postwar era also witnessed the rapid depopulation of rural Sweden, as industry and commercial concerns in the cities lured workers from the hinterlands.

Despite fears of provoking Soviet suspicions, Sweden accepted Marshall Plan aid and in 1951 also adopted the U.S. Cold War initiative that called for an embargo of strategic commodities and products to the Eastern bloc. Sweden also put recognition of the German Democratic Republic (GDR, East Germany) on hold until 1972 in accordance with the general Western view that recognition could be seen as a hostile act against the Federal Republic of Germany (FRG, West Germany), a major trading partner.

In the areas of trade and other transnational interactions, Sweden did align itself with the West. Swedish policymakers thus created a tension between nonalignment and economic necessity. The European Council provided one arena for interacting with other democracies without being tied to a bloc. The European Free Trade Association (EFTA) allowed for free trade outside the more politicized European Economic Community (EEC), which Swedish officials refused to join because it would contradict nonalignment.

As East-West tensions eased beginning in the mid-1960s, many nonaligned states had more freedom of action of foreign affairs. Accordingly, the Social Democratic government moved from pure realpolitik to a more idealistic foreign policy. At the core of this reorientation were expectations of a new economic world order, decolonization, nuclear disarmament, and the curbing of great power influence. The move away from realpolitik became most evident at the UN by Swedish participation in peacekeeping missions in the Middle East and the Congo and by Dag Hammarskjöld's posting as UN secretary-general. Indeed, rapid decolonization swelled the number of nonaligned states and broadened the appeal of Swedish foreign policy.

Swedish leaders did not shy away from confronting the United States. Prime Minister Olof Palme spoke out fiercely against the Vietnam War. Indeed, after the U.S. Christmas Bombings of Hanoi in December 1972, Palme compared the incident to the Holocaust. President Richard M. Nixon's administration was outraged and withheld its ambassador from Stockholm until 1974. Sweden also provided asylum to U.S. draft dodgers seeking to escape service in Vietnam, a policy that particularly rankled Washington.

In 1976, U.S.-Swedish relations improved markedly when the political Right gained power under Prime Minister Thorbjörn Fälldin. The Peasant Party, to which Fälldin belonged, had changed its name to the Center Party and simultaneously aligned itself with the political Right. Still, no major policy

changes occurred, although the idealism of the Social Democrats was drastically toned down.

With Cold War tensions already on the rise again in the late 1970s, the Swedish government condemned the 1979 Soviet invasion of Afghanistan and the imposition of martial law in Poland in 1981. At the same time, dramatic events were also unfolding closer to home. In October 1982, a Soviet submarine ran aground outside the Karlskrona naval base in southern Sweden. Moscow acknowledged the undeniable fact of the grounded sub (which the Soviets blamed on a damaged navigation system) but denied that there had been any systematic Soviet violation of Swedish territorial waters. Nonetheless, Soviet intrusions by submarines into Swedish waters continued.

When the Social Democrats and Palme regained power in 1986, Swedish officials withdrew their protests of Soviet submarine violations and announced an upcoming state visit to Moscow. However, Palme was assassinated in February 1986, and the trip was made by his successor, Ingvar Karlsson, in 1987. The rapprochement between the Soviet Union and Sweden was facilitated by new Soviet leader Mikhail Gorbachev's reforms.

The end of the Cold War transformed the Baltic Sea from a part of the Iron Curtain to an increasingly important line of communication between Sweden and the former Eastern bloc countries. As such, Sweden's influence in the region grew. However, friction was also apparent. Estonia, Latvia, and Lithuania harbored a grudge toward Sweden for its 1940 recognition of the Soviet takeover of these republics and had not forgotten Sweden's forced repatriation of Baltic refugees back to the Soviet Union in 1945. There was also some Baltic discontent over Stockholm's tepid support during the 1989–1991 struggles for independence. Baltic skepticism toward Sweden also had deep historical roots, as it was here that Sweden had vied with Russia for Baltic supremacy in the seventeenth and early eighteenth centuries.

With the end of the Cold War, Sweden no longer regarded the European Union (EU), the successor of the EEC, as part of a political bloc to which membership on their part would be a breech of their nonalignment policy. Thus, Sweden joined the EU after a referendum in 1994.

At the end of the twentieth century, government interventionism and large-scale industrial structures marked a troubled Swedish economy. It faced the challenge of globalization and demands for harmonizing with EU standards. Unemployment has been comparatively high by Scandinavian standards, placing additional burdens on social services. Foreign interests have purchased Swedish trademarks such as Volvo and Saab, and production has moved to countries in which labor costs are lower. Fearing unemployment and diminished benefits, Swedish trade unions have not always been cooperative in making necessary sacrifices in order to make Sweden's industry more competitive.

Frode Lindgjerdet

See also
Erlander, Tage; Hammarskjöld, Dag; Palme, Olof; Scandinavia; Sweden, Armed Forces; Vietnam War Protests

References
Andrén, Nils. *Maktbalans och alliansfrihet* [Balance of Power and Freedom of Alliances]. Stockholm: Nordstedts Juridik, 1996.
Bjereld, Ulf, and Ann-Marie Ekengren. *Cold War Historiography in Sweden.* Odense: University Press of Southern Denmark, 2004.
Hanhimäki, Jussi. *Scandinavia and the United States: An Insecure Friendship.* New York: Twayne, 1997.
Lundestad, Geir. *America, Scandinavia and the Cold War.* Oslo: Universitetsforlaget, 1982.

Sweden, Armed Forces

In 1945, the Swedish Army lacked the capability of fighting a mechanized opponent in open terrain. The Swedish Navy and the Swedish Air Force had been expanded and were relatively modern in 1945, but the army was widely dispersed in a large number of units defending different parts of Swedish territory rather than maintaining fewer, more modernized, and well-equipped units. This problem worsened during the 1970s and 1980s.

Sweden's war planning prepared for a combined Soviet coastal and airborne attack directed toward eastern Sweden around Stockholm, eventually followed by landings in southern Skåne as well as on the island of Gotland and in Gothenburg in western Sweden. In some scenarios, a land invasion across the Finnish border was also regarded as a potential threat. From the early 1960s, relatively more emphasis was placed on preparations to defend the most northern parts of Sweden. Here the fortress of Boden was supported by lines of fortifications along the rivers in northern Sweden. Other large systems of modern fortifications were built, especially in the Stockholm archipelago, while along the shores of Skåne in southern Sweden no fewer than 600 fortifications built during 1939–1945 were utilized during most of the Cold War.

Sweden's policy of neutrality prevented any formal ties with the North Atlantic Treaty Organization (NATO), but Sweden secretly established multilateral military cooperation with Denmark, Norway, the United Kingdom, and the United States. Swedish air bases were prepared to receive U.S. strategic bombers, plans were made for receiving oil and other strategic goods via Trondheim in Norway, and the communication system of the Swedish Air Force was connected with the U.S. air base in Wiesbaden in the Federal Republic of Germany (FRG, West Germany). It is believed that Sweden also maintained intelligence cooperation with other Western nations and, beginning in 1960, was tacitly protected by the U.S. nuclear umbrella.

In the late 1940s, Swedish armed forces consisted of 850,000 conscripts, approximately 60,000 professionals, and more than 100,000 volunteers. The total military structure comprised 36 army brigades, 33 large surface warships, 24 submarines, and 50 air force divisions with 1,000 airplanes. A large armaments industry included artillery systems from Bofors, aircraft from Saab, and surface ships from the Karlskrona shipyard. From 1960 on, the navy developed the concept of a lighter navy, in which the 2 cruisers and 15 destroyers were sequentially replaced by smaller but more powerful units. With the parliamentary defense budget decisions of 1968 and 1972, the military establishment was expected to do more with less. This resulted in severe organizational cutbacks and canceled training exercises, especially for the air force and navy, and the postponement of equipment replacement for the army. Instead, the need to defend a large area of territory took priority over further modernization and training. During 1956–1994, 70,000 Swedish soldiers participated in peacekeeping missions for the United Nations (UN) in the Middle East (1956–1994), the Congo (1960–1964), and Cyprus (1964–1987).

As late as 1982, Sweden could mobilize 850,000 men in twenty-eight army brigades, forty-eight naval ships (including twelve submarines), and twenty-three to twenty-four air force divisions. But of the twenty infantry brigades, only eight were regarded as modern, meaning that they could be employed for offensive operations. The remainder could only be used for defensive tasks. In 1992, the infantry brigades were reduced to seventeen, and the total personnel in the armed forces amounted to 750,000.

As early as 1954, instructions had been issued as to how Swedish troops should deploy in case of a nuclear attack by the Soviets. During the 1950s, the Swedish military establishment began demanding the development of a Swedish nuclear deterrent. After serious and protracted debate, however, all such plans were scrapped in 1968.

For most of the Cold War period, the Swedish Air Force was among the world's most modern and powerful. In the 1950s, it numbered some 1,000 aircraft, produced by domestic manufacture. Many of these planes were in hardened sites, and the Swedes developed a widespread system of airstrips that would make use of the Swedish highway system in order to make it difficult for an attacker to wipe out the majority of aircraft in a first strike. The chief task of the air force and navy was to meet and defeat in the Baltic Sea any invasion force before it could reach Sweden itself. Training in close air support for ground forces was thus not a priority.

Lars Ericson

See also

Finland; Scandinavia; Sweden; Whisky on the Rocks Crisis

References

Agrell, Wilhelm. *Fred och fruktan: Sveriges säkerhetspolitiska historia, 1918–2000* [Peace and Fear: The History of Sweden's Security Policy, 1918–2000]. Lund: Historiska media, 2000.

Dörfer, Ingemar. *System 37 Viggen: Arms Technology and the Domestication of Glory.* Oslo: Universitetsforlaget, 1973.

Ericson, Lars. *Svensk militärmakt: Strategi och operationer i svensk militärhistoria under 1,500 år* [Swedish Military Power: Strategy and Operations in Swedish Military History during 1,500 years]. Stockholm: National Defence College, 2003.

Wallerfelt, Bengt. *Si vis pacem . . . para bellum: Svensk säkerhetspolitik och krigsplanläggning 1945–1975* [Swedish Defense Policy and War Planning, 1945–1979]. Stockholm: Probus, 1999.

Świarło, Józef (1915–1985?)

Officer in the Polish security apparatus and one of the most celebrated of communist defectors. Józef Świarło was born Izak Fleischfarb on 1 January 1915 in Medyna (Eastern Galicia), the son of a Jewish low-ranking civil servant. He completed only primary school. During 1932–1938, he was an active member of a communist youth organization in Kraków and was twice arrested for his political activities.

In 1938 Fleischfarb was drafted into the Polish Army. Captured by the German Army in their invasion of Poland in September 1939, he escaped and made his way to eastern Poland, which had been incorporated into the Soviet Union. In 1943 he joined the communist-organized Polish Army, and in November 1944 he was transferred to the Ministry of Public Security, where he worked with the Soviet Komitet Gosudarstvennoi Bezopasnosti (KGB).

In postwar Poland, the Soviets coerced Jews to change their Yiddish names to Polish names, and Izak Fleischfarb became Józef Świarło. During 1945–1948 he held key posts in the regional structure of the security apparatus, and in October 1948 he was transferred to the central offices to work in a unit specially created for dealing with the Polish Communist Party. Dependable and distinguished for his abilities, he was entrusted with such tasks as the arrests of Władysław Gomułka and Cardinal Stefan Wyszyński.

On 5 December 1953, while on an official trip to Berlin, Świarło found his way to U.S. authorities, defected, and was transported to the United States, where the Central Intelligence Agency (CIA) used him for propaganda purposes. In September 1954 he was granted political asylum, which was trumpeted by the U.S. government. Radio Free Europe broadcast more than 100 of Świarło 's programs titled *Behind the Scenes of the Security and the Party,* and in 1955 more than 800,000 copies of a brochure based on the broadcasts were

scattered on Polish territory as part of the CIA's largest balloon campaign, Operation SPOTLIGHT. Świarło's revelations forced Polish authorities to reorganize the security apparatus and to discharge or arrest several high-ranking Polish security officials.

Świarło continued to reside in the United States under an assumed name and with CIA protection, essentially a non-person. He died possibly in New York City in May 1985.

Andrzej Paczkowski

See also

Gomułka, Władysław; Poland; Radio Free Europe and Radio Liberty; Wyszyńki, Stefan, Cardinal

References

Gluchowski, L. W. "The Defection of Josef Swiatlo and the Search for Jewish Scapegoats in the Polish United Workers' Party, 1953–1954." *Inter Marium* 3(2) (1999): 2–32.

Kaminski, Bartlomiej. *The Collapse of State Socialism: The Case of Poland.* Princeton, NJ: Princeton University Press, 1991.

Michie, Allan A. *Voice through the Curtain: The Radio Free Europe Story.* New York: Dodd, Mead, 1963.

Schatz, Jaff. *The Generation: The Rise and Fall of the Jewish Communists of Poland.* Berkeley: University of California Press, 1991.

Switzerland

West European nation encompassing 15,942 square miles, about twice the size of the U.S. state of New Jersey. Switzerland is bordered by Italy to the south, France to the west, and Germany and Austria to the north and east. The Swiss population in 1945 was 4.428 million people. By the end of World War II, Switzerland's neutrality during the conflict and its role as a financial and commercial center for Nazi Germany assured strained relations with both the United States and the Soviet Union. The Swiss were internationally isolated and viewed integration and multilateralism warily. Their long-standing tradition of neutrality was at odds with the multilateral collectivism of the United Nations (UN). In 1946, Switzerland determined that it could not join the UN without having its neutrality explicitly recognized.

In 1954, the Swiss promulgated the so-called Bindschedler Doctrine, specifically outlining the nation's neutral position in peacetime. This doctrine strictly differentiated between the political and technical aspects of international affairs. Thus, while Switzerland would keep aloof from political and military alliances, it would play an active role in international economic, humanitarian, and technical organizations, displaying its commitment to international solidarity. During the Cold War, Swiss foreign policy hence pursued economic integration without political encumbrances.

Swiss Cold War security policy, with its emphasis on autonomous national defense by a militia army, was derived from the principle of armed neutrality. The concept of the citizen-in-arms was an important part of Swiss life and provided for a large army despite the nation's small population. At peak strength, the Swiss Army could field 600,000 soldiers.

During the early Cold War, Switzerland sided with the West and indirectly profited from the nuclear umbrella of the United States and the North Atlantic Treaty Organization (NATO). Under Federal Councilor Max Petitpierre (1945–1961), the Swiss government emphasized that the nation was ideologically aligned with the West, although it remained militarily neutral.

As a small landlocked country, Switzerland relied heavily on international trade. Therefore, with the exception of the subsidized agricultural sector, it supported the reduction of trade tariffs. Switzerland remained prosperous throughout the Cold War, depending on industrial exports such as textiles, chemicals, and engineering-related products. Switzerland also kept its place as an international financial center. Because the Swiss eschewed a large welfare state, their economy weathered the economic storms of the 1970s and 1980s rather well. The nation boasted comparatively low inflation,

low unemployment, and positive growth and productivity. In addition, labor-management relations remained positive and nonconfrontational, which added to Swiss economic stability.

Swiss politics are unique in that parties are highly decentralized and are focused on local rather than national issues. Although all the major parties are represented at the national level, they tend to be fixated on local constituencies and their particular interests, which dilutes the political system at the federal level. There is also a plethora of political parties in Switzerland that are decidedly balkanized by the large number of religious and linguistic cleavages throughout the country. Large French, German, and Italian-speaking populations help account for the great diversity in the political process. The four largest political parties in Switzerland are the Social Democratic Party (SPS), the Swiss People's Party (SVP), the Radical Party (FDP), and the Christian Democratic Party (CVP).

The Cold War accorded Switzerland an intermediary role in the East-West conflict. Switzerland provided its mediation services offices to both East and West, including offers to

Sir Anthony Eden (*right*) and Swiss President Max Petitpierre review a Swiss Honor Guard in Geneva in 1955. (Library of Congress)

mediate a settlement to both the 1967 and 1973 Arab-Israeli conflicts. In 1953, Switzerland engaged in the Korean War cease-fire agreement through two international commissions. Swiss neutrality was further recognized when the Soviet Union suggested in 1955 that Austria should develop a neutrality of the kind practiced by the Swiss.

Switzerland also took on international mandates to act as a protecting power, such as in representing U.S. interests in Cuba after 1961. In addition, Geneva served many times as a center for international negotiations. In 1985, for example, Geneva was the site of the historic summit between U.S. President Ronald Reagan and Soviet leader Mikhail Gorbachev. Switzerland also hosted the humanitarian offices of the Geneva-based International Committee of the Red Cross, which aims at assisting civilian victims of war.

In the 1970s, under Foreign Minister Pierre Graber (1970–1978), Swiss foreign policy became more active and multilateral. The Swiss Federal Council's landmark 1973 Security Report envisioned political participation in international security organizations such as the Conference on Security and Cooperation in Europe (CSCE). Switzerland played an important role in the CSCE together with other neutral and nonaligned nations.

During the Cold War and beyond, Switzerland's relationship with an increasingly united Western Europe was often troubled. Switzerland joined the Organization for European Economic Cooperation (OEEC) in 1948 and, with great delay, the Council of Europe in 1963. Yet Swiss relations with Europe became more difficult after the European Free Trade Association (EFTA), founded in 1960 with Switzerland as an active member, lost its importance in the 1970s with British entry into the European Economic Community (EEC).

After a late, even if most-narrow, referendum in favor of joining the United Nations (UN) in March 2002 (in 1986, a vast majority of Swiss voters had still voted against such an entry), Switzerland's major challenge in the twenty-first century remains the shaping of its relationship with a dynamically proceeding European Union (EU).

Christian Nuenlist

See also
Europe, Western; European Union; Security and Cooperation in Europe, Conference on

References
Gabriel, Jürg Martin, and Thomas Fischer, eds. *Swiss Foreign Policy, 1945–2002*. New York: Palgrave Macmillan, 2003.
Katzenstein, Peter. *Corporatism and Change: Austria, Switzerland and the Politics of Change*. Ithaca, NY: Cornell University Press, 1984.
New, Mitya, ed. *Switzerland Unwrapped: Exposing the Myths*. London: Tauris, 1997.
Spillmann, Kurt R., et al. *Schweizer Sicherheitspolitik seit 1945: Zwischen Autonomie und Kooperation* [Swiss Security Policy since 1945: Between Autonomy and Cooperation]. Zürich: Verlag Neue Zürcher Zeitung, 2001.

Swords to Ploughshares Movement

Independent peace movement begun in the German Democratic Republic (GDR, East Germany) in 1980. "Swords to ploughshares" is a biblical quotation from the Book of Micah 4:3 and the Book of Isaiah 2:4. The movement's symbolic motto is depicted by sculptor Evgeniy Vuchetich's statue "Let Us Beat Swords into Ploughshares," donated by the Soviet Union to the United Nations (UN) Headquarters in New York in 1959.

During the preparations for the first Peace Decade in 1980, a ten-day period of peace activities conducted by the East German Union of Evangelical Churches, youth vicar Harald Bretschneider first used the symbol to summon all Christians to attend nationwide prayers. He also connected the symbol to the pacifist campaign "Make Peace Without Weapons" and to various peace movements in the West.

The symbol was made into cloth badges and was eagerly worn by many East German youths, who used it as a silent protest against the militarization of East German society. From 1980 on, peace groups formed within many churches in East Germany. They demonstrated against the presence of Soviet missiles on East German soil as well as against the degradation of the environment caused by industrial waste. Consequently, in November 1981 East German officials banned the wearing of the badges. The government considered it subversive to its so-called communist peace politics.

Peace activists both in and outside East German churches were labeled as subversive elements. Many youths who persisted in wearing the badges were harassed by the secret police (Stasi), banned from their final exams, and even prosecuted. The East German regime managed to prevent these groups from maturing into political movements, at least for a time. Pacifist and ecological groups remained at the grassroots level and were closely observed by the Stasi. Nevertheless, in the summer and fall of 1989, the opposition peace groups formed the nucleus of the mass protests against the government, which in turn brought an end to communism and the division of Germany.

Beatrice de Graaf

See also
German Democratic Republic; Human Rights; Peace Movements; Stasi

References
Pfaff, Steven. "The Politics of Peace in the GDR: The Independent Peace Movement, the Church, and the Origins of the East German Opposition." *Peace & Change* 25(3) (July 2001): 280–300.
Schroeder, Klaus. *Der SED-Staat: Partei, Staat und Gesellschaft* [The SED-State: Party, State and Society]. München: Carl Hanser, 1998.
Sandford, John. *The Sword and the Ploughshare: Autonomous Peace Initiatives in East Germany*. London: Merlin Press/European Nuclear Disarmament, 1983.

Silomon, Anke. *"Schwerter zu Pflugscharen" und die DDR: Die Friedensarbeit der evangelischen Kirchen in der DDR im Rahmen der Friedensdekaden 1980 bis 1982* ["Swords to Ploughshares" and the GDR: The Peace Activities of the Evangelical Churches in the GDR within the Framework of the Peace Decades 1980 to 1982]. Göttingen: Vandenhoeck and Ruprecht, 1999.

Symington, William Stuart, III (1901–1988)

U.S. senator, secretary of the U.S. Air Force, and chairman of the National Security Resources Board (NSRB). Born in Amherst, Massachusetts, on 26 June 1901, Stuart Symington enlisted in the U.S. Army artillery in 1918, eventually earning a commission. Following demobilization after World War I, he attended Yale University, graduating in 1923. He cultivated a highly successful business career as a corporate troubleshooter and eventually ran several companies, most notably St. Louis-based Emerson Electric Manufacturing from 1938 to 1945.

In 1946 Symington became assistant secretary of war for air, and in 1947 President Harry S. Truman named him the first secretary of the air force. As such, Symington lobbied hard for the B-36 bomber and exclusive air force control of strategic nuclear weapons. He resigned in April 1950, just prior to the Korean War, to protest cuts in the air force budget. Within weeks, Truman had appointed him chairman of the NSRB (an arm of the National Security Council), a post he held until April 1951.

In 1952 Symington ran successfully for the first of four terms as U.S. senator from Missouri. He served on the McCarthy Permanent Investigations Subcommittee and often engaged in public battles with its chair, particularly during the 1954 hearings on communist influence in the army. As a prominent member of the Senate Armed Services Committee, Symington remained a leading advocate of the air force and a strong national defense. When the Soviets unveiled their first intercontinental ballistic missile (ICBM), followed by the *Sputnik 1* launch in October 1957, Symington became the watchdog for alleged American deficiencies in ICBM development. He repeatedly criticized President Dwight D. Eisenhower's failure to match Soviet missile development. Symington's attacks led to spurious charges of a missile gap between the Soviet Union and the United States, which the Democrats exploited in the 1960 presidential election.

When John F. Kennedy became president, Symington supported a larger American presence in Vietnam and he voted for the Gulf of Tonkin Resolution in August 1964. Subsequently reevaluating his position based on the escalating costs of the Vietnam War, he argued that Washington should either lift restrictions on the use of airpower in Vietnam or withdraw entirely from the conflict. By 1968, seeing no chance of victory, he turned against the war. In his last term, he was a leading critic of President Richard M. Nixon's secret war in Laos. In 1971 Symington characterized it as a war "waged under executive privilege," and he helped secure passage of legislation limiting military involvement in Laos. He also argued for greater congressional oversight of the Central Intelligence Agency (CIA).

Symington retired from the Senate in December 1976 and died in New Canaan, Connecticut, on 14 December 1988.

Thomas D. Veve

See also
Johnson, Louis Arthur; Missile Gap; Missiles, Intercontinental Ballistic; Nixon, Richard Milhous; *Sputnik;* Truman, Harry S.; Vietnam War

References
Barlow, Jeffrey G. *Revolt of the Admirals: The Fight for Naval Aviation, 1945–1950.* Washington, DC: Naval Historical Center, 1994.
Hogan, Michael J. *A Cross of Iron: Harry S. Truman and the Origins of the National Security State, 1945–1954.* New York: Cambridge University Press, 1998.
McFarland, Linda. *Cold War Strategist: Stuart Symington and the Search for National Security.* Westport, CT: Praeger, 2001.
Watson, George M., Jr. *Secretaries and Chiefs of Staff of the United States Air Force: Biographical Sketches and Portraits.* Washington, DC: U.S. Government Printing Office, 2001.

Syria

Arab nation in the Middle East covering 71,498 square miles, just slightly larger than the U.S. state of North Dakota. The Syrian Arab Republic, with a 1945 population of approximately 3.2 million people, borders on Jordan and Israel to the south, Lebanon and the Mediterranean Sea to the west, Turkey to the north, and Iraq to the east. For much of its history, Syria was dominated by larger powers. It was part of the Ottoman Empire until 1920, and its economy and educational system had left its populace in relative destitution. In 1920, France received a League of Nations mandate over both Syria and neighboring Lebanon. However, French rule there resulted in repeated uprisings—particularly among the Druze. After a tortuous series of negotiations that began in the late 1920s, Syria was granted considerable autonomy in 1936. To fulfill previous agreements, France announced the formation of an independent Syrian republic in September 1941 with Shukri al-Kuwatl as its president. Syria became fully independent on 1 January 1944.

Syria took part in the failed Arab war against Israel during 1948–1949. A member of the Arab League, Syria was a vociferous opponent of Israeli statehood. The defeat in the war and disagreement over Syria's potential union with Iraq torpedoed al-Kuwatl's government. There were three coups in 1949, the last one headed by Lieutenant Colonel Adib al-Shishakli, who governed with a heavy hand until 1954. Al-Shishakli was ousted in 1954, and late that year elections were held to determine the makeup of the new government. In the end, a three-party coalition (People's, National, and Baath Parties) emerged with National Party chief Sabri al-Asali as head of the government. In the succeeding years, the Baathists, who combined Arab nationalism with socialist policies, became the most powerful political force in Syria. As such, Syria entered into economic and military agreements with the Soviet Union.

In February 1958, Syria and Egypt joined to form the United Arab Republic (UAR). Within a year Egypt's intention to dominate the UAR became obvious, which forced yet another coup against the Syrian government in September 1961. Carried out by a group of military officers, the coup plotters pulled Syria out of the UAR and established the Syrian Arab Republic. In December 1961 elections for a national assembly occurred, and the body chose two conservative People's Party members to lead the new regime. Another coup in late 1962 again toppled the government.

In 1963, a joint Baath-military government came to power. The new government nationalized most industrial and large commercial concerns and engaged in land reforms that redistributed land to the peasants. Meanwhile, Syria continued to cultivate relations with the Soviet bloc. A schism in the Baath Party resulted in more instability, and in 1966 the radical wing of the party staged a coup and installed Yusseff Zayen as prime minister. Nureddin al-Attassi became president. This new regime tightened Syria's ties with the Soviets and Egyptians.

Syria fought yet another war with Israel in June 1967. This time, its defeat included the loss of the Golan Heights to the Israelis. The outcome of the war ultimately brought General Hafez al-Assad to power in 1970. An ardent Baath nationalist, Assad sought to increase ties to other Arab states, deemphasize Syrian reliance on the Soviet Union, and defeat Israel.

In early 1971, Assad was elected president. He would rule the country until his death in 2000. Over the next several years following his election, he modernized the Syrian Army and engaged in modest economic reforms, while the Baath Party gained even more strength. Befitting his Baathist philosophy, the state played a central role in economic planning and implementation. It must be noted, however, that Assad's tactics could be brutal and that there was little room for dissent or democracy in Syria. Syria was involved in a fourth

Arab-Israeli war in October 1973. After initial successes, and although Syrian forces this time fought well, they were nonetheless driven back beyond their original positions.

In the late 1970s and 1980s, Sunni Muslim fundamentalists began challenging the Baath Party's secular outlook. During 1976–1982, urban areas all across Syria became hotbeds of political unrest. Assad brutally crushed a February 1982 uprising by the Muslim Brotherhood in Hama, and troops killed several thousand people.

Assad also sent his army into Lebanon in 1976, ostensibly as a peacekeeping force during the civil war there. The troops stayed on, however, Assad siding with the Muslims who were fighting Christian militias. By the mid-1980s, Assad's forces had become the preponderant political and military force in Lebanon. Syrian troops were not withdrawn from Lebanon until 2005.

At the same time, the 1980s saw the Assad regime taking harder-line Arab positions and moving closer to the Soviets. Assad's get-tough approach in regional politics included his funding and encouragement of terrorism. Assad, who was always in the end a pragmatist, sought to ameliorate relations with the West as the Soviet Union began to implode in 1990. When Iraq invaded Kuwait in August 1990, Assad was the first Arab leader to denounce the attack. His government also provided 20,000 troops to the international coalition that defeated Iraqi forces in the 1991 Persian Gulf War.

In 1991, Assad's government entered into peace negotiations with Israel, although the process broke down with no firm agreement in January 2000. In June 2000, Assad died unexpectedly after thirty years in office. He was succeeded by his son, Bashar al-Assad, who was carefully groomed as the heir apparent. Allegedly a free-market proponent, the younger Assad attempted some economic and political reforms, but the process has been fraught with setbacks and obstacles. In 1998, 65 percent of all Syrian revenues came from petroleum products.

Paul G. Pierpaoli Jr.

See also
Arab-Israeli Wars; Arab Nationalism; Assad, Hafez; Lebanon; Middle East; Persian Gulf War; Radical Islam

References
Maoz, Moshe, and Avner Yaniv, eds. *Syria under Assad: Domestic Constraints and Regional Risks.* London: Croom Helm, 1987.
Pipes, Daniel. *Greater Syria: The History of an Ambition.* New York: Oxford University Press, 1990.
Seale, Patrick. *Assad of Syria: The Struggle for the Middle East.* Berkeley: University of California Press, 1988.

T

Taft, Robert Alphonso (1889–1953)

U.S. senator (1939–1953) and unsuccessful candidate for the Republican presidential nomination (1940, 1948, 1952). Born in Cincinnati, Ohio, on 8 September 1889, the eldest son of the future Republican President William Howard Taft and his wife Helen Herron Taft, Robert Taft attended the Taft School for Boys in Watertown, Connecticut, and graduated from Yale University (1910) and Harvard Law School (1913). From 1914 onward Taft practiced law in Cincinnati, where he soon became active in Republican politics. Hostile to most New Deal domestic measures of the 1930s, by the time he won election to the Senate for Ohio in 1938 he was firmly identified with his party's conservative wing.

Taft was equally critical of President Franklin D. Roosevelt's foreign policies. When World War II began, Taft opposed American aid to the Allies, supporting the America First policies enunciated by ex-President Herbert Hoover and others and insisting that war would destroy American civil liberties and that Germany posed no danger to the Western Hemisphere. Following the U.S. entry into the war, Taft constantly assailed what he viewed as the excesses of domestic controls and propaganda while opposing the creation of a world bank or any other international organization apart from the United Nations (UN).

By 1946 Taft, nicknamed "Mr. Republican," had become a major figure within the cross-party conservative coalition that effectively dominated Congress. Immune to appeals for bipartisanship, as the Cold War developed he opposed high defense expenditures, voted in 1946 against the large American loan to Britain; complained that American military and economic support for Greece, Turkey, and the Marshall Plan were all too expensive; and opposed the creation of the North Atlantic Treaty Organization (NATO). He believed that America's atomic weapons safeguarded it from any foreign attack and that his country should not commit troops outside the Western Hemisphere.

When the Korean War began, Taft, de facto though not official leader of a Republican Senate majority, exploited the war to shore up both his party's and his own political fortunes in the impending 1952 presidential campaign, which the Republicans were determined not to lose as they had unexpectedly done to Truman in 1948. Taft reluctantly supported Truman's initial decision to commit forces to Korea, but after communist China's intervention in late 1950, Taft accused the president of mishandling the war. Taft also deplored the administration's failure to seek either a formal declaration of war or a congressional resolution authorizing the use of force in Korea. He laid much of the responsibility for the war on the administration's "bungling and inconsistent foreign policy." Taft even suggested that the United States might be well advised to withdraw from Korea and base its defenses upon a line running through the island positions of Taiwan and Japan. When Truman recalled General Douglas MacArthur in the spring of 1951, Taft defended the general, abandoning his customary restraint and publicly advocating MacArthur's preferred and highly provocative measures of bombing Chinese supply lines in Manchuria and including Guomindang (GMD, Nationalist) troops from the Republic of China (ROC) on Taiwan in UN forces.

Even though Taft found the extremist tactics of Senator Joseph R. MacCarthy personally distasteful, he tolerated them, believing that they would enhance the Republican Party's

Ohioan Robert Taft, son of President William Howard Taft, was known as "Mr. Republican," a title that reflected his prominence as a powerful leader in the Senate but also characterized the values of the middle America he represented and held dear. His isolationist position prevented him from gaining the Republican nomination for president in either 1948 or 1952, but he remained influential. (Library of Congress)

chances of victory. Campaigning for the 1952 Republican nomination, which he lost to the internationalist war hero Dwight D. Eisenhower, Taft harped constantly on the refrain that the Democratic administration had blundered unnecessarily into an expensive war that it could neither win nor end with honor, a theme that Eisenhower and other Republican candidates continually repeated. Named Republican majority leader after the election, a mellower Taft unsuccessfully attempted to rein in the excesses of McCarthyism. Taft died of cancer in New York City on 31 July 1953.

Priscilla Roberts

See also

Eisenhower, Dwight David; Greek Civil War; Hoover, Herbert Clark; Korean War; MacArthur, Douglas; Marshall Plan; McCarthy, Joseph Raymond; McCarthyism; North Atlantic Treaty Organization, Origins and Formation of; Roosevelt, Franklin Delano; Truman, Harry S.; United Nations

References

Caridi, Ronald J. *The Korean War and American Politics: The Republican Party As a Case Study.* Philadelphia: University of Pennsylvania Press, 1968.

DeJohn, Samuel, Jr. "Robert A. Taft, Economic Conservatism, and Opposition to United States Foreign Policy, 1944–1951." Unpublished PhD diss., University of Southern California, 1976.

Matthews, Geoffrey. "Robert A. Taft, the Constitution and American Foreign Policy, 1939–53." *Journal of Contemporary History* 17(3) (July 1982): 507–522.

Patterson, James T. *Mr. Republican: A Biography of Robert A. Taft.* Boston: Houghton Mifflin, 1972.

Taft, Robert A. *A Foreign Policy for Americans.* Garden City, NY: Doubleday, 1951.

Wunderlin, Clarence E., Jr., ed. *The Papers of Robert A. Taft.* 2 vols. to date. Kent, OH: Kent State University Press, 1997–.

Taiwan Strait Crisis, First (1954–1955)

Shelling of offshore Chinese islands in the Taiwan Strait from 3 September 1954 to 1 May 1955, initiated by the People's Republic of China (PRC). The PRC's birth in October 1949 did not signify complete victory in the Chinese Civil War, at least not in the mind of PRC Chairman Mao Zedong. Jiang Jieshi's Guomindang (GMD, Nationalist) government still retained control of Taiwan and a number of the offshore islands in the Taiwan Strait, and Jiang continued to harbor quixotic ideas of retaking Mainland China. Mao in turn wished to complete his victory by capturing Taiwan and crushing the GMD. In fact, both Mao and Jiang had devised military plans to carry on the civil war so as to liberate the territories held by the other. The Korean War, however, had temporarily put these plans aside.

The first sign of a resumption in the civil war occurred in summer 1954. In August, Jiang deployed troops to the Jinmen and Matzu islands, known to Westerners as Quemoy and Matsu, two clusters of small islands located 8 miles off Mainland China's southeastern coast. At the same time, ongoing negotiations in Manila for a Southeast Asian mutual defense treaty, initiated by the United States during the Geneva Conference in April 1954, were about to conclude. Rumors flew that Jiang's GMD and the United States were working on a mutual defense pact aimed at the PRC. Seeing these moves as unwarranted provocation by the West, Mao was determined to stage a military showdown. On 3 September 1954, he ordered an artillery bombardment of Jinmen from Fujian Province, beginning the initial phase of the First Taiwan Strait Crisis, which endured until late October. In the process, both Jinmen and Mazu suffered heavy bombardment.

The second phase began on 1 November and ended four days later, when PRC forces shelled and raided the Dachen and Yijiangshan islands off Mainland China's Zhejiang Province, north of Taiwan. Afterward, China's bombardment subsided and resumed periodically on a limited scale while the PRC's government awaited U.S. and Taiwanese reactions. In the midst of the crisis, the U.S. Congress passed the Mutual Defense Treaty on 2 December 1954, which promised defensive aid to Taiwan. The PRC strongly protested the U.S. commitment to Taiwan, a stance that later secured the PRC's success at the Bandung Conference in April 1955.

The crisis reached a new zenith when PRC forces resumed heavy bombardment of the Dachens on 10 January 1955 and seized Yijiangshan on 18 January 1955. To halt further PRC advances, the U.S. Congress passed the Taiwanese (Formosan) Resolution on 24 January 1955, which authorized the use of U.S. military force to fight further hostile Chinese communist movements. Determined to avoid a direct confrontation with the United States, Mao ordered the shelling scaled back. At the same time, Washington also wished to prevent a full military confrontation, as it was not prepared to defend all of the offshore islands in the Taiwan Strait.

The stalemated crisis finally drew to a close in late April 1955, upon an initiative from the PRC. On 23 April 1955, Premier and Foreign Minister Zhou Enlai declared at the Bandung Conference that the PRC had no desire to engage the United States in a war and was ready to negotiate an end to the standoff. To show its good faith, the PRC stopped all bombing of the offshore islands on 1 May 1955, which effectively ended the First Taiwan Strait Crisis. Shortly thereafter, the PRC and the United States agreed to hold ambassadorial talks to resolve the Taiwan question. The talks began on 1 August 1955 in Geneva between the Chinese ambassador to Poland, Wang Bingnan, and the U.S. ambassador to Poland, Alexis U. Johnson. The Sino-American Ambassadorial Talks

deadlocked, however, and were suspended in December 1957. In September 1958, the Second Taiwan Strait Crisis broke out, which resulted in another Sino-American confrontation.

Law Yuk-fun

See also

Bandung Conference; China, People's Republic of; China, Republic of; Chinese Civil War; Jiang Jieshi; Jinmen and Mazu; Mao Zedong; Taiwan Strait Crisis, Second; Wang Bingnan; Zhou Enlai

References

Christensen, Thomas J. *Useful Adversaries: Grand Strategy, Domestic Mobilization, and Sino-American Conflict, 1947–1958.* Princeton, NJ: Princeton University Press, 1996.

Garver, John W. *The Sino-American Alliance: Nationalist China and the American Cold War Strategy in China.* Armonk, NY: Sharpe, 1997.

Soman, Appu K. *Double-Edged Sword: Nuclear Diplomacy in Unequal Conflicts; The United States and China, 1950–1958.* Westport, CT: Praeger, 2000.

Stolper, Thomas E. *China, Taiwan, and the Offshore Islands.* Armonk, NY: Sharpe, 1985.

Tucker, Nancy Bernkopf, ed. *Dangerous Strait: The U.S.-Taiwan-China Crisis.* New York: Columbia University Press, 2005.

Taiwan Strait Crisis, Second (1958)

Artillery bombardment of the offshore islands in the Taiwan Strait from 23 August to 25 October 1958, initiated by the

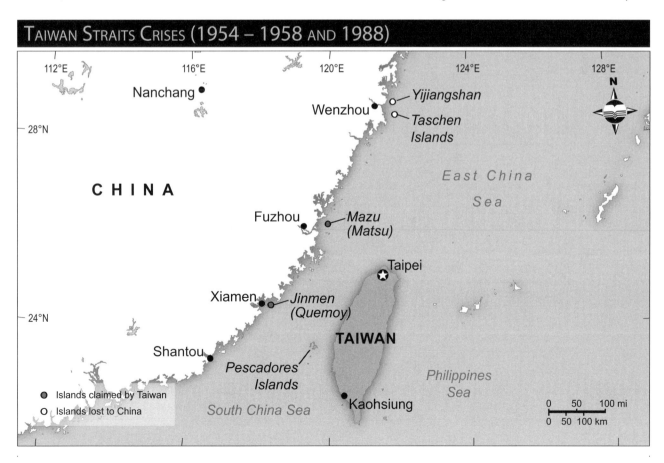

TAIWAN STRAITS CRISES (1954 – 1958 AND 1988)

People's Republic of China (PRC). Unlike the First Taiwan Strait Crisis (1954–1955), the Second Taiwan Strait Crisis may be attributed to PRC Chairman Mao Zedong's desire to enhance his country's international standing in view of its growing diplomatic isolation. This isolation was chiefly a result of poor relations with the United States and a deteriorating rapport with its erstwhile ally, the Soviet Union. Sino-American ambassadorial talks following the Bandung Conference and the First Taiwan Strait Crisis had been suspended in late 1957 because of irreconcilable positions over Taiwan. By mid-1958, after Soviet Premier Nikita Khrushchev's Beijing visit and his advocacy of peaceful coexistence with the West, Mao realized that the Soviet Union could not be counted on to lead the communist bloc. Mao was thus emboldened to pursue his own independent course in hopes of establishing himself as the true leader of the socialist world.

International events during July 1958 provided Mao with the perfect opportunity to test his mettle. The United States sent troops to intervene in Lebanon's civil disorder, and Britain deployed troops to quell uprisings in Jordan. Meanwhile, Taiwanese President Jiang Jieshi ordered his military on alert, which the PRC perceived as provocation. In response, on 23 August 1958 Mao ordered the shelling of Jinmen and Mazu, known to Westerners as Quemoy and Matsu, two island groupings 8 miles off Mainland China's southeastern coast. Mao rationalized his actions as providing moral support to

the Middle East's "anti-imperialist struggles." Several days after the bombing began, the United Nations (UN) General Assembly passed a resolution requesting the withdrawal of Anglo-American troops from the Middle East. Mao played this up by publicly denouncing "continuing U.S. imperialism" in the Taiwan Strait. He also restated the PRC's claim of sovereignty over Taiwan and its offshore islands. At the same time, he momentarily drew closer to the Soviet Union when Khrushchev gave his full support to the PRC's claims over the offshore islands.

Soviet support, as it turned out, was halfhearted. Disturbed by Mao's seemingly irrational and independent conduct, Khrushchev decided to rescind his earlier promise of sharing nuclear secrets with the PRC. Unlike in the First Taiwan Strait Crisis, the United States was fully prepared to defend Taiwan and the offshore islands. In a show of force, the United States deployed additional air and naval forces to protect the Taiwan Strait, and as a result, American and Chinese forces exchanged fire. The United States and the PRC appeared to be headed for a full-fledged conflict, which was not what Mao had intended. He had only wanted to keep the Taiwan question in play by applying what he called his noose strategy. He viewed the Jinmen as nooses constraining the United States, with Taiwan as another more distant noose. He reasoned that America, by committing itself to the defense of these three areas, had put a rope around its neck by trapping

A house on Jinmen destroyed by People's Republic of China (PRC) shelling, 1 October 1958. (John Dominis/Time Life Pictures/Getty Images)

itself in the Taiwan Strait. This, he thought, would not only stretch U.S. resources but would also provide the PRC with the upper hand in the region.

Having successfully hooked the U.S. on the nooses, Mao decided to ease tensions in the Taiwan Strait. On 6 September 1958, the PRC proposed the resumption of the Sino-American Ambassadorial Talks, which finally reconvened at year's end. On 5 October 1958, the PRC issued the "Message to the Compatriots in Taiwan," restating the PRC's claim to sovereignty over the Taiwan Strait and its willingness to settle the crisis by peaceful means. On 25 October 1958, the PRC issued the "Second Message to the Compatriots in Taiwan," announcing that the shelling of the Jinmen would be restricted to odd-numbered days and would be limited by certain conditions, which helped defuse the Second Taiwan Strait Crisis. Periodic bombardment continued until 9 January 1959, when Mao lifted the shelling orders.

Law Yuk-fun

See also
Bandung Conference; China, People's Republic of; China, Republic of; Jiang Jieshi; Jinmen and Mazu; Khrushchev, Nikita; Mao Zedong; Taiwan Strait Crisis, First

References
Christensen, Thomas J. *Useful Adversaries: Grand Strategy, Domestic Mobilization, and Sino-American Conflict, 1947–1958.* Princeton, NJ: Princeton University Press, 1996.
Garver, John W. *The Sino-American Alliance: Nationalist China and the American Cold War Strategy in China.* Armonk, NY: Sharpe, 1997.
Li, Xiaobing, and Hongshan Li, eds. *China and the United States: A New Cold War History.* Lanham, MD: University Press of America, 1998.
Soman, Appu K. *Double-Edged Sword: Nuclear Diplomacy in Unequal Conflicts; The United States and China, 1950–1958.* Westport, CT: Praeger, 2000.
Stolper, Thomas E. *China, Taiwan, and the Offshore Islands.* Armonk, NY: Sharpe, 1985.
Tucker, Nancy Bernkopf, ed. *Dangerous Strait: The U.S.-Taiwan-China Crisis.* New York: Columbia University Press, 2005.

Tanaka Kakuei (1918–1993)

Japanese politician and prime minister (1972–1974). Born in Niigata Prefecture on 4 May 1918 to a poor family that raised cattle, Tanaka Kakuei moved to Tokyo at age fifteen and established his own construction company, which became very successful during World War II. He was elected to the lower house of the Diet in 1947 and served as secretary-general of the conservative Liberal Democratic Party (LDP) during 1965–1966 and 1968–1971.

Tanaka held several cabinet positions, including minister of finance (1962–1965) and minister of trade and industry (1971–1972). He succeeded Satō Eisaku as prime minister in July 1972.

The advent of Soviet-American détente and America's opening of relations with the People's Republic of China (PRC) beginning in the early 1970s gave Tanaka a chance to improve Japanese relations with both the Soviets and Chinese. After President Richard M. Nixon's historic February 1972 visit to the PRC, Tanaka visited Beijing in September 1972, meeting with Prime Minister Zhou Enlai and establishing diplomatic relations with the PRC. Tanaka also visited Moscow in October 1973, although a joint Japanese-Soviet communiqué issued at the end of the meeting indicated minor progress in improving relations between the two nations.

The 1973–1974 oil crisis presented diplomatic difficulties for Tanaka. Although U.S. Secretary of State Henry A. Kissinger visited Japan in November 1973 to unite the Western powers behind a single policy to deal with the crisis, Japan moved its Middle East policy toward a more pro-Arab stance to ensure a continued flow of oil.

Tanaka was forced to resign as prime minister in December 1974 over alleged financial mismanagement. He was arrested in 1976 and charged with accepting 500 million yen in bribes from the Lockheed Corporation. Even after his conviction in 1983, he continued to lead the LDP's largest faction and thus influenced Japanese politics until his health declined in 1985. Tanaka died in Tokyo on 16 December 1993.

Iikura Akira

See also
Détente; Japan; Satō Eisaku

References
Babb, James. *Tanaka: The Making of Postwar Japan.* Harlow, UK: Longman, 2000.
Buckley, Roger. *US-Japan Alliance Diplomacy, 1945–1990.* New York: Cambridge University Press, 1992.
Hosoya Chihiro and A50 Editorial Committee, eds. *Japan and the United States: Fifty Years of Partnership.* Tokyo: Japan Times, 2001.
Schaller, Michael. *Altered States: The United States and Japan since the Occupation.* Oxford: Oxford University Press, 1997.
Welfield, John. *An Empire in Eclipse: Japan and the Postwar American Alliance System; A Study in the Interaction of Domestic Politics and Foreign Policy.* London: Athlone, 1988.

Tank Warfare

Despite those who believed that the atomic bomb had rendered conventional weapons obsolete, tanks—also known as armored fighting vehicles (AFVs)—saw wide service after World War II. The Soviet Union in particular saw AFVs as an essential element in forces that would engage the North Atlantic Treaty Organization (NATO) on the plains of Central and Eastern Europe.

One lesson learned in World War II was the need for all military components in a military force to be as mobile as the tanks. This led to the introduction of armored personnel carriers (APCs) to transport infantry but also to mount antiaircraft weapons, rockets, and mortars. The Soviets led in this development. Their Boevaia Mashina Pekhoti (BMP, Combat Infantry Vehicle) series was the first infantry fighting vehicle in the world. Infantry could now fight from within the vehicle, and some BMPs mounted a powerful gun and carried antitank missiles, enabling them to provide effective close infantry support. Self-propelled guns also continued in wide use.

In modern wars, armor, infantry, and artillery work together as a team in battle. Infantry and armor provide mutual support and protection. Tanks without accompanying infantry are vulnerable to enemy tank-killer weapons, while infantrymen in turn fall prey to small arms, machine guns, and other direct-fire weapons. Infantrymen and artillery help to protect the tanks from the tank killers, and the tanks engage enemy direct-fire weapons and armor. Offensive tactics envision armor employed en masse, in large formations to overwhelm an enemy and make deep penetrations.

The Soviet Union planned to utilize its far larger numbers of AFVs offensively. The Soviets thus opted for fast, maneuverable tanks with excellent firepower. Nuclear, biological, and chemical (NBC) protection was a low priority. The Western powers, assuming that they would be standing on the defensive against far larger Soviet formations, adopted defensive tactics. The British gave top priority to firepower, followed closely by protection for the tank crews as the second priority and then mobility as the third priority. As a result, the British fielded some of the heaviest tanks of the Cold War era. The Americans adopted a middle position. Speed and maneuverability held top priority, followed by firepower second and protection third.

In the late 1950s, the Soviet Union gradually moved away from nuclear warfare doctrine back to maneuver warfare. By the 1970s, the doctrine of the deep battle held sway in Soviet military thinking. Soviet armor doctrine evolved into something akin to that of World War II. Other forces would open gaps in an enemy front, which would then be exploited by massed armor formations, up to that point held in reserve. Armor columns would then drive deep into the enemy rear areas.

American and NATO strategy relied on firepower and slow withdrawal to inflict maximum punishment on Warsaw Pact attacking forces. This doctrine shifted in the 1980s in the Air-Land Battle concept combining airpower, air mobility, and armor in a united offensive strategy in which NATO forces planned to outmaneuver and outfight the Warsaw Pact armies.

Although the dreaded confrontation between the Warsaw Pact and NATO forces did not occur, Soviet tanks saw action in the restive satellite states, helping to quell an uprising in the German Democratic Republic (GDR, East Germany) in 1953 and to crush the 1956 Hungarian Revolution. The almost completely bloodless 1968 occupation of Czechoslovakia that ended the Prague Spring involved some 2,000 Warsaw Pact tanks, the largest deployment of armor in Europe during the Cold War. Tanks also took part in fighting in the former Yugoslavia at the end of the Cold War.

In Asia, tanks participated in the Chinese Civil War (1946–1949) and in the Korean War (1950–1953), notable as the first clash between U.S. and Soviet armor. At the beginning of the conflict, the Korean People's Army (KPA, North Korean Army) had a tremendous advantage in military hardware, including some 150 T34/85 medium tanks. The Army of the Republic of Korea (ROK, South Korea) had no tanks at all. The United States first deployed M24 Chaffee light tanks, hastily dispatched from Japan. The arrival in Korea of more powerful M4 Shermans and M26 Pershings, along with the 3.5-inch bazooka antitank rocket, helped turn the tide against the KPA armor. Korea's terrain precluded large tank battles, although each side employed tanks as mobile pillboxes in dug-in positions for long-range pinpoint sniping fire against enemy positions.

Tanks also took part in the long Indochina War (1946–1954). They were, however, largely useless in the interior jungles. The French flew ten M24 Chaffees into Dien Bien Phu and assembled them there to take part in the most important battle of the war, but they could not prevent the French defeat.

Tanks participated in the Vietnam War (1957–1975). Army of the Republic of Vietnam (ARVN, South Vietnamese) Army forces utilized the M24 Chaffee. After American forces entered the fighting in 1965, the United States deployed some 600 tanks to Vietnam. Although some lighter tanks—such as the M551 Sheridan and M50A1 Ontos—proved ill-suited for the Vietnam combat environment, the M48A3 Patton MBT (main battle tank) was widely employed in search and destroy missions, where it came to be known for its jungle-busting ability in clearing paths through dense vegetation. Its 90mm main gun proved an effective bunker buster, and its tracks and great weight could survive mines and grind down bunkers. Tanks helped protect convoys, secure lines of communication (LOCs), and protect bases and also served as a rapid-reaction force.

Communist AFVs, chiefly the Soviet PT-76 light amphibian tank, were deployed mostly during the conflict's last few years and primarily in an offensive role. People's Army of Vietnam (PAVN, North Vietnamese Army) forces deployed some 100 T-34 and T-54 Soviet-supplied tanks in their unsuccessful invasion of the Republic of Vietnam (RVN, South Vietnam) in the spring of 1972 and lost 80 percent of them. In the final 1975 communist offensive, PAVN armor units with

A flamethrower tank during training in Korea. (U.S. Department of Defense)

Soviet T-54s and T-55s, now better trained and integrated with infantry and artillery, proved an important element in the swift conquest of South Vietnam.

Tanks fought in the three wars between India and Pakistan, especially in 1965 and 1971. In the 1965 war, principally around Chamb and Shakargarth, India and Pakistan each deployed more than 1,000 tanks. In the ensuing heavy fighting, Pakistan lost some 300 tanks, India perhaps half that number.

Many governments used tanks to keep their own population in check. No more powerful image of the tank in the Cold War exists than that of Wang Weilin, the so-called "Tank Man," placing himself in front of and temporarily halting a line of Chinese NORINCO Type 69/59 MBTs on their way to crush the June 1989 student protest movement in Beijing's Tiananmen Square.

In the Middle East, tanks saw widespread service in Arab-Israeli wars, in the Iran-Iraq War (1980–1988), and in the

Soviet occupation of Afghanistan (1979–1989). Perhaps no other conflicts of the period captured the world's imagination as did the numerous wars in the Middle East, which saw some of the largest tank battles in history and proved useful laboratories concerning the design and employment of armored fighting vehicles. For the most part, the Soviet Union acted as chief supporter and arms supplier to the Arab states, and the Western powers, particularly the United States and France (at least until after the 1967 War) supported Israel. The fighting in the Middle East also saw the beginning of a new age in warfare with the first employment of antitank and antiship missiles.

In its war for independence, Israel initially had only a small armored force of pre–World War II French Hotchkiss light tanks, World War II British Cromwells, and U.S. Shermans, the latter purchased from Italy and the Philippines. These faced the far more numerous tanks of Lebanon, Syria, Jordan, Egypt, and Iraq. After 1949, the Israel Defense Forces (IDF) invested heavily in tanks, and the Jewish state became one of the most skillful practitioners of armored warfare in history. In collusion with France and Britain against Egypt in 1956, Israeli Super Shermans and French tanks rolled across the Sinai Peninsula in only four days, defeating a far larger Egyptian force of Shermans, British Centurions, and some Soviet JS-3s but also 230 Soviet T-34/85s and a number of armored personnel carriers and self-propelled guns.

In June 1967, Israel again used its highly mechanized forces to launch a devastating preemptive strike against Egypt and Syria. Israeli tactics were similar to those employed by the Germans in their Blitzkrieg of World War II. Tanks would break through the enemy front and then push forward, closely followed by mechanized infantry that would engage enemy forces. This armored thrust was followed by motorized infantry to mop up what remained of enemy resistance in order to allow the vital supply column to proceed forward. Rapid Israeli envelopments allowed the numerically inferior Israeli armored forces to take the heavier Arab tanks from the rear and make short work of the Arab armies. Israel had some 800 tanks, while Egypt, Saudi Arabia, Jordan, Kuwait, Syria, Lebanon, and Iraq had a combined strength of perhaps 2,500 tanks. Of 1,200 Egyptian tanks before the war, 820 were lost. Israeli armor losses amounted to 122 tanks, many of which were repaired and returned to battle.

In the 1973 Yom Kippur War, the tables were almost turned, thanks to Israeli complacency and new Egyptian tactics. Israel had invested heavily in the Bar Lev Line, a static defensive front along the eastern bank of the Suez Canal, in effect rejecting maneuver tank warfare in which the bulk of armored forces are held back in mobile reserve. Egyptian troops struck in force across the Suez Canal, while Syrian troops simultaneously invaded the Golan Heights. These offensives caught the Israeli defenders completely off guard. On the Golan Heights, Syria deployed 1,400 tanks including Soviet T-34s, T-54s, and the latest T-64 model. To break through the thick Israeli minefields and defenses, the Syrians also utilized specialized armor vehicles such as flail tanks, bridge-layers, and engineer tanks. At the end of four days of savage fighting, however, Israeli forces (which included only 177 tanks) centered on British Centurions defeated the attacking Syrians.

With 1,700 tanks and another 2,500 armored vehicles, the Egyptian force on the Suez front was even larger. The Egyptians pushed across the canal with two armies and more than 1,000 tanks. The Egyptians promptly inflicted heavy losses on the counterattacking Israelis, releasing barrages of shoulder-fire missiles and in two days destroying 260 Israeli tanks. This success emboldened Egyptian President Anwar Sadat, who decided on a deeper penetration of the Sinai. But this took Egyptian forces beyond the range of their surface-to-air (SAM) missile cover. The Egyptian offensive on 14 October involved more than 2,000 tanks on both sides, making it

Wang Weilin, known as the "Tank Man," slowing the progress of tanks on the Avenue of Eternal Peace in Beijing during the crushing of the Tiananmen Square uprising, 5 June 1989. (Reuters/Corbis)

second in history only to the World War II Battle of Kursk in numbers of tanks engaged. The Israelis brought up reinforcements but were still outnumbered two to one in tanks, a disadvantage offset by superior hardware and training and the involvement of the Israeli Air Force. The Israelis not only stopped the Egyptian advance but also destroyed some 500 of their tanks.

Israeli forces then crossed over the canal and were in a position to inflict a resounding defeat on the Egyptians when a cease-fire went into effect. Israel won the Yom Kippur War but at a high cost, including the loss of 830 tanks. Many analysts concluded that the Yom Kippur War spelled the end of the tank era, as small, wire-guided missiles and rocket-propelled grenades (RPGs) had caused about a third of Israeli armor losses. The conclusion proved premature.

Israeli tanks, most notably their superb new Merkava MBT, took part in the invasion of Lebanon in 1982 and destroyed the Syrian 1st Armored Division. Although there were no interstate wars involving Israel thereafter, tanks and other AFVs continued to play a key role in intrastate operations as perhaps the most visible component of Israeli security operations against the Palestinian uprising.

Despite the proliferation of new antitank weapons and predictions that the day of the tank was over, when the Cold War came to a close with the collapse of the Soviet Union, AFVs were still very much a part of the world's military establishments.

Spencer C. Tucker

See also
AirLand Battle; Arab-Israeli Wars; Dien Bien Phu, Battle of; India-
Pakistan Wars; Iran-Iraq War; Korean War; Persian Gulf War;
Vietnam War

References
Foss, Christopher F., ed. *The Encyclopedia of Tanks and Armored
Fighting Vehicles: The Comprehensive Guide to Over 900 Armored
Fighting Vehicles from 1915 to the Present Day.* San Diego, CA:
Thunder Bay Press, 2002.
Miller, David. *The Great Book of Tanks: The World's Most Important
Tanks from World War I to the Present Day.* St. Paul, MN: MBI
Publishing, 2002.
Tucker, Spencer C. *Tanks: An Illustrated History of Their Impact.*
Santa Barbara, CA: ABC-CLIO, 2004.

Tanks

Tanks, often referred to loosely as armor, armored fighting
vehicles (AFVs), or tracks, are tracked and armored fighting
vehicles armed with a high-velocity, flat-trajectory main gun
for direct-fire engagement. This distinguishes them from
artillery, which primarily employs indirect fire. Conceived
in World War I as a means of ending the bloody stalemate of
trench warfare, tanks were first employed by the British in
September 1916 during the Battle of the Somme. They came
into their own during World War II.

Among tank developments in the Cold War period was the
end of the heavy tank in the 1950s. Technological advances
allowed their functions to be performed by lighter, more
maneuverable, and less expensive MBTs (main battle tanks),
combining the old World War II medium and heavy tanks.
Guns increased in caliber from 76mm, 88mm, and 90mm at
the end of World War II to 105mm and even 120mm. Tanks
appeared in a bewildering array of models. Their many variants included bridge-layers, flamethrowers, and engineer and
tank recovery vehicles. In addition to their main guns, tanks
mounted one or more machine guns for antiaircraft protection and for engaging personnel and thin-skinned vehicles.

During the Cold War, tanks received improved engines
and were capable of higher speeds. Systems also developed
to provide protection for crews against the new threats posed
by nuclear, biological, and chemical (NBC) attack. New sights,
night vision equipment, improved laser rangefinders and
thermal imaging systems, and more powerful guns and projectiles also came into widespread use. In the ongoing race
between projectiles and armor, more effective armor emerged
in the form of layers of steel interspersed with ceramic-based
light alloys providing excellent protection against both kinetic
and chemical energy rounds.

United Kingdom. The United Kingdom possessed a number of tanks from World War II that saw extended postwar
service. Among these was the Comet (A34), with a 77mm main

gun. It fought in the Korean War and remained in service
until the early 1960s. The Centurion (A47) remained the principal British main battle tank of the first decades of the Cold
War. The Centurion Mk VII mounted a 105mm main gun.
It was widely exported and saw combat service in Korea,
the Middle East, southern Africa, Pakistan, and Vietnam.
It remained in service until 1969. The heavy A22 Churchill
Infantry tank, first mounting a 75mm and later a 95mm main
gun, fought in Korea.

The threat posed by Soviet heavy tanks in Europe led the
British to develop the Conqueror heavy tank. Entering service in 1956, it mounted a 120mm gun. A new tank also mounting a 120mm main gun, the Chieftain Mark V MBT, came on
line in 1963. Chieftains were exported to Iran, Kuwait, Jordan, and Oman. The chief British MBT of the 1980s was the
Challenger, introduced in 1983. It mounted a 120mm rifled
gun and performed well in the 1991 Persian Gulf War. Among
tanks built specifically for export were the Vickers Mk I MBT
(1964) with a 105mm main gun, sold to Kuwait and to India;
an improved model Vickers Mk III MBT (1973), sold to Kenya
and Nigeria; and the Khalid MBT (1981) with a 120mm gun,
sold to Jordan.

France. In the immediate post–World War II period,
France relied extensively on World War II equipment, on U.S.
tanks supplied to the French Army at the end of the war but
also on stocks of captured German tanks, most notably the
Panther. The most successful of French-designed tanks was
the excellent lightweight, air-transportable AMX-13. Introduced in 1952 with production continuing into the 1980s, it
had an automatic loader for its long-barreled 75mm main gun,
later upgraded to 90mm and then 105mm. The French sold
the AMX-13 widely abroad, including to Israel.

Until the mid-1950s, both France and the Federal Republic of Germany (FRG, West Germany) relied chiefly on the
U.S. M47 Patton as their MBT. These nations and Italy then
decided to develop a lighter and more powerful MBT for their
common use. The Germans produced the Leopard, while
the French developed the AMX-30. It entered production in
1966 and mounted a powerful 105mm main gun along with
a coaxial 20mm cannon. A large number of AMX-30s were
sold abroad, including to Spain.

West Germany. When the West German government was
permitted to rearm in 1955, it initially employed the U.S. M47
Patton as its MBT. With the failure of the joint French-
German tank project, however, West Germany developed the
Leopard. Produced during 1965–1984, it was also built under
license in Italy. Mounting a 105mm gun, the Leopard 1 sacrificed armor protection for speed and maneuverability. This
reliable, effective MBT attracted a number of foreign pur-
chasers and was exported to a number of Western nations.

United States. Initially, the United States continued a
number of its World War II tanks in service. The 75mm-gun

A British Challenger main battle tank moves into a base camp with other Allied armor during Operation DESERT STORM, 28 February 1991. (U.S. Department of Defense)

M24 Chaffee was the main U.S. light tank until 1953. It was the first U.S. tank to enter the Korean War and saw wide service abroad in other armies during the entire duration of the Cold War. France employed it in Indochina, and Nationalist China modified its M24s with a 90mm main gun.

The M41 Walker Bulldog replaced the Chaffee. One of the first U.S. tanks to be designed around a suitable engine, rather than designing the tank first and then trying to find an engine to suit, it mounted a 76mm main gun. Widely exported, it saw extensive and long service in many armies.

In the 1960s the U.S. Army tried to counter the growing weight of tanks with the M551 Armored Reconnaissance/ Airborne Assault Vehicle (AR/AAV) Sheridan, a lightweight, air-transportable armored vehicle with a heavy gun capable of knocking out any known tank. It mounted a 152mm gun, designed to fire the Shillelagh HEAT missile or combustible cartridge case conventional projectiles. The M551, although strictly speaking not a tank, was nonetheless used as one but had only limited armor protection. The Sheridan experienced numerous problems and did not enter service until 1968. It served in Vietnam but was poorly protected against enemy mines. The Sheridan remained in service with the 82nd Air-

borne Division into the 1990s and saw service both in Panama in 1989 and in the Persian Gulf War.

Sherman M4A3 and M4A3E8 medium tanks, the mainstay of U.S. armored forces at the end of World War II, fought with the United Nations Command (UNC) forces in Korea. There were many models and variants of the basic design, including dozers, 105mm howitzers, rocket launchers, tank retrievers, and flamethrowers. A great many Shermans were exported to other countries after World War II. Israeli Shermans, which were kept in operation for decades from a wide variety of sources, were also armed with an equally wide panoply of weapons, including antiradiation missiles. The French upgraded a number of Israeli Shermans with 75mm and 105mm main guns. Known as M50 and M51 Super Shermans, these fought modified M4 Egyptian Army Shermans in the 1973 Yom Kippur War.

The M26 Pershing tank, which entered service only in the last few months of the war in Europe, fought in Korea. Pending introduction of a new medium tank, World War II M26 Pershings were converted into the M46 medium with a new V-12 engine and cross-drive transmission. The M46 was unofficially known as the Patton, the name later officially bestowed on the M47. The M46 and the M26 bore the brunt of armor combat in Korea. The M46 had many of the same basic characteristics of the M26 and mounted a 90mm main gun.

The Korean War caught the U.S. Army in the midst of developing a new medium tank. The T42 design was not ready, but its turret and new gun were. As a stopgap measure, these were then adapted to the M46 hull, in effect the old World War II M26 with a new engine and other upgrades. This marriage of convenience became the M47 Patton. Mounting a 90mm gun, it entered service in 1952 and proved a successful design. Although it did not serve in the Korean War, it saw extensive service life in other armies, including in West Germany, France, Iran, Pakistan, the Republic of Korea (ROK, South Korea), and Yugoslavia.

The M48 Patton II MBT was rushed into service as a consequence of the Korean War and Soviet pressure on Berlin. Entering service in 1952, it was a brand-new design with new hull, turret, tracks, suspension, and transmission. The M48 was one of the most important of post–World War II tanks. Although it saw considerable service during the Vietnam War, this was rarely against communist armor. In Middle Eastern fighting with the Israeli Army, the M48 achieved an enviable record against its Soviet counterparts. It too was widely exported.

The M60 was essentially a refinement of the M48 begun in the late 1950s. Later, a number of M48s were rebuilt as M48A5s, essentially M60s, making the two virtually indistinguishable. The first M60 prototypes appeared in 1958. The M60 entered production in 1959 and service in 1960. It mounted the new British L7A1 105mm (4.1-inch) gun (known in the U.S. as the M68). The M60 also had a new fire-control system. The new tank weighed nearly 116,000 pounds and had a four-man crew. Its 750hp engine produced a maximum tank speed of 30 miles per hour. Armament consisted of the 105mm gun and two machine guns. Variants included the M60A1, with a new turret; the M60A2, which had a new turret with the 152mm gun/launcher developed for the M551 Sheridan; and the M60A3, which returned to the 105mm gun but with a thermal barrel jacket, a new fire-control computer with laser rangefinder, infrared searchlight, and night vision equipment. Most M60A1s were later modified to M60A3s.

The M60 was first supplied to U.S. Army units in Germany. Although no longer in U.S. active military service, the M60 was the principal U.S. main battle tank for twenty years, until the introduction of the M1 Abrams. The M60 saw combat in the Arab-Israeli wars and in the Persian Gulf War, when it served with the U.S. Marine Corps and the Saudi Arabian Army. A number of M60s remain in reserve and in the armed forces of many nations.

The M60's replacement, the M1A1 and M1A2 Abrams, is today probably the top main battle tank in the world. It began during a search by West Germany and the United States for a new MBT that could defeat the vast number of tanks that the Soviets might field in an invasion of Central Europe. The first production model M1 came off the assembly line in 1980. The M1 was a revolutionary design and also a sharp departure from previous U.S. tanks. The M1 was more angular, with flat-plate composite Chobham-type armor and with armor boxes that could be opened so that the armor could be changed according to the threat.

After initial M1 production had begun, the army decided to arm the M1 not with a 105mm but with a German-designed 120mm smoothbore gun. It was first available in 1984, and the first M1A1 with this new armament was delivered in 1985. The M1A1HA introduced new steel-encased, virtually impenetrable, depleted-uranium armor. Kuwait and Saudi Arabia bought the Abrams. Egypt produced more than 500 under a coproduction arrangement.

Soviet Union. The Soviet Union ended World War II with a large inventory of AFVs. Their excellent T-34/85 remained in production until the late 1940s. In 1947 the Soviets introduced an upgraded model, the T-34/85 II, that remained the principal Soviet MBT into the 1950s. Produced under license in both Poland and Czechoslovakia in the 1950s, it was widely exported, and production did not cease until 1964.

The T-34/85 II saw extensive service in the Korean War with the Korean People's Army (KPA, North Korean Army). It also fought in the successive Middle East wars and in Africa, and it saw combat as recently as the Yugoslav wars of the 1990s.

As noted, the Soviets led in the post–World War II development of armored personnel carriers (APCs) and modified them to carry a variety of weapons. These were gradually replaced by the Bronirovanniy Transportnaya Rozposnania (BTR, armored wheeled transporter) series of eight-wheeled APCs through missile-armed Boevaya Razvedyvatnaya Descent Mashina (BRDM, airborne combat reconnaissance vehicle) scout cars and the BMP series of personnel carriers. The BMPs mounted a large gun capable of providing effective support to dismounted infantry. They also carried antitank missiles and were constructed so as to allow infantry to fight from inside the vehicle, which distinguished this infantry fighting vehicle (IFV) from the less-capable APCs.

Along these lines the Soviets developed the PT-76 light tank, which had no equivalent in the West. As large as an MBT, the PT-76 was, however, thinly armored and was developed chiefly to lead amphibious assaults and conduct reconnaissance. Easily identifiable by its pointed nose and low, round turret with sloped sides and flat roof, the PT-76 was an amphibian without any preparation. Movement through water was accomplished by means of water jets from the rear of the hull. Mounting a 76.2mm main gun, the PT-76 entered service in 1955 and continued in Soviet service until 1967. It

A Soviet T-55 main battle tank, 29 September 1989. (U.S. Department of Defense)

saw wide service in the armies of Soviet bloc countries but also was widely exported to Africa, the Middle East, Asia, and Latin America. It fought in the Vietnam War, in the 1965 India-Pakistan War, and in conflicts in Africa. It continued in wide service well past the Cold War.

The IS-3 (Josef Stalin-3) remained the principal Soviet heavy tank immediately after World War II. The first postwar Soviet MBT, introduced in 1948, was the formidable T-54, itself a refinement of the T-44, the short-lived redesign of the T-34/85 at the end of World War II. It mounted a 100mm main gun.

The T-55, a follow-on T-54, appeared in 1958. Among many improvements was a more powerful engine. The T-54/T-55 had a long service life. Production continued until 1981, with a phenomenal 95,000 tanks manufactured, more than any other tank in history. Both the Chinese and Romanians produced copies. Even at the end of the Cold War, T-54/T-55s constituted some 38 percent of Soviet tank strength and as much as 86 percent of non-Soviet Warsaw Pact armor. Reliable and relatively inexpensive, the T-54/T-55 was exported to more than thirty-five other nations. The T-54/T-55s had a mixed combat record. While sufficient to crush the 1956 Hungarian Revolution, they were not successful against Western-supplied Israeli armor in the 1967 Six-Day War or Coalition tanks in the 1991 Persian Gulf War.

In 1953 the Soviets introduced their last heavy tank, the T-10 Lenin. It was basically an enlarged IS with a 122mm main gun. Expensive to build, heavy, and difficult to maintain, the T-10 was phased out in the mid-1960s in favor of the T-62, but it nonetheless equipped a number of Warsaw Pact armies and was exported to both Egypt and Syria.

The successor tank to the T-54/T-55 was the follow-on T-62 of 1961, which remained in first-line Soviet service for two decades. Similar in layout and appearance to the T-55, the T-62 introduced a number of improvements. It also mounted the new, larger 115mm smoothbore main gun, the first smoothbore tank gun in the world. Its gun enabled the T-62 to fire armor-piercing, fin-stabilized discarding sabot rounds that could destroy any tank at ranges of under 1,500 meters. Nonetheless, the gun could only fire four rounds a minute, and its automatic spent-case ejection system was a danger to the crew.

The Soviets built some 20,000 T-62s, and it was the principal Soviet MBT of the 1960s and much of the 1970s. It constituted 24 percent of Soviet tank strength at the end of the Cold War. T-62s were also built in large numbers by the

People's Republic of China (PRC), Czechoslovakia, and the Democratic People's Republic of Korea (DPRK, North Korea). The T-62 had a checkered combat record. Many were exported to the Middle East, where they proved vulnerable to hostile fire.

While the T-62 was simply an improvement of the T-55, the next Soviet MBT, the T-64, was a new design and a significant advance in firepower, armor protection, and speed. It entered production in 1966 and was designed to replace both the T-54/T-55 series and the T-62. Initially it was armed with a 115mm gun, but Soviet designers decided that the tank was undergunned against the U.S. M60A1, so they upgraded the definitive version T-62A to a more powerful 125mm smoothbore. The T-62B version could fire the 4,000-meter-range Songster antitank guided missile. The new tank experienced numerous reliability problems and was never exported.

The T-72 of 1971 proved to be both more reliable and far cheaper to produce. Similar in appearance to the T-64, it utilized the same gun, suspension, and track. Although its enormous 125mm smoothbore main gun allows the T-72 to fire projectiles with great destructive capability, ammunition flaws mean that the gun has a reputation for inaccuracy beyond about 1,500 meters. The gun is stabilized, allowing it to fire on the move, but is only truly effective at short ranges, and most crews halt the tank before firing. This put the T-72 at an enormous disadvantage against Western tanks with far superior gun-stabilization systems.

A large number of T-72 variants have appeared, offering an improved diesel engine, improved armor, and better sights. The T-72 currently equips not only the Russian Army and the armies of the former Warsaw Pact states but is also widely employed in the Middle East and Africa. It has been produced under license in Czechoslovakia, India, Iran, Iraq, Poland, and the former Yugoslavia. It is in fact the world's most widely deployed tank. Despite its many sales, the T-72 has not fared well in battle.

Both Iran and Iraq employed T-72s during their eight-year war in the 1980s, but there is little information about their effectiveness. Iraq counted some 1,000 T-72s in its inventory during the Persian Gulf War, but they were easily defeated by the U.S. M1A1 Abrams, which was able to take on the T-72 and destroy it at twice the effective range of the T-72's main gun. No M1A1s were destroyed by Iraqi tank fire. Despite these failings, it should be remembered that the T-72 was not designed to defeat Western armor—that was to be left to the T-64 and T-80. Rather, it was intended as a relatively inexpensive MBT that would be reliable and easy to maintain and could be widely exported. It met these criteria well.

The T-80 was the MBT designed to take on and destroy U.S. and other Western tanks. The last Soviet Union MBT, it appeared in prototype in 1976 but did not enter production until 1980. It was basically the follow-on to the T-64 with the flaws corrected, including a new engine and suspension system. It is armed with the 125mm smoothbore gun and two machine guns and is protected by composite explosive-reactive armor. The T-80 continues in production both in Russia and Ukraine. It has gone through upgrades and has been sold to China, Pakistan, and South Korea.

Israel. Tanks were essential weapons on the relatively flat and open terrain of the Middle East. The first Israeli armored vehicles were a hodgepodge of converted trucks and buses. In the 1948–1949 War for Independence, Israel had few tanks available. The United States provided a number of World War II-vintage M4 Shermans, and the Israelis also secured surplus Shermans from other armies. These saw long service, undergoing a bewildering succession of upgrades, including heavier guns, improved engines, and modified turrets. Once they had reached the limit of possible improvements, a number were turned into self-propelled guns. Indeed, improvisation became a hallmark of the Israeli military. The British Centurion, one of the world's most successful tank designs, underwent upgrades in Israel beginning in 1967 to improve its range but also to improve crew protection, in which Israel probably led the world.

France also supplied AMX-13 light tanks (until France cut off arms shipments to Israel in 1967). Other tanks in the Israel Defense Forces (IDF) included the British Centurion and the U.S. M47 and M60 MBTs.

Remodeled M60s are designated the Magach 6, 7, and 8. The Magach 7s and 8s fitted with a 120mm smoothbore gun are known as the Sabra. Israel offered this tank to Turkey and also converted a number of Turkish M60s to Sabras.

In their wars, the Israelis captured large numbers of Soviet T-54 and T-55 tanks from the Arab armies. These were modified and added to the Israelis' inventory. Improvements included a new 105mm rifled gun, improved armor, and new fire-control systems.

In the 1970s, Israel began development of its own tank. Known as the Merkava, it entered service in 1978. Built on lessons learned in previous wars, the primary concerns in its design were firepower and armor protection. The Merkava underwent continued upgrades, with the Mk 2 appearing in 1983 and Mk 3 in 1990. One of the world's most powerful tanks, it also affords perhaps the best crew protection. The Mk 1 mounts a 105mm gun and also has a 60mm mortar in the turret roof. The Mk 2 has the same armament but improved armor and a new fire-control system. These two models were superseded by the Mk 3, introduced in 1990.

Tanks are expensive and difficult to design and manufacture, and the Arab states lacked such capability. Egypt manufactured tanks under license and produced an excellent APC. Saudi Arabia has also produced light armored vehicles. But for the most part, the Arab states have chosen to rely on foreign-manufactured AFVs.

Iran. Iran was forced, both because of its isolation from much of the world as a result of its Islamic fundamentalist government and a long war with neighboring Iraq, to manufacture its own tanks. One of its projects was to upgrade Soviet T-54 and T-55 tanks captured during the long Iran-Iraq War. Known as the T-72Z Safir-74, this tank incorporates a 105mm rifled gun. The Zulfiqar MBT, however, combines components of the U.S. M48 and M60 and Russian T-72 tanks. The Iranians also produce their own APCs.

India and Pakistan. Aside from the Middle East, the largest Cold War–era tank battles occurred on the Indian subcontinent. Originally, both armies were equipped with World War II-vintage U.S. M4 Shermans. India secured from France the AMX-13 light tank and from Britain the Centurion MBT. Pakistan acquired the U.S. M24 Chaffee light tanks and the M48 MBT. These AFVs were the principal tanks of the first war fought between India and Pakistan in 1965. In their 1971 war, Pakistan also deployed Type 59 tanks from China, and India used T-55 tanks from the Soviet Union.

Following the 1971 war, India took steps to develop its own MBT. Beginning in 1974, India began design work on the Arjun. While the Arjun was undergoing development, India proceeded with local production of a Vickers MBT design, the Vijayanta (Victory) and the Soviet T-72. As the arms race on the Indian subcontinent intensified, Pakistan developed the MBT-2000 Al Khalid beginning in 1988.

China. China produced no tanks of its own during World War II or the civil war that followed. After the communist victory in 1949, China acquired a number of T-54s, and China simply copied these for its first tank, the T-59. Developed by NORINCO (China North Industries Corporation) in 1959, the T-59, a virtual copy of the Soviet T-54 with modifications, mounted a 100mm smoothbore gun. In the early 1980s a Type II appeared with the substitution of a 105mm rifled main gun. China exported the Type 59 widely. It remains in service in China and in many countries of the Middle East, Southeast Asia, and Africa. Western companies have since upgraded a number of these tanks.

The first Chinese indigenous AFV was the Type 62 light tank of 1962. In essence a reduced version of the T-59, it mounted an 85mm main gun. Most remain in service. The T-62 was exported to Albania as well as to Africa and other Asian states, with Vietnam the principal recipient.

Chinese armor doctrine copied that of the Soviet Union in placing reliance on large numbers of light amphibious tanks. The Chinese Type 63 light tank improved on the Soviet PT-76 but mounted the same 85mm main gun armament.

The next Chinese MBT design was the NORINCO Type 69. Believed to have appeared first in 1969, it was first seen in public in a parade in 1982. The Type 69 MBT employed the same basic design of the Type 59 but soon received the more accurate 100mm rifled gun. The subsequent Type 79 was vir-

tually a Type 69 but with the 105mm gun. A number of Type 69 tanks were exported to Iran and Iraq. Completely outclassed by the U.S. M1A1 Abrams and British Challenger MBTs, a large number of Iraqi Type 69s were destroyed in the 1991 Persian Gulf War.

The NORINCO Type 80 introduced many improvements. Much of the world first saw the Type 69, believed to have entered production in 1985, in scenes of Chinese tanks crushing the prodemocracy student movement in Tiananmen Square, Beijing, in 1989. It incorporated a 105mm gun that could fire both Chinese and Western ammunition and an improved fire-control system.

Japan. As with West Germany, Japan rearmed only as a consequence of the Cold War. Japan did not produce a post–World War II tank until 1962. Its Type 61 MBT for the Japanese Ground Self-Defense Force (GDF) closely followed the U.S. M48 Patton, mounting a 90mm main gun. Its successor, the Type 74 MBT with 105mm gun, entered service in 1975.

Melissa Hebert and Spencer C. Tucker

See also
AirLand Battle; Tank Warfare
References
Foss, Christopher F., ed. *The Encyclopedia of Tanks and Armored Fighting Vehicles: The Comprehensive Guide to Over 900 Armored Fighting Vehicles from 1915 to the Present Day.* San Diego, CA: Thunder Bay Press, 2002.
Hogg, Ian V. *The Greenhill Armoured Fighting Vehicles Data Book.* London: Greenhill, 2000.
Miller, David. *The Great Book of Tanks: The World's Most Important Tanks from World War I to the Present Day.* St. Paul, MN: MBI Publishing, 2002.
Tucker, Spencer C. *Tanks: An Illustrated History of Their Impact.* Santa Barbara, CA: ABC-CLIO, 2004.

Tanner, Väinö Alfred (1881–1966)

Finnish politician, Social Democratic Party (SDP) leader, and prime minister (1926–1927). Born in Helsinki on 12 March 1881, Väinö Tanner was the son of a railway worker. After his secondary education in Helsinki in 1900, he completed a year of business school in 1901, then worked for corporations in Hamburg, Turku, and Viborg before entering law school at the University of Helsinki. Graduating in 1911, he then practiced law until 1915 while playing a leading role in the cooperative movement. In 1918, he became chairman of the Finnish Social-Democratic Party. He struggled to defend Finnish freedom and democracy first against the threats posed by the right wing in Finland and then from the Soviet Union during and after World War II.

Tanner was instrumental in concluding the 1920 Tartu Treaty and the 1940 Moscow Treaty, both of which eased Finland's relationship with the Soviet Union. He transformed the SDP into a party that offered a Scandinavian brand of socialism. His pragmatic leadership helped heal the wounds of the civil war following World War I, and he led his party to power in 1926 and again in 1937. He served as premier of Finland from December 1926 to December 1927.

When the Winter War with the Soviet Union began in November 1939, as foreign minister Tanner championed his government's resistance to Soviet demands. A cabinet minister throughout World War II, he helped rally the Finnish working class behind the war effort.

Following World War II, Moscow considered Tanner its greatest nemesis. On Soviet insistence, in 1946 a Finnish court sentenced him to five and a half years of imprisonment under the vague charge of "war responsibility." Pardoned in 1949, he made an energetic political comeback and was reelected chairman of his party in 1957. Suspicious of Tanner's attempts to oust Urho Kekkonen from the presidency, in October 1961 Soviet leader Nikita Khrushchev staged the so-called Note Crisis in which he demanded that Finland reaffirm its neutrality. This secured the reelection of the incumbent president after his quick moves to placate the Soviets.

In 1963 Tanner retired from the chairmanship of the SDP. He died in Helsinki on 19 April 1966.

Silviu Miloiu

See also
Finland; Kekkonen, Urho
References
Allison, Roy. *Finland's Relations with the Soviet Union, 1944–1984.* London: Macmillan, 1985.

Jussila, Osmo, Seppo Hentila, and Jukka Nevakivi. *From Grand Duchy to a Modern State: A Political History of Finland since 1809.* London: Hurst, 1999.

Rintala, Marvin. *Four Finns: Political Profiles.* Berkeley: University of California Press, 1969.

Tanzania

East African nation. Tanzania covers 364,898 square miles and is bordered by Uganda and Kenya to the north; Burundi, Rwanda, and Congo to the west; Mozambique, Zambia, and Malawi to the south; and the Indian Ocean to the east. A former German protectorate, subsequently under British administration after World War I, Tanzania achieved its current form in 1964, after Zanzibar and Tanganyika joined. Because the nation was a conglomeration that did not exist in 1945, there is no population data from that year. Tanzania's population was 12.3 million people in 1967, the first year of an official census.

In accordance with the 1885 Berlin Conference, a territory coinciding roughly with modern Tanzania was declared a German protectorate, while Zanzibar and Pemba became British protectorates. As a result of World War I, German East Africa, named Tanganyika in 1920, was placed under a League of Nations mandate, with Great Britain as the administering power. In 1922 the Tanganyika Civil Service Association (TCSA) was founded, and in 1929 the Tanganyika African Association (TAA) was created. In 1954, these groups merged into the singular Tanganyika African National Union (TANU), under the leadership of Julius Nyerere.

Since 1954, when TANU was allowed to function as a political organization, Nyerere's leadership turned it into the main political force in the country. From 1955 on, it also gained the support of the Tanganyika Federation of Labor (TFL), established by Rashidi Kawawa. Worried that TANU would agitate for independence, the British attempted to counterbalance the growing power of the organization by backing the Tanganyika United Party (TUP). Nevertheless, in the 1959–1960 general elections, TANU emerged as the winning political party, and Nyerere became chief minister and then prime minister when Tanganyika became independent in 1961. Kawawa became prime minister in 1962, and Nyerere went on to become president of the new republic.

Neighboring Zanzibar, after becoming a sultanate in 1963, witnessed the triumph of the Afro-Shirazi Party (ASP) under Abeid Karume, an ally of TANU, over the minority coalition that had been formed by the Zanzibar Nationalist Party (ZNP) and the Zanzibar and Pemba People's Party (ZPPP). In 1964, Tanganyika and Zanzibar formed a union, with the new political entity named Tanzania. Karume became vice president under Nyerere.

Tanzania adopted a new constitution in 1965. Nyerere remained president of the now one-party state and held power until 1985. Over two decades, he oriented the country toward socialism, with the aim of self-reliance. He tried to achieve this through the exploitation of native agriculture, concentrating the means of production in the hands of workers; state control of industry, inculcating the spirit of *Ujamaa* (brotherhood) that opposed human exploitation; and the redistribution of income. He also eschewed foreign aid, arguing that it brought with it binding, long-term commitments. His socialist policies took written form in the 1967 Arusha Declaration.

In 1972, Kawawa was reappointed prime minister, and Karume was assassinated. Karume's successor, Aboud Jumbe, extended the powers of the ASP, and in 1979 the Supreme Revolutionary Council of Zanzibar adopted a separate constitution. In February 1977, TANU and ASP merged to form the Chama Cha Mapinduzi (CCM, Revolutionary Party) with Nyerere as chairman.

Deteriorating economic conditions saw half the members of the National Assembly lose their seats in the 1980 elections. In 1984, the presidential term was reduced to two years, giving more power to the National Assembly. The next year, Nyerere was forced to retire amid a serious economic crisis.

Nyerere staged something of a comeback, however, and was reelected chairman of the CCM for a five-year term in October 1987. In 1990, Nyerere's CCM initiated a broad campaign against government corruption. The issue of democracy, which had been raised several times since he left office, was raised once more in December 1991, when a presidential commission recommended the establishment of a pluralistic political system. Finally, in 1995, multiparty legislative elections were held, and a democratically elected parliament came into being.

Abel Polese

See also

Africa; Nyerere, Julius Kambarage

References

Africa South of the Sahara. 32nd ed. London: Europa Publications, Taylor and Francis Group, 2003.

McHenry, Dean E., Jr. *Limited Choices: The Political Struggle for Socialism in Tanzania.* Boulder, CO: Lynne Rienner, 1994.

Rugumanu, Severine M. *Lethal Aid: The Illusion of Socialism and Self-Reliance in Tanzania.* Trenton, NJ: Africa World Press, 1996.

Taylor, Maxwell Davenport (1901–1987)

U.S. Army general, chairman of the Joint Chiefs of Staff (JCS), ambassador, and presidential consultant. Born in Keytesville, Missouri, on 26 August 1901, Maxwell Taylor graduated from the U.S. Military Academy, West Point, in 1922 and was commissioned in the engineers. In 1926 he transferred to the field artillery. A talented linguist, he taught French and Spanish for five years at West Point before graduating from the Command and General Staff College, Fort Leavenworth, Kansas, in 1935. He then was an assistant military attaché in Japan.

Taylor graduated from the Army War College in 1940 and served on the staff of Army Chief of Staff General George C. Marshall and was promoted to lieutenant colonel. In July 1942, Taylor became chief of staff of the 82nd Airborne Division as a colonel. In December he was advanced to brigadier general and assumed command of the divisional artillery. He fought in Sicily and, in September 1943, carried out a mission behind enemy lines to Rome, determining that a planned airborne drop there was not feasible.

In March 1944, Taylor assumed command of the 101st Airborne Division. Promoted to major general in March 1944, he participated with his division in the Normandy invasion and then in Operation MARKET-GARDEN, the failed attempt to seize a crossing over the Rhine at Arnhem, in which he was wounded. He was in Washington when the Battle of the Ardennes (also known as the Battle of the Bulge) began on 16 December 1944 but rejoined his division on 25 Decem-

U.S. Army General Maxwell D. Taylor was one of America's most distinguished military leaders. During the Cold War, he was sharply critical of U.S. reliance on nuclear weapons at the expense of conventional forces and advocated flexible response for fighting limited wars. (Harry S. Truman Library)

ber and fought with it in the remainder of that battle and in the Ruhr.

In September 1945, Taylor became superintendent of West Point and initiated a number of curriculum changes. Between 1949 and 1951 he headed the Berlin Command. In 1951 he was promoted to lieutenant general and became deputy chief of staff for Operations and Training. In February 1953 he assumed command of the Eighth Army in Korea as a full general. He was then commanding general of the Army Forces Far East in 1954 and commander in chief of the Far East Command in 1955.

Taylor served as army chief of staff during 1955–1959. His views differed sharply from President Dwight D. Eisenhower's strategy of massive retaliation. Taylor urged greater emphasis on conventional forces and the ability to fight limited wars, which later became known as flexible response. Retiring in 1959, he expressed his views publicly in his book *The Uncertain Trumpet,* which caught the attention of John F. Kennedy.

President Kennedy brought Taylor from retirement to serve as his military advisor during 1961–1962. Taylor advocated the dispatch of 8,000 U.S. ground combat troops to the

Republic of Vietnam (RVN, South Vietnam). Kennedy then appointed Taylor chairman of the JCS, a post he held during 1962–1964. Named by President Lyndon Johnson as ambassador to South Vietnam (1964–1965), Taylor urged escalation of the war through bombing of the Democratic Republic of Vietnam (DRV, North Vietnam) as a means to bring North Vietnam to the negotiating table. For the remainder of his life, he defended U.S. policies in Vietnam and blamed America's defeat there on the media. He was president of the Institute for Defense Analysis during 1966–1969 and president of the Foreign Intelligence Advisory Board during 1965–1970. Taylor died in Washington, D.C., on 19 April 1987.

Spencer C. Tucker

See also

Eisenhower, Dwight David; Flexible Response; Johnson, Lyndon Baines; Kennedy, John Fitzgerald; Marshall, George Catlett; McNamara, Robert Strange; Ridgway, Matthew Bunker; United States Army; Vietnam War

References

Buzzanco, Robert. *Masters of War: Military Dissent & Politics in the Vietnam Era.* New York: Cambridge University Press, 1996.

Halberstam, David. *The Best and the Brightest.* New York: Random House, 1972.

Kinnard, Douglas. *The Certain Trumpet: Maxwell Taylor and the American Experience in Vietnam.* Washington, DC: Brassey's, 1991.

Taylor, John M. *General Maxwell Taylor: The Sword and the Pen.* New York: Doubleday, 1989.

Taylor, Maxwell D. *Responsibility and Response.* New York: Harper, 1967.

———. *Swords and Plowshares.* New York: Norton, 1972.

———. *The Uncertain Trumpet.* New York: Harper, 1959.

Teller, Edward (1908–2003)

U.S. atomic scientist, known as the father of the hydrogen bomb. Born in Budapest, Hungary, on 15 January 1908 to a Jewish family, Edward Teller received his doctorate in theoretical physics from the University of Leipzig in 1930. He immigrated to the United States in 1935. During World War II he worked at Los Alamos, New Mexico, on the Manhattan Project, which produced the world's first atomic bomb in 1945. After the Soviets tested their first atomic weapon in August 1949, Teller strongly pushed for a hydrogen bomb program, which President Harry S. Truman authorized in January 1950.

Teller's advocacy of the hydrogen bomb alienated him from many other nuclear scientists, who did not see the need for such a weapon and worried that production of one would lead inexorably to a nuclear arms race. In late 1950 Teller left Los Alamos for the Lawrence Livermore Laboratory in California when he was not selected to head the hydrogen bomb project. He served as associate director of the laboratory during 1953–1958 and director during 1958–1960. While he was

director, the lab worked on the nuclear warhead for the U.S. Navy's new Polaris missile.

In 1954, the Atomic Energy Commission (AEC) denied Robert Oppenheimer, head scientist on the Manhattan Project, a renewal of his government security clearance. Teller had testified at AEC hearings against Oppenheimer, furthering the rift between himself and much of the scientific community. Undeterred by this, Teller spent his life devoted to scientific advancement and was an advocate of strong national defenses. During the 1980s, he ardently supported President Ronald Reagan's Strategic Defense Initiative. Teller was awarded the Presidential Medal of Freedom in July 2003. He died in Stanford, California, on 9 September 2003.

Valerie Adams

See also

Hydrogen Bomb; Missiles, Polaris; Nuclear Arms Race; Oppenheimer, Robert

References

Goodchild, Peter. *Edward Teller: The Real Dr. Strangelove.* Cambridge: Harvard University Press, 2004.

Herken, Gregg. *Brotherhood of the Bomb: The Tangled Lives and Loyalties of Robert Oppenheimer, Ernest Lawrence, and Edward Teller.* New York: Holt, 2002.

Rhodes, Richard. *Dark Sun: The Making of the Hydrogen Bomb.* New York: Simon and Schuster, 1995.

Teller, Edward, and Judith Shoolery. *Memoirs: A Twentieth Century Journey in Science and Politics.* New York: Perseus, 2001.

Templer, Sir Gerald (1898–1979)

British field marshal. Born in Colchester on 11 September 1898, Gerald Walter Robert Templer was educated at Wellington College and Sandhurst Military Academy in 1916, when he was commissioned in the Royal Irish Fusiliers. He then saw combat service in France. Between the world wars he served in both the Middle East and England and graduated from the Staff College in 1929. At the outbreak of World War II, he was assigned to the intelligence section in the War Office. In November 1940 he was appointed to command a brigade, and in April 1941 he took command of the 47th Division as a temporary major general. In September 1942 he commanded II Corps, part of the British home defense, becoming the youngest lieutenant general in the army. However, ten months later he requested command of a field division and reverted to major general. In October 1943 he was assigned command of the 56th Division in Italy, which he led at Volturno River, Monte Camino, and Anzio. He was sent home the following August to recuperate after being wounded when his vehicle hit a mine.

In 1945 Templer was named director of civil affairs/military government in the British occupation zone in Germany. The following year he returned to the War Office, where he served successively as director of Military Intelligence and vice chief of the Imperial General Staff. He was promoted to lieutenant general in April 1948 and to general in June 1950. In 1952, following two years as chief of the Eastern Command, he was personally chosen by Prime Minister Winston Churchill to become high commissioner in Malaya, then in the midst of the Malayan Emergency.

To restore order in Malaya, Templer selectively built on his predecessors' initiatives while insisting on strict discipline and implementation of reforms, most notably in the police, intelligence, and information services. This approach was closely associated with what became known as the hearts and minds philosophy of counterinsurgency. By the time of his departure in 1954, the insurgents had essentially been defeated. He subsequently served as chief of the Imperial General Staff from 1955 to 1958 and was promoted to field marshal in November 1956. Templer died in London on 25 October 1979.

George M. Brooke III

See also
Anticolonialism; Churchill, Winston; Communist Revolutionary Warfare; Malayan Emergency; Southeast Asia

References
Cloake, John. *Templer, Tiger of Malaya.* London: Harrap, 1985.
Stubbs, Richard. *Hearts and Minds in Guerrilla Warfare: The Malayan Emergency, 1948–1960.* Oxford: Oxford University Press, 1989.

Territorial Changes after World War II

World War II and the attendant postwar settlements produced major territorial changes. In Europe, Germany was divided into four occupation zones, as was the capital city of Berlin. In a few years, these gave way to the Federal Republic of Germany (FRG, West Germany) and the German Democratic Republic (GDR, East Germany). Germany was not reconstituted as a whole nation until 1990 and the end of the Cold War.

Germany lost all territory that it had taken during the war. France secured the small border areas of Tenda and Briga. France also temporarily secured control of the coal-rich Saar region. Paris sacrificed efforts to secure the Saar permanently in return for a rapprochement with Bonn. Following a plebiscite in November 1955 in which Saarlanders voted two to one to reject internationalization, the Saar joined West Germany in 1957.

Poland's postwar borders had been the topic of much rancor and debate in the wartime meetings of Allied leaders at Tehran (November–December 1943) and Yalta (February 1945). Germany lost all of former East Prussia to the Soviets

and Poles. The Soviet Union annexed Königsberg (renamed Kaliningrad), Memel (now Klaipeda), and northern East Prussia, with the remainder of the province going to Poland. West of the former Polish corridor, Germany was forced to cede to Poland all German territory up to the Oder and Neisse Rivers as well as the city of Stettin east of the Oder. The Western powers agreed to only a temporary administration of this territory, pending a formal German peace treaty. Nonetheless, the arrangement became permanent and was formally recognized as such in the signing of a peace treaty with Germany in 1991.

Territory taken from Germany and given to Poland was to compensate that country for the loss of much of its eastern territory to the Soviet Union. The Western powers had agreed at Yalta that the Soviet western frontier should be the old Curzon Line, set as the boundary between Poland and Russia by a commission of the Western powers in 1919. The settlement of Poland's postwar frontiers thus moved Poland west, but it also eliminated the old Polish corridor and the territorial division of Germany that had been the stated cause of the German invasion of Poland in 1939, marking the beginning of World War II in Europe.

Without treaty or agreement by the Western powers, the Soviet Union also annexed the Baltic states of Estonia, Latvia, and Lithuania (which had been extended eastward in 1939 to include Vilnius). The Soviets had forcibly annexed these three states in 1940. Finland was forced to cede to the Soviet Union the Karelian Isthmus and the Arctic seaport of Petsamo (now Pechenga). This latter gave the Soviet Union a frontier with Norway. The Soviet Union also secured from Finland a fifty-year lease on a naval base at Porkkala.

The Allies agreed in 1943 that Czechoslovakia, declared a belligerent state on the Allied side, was to be returned to its pre-1938 Munich Agreement frontiers, but in November 1944, with the Red Army in occupation, a self-proclaimed council met in sub-Carpathian Rus' (which the Paris Peace Conference had awarded to the new state of Czechoslovakia in 1919 in order to provide a land link with Romania) and declared its desire to be reunited with the "Soviet Ukrainian motherland." This "voluntary" action was confirmed by a bilateral treaty between the Soviet Union and Czechoslovakia in June 1945.

In east-central Europe, the victorious powers rejected Hungary's claims to retain control of Transylvania. That area was returned to Romania, and Hungary shrunk back to its 1919 Treaty of Trianon borders, with the exception of a small bit of land south of the Danube near Bratislava, which went to Czechoslovakia.

Romania recovered its prewar western boundary, with the return of Transylvania. In the 1947 Treaty of Paris, however, it was forced to yield to the Soviet Union both Bessarabia and northern Bukovina. Romania was also compelled to recog-

East Germans drive through Checkpoint Charlie in Berlin as they take advantage of relaxed travel restrictions to visit the Federal Republic of Germany (FRG, West Germany) West Germany, November 1989. (U.S. Department of Defense)

nize the loss in 1940 to Bulgaria of the southern Dobrudja, including the Danubian port of Silistra.

Italy's frontiers were also redrawn. In addition to losing some small territory to France, the 1947 treaty recognized the Yugoslavian acquisition of all former Italian land east of the Adriatic Sea. This included the Dalmatian city of Zadar (Zara) and the Adriatic islands of Cres (Cherso), Lošinj (Lusino), and Lastovo (Lagosta) as well as the long-contested city of Rijeka (Fiume) and, to the north, western Slovenia and part of Istria. The chiefly Italian city of Trieste was initially declared a free territory and was administered by Anglo-American forces. Trieste was finally incorporated into Italy in 1954. The 1947 treaty also awarded Italy's Dodecanese Islands to Greece, and Italy lost sovereignty over its North African colonies of Libya, Ethiopia, Eritrea, and Italian Somaliland.

In Asia, the victorious Allies had agreed early on that Japan would be reduced to its home islands. At the Yalta Conference, in return for a Soviet pledge to enter the war against Japan "two or three months" after the defeat of Germany, the Allies agreed that the Soviet Union would receive South Sakhalin Island (lost by Russia to Japan following the 1904–1905 Russo-Japanese War), concessions in the port of Darien, the return of Port Arthur as a Soviet naval base, and control over railroads leading to these ports. The Kurile Islands, which had never been in Russian possession, also passed to the Soviet Union. In the early 1950s, the Soviet Union returned to the People's Republic of China (PRC) the various concessions granted to it in Chinese territory.

Also as a result of World War II, China regained sovereignty over Manchuria, Taiwan (Formosa), and the Pescadores Islands, while Outer Mongolia continued to be independent of China. In effect, these concessions sanctioned the replacement of Japanese imperialism with Soviet domination, but the Western leaders believed this a necessary evil to secure timely Soviet entry into the Pacific war. The allies also agreed that Korea would in due course be restored to independence. Soviet forces were to disarm Japanese forces north of the 38th Parallel, while American forces would do the same south of the 38th Parallel.

The former German islands mandated to Japan after World War I now passed to U.S. control. These were the Gilbert, Caroline, and Northern Mariana Islands. They became a U.S. Trust Territory in 1947. The Japanese islands of Iwo Jima and Okinawa were taken from Japan but were restored in 1968 and 1972, respectively. Guam, taken by the United States in 1898 and occupied by Japan during the war, was restored to U.S. control. It became an incorporated territory of the United States in 1950. The United States granted independence to the Philippines in 1946.

Other territorial changes occurred indirectly as a result of the war. Within a few years of the end of the war, decolonization had wrought great changes in Africa, Asia, and the Middle East. The former French colonies of Lebanon and Syria retained the independence they had gained during the war, for instance. Jordan became a sovereign state in 1946. The European powers, spurred by the horrors of the Holocaust, also supported the creation of a Jewish national homeland (Israel) in the former British mandate of Palestine. This initiative, which was mediated by the United Nations (UN) in 1948, remains one of the most controversial territorial changes stemming from World War II.

Independence came gradually to African and Asian nations, and not without conflict. This movement was largely a result of the Atlantic Charter of August 1941 that called for the self-determination of peoples; pressure on the colonial powers by the Soviet Union and the United States; the occupation of Asian territories by Japan; and the weakened positions of Britain, France, Belgium, and the Netherlands immediately after the war. Within a decade of the end of the war, these circumstances would lead to the dismantling of most of the European colonial empires and to more than a few wars.

Spencer C. Tucker

See also
World War II, Allied Conferences

References
Black, Cyril E., et al. *Rebirth: A History of Europe since World War II.* Boulder, CO: Westview, 1992.

Churchill, Winston S. *The Second World War,* Vol. 6, *Triumph and Tragedy.* Boston: Houghton Mifflin, 1953.

Fischer, Louis. *The Road to Yalta: Soviet Foreign Relations, 1941–1945.* New York: Harper and Row, 1972.

Gardner, Lloyd C. *Spheres of Influence: The Great Powers Partition Europe, from Munich to Yalta.* Chicago: Ivan R. Dee, 1993.

Nadeau, Remi A. *Stalin, Churchill, and Roosevelt Divide Europe.* New York: Praeger, 1990.

Wheeler-Bennett, John, and Anthony J. Nicholls. *The Semblance of Peace: The Political Settlement after the Second World War.* New York: Norton, 1974.

Terrorism

The 11 September 2001 terrorist attacks on the United States brought the issue of terrorism to the forefront of global consciousness, yet politically motivated violence is nothing new. During the Cold War, the instances of both domestic and international terrorism were ample, with no region of the world free from its dangers. And while terrorism is rightfully considered a great modern evil, to ignore the fundamentally political nature of such violence is to miss the central point of its occurrence, especially within the context of the ideological, postcolonial politics of the Cold War.

In very general terms, terrorism involves the use of violence (or the threat thereof) against mainly civilian targets for political ends. The goal is to either coerce a government into radically altering policy or to intimidate the public into abandoning support for the existing regime. Specific definitions of terrorism vary depending on the particular governmental or scholarly agendas, and terrorists themselves often claim to be revolutionaries, reluctant warriors, or freedom fighters. Additionally, some scholarship—primarily leftist in orientation—seeks to define virtually all military action as terrorism, but to do so only obfuscates the issue. Illegitimate state-sponsored violence can more appropriately be classified as either war crimes or genocide.

Terrorism throughout the Cold War impacted all regions of the world, but it can best be grouped into three distinct yet overlapping categories: the nature of Cold War competition made ideological groups, predominantly Marxist groups, most prevalent; several prominent ethnonational separatist groups must be considered; and a host of Middle Eastern terrorist groups emerged, most of which were initially motivated by Arab nationalist causes but became increasingly Pan-Islamic or religiously based as the Cold War evolved. In addition, state-sponsored terrorism was an aspect of the Cold War, but it is an issue that deals more with sources of funding and support for terrorism rather than being a motivating factor for political violence.

Widespread student revolts in Europe and the United States in the late 1960s signified the ascendancy of the New Left, which was young, radical, and founded upon an ideology that was revolutionary rather than reformist. The terrorists who emerged from this movement had romantic notions of working-class struggles, even if they themselves were almost exclusively from middle-class backgrounds.

Typical of this lack of proletarian credentials was the Weather Underground Organization (also known as the Weathermen) in the United States. An offshoot of the Students for a Democratic Society (SDS), the Weathermen were essentially embroiled in an identity crisis, motivated by boredom and a desire for excitement. This was in direct contrast to members of the Black Panthers, who as products of America's inner cities were more authentically radical and could more genuinely connect their struggle with the plight of the oppressed in the developing world.

In Europe, several groups established a sort of European International, a loose but coordinated federation of leftist groups united against North Atlantic Treaty Organization (NATO) imperialism. These groups often received logistical and matériel aid from the Soviet Union via its East European satellites. In the Federal Republic of Germany (FRG,

West Germany), the Red Army Faction (RAF), also known as the Baader-Meinhof Gang, grew out of a rejection of postwar capitalist consumerism but also considered itself the champion of the oppressed developing world. Aligned with the RAF was France's Action Directe (AD). Together these two groups sought to establish a network of West European revolutionaries who would fight on behalf of developing-world victims of Western imperialism. The Italian Red Brigades was also included in this milieu, but it went further by attempting to form alliances with terrorists in Ireland and Spain (whose causes were entirely different in nature). An organization known as November 17 (N17) followed the Marxist, anti-Western model in Greece but had an additional and more specific grievance against the United States, which they blamed for the Turkish occupation of Cyprus. In Eastern Europe, however, strong police states effectively negated any chance for the rise of such revolutionary movements.

The Japanese Red Army (JRA) shared N17's explicit anti-Americanism. Founded in large part upon a rejection of the United States–Japan Security Treaty, the JRA had explicit ties to European terrorists but also maintained connections with Middle Eastern terrorists. The JRA was more internationalist in its worldview than its European counterparts.

Communist revolutionary fervor was quite evident in Latin America, where virtually every nation was affected. Uruguay, Argentina, Brazil, and Venezuela were all plagued with guerrilla armies, but in contrast to European terrorism, violence in Latin America was founded upon genuine peasant uprisings. A more organized urban guerrilla warfare substituted for the clandestine student-oriented groups in Western Europe. Colombia watched guerrilla warfare quickly turn from revolutionary insurgency into the narcoterrorism that defines the Revolutionary Armed Forces of Colombia (FARC) today, whereas in Peru, Sendero Luminoso (Shining Path) remains and is often cited as the prototype of a Marxist insurgency group. Shining Path can also be likened to the many ethnonational groups, but their claims in this regard were always secondary to the group's revolutionary goals.

In the United States, Western Europe, and Latin America, the revolutionaries overestimated the salience of their Marxist ideology, and as a result they never received significant public support. Russian revolutionaries Vladimir Lenin and Leon Trotsky had warned against the use of revolutionary terrorism because, they believed, it lacked a genuine connection to the working-class struggle. The radical terrorists of the late 1960s favored immediate action. In the end, because of often indiscriminate violence, such movements tended to reduce rather than increase popular support for the Left.

The second category of Cold War terrorism, ethnonational separatists, typically operated within an existing state but made irredentist claims based on the shared perception that the territory was the group's ancestral homeland. During the Cold War, many of these groups claimed some form of Marxist solidarity, but in fact their true motivations were entirely nationalistic. Ethnonational groups have been far more prolific than their ideological counterparts, and their longevity has been generally greater. In several cases, however, they have operated in democratic nations, which limited the amount of public sympathy they received, even among coethnics.

Perhaps the earliest Cold War example of this type of terrorism are the Zionist terrorists of the Irgun and Stern Gang, who undertook terrorist operations against both British and Arab targets in Palestine prior to the creation of the state of Israel in 1948 but disbanded after 1948 because such clandestine groups are unnecessary once they achieve their goal.

One of the more recognizable of all terrorist groups is the Irish Republican Army (IRA), perhaps because its demand that Northern Ireland be reunified with the Republic of Ireland calls into question two of the pillars of Western Cold War dogma: the pluralist assumptions of representation and self-determination. Similarly, Euzkadi ta Askatasuna (ETA, Basque Homeland and Liberty) seeks an independent state in the Basque region of Spain (and a small portion of France), but their suppression under Spanish dictator Francisco Franco and Spain's subsequent granting of semiautonomy to the region lessened the appeal of their cause.

It is inexplicable that the most deadly of all terrorist groups, the Liberation Tigers of Tamil Eelam (LTTE, Tamil Tigers), is relatively unknown. The LTTE seeks to annex the northern portion of Sri Lanka, a territory they claim as the Tamil homeland. It is estimated that the Tamil Tigers have killed more than 50,000 people to date, most notably two world leaders, Indian Prime Minister Rajiv Gandhi in 1991 and Sri Lankan President Ranasinghe Premadasa in 1993.

Equally inexplicable is that there is one terrorist group that was entirely successful in achieving its political goals, which were anticolonial rather than separatist. The National Liberation Front (FLN) managed to drive French colonial forces out of Algeria and established itself as the new Algerian government.

While it is true that most, if not all, ethnonational separatist groups have relied on one another in a type of international network of matériel support, it is a mistake to conclude from this that during the Cold War they were not completely autonomous. Connections and mutual support existed, but this was not international terrorism as it is properly defined.

The third category of Cold War terrorism, Middle Eastern terrorism, is perhaps the most difficult to define because violence in the Middle East has been based on a combination of ideology, Arab nationalism, and what is aptly described as political religion. Contrary to popular belief, much Middle Eastern terrorism has until relatively recently been limited to Arabs attacking other Arabs. Palestinians have attacked Jordanians, Iraqis and Syrians have fought one another, and the

Lebanese Civil War pitted Iranian and other Shiite Muslims against Lebanon's Christian majority as well as Sunni Muslims. Iranian support gave rise to Hezbollah (Party of God), which in a 1983 act of international terrorism killed 241 U.S. servicemen in a truck bombing at a Marine barracks in Beirut. Thus, the distinction between terrorist typologies is easily blurred.

One group that especially typifies the difficulty in categorizing Middle Eastern terrorist groups is the Kurdistan Workers' Party (PKK), which is at once Marxist, separatist, and Arab nationalist (not Islamic) in orientation. There is also the Abu Nidal Organization (ANO), which operated much like a terrorist contractor or gun for hire and was often employed by one Middle Eastern interest against another.

However, the more obvious and virulent strain of such violence is that between Arabs and Jews. After World War II, several hundred thousand Palestinians (estimates range from 500,000 to more than a million) were forcibly removed from their homes to facilitate the creation of Israel. Thus, it is no surprise that much Middle Eastern antipathy is aimed at Israelis and Americans, who are seen as Israel's unstinting benefactor.

Throughout the Cold War, the most prominent of these groups was the Palestine Liberation Organization (PLO) and its ancillary organization, the Popular Front for the Liberation of Palestine (PFLP). While there had been prior attacks against Israeli settlements and minor border skirmishes, Palestinian groups began their campaign in earnest after the 1967 War and the Israeli occupation of the West Bank. The PLO acted as an umbrella organization, receiving funds from Arab oil states and channeling them to its secondary partners. Most notably, Black September, a commando unit of the PLO and PFLP, was responsible for the deaths of eleven Israeli athletes at the 1972 Munich Olympics. This event effectively brought the Palestinian cause as well as international terrorism to the attention of the global community. Objectively, though, Palestinian terrorism has been highly ineffective. Any tactical/operational successes were mitigated by Israeli (and others') countermeasures. Yet Palestinian terrorism was effective in unifying among the Arab peoples the anti-Israeli and anti-American sentiments that continue today.

While the universal hope was that the end of the Cold War would usher in a new era of peace, the fall of the Soviet Union simply eliminated the financial support and ideological vali-

Armed police drop into position on a terrace directly above the apartments where members of the Israeli Olympic team were being held hostage by Arab Black September terrorists in Munich, 5 September 1972. The attack ended in a shootout with German police. (Bettmann/Corbis)

dation for one particular type of terrorism. It did nothing, however, to alter the nature of the grievances of the working classes or the genuinely oppressed, and it actually may have removed some constraints on violence, allowing terrorists to become more global and deadly in scope. Indeed, Middle East-based terrorism expounding political religion as its ideological basis may have been aided and emboldened by the end of the Cold War. Whereas both the Soviets and Americans sought to restrain violence in the Middle East during the Cold War, with the Soviet Union gone, an important countervailing force has been lost. Politically motivated violence has not abated but instead has merely changed forms.

Matthew O'Gara

See also
Arab-Israeli Wars; Basque Separatism; Black Panthers; Communist Revolutionary Warfare; Decolonization; Eurocommunism; Irish Republican Army; Latin America, Popular Liberation Movements in; Nationalism; Radical Islam; Red Army Faction; Red Brigades; Shining Path; Weathermen

References
Hoffman, Bruce. *Inside Terrorism.* New York: Columbia University Press, 1998.
Hudson, Rex A. *Who Becomes a Terrorist and Why.* Guilford, CT: Lyons, 2002.
Laqueur, Walter. *The New Terrorism: Fanaticism and the Arms of Mass Destruction.* Oxford: Oxford University Press, 1999.
O'Neill, Bard E. *Insurgency & Terrorism: Inside Modern Revolutionary Warfare.* Dulles, VA: Brassey's, 1990.
Whittaker, David J. *The Terrorism Reader.* New York: Routledge, 2003.

Tet Offensive (1968)

Military offensive by the People's Army of Vietnam (PAVN, North Vietnamese Army) and the Viet Cong (VC) that proved to be a critical turning point of the American war in Vietnam. Beginning early on 30 January 1968, the Vietnamese new year (Tet) truce was broken when Viet Cong forces attacked 13 cities in the central region of the Republic of Vietnam (RVN, South Vietnam). By the end of the day on 31 January, the communists had attacked 5 of 6 cities, 36 of 44 provincial capitals, and 64 of 245 district capitals. In one of the boldest attacks, a VC platoon managed to penetrate the grounds of the U.S. embassy in Saigon for several hours. Although U.S. troops repelled the incursion, this bold challenge to American power in the heart of Saigon gained wide publicity, especially in the U.S. press.

In heavy fighting over the next several days, all the attacks throughout South Vietnam were countered by U.S. and Army of the Republic of Vietnam (ARVN, South Vietnamese Army) forces. The communist attackers incurred heavy casualties. The most bitter and prolonged fighting occurred in the city of Hue, where the communists made a major investment of forces, and in Cholon, the Chinese section of Saigon. In these locations fighting raged for weeks, and in Hue much of the city was destroyed.

Militarily, the Tet Offensive failed to achieve Hanoi's military objectives. PAVN commander General Vo Nguyen Giap, although not completely in agreement with the decision to launch the offensive, believed that the plan might break the bloody stalemate between his troops and the large American expeditionary force. By launching a general offensive of simultaneous attacks throughout South Vietnam, the Democratic Republic of Vietnam (DRV, North Vietnam) hoped that the ARVN would collapse and that South Vietnamese civilians would join the VC in a general uprising against Saigon. With its puppet government overthrown, the North Vietnamese government reasoned, the United States would be unable to continue the war. Initially, the scheme worked well. In several well-conceived diversions by Giap's troops, including the siege of the Khe Sanh Marine base, he lured several U.S. units to outlying areas. Meanwhile, he secretly supplied VC units and moved them into position for attacks on the cities and towns.

One of the myths of the Tet Offensive is that it caught U.S. and ARVN forces by surprise. The U.S. command anticipated the offensive but not its timing and intensity. U.S. commanders did not think that the communists would alienate the South Vietnamese population by attacking during Tet, nor did they anticipate that the communists would mount an offensive with all their available forces. As the offensive unfolded, however, the ARVN fought surprisingly well, no uprising occurred, and the PAVN and VC suffered perhaps 45,000 casualties, half of the force engaged. The VC units were so decimated that troops from North Vietnam had to take over most of the combat operations for the remainder of the war.

The offensive compounded problems for the South Vietnamese government, as it dramatically increased the number of refugees. It also proved to be both a strategic and public relations success for the South Vietnamese government, because the magnitude of the attack led Washington to begin a reassessment of costs and objectives in the war. Spokesmen for President Lyndon B. Johnson's administration, including the commander of U.S. forces in Vietnam, General William Westmoreland, had claimed right before Tet that the end of the war was in sight, but the offensive led many to challenge that claim. Westmoreland saw in the Tet Offensive an opportunity and requested 206,000 additional troops to mount a decisive counteroffensive. When news of his request appeared in the *New York Times,* however, many Americans interpreted it as an act of desperation and began demanding an end to the escalation. President Johnson, stunned by the ferocity and scope of the offensive and counseled by a number of his

TET OFFENSIVE, 1968

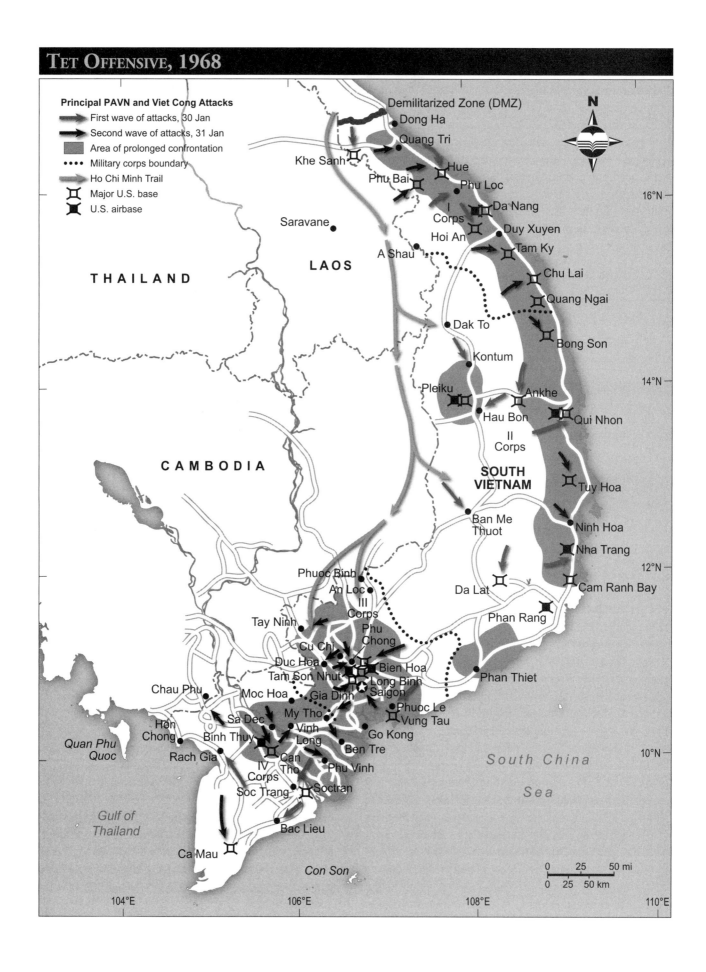

Principal PAVN and Viet Cong Attacks
- First wave of attacks, 30 Jan
- Second wave of attacks, 31 Jan
- Area of prolonged confrontation
- Military corps boundary
- Ho Chi Minh Trail
- Major U.S. base
- U.S. airbase

THAILAND

LAOS

CAMBODIA

SOUTH VIETNAM

Demilitarized Zone (DMZ)

Dong Ha
Quang Tri
Khe Sanh
Phu Bai
Hue
Phu Loc
I Corps
Da Nang
Hoi An
Duy Xuyen
Tam Ky
Chu Lai
Quang Ngai
Bong Son
Saravane
A Shau
Dak To
Kontum
Pleiku
Ankhe
Hau Bon
Qui Nhon
II Corps
Ban Me Thuot
Tuy Hoa
Ninh Hoa
Nha Trang
Da Lat
Cam Ranh Bay
Phuoc Binh
An Loc
III Corps
Tay Ninh
Phu Chong
Cu Chi
Duc Hoa
Bien Hoa
Tam Son Nhut
Long Binh
Gia Dinh
Saigon
Moc Hoa
Chau Phu
My Tho
Phuoc Le
Vung Tau
Sa Dec
Vinh Long
Go Kong
Hon Chong
Binh Thuy
Ben Tre
Phan Rang
Phan Thiet
Rach Gia
Can Tho
Phu Vinh
IV Corps
Soc Trang
Soctran
Bac Lieu
Ca Mau

Quan Phu Quoc

Gulf of Thailand

South China Sea

Con Son

| 0 | 25 | 50 mi |
| 0 | 25 | 50 km |

16°N
14°N
12°N
10°N

104°E   106°E   108°E   110°E

advisors against a widening of the war, denied Westmoreland's request.

In a nationally televised address on 31 March 1968, Johnson announced to a stunned nation that he was limiting the bombing of North Vietnam, calling for negotiations, and bowing out of the 1968 presidential election. The Tet Offensive did not end the American war, but it dramatically contradicted the Johnson administration's optimistic claims that the war was all but won. It also helped contribute to Richard M. Nixon's close victory in the November 1968 election. Although the fighting in Vietnam continued for another four years, the Tet Offensive marked a watershed in America's involvement in the war as well as in the tenor of American politics.

James H. Willbanks

See also
Johnson, Lyndon Baines; Vietnam; Vietnam War; Vo Nguyen Giap; Westmoreland, William Childs

References
Arnold, James R. *Tet Offensive 1968: Turning Point in Vietnam.* Westport, CT: Praeger, 2004.
Braestup, Peter. *Big Story.* Boulder, CO: Westview, 1977.
Gilbert, Marc Jason, and William Head, eds. *The Tet Offensive.* Westport, CT, and London: Praeger, 1996.
Hoang Ngoc Lung. *General Offensives of 1968–69.* Washington, DC: U.S. Army Center of Military History, 1981.
Oberdorfer, Don. *Tet! The Turning Point in the Vietnam War.* Baltimore: Johns Hopkins University Press, 2001.
Schmitz, David F. *The Tet Offensive: Politics, War, and Public Opinion.* Lanham, MD: Rowman and Littlefield, 2005.

Thailand

Southeast Asian nation covering 198,455 square miles, roughly the size of France. Thailand is bordered by Burma (Myanmar) to the north and west, Laos to the northeast, Cambodia due east, and Malaysia and the Gulf of Thailand to the south. In 1945 the nation had a population of roughly 19 million people. The only Southeast Asian country never colonized, Thailand largely avoided the divisions that consumed other states in the region. It was nonetheless center stage during the Cold War as America's forward base against communist expansion. Despite communist victories throughout Indochina, Thailand became a relatively stable, noncommunist, and prosperous country.

Thailand allied with Japan during World War II, but its position was ignored by the United States, which instead recognized an exile government in Washington. The United States also opposed Allied demands on Thailand after the war, protecting it from European colonialism. American interests developed further with the communist revolution in China and the Korean War (1950–1953). Concerned that Southeast Asia

would fall to communism like dominoes, Washington began economic and military aid programs in the region. The Americans also sponsored strong anticommunist leaders. In Thailand, this brought back to power Phibun (Phibunsongkhram), who ruled during 1938–1944 and 1948–1957. Washington valued Phibun's anticommunism, ignored his previous ties to Japan, and welcomed the return of his military rule.

In 1950 Thailand joined the U.S. Military Defense Assistance Program. President Harry S. Truman then sent a Military Advisory Assistance Group to Bangkok. By 1953 American aid to Thailand exceeded $56 million per year. Washington also helped Thailand secure the first World Bank loan in Southeast Asia and funded extensive expansions of Thai transportation and communication networks. This aid led to an intimate relationship predicated on the containment of communism. For the United States, Thailand represented a stable ally and a base for military operations in the region. Thailand hosted myriad clandestine operations through which the United States established logistical and intelligence networks during the Vietnam War. Thailand also became the headquarters of the Southeast Asia Treaty Organization (SEATO).

For Thailand, the United States represented more than a wealthy benefactor. Economic incentives unquestionably motivated Thai leaders. Connections with Washington also legitimized military government. However, the Thais were no mercenaries. Communism threatened not only the country but also Thai culture. Deeply reverent of the monarchy and the Buddhist faith, most Thais considered communism anathema. Moreover, behind communist threats loomed the ancient specter of Chinese domination. Countering these concerns necessitated close relations with the Americans.

Particularly worrisome to Thailand was chaotic Laos, which by the early 1960s was partly controlled by the communist Pathet Lao. To help navigate the labyrinthine world of Lao politics, the United States depended on Thai Prime Minister Sarit Thanarat (1958–1963). Part Lao, Sarit wielded considerable influence in the region. He also supported factions without American support, as he did in troubled Cambodia. To secure neutrality in both countries, the United States required Thai assistance, which was difficult given Bangkok's concern about its neighbors.

Another threat manifested itself in a communist insurgency in Thailand's remote northeastern region. Although smaller than other Southeast Asian movements, the insurgency alarmed Thai and U.S. officials. Concerned about Laos and disenchanted with SEATO, Sarit lobbied Washington for a bilateral security agreement. In March 1962, President John F. Kennedy's administration responded with the Rusk-Thanat Agreement, which was not, however, a formal alliance, much to Thai dismay.

Based on the agreement, 6,500 U.S. Marines landed in Thailand in May 1963 when communist advances in Laos precipitated a tense standoff along the Mekong River. Although war was averted and U.S. forces were quickly withdrawn, the deployment led to expanded military facilities and operations in Thailand, with air bases taking top priority. During 1960–1966 six major bases were built with U.S. assistance. During December 1965–November 1968, 1,500 weekly bombing runs originated in Thailand, 80 percent of ordnance dropped on the Democratic Republic of Vietnam (DRV, North Vietnam) and Laos in Operations ROLLING THUNDER and BARREL ROLL, respectively.

Thai officials continually denied existence of the bases and maintained that the 25,000 U.S. servicemen in Thailand by 1967 were simply advisors. In fact, Thailand was very much part of the American war in Vietnam. Under Prime Minister Thanom Kittikachorn (1963–1973), 11,000 Thai soldiers—15 percent of the armed forces—served in Vietnam, while approximately 22,000 fought in Laos, comprising much of the strength of irregular forces there. Thailand also hosted American servicemen on leave, generating $22 million annually in revenues from rest and relaxation facilities.

Congressional scrutiny ultimately undermined U.S.-Thai relations. So too did failure in Vietnam. In 1966 Thai leaders

considered dialogue with Hanoi and Beijing and by 1969, resigned to U.S. disengagement, sought an independent regional policy. That August, Thanom announced the end of Thai participation in Vietnam and asked President Richard M. Nixon to remove U.S. forces from Thailand.

However, many covert Thai operations continued. Some American soldiers remained, and Thai air bases were still used. Many Thais resented this presence, especially while Nixon pursued détente with China and peace talks with North Vietnam. Demands for foreign policy change and domestic reform culminated in violent protests in October 1973. Only through the intervention of King Bhumipol was major conflict averted. Thanom fled the country in the fall of 1973, and a new civilian government opened talks with Hanoi and Beijing. After the fall of Saigon and Cambodia in 1975, another revolution developed in October 1976, bringing military government back to Thailand.

The communist threat, however, had subsided, and the 1978 Vietnamese invasion of Cambodia and the 1979 Sino-Vietnamese War revealed serious divisions between communists. Moreover, the insurgency in Thailand waned. Thereafter, economic development became the priority, and Thailand

Demonstrating students hurling tear gas canisters back at Thai Army tanks attempting to disperse them on 14 October 1973. Antigovernment riots that left 400 people dead toppled the ten-year-old military regime of Field Marshall Thanom Kittikachorn. (Bettmann/Corbis)

in the 1980s underwent a radical transformation, becoming one of Asia's economic tigers. Security and prosperity led to democratic reforms, which became the focus of the 1990s.

With a more homogeneous population, Thailand avoided ethnic tensions seen elsewhere in Southeast Asia. Buddhism and the monarchy undoubtedly helped stabilize Thai politics. Shrewd diplomacy and the economic benefits of U.S. aid also factored into Thailand's success. Indeed, it emerged from the Cold War more unified and prosperous than most Southeast Asian nations.

Arne Kislenko

See also

Association of Southeast Asian Nations; Bhumipol Adulyadej, King of Thailand; Cambodia; Cambodia, Vietnamese Occupation of; Domino Theory; Laos; Southeast Asia; Southeast Asia Treaty Organization; Vietnam War

References

Fineman, Daniel. *A Special Relationship: The United States and Military Government in Thailand, 1947–1958.* Honolulu: University of Hawaii Press, 1997.

Kislenko, Arne. "Bamboo in the Shadows: Relations between the United States and Thailand during the Vietnam War." Pp. 197–219 in *America, the Vietnam War and the World: Comparative and International Perspectives,* edited by Andreas W. Daum, Lloyd C. Gardner, and Wilfried Mausbach. New York: Cambridge University Press, 2003.

———. "Bending with the Wind: The Continuity and Flexibility of Thai Foreign Policy." *International Journal* 57(4) (Autumn 2002): 537–561.

Randolph, R. Sean. *The United States and Thailand: Alliance Dynamics, 1950–1985.* Berkeley: Institute of East Asian Studies, University of California Berkeley, 1986.

Wyatt, David K. *Thailand: A Short History.* New Haven, CT: Yale University, 1982.

Thatcher, Margaret (1925–)

British politician and prime minister (1979–1990). Born in Grantham, Lincolnshire, on 13 October 1925, Margaret Hilda Roberts attended Kesteven and Grantham High School for Girls, then read chemistry at Somerville College, Oxford, becoming president of the Oxford University Conservative Association. Upon graduation in 1947, she worked as a research chemist and in 1951 was called to the bar as a lawyer. In 1951 she married Denis Thatcher, a wealthy businessman.

After two failed attempts, in 1959 Margaret Thatcher won election to Parliament as Conservative member for Finchley. In 1961 she was parliamentary secretary at the Ministry of Pensions and in 1970 secretary of state for education and science under Edward Heath until his government lost the 1974 election to Harold Wilson's Labour Party. The following year, Thatcher became Conservative leader, the first woman to

Known as the "Iron Lady," Margaret Thatcher was Britain's first woman prime minister (1979–1990). As leader of the Conservative Party, Thatcher was a strong ally of U.S. President Ronald Reagan. (Corel)

head either major British political party, and after four years, during which she broke decisively with the centrist consensus on the mixed economy and welfare state that had dominated all British governments since 1945, led her party to electoral victory over Labour Prime Minister James Callaghan in 1979. This was the first of three successive general election triumphs for Thatcher, the others occurring in 1983 and 1987.

As British prime minister—the first woman to hold that position—Thatcher used monetarist measures to moderate the prevailing high inflation of the 1970s, cut taxes dramatically, trim back the welfare state, privatize many nationalized industries, and drastically curtail the power of labor in bitter confrontations with major trade unions. Far more ideological than her predecessors, she accepted double-digit unemployment rates, which peaked at 3 million in the early 1980s, and the consequent short-term political unpopularity as the inevitable price of such policies.

Strongly anticommunist in outlook, while still in opposition in 1976 Thatcher had assailed Soviet policies for opposing "genuine détente" through intervention in Angola and opposed any weakening of the North Atlantic Treaty Organization (NATO). Dubbed the "Iron Lady" by the Soviet press, she accepted the sobriquet with pride and worked to strengthen British defenses and repair strained relations with the United States. She consciously modeled herself on Winston Churchill, another maverick Conservative prime minister who supported tough foreign policies. Her uncompromising rhetoric, strong principles, and forceful personality soon made her a major international figure, admired by conservatives and often reviled by liberals.

From early 1981, Thatcher worked closely with U.S. President Ronald Reagan, whose political views on both domestic and international issues coincided almost exactly with her own, and the two soon developed a warm friendship. Internationally, she almost always backed the United States, even when Reagan's fiercely antiterrorist and anticommunist policies toward such countries as Libya, Nicaragua, and Chile generated considerable domestic and foreign criticism. She did, however, break with Reagan over his 1983 invasion of Grenada, a British Commonwealth country, and refused to endorse the economic sanctions that the U.S. Congress imposed, albeit without Reagan's backing, on apartheid South Africa. She consistently backed NATO, endorsing the controversial 1979 decision to deploy nuclear-armed intermediate-range cruise missiles in Western Europe and replace Britain's Polaris submarine fleet with modern Trident II submarines. In doing so, she ignored protests, including the revival of the Campaign for Nuclear Disarmament and the encampment of protestors for several years outside the American air base of Greenham Common, Berkshire. Splits within the Labour Party over defense and British membership in NATO contributed to Thatcher's subsequent reelection victories.

While taking a tough line on defense and rearmament, initially Thatcher concentrated on economic and domestic issues, leaving her foreign secretary, Lord Carrington, responsible for handling such thorny issues as negotiating a settlement in Zimbabwe (Rhodesia) in 1980 that replaced the state's breakaway white government with one dominated by Africans. From 1982, however, when against much advice she chose to send a military expedition to the South Atlantic to regain the British-controlled Falkland Islands after their seizure by Argentina, Thatcher became far more active in international affairs. She played a major part in negotiating the 1984 Joint Declaration whereby, against her own initial instincts, Britain agreed to return Hong Kong to the People's Republic of China (PRC) in 1997. Always somewhat suspicious of the European Community (EC), she did not withdraw Britain from membership but undertook hard bargaining to ensure that Britain's overall budgetary contributions to the EC declined substantially.

During the early 1980s, Thatcher's relations with Soviet leaders Leonid Brezhnev, Yuri Andropov, and Konstantin Chernenko were frosty. Meeting Mikhail Gorbachev in December 1983 shortly before he became Soviet Communist Party secretary, she quickly developed a rapport with him and urged Reagan to give credence to Gorbachev's calls for major reductions in nuclear and conventional forces as well as his attempts at economic reform. Interestingly, fearing that Gorbachev's political survival was precarious and that more hardline Soviet officials might well replace him, Thatcher was more cautious than Reagan in sanctioning such reductions, including the 1987 Intermediate-Range Nuclear Forces (INF) Treaty, and urged the Western alliance to proceed relatively slowly. She was therefore somewhat uncomfortable with the sweeping agreements that Reagan and Gorbachev reached at Reykjavík in 1986, a meeting that, like several others between Gorbachev and Presidents Reagan and George H. W. Bush, she did not attend.

Well-founded doubts over the effectiveness of the Strategic Defense Initiative (SDI) system of antinuclear defenses that Reagan favored made Thatcher reluctant to dismantle both nuclear weapons and antinuclear defenses. Memories of German involvement in two world wars also led her to unavailingly oppose the unification of the German Democratic Republic (GDR, East Germany) and the Federal Republic of Germany (FRG, West Germany). In the summer of 1990, she reportedly urged President Bush to remain firm in opposition to the seizure of Kuwait by President Saddam Hussein of Iraq, support that many believed contributed to Bush's decision to launch a war against Iraq the following year, a conflict in which British forces participated.

In November 1990, Conservative opposition to Thatcher's domestic policies, especially the highly unpopular new poll tax, created a rebellion within her own party that forced her from office. Ennobled as Baroness Thatcher, she then published several volumes of memoirs and speeches, made numerous public addresses, and somewhat ineffectively attempted to pressure her successors to follow her policies. She opposed any further strengthening of the European Union (EU) but strongly supported the continuation and enlargement of NATO. She also established a foundation to promote and encourage her free enterprise and antisocialist political views. In failing health by the early twenty-first century, in June 2004 she nonetheless insisted on attending her old friend Reagan's funeral and burial services, for which she had recorded a eulogy lauding his domestic and international achievements. Although her own country lacked the superpower status of the United States, much of her praise of Reagan's courage, determination, and political skills was equally applicable to Thatcher herself.

Priscilla Roberts

See also

British Commonwealth of Nations; Bush, George Herbert Walker; Callaghan, James; Détente; Falklands War; Gorbachev, Mikhail; Greenham Common; Grenada Invasion; Heath, Edward; Intermediate-Range Nuclear Forces Treaty; Iraq; Kuwait; Missiles, Cruise; Missiles, Intermediate-Range Ballistic; Missiles, Polaris; North Atlantic Treaty Organization, Origins and Formation of; Nuclear Weapons, Tactical; Reagan, Ronald

Wilson; Reykjavík Meeting; Soviet Union; Strategic Defense
Initiative; Submarines; United Kingdom; United States; Wilson,
James Harold; Zimbabwe

References
Campbell, John. *Margaret Thatcher*, Vol. 1, *The Grocer's Daughter*.
London: Jonathan Cape, 2000.
———. *Margaret Thatcher*, Vol. 2, *Iron Lady*. London: Jonathan
Cape, 2003.
Cannadine, David. *In Churchill's Shadow: Confronting the Past in
Modern Britain*. New York: Oxford University Press, 2003.
Evans, Brendan. *Thatcherism and British Politics, 1975–1999*.
Stroud, Gloucestershire, UK: Sutton, 1999.
Evans, Eric J. *Thatcher and Thatcherism*. 2nd ed. New York:
Routledge, 2004.
Jenkins, Peter. *Mrs. Thatcher's Revolution: The Ending of the
Socialist Era*. Cambridge: Harvard University Press, 1988.
Sharp, Paul. *Thatcher's Diplomacy: The Revival of British Foreign
Policy*. New York: St. Martin's, 1997.
Smith, Geoffrey. *Reagan and Thatcher*. New York: Norton, 1991.
Thatcher, Margaret. *Downing Street Years*. New York: HarperCollins,
1993.
———. *The Path to Power*. New York: HarperCollins, 1995.

Thompson, Llewelyn Edward, Jr. (1904–1972)

American career diplomat and one of the premier U.S. Cold War Soviet experts. Born the son of a sheep rancher on 24 August 1904 in Las Animas, Colorado, Llewelyn Thompson graduated from the University of Colorado in 1928 and joined the Foreign Service the following year. His first appointment to Moscow came in 1941, during which time he endeared himself to Muscovites by staying on during the grim Nazi siege of 1941–1942. In 1944 he was sent to London, and in 1946 he returned to Washington to take on senior posts in East European and European affairs.

In 1950 Thompson went to Rome and was then appointed high commissioner and ambassador to Austria (1952–1956), his most productive years as a Cold War diplomat. His tenacious skills as a negotiator contributed both to a settlement of the Trieste issue in 1954 and the signing of the Austrian State Treaty in May 1955, both milestones in East-West diplomacy. He went on to serve during 1957–1961 as ambassador to Moscow, where he secured Soviet leader Nikita Khrushchev's personal trust. This served Thompson well as an advisor to Presidents Dwight D. Eisenhower and John F. Kennedy during Cold War crises over Berlin and Cuba between 1958 and 1962.

Thompson facilitated Khrushchev's visit to America in 1959 as well as U.S.-Soviet summits in Paris (1960) and Vienna (1961). Thompson returned to Washington in 1962 and was appointed ambassador-at-large. During the 1962 Cuban Missile Crisis, he exerted a moderating influence in White House Executive Committee meetings. Involved in many crucial nuclear arms talks, President Lyndon B. Johnson appointed Thompson ambassador to Moscow for a second time in 1966, a post he held until 1969, making him the longest-serving ambassador to Moscow in American history. Thompson died in Bethesda, Maryland, on 6 February 1972.

Günter Bischof

See also
Austria; Austrian State Treaty; Berlin Crises; Cuban Missile Crisis; Eisenhower, Dwight David; Kennedy, John Fitzgerald; Khrushchev, Nikita; Nuclear Arms Race; Soviet Union; Trieste; Vienna Conference

References
Beschloss, Michael R. *The Crisis Years: Kennedy and Khrushchev,
1960–1963*. New York: HarperCollins, 1991.
Bischof, Günter. *Austria in the First Cold War, 1945–1955: The
Leverage of the Weak*. London: Macmillan, 1999.
Garthoff, Raymond L. *A Journey through the Cold War: A Memoir
of Containment and Coexistence*. Washington, DC: Brookings
Institution Press, 2001.
Mayers David. *The Ambassadors and America's Soviet Policy*. New
York: Oxford University Press, 1995.

Thompson, Sir Robert (1916–1992)

British counterinsurgency expert. Born on 12 April 1916 in Charlwood, Robert Grainger Ker Thompson was educated at Marlborough and Sidney Sussex College, from which he graduated in 1938. Later that same year he was posted as a Malayan Civil Service (MCS) cadet. During 1942–1944 he served as Royal Air Force liaison officer with Orde Charles Wingate's Chindits, rising to wing commander. In 1946 he returned to the MCS as assistant commissioner of labor in Perak. During the Malayan Emergency (1948–1960), he was closely involved with the successful effort to defeat the insurgents, and he advanced up the MCS ranks, becoming permanent secretary for defense in 1959.

In September 1961, now retired from the MCS, Thompson went to the Republic of Vietnam (RVN, South Vietnam) as head of a small British Advisory Mission (BRIAM) to President Ngo Dinh Diem. Thompson established cordial relations with the Americans, but he was unable to convince the Vietnamese to adopt the approach that had worked in Malaya, and BRIAM was subsequently dissolved in 1965. Later that year he was hired as a consultant by the RAND Corporation and wrote *Defeating Communist Insurgency*, which compared Malaya and Vietnam and established principles for defeating similar insurgencies. He severely criticized President Lyndon B. Johnson's Vietnam War strategy, adopted in 1966, as a failure to understand the nature of the war. In *No Exit from*

Vietnam (1968), Thompson explained how the Americans'
flawed policy had led to the January 1968 Tet Offensive. In
1969 he was hired as an independent observer by President
Richard M. Nixon, whose new strategy for Vietnam was more
attuned to Thompson's ideas. Thompson remained an observer until the collapse of South Vietnam in April 1975.
However, his disillusionment with the 1973 Paris Agreement
led him to conclude that the lack of American will to enforce
it was the ultimate cause of defeat. Thompson died on 16 May
1992 in Winsford, England.

George M. Brooke III

See also

Communist Revolutionary Warfare; Johnson, Lyndon Baines;
    Malayan Emergency; Ngo Dinh Diem; Nixon, Richard Milhous;
    RAND Corporation; Tet Offensive; Vietnam War

References

Thompson, Robert. *Defeating Communist Insurgency: The Lessons
    of Malaya and Vietnam.* New York: Praeger, 1966.
———. *Make for the Hills: Memories of Far Eastern Wars.* London:
    Leo Cooper, 1981.
———. *No Exit from Vietnam.* New York: McKay, 1968.

Thorez, Maurice (1900–1964)

French politician and leader of the French Communist Party
(PCF) during 1930–1964. Born in Noyelle-Godault in the
Pas-de-Calais region of northern France, the son of an impoverished coal miner, on 28 April 1900, Maurice Thorez
attended only a few years of primary school before he became
a coal miner at age twelve. He joined the PCF in 1920, became
a local party secretary in 1923, and rose to secretary-general
of the party in July 1930. He would lead the PCF until his death
in 1964, taking a staunchly Stalinist line and resisting the
currents of reform associated with Eurocommunism in Italy
and other European countries.

Thorez was elected to the French Chamber of Deputies in
1932 and served until 1939. In 1934, he abandoned the class-
against-class strategy of the 1920s and adopted a new policy
of cooperation with the socialists, a shift that culminated in
communist support for the Popular Front government of Léon

Maurice Thorez, leader of the French Communist Party, October 1947. (Bettmann/Corbis)

Blum following the legislative elections of 1936. The key objectives of the policy shift were to block the spread of fascism to France and to support the Soviet Union internationally.

With the conclusion of the nonaggression pact of 23 August 1939 between Germany and the Soviet Union and the outbreak of World War II barely a week later, the PCF adopted a new political line dictated by the Comintern that denounced the war as a clash of rival imperialisms. Thorez was mobilized into the French Army but, on Comintern orders, deserted and made his way to Moscow, leaving Jacques Duclos in charge of the party. Thorez remained in Moscow until November 1944, even as the PCF, following the June 1941 German attack on the Soviet Union, emerged as a leading force in the French Resistance.

After the French liberation in August 1944, Thorez was once more elected to the French Chamber of Deputies and served as minister and deputy prime minister in the tripartite (communist-socialist–Christian Democratic) governments of November 1945–November 1947. With the establishment of the Cominform in September 1947, Soviet leader Josef Stalin effectively compelled the PCF once more to turn sharply to the Left. Thorez subsequently confessed that the PCF had erred in cooperating with other political forces, and he mobilized the party to combat French participation in the Marshall Plan and the North Atlantic Treaty Organization (NATO).

In December 1950, Thorez suffered a stroke and went to Moscow for treatment. He returned to France in April 1953, following the death of Stalin the previous month. Thorez strongly resisted Soviet leader Nikita Khrushchev's de-Stalinization campaign when it was launched in late 1956, not least because Thorez himself had established a personality cult patterned after Stalin's that went back to his 1937 fictionalized autobiography *Fils du Peuple* (Son of the People).

Thorez strongly opposed General Charles de Gaulle's return to power in May 1958, calling for unity with the socialists that paved the way for the union of the Left in the 1980s. Throughout Thorez's tenure, the electoral base of the PCF remained remarkably constant. The party received 28.6 percent of the vote in the national elections of 1946, 25.6 percent in 1951, and 25.7 percent in 1956. This support fell to 18.9 percent in 1958, following de Gaulle's return to power, but rebounded to 21.7 percent in 1962. Thorez died on 12 July 1964 while en route to a vacation at a dacha on the Soviet Black Sea coast.

John Van Oudenaren

See also
Duclos, Jacques; France
References
Sirot, Stéphane. *Maurice Thorez.* Paris: Presses de la Fondation Nationale des Sciences Politiques, 2000.
Tiersky, Ronald. *French Communism, 1920–1972.* New York: Columbia University Press, 1974.

Threshold Test Ban Treaty (1974)

The Threshold Test Ban Treaty (TTBN), signed on 3 July 1974 between the United States and the Soviet Union, set limitations on underground nuclear tests. The TTBN followed the 1963 Partial Teat Ban Treaty (PTBT). The TTBN limited the size of any nuclear test by setting a ceiling threshold of 150 kilotons for any underground nuclear test. This limit was designed specifically to prevent both the Soviets and Americans from developing warheads that would allow for a first-strike capability. Treaty terms included provisions for exchange of data and designation of the test sites. Complementing the TTBN was the Peaceful Nuclear Explosions (PNE) Treaty, signed in April 1976.

Critics of the TTBN focused on Soviet violations; the 150 kiloton limit, which many regarded as too high; and the lack of adequate verification procedures. Following agreement on the latter in July 1990, the U.S. Senate ratified both the TTBN and the PNE in December 1990.

Spencer C. Tucker

See also
Nuclear Arms Race; Nuclear Tests
References
Graham, Thomas, Jr., and Damien J. LaVera. *Cornerstones of Security: Arms Control Treaties in the Nuclear Era.* Seattle: University of Washington Press, 2003.
U.S. Arms Control and Disarmament Agency. *Arms Control and Disarmament Agreements: Texts and Histories of the Negotiations.* Washington, DC: U.S. Government Printing Office, 1990.

Tiananmen Square (4 June 1989)

A large public plaza in Beijing, capital of the People's Republic of China (PRC), Tiananmen Square, literally meaning "Gate of Heavenly Peace," has been the site of student movements since the 1919 May Fourth Movement. The Tiananmen Square protests of 15 April–4 June 1989 were of the utmost importance in both their domestic and international contexts. The protests began on 15 April when Beijing's students gathered in the square, mourning the death of Hu Yaobang, former secretary-general of the Chinese Communist Party (CCP) during 1980–1987. That Hu was ousted from office in January 1987 because of his sympathetic stance toward the prodemocracy student movement of 1986 helped transform mourning activities into a series of nationwide student demonstrations. Students renewed their calls for immediate democratization and demanded direct dialogues with senior leaders. The movement employed mass sit-ins, boycotts of classes, public forums, bicycle demonstrations, and hunger strikes.

On 4 May 1989, organized prodemocracy demonstrations occurred in fifty-one Chinese cities. Other sectors also expressed their discontent with the CCP. Coincident with the visit of Soviet leader Mikhail Gorbachev in mid-May, the protests received global media coverage.

The worldwide attention and escalation of the student movement irritated PRC leaders. The handling of students' demands renewed the factional struggles between the liberal reformers and the conservatives, whose origins dated to 1979, when the paramount leader Deng Xiaoping introduced a market economy and open-door policy to modernize China. This time, the struggle was personalized by the liberal reformist CCP Secretary-General Zhao Ziyang and the conservative hard-liner Premier Li Peng. Zhao preferred a conciliatory stance, arguing that the protest was of a patriotic nature and that political reform should be accelerated to facilitate economic modernization. Li, by contrast, insisted on clear-cut coercive measures to disperse the demonstrators and restore stability.

Although away from the front line since the early 1980s, Deng remained highly influential as the chairman of the Central Military Commission. Fearing that his economic program would be jeopardized, he supported Zhao's soft-line, accommodating posture. The government's dialogues with students, however, proved fruitless. With no sign that the protests would soon end, Deng's patience was exhausted, and he decided to adopt Li's hard-line approach.

On 20 May 1989, Li declared martial law in Beijing, ordering the People's Liberation Army (PLA) to clear Tiananmen Square on the condition that no bloodshed occur. Owing to the students' blockade, the army stopped on the outskirts of Beijing city, resulting in a stalemate for the rest of the month. Meanwhile, the government was preoccupied with two issues: preparing a change in leadership to end the factional struggles and regaining Tiananmen Square to end the protests. On 28 May, Zhao was placed under house arrest and was replaced by Jiang Zemin, the party secretary of the Shanghai Municipal Committee, whose decisive action in closing down a newspaper for reporting the Tiananmen Square protests drew the conservatives' attention.

After consulting retired elder statesmen such as Li Xiannian, Bo Yibo, and PRC President Yang Shangkun, Deng finally agreed on more forceful means to end the standoff, implying the clearance of the square at all costs. On 2 June, Yang ordered a military crackdown on the student demonstrators and the clearance of Tiananmen Square on the grounds that an alleged counterrevolutionary riot was fermenting and that continued instability would retard economic reform. On 4 June at midnight, the PLA marched into the square, and by dawn it had fulfilled its orders, thereby ending the seven-week-long protests. Because of a press blackout, the estimated deaths and injuries on that night vary from 240 to 10,000.

To prevent a recurrence, on 9 June the government ordered the arrest of all student leaders and activists. Some leaders, such as Wang Dan, were arrested and sentenced to long prison terms, while others such as Chai Ling and Wuer Kaixi fled abroad. On 10 June, the PRC claimed that a total of 468 "troublemakers" had been arrested and that calm had been restored in Beijing.

The PRC's use of the PLA to suppress the student demonstrations stunned the world. Some contemporaries labeled the incident the Tiananmen Massacre. Foreign condemnations, including those from the Soviet bloc, flooded in, followed by a number of punitive sanctions, including the suspension of arms sale to China, the linking of human rights issues to the PRC's entry into the World Trade Organization (WTO), and economic embargoes. From a broader perspective, the legacy of the Tiananmen Square protests was twofold. In the PRC, the protests enabled the conservatives to gain the upper hand. In November 1989, Deng relinquished his remaining post to Jiang, passing the ruling power to the third generation, and his economic modernization was slowed down. In the Cold War context, there is a consensus that the Tiananmen Square protests in some ways inspired the liberation of Eastern Europe from Soviet control, precipitating the Cold War's end.

Law Yuk-fun

See also

China, People's Republic of; Deng Xiaoping; Hu Yaobang; Li Peng; Yang Shangkun; Zhao Ziyang

References

Blecher, Marc J. *China against the Tides: Restructuring through Revolution, Radicalism and Reform.* London: Continuum, 2003.

Evans, Richard. *Deng Xiaoping and the Making of Modern China.* Rev. ed. London: Penguin, 1997.

Nathan, Andrew J., and Perry Link, eds. *The Tiananmen Papers: The Chinese Leadership's Decision to Use Force against Their Own People—In Their Own Words.* New York: Public Affairs Press, 2001.

Tibet

A provincial-level administrative region of the People's Republic of China (PRC) since 1951, officially known as the Xizang Autonomous Region, with the capital at Lhasa. Tibet covers an area of 461,700 square miles and is located in southwestern China. It is bordered on the south by Myanmar, India, Bhutan, and Nepal; on the west by India; and on the east and north by the PRC. It had a 1945 population of some 4–5 million people.

With the introduction of Indian Buddhism in the seventh century, Tibet grew into an independent theocracy. In the seventeenth century, the Yellow Hat sect gained supremacy and practiced Lamaism, a hierarchical organization of Tibetan

Buddhist monks (lamas). Atop the hierarchy was the Dalai Lama, both the spiritual and political head of Tibetans. Just below him was the Panchen Lama.

Isolated Tibet was forced to open itself to the world in 1904 by the British, who sought to secure a trade route to China and erect a buffer against Russian expansion into British India, bordering on the south of Tibet. In 1907 Britain, Russia, and China agreed on Chinese sovereignty over Tibet and pledged noninterference in Tibetan affairs. Tibet declared its independence in late 1911 after the overthrow of China's ruling Qing dynasty. Although the two post-Qing successors, the Nationalist Chinese (1912–1949) and the Chinese communists since 1949, refused to acknowledge Tibetan independence, Tibet's resumption of Lamaism remained undisturbed, strengthening Tibetans' visions of lasting independence.

A year after the PRC's birth in October 1949, Chinese communist leaders sent 80,000 troops into Tibet in October 1950. Unable to defend his people, the fourteenth Dalai Lama unsuccessfully appealed to the United Nations (UN), the United States, Britain, and India for assistance. In May 1951, the Tibetan government reluctantly accepted the PRC's 17-Point Agreement for the Peaceful Liberation of Tibet, which instituted a joint Chinese-Tibetan authority. This promised Tibetans apparent autonomy.

To modernize and continue the socialist revolution, during the early 1950s PRC officials implemented a number of measures that brought Tibetan autonomy into question. These modernization efforts included land reform, heavy industrialization, the introduction of secular education, the opening of Tibet through construction of nationwide communication networks, and a purge of anti-PRC officials. Tibetans found these measures antithetical to their traditional practices of feudalism and socioeconomic simplicity and threatening to Tibetan homogeneity. Tibetans, who considered themselves a unique race, responded with a series of anti-Chinese revolts, transforming the Tibet question into an interethnic dispute between Tibetans and the Han Chinese.

Meanwhile, the U.S. Central Intelligence Agency (CIA) capitalized on Tibetan disaffection to advance American strategic interests. In early 1956, the CIA began to provide military training to Tibetan rebels. In autumn 1957, the CIA launched a covert operation by air-dropping into Tibet U.S.-trained Tibetan rebels along with American-made weapons and radios. This Tibetan-CIA operation led to a full-scale rebellion in Lhasa in March 1959. Chinese leaders deployed 40,000 troops to put down the rebellion, resulting in nearly 8,700 Tibetan deaths and the exile of the Dalai Lama to India. To resolve the Tibet question, the PRC named the tenth Panchen Lama as Tibet's acting head while concurrently preparing Tibet as an autonomous administrative region. In 1965, the PRC replaced Tibet's theocracy with a Chinese communist administration, making it an Autonomous Region.

A Chinese soldier keeps watch in a village in Tibet. China sent troops into Tibet in 1950 and controlled it thereafter. (Corel)

With CIA assistance, the Dalai Lama and 80,000 followers settled in northern India, where they founded the Government of Tibet in Exile at Dharamsala. The Dalai Lama internationalized the Tibet question by appealing to the UN, successfully securing two Tibet resolutions in 1961 and 1965 denouncing the PRC's violation of human rights in the March 1959 rebellion. Since then, the Dalai Lama has pursued an active posture in international affairs, championing Tibet's independence and self-determination, human rights, and peace and freedom.

After 1959, the Americans reversed their previous indifference to the Tibet question and publicly supported Tibetan independence. The CIA remained active in Tibet, chiefly in intelligence gathering, especially concerning the PRC's nuclear program in the neighboring Xinjiang Province. In Tibet, the anti-Chinese movement continued after the 1959 rebellion, and the PRC has responded with periodic crackdowns. The Cultural Revolution (1966–1976) marked the low point of the Tibetan-Chinese relationship, during which religious practices were condemned, monasteries were destroyed, and monks and nuns were persecuted. This triggered a massive exodus of Tibetans to India, Nepal, and Bhutan.

Two breakthroughs regarding the Tibet question were realized in the 1970s. First, to facilitate the Sino-American rapprochement, the CIA diminished its assistance to Tibetan rebels beginning in 1969. This ended altogether in 1974. Shortly before the establishment of formal Sino-American diplomatic relations, in 1978 the U.S. government recognized Tibet as part of China, thus reducing the issue to an internal Chinese affair. Second, PRC leaders moderated their policy toward Tibet after 1976. On the one hand, the government implemented a number of reforms to modernize Tibet, intending to win Tibetans' approval by raising their living standards. To curb Tibetan rebels, the PRC allowed a certain degree of religious freedom while also relocating huge numbers of Han Chinese to Tibet, intending to keep Tibetans under control through assimilation. The Tibetan cause attracted support and publicity from a number of international celebrities, such as the American movie star Richard Gere. In the 1990s, a dramatic dispute over which of two young boys was the rightful candidate to succeed as Panchen Lama, the second most influential Tibetan Buddhist figure, damaged Sino-Tibetan relations.

On the other hand, the PRC signaled its willingness to resolve the Tibet question with the Tibetan government-in-exile. Negotiations between the PRC and the Dalai Lama's exiled government began in 1979 but broke off in 1988 due to irreconcilable differences. In the early twenty-first century, the Tibet question remained unresolved.

Law Yuk-fun

See also
China, People's Republic of; Dalai Lama; Panchen Lama
References
Barnett, Robert, ed. *Resistance and Reform in Tibet.* Bloomington: Indiana University Press, 1994.
Conboy, Kenneth, and James Morrison. *The CIA's Secret War in Tibet.* Lawrence: University of Kansas Press, 2003.
Dalai Lama. *Freedom in Exile: The Autobiography of the Dalai Lama.* New York: HarperCollins, 1990.
Grunfeld, A. Tom. *The Making of Modern Tibet.* Armonk, NY: Sharpe, 1996.

Tildy, Zoltán (1889–1961)

Hungarian politician, prime minister (1945–1946), and president of Hungary (1946–1948). Born in Losonc on 18 November 1889, Zoltán Tildy studied theology at the Protestant Theological Academy in Pápa, Hungary, then worked as a protestant minister and teacher until 1946. In 1930 he had cofounded the Independent Smallholders' Party, becoming its chairman in 1945. His engagement with politics and the cause of rural welfare dated back to 1917, when he joined the National Independence and Peasant Party.

Following the November 1945 elections, Tildy was chosen premier, leading the coalition government until 31 January 1946. On 1 February 1946 he became the president of the newly declared republic. However, in August 1948 he was forced to resign after his son-in-law Viktor Csornoky was arrested, charged with spying for the West, and executed. Tildy remained under house arrest until May 1956.

During the 1956 Hungarian Revolution, Tildy acted as minister of state in Imre Nagy's short-lived reform government. Following the failed revolution, Tildy was imprisoned for six years for his role in the 1956 uprising. Because of advanced age and poor health, he was released in April 1959. Tildy died in Budapest on 4 August 1961.

Anna Boros-McGee

See also
Europe, Eastern; Hungarian Revolution; Hungary; Nagy, Imre
References
Haas, György. *Diktatúrák árnyékában: Tildy Zoltán élete* [In the Shadow of Dictatorships: The Life of Tildy Zoltán]. Budapest: Magyar Napló, 2000.
Roman, Eric. *The Stalin Years in Hungary.* Lewiston, NY: Edwin Mellen, 1999.

Tito, Josip Broz (1892–1980)

Yugoslav communist leader, major figure in the Yugoslav resistance during World War II, and leader of Yugoslavia. Born on 7 May 1892 into a peasant family in the village of Kumrovec in Croatia on the border with Slovenia (then part of Austria), Josip Broz was one of fifteen children of a Croat blacksmith and a Slovene mother. Much of his early life remains obscure. With little formal education, he became a metalworker and machinist. Active in the Social-Democratic Party, he was drafted into the Austro-Hungarian Army in 1913. He fought in World War I and rose to the rank of sergeant, commanding a platoon in a Croatian regiment before being captured in 1915 on the Russian Front.

While in the camp, Broz became fluent in Russian. Released following the March 1917 Revolution, he made his way to Petrograd, where he joined the Bolsheviks but was imprisoned until the Bolsheviks took power in October 1917. He fought on the communist side in the Russian Civil War but returned to Croatia in 1920 and helped organize the Yugoslav Communist Party (YPJ). Rising rapidly in responsibility and position, he became a member of the YPJ Politburo and Central Committee. It was at this time that he took the pseudonym of "Tito" to conceal his identity. He was imprisoned from 1929 to 1934. In 1937 Stalin appointed Tito to head the YPJ as its secretary-general. Tito knew little of communist ideology, but Stalin was interested in loyalty.

Dedicated Yugoslav communist Josip Broz Tito led the Partisan guerrilla movement against the German occupiers of his country during World War II. Tito then crushed all opposition and ruled Yugoslavia until his death in 1980. (Library of Congress)

Following the German invasion of Yugoslavia in April 1941, Tito took command of the communist Partisan resistance movement with the twin goals of fighting the Axis occupiers and then seizing power in Yugoslavia once the Allies had won. Tito and the Partisans did not hesitate to attack German garrisons, sparking retaliation and the execution of many more innocent hostages than Germans slain. Tito's Partisans became archrivals of the Serb-dominated Četniks (Chetniks) led by General Draža Mihajlović, minister of war in the Yugoslav government-in-exile in London. The Četniks eschewed the types of attacks undertaken by the Partisans, rightly fearing German reprisals. In a controversial decision that had far-reaching repercussions for the future of Yugoslavia, in 1943 the British government, which headed the Allied effort to assist the Yugoslav resistance, shifted all support to the Partisans.

By the end of the war, the Partisans had grown to a force of 800,000 people and had in fact liberated most of Yugoslavia themselves, placing Tito in a strong bargaining position with

Stalin. Tito attempted to annex the southern provinces of Austria, moving Yugoslav forces into Carinthia, but was prevented in this design by the timely arrival of the British V Corps and was convinced to quit Austrian territory in mid-May 1945.

Tito extracted vengeance on the Croats, many of whom had been loyal to the Axis, as had many Slovenes. Perhaps 100,000 people who had sided with the Axis occupiers were executed by the Partisans without trial within weeks of the war's end. The majority of German prisoners taken in the war also perished in the long March of Hate across Yugoslavia.

With the support of the Red Army, Tito formed the National Front and consolidated his power. Although superficially there appeared to be a coalition government in Yugoslavia, Tito dominated. In the November 1945 elections for a constituent assembly, the National Front headed by the Partisans won 96 percent of the vote. The assembly promptly deposed Peter II and proclaimed a republic. Yugoslavia's new constitution was modeled on that of the Soviet Union. Tito elaborated the twin ideas of national self-determination for Yugoslavia's nationalities and a strong, centralized communist party organization that would be the sole political expression of each national group's will. Under Tito, Yugoslavia became a federal republic, a beneficial change for a country that had suffered severely from rivalries among its various peoples. Tito also nationalized the economy and built it on the Soviet model.

Following the war, Tito had General Mihajlović and some other leading Četniks put on trial under trumped-up charges of collaboration with the Germans. Despite vigorous Western protests, they were executed in July 1946. Equally destructive of European goodwill was the sentencing of Archbishop Aloysius Stepinac to life imprisonment for his anticommunist role during the war.

For thirty-five years, Tito held Yugoslavia together by ruling as a despot. In a departure from his past record of sharing hardships with his men, once in power he developed a taste for a luxurious lifestyle. He muzzled dissent, but repression and fear of outside powers, chiefly the Soviet Union, solidified his rule.

In 1948 Yugoslavia was expelled from the international communist movement. The break sprang in large part from Tito's desire to form under his leadership a Balkan confederation of Yugoslavia, Albania, and Bulgaria. There were also differences with Moscow over Yugoslav support for the communist side in the Greek Civil War, as Moscow lived up to its bargain with Winston Churchill during the war not to contest British control in Greece.

The break with Moscow and fears of a Russian invasion led Tito to build up a large military establishment. In this he was assisted by the West, chiefly the United States. By the time of Tito's death in 1980, the Yugoslav standing army and reserves totaled 2 million men. To protect his freedom of movement, Tito also joined Yugoslavia to the Non-Aligned Movement, and in the 1960s he became a leader of this group along with Gamal Abdel Nasser of Egypt and Jawaharlal Nehru of India.

Before the break, Tito was as doctrinaire as Stalin. After the schism, Tito became more flexible. He allowed peasants to withdraw from cooperative farms and halted the compulsory delivery of crops. He decentralized industry by permitting the establishment of workers' councils with a say in running the factories. He permitted citizens more rights in the courts and limited freedom of speech, and he opened cultural ties with the West and released Archbishop Stepinac (although he was not restored to authority). In 1949 Tito even wrote an article in the influential American journal *Foreign Affairs* titled "Different Paths to Socialism," giving birth to polycentralism.

By 1954, however, reform had ended. Tito reacted sharply to Milován Djilas's proposal to establish a more liberal socialist movement in the country that would in effect turn Yugoslavia into a two-party state. Djilas's book, *The New Class* (1957), charged that a new class of bureaucrats exploited the masses as much as or more than their predecessors. Djilas was condemned to prison. Meanwhile, financial problems multiplied. By the end of the 1970s, inflation was surging, Yugoslavia's foreign debt was up dramatically, its goods could not compete in the world marketplace, and there were dramatic economic differences between the prosperous North and impoverished South that threatened to break up the state.

As long as Tito lived, Yugoslavia held together. In 1974, Tito had set up a complicated collective leadership. The constitution of that year provided for an association of equals that helped to minimize the power of Serbia, diminish Yugoslavia's ethnic and religious hatreds and rivalries, and keep the lid on nationalism. There was a multiethnic, eight-man State Presidency representing the six republics and two autonomous regions. Each of the six republics had virtual veto power over federal decision making. Djilas claimed that Tito deliberately set things up so that after his death, no one would ever possess as much power as he did.

Tito died in Lubljana on 4 May 1980. With the collapse of the Soviet Union and Eastern Europe and the end of the threat of Soviet invasion and with the discrediting of communism, the federal system that Tito had put together came apart in bloodshed and war.

Spencer C. Tucker

See also
Djilas, Milován; Mihajlović, Dragoljub Draža; Soviet-Yugoslav Split; Yugoslavia; Yugoslavia, Armed Forces

References
Djilas, Milován. *Tito.* New York: Harcourt Brace Jovanovich, 1980.
Pavlowitch, Steven K. *Tito, Yugoslavia's Great Dictator: A Reassessment.* Columbus: Ohio State University Press, 1992.

Roberts, Walter R. *Tito, Mihailović, and the Allies, 1941–1945.* New Brunswick, NJ: Rutgers University Press, 1973.
West, Richard. *Tito and the Rise and Fall of Yugoslavia.* New York: Carroll and Graf, 1994.
Wilson, Duncan. *Tito's Yugoslavia.* New York: Cambridge University Press, 1979.

Tlatelolco Treaty (1967)

Treaty signed by Latin American nations in 1967 banning nuclear weapons from the region. In the middle of the Cold War, Latin America decided to determine its own destiny by creating a Latin American Nuclear Weapon Free Zone via the Tlatelolco Treaty (Treaty for the Prohibition of Nuclear Weapons in Latin America), which was signed on 14 February 1967 in Mexico City. It entered into force on 25 April 1968 and was endorsed by the United Nations (UN) that December. The treaty obligates signatories not to acquire or possess nuclear weapons or to permit the storage or deployment of nuclear weapons on their territories. The agreement was expanded in 1990 to include the Caribbean basin states, at which time its title was amended to read Treaty for the Prohibition of Nuclear Weapons in Latin America and the Caribbean. Cuba became the last of thirty-three eligible states to ratify the treaty on 26 October 2002, when it then came into full force throughout the region. The treaty's geographic boundaries encompass all signatory states and large sectors of the Pacific and Atlantic Oceans. Alfonso García Robles and Alva Myrdal received the Nobel Peace Prize in 1982 for their efforts in promoting the treaty.

The Tlatelolco Treaty called for the creation of the Agency for the Prohibition of Nuclear Weapons in Latin America and the Caribbean (OPANAL), located in Mexico City. OPANAL has been recognized by the UN for its unprecedented cooperation with the International Atomic Energy Agency (IAEA) in jointly providing the institutional framework for compliance and verification. All parties to the Tlatelolco Treaty commit themselves to the IAEA's safeguard agreements. OPANAL's council meets every two months, and a general conference of all member states takes place every two years. Should OPANAL note a case of noncompliance with the treaty, it first draws attention to that violation to the party involved. If that does not result in compliance and the violation endangers peace and security in the region, OPANAL can take the matter to the UN Security Council, the UN General Assembly, and the IAEA.

The covenant shares several provisions with other regional nuclear weapons–free zone (NWFZ) treaties. They prohibit member states from manufacturing, producing, possessing, testing, acquiring, receiving, and deploying nuclear weapons. All of the treaties also include provisions for security assurances from nuclear weapons states to the treaties' members. And the treaty commits its Latin American signatories to use nuclear energy solely for peaceful purposes.

There are two additional protocols to the Tlatelolco Treaty. The first binds those overseas countries with territories in the region to the terms of the treaty. This includes the United Kingdom, France, the Netherlands, and the United States. The second requires the world's declared nuclear weapons states to refrain from undermining the nuclear free status of the region. That protocol has been signed and ratified by the United States, the United Kingdom, France, the People's Republic of China (PRC), and Russia.

The Tlatelolco Treaty formed the basis for several other regional NWFZ treaties, which together have effectively denuclearized most of the Southern Hemisphere. Those include the 1985 Treaty of Rarotonga for the South Pacific; the Treaty of Bangkok (1995), which created an NWFZ for Southeast Asia; and the 1996 Treaty of Pelindaba for Africa. Arguably the first NWFZ was created by the Treaty of Antarctica in 1959. Proponents view nuclear weapons–free zones as steps toward a nuclear weapons–free world. NWFZs can also be seen as instruments of both nonproliferation and disarmament because they have, as in the case of Argentina and Brazil, caused states to abandon their nuclear weapons programs.

Jeffrey A. Larsen

See also
Americas; Arms Control; Nuclear Arms Race
References
Confidence- and Security-Building Measures in the Americas: A Reference Book of Hemispheric Documents. Washington, DC: Arms Control and Disarmament Agency, September 1998.
Robles, Alfonso Garcia. *The Latin American Nuclear-Weapon–Free Zone.* Occasional Paper 19. Muscatine, Iowa: Stanley Foundation, May 1979.
Serrano, Monica. *Common Security in Latin America: The 1967 Treaty of Tlatelolco.* London: Institute of Latin American Studies, 1992.

Todorov, Stanko (1920–1976)

Bulgarian politician and prime minister. Born in Klenovik, Bulgaria, on 10 December 1920, Stanko Todorov attended only primary school and then apprenticed as a tailor. By age sixteen, he was politically active and had joined both the leftist Worker Youth Federation (RMS) and the tailors' union. Todorov served in the Bulgarian Army in World War II during 1941–1943 but deserted and joined the illegal Bulgarian Communist Party (BCP). He was a key leader in the September 1944 rebellion that formally ended Bulgaria's monarchy and established the People's Republic of Bulgaria.

Later in the 1940s, Todorov remained active in the RMS and BCP, holding increasingly prominent positions in both organizations. During 1952–1957 he served as minister of agriculture. In 1954 he was elected to the BCP's Central Committee and in 1957 became its secretary. During 1959–1962 he served as deputy chairman of the Council of Ministers, led the National Planning Commission, and represented Bulgaria in the Comecon. By 1962 he was also a full member of the Politburo.

In 1971, BCP chief Todor Zhivkov became the new Bulgarian head of state, which left Todorov as prime minister and head of the Council of Ministers. Over the next ten years, he improved relations with the Federal Republic of Germany (FRG, West Germany) in an attempt to stimulate trade with the West. He resigned as council president and prime minister in 1981 to become parliamentary president. In 1988 he was ousted from the Politburo. By then, he had become a proponent of Mikhail Gorbachev's perestroika policies although favoring a more gradual approach than that of the Soviet Union. Todorov's support of perestroika no doubt marginalized him within the BCP. As communist regimes began to fall in Central Europe, he was reelected to parliament in 1990. His health quickly failed, however, and he withdrew from public life within months of election. Todorov died in Sofia on 17 December 1996.

Luc Stenger

See also
Bulgaria; Comecon; Europe, Eastern; Gorbachev, Mikhail; Perestroika; Zhivkov, Todor
References
Hristov, Hristo. *A History of Bulgaria.* Sofia: Sofia Press, 1995.
Starr, Richard F. *Communist Regimes in Eastern Europe.* Stanford, CA: Hoover Institution Press, 1988.
Todorov, Stanko. *Do vurkhovete na vlastta: Politicheski memoari* [At the Summit of Power: Political Memoirs]. Sofia: Izdatelska kushta "Kristo Botev," 1995.

Togliatti, Palmiro (1893–1964)

Italian politician and general secretary of the Italian Communist Party (PCI) during 1927–1964. Born in Genoa on 26 March 1893, Palmiro Togliatti graduated from the University of Turin in 1915 with a degree in law. While a student there, he joined the Italian Socialist Party (PSI). He served as an officer in the Italian Army health corps in World War I.

In 1917 Togliatti became a reporter for the socialist press. After the war, in 1919 he helped establish the left-wing weekly *L'Ordine Nuoro* (The New Order) and, together with Antonio Gramsci, Togliatti bolted from the PSI in 1921 and founded the PCI, becoming a member of its Central Committee in 1922. Arrested repeatedly and held for brief periods, in 1926

Palmiro Togliatti was one of the founders of the Italian Communist Party. As its general secretary during 1927–1964, Togliatti built the party into the most powerful communist party in Western Europe. (Library of Congress)

Togliatti left Italy for the Soviet Union to escape fascism, becoming secretary of the PCI in 1927. He fought briefly in the Spanish Civil War of 1936–1939. In Moscow, he became closely associated with Soviet dictator Josef Stalin.

During his exile, Togliatti studied the phenomenon of fascism as a mass movement. This and his reading of Gramsci's theories on hegemony guided his postwar leadership of the PCI. His policies helped turn the PCI into a political force that appealed to many Italians. In April 1944, in the wake of negotiations between the Soviets and the Pietro Badoglio government, Togliatti returned to Italy and declared his willingness to unite the PCI with other antifascist forces to accomplish the liberation of the country, postponing to the end of the war any decision on the institutional future of Italy.

The importance of the PCI in the delicate balance of Italian politics increased when Togliatti made clear that his party would follow a parliamentary rather than a revolutionary road to socialism. He saw the continuation of the wartime alliance with other antifascist forces—particularly the Christian Democrats (DC)—as the best way to establish the PCI as a legitimate political force. His efforts were shattered, however, by the deepening Cold War and the 1947 expulsion of the PCI from the government. Thereafter, the party followed a more

confrontational course, albeit without returning to revolutionary tactics. The PCI's 1948 electoral defeat prevented it from returning to power but nevertheless left it as the main opposition force to the DC for the next forty years.

After escaping a 1948 assassination attempt, Togliatti aimed at establishing the party at the grassroots level. He was somewhat critical of Soviet leader Nikita Khrushchev's denunciation of Stalin in 1956 and he condemned the Hungarian uprising while walking a delicate balance of trying to encourage some autonomy for the party within the limits of a strong loyalty to the Moscow. Togliatti expressed his policy of autonomy in the Yalta memorandum, the last document he wrote before his death at Yalta on 24 August 1964 while vacationing in the Crimea.

Leopoldo Nuti

See also
Berlinguer, Enrico; De Gasperi, Alcide; Italy; Nenni, Pietro
References
Agosti, Aldo. *Palmiro Togliatti.* Torino, Italy: UTET, 1996.
Bocca, Giorgio. *Palmiro Togliatti.* 2 vols. Rome, Italy: L'Unità, 1992.
Serfaty, Simon, and L. Gray, eds. *The Italian Communist Party Yesterday, Today, and Tomorrow.* Westport, CT: Greenwood, 1980.
Urban, Joan B. *Moscow and the Italian Communist Party: From Togliatti to Berlinguer.* Ithaca, NY: Cornell University Press, 1986.

Tökés, László (1952–)

Protestant minister of Hungarian ancestry residing in Transylvania (Romania) who helped trigger the overthrow of the Romanian government of Nicolae Ceauşescu in 1989. Born on 1 April 1952 in Cluj, Romania, László Tökés graduated from the Protestant Theological Institute in 1975. During 1975–1984 he worked as an assistant pastor in Braşov and Dej. In 1984 he was discharged from his duties for political reasons.

In 1986 Tökés was reinstalled in Timişoara, first as chaplain and then as pastor of a small Hungarian Reformed church. In November 1989 the Reformed Church of Romania, under pressure from the Romanian Communist Party, decided to banish him from Timişoara and threatened him with deportation. Residents of Timişoara soon began gathering outside Tökés's residence to demonstrate their support for him. On 15 December 1989, the police broke through the crowd, seized Tökés, and exiled him to Mineu, Romania. The crowd then moved to the main square of the city, where the demonstration evolved into a full-scale assault against the Romanian communist government during 16–20 December 1989, interrupted by military intervention that left 122 dead. Rioting there led to violence in Bucharest, culminating in the collapse of the communist regime in Romania on 22 December.

In 1990 Tökés was appointed bishop of the Királyhágó-mellék Diocese in Romania and commenced doctoral studies at the Theological Academy in Debrecen, Hungary. During 1990–1991 he studied in the United States. He is the honorary president of both the Democratic Union of Ethnic Hungarians in Romania and the Hungarian World Federation. In recognition of his commitment to democracy and the role he played in Romanian politics, in 1999 the Hungarian government awarded Tökés the Grand Cross of the Republic of Hungary.

Anna Boros-McGee

See also
Ceauşescu, Nicolae; Europe, Eastern; Grósz, Károly; Hungary; Németh, Miklós; Romania
References
Corley, Felix. *In the Eye of the Romanian Storm: The Heroic Story of Pastor László Tökés.* Old Tappan, NJ: F. H. Revell, 1990.
Tökés, László. *The Fall of Tyrants: The Incredible Story of One Pastor's Witness, the People of Romania, and the Overthrow of Ceausescu.* Wheaton, IL: Crossway Books, 1990.

Tomášek, František (1899–1992)

Archbishop of Prague. František Tomášek was born in Studénka, Moravia, on 30 June 1899, the son of a teacher. He served in the Austro-Hungarian Army during World War I, after which he entered the Roman Catholic seminary in Olomouc. He was ordained in 1922. He received two doctorates in theology from and taught at the Theological Faculty of Saints Cyril and Methodius in Olomouc before the Germans and later the communists closed the school in 1940 and 1948, respectively.

Shortly after Tomášek became bishop of Buto and auxiliary bishop of Olomouc in 1949, Czechoslovak authorities arrested him on antigovernment charges and sent him to a labor camp. Following his release in 1954, he served as a parish priest until 1965. The Czechoslovak government permitted him to attend the Vatican Council II in Rome during 1962–1965.

When the communists refused to allow Archbishop Josef Beran to return to Prague from Rome in 1965, Tomášek became the apostolic administrator of the archdiocese. He supported the 1968 Prague Spring reforms, attempted to revitalize the Roman Catholic Church in Czechoslovakia, and urged religious freedom. After the Warsaw Pact invasion ended the Prague Spring, he discreetly sought concessions from the government and openly criticized Charter 77, much to the dismay of Czechoslovak dissidents.

In 1976 Pope Paul VI secretly named Tomášek cardinal and archbishop of Prague, publicly releasing the news in 1977. With the election of Pope John Paul II in October 1978,

Tomášek attacked the government-sanctioned organization of priests in Czechoslovakia and, in 1985, led the celebrations of the 1,100th anniversary of the death of St. Methodius.

In 1988, Tomášek supported a petition demanding religious freedom in Czechoslovakia and actively backed the 1989 Velvet Revolution by celebrating the first televised mass in Czechoslovakia, on 21 November 1989. In 1990 he hosted John Paul II's visit to Czechoslovakia. Tomášek retired in 1991 and died in Prague on 4 August 1992.

Gregory C. Ference

See also
Beran, Josef; Charter 77; Czechoslovakia; Prague Spring
References
Prague Winter: Restrictions on Religious Freedom in Czechoslovakia Twenty Years after the Soviet Invasion. Washington, DC: Puebla Institute, 1988.
Hartman, Jan. *Kardinál Tomášek Generál bez vojska?* [Cardinal Tomášek: A General without an Army?]. Prague: Vyšehrad, 2003.

Tonkin Gulf Incidents and Resolution (August 1964)

On 2 August 1964, Democratic Republic of Vietnam (DRV, North Vietnam) torpedo boats attacked the U.S. Navy destroyer *Maddox* while it was on a DESOTO electronic intelligence–gathering patrol in international waters in the Gulf of Tonkin some 28 miles off the North Vietnamese coast. This was probably the consequence of two Republic of Vietnam (RVN, South Vietnam) PT boat attacks on 31 July, a fact unknown to Captain John Herrick of the *Maddox*. The South Vietnamese PT boat raids were part of OPLAN (operations plan) 34A harassment activities run by the Military Assistance Command, Vietnam (MACV), against North Vietnam.

Captain Herrick sought approval from commander of U.S. forces in the Pacific Admiral Ulysses Grant Sharp to terminate his patrol. Sharp feared that this might call into question U.S. resolve or the right to steam in international waters, and he secured permission from the Joint Chiefs of Staff (JCS) to strengthen the patrol by adding a second destroyer, the *Turner Joy,* to Herrick's command.

On 3 August another OPLAN 34A raid took place, and on the next night Herrick reported a possible torpedo boat attack on the two destroyers. Almost all of those on the two destroyers believed that an attack of up to two hours had occurred, but there were no visual sightings of North Vietnamese patrol craft in the area. Only hours after learning of the American claim of a second attack, the North Vietnamese government issued a public denial, a position that it has maintained ever since.

In February 1968, U.S. Secretary of Defense Robert S. McNamara testified before the Senate Foreign Relations

Committee in closed session and said that he had "un-impeachable" proof of a second attack. In November 1995, however, he met with General Vo Nguyen Giap, former North Vietnamese defense minister, in Hanoi. Giap confirmed the first attack, which he said was the work of "a local coast guard unit," but he denied that there had been any second attack. He also charged President Lyndon Johnson's administration with a deliberate plan to fabricate the attack in order to seek the approval of Congress for the war.

Undoubtedly, there was no attack on 4 August. The reports of it are probably attributable to stormy weather, evasive maneuvering, and inexperienced and fatigued radar and sonar operators. On the other hand, there is no evidence to support Giap's charge that the Johnson administration knowingly faked the incident to escalate the war. It was a genuine mistake rather than a deliberate deception.

In Washington, President Johnson and U.S. military leaders did not want the North Vietnamese leadership to equate lack of U.S. response with lack of resolve, especially as Johnson was then locked in an election campaign against Republican hawk and airpower advocate Senator Barry Goldwater. Secure in his belief of an attack, Johnson also wanted to be able to announce a U.S. military response on the evening television news. Despite a radio message from Herrick that "review of action makes many reported contacts and torpedoes fired appear doubtful" and a later message to Sharp that "details of action present a confusing picture," on 5 August Johnson ordered Operation PIERCE ARROW, a retaliatory U.S. Navy strike against North Vietnamese coastal naval facilities.

As it turned out, Johnson's public announcement came before some of the U.S. aircraft from the carriers *Ticonderoga* and *Constellation* had reached their targets—oil storage tanks and torpedo boat bases at Thanh Hoa, Hoa Ngu, Vinh, and Quang Khe. U.S. aircraft flew sixty-four sorties. Two planes were shot down, with one pilot killed and the other captured.

Even before the incidents, Johnson had told congressional leaders of his intention to seek a resolution of support for his Southeast Asia policy. Such a request reached Congress on 5 August. Two days later, Congress passed the Tonkin Gulf Resolution by a vote of 416–0 in the House and 88–2 in the Senate.

The resolution styled North Vietnamese attacks on U.S. ships as "part of a deliberate and systematic campaign of aggression . . . against its neighbors and the nations joined with them in the collective defense of their freedom." It authorized the president to take those steps necessary "to repel any armed attack against the forces of the United States and to prevent any further aggression." It also held that the United States regarded the maintenance of peace and security in Southeast Asia as "vital to the national interest and to world peace" and was thus "prepared, as the president determines, to take all necessary steps, including the use of armed force, to assist any member or protocol state of the Southeast Asia Collective Defense Treaty requesting assistance in defense of its freedom."

In effect what became known as the Tonkin Gulf Resolution gave Johnson blanket authority to wage war in Vietnam without a formal declaration of war. Contrary to later charges, the implications of the resolution were fully, albeit briefly, aired before the vote.

Following the public revelation of President Richard M. Nixon's clandestine bombing of Cambodia, Congress rescinded the resolution in June 1970. In 1973, Congress passed the War Powers Act, which quite specifically prescribed the president's power to wage war and the role of Congress in any such endeavor. Unlike the carte blanche wording of the Tonkin Gulf Resolution, the War Powers Act was very deliberate in its attempt to avoid another Vietnam.

Spencer C. Tucker

See also
Johnson, Lyndon Baines; Nixon, Richard Milhous; Vietnam War
References
Herring, George C. *America's Longest War: The United States and Vietnam, 1950–1975.* 4th ed. New York: McGraw-Hill, 2001.
Moïse, Edwin E. *Tonkin Gulf and the Escalation of the Vietnam War.* Chapel Hill: University of North Carolina Press, 1996.
Tucker, Spencer C. *Vietnam.* Lexington: University Press of Kentucky, 1999.

Touré, Ahmed Sékou (1922–1984)

Nationalist African premier (1958) and president (1959–1984) of the Republic of Guinea. Born in Faranah, Guinea, on 9 January 1922 to a poor family, Ahmed Sékou Touré worked for the postal service and helped organize a union of its workers in 1945, which he then headed. In 1952 he became the head of the Partie Démocratique de Guinée (PDG, Democratic Party of Guinea). In 1954 he was elected president of the General Confederation of African Workers, and in January 1956 he was elected mayor of the capital city of Conakry and Guinea's representative to the French National Assembly. In November 1957 he became vice premier of Guinea, and in July 1958 he became premier.

In May 1958, the French Fourth Republic had collapsed and Charles de Gaulle came to power. The new constitution of the Fifth Republic established the French Community in place of the former French Union, and de Gaulle called on the French African states to vote on the new constitutional arrangement. A vote of no would mean independence. With much of French Africa desperately poor and dependent on aid from Paris, the vote was expected to be favorable.

Touré opposed membership in the French Community, however. He claimed that "dignity" was more important, and

Ahmed Sékou Touré, the nationalist who became the first president of independent Guinea in 1959. His defiant attitude ended ties with France. (UPI-Bettmann/Corbis)

the end of the 1970s, he established closer relations with the Muslim world and cemented relationships with those states and with Islamic organizations. His hold on power was weakened by two assassination attempts, in June 1969 and April 1971. Constantly reelected president (for the fifth time in 1982), Touré was visiting Saudi Arabia when he became ill from a heart aliment. He preferred to go to the United States for treatment and died in Cleveland, Ohio, on 24 March 1984.

Spencer C. Tucker

See also
Africa; France
References
Adamolekun, 'Ladipo. *Sekou Toure's Guinea: An Experiment in Nation Building.* London: Methuen, 1976.
Diallo, A. A. *La Vérité du ministre: Dix ans dans les Geôles de Sékou Touré.* Paris: Calmann-Lévy, 1985.
Marton, Imre. *The Political Thought of President Ahmed Sekou Touré.* Conakry, Guinea: Press Office, 1977.
Skurnik, W. A. E. *African Political Thought: Lumumba, Nkrumah, Touré.* Denver, CO: University of Denver, 1968.

that there could "be no dignity without true liberty." The community would still mean a degree of French control, and as Touré put it, "We prefer poverty in freedom to riches in slavery." The charismatic Touré helped stay the vote in Guinea. On 28 September 1958, Guinea was the only state in French Africa to vote against the constitution. The negative vote was by an overwhelming 95 percent majority.

Guinea received its independence on 2 October 1958. In national elections that same year, Touré's PDG won fifty-seven of sixty seats. He became president of Guinea in January 1959. He then pushed through a new constitution that made the PDG the sole legal political party.

Touré immediately moved Guinea into the socialist camp. Relations with France deteriorated and were broken off altogether in 1965, not to be renewed until 1975. In 1978 French President Valéry Giscard d'Éstaing undertook a state trip to Guinea, and Touré reciprocated with a visit to Paris in 1982.

Touré sought to follow a nonaligned foreign policy. Thus, during the Cuban Missile Crisis of 1962, he refused to allow Soviet aircraft to refuel in Guinea during flights to Cuba. At

Transylvania

During the Cold War, a part of Romania bounded to the north and east by the Carpathian Mountains, the Transylvanian Alps to the south, and the Alpuseni Mountains to the west. An area of some 21,000 square miles, Transylvania became part of Hungary by 1911. In the 1920 Treaty of Trianon, the victorious Allies forced defeated Hungary to cede Transylvania to Romania. In order to reward Hungary for acceding to the Axis, German dictator Adolf Hitler in the Second Vienna Accord of August 1940 restored northern Transylvania to Hungary. When Romania withdrew from the Axis in August 1944, declared war on Germany, and signed an armistice with the Soviet Union, the restitution of northern Transylvania was part of the agreement. It was formally restored to Romania in the Paris peace treaties of 1947.

Transylvania's population in 1948 was 3.75 million Romanians, 1.48 million Hungarians, 331,000 Germans, and 30,000 Jews. Roma and other ethnic groups made up 197,000. Many thousands of Germans and Jews who had not fled or been exterminated during World War II left Transylvania during the communist era. By 1977, only 8,000 Jews remained, and by 1989, just 130,000 Germans were left. The Hungarian minority was thus the main target of what Romanian President Nicolae Ceaușescu called homogenization, whereby migration, chiefly into Hungarian areas, altered the population balance. Although the 1948 constitution promised Hungarian language and educational rights and a Hungarian Autonomous Region was established in 1952, Hungarian rights were soon curtailed, particularly after the 1956 Hungarian

Revolution. In 1959, the Hungarian Bolyai University of Cluj merged with the Romanian Babeş University, and in 1968 the autonomous region was eliminated. Decrees in the 1970s narrowed Hungarian educational opportunities, limited the size of Hungarian newspapers, and made all archival materials state property and subject to collection and confiscation.

By signing the 1975 Helsinki Final Act, Ceauşescu opened himself to international criticism. From 1977 on, protests grew, and many were brutally silenced by the Securitate (secret police). Nevertheless, letters from Károly Király, a prominent member of the Romanian Communist Party (PCR), reached the Committee for Human Rights in Romania (CHRR), established in New York City to monitor violations of the Helsinki agreements. Király was forced into internal exile. Ethnic conflict was exacerbated in the 1980s with the launch of underground periodicals and a spate of anti-Hungarian literature. Soviet and Hungarian government officials began to criticize Romanian treatment of minorities. During his May 1987 visit to Romania, Soviet Premier Mikhail Gorbachev stressed the need for friendship among ethnic groups. The following year, however, Ceauşescu's systematization campaign, whereby villages were razed and their inhabitants resettled in agro-industrial complexes, led to a massive anti-Romanian demonstration in Budapest. Ceauşescu responded by closing the Cluj Hungarian consulate and expelling a Hungarian delegate from Bucharest. Concurrently, a steady flow of Transylvanian refugees, mainly Hungarian, entered Hungary in numbers that peaked at 25,000 during the first eight months of 1989.

Fittingly, the revolt that toppled the Ceauşescu regime began in Transylvania, where a vigil in support of László Tökés, a dissident Reformed Church pastor in Timişoara, turned into a major demonstration during 16–20 December 1989, interrupted briefly by military intervention that left 122 dead. Inspired by the events in Timişoara, an uprising in Bucharest two days later led to the flight, arrest, and execution of Ceauşescu on 25 December 1989.

Relations between Romania and Hungary improved markedly following a 1996 bilateral treaty in which each state renounced any territorial claims on the other and committed both to respecting the rights of ethnic minorities.

Anna M. Wittmann

See also
Ceauşescu, Nicolae; Gorbachev, Mikhail; Helsinki Final Act; Hungarian Revolution; Hungary; Romania; Securitate; Tökés, László

References
Cadzow, John F., et al., eds. *Transylvania: The Roots of Ethnic Conflict.* Kent, OH: Kent State University Press, 1983.
Joó, Rudolf, and Andrew Ludanyi, eds. Translated by Chris Tennant. *The Hungarian Minority's Situation in Ceauşescu's Romania.* Boulder, CO: Westview, 1994.

Triad

U.S. strategic nuclear force comprised of three components: manned bombers, land-based intercontinental ballistic missiles (ICBMs), and submarine-launched ballistic missiles (SLBMs). The nuclear delivery capability of the United States originally relied upon the long-range bomber force of the Strategic Air Command (SAC). During the late 1950s, the strategic delivery force began to expand to include U.S. Air Force–controlled ICBMs and the U.S. Navy's SLBMs. The early triad structure was a natural evolution of new technological capabilities, but military planners also developed a strong strategic rationale based on the realities of each type of weapon system and the need to create a stable deterrent force structure.

The manned bomber force was the most accurate delivery platform. Additionally, bombers provided the most flexibility. Aircraft could be launched or forward-deployed as a show of force, and having a crew in the loop allowed bombers to be recalled or redirected while in flight. The bombers could also conduct visual assessments of targets or search for specific types of targets in a general area to counter new or mobile targets. But bombers had major vulnerabilities. They could be attacked before they launched, especially by missiles, and the aircraft were relatively vulnerable to air defense systems. Bombers were also relatively slow, taking many hours to deliver nuclear weapons over intercontinental ranges.

The ICBM force provided the capability for rapid strikes against enemy targets, with flight times of approximately thirty minutes, and the ability to maintain a large percentage of the force in a high-alert status. Although the land-based missiles were potentially vulnerable due to their fixed locations, they could be launched relatively quickly before being hit and were often placed in hardened silos for protection. Mobile ICBM options were developed in response to improved Soviet accuracy but were not deployed. Early ICBMs were much less accurate than bombers, although the differences were significantly reduced over time. The submarine force was the most survivable of the three systems. Although communications with the submarines were initially a concern and accuracies were initially below those of the other two legs of the triad, these performance issues were steadily rectified over time.

The triad's offensive capability was melded together in the Single Integrated Operations Plan by the Joint Strategic Target Planning Staff, which was colocated with SAC headquarters. The use of different weapons delivery platforms complicated the defensive preparations of the Soviet Union, the primary target of American strategic nuclear planning.

More importantly, the varying characteristics of the three weapons systems made an effective enemy attack, especially a surprise attack, much more difficult. Although the Soviet force structure was also referred to as a triad, that structure was much less balanced and relied heavily on land-based ICBMs, with a secondary capability in SLBMs, and a limited long-range bomber force. The American triad and its contribution to nuclear deterrence was the foundation of geopolitical stability and military balance during the Cold War.

Jerome V. Martin

See also

Bombers, Strategic; Missiles, Intercontinental Ballistic; Missiles, Polaris; Missiles, Poseidon; Missiles, Submarine-Launched Ballistic; United States Air Force

References

Arkin, William M., Thomas B. Cochran, and Milton M. Hoenig. *U.S. Nuclear Forces and Capabilities,* Vol. 1, *Nuclear Weapons Databook.* Cambridge, MA: Ballinger, 1983.

Collins, John M. *U.S.-Soviet Military Balance: Concepts and Capabilities, 1960–1980.* New York: McGraw-Hill, 1980.

Kahan, Jerome H. *Security in the Nuclear Age: Developing U.S. Strategic Arms Policy.* Washington, DC: Brookings Institution Press, 1975.

Trieste

Italian city at the northern head of the Adriatic Sea near the border with Yugoslavia (now Slovenia and Croatia) whose sovereignty was hotly contested between Italy and Yugoslavia. Securing Trieste from the Austro-Hungarian Empire was one of the main objectives of Italian intervention in World War I, which explains the emotion bound with its name among many Italians. Mainly surrounded by hills that have limited its size, Trieste became important when it was occupied at the end of World War II by the Yugoslav Partisans, led by veteran communist Josip Broz Tito. Meanwhile, the British and Americans pushed the 2nd New Zealand Armored Division to Trieste to prevent Yugoslavia from securing full control of the city's important harbor. Some observers saw in this development the first sign of the forthcoming Cold War.

The Yugoslav occupation elicited violence against the majority Italian population and against noncommunist Slovenians, but an agreement brokered between the British and Tito's representatives on 8 August 1945 restored at least partial order. The former Italian territory now under Yugoslav control was divided into two areas by the Morgan Line. The British and Americans occupied the western zone comprising Trieste Harbor, and the Yugoslavs controlled the eastern territory, which contained important strategic natural resources such as mercury, bauxite, and coal.

Trieste straddled two worlds: the Eastern communist bloc and the Western democratic bloc. Certainly, the Soviet Union supported communist Yugoslavia's claims on the region. For their part, the Allies actually encouraged Tito in the sense that they assisted him economically and diplomatically following his 1948 break with the Soviet Union.

The Yugoslavs reinforced their troop presence in the area, and in 1951 the Italians deployed the first groups of former partisans in a covert stay-behind organization known as "O," which later would be integrated into the Gladio organization under the control of the Central Intelligence Agency (CIA) and the North Atlantic Treaty Organization (NATO).

In the Paris Peace Treaty signed on 10 February 1947 between Italy and the Allies, Yugoslavia secured the Istrian Peninsula, forcing some 250,000 Italians to abandon the area and find refuge in Italy. The Trieste area was designated a Free Territory under the administration of the United Nations (UN). Meanwhile, Yugoslavs killed perhaps 10,000 Italians in the *foibe* (karstic sinkholes), which were effective natural cemeteries.

Because neither Italy nor Yugoslavia could agree on a governor for Trieste, the area was divided into area "A" (from Duino to Trieste) and area "B" (Capodistria to Cittanova). On several occasions, the Italian population of Trieste protested against the Allied occupation, resulting in civilian fatalities when British troops overreacted to the demonstrations. At the same time, Yugoslavia continued to threaten the annexation of area "B."

According to some historians, the Italian government mounted covert paramilitary operations in Istria that were designed to discourage Yugoslavia's aspirations and plans regarding annexation. The Trieste crisis also played an important role in Italian domestic politics because it fueled Italian right-wing movements. Several youth organizations volunteered to mount strong protests against Tito and the Allied occupation of the city.

Finally, an agreement was signed in London on 10 May 1954 stipulating that Istria was to be administered by Yugoslavia and Trieste by Italy, with mutual respect of minority rights. This led to the Anglo-American withdrawal of troops from Trieste, which now passed to Italian sovereignty. On 10 December 1975, Italy and Yugoslavia signed the Osimo Treaty that finalized the border permanently with only a few slight modifications.

The dissolution of Yugoslavia after the Velvet Revolution of 1989–1990 did not change the Trieste situation. In June 1991, war broke out in the former Yugoslav territories, which led to the end of the Yugoslav federal state, as Croatia and Slovenia gained their independence. Both declared that they

A young resident of Trieste waves the Italian tricolor flag, celebrating the return of that port city to Italy, 10 October 1954. (Bettmann/Corbis)

would respect the Yugoslav state's legacy and would therefore honor the Osimo Treaty. Italian Foreign Minister Emilio Colombo expressed Italy's satisfaction with this decision.

Alessandro Massignani

See also
Gladio; Italy; Paris Peace Conference and Treaties; Tito, Josip Broz; Yugoslavia

References
Brogi, Alessandro. *A Question of Self-Esteem: The United States and the Cold War Choices in France and Italy, 1944–1958.* Westport, CT: Praeger, 2002.

De Leonardis, Massimo. *La diplomazia "Atlantica" e la soluzione del problema di Trieste (1952–1954).* [Atlantic Diplomacy and the Resolution of the Trieste Problem (1952–1954)]. Naples, Italy: Esi, 1992.

Rabel, Roberto G. *Between East and West: Trieste, the United States and the Cold War, 1941–1954.* Durham, NC: Duke University Press, 1988.

Trilateral Commission

Private, nonpartisan, multinational organization founded in 1973 that advises and supplements the work of national governments and international organizations with the goal of increasing interregional and international cooperation, particularly in the areas of economic development and globalization. In 1973, a group of influential American citizens decided that the world's industrialized democracies had to bring more coherence and cooperation to the international system, which at the time was experiencing severe economic and political dislocations. The founding member of the Trilateral Commission, David Rockefeller, who controlled much of the Rockefeller family fortune and worldwide empire, decided to establish the commission upon reading national security expert Zbigniew Brzezinski's *Between Two Ages* (1971), which called for an alliance among Europe, North America, and Japan to stabilize a rapidly changing world.

At the time, governments were not cooperating as closely as they had in the first two decades of the Cold War. America's economic and political dominance was slipping, the bipolarity of the Cold War was giving way to a multipolar international system, and nations such as Japan were becoming economic superpowers in their own right. Meanwhile, the Soviet Union's military power seemed to be growing; Cuba was promoting and supporting insurgencies in Africa; oil-producing nations, especially in the Middle East, were dominating the world economy; and Western Europe seemed to be fragmenting. The Trilateral Commission's original members represented Europe, Japan, Canada, and the United States.

Rockefeller had held a series of meetings in 1972 to broach the idea of the Trilateral Commission to the international Bilderberg Group. Sensing agreement that the commission was a necessary counterbalance to the rapid changes in the world's geopolitical system, Rockefeller and Brzezinski handpicked the first members, including Jimmy Carter, who proceeded to appoint trilateralists to key government positions when he became president in 1977. Carter also promoted the trilateralist agenda during his four-year term in office. The commission formally began in November 1973.

By the commission's thirtieth anniversary, the international system had become fully globalized. Over the years, the Trilateral Commission broadened its membership, with the Japan Group becoming the Pacific Asian Group. Mexico joined North America, and the European Union (EU) group matched the enlarging EU itself. Members also represent specialized areas, not just nations or regions.

The commission has 350 members from the public sector, academia, organized labor, business, nongovernmental organizations (NGOs), and the media. Prominent members at one time or another have included Carter, Bill Clinton, Henry Kissinger, and other influential politicians and businesspeople. Commission members meet annually and issue reports that the commission later publishes.

Conspiracy theorists have asserted that the Trilateral Commission is the means by which the ruling class maintains its power and prevents the changing world from usurping its power and wealth. Some argue that it controls the leaders of emerging nations, for instance, to ensure that they do not upset the system by redistributing wealth or power. The conspiracy theorists view the Trilateral Commission as a dark and sinister cabal controlling the world by creating a police state devoted to the interests of world capitalism or, more familiarly, the New World Order. Some right-wing Christian fundamentalist groups claim that the Trilateral Commission is really a shadow government that works in tandem with the United Nations (UN) to bring about a world government.

Such theories do not hold up. The work of the Trilateral Commission has proven to be a helpful endeavor for nations and supranational organizations around the world.

John H. Barnhill

See also
Brzezinski, Zbigniew; Carter, James Earl, Jr.; Kissinger, Henry
References
Brzezinski, Zbigniew. *Between Two Ages.* New York: Viking, 1971.
Gill, Stephen. *American Hegemony and the Trilateral Commission.* New York: Cambridge University Press, 1990.
Sklar, Holly, ed. *Trilateralism, the Trilateral Commission, and Elite Planning for World Management.* Boston: South End Press, 1980.

Trudeau, Pierre (1919–2000)

Canadian Liberal Party politician and prime minister (1968–1979, 1980–1984). Born in Montreal on 18 October 1919, Pierre Elliott Trudeau received his BA degree from College Jean de Brébeuf in 1940 and earned a law degree in 1943 from the University of Montreal and a master's degree in political economy from Harvard University in 1945. After working chiefly as a lawyer and law professor, he was elected to the Canadian House of Commons in 1965. In 1967 he became both minister of justice and attorney general in the Lester Pearson cabinet. In 1968, Trudeau became prime minister and leader of the Liberal Party. With the exception of a brief ten-month interlude during 1979–1980, he remained prime minister until 1984, casting a long shadow on Canadian politics that endures to this day.

As prime minister, Trudeau sought increased independence from U.S. political and economic hegemony. As such, his government frequently parted company with the United States on foreign policy. In 1970 the Trudeau government officially recognized the People's Republic of China (PRC), and Trudeau embarked on a lifelong campaign for nuclear disarmament, leading efforts to ensure nuclear nonproliferation. Also in 1970, faced with terrorist attacks by the radical Quebecois separatist group Front de la libération de Québec (Liberation Front of Quebec), Trudeau briefly invoked martial law to diffuse the crisis. Although quite popular, he weathered several political storms throughout the 1970s, many of which revolved around economic policy. As with other Western nations in that era, Canada experienced periods of high unemployment and inflation, made worse by the 1973–1974 oil crisis.

Perhaps Trudeau's most significant impact as it relates to the Cold War was to distance Canada from the Western orbit so as to become more involved in the developing world. In doing so, the Trudeau government left Canada's armed forces chronically underfunded, much to the chagrin of the United States and the North Atlantic Treaty Organization (NATO). By the late 1970s, Trudeau's vision of a quasi-neutral Canada was shaken by its NATO partners, who had begun to suggest that if Canada did not wish to participate in collective security, then Europe might look elsewhere when it came to trade. Thus, in the early 1980s small increases in defense spending were implemented to mollify the Europeans and Americans. In 1983, however, when he undertook his Peace Initiative, convinced that the world stood at the brink of nuclear war, he once more raised the hackles of Canada's defense partners. Trudeau retired from politics in 1984 and died on 28 September 2000 in Montreal.

Paul G. Pierpaoli Jr.

See also
Canada; North Atlantic Treaty Organization, Origins and Formation of

References
Cuthbertson, Brian. *Canadian Military Independence in the Age of the Superpowers.* Toronto: Fitzhenry and Whiteside, 1977.

Granatstein, J. L., and Robert Bothwell. *Pirouette: Pierre Trudeau and Canadian Foreign Policy.* Toronto: University of Toronto Press, 1990.

Trudeau, Pierre Elliot. *Memoirs.* Toronto: McClelland and Stuart, 1993.

Rafael Trujillo was the dominant political figure of the Dominican Republic from 1930 to 1961. Trujillo's strong anticommunist stance engendered support from the United States, despite his despotic rule. (Library of Congress)

Trujillo, Rafael Leónidas (1891–1961)

President and dictator of the Dominican Republic (1930–1938, 1942–1952). Born in San Cristóbal on 24 October 1891, Rafael Leónidas Trujillo received only a rudimentary education. Trained by U.S. Marines during the American occupation of the Dominican Republic (1916–1924), he rose in 1925 to the rank of colonel in the National Guard, which the Americans had helped establish. In 1927 he was promoted to the rank of brigadier general.

Trujillo came to power in 1930 after a coup against President Horacio Vásquez. Almost immediately, Trujillo put in place a repressive dictatorial regime and promoted a cult of personality that rivaled any of the world's worst despots. He tried to modernize the country, but widespread graft and corruption in his government blunted the effort. In an attempt to "lighten" the population, he invited Jews to immigrate to the Dominican Republic and ordered the purging of Haitian workers. During 1937 alone, he was responsible for the deaths of some 15,000 Haitians.

Trujillo, a rabid anticommunist, allowed the Dominican Communist Party (PCD) to exist until 1947, when at the suggestion of the United States he outlawed the party. He gained financial support from the United States and other Western nations to modernize the Dominican Republic but also siphoned off vast amounts of government funds for his personal use. Through his extended family—much of which reaped a small fortune from his financial shenanigans— Trujillo controlled most of the nation's industry and commerce. It is worth noting that while he held the presidency in name for some eighteen years, he was firmly in control at all times, preferring to work behind the scenes while a pliant puppet occupied the post of president. Trujillo enjoyed the support of the island's powerful "100 Families" until 1960, when he ordered the three socialite Mirabal sisters killed for their part in a plot against him.

The year 1960 also saw Trujillo lose the support of some of his powerful international patrons, including the United States. His henchmen were nearly successful in assassinating Venezuelan President Rómulo Betancourt in 1960, forcing the United States to withdraw much of its support to the Dominican Republic. On 30 May 1961, members of the Dominican military assassinated Trujillo in Ciudad Trujillo (Santo Domingo). His son Ramfis tried to assume power but was exiled following a coup. Nonetheless, Trujillo's supporters continued to exercise power in the country until well beyond the Cold War era. Joaquín Balaguer, who had served under Trujillo, secured the presidency several times until the United Nations (UN) brokered a deal forcing him to step down permanently in 1996.

Paul G. Pierpaoli Jr. and David H. Richards

See also
Balaguer Ricart, Joaquín Antonio; Dominican Republic
References
Roorda, Eric Paul. *The Dictator Next Door: The Good Neighbor Policy and the Trujillo Regime in the Dominican Republic, 1930–1945.* Durham, NC: Duke University Press, 1998.
Wiarda, Howard J. *Dictatorship and Development: The Methods of Control in Trujillo's Dominican Republic.* Gainesville: University of Florida Press, 1970.

Truman, Harry S. (1884–1972)

U.S. senator (1935–1944), vice president (January–April 1945), and president (1945–1953). Born in Lamar, Missouri, on 8 May 1884, Harry S. Truman worked as a construction timekeeper, bank teller, and farmer before seeing combat in World War I as an artillery captain in France. He then opened a clothing store in Kansas City, but it soon failed, leaving him with large debts. He won election as county judge in 1922 with the backing of the political machine of Tom Pendergast in nearby Kansas City. Truman's record of efficiency and fair-mindedness earned him considerable praise. A Democrat, he was elected to the U.S. Senate in 1934, where colleagues appreciated his hard work, modesty, and amiability. Reelected in 1940, he gained national prominence during World War II as chair of a Senate committee investigating corporate waste, bureaucratic incompetence, contractor fraud, and labor abuse in the defense industry.

Truman, the surprise choice for the vice presidential candidate on President Franklin D. Roosevelt's successful 1944 reelection ticket, had no international experience when he assumed the presidency upon Roosevelt's death in April 1945. Truman closely guarded his authority and took actions that were decisive and at times impulsive. This was especially true in foreign affairs, where he immediately faced the challenge of emerging discord with the Soviet Union. As a senator,

Democrat Harry Truman became president of the United States in April 1945 following the death of President Franklin Roosevelt. Truman oversaw the end of World War II, took the decision to drop the atomic bomb, and decided to come to the aid of the Republic of Korea (ROK, South Korea) in June 1950. In many ways, his policies helped to shape the postwar world. (Library of Congress)

Truman had favored wartime aid to the Soviets but suggested shifting U.S. support to the Nazis once communist forces had the advantage. Only days into his presidency, he sharply rebuked Soviet Foreign Minister Vyacheslav I. Molotov, sternly lecturing him about trying to dominate Poland. This contretemps was a harbinger of Truman's hard-line policy toward the Soviet Union.

In July 1945, Truman and Soviet leader Josef Stalin met at the Potsdam Conference but did not reach agreement on any major issues. While there, the president received word that the test explosion of an atomic bomb had succeeded, although he only made an ambiguous reference about this to Stalin. Truman subsequently ordered atomic attacks on two Japanese cities in August. His justification was to save lives, but he may have also used Hiroshima and Nagasaki to intimidate the Soviets and keep them out of the Pacific war. Just before Japan surrendered, the Soviets entered the war in the Pacific, resulting in Korea's division into two zones of occupation. Truman rejected Stalin's request for a similar arrangement in Japan, appointing General Douglas MacArthur to implement sweeping reforms there under complete U.S. control. After 1947, a reverse course in U.S. policy transformed Japan into an anticommunist bulwark in Asia and a security partner of the United States in the Cold War.

Meanwhile, Truman struggled to end the civil war in China between the Guomindang (GMD, Nationalists) and the CCP led by Mao Zedong. Late in 1945, Truman sent General George C. Marshall to negotiate a cease-fire and a political settlement, which never took hold. Marshall returned home in early 1947, became secretary of state, and advised Truman to disengage from China. By then, Truman had decided to implement the containment policy against the Soviet Union.

Truman's application of pressure at the United Nations (UN) had forced Soviet withdrawal from Iran in 1946. His Truman Doctrine speech in March 1947 called for U.S. aid to any nation resisting communist domination. Congress then approved Truman's request for $400 million for Greece (to suppress a communist insurgency) and Turkey (to check Soviet advances). A proposal in June 1947 to help Europe avert economic collapse and keep communism at bay led to the Marshall Plan, an ambitious and successful endeavor that helped reconstruct war-torn economies.

Stalin's reaction to Truman's successes greatly intensified the Cold War, beginning early in 1948 with the communist coup in Czechoslovakia. The Soviets then blockaded West Berlin to force U.S. and British abandonment of the city, but Truman ordered an airlift of food and supplies that compelled Stalin to restore access one year later. Countering the Soviet threat led to the 1949 creation of the North Atlantic Treaty Organization (NATO) and a U.S. commitment of military defense for Western Europe. Truman sent U.S. troops and huge amounts of military assistance across the Atlantic, but he refused to replicate this policy in China, resisting Republican pressure to expand support for Jiang Jieshi's Nationalist regime. This led to charges that Truman had allowed disloyal American diplomats to undermine the Nationalists and lose China after the communists triumphed in October 1949. The Soviet explosion of an atomic bomb that September only increased popular anxiety in the United States. As fears of internal subversion grew, Truman appeared to be soft on communism when Senator Joseph R. McCarthy, an obscure Wisconsin Republican, charged that 205 communists worked in the State Department.

Early in 1950, Truman approved development of a hydrogen bomb but initially refused to implement National Security Council Report NSC-68, which called for massive rearmament. He would not approve NSC-68 until September of that year. When the Democratic People's Republic of Korea (DPRK, North Korea) attacked the Republic of Korea (ROK, South Korea) in June, Truman committed troops because he believed that Stalin had ordered the invasion and that inaction would encourage more expansionist acts. He then

ordered military protection for Jiang's regime on Taiwan and greater support for the anticommunist efforts of the British in Malaya and the French in Indochina. Even before MacArthur, whom he had named UN commander, had halted the invasion, Truman approved an offensive into North Korea that provoked Chinese intervention. Truman's courageous decision to recall MacArthur in April 1951 for trying to widen the war was highly unpopular but won acclaim from most military observers and European allies. Armistice talks began in July 1951 but deadlocked after Truman refused to force repatriation of communist prisoners. Unable to end the Korean War, he had made the Cold War more dangerous and intense with the implementation of NSC-68, military strengthening of NATO, and the rearming of the Federal Republic of Germany (FRG, West Germany).

Truman left office in January 1953 and returned to Independence, Missouri, to write his memoirs. He died on 26 December 1972 in Kansas City, Missouri.

James I. Matray

See also

Acheson, Dean Gooderham; Berlin Blockade and Airlift; Chinese Civil War; Containment Policy; Greek Civil War; Korean War; Marshall Mission to China; Marshall Plan; McCarthyism; National Security Council Report NSC-68; North Atlantic Treaty; North Atlantic Treaty Organization, Origins and Formation of; Stalin, Josef; Truman Doctrine; Truman Loyalty Program

References

Donovan, Robert J. *Conflict and Crisis: The Presidency of Harry S. Truman, 1945–1948.* New York: Norton, 1977.
———. *Tumultuous Years: The Presidency of Harry S. Truman, 1949–1953.* New York: Norton, 1982.
Hamby, Alonzo L. *Man of the People: A Life of Harry S. Truman.* New York: Oxford University Press, 1995.
McCullough, David. *Truman.* New York: Simon and Schuster, 1992.

Truman Doctrine (12 March 1947)

U.S. foreign policy doctrine enunciated by President Harry S. Truman that formally committed the United States to fight communist expansionism abroad. On 12 March 1947, President Truman addressed a joint session of Congress and stated: "I believe that it must be the policy of the United States to support free peoples who are resisting attempted subjugation by armed minorities or by outside pressures." He was of course referring to communist "pressures" and thereby committed the United States to uphold the containment policy, which pledged that all necessary measures would be taken to check the spread of communism and Soviet influence.

The catalyst for the Truman Doctrine had been Britain's February 1947 announcement that it could no longer afford to provide military or financial support to Greece and Turkey.

This meant that these nations might fall to communism, and this was especially true for Greece, whose pro-Western government was fighting a communist guerrilla insurgency in the northern part of the country.

The eastern basin of the Mediterranean, including the Middle East, had historically been under British influence since the nineteenth century. The area was still important to Britain after World War II, but it took on great importance in light of the developing Cold War. Soviet presence in the region would jeopardize the ability of the Western powers to launch strategic air strikes on the Soviet Union from bases in the area. The defense of the region had been a British preserve and rested on British military bases, the largest of which was in Egypt. British power was declining, however, while at the same time Soviet activity in the region seemed on the increase.

The Soviet Union had demanded that the Turkish government change the rules governing ship movements through the Dardanelles and allow it to participate, along with other Black Sea nations, in the defense of the straits. The U.S. interpretation of the Soviets' demand was that they intended to secure hegemony over Turkey, build bases there, and then gain control over Greece. From there it could dominate much of the Middle East and the eastern Mediterranean. The demand in itself was of relatively minor importance because it was made in the form of a diplomatic note, not supported by any explicit or implicit military threats.

For planners in Washington, there seemed to be a power vacuum in the region, the result of Britain's declining strength. Britain was providing military aid to Turkey, but the U.S. Joint Chiefs of Staff (JCS) thought that because of its strategic importance and in order to increase its ability to meet Soviet aggression, the United States should increase its economic and military aid to Turkey. As long as the British furnished military assistance, however, the Truman administration would provide only economic aid.

American attitudes toward the situation in Turkey were linked to the situation in Greece. Like Turkey, Greece was considered a barrier between the Soviet Union and the Mediterranean. The struggle in Greece was not one inspired by the Soviet Union but rather resulted from conflict between rightists seeking to restore the monarchy who were also failing to tackle the grave economic situation and left-wing parties seeking to install a communist regime. Washington, however, chose to view the Greek Civil War through the lens of the Cold War. A loss in Greece to the communists would not only result in a victory for the Soviets but, it was argued, would also open the entire region to communist subversion. Thus, the Americans could not tolerate the establishment of a communist regime in Athens whether or not it was inspired by Moscow. Despite the shortcomings of the anticommunist Greek government, the Truman administration now moved to provide assistance to it. The decisive turning point came

with London's announcement in February 1947 that Britain would be unable to continue its support to Greece and Turkey. It was obvious to U.S. State Department officials that the United States had to fill the breach. While preparing the draft legislation for the 1947 Greco-Turkish aid package, however, Undersecretary of State Dean Acheson found it difficult to justify the assistance request for Turkey, as it was not under a direct threat from either the Kremlin or an indigenous communist insurgency. Acheson also knew that Congress was in no mood to approve a large foreign aid request without proper justification, as it was engaged in efforts to curtail spending and pay down the national debt accrued during World War II. Also, Moscow was issuing conciliatory messages, further reducing the incentive in Congress to take strong measures against the Soviet Union.

Truman and his advisors, determined to provide military and economic assistance to both Greece and Turkey, had to find a way to sell this foreign aid package to Congress. Just prior to Truman's speech, Acheson described to the congressional leadership in stark terms the implications of Soviet domination over the eastern Mediterranean and the worldwide geopolitical consequences of such a scenario. In response, Republican Senator Arthur H. Vandenberg, a formerly steadfast isolationist, informed Truman that if he were to present his request to Congress in the manner that had been used by Acheson, he and the majority of Congress would support the aid deal. As a result, Truman's request for a $400 million aid package earmarked for Turkey and Greece was presented in the Cold War terms of a struggle "between alternate ways of life," marking the emergence of the Truman Doctrine, which came to represent a concerted long-term effort to resist communist aggression around the world. Vandenberg kept his promise. The Greco-Turkish aid package was speedily approved.

David Tal

See also

Acheson, Dean Gooderham; Containment Policy; Greek Civil War; Middle East; Truman, Harry S.; Turkey; Vandenberg, Arthur Hendrick

References

Kuniholm, Bruce R. *The Origins of the Cold War in the Near East.* Princeton, NJ: Princeton University Press, 1980.

Lafeber, Walter. *America, Russia and the Cold War, 1945–2002.* Updated 9th ed. New York: McGraw-Hill, 2004.

Leffler, Melvyn P. *A Preponderance of Power: National Security, the Truman Administration, and the Cold War.* Stanford, CA: Stanford University Press, 1992.

Truman Loyalty Program (1947)

Program launched by U.S. President Harry S. Truman requiring federal employees to take an oath of loyalty to the government, which enabled federal agencies to investigate employees and, if warranted, dismiss them for activities considered suspect. In the first years after World War II, as fears of malfeasant Soviet power abroad and communist subversion at home mounted, the politics of anticommunism became a potent weapon. Charges that Soviet spies or disloyal Americans were serving in important government posts began to circulate, and the Truman administration was powerless to stop the largely untruthful allegations. Soon, a Red Scare set in, and Truman felt obliged to take action to quell the resultant paranoia.

The Democrats lost control of Congress to the Republicans in 1946, putting great pressure on Truman, a Democrat. At the same time, the House Un-American Activities Committee (HUAC) was uncovering alleged communist subversion in nearly all American institutions, including the government. Under political pressure from the Republicans and the right wing of his own party, Truman ordered the Department of Justice to develop a list of possibly subversive government employees, who were then required to sign a loyalty oath. Truman unwittingly added to the general atmosphere of paranoia by feeding the flames of anticommunist fervor.

The Loyalty Program established by Executive Order 9835 on 21 March 1947 mandated that all federal employees be subjected to background checks and sign a pledge of loyalty to the U.S. government. To aid in this endeavor, loyalty boards in each of the federal agencies were created. These boards performed security checks and background investigations. The loyalty review boards investigated more than 3 million federal workers, of whom roughly 3,000 were forced to resign or lost their jobs without indictment. Truman personally fired 212 executive-level employees. Soon, the loyalty oath program spread to other government agencies, especially in education.

At the time, the program seemed to some, at least, to be a violation of civil liberties and an infringement on Americans' constitutionally guaranteed rights. In the federal government, employees lost their right to openly criticize U.S. foreign policy, own books on socialism, or attend certain foreign films. In 1951, under Executive Order 10241, if the government had "reasonable" grounds for believing that a person was disloyal, it could fire that person.

When Truman left office in January 1953, McCarthyism was in full swing. Truman's Executive Orders 9835 and 10241 and Public Law 733 were precedents for Executive Order 10450 on 17 April 1953, which President Dwight Eisenhower used to purge additional alleged subversives or security risks from the government. As a result, 600 federal workers resigned, and 1,500 more were fired.

In 1947, Julia Steiner of the Los Angeles County Library System, along with two unions, tried to obtain an injunction prohibiting supervisors from asking employees about reading interests, political views, or past associations. This challenge became the first of thirty-three cases to eventually challenge the entire Loyalty Program. From the 1950s into the late 1960s, a series of court cases gradually dismantled the various elements of the Truman-Eisenhower loyalty oath programs, largely on procedural grounds. But the concept of a loyalty oath was not overturned.

In 1972 the U.S. Supreme Court reaffirmed the legitimacy of loyalty oaths, which remain in use, most commonly by licensing boards and in public education. While the issue of such oaths has become muted, it is clear that Truman's original 1947 action helped set the stage for the corrosive politics and excesses of the McCarthy era (1950–1954) and the attendant civil liberty violations that ensued.

John H. Barnhill

See also
Civil Liberties in the United States; McCarthy, Joseph Raymond; McCarthyism; Truman, Harry S.

References
Fariello, Griffin. *Red Scare: Memories of the American Inquisition: An Oral History.* New York: Norton, 1995.
Freeland, Richard M. *The Truman Doctrine and the Origins of McCarthyism: Foreign Policy, Domestic Politics, and Internal Security, 1946–1948.* New York: New York University Press, 1985.
McCullough, David. *Truman.* New York: Simon and Schuster, 1992.
Morgan, Ted. *Reds: McCarthyism in Twentieth-Century America.* Westminster, MD: Random House, 2003.
Pemberton, William E. *Harry S. Truman: Fair Dealer and Cold Warrior.* Boston: Twayne, 1989.
Reichard, Gary. *Politics As Usual: The Age of Truman and Eisenhower.* Arlington Heights, IL: Harlan Davidson, 1988.

Tuđman, Franjo (1922–1999)

Yugoslav military officer and first president of the Republic of Croatia (1990–1999). Born in Veliko, Trgovišće, in the Kingdom of Serbs, Croats, and Slovenes (now Croatia) on 14 May 1922, Franjo Tuđman attended secondary school in Zagreb and graduated from the Military Academy in Belgrade in 1957.

Tuđman worked in the Yugoslav Ministry of National Defense during 1945–1961, becoming one of the youngest generals in the Yugoslav Army in 1960. He left active military service the next year and began a new career as head of the Institute for the History of the Labor Movement of Croatia (1961–1967). During 1963–1967 he was also an associate professor of history at Zagreb University, where he earned a doctorate in political science in 1965.

Tuđman was a member of the Socialist Republic of Croatia's parliament during 1965–1969. After participating in the Croatian Spring movement, he was imprisoned for two years beginning in October 1972. He was again imprisoned during 1981–1984 for his political activities aimed at Croatian independence.

In 1989 Tuđman was one of the founding members of the Croatian Democratic Union (HDZ). After the HDZ won the first democratic elections in 1990, he joined the parliament, which designated him president of the new Republic of Croatia. In 1991 Tuđman led his country to full independence from Yugoslavia and in the subsequent war with Serbia, which lasted until 1995 and claimed thousands of lives.

Tuđman was reelected president in direct elections in 1992 and 1997. His regime was characterized by both significant human rights abuses and political repression. In 1995 he signed the Dayton Agreement but refused to cooperate with the International Criminal Tribunal. Tuđman died on 10 December 1999 in Zagreb.

Lucian N. Leustean

See also
Yugoslavia; Yugoslavia, Armed Forces
References
Goldstein, Ivo. *Croatia: A History*. Translated by Nikolina Jovanovic. London: Hurst, 1999.
Tanner, Marcus. *Croatia: A Nation Forged in War*. New Haven, CT: Yale University Press, 2001.

Tunisia

North African nation. The Republic of Tunisia, an overwhelmingly Sunni Muslim nation, covers 63,170 square miles, about twice the size of the U.S. state of South Carolina, and had a 1945 population of approximately 3 million people. Tunisia borders Algeria to the west, Libya to the south, and the Mediterranean Sea to the east and north. Until the late nineteenth century, Tunisia had been dominated by various larger powers as well as Arab and Berber dynasties. In 1881, the French signed an agreement with the bey, the local Tunisian ruler, establishing a French protectorate there. Prior to that, Tunisia had been part of the Ottoman Empire. Tunisian culture was greatly affected by the long period of French colonial rule, which did not officially end until 1956.

Following World War II, a strong nationalist movement in Tunisia engaged in a protracted struggle against French colonial rule. On 20 March 1956, following arduous, delicate, and behind-the-scenes negotiations, an independence protocol was signed by French Foreign Minister Christian Paul Francis Pineau and Tunisian Prime Minister Tahar ben Amara. On 25 July 1957, the Tunisian Constituent Assembly ousted the bey, Muhammad VIII al-Amin, who was sympathetic to France and had long been unpopular; declared the formation of the Tunisian Republic; and elected Habib Bourguiba as president.

Bourguiba, who ruled until 1987, was decidedly pro-Western in his ideas and foreign policy. He also maintained cordial relations with France. As he tried to transform Tunisia into a modern, democratic state, he was backed by the majority of young, Westernized Tunisian intellectuals. His main political support came from the well-organized Neo-Destour Party, which he had founded in 1934, that constituted the country's chief political force.

Bourguiba was not without political rivals, however. Early in his presidency, he was strongly challenged by Salah ben Youssef, who leaned toward Egypt and Pan-Arabism and who championed the continuation of Tunisia's ancient Islamic traditions. Youssef was generally supported by conservative, wealthy urbanites and traditionalist Muslims.

The constitution of Tunisia was introduced in 1959 and amended in 1988. It provides for a presidential system not unlike that of the current French Fifth Republic. The president is elected by popular vote for a five-year term, while the prime minister is appointed by the president.

During the Cold War, Tunisia aligned itself squarely with the West and was considered a strong American ally. During the June 1967 Arab-Israeli War, for example, Bourguiba refused to sever relations with the United States over its support of Israel, despite considerable pressure to do so from other Arab states.

In spite of its support of Western-style democracy, the Bourguiba regime exerted strong, centralized authority. The economy was closely controlled by Tunis, and as fears of Islamic fundamentalism increased, especially after the late 1970s, the government increasingly relied on censorship and illegal detentions to smother radical movements. Bourguiba's heavy-handedness and frail health combined to bring about his ouster on 7 November 1987 during a bloodless coup led by General Zine al-Abidine Ben Ali, who succeeded him as president.

In recent years, under Ben Ali's tenure, Tunisia has taken a moderate, nonaligned stance in its foreign relations. Domestically, it has sought to diffuse rising pressures for a more open political system while at the same time dealing with increased Islamic fundamentalist activities and growing anti-Western sentiments. These efforts have resulted in significant government-sponsored repression and a deteriorating human rights record.

Tunisia's principal industries have been agriculture, mining, tourism, and light manufacturing. Petroleum is the chief mineral resource. Government control of economic affairs, while still heavy, has gradually moved toward privatization, simplified tax codes, and a more prudent approach to debt management. Since the late 1990s, Tunisia's economy has witnessed significant growth, which has begun to attract foreign investment. In 1995, Tunisia also signed an agreement with the European Union (EU) to remove trade barriers over the next decade. Broader privatization, increased government efficiency, and further reductions in the trade deficit are among the challenges that still lie ahead.

Nilly Kamal and Mark Sanders

See also
Africa; Arab Nationalism; Bourguiba, Habib; Decolonization; France

References
Geyer, Georgie Anne. *Tunisia: The Story of a Country That Works.* London: Stacey International, 2002.
Mosaad, Niveen, and Ali Helal. *Al-Nozom Al-Siaseya Al-Arabya Kadaya Al-Estemrar wa Al-Taghaior* [Arab Political Systems: Issues of Continuity and Change]. Beirut: Center for Arab Unity, 1999.
Perkins, Kenneth. *A History of Modern Tunisia.* New York: Cambridge University Press, 2004.
Salem, Norma. *Habib Bourguiba, Islam, and the Creation of Tunisia.* London: Croom Helm, 1984.

Turkey

Straddling both Europe and Asia Minor, Turkey occupied an important strategic position during the Cold War. With an area of 300,948 square miles, Turkey is larger than the U.S. state of Texas. European Turkey borders Greece and Bulgaria to the east and north, while in Asia Minor it shares common borders with Georgia to the northwest, Armenia and Iran to the east, and Syria and Iraq to the south. Its 1945 population was some 18.79 million people, while at the end of the Cold War in 1990 it had grown to some 56.47 million people.

In the early-modern period, the Ottoman Empire controlled the Balkans and on two occasions threatened Vienna. The empire also dominated the Middle East and North Africa. Turkish power receded in the nineteenth century, however. Regarded as the "Sick Man of Europe," the Ottoman Empire was forced to yield most of its territory in the Balkans. The empire was also on the losing side in World War I and suffered substantial territorial losses, especially in the Middle East.

Turkey became a republic in October 1923 with the abolition of the sultanate. Domestically, Turkey had been a secular state since 1924, but it was hardly a democracy. Only one political group, the Republican People's Party, was permitted.

The father of modern Turkey, Mustafa Kemal, known as Atatürk ("the father of the Turks"), mounted a successful military effort against the Greeks, whose army had occupied western Anatolia (including Izmir/Smyrna) after World War I. Atatürk also carried out a rapid and enforced Westernization, insisting on strict separation of religion and state. In 1924 religious instruction in the schools was forbidden. Turkish replaced Arabic as the national language, and the nation adopted Roman letters. Islamic law was abolished in favor of a new civil code.

Atatürk died in 1938. Premier Ismet Inönü, his closest associate, succeeded him as leader of the nation and the Republican People's Party. Inönü was reelected president in 1943. He and other Turkish leaders were determined to maintain Turkish neutrality in World War II. They kept the large Turkish Army mobilized, alarmed by the ambitions of Germany and the Soviet Union and especially concerned that the two might combine against Turkey. Italian ambitions in the Balkans were also a concern.

Once the Germans controlled the Balkans, in June 1941 Ankara signed a Treaty of Territorial Integrity and Friendship with Germany that offered economic concessions. Inönü, however, strongly resisted pressure from Berlin to enter the war on its side. As soon as the Allies were ascendant, Turkey resumed its pro-Western position, although it also resisted pressure from the United States and Britain to join them in the war. Not until February 1945 did Turkey declare war on Germany, and this was done to assure membership in the United Nations (UN).

Following the war, the Soviet Union applied tremendous pressure on Turkey in an effort to annex Kars and Ardahan. These two northeastern Turkish provinces had long been in contention between the two states. Moscow also demanded a share of control over the defense of the straits connecting the Black Sea to the Mediterranean (the Bosporus, Sea of Marmara, and the Dardanelles).

Soviet pressure on Turkey along with the communist threat to Greece led to the 1947 Truman Doctrine and U.S. aid. Turkey sought to join the North Atlantic Treaty Organization (NATO) at its founding in 1949 but was rebuffed. Not until Turkey hinted that it might pursue a neutral course was it admitted to NATO membership, along with Greece, in 1952.

In fulfillment of its obligations to defend the West, Turkey sent a brigade to fight on the UN side in the Korean War (1950–1953). There, Turkey established an excellent combat record. Turkey also provided bases to the United States for communications intelligence gathering on the Soviet Union and in 1955 joined the Baghdad Pact.

Internally, Turkey struggled to achieve a Western economy and style of government. After World War II, Inönü allowed the formation of a genuine second political party. The 1946 elections were held so abruptly, however, that the new Democratic Party, led by Celal Bayar, lacked time to organize properly and was only able to secure 63 of 465 seats.

In the 1950 elections, by contrast, the Democratic Party won a landslide victory, taking 408 seats to only 69 for the Republican People's Party. Bayar became the president, with Adnan Menderes as premier. The Democratic Party held power until 1960 and emphasized private enterprise. Under the leadership of Menderes, Turkey embarked on an economic development program. Agrarian reform had already been introduced by the previous regime, but the Menderes gov-

Voter placing ballot in box during voting in Istanbul, Turkey, 1950. Following the legalization of multiple political parties in 1946, the Democratic Party, which promoted political and economic liberalism, quickly rose to power and dominated the Turkish government throughout the 1950s. (Library of Congress)

ernment continued the process of breaking up the large estates, government holdings, and ecclesiastical lands and transferring these to the peasants. It also sought to introduce modern farming methods, with agricultural production doubling over the next decade. As more than 80 percent of the Turkish population lived in the countryside, the benefits of these reforms, including new roads and rural electrification, provided a powerful base for the Democratic Party. Some state-owned industries were also turned over to private ownership, and new factories were built to produce sugar, textiles, cement, and steel.

Rapid development, however, brought both large government deficits and inflation. Some $3 billion in U.S. aid as well as loans from Europe drove up both prices and the cost of living. As its unpopularity increased in the cities, the Menderes government began to restrict political liberties. It won an easy election victory in 1954, but only repressive measures kept it in power thereafter. Then, in 1957, all other Turkish political parties combined against the government. The government struck back by declaring this illegal and denying the opposition access to the media.

In May 1960 the Turkish armed forces stepped in, seizing power. The armed forces repeated this process two more times, in 1971 and in 1980. Much to its credit, each time the army also peacefully relinquished power. General Cemal Gürsel headed the new government, made up chiefly of younger army officers. In 1961 the government submitted for voter approval a new constitution that established a bicameral parliament and proportional representation, along with a constitutional court. New elections gave the Republican People's Party 173 of 450 seats in the national assembly, and Inönü became premier. Unfortunately, the system of proportional representation led to many small blocs in parliament and political stalemate. At first the Republican People's Party and the Justice Party (successor to the Democrat Party) shared power, but in 1962 Inönü formed a new ministry made up of members of the Republican People's Party and smaller political parties. The Cuban Missile Crisis of October 1962 affected Turkey, for as part of the settlement President John F. Kennedy agreed to remove obsolete U.S. Jupiter missiles from Turkey.

Seemingly intractable problems remained in regard to a large foreign debt and annual budget deficits. Help came in the form of a $100 million loan from a consortium of twelve nations. Turkey also benefited from admission as an associate member of the European Economic Community (EEC) in 1963. The Turks resented the fact that they could not secure full membership, a consequence not only of Turkey's economic problems but also of concerns among many West Europeans that Turkey was a Muslim nation.

Early in 1965, the Justice Party brought down the government in a vote of no-confidence, and Inönü again relinquished power. Elections later that year gave the Justice Party 240 seats and the Republican People's Party only 134 seats of 450 in the assembly. Süleyman Demirel became premier. The Justice Party continued to draw the bulk of its support from the countryside, conservative Muslims, and part of the middle class, while the Republican People's Party drew its support chiefly from the cities.

In March 1971, with Turkey sharply polarized between Right and Left and strikes occurring, the military again seized power. The generals modified the constitution, and in October 1973 new elections brought an odd coalition of leftists and Islamists to power.

A crisis with Greece over the island of Cyprus complicated matters. In July 1974, Greeks on the island seized power in order to reunite Cyprus with Greece. The Turkish government appealed to the British for a joint military intervention, but London refused. That same month, Turkey sent 40,000 troops to northern Cyprus. They drove out some of the Greeks there and occupied 37 percent of the island. Turkish troops remain on the island, with Ankara claiming that they are there to protect the Turkish Cypriot community. Talks to resolve the impasse have been unsuccessful, and the Turks have set

Turkish fishermen in the Marmara Sea using nets made possible as a result of Marshall Plan assistance, 1951. (National Archives and Records Administration)

up a de facto Turkish Cypriot state. With Greece and Turkey longtime enemies, concern remained through the Cold War and afterward that these two NATO members might go to war with each other. The Turks believed that their allies, particularly the United States, had let them down, and by the mid-1960s Ankara was distancing itself a bit from Washington and seeking improved ties with Moscow. A U.S. embargo on the sale of arms to Turkey plunged relations between the United States and Turkey to a new low.

Turkey benefited from the Islamic Revolution in Iran and the Soviet invasion of Afghanistan, both in 1979. That same year the United States substantially increased its assistance to Turkey. Aid went from $300 million a year to $500 million. The United States also continued to maintain military bases in Turkey.

For most of the 1970s, the government was run by the left-of-center Republican People's Party headed by Bulent Ecevit

or, at the end of the decade, Demirel's rightist Justice Party. As neither party was able to win a majority in parliament, both were forced to form uneasy alliances with smaller parties and independents. Meanwhile, many of Turkey's fundamental problems went unaddressed.

In September 1980 the army, led by Chief of Staff General Kenan Evren, again took power. The junta dissolved parliament, suspended the constitution and some civil liberties, and arrested Premier Demirel and more than 100 other politicians. The army also arrested thousands of suspected terrorists and executed a number of them. The army's action had again been sparked by political infighting; neglect of the nation's serious economic problems, including an inflation rate of nearly 100 percent a year; and right- and left-wing terrorists who had killed more than 2,000 people in 1980 alone. The generals were particularly concerned with the rise of Islamic fundamentalism in view of recent events in Iran.

The army takeover led to Turkey's expulsion from the Parliamentary Assembly of the Council of Europe, a halt in negotiations with the EEC, and investigations by the European Commission on Human Rights in Strasbourg. But General Evren saw himself as a leader in the mold of Atatürk. In 1982 Evren became president for a seven-year term in a referendum that was also a vote for a new constitution. The referendum received a 92 percent favorable vote. The new constitution was framed to increase presidential powers and, in the case of the Grand National Assembly, the Turkish parliament, to encourage the development of a stable two-party system.

In the 1983 parliamentary elections, the party favored by the military, the Nationalist Democratic Party, came in third. The big winner was the Motherland Party, led by Turgut Özal, that won an absolute majority in the Grand National Assembly, the first party to enjoy such power since the 1960s. Özal put the nation back into financial order and created a free market economy. In 1985 Turkey was readmitted into the Council of Europe. There was some resentment toward the West, with Turkey's leaders believing that their allies had failed to appreciate the situation that had necessitated military rule.

In 1989 there was a crisis with neighboring Bulgaria when that country drove out many members of its Turkish minority (1.5 million people out of a total population of 10 million) into Turkey. Turkey did benefit from the crisis over Iraq's seizure of Kuwait. Özal was quick to join his country to the anti–Saddam Hussein coalition, but Turkey suffered economically. By November 1990, rigid enforcement of the economic blockade had cost Turkey an estimated $3 billion in revenues, chiefly from shutting down an oil pipeline through the country.

Turks resented the phobia expressed by many Americans and West Europeans toward its Muslim identity and what it perceived as a lack of support for Ankara's efforts to stamp out demands for autonomy by its Kurdish minority (20 percent of the country's overall population) in southern Turkey. This was evident in Operation STEEL CURTAIN in March 1995, when Turkey sent 35,000 troops into the Kurdish zone of northern Iraq in an effort to trap several thousand guerrillas and halt cross-border raids by the Marxist Kurdish Workers' Party (PKK). The PKK had been fighting for more than a decade in southeastern Turkey to establish a separate Kurdish state. More than 15,000 people had been killed since 1984, and Turkey mounted the military campaign in an effort to wipe out the movement. Economic problems in the cities also led to a rise in Muslim fundamentalism, perhaps the greatest threat to the secular Turkish state. At the end of the Cold War, Turkey nonetheless remained committed to NATO and sought to become a full-fledged member of the European Community.

Cem Karadeli and Spencer C. Tucker

See also
Cyprus; Demirel, Süleyman; European Economic Community; Greece; İnönü, Ismet; Menderes, Adnan; North Atlantic Treaty Organization, Origins and Formation of; Özal, Turgut
References
Ahmad, Feroz. *Turkey: The Quest for Identity.* Oxford, UK: One World, 2003.
Deringil, S. *Turkish Foreign Policy during the Second World War.* Cambridge: Cambridge University Press, 1989.
Kinzer, Stephen. *Crescent and Star: Turkey between Two Worlds.* New York: Farrar, Straus and Giroux, 2001.
Mango, Andrew. *The Turks Today: Turkey after Ataturk.* London: John Murray, 2005.
Zuercher, Erik Jan. *Turkey: A Modern History.* London: Tauris, 1997.

Turkey, Armed Forces

The Turkish armed forces consist of the Territorial Army, Navy, Air Force, and the Gendarmerie. The last is used for policing duties in rural areas. Turkey's armed forces played important roles during the Cold War both in Turkish domestic developments and internationally.

The Turkish military remained fully mobilized during World War II. Following Soviet pressure on Turkey at the end of the war and the country's alliance with the West, Turkey sent a brigade to fight in the Korean War. Commanded by Brigadier General Tahsin Yazici, the brigade was attached to the U.S. 25th Infantry Division and secured an enviable reputation for its fighting ability. Turkish military involvement in the Korean War helped improve the Turkish image in the West. However, Turkey did not become a member of the North Atlantic Treaty Organization (NATO) until February 1952.

With NATO membership, the role of the Turkish armed forces changed from protecting the country and safeguarding Westernization to active involvement in NATO. Turkey received substantial military assistance from the United States to modernize its armed forces and achieve NATO compatibility. The army also saw itself as the guarantor of law and order in the nation, and three times it seized power: in 1960, 1971, and 1980. Each time, once order had been restored and much to its credit, the military voluntarily relinquished power back to an elected civilian government.

In the late 1960s, with the rise of tension with Greece over Cyprus, Turkey began a military modernization effort aimed at producing its own warships, landing ships, and other military equipment. In 1974, when Greeks on Cyprus tried to bring about union of the island with Greece, Turkish forces invaded the island. Some 35,000 troops were deployed in the operation, which seized 37 percent of the island. Some 30,000 Turkish troops remain in northern Cyprus.

Turkish military intervention in Cyprus led the U.S. Congress in February 1975 to impose an embargo on the sale of military equipment to Turkey. As a result, the Turkish government declared the suspension of the 1969 U.S.-Turkish Defense Cooperation Agreement and announced that the Turkish armed forces would have complete control and jurisdiction over American bases and installations in Turkey. A new Defense Cooperation Agreement was concluded on 26 March 1976, but the U.S. embargo continued until 1978.

In 1985, Turkey embarked on an ambitious ten-year, $10 billion military modernization program. In 1990, Turkey had an army of approximately 800,000 men, the second-largest standing force in NATO, plus several hundred thousand more in the reserves. Resentment toward the United States lingered, especially over the 10–7 rule imposed by Washington. The rule required that Greece receive $7 in U.S. military aid for every $10 for Turkey.

The Turkish Army consists of four armies, ten army corps, two mechanized infantry division headquarters, one infantry division, one infantry training division, fourteen mechanized infantry brigades, fourteen armored brigades, twelve infantry/domestic security brigades, five commando brigades, and five training brigades. The Turkish Air Force is composed of nineteen fighter squadrons as well as two reconnaissance, five training, six transport, one tanker, and eight surface-to-air missile (SAM) squadrons. It has the largest number of F-16 fighters after the United States. The Turkish Navy deploys twenty-one frigates, twenty-two mine countermeasures support ships, twenty-one cruise missile gunboats, thirteen submarines, fifty-two landing craft, twenty-three naval patrol airplanes and helicopters, and one amphibious Marine Corps brigade.

The Turkish armed forces can field an army corps of 40,000–50,000 troops for joint operations on very short notice and can transfer a force of five to six battalions over a long distance in limited time through night and day airborne assault. In the wake of the Cold War, the Turkish armed forces actively participated in United Nations (UN) peacekeeping activities in such locations as Bosnia-Herzegovina, Kosovo, and Afghanistan.

Cem Karadeli

See also

Cyprus; North Atlantic Treaty Organization, Origins and Formation of; Turkey

References

Jenkins, Gareth. *Context and Circumstance: The Turkish Military and Politics.* Adelphi Papers, Vol. 337. London: ISS, 2001.

Kinzer, Stephen. *Crescent and Star: Turkey between Two Worlds.* New York: Farrar, Straus and Giroux, 2001.

Olcaytu, Turhan. *Türk Silahlı Kuvvetleri ve Atatürkçülük* [The Turkish Armed Forces and Kemalism]. Ankara: GKB, 1973.

Twentieth Party Congress (February 1956)

The February 1956 meeting of the governing body of the Communist Party of the Soviet Union (CPSU) that formally denounced Stalinism. Theoretically the ruling body of the CPSU, the party congress was usually a pro forma, ceremonial event. However, the Twentieth Party Congress, held in Moscow, was a watershed in the history of international communism and the Cold War. In his celebrated so-called secret speech, First Secretary of the CPSU Nikita Khrushchev revealed to dumbstruck delegates that the late Soviet leader Josef Stalin was a bloodthirsty criminal responsible for systematic killing and mass terror instead of a wise and beneficent ruler to be adored and idolized.

Khrushchev delivered his speech in the very early hours of 25 February 1956 to a closed session of the congress from which all foreign delegates had been excluded. Khrushchev himself was largely responsible for the decision to issue a stinging denunciation of Stalin's rule. It had been opposed by the overwhelming majority in the presidium, who did manage to prevent the incorporation of the speech into Khrushchev's formal, open report. Khrushchev limited his comments to Stalin's use of terror against "loyal communists" after 1934. Revelation of Stalin's "violations of socialist legality" (the term "crimes" was avoided) was restricted to abuses against the party elite. Khrushchev went on to speak approvingly of Stalin's struggle against Trotskyist and Bukharinist "oppositionists" in the 1920s and during the industrialization drive. Khrushchev did not question the one-party system, land collectivization, or the command economy, all of which he sought to preserve.

In spite of these limitations, the speech was a political bombshell, exposing the mechanism of terror and the system of arbitrary rule that had dominated the Soviet Union for thirty years. Khrushchev employed dozens of government papers and a wealth of detail to document the brutal character of Stalin's reign of terror. One such document, which Khrushchev read aloud, was a letter from a Politburo member whose spine was broken by his interrogator. Khrushchev convincingly demonstrated that the history of the CPSU under Stalin consisted of a pattern of criminal acts, unlawful mass deportations of non-Russian peoples, political errors such as the break with Josip Broz Tito's Yugoslavia, inept leadership, the methodical falsification of history directed by Stalin himself, and the abandonment of Leninist principles of collective leadership in favor of the cult of personality. In short, Khrushchev entirely debunked the mystical aura that surrounded Stalin.

The allegedly secret speech, deliberately leaked to a Western correspondent through a former Komitet Gosudarstvennoi Bezopasnosti (KGB) official, has long overshadowed the rest of the Twentieth Party Congress's proceedings. Yet Khrushchev's 14 February open speech on peaceful coexistence with the West was almost as significant. He jettisoned the classic thesis of Marxism-Leninism, namely that war with the West was inevitable as long as capitalism survived. He also called for nonviolent competition between capitalism and communism; argued that communism would inevitably prevail over capitalism because it was a fairer system; acknowledged that there were different transitional forms from capitalism to socialism, including the parliamentary route of free elections; and insisted that the Soviet Union did not seek to export revolution.

The implications of Khrushchev's secret and public speeches reinforced each other with overwhelming effect. On the one hand, Stalin's authoritarian methods were discredited; on the other hand, a peaceful, parliamentary road to socialism was acclaimed. For authoritarian communist parties such as those in Albania, the People's Republic of China (PRC), and the Democratic People's Republic of Korea (DPRK, North Korea), this was heresy, but for others, such as Poland's, it was liberating. The nation most profoundly affected by the Twentieth Party Congress was Hungary. Within the Hungarian Workers' Party, a movement seeking greater democratization and national independence soon gathered momentum. In July 1956, Hungary's first secretary of the Central Committee, Mátyás Rákosi, was dismissed. In early October, László Rajk and other Hungarian victims of the 1949 Stalinesque trials were paid tribute, and in late October the new regime of Imre Nagy replaced that of Ernő Gerő. Unfortunately, however, the Budapest uprising of 1956 was soon quashed by the Soviet Army.

The Twentieth Party Congress did not reverberate only in Eastern Europe. It also shattered the chimera of ideological continuity between 1917 and 1956. In so doing, it created the possibility for a new, more independent direction for world communist movements.

Phillip Deery

See also

Hungarian Revolution; Khrushchev, Nikita; Soviet Union; Stalin, Josef; Yugoslavia

References

Filtzer, Donald. *The Khrushchev Era: De-Stalinisation and the Limits of Reform in the USSR, 1953–1964.* Basingstoke, UK: Macmillan, 1993.

Markwick, Roger D. *Rewriting History in Soviet Russia: The Politics of Revisionist Historiography, 1956–1974.* Basingstoke, UK: Palgrave, 2001.

Rigby, T. H., ed. *The Stalin Dictatorship: Khrushchev's "Secret Speech" and Other Documents.* Sydney: Sydney University Press, 1968.

Taubman, William. *Khrushchev: The Man and His Era.* New York: Norton, 2003.

Twining, Nathan Farragut (1897–1982)

U.S. Army and Air Force general, air force chief of staff during 1953–1957, and chairman of the Joint Chiefs of Staff (JCS) during 1957–1960. Born in Monroe, Wisconsin, on 11 October 1897, Nathan Farragut Twining was called up for National Guard duty in Mexico in 1916. During World War I he briefly attended the U.S. Military Academy, West Point; received a commission; and remained in the army. In the early 1920s he became interested in aviation and, after receiving flight training, formally transferred to the U.S. Air Service in 1926.

General Nathan F. Twining was the first U.S. Air Force general to be appointed chairman of the Joint Chiefs of Staff (1957–1960). He expanded the Strategic Air Command and supported the massive retaliation strategies of the Eisenhower administration. (Library of Congress)

In the 1930s he served on aviation bases in Hawaii, Texas, and Louisiana and studied at various army schools.

From August 1940, Twining held assorted staff positions in Washington, D.C., transferring as a brigadier general to the South Pacific in July 1942 to become chief of staff of army ground and air forces. Promoted to major general in 1943, he commanded the new Thirteenth Air Force in the Solomon Islands campaign and, in 1944 and 1945, the Fifteenth Air Force, based in southern Italy, that mounted numerous raids against German and Balkan targets, especially oil refineries, and provided air support for ground campaigns in Italy and southern France. Promoted to temporary lieutenant general, at the end of the war Twining commanded the Twentieth Air Force in the final bombing of Japan.

After holding postwar commands in Ohio and Alaska, Twining was promoted to full general and became U.S. Air Force vice chief of staff in 1950, later succeeding Hoyt S. Vandenberg as chief of staff. Under Twining, the Strategic Air Command (SAC) expanded, acquiring B-52 and XB-70 bombers to become the keystone of the massive retaliation nuclear strategy favored by President Dwight D. Eisenhower. Twining also forcefully advocated developing assorted intercontinental ballistic missile (ICBM) programs, including Jupiter and Atlas missiles and Polaris submarine-launched weapons, as part of a full and coordinated American nuclear defense strategy.

A hard-liner, Twining opposed the decreases in conventional defense forces envisaged by Eisenhower's 1953 New Look defense strategy. In 1957, Twining's repeated assertions of a bomber gap between the United States and the Soviet Union persuaded Congress to increase air force appropriations by $1 billion. Like JCS Chairman Arthur W. Radford, whom he succeeded in 1957, Twining unsuccessfully advocated a nuclear strike against communist Viet Minh forces during the 1954 siege of Dien Bien Phu in Indochina and also supported an uncompromising American commitment to defend Taiwan. By the late 1950s, some critics questioned his reliance on nuclear weapons, preferring a more flexible response capacity.

Twining retired in 1960, subsequently supporting American involvement in Vietnam, advising Republican presidential candidate Barry Goldwater in the 1964 election, and in the book *Neither Liberty nor Safety* (1966) fiercely criticizing President Lyndon Johnson's reluctance to modernize American nuclear weaponry. In the 1970s he opposed the Strategic Arms Limitation (SALT) and Anti-Ballistic Missile (ABM) Treaties, arguing that they compromised American national security. Twining died at Lackland Air Force Base in San Antonio, Texas, on 29 March 1982.

Priscilla Roberts

See also

Anti-Ballistic Missile Treaty; Dien Bien Phu, Battle of; Eisenhower, Dwight David; Goldwater, Barry Morris; LeMay, Curtis Emerson; Missiles, Intercontinental Ballistic; Missiles, Polaris; New Look Defense Policy; Radford, Arthur William; Strategic Arms Limitation Talks and Treaties; United States Air Force; Vandenberg, Hoyt Sanford; Vietnam War

References

McCarley, J. Britt. "General Nathan Farragut Twining." Unpublished PhD diss., Temple University, 1989.

Moody, Walton S. *Building a Strategic Air Force.* Washington, DC: Air Force Museums and History Program, 1996.

Mrozek, Donald J. "Nathan F. Twining: New Dimensions, a New Look." Pp. 257–280 in *Makers of the United States Air Force.* Edited by John L. Frisbee. Washington, DC: U.S. Government Printing Office, 1987.

Schnabel, James, et al. *The History of the Joint Chiefs of Staff: The Joint Chiefs of Staff and National Policy.* 7 vols. to date. Washington, DC: Historical Division, U.S. Joint Chiefs of Staff, 1986–2000.

Webb, Willard J. *The Chairmen of the Joint Chiefs of Staff.* Washington, DC: Historical Division, U.S. Joint Chiefs of Staff, 1989.

Tydings Committee (1950)

U.S. Senate subcommittee investigation during March–July 1950 of Republican Senator Joseph R. McCarthy's allegations of communist subversion in the U.S. Department of State. The U.S. Senate Subcommittee on the Investigation of Loyalty of State Department Employees, or the Tydings Committee, was created in February 1950 and formally convened on 8 March. Under the chairmanship of Democratic Senator Millard E. Tydings of Maryland, the subcommittee held thirty-one days of hearings and heard from thirty-four witnesses.

On 9 February 1950, McCarthy had stated in a public address that there were 205 State Department employees who were communists. In subsequent presentations, that number fluctuated from 57 to the original 205. McCarthy proceeded to take his claims to the floor of the Senate, forcing the Democratic Party (then in the majority) to take action.

The committee's first witness was Senator McCarthy. Before the Wisconsin senator was able to complete his opening statement, Tydings demanded that he provide the name of one of the alleged communists. McCarthy refused, and after Tydings proceeded to badger the witness, Republican Senator Henry Cabot Lodge, Jr. requested that McCarthy be allowed to present his charges as he saw fit.

During the second week of hearings, McCarthy provided the subcommittee with a list of eight names, seven of which were individuals with connections to the State Department who, he alleged, had "pro-communist proclivities" or had given "pro-Soviet" advice. One of those on the list was Owen J. Lattimore, a Johns Hopkins University professor who had been a White House advisor to Nationalist Chinese leader Jiang Jieshi during World War II. In response to this charge, Tydings obtained Lattimore's file from the State Department and reported to the panel on 23 March that Lattimore had no present connection to the department.

McCarthy supported his claims against Lattimore with a witness named Louis F. Budenz, a former editor of the *Communist Daily Worker*. Budenz testified that he had been told that Lattimore was a communist but that Lattimore probably was not a spy. Lattimore appeared before the committee on 6 April and dismissed Budenz's accusations as "gossip and hearsay." Although Budenz's testimony did not prove that Lattimore was disloyal, it did suggest to many media observers that McCarthy's charges might have had at least some merit.

The Tydings Committee's investigation was hindered by the inability to obtain loyalty files held by President Harry Truman's administration, which claimed executive privilege in refusing to release them. On 4 May, Truman finally agreed to allow the committee access to the files. The committee Democrats found no evidence in them to support McCarthy's charges. However, Republican senators claimed that the files were not tamper-proof and that the lack of findings proved nothing.

The final phase of the Tydings investigation involved a review of the *Amerasia* spy case. Several employees of *Amerasia*, a journal of Far Eastern affairs, were found to be in possession of classified documents concerning U.S. policy in China. In 1945, six people were arrested on conspiracy and espionage charges related to some 1,000 stolen classified government documents. Three of those arrested—Andrew Roth, Emmanuel Larsen, and John Stewart Service—were govern-

ment officials. The committee reviewed the entire history of the affair and heard testimony from Larsen. The committee reached the conclusion that the federal government had handled the *Amerasia* case properly and that no agency was derelict in investigating the charges.

After four months of hearings, the committee released its report on 17 July. The report was critical of McCarthy and concluded that the available evidence supported none of the senator's charges. Only the Democrats signed the report. The Senate debate on the report was bitter and partisan, with Republicans accusing Tydings of leading a "scandalous and brazen whitewash of treasonable conspiracy." In the end, the committee's report only provided McCarthy and McCarthyism more fodder.

John David Rausch Jr.

See also
Espionage; McCarthy, Joseph Raymond; McCarthy Hearings; McCarthyism; Truman Loyalty Program

References
Fried, Richard M. *Men against McCarthy*. New York: Columbia University Press, 1976.
Griffith, Robert. *The Politics of Fear: Joseph R. McCarthy and the Senate*. 2nd ed. Amherst: University of Massachusetts Press, 1987.
Keith, Caroline. *"For Hell and a Brown Mule": The Biography of Senator Millard E. Tydings*. Lanham, MD: Madison Books, 1991.
Klehr, Harvey, and Ronald Radosh. *The Amerasia Spy Case: Prelude to McCarthytism*. Chapel Hill: University of North Carolina Press, 1996.

U

U Nu (1907–1995)

Burmese nationalist and prime minister (1948–1956, 1957–1958, 1960–1962). Born in Wakema on 25 May 1907, U Nu secured a BA degree from the University of Rangoon in 1929 and served as headmaster and superintendent of the Pantanaw National High School. In 1936 he was expelled from the University of Rangoon law school along with fellow nationalist Aung San for his anti-British political activity. Imprisoned in 1942 by British authorities, Nu was released upon the Japanese occupation of Burma. He subsequently served as foreign minister in the Baw Maw Japanese-sponsored puppet government while retaining links with resistance guerrillas.

Following the war, Nu became vice president of the Anti-Fascist People's Freedom League (AFPFL) and was also unanimously elected president of the Constituent Assembly in June 1947. When Aung San, then deputy chairman of the interim government, was assassinated in the summer of 1947, Nu succeeded him at the colonial governor's request. Nu worked to hasten Burmese independence and signed the independence treaty with British Prime Minister Clement Attlee on 17 October 1947. Nu began serving as independent Burma's first prime minister on 4 January 1948 while introducing parliamentary democracy.

Nu was immediately confronted with a war-ravaged economy, communist subversive activity, and ethnic strife. Burma's neutrality in the Chinese Civil War was compromised when Chinese Guomindang (GMD, Nationalist) troops launched raids from Burmese territory, forcing Nu's government to lodge a protest with the United Nations (UN). He resigned in 1956 and returned to power in 1957 but was ultimately forced to yield to General Ne Win and the Burmese military in 1958, which headed a caretaker government until April 1960. Nu returned to power when his party won the February 1960 elections, but civil unrest persisted. This instability enabled Ne Win to stage a coup on 2 March 1962.

Nu was imprisoned until 1966 and then fled in exile to Bangkok, where he attempted to organize a prodemocratic, anti–Ne Win movement under the United National Liberation Front in 1969. Nu shifted his base of operations to India during 1974–1980 and, on assurances from Ne Win, returned to Burma (now Myanmar) in 1980. Following increased government repression, on 8 August 1988 Nu announced the establishment of a largely symbolic provisional government. In 1989 he was arrested and was kept under house arrest until 1992. Nu died in Yangon (Rangoon) on 14 February 1995.

Udai Bhanu Singh

See also
Aung San Suu Kyi; Burma

References
Butwell, Richard. *U Nu of Burma.* Stanford, CA: Stanford University Press, 1963.
U Nu. *U Nu, Saturday's Son.* New Haven, CT: Yale University Press, 1975.

U Thant (1909–1974)

Burmese politician and secretary-general of the United Nations (UN) during 1961–1971. Born in Pantanaw, Burma, on 22 January 1909, U Thant worked as an educator and freelance journalist before going into government service. During 1947–1957 he served as press director of the government

Burmese politician U Thant served as secretary-general of the United Nations during the turbulent period of 1961–1971. (Corel)

of Burma, director of national broadcasting, secretary to the Ministry of Information, secretary of projects in the Office of Prime Minister, and executive secretary of Burma's Economic and Social Board. In 1957 he became Burma's representative to the UN. He quickly became a leading figure in the UN effort to broker a solution to the war in Algeria. As a moderate neutralist, he was elected to complete the term of UN Secretary-General Dag Hammarskjöld, who died in a September 1961 plane crash.

As secretary-general, Thant preferred quiet diplomacy and tended to rely more heavily on superpower initiatives than had his predecessor. But he could also be quite forceful in policy implementation, as in the case of the UN effort to end the secession crisis involving the Congolese province of Katanga. When U.S. President John F. Kennedy sponsored a plan for national reconciliation in the Congo, Thant adopted the idea, which became known as the U Thant Plan. It was Thant's decision to send UN forces into Katanga on two occasions, once in November 1961 and again in December 1962, that finally ended the secession of Katanga and helped reunify the Congo.

In other crises, Thant helped facilitate negotiations between the Netherlands and Indochina over West New Guinea in 1962, sent a UN observation mission to Yemen in 1963, and initiated a 1963 fact-finding mission to North Borneo (and Sarawak) regarding its recent inclusion in the Federation of Malaysia. His most notable successes included sending UN peacekeeping forces to Cyprus in 1964 and his 1965 brokering of a cease-fire in the 1965 Indo-Pakistani war over Kashmir.

At the height of the Cold War, however, Thant's efforts were at times marginalized. In the midst of the 1962 Cuban Missile Crisis, he sent identical appeals to President Kennedy and Soviet leader Nikita Khrushchev to end the crisis. Those appeals were ignored. Thant's attempts after 1963 to sponsor negotiations among the United States, the Democratic Republic of Vietnam (DRV, North Vietnam), and the Soviet Union were continually rebuffed by Presidents Lyndon B. Johnson and Richard M. Nixon. Thant made his most controversial decision as UN secretary-general in 1967, when Egyptian President Gamal Abdel Nasser asked him to withdraw the UN Emergency Force from the Sinai. Believing that he had little choice but to pull out the UN troops, Thant unwittingly opened the way for the Six-Day War, ultimately weakening the UN's role in the Middle East. He retired from the UN in December 1971, at the end of his term of office. Thant died on 25 November 1974 in New York City.

Lise Namikas

See also

Arab-Israeli Wars; Cuban Missile Crisis; Cyprus; Hammarskjöld, Dag; United Nations; Vietnam War

References

Firestone, Bernard J. *The United Nations under U Thant, 1961–1971.* Lanham, MD: Scarecrow, 2001.

Nassif, Ramses. *U Thant in New York, 1961–1971: Portrait of the Third U.N. General-Secretary.* New York: St. Martin's, 1988.

U Thant. *View from the UN.* New York: Doubleday, 1977.

U-2 Incident (May 1960)

A period of heightened Soviet-U.S. tensions precipitated by the Soviet Union's 1 May 1960 downing of an American U-2 reconnaissance plane that was clandestinely taking high-altitude photographs of Soviet defense installations. The plane's wreckage, together with the confession of the captured pilot, offered irrefutable proof of previously unacknowledged American surveillance of the Soviet Union. The incident increased international tensions and caused Soviet leader Nikita Khrushchev to cancel a much-anticipated summit with U.S. President Dwight D. Eisenhower.

Because the closed nature of Soviet society made it difficult to determine that nation's military capabilities, in 1954 Eisenhower secretly ordered the fabrication of a small num-

Official Soviet photo showing people viewing the wreckage of a Turkey-based U.S. U-2 reconnaissance plane shot down over Soviet territory, 1 May 1960. (Bettmann/Corbis)

ber of special reconnaissance aircraft, built by Lockheed and dubbed the U-2, to secretly overfly the Soviet Union. The U-2 was an engineering marvel, essentially a glider outfitted with a jet engine and capable of flying at 70,000 feet and more than 4,000 miles without refueling. On 4 July 1956, civilians under contract with the Central Intelligence Agency (CIA) began piloting U-2 aircraft on twenty-four missions over the Soviet Union, taking photographs and gathering other electronic data. The U-2 overflights showed that the Soviets had been exaggerating their bomber and missile capabilities. Eisenhower feared that revelation of the flights could be considered a hostile action, but he believed that the need to obtain intelligence outweighed the potential risks of the U-2 program.

Although initial studies suggested that the Soviet Union's defenses would be incapable of reliably tracking or attacking the U-2s at their normal flying altitude, the planes were nevertheless monitored closely and were frequently targeted by Soviet interceptors and surface-to-air missiles (SAMs). The Soviets lodged objections with the United States after the early flights but did not complain publicly, probably because of their reluctance to acknowledge their inability to destroy the planes.

In February and March 1960, having authorized only four overflights since 1958, Eisenhower approved two missions for the coming weeks. Although he was worried about harming East-West rapport on the eve of a summit among American, Soviet, British, and French leaders scheduled to begin on 16 May in Paris, he was convinced of the need to gather details about recent Soviet intercontinental ballistic missile (ICBM) developments before the meeting. Midway through the second of these flights, the U-2 jet piloted by Francis Gary Powers was shot down by Soviet air defenses, and he parachuted into Soviet hands. The Soviets also collected—largely intact—the camera and other remnants of the plane.

To Khrushchev, this overflight was a particular affront because it occurred on a communist holiday (May Day) and because he saw it as an intentional presummit provocation. Correctly assuming that the United States did not know that the Soviets had captured Powers and secured incriminating aircraft components, Khrushchev set out to embarrass the Eisenhower administration. After the United States announced that the downed plane was a weather research aircraft, the Soviet leader publicly revealed the damning evidence to the contrary and announced his intent to try Powers for espionage. The eventual confirmation of the Americans' activities and their attempts to cover them up created an international sensation and torpedoed the forthcoming Paris summit.

Eisenhower tried to explain the overflights as regrettable infringements upon Soviet sovereignty that were nonetheless necessary to understand Soviet military capacity. He hoped that the summit would continue as planned and thus allow his presidential term to conclude on a high note by building upon the improved relations that had resulted from Khrushchev's celebrated 1959 visit to the United States. Some of Eisenhower's advisors thought that the CIA had been ill-prepared for the possibility of a downed plane and failed to advise the president of the likelihood of an interception, especially given persistent Soviet efforts to achieve such. Some aides proposed that Eisenhower avoid responsibility by claiming that the overflights occurred without his authorization, a suggestion the president rejected because it would improperly place blame on subordinates and would incorrectly suggest that underlings had the latitude to authorize such significant activity. Some officials, not privy to the details of what to do if captured, blamed Powers for allowing himself to be taken prisoner and too readily admitting to his activities.

While it is more difficult to assess Soviet reactions, many U.S. analysts believe that Khrushchev shared Eisenhower's quest for relaxed relations but faced resistance from hardliners in the Kremlin. This forced Khrushchev to balance anger with interest in a rapprochement, although he did lash out against Pakistan and Norway, nations that he knew had facilitated some U-2 missions. When he arrived in Paris putatively for a preliminary meeting, he made it clear that he would not assent to the formal convening of the summit without a public apology from Eisenhower. The U.S. leader refused, although he renounced any further aircraft overflights. This stance was unacceptable to Khrushchev, who therefore refused to participate in the summit and canceled arrangements for Eisenhower's state visit to the Soviet Union.

Although global reaction varied as to which party was responsible for the meeting's failure (some believed that Khrushchev exaggerated his position for propaganda purposes), Eisenhower considered it a great loss. After an August 1960 show trial, Powers was sentenced to ten years' imprisonment. In February 1962, however, he was traded for Colonel Rudolf Abel, a Soviet spy being held in U.S. custody. Subsequent investigations determined that Powers had acted properly during his mission and time in captivity. By the late summer of 1960, U.S. photographic intelligence of the Soviet Union began to rely on secret orbiting satellites that passed over Soviet territory. Because they traveled through space, international law did not consider them violations of sovereign airspace.

Christopher John Bright

See also
Eisenhower, Dwight David; Khrushchev, Nikita; Paris Conference; Powers, Francis Gary; U-2 Overflights of the Soviet Union
References
Beschloss, Michael R. *Mayday: Eisenhower, Khrushchev, and the U-2 Affair.* New York: Harper and Row, 1986.
Pedlow, Gregory W., and Donald Welzenbach. *The CIA and the U-2 Program, 1954–1974.* Washington, DC: Central Intelligence Agency, 1998.
Powers, Francis Gary, with Curt Gentry. *Operation Overflight: A Memoir of the U-2 Incident.* Washington, DC: Brassey's, 2004.

U-2 Overflights of the Soviet Union

In the early days of the Cold War, British and American aircraft and U.S. balloons flew over Soviet territory to obtain otherwise unavailable details about Soviet military capabilities. While most of these overflights were known to the Soviets, none of them were acknowledged to be reconnaissance missions until the United States took belated responsibility for a U-2 spy plane shot down over the Soviet Union on 1 May 1960. The use of piloted aircraft to obtain detailed intelligence information was supplanted shortly thereafter by orbiting space satellites.

The closed nature of Soviet society allowed the West little understanding of Soviet military preparations at the Cold War's onset. There was great concern in the West about a possible surprise Soviet attack on Europe, North America, or elsewhere, particularly after September 1949 and the detonation of the first Soviet atomic weapon. Thus, American and British officials considered aerial reconnaissance a military necessity, albeit potentially provocative and a violation of Soviet airspace.

Beginning in 1949, various types of specially modified aircraft took high-altitude photographs of Soviet air bases and other defense installations or used radar to map strategic areas. Some aircraft also recorded electronic signals emanating from Soviet radar stations and other facilities, allowing them to be precisely located and their specific functions determined. Hundreds of these risky flights were undertaken. One program operated occasionally just inside Soviet borders. Other flights routinely penetrated further into Soviet airspace. In one particularly ambitious effort in 1956, twenty-one U.S. Air Force reconnaissance aircraft flew 156 missions over Siberia in the course of seven weeks, including one mission that involved six RB-47E aircraft flying abreast in broad daylight. All returned safely.

In other instances, however, the Soviet Union and its allies reacted with hostility to such incursions. From 1949 to 1969,

A Lockheed U-2 Dragon Lady spy plane in flight. (U.S. Air Force)

sixteen American planes were shot down and 163 crew members killed. The Soviets also lodged vigorous diplomatic protests, but the British and American governments claimed that the aircraft were engaged in weather research or other innocuous activities and had not intentionally crossed into Soviet territory.

In order to reduce dangers to crewmen and decrease the likelihood of interceptions, the United States briefly used high-flying unmanned balloons to supplement its photographic intelligence efforts. In Project GENETRIX during January and February 1956, 516 balloons were sent aloft from the Federal Republic of Germany (FRG, West Germany), Scotland, and Turkey. The balloons were carried by the prevailing winds higher than the maximum ceiling of most Soviet interceptor aircraft. After leaving Soviet airspace, exposed film canisters were ejected and then recovered in midair by awaiting aircraft. Only thirty-four GENETRIX film loads were recovered and produced usable photographs. The balloons carrying the remainder either failed, descended prematurely, traveled off course, or were shot down. This short-lived balloon program nonetheless provided an understanding of high-altitude wind currents, Soviet radars, and interception techniques. All were details helpful in preparing for U-2 overflights of the Soviet Union that were to begin a few months later.

In 1954, the Central Intelligence Agency (CIA) placed intelligence operative Richard W. Bissell in charge of developing and operating the secret U-2 spy plane. The U-2 was designed by Kelly Johnson, of the Lockheed Corporation, who had also designed many other aircraft, including the P-38 and F-104 fighters. The U-2, the first prototype of which was launched in 1956, was a reconnaissance aircraft with photographic and electronic surveillance capabilities designed to overcome limitations posed by other planes. The exceedingly light plane was modeled after a glider and was equipped with a jet engine, allowing it to fly at very high speeds. With a maximum speed of more than 530 mph, the U-2 cruised at 70,000 feet—beyond the range of Soviet fighters or surface-to-air missiles (SAMs)—and could travel more than 4,000 miles on a single load of fuel. These features made the plane seemingly immune to attack and maximized intelligence gathering.

President Dwight D. Eisenhower approved the first U-2 mission over the Soviet Union on 4 July 1956. The unarmed aircraft were operated by the CIA and flown by former U.S. Air Force pilots under contract with the CIA. Civilian rather than military aircraft and crews were used so that if the Soviets learned about the flights, they might consider them less threatening. This thinking proved prescient, because the Soviets tracked nearly every U-2 incursion, finally downing one with near misses by three SAMs detonated below the aircraft on 1 May 1960. The Soviets retrieved a substantial amount of the aircraft's wreckage and equipment. Coupled with the capture of pilot Francis Gary Powers and his admission of the flight's purpose, the downing of the U-2 forced the United States to concede publicly that it had been conducting aerial reconnaissance of the Soviet Union, although the scope and extent of the effort were not specified.

The data gathered by the U-2 and other reconnaissance programs was an enormous intelligence windfall that helped shape Western military planning and diplomacy at the time. For example, for the limited number of individuals privy to such information, the data helped confirm the absence of a missile gap between the Soviet Union and United States. The persistent overflights also may have influenced the advent of certain Soviet armaments. For example, the prospect of countering increasingly higher- and faster-flying planes required the development of more capable fighter interceptors and antiaircraft weapons. This, in turn, led the United States to rely more on reconnaissance satellites invulnerable to these arms.

Christopher John Bright

See also

Bissell, Richard Mervin, Jr.; CORONA Program; Missile Gap; Open Skies Proposal; Powers, Francis Gary; U-2 Incident

References

Burrows, William E. *By Any Means Necessary: America's Secret Air War in the Cold War.* New York: Farrar, Straus and Giroux, 2001.

Hall, R. Cargill. "The Truth about Overflights: Military Reconnaissance Missions over Russia before the U-2." *Military History Quarterly* 9(3) (Spring 1997): 24–39.

Jenkins, Dennis R. *Lockheed U-2 Dragon Lady.* North Branch, MN: Specialty Press, 1998.

Lashmar, Paul. *Spy Flights of the Cold War.* Annapolis, MD: Naval Institute Press, 1996.

Pedlow, Gregory W., and Donald Welzenbach. *The CIA and the U-2 Program, 1954–1974.* Washington, DC: Central Intelligence Agency, 1998.

Peebles, Curtis. *Shadow Flights: America's Secret War against the Soviet Union: A Cold War History.* Novato, CA: Presidio, 2001.

———. *Twilight Warriors: Covert Air Operations against the USSR.* Annapolis, MD: Naval Institute Press, 2005.

Taubman, Philip. *Secret Empire: Eisenhower, the CIA, and the Hidden Story of America's Space Espionage.* New York: Simon and Schuster, 2003.

Uganda

East African nation covering an area of 91,135 square miles, about twice the size of the U.S. state of Pennsylvania. The Republic of Uganda borders the Democratic Republic of the Congo to the west, Sudan to the north, Kenya to the east, and Rwanda and Tanzania to the south. Uganda's economy was largely agricultural, and its major exports included coffee and cotton. The nation demonstrated the defining influence of European colonialism on African national boundaries. Formerly part of the British Empire, Uganda gained its independence in 1962. The history of the nation during the Cold War serves as an excellent example of the difficulties faced by much of postcolonial Africa, including instability, internal division, authoritarian government, and civil war.

In the decades after World War II, European colonialism quickly faded, creating dozens of new states by 1970. In Britain's African possessions, local resistance movements accelerated the independence process. The Mau Mau rebellion in Kenya in the early 1950s led the British to plan for the gradual independence of their African colonies over a period of two to three decades. However, further unrest in Malawi and East Africa in 1959 and 1960 forced them to expedite the process. As a result, Uganda and other nations acquired independence in the early 1960s without the established institutions necessary for a stable transfer of power. This institutional weakness, coupled with the multiethnic character of the new nations, created a serious threat of internal conflict.

Uganda's situation at the time of independence appeared promising. Prime Minister Milton Obote presided over the various groups within the country. The largest of these, the Buganda, enjoyed semiautonomous status in their homeland of Buganda; a role for their traditional ruler, the Kabaka; and a separate parliament, the Lukiiko. Obote sought greater power, however, and in 1966 he dissolved the National Assembly and produced a new constitution concentrating authority in his own hands. During the same period, he acted against the autonomy of the Buganda, removing the authority of the Kabaka and sending troops against the parliament. He formally eliminated the separate status of Buganda in 1967.

Obote had appointed Idi Amin head of the army in 1966. Amin, a former member of the British colonial army, had risen in status as a result of independence and the lack of trained officers in Uganda. In 1971, he took advantage of Obote's absence from the country and staged a successful coup with the support of the military. As a result of Obote's concentration of power, no institution existed to stand in Amin's way. Amin acted ruthlessly and began the systematic elimination of Obote's supporters. Because Obote's roots lay with the Langi and Acholi tribes of northern Uganda, Amin also ordered the wholesale slaughter of those groups. Over the eight years of his regime, hundreds of thousands of people were killed, as Amin eliminated anyone who appeared to oppose him.

As a former subject of British colonialism, Amin also sought to act against imperialism and its vestiges. He delighted in humiliating the remnants of Uganda's British community.

More importantly, in 1972 he expelled much of the Asian population, immigrants from other areas of the British Empire (mostly India) who had gone to Uganda during the years of British rule. Asians were resented because of their prosperity and because the British had given them preferential treatment. Amin gained popularity by forcing them to leave and confiscating their property. He used the proceeds of the seizures to buy the support of the army. The departure of as many as 60,000 Asians, including much of the business and professional sectors, took a catastrophic toll on the already fragile economy.

Amin also tried to make a mark on the world stage as an opponent of Western imperialism. He purchased weapons from the Soviet Union and secured support from Saudi Arabia and Libya. His most well-known venture involved his participation in the hijacking of an Air France flight on 27 June 1976. Pro-Palestinian terrorists seized the plane and forced it to fly to Entebbe Airport in Uganda, where they held 105 Israeli and Jewish passengers hostage (the non-Jewish passengers were released) and demanded the release of prisoners held by Israel. The Israelis agreed to negotiate but used the time to plan a daring rescue attempt. Two hundred Israeli soldiers landed at Entebbe, killed the terrorists, and successfully recovered the hostages on 3 July. Three hostages died in the operation. In the process, Amin's force of Soviet MiG fighters was destroyed.

In 1979, in an attempt to retain control of the army, Amin allowed the looting of parts of northern Tanzania. When the Tanzanian Army responded with an invasion of Uganda, Amin was forced into exile in Saudi Arabia. Obote resumed power in 1980, but his electoral victory was contested, and violence quickly broke out. Like Amin, he used ruthless force to eliminate his opponents. Again, thousands were killed. When Obote fell from power in 1985, Uganda lay in ruins, gutted by twenty years of authoritarian rule and internal violence. In 1986 Yoweri Museveni was declared president amid a chaotic power struggle and continues to serve in that position. In the years following his election, Uganda's economy experienced an impressive recovery. Museveni cracked down on corruption and invested millions in education and public health. Despite Uganda's economic miracle, it remains one of Africa's poorest countries.

Robert Kiely

See also

Africa; Amin, Idi; Anticolonialism; Decolonization; Entebbe Raid; Mau Mau; Obote, Apollo Milton

References

Measures, Bob, and Tony Walker. *Amin's Uganda.* London: Minerva, 1998.

Meredith, Martin. *The Fate of Africa.* New York: Public Affairs Press, 2005.

Ofcansky, Thomas. *Uganda: Tarnished Pearl of Africa.* Boulder, CO: Westview, 1996.

Ukraine

Former Soviet republic located in Eastern Europe that declared its independence from the Soviet Union on 24 August 1991. Ukraine had an estimated 1945 population of nearly 40 million people and covers 233,089 square miles, making it roughly twice the size of the U.S. state of Arizona. Ukraine is bordered by Belarus to the north; Russia to the north, northeast, and east; the Sea of Azov and the Black Sea to the south; Moldova and Romania to the southwest; and Hungary, Slovakia, and Poland to the west. Throughout history, Ukraine's position as a strategic frontier region has brought repeated invasions and constantly shifting borders as well as a rich cultural heritage.

The country's geographic position on the southwestern border of the Soviet Union clearly gave it a vital role during the Cold War. Throughout the Cold War, Ukrainians had the distinction of being the largest European population without an independent state. It is impossible to understand the role of Ukraine and the Ukrainians during the Cold War without at least some passing reference to pre–Cold War Ukrainian history. The most important aspects of this relevant to the Cold War period include Ukraine's position as a battleground of empires and ideas and the country's long and often troubled association with Russia. During the 1917 Russian Revolutions and ensuing civil war, Ukrainians attempted to establish an independent state, which was ultimately defeated by the Bolsheviks. Ukrainian lands were thereby divided between Poland and the newly established Soviet Union in the early 1920s.

The political, economic, and social upheavals of the revolutionary era in Ukraine were followed by the forced collectivization of agriculture under Soviet dictator Josef Stalin, which resulted in a devastating man-made famine that claimed the lives of millions of Ukrainians during 1932–1933. This demographic and humanitarian disaster was then quickly succeeded by extensive purges of the Ukrainian Communist Party, which led to further population losses especially among the educated elite.

In September 1939, in the wake of the German invasion of Poland and in accordance with the terms of the Molotov-Ribbentrop Pact, Stalin moved Soviet forces into eastern Poland, which was largely inhabited by Ukrainians and Belarusians. Ukrainians suffered tremendously during the war, and Ukraine became one of the major sites for the extermination of European Jewry during the Holocaust. The reunification of the two parts of Ukraine under Soviet rule in 1939 was made permanent at the end of World War II when the Western Allies accepted Stalin's plan to move Poland's border with Germany significantly west to compensate for the loss of western Ukraine and western Belarus.

Ukrainian resistance to both Nazi and Soviet rule during the war, led by both the Organization of Ukrainian Nationalists (OUN) and the Ukrainian Partisan Army (UPA), continued well into the 1950s, until a combination of internal friction and Soviet countermeasures resulted in the defeat of the insurgents. Polish and Soviet armed forces undertook extensive anti-insurgency operations, which were accompanied by ethnic cleansing throughout the border regions.

Ukraine figured prominently in the early stages of the Cold War, as Stalin attempted to ensure a large Soviet presence at the newly created United Nations (UN). Despite Western refusal to allow Stalin's demand that each of the Soviet republics enjoy individual representation at the UN, Ukraine and Belarus were granted seats in the UN General Assembly. Ukrainian diplomats were completely subordinated to the policies laid down by the Soviet leadership in Moscow, however.

Throughout the 1950s, the Ukrainian Diaspora, many Ukranians had become refugees during World War II, attempted to draw attention to the situation in their homeland, most notably through the founding of the Anti–Bolshevik Bloc of Nations (ABN), which had ties to other organizations representing the subject nationalities of the Soviet Union.

During the late 1940s and the 1950s, Ukraine underwent extensive social, political, and economic change. Shifting borders, enormous loss of life, and extensive wartime destruction of both the industrial and agricultural infrastructure created difficult living conditions in the Ukrainian countryside as well as in the major cities. Nevertheless, by the 1960s Ukraine had begun to recover economically, and living standards were on the rise. Politically, however, the situation in Ukraine remained tense, especially in the aftermath of the 1968 Soviet invasion of Czechoslovakia, which quashed the Prague Spring and increased Ukrainian dissatisfaction with Soviet rule. An active dissident movement opposed to Soviet rule developed in Ukraine, and many activists were arrested and sentenced to long terms of imprisonment in the gulags.

By the 1970s, Ukrainian political, social, and economic life mirrored trends elsewhere in the Soviet Union and also suffered under Soviet leader Leonid Brezhnev's Era of Stagnation. A Brezhnev loyalist, Volodymir Shcherbitsky, replaced the leader of the Ukrainian Communist Party, Petro Shelest, and restored obedience to Moscow. This state of affairs continued well into the 1980s, until the advent of Mikhail Gorbachev as general secretary of the Communist Party of the Soviet Union (CPSU) in 1985. A major catalyst for change in

Demonstrators marking the fifth anniversary of the 1986 Chernobyl nuclear power plant disaster. (Chuck Nacke/Time Life Pictures/Getty Images)

Ukraine was the April 1986 nuclear disaster at the Chernobyl nuclear power plant in the north of the country near the border with Belarus. The immediate impact of Chernobyl was to irradiate large parts of the surrounding area and its population, creating a human and environmental tragedy of unprecedented proportions. Gorbachev's failure to adequately respond to Chernobyl drew increased attention to the failings of the Soviet system. Soon, there were increased calls for dramatic reform throughout Ukraine.

As Gorbachev's glasnost and perestroika reforms developed and as people in the Soviet Union, including Ukraine, were freer to discuss the issues confronting Soviet society, a nascent democratic movement, called the Rukh National Movement for Perestroika (also known as the People's Movement), was formed in Ukraine by the Writers' Union in 1989. Rukh led the drive for reform and eventually Ukrainian independence. Shcherbitsky was removed as leader of the Ukrainian Communist Party and was replaced by Leonid Kravchuk, who went on to become Ukraine's first president. In the March 1990 Supreme Soviet elections, Rukh and its allies did relatively well at the polls. By July 1990, the Ukrainian Supreme Soviet, in defiance of Moscow and the central Soviet authorities, declared the economic and political sovereignty of Ukraine. This tense and anomalous situation of being a sovereign country within the Soviet Union was finally resolved in August 1991 in the aftermath of the failed coup attempt against Gorbachev. On 24 August 1991, Ukraine declared itself fully independent.

Robert Owen Krikorian

See also

Brezhnev, Leonid; Chernobyl; Glasnost; Gorbachev, Mikhail; Gulags; Perestroika; Prague Spring; Soviet Union; Stalin, Josef

References

Magocsi, Robert. *A History of Ukraine.* Toronto: University of Toronto Press, 1996.

Subtelny, Orest. *Ukraine: A History.* Toronto: University of Toronto Press, 1994.

Szporluk, Roman. *Russia, Ukraine and the Breakup of the Soviet Union.* Stanford, CA: Hoover Institution Press, 2000.

Ulbricht, Walter (1893–1973)

Head of the German Democratic Republic (GDR, East Germany) during 1949–1971. Born in Leipzig on 30 June 1893, Walter Ulbricht was the son of a tailor, and both his parents were members of the German Social Democratic Party (SPD). After serving in the German Army during World War I from 1915 to 1918, Ulbricht migrated to the radical wing of the party during the German Revolution of 1918–1919 and became a founding member of the German Communist Party (KPD).

In 1924, Ulbricht left Germany to attend Communist International (Comintern) courses in Moscow. On his return in 1926, he was elected to the state parliament of Saxony. He subsequently won election to the national parliament in 1928 and served there until 1933. He fled Germany when Adolf Hitler came to power, moving first to Paris and then to Prague. Ulbricht also fought with the International Brigades on the Republican side in the Spanish Civil War. He then fled to Moscow in 1938.

In the Soviet Union during World War II, Ulbricht and many other national communist leaders trained in preparation for their return after the war. Ulbricht returned to Germany with the Soviet Red Army in 1945 and established his group as the core of the revived KPD. Supported by the Soviet Military Administration, Ulbricht and Wilhelm Pieck negotiated a merger with the SPD in the Soviet zone of Germany, forming the Socialist Unity Party (SED). Ulbricht emerged as secretary-general of the party and led the drive to embed Soviet-style policies. When the East German government was formed in October 1949, the leading role of the SED was enshrined in the constitution and Ulbricht became deputy premier.

Ulbricht worked behind the scenes but was generally acknowledged as the real power within East Germany. Along with Willi Stoph, Ulbricht managed a purge of the SED, leaving hard-line communists in all the key positions in both the party and the government. He adopted hard-line Stalinist policies, promoting rapid industrialization and the collectivization of agriculture.

After the death of Stalin in 1953, it appeared that Ulbricht might fall from power when he refused to implement reforms suggested by the new Soviet leadership. His intransigence sparked riots in East Berlin and across East Germany on 16–17 June 1953, and Red Army tanks had to be called in to restore order.

Ironically, the threat of rebellion wedded the Soviet leadership more firmly to Ulbricht. He was one of the main forces behind the 1955 formation of the Warsaw Treaty Organization, designed to counter the North Atlantic Treaty Organization (NATO) and the perceived Western threat to East German government. When Pieck, who had been elected president of East Germany in 1949, died in 1960, Ulbricht assumed the title of head of state. Not until after the construction of the Berlin Wall in August 1961 did he institute even limited reforms.

The New Economic System of 1963 was designed to free up market forces within East Germany while maintaining the SED's constitutional grip on political power. Instead, the economy stagnated, and critics of the SED regime who might have immigrated to the Federal Republic of Germany (FRG, West Germany) now emerged within East Germany. Ulbricht refused to compromise, and when Warsaw Pact forces entered

Czechoslovakia to suppress the reforms of the Prague Spring, Ulbricht dispatched a division to assist. By 1970, however, it was clear that hc was out of touch and out of favor among the East German leadership. Erich Honecker, long recognized as the "crown prince" of the SED, effectively organized Ulbricht's ouster in 1971. Ulbricht remained as head of state, but Honecker became secretary-general of the SED and the real power in East German government.

Ulbricht died in the Berlin suburb of Döllnsee on 1 August 1973. His legacy is that of a true Cold Warrior who clung to Stalinist policies regardless of cost. His insistence on collectivization and industrialization in the 1940s and 1950s nearly broke the fledgling state's economy. By 1961, Ulbricht's regime was forced to imprison its own citizens behind the Berlin Wall. Because of such decisions, East Germany remained largely isolated under his regime, a symbol of the deep divisions of the Cold War.

Timothy C. Dowling

See also

Berlin Crises; Berlin Wall; German Democratic Republic; Honecker, Erich; North Atlantic Treaty Organization, Origins and Formation of; Pieck, Wilhelm; Stalin, Josef; Warsaw Pact

References

Frank, Mario. *Walter Ulbricht: Eine deutsche Biografie.* Berlin: Siedler, 2001.

Major, Patrick, and Jonathan Osmond, eds. *The Workers' and Peasants' State: Communism and Society in East Germany under Ulbricht, 1945–1971.* Manchester, UK: Manchester University Press, 2002.

Podewin, Norbert. *Ulbrichts Weg an die Spitze der Macht: Stationen zwischen 1945 und 1954* [Ulbricht's Path to the Pinnacle of Power: Situations between 1945 and 1954]. Berlin: Helle Panke, 1998.

Stern, Carola (pseud.) *Ulbricht: A Political Biography.* London: Pall Mall Press, 1965.

Ulbricht, Lotte. *Mein Leben: Selbstzeugnisse, Briefe und Dokumente* [My Life: Self-witness, Letters and Documents]. Berlin: Das Neue Berlin, 2003.

Union of Soviet Socialist Republics

See Soviet Union

United Kingdom

In the early 1960s, former U.S. Secretary of State Dean Acheson controversially stated that Britain had "lost an empire and failed to find a role." Britain's post-1945 foreign policies were driven by the desire to maintain, insofar as possible, great-power status, which made it crucial to forge a special relationship with the United States whereby Britain could obtain economic and military assistance from the United States, not least in implementing anti-Soviet policies in Europe. Although Britain was usually the closest U.S. ally, British leaders often found galling their new disparity in status, as the United States replaced Britain as the world's strongest power.

By 1943, British leaders were apprehensive that when World War II ended, Soviet military power and territorial holdings would be greatly enhanced, allowing the communist Soviet Union to dominate much of Eastern Europe. In October 1944, British Prime Minister Winston Churchill negotiated an informal percentages agreement with Soviet Premier Josef Stalin whereby the two leaders delineated their countries' respective spheres of influence. At the February 1945 Yalta Conference, Churchill and U.S. President Franklin D. Roosevelt both acquiesced in effective Soviet domination of most of Eastern Europe. The three leaders also agreed to divide Germany into three separate occupation zones, to be administered by their occupying military forces but ultimately to be reunited as one state. In April 1945, Churchill unavailingly urged American military commanders to disregard their existing understandings with Soviet forces and take and—he apparently hoped—retain Berlin, the symbolically important German capital.

Churchill's successor as prime minister, Labour Party leader Clement Attlee, and his foreign secretary, Ernest Bevin, a firmly anticommunist trade unionist, were equally strong advocates of a policy of firm resistance to Soviet expansion in Europe. Their position, however, was one of relative weakness, as Britain ended the war near bankruptcy, heavily indebted to the United States for Lend-Lease aid—obligations canceled in return for British pledges to dismantle the sterling area—and faced with heavy and expensive military commitments in Germany, Japan, and Greece and around its far-flung empire. London's foreign debt increased sevenfold during the war, standing at £13.3 billion in June 1945. To finance the war, the British had liquidated most of their overseas investments, and the country was running a substantial adverse balance of trade, while wartime bombing had badly damaged existing factories and plants, squeezing Britain's export capacities. In addition, the new Labour government sought to institute ambitious social welfare policies. Without U.S. assistance, Attlee and Bevin believed, Britain's foreign policy goals would remain unattainable.

In 1945, Britain still ruled the greatest empire in history, significant portions of which in Asia were regained in the last months of the war. Budgetary considerations and the desire to allay American anticolonialist sentiment mandated the speedy jettisoning of much of the empire, as did the Labour Party's stated anti-imperialist outlook and the strength of nationalist sentiment, especially in India. In February 1946, Attlee proudly announced plans to grant that country full independence in the near future. This occurred in August 1947, with the largely Muslim northwestern and northeastern provinces choosing to separate from the predominantly Hindu remainder, leaving what became Pakistan. Within a few years, Burma followed suit, although Britain retook and retained for some years those Asian colonies—Malaya, Singapore, and Hong Kong—whose continued possession and administration remained economically profitable.

British initiatives and prompts were highly significant to the making of early U.S. Cold War policies. Conscious of British weakness, especially vis-à-vis the newly menacing Soviet Union, with its power now ensconced across Central and Eastern Europe to the Elbe, Attlee sought to encourage the United States to maintain a close Anglo-American alliance. He was privy to and endorsed Churchill's intention to sound these themes in a major address in the United States, which Churchill did in his famous February 1946 "Sinews of Peace" speech (also known as the "Iron Curtain" speech) at Fulton, Missouri.

By late 1946, budgetary problems left British leaders little alternative but to reduce expensive military commitments. They chose to do so in Greece and Turkey. Greece was facing a major internal communist insurgency, while Turkey was experiencing heavy Soviet pressure for rights to the strategic Dardanelles straits. Attlee and Bevin privately informed President Harry S. Truman and Secretary of State George Marshall of their intention to withdraw sometime before the public announcement, which became the occasion for Truman's February 1947 speech (known as the Truman Doctrine), placing U.S. aid to Greece and Turkey in the broader context of a worldwide anticommunist strategy.

The harsh winter of 1946–1947 caused economic difficulties and generated unrest across Western Europe, bringing further British pleas for U.S. aid. This helped to generate the Marshall Plan, a coordinated program for European economic recovery. British acquiescence in the merging of their and the American occupation zone of Germany and the area's inclusion in the Marshall Plan were contributing factors in the 1948–1949 Berlin Blockade. Attlee and Bevin, already instrumental in establishing a Western European Union defense pact under the March 1948 Treaty of Brussels, urged that only if the United States itself joined a defensive pact would Europe feel secure. This in turn led to the North Atlantic Treaty, signed in Washington in April 1949 by the United States, Canada, and ten West European states. The members of the resultant North Atlantic Treaty Organization (NATO) pledged to come to each other's defense should one be attacked.

By 1950, major differences existed between the United States and Britain on Asian policy over Hong Kong, Indo-china, anticolonialism, and especially the new communist People's Republic of China (PRC). Britain, unlike the United States, pragmatically accorded the PRC almost immediate recognition and traded extensively with it. The Korean conflict gave British leaders an opportunity to demonstrate their continuing loyalty and regain the international status that Britain's economic problems and the 1949 devaluation of the pound had eroded. Due to Bevin's poor health and eventual death, during the Korean crisis Attlee was central to British policymaking. Urged on by his ambassador in Washington, Sir Oliver Franks, in July 1950 Attlee overrode his reluctant chiefs of staff and committed British troops to the American-led United Nations (UN) forces.

British officials welcomed the massive American enhancement of NATO forces that quickly resulted from the Korean conflict. Fearful, however, of UN commander General Douglas MacArthur's bellicose rhetoric on the potential use of nuclear weapons, they welcomed his removal. Churchill, who regained office in 1951, rejoiced when his old colleague Dwight David Eisenhower, former World War II commander of Allied forces in Europe, became president of the United States in 1953. Fearful of the destructive consequences of nuclear war, especially since both the Americans and the Soviets were developing thermonuclear weapons and since Eisenhower's New Look defense strategy relied primarily upon nuclear rather than conventional forces, Churchill urged Eisenhower to seek rapprochement and arms control agreements with the Soviet Union—advice that reinforced Eisenhower's own proclivities and contributed to his search for coexistence with the new Soviet general secretary, Nikita Khrushchev. Although Eisenhower probably only used this as a convenient excuse to justify his own preexisting inclinations, he cited Churchill's refusal in 1954 to join the United States in mounting air strikes to relieve beleaguered French forces at Dien Bien Phu as the reason that the American government declined to intervene there and help the French continue the conflict.

In 1956, nonetheless, Eisenhower made Britain's reduced status and dependence upon the United States humiliatingly apparent. In 1953 the nationalist Gamal Abdel Nasser took power in Egypt. Initially, he sought both military and economic aid from the United States, but the Israeli lobby pressured Congress to deny aid, whereupon Nasser obtained arms from the Soviet bloc. This, in turn, led U.S. Secretary of State John Foster Dulles in 1956 to rescind an earlier American pledge to provide Nasser with funding for his Aswan Dam project, whereupon Nasser nationalized the Suez Canal, co-owned by the British and French governments. While joining Dulles in negotiations to resolve the crisis, Britain and France secretly collaborated with Israel on war against Egypt to regain the canal, mounting an invasion in early November 1956, just prior to the U.S. presidential election. Dulles and Eisenhower

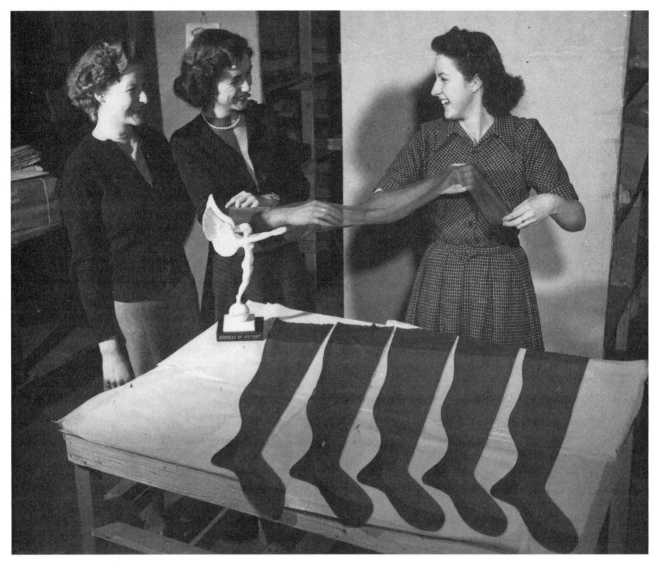

Marshall Plan aid benefited all segments of society. Here, new machinery financed under the plan helps the T. S. Cunningham Nylon Factory in Scotland increase production. The new production rate is represented by the five stockings on the table, while the old rate is shown in the single stocking, held by the women. (National Archives and Records Administration)

exerted financial and military pressure on all three powers to withdraw, which they eventually did, but the episode greatly embittered Anglo-American relations.

Anthony Eden's successor as prime minister, the half-American Harold Macmillan, an old wartime colleague of Eisenhower's who was also connected by marriage to John F. Kennedy, valiantly attempted to restore the relationship. From 1957 to 1962, the two countries signed a series of defense agreements on the sharing of nuclear information, according Britain exclusive rights to use American nuclear technology in return for U.S. rights to deploy military weapons on British bases. The United States also promised Skybolt missiles and then sold Polaris missiles to Britain. In addition, in 1959 Eisenhower finally committed the United States to defend the British colony of Hong Kong, once an embarrassing colonial survival, now a free world bastion.

As they became increasingly embroiled in both the Middle East and Asia, American leaders perceived Britain's military forces and imperial holdings as useful adjuncts to their own undertakings. Between 1948 and 1960, British troops successfully suppressed a communist insurgency in Malaya, after which the country received its independence. Plagued by various financially and militarily burdensome nationalist and guerrilla movements in many of Britain's African colonies, in 1960 Macmillan publicly announced that in response to "winds of change," Britain would speedily grant independence to its remaining colonies, a pledge largely fulfilled by 1970. During the 1960s, growing U.S. military involvement in Vietnam helped to divide the United States from its European NATO allies, all of whom ignored forceful American requests to commit military forces to the conflict, in part because of strong domestic political opposition and major antiwar protests.

Britain did, however, provide intelligence information and logistical support to U.S. forces in Vietnam. In addition, British Prime Minister Harold Wilson cited British anticommunist efforts in Malaysia and Indonesia as major contributions supplementing American efforts elsewhere in Southeast Asia. President Lyndon B. Johnson's administration deplored Britain's 1967 decision to withdraw British military forces east of the Suez and the near-contemporaneous devaluation of the pound, which undercut U.S. efforts to maintain the post–World War II Bretton Woods international exchange system of fixed-rate currencies. Johnson was nonetheless grateful these had not come earlier.

Wracked by major economic and social problems for much of the 1970s, Britain was less significant to American foreign policy, and the relationship languished. Conservative Prime Minister Edward Heath (1970–1974) looked toward Europe, not the United States. He finally succeeded in negotiating British entry into the European Economic Community (EEC) in 1973, after two earlier failed attempts during the 1960s. Many believed that this marked a permanent reorientation of British foreign policy in favor of Europe at the expense of both the United States and the British Commonwealth. The Labour government that replaced Heath in 1974 faced serious internal problems, including a strong party faction favoring withdrawal from NATO. So severe were British economic difficulties that in 1976 the country had to seek a substantial and humiliating loan from the International Monetary Fund (IMF). This was granted only in return for major cuts in British public spending.

In 1979, however, the right-wing Conservative Party politician Margaret Thatcher won election as prime minister. She was determined to restore British greatness and the free market and was staunchly anticommunist and pro-American in outlook. The more jovial but equally ideological Ronald Reagan, elected U.S. president in November 1980, admired and respected her as an intellectual soul mate. They soon forged a close political and personal friendship. Initially, the two embarked on firmly anti-Soviet policies, cutting social welfare spending but increasing defense budgets. In the 1982 Falklands War, Thatcher's determination to resist Argentine seizure of British-owned islands won Reagan's admiration and ultimately received significant military and intelligence support from his administration. The two governments cooperated closely on defense and other issues. Thatcher was the only European leader to support Reagan's 1986 bombing of the Libyan capital of Tripoli, an action taken in retaliation for alleged terrorist activities. She also overrode substantial domestic opposition to stationing short- and intermediate-range American nuclear-armed cruise missiles on British soil, symbolized by the camp that antinuclear protestors established in 1980 and maintained for several years outside Greenham Common Air Base in Berkshire.

British Prime Minister Margaret Thatcher with President Ronald Reagan at the Camp David presidential retreat in Maryland, 6 November 1986. (Ronald Reagan Library)

After the reformist Mikhail Gorbachev became Soviet general secretary in March 1985, Thatcher met with him and urged Reagan to have faith in his expressed desire to moderate the Cold War. Her prompts apparently weighed heavily with Reagan in his own subsequent meetings with Gorbachev, which began the process of Soviet-American rapprochement that eventually brought an end to the Cold War. When Iraqi dictator Saddam Hussein annexed Kuwait in 1990, Thatcher reputedly helped to persuade President George H. W. Bush, Reagan's successor, to stand firm. Her successor, John Major, dispatched the second-largest military contingent—after that of the United States—to the consequent 1991 Persian Gulf War.

This pattern continued even after the Cold War ended, with Britain the most reliable military ally of the United States. Having forged a close relationship with President William "Bill" Clinton, British Prime Minister Tony Blair developed an equally strong bond with President George W. Bush, breaking with much of his own Labour Party to join the war against Iraq in 2003. Regardless of political affiliation, and temporary estrangements notwithstanding, from 1945 onward most British prime ministers looked to the United States as their perennial and most reliable ally.

Priscilla Roberts

See also

Anticolonialism; Attlee, Clement Richard, 1st Earl; Bevin, Ernest; British Commonwealth of Nations; Churchill, Winston; Containment Policy; Decolonization; Douglas-Home, Sir Alexander Frederick; Eden, Sir Anthony, 1st Earl of Avon; Eisenhower, Dwight David; Elizabeth II, Queen of England; European Economic Community; European Integration Movement; Foot, Michael; Gaitskell, Hugh; George VI, King of Great Britain; Germany, Federal Republic of; Gorbachev, Mikhail; Greenham Common; Healey, Denis; Heath, Edward; Heseltine, Michael; Hong Kong; India; Indonesia; International Monetary Fund; Johnson, Lyndon Baines; Kennedy, John Fitzgerald; Khrushchev, Nikita; Korean War; Lloyd, Selwyn; Macmillan, Maurice Harold; Malayan Emergency; Marshall Plan; MI5; MI6; Missiles, Polaris; Missiles, Poseidon; Nasser, Gamal Abdel; Nixon, Richard Milhous; North Atlantic Treaty; North Atlantic Treaty Organization, Origins and Formation of; Reagan, Ronald Wilson; Roosevelt, Franklin Delano; "Sinews of Peace" Speech; Singapore; Skybolt Affair and Nassau Conference; Soviet Union; Stalin, Josef; Suez Crisis; Thatcher, Margaret; Truman, Harry S.; Vietnam; Vietnam War; Vietnam War Protests; Wilson, James Harold; World War II, Allied Conferences

References

Baylis, John. *The Diplomacy of Pragmatism: Britain and the Formation of NATO, 1942–1949.* Kent, OH: Kent State University Press, 1993.

Blackwell, Michael. *Clinging to Grandeur: British Attitudes and Foreign Policy in the Aftermath of the Second World War.* Westport, CT: Greenwood, 1993.

Charmley, John. *Churchill's Grand Alliance: The Anglo-American Special Relationship, 1940–57.* New York: Harcourt Brace, 1995.

Deighton, Anne, ed. *Britain and the First Cold War.* New York: St. Martin's, 1990.

Dimbleby, David, and David Reynolds. *An Ocean Apart: Britain and the United States in the Twentieth Century.* New York: Random House, 1998.

Dockrill, Saki. *Britain's Retreat from East of Suez: The Choice between Europe and the World.* New York: St. Martin's, 2002.

Greenwood, Sean. *Britain and the Cold War, 1945–91.* New York: St. Martin's, 2000.

Hathaway, Richard M. *Great Britain and the United States: Special Relations since World War II.* Boston: Twayne, 1990.

Hennessy, Peter. *The Secret State: Whitehall and the Cold War.* London: Allen Lane/Penguin, 2002.

Keeble, Sir Curtis. *Britain, the Soviet Union, and Russia.* 2nd ed. New York: St. Martin's, 2000.

Kent, John. *British Imperial Strategy and the Origins of the Cold War, 1944–49.* Leicester, UK: Leicester University Press, 1993.

Lee, Sabine. *Victory in Europe? Britain and Germany since 1945.* New York: St. Martin's, 2001.

Ovendale, Ritchie. *The English-Speaking Alliance: Britain, the United States, the Dominions, and the Cold War, 1945–1951.* Boston: Allen and Unwin, 1985.

Renwick, Sir Robin. *Fighting with Allies: America and Britain in Peace and at War.* New York: Random House, 1996.

Sharp, Paul. *Thatcher's Diplomacy: The Revival of British Foreign Policy.* New York: St. Martin's, 1997.

Smith, Geoffrey. *Reagan and Thatcher.* New York: Norton, 1991.

Taylor, Peter J. *Britain and the Cold War: 1945 As Geopolitical Transition.* London: Pinter, 1990.

Woods, Randall Bennett. *A Changing of the Guard: Anglo-American Relations, 1941–1946.* Chapel Hill: University of North Carolina Press, 1990.

Young, John W. *Britain and European Unity, 1945–1999.* 2nd ed. New York: St. Martin's, 2000.

United Kingdom, Air Force

During the Cold War, Britain's Royal Air Force (RAF) paralleled the narrowing in focus of Britain's overseas commitments and the reduction of its armed forces. Two predominant forces that shaped the RAF were sharp downsizing and spiraling technological sophistication, which combined to transform the 1945 great power air arm into the only second-tier air force capable of global operations by 1991.

The RAF's contraction from its World War II end strength of 1 million men to only 89,000 by 1991 had a number of important effects. Foremost, the end of conscription in 1960, coupled with ever more complex aircraft, accelerated the professionalization of the service. Additionally, fewer resources and Britain's narrowing strategic interests eliminated most overseas postings outside the United Kingdom after the withdrawal from east of the Suez in 1967.

The growing technological sophistication of airpower also decisively shaped the postwar RAF. The advent of jet technology and swept wings in the 1940s, supersonic flight, electronic warfare, British nuclear weapons and variable-geometry aircraft in the 1950s, and terrain-following flight in the 1960s presented too hostile an environment for most of the British aeronautical industry. Radical downsizing and consolidation reduced Britain's industry to a handful of companies. The cancellation of the TSR.2 in 1965 forced cooperation with allied powers in projects such as the Jaguar and Tornado or wholesale adoption of American weapon systems such as the F-111 and C-130. Despite the evisceration of Britain's aeronautical industry, the RAF remained capable of applying cutting-edge technology and by 1991 was one of only a handful of powers capable of worldwide operations with precision munitions.

The initial role of the RAF in the postwar world emanated from its heritage as a strategic bombing force. Following a 1947 decision to develop an independent nuclear program, the RAF engaged in a tortuous process of developing both usable weapons and the platforms capable of delivering them. Britain achieved the former in a test at the Monte Bello Islands in 1952, but the latter turned out to be more problematic. Although Lincolns (upgraded wartime Lancasters) and Washingtons (U.S.-loaned B-29s) provided an interim nuclear delivery capability, they were ultimately unsatisfactory in the long run. A ten-year development cycle resulted in a generation of swept-wing, all-jet V-bombers—the Valiant, Vulcan, and Victor—that by 1957 were only marginally capable of penetrating Soviet air defenses. An attempt to evade Soviet surface-to-air missile (SAM) systems by switching from high- to low-altitude penetration exceeded the design capacity of the V-bombers and mandated their phased withdrawal from frontline strategic service beginning in 1964. That together with the cancellation of the Anglo-American Skybolt tactical missile that was to extend the V-bomber's strike range and the offer of the U.S. Polaris submarine-launched ballistic missile (SLBM) to the Royal Navy (RN) all but ended the RAF's strategic role.

As a result, in a general overhaul reflecting changed missions and resource constraints, the RAF drastically reorganized at the end of the 1960s. The dissolution of Bomber and Fighter Commands in 1968 and the creation of the Strike Command was followed by the RN's Polaris-equipped submarines formally assuming responsibility for the British nuclear deterrent in 1969.

Despite the eclipse of the RAF's strategic role, both before and after 1969 it played an active part in almost every British military operation. After teaming with the U.S. Air Force in the 1948–1949 Berlin Airlift, the RAF successfully aided in defeating insurgencies in Malaya, Cyprus, and Kenya. The strength required for the former precluded large-scale conventional involvement in the Korean War. While fighting instability in erstwhile colonies during the 1950s, the RAF also participated in Britain's military campaign during the 1956 Suez Crisis, effectively destroying the Egyptian Air Force in two days. Smaller conventional operations punctuated the 1960s, including the defense of Kuwait in 1961, extended deployments to contain Indonesia during 1963–1966, and the evacuation of Aden in 1967, a part of the overall withdrawal from east of the Suez.

The slow pace of the 1970s erupted into a major independent campaign in 1982 against Argentina over the Falkland Islands. Operation CORPORATE, which featured joint RN-RAF operations more than 8,000 miles from Britain and required robust logistics, highlighted the RAF as the only European air force still capable of projecting force outside the region. During the 1991 Gulf War, the RAF again showed its prowess by adapting low-level, high-speed delivery techniques developed for the European theater to destroy Iraqi air defenses. Both the RAF's 6,000-plus sorties and extensive Special Air Service operations were a critical component of the Coalition's swift victory. The RAF's performance in the Gulf War underscored its role as a uniquely capable Cold War force that adroitly

projected regional and global airpower to advance British and allied interests.

Edward Kaplan

See also
Anticolonialism; Atomic Bomb; Berlin Blockade and Airlift; Bombers, Strategic; British Army; Hydrogen Bomb; Malayan Emergency; Missiles, Polaris; Missiles, Submarine-Launched Ballistic; Suez Crisis; United Kingdom; United Kingdom, Royal Navy

References
Freedman, Lawrence. *The Evolution of Nuclear Strategy.* 3rd ed. Houndmills, UK: Palgrave Macmillan, 2003.
James, A. E. Trevenen. *The Royal Air Force: The Past 30 Years.* London: Macdonald and Jane's, 1976.
Kaplan, Edward Andrew. "With a Bloody Union Jack on Top: The First Generation British Atomic Deterrent." Unpublished master's thesis, University of Calgary, 1995.
Taylor, John W. R., and Philip John Richard Moyes. *Pictorial History of the R.A.F.* London: Allan, 1968.
Taylor, N. E. *A Short History of the Royal Air Force.* London: Ministry of Defence, 1994.

United Kingdom, Army

The period of the Cold War was punctuated by a number of small wars for the British Army. British troops were deployed in conflicts around the world, including Java and Sumatra (1945), India (1945–1948), Palestine (1945–1948), Malaya (1948–1960), Korea (1950–1953), the Suez Canal (1951–1956), Kenya (1952–1960), Cyprus (1955–1959), Aden and Radfan (1955–1967), Borneo (1962–1966), Oman (1969–1976), the Falkland (Mariana) Islands (1982), and the Persian Gulf (1990–1991). During this period, the British Army was awarded a total of twenty-three battle honors for action in the Korean War, the Falklands War, and the Persian Gulf War.

Following World War II, Britain found itself weighed down by its postwar obligations, colonial holdings, and the outbreak of the Cold War. The British Army of the Rhine, comprising some 50,000 troops in three divisions, participated in the Allied occupation of Germany. An additional 3,000 troops were stationed in divided Berlin. There was often a colonial/Cold War overlap, such as when Britain faced problems with the Soviet Union in Germany while dealing with independence movements in India, Palestine, and Malaya.

The British Army at the close of World War II numbered 2.931 million men. By August 1947, it had shrunk to a little more than 750,000 men. Even so, the peace dividend was limited. Although military spending dramatically decreased in the initial postwar years, imperial overstretch combined with the Cold War led to defense expenditures taking up a significant portion of the total British budget; indeed, in the 1948–1954 period, defense allocations took up 22–42 percent

British troops on patrol in Calcutta, India, following riots that claimed the lives of 250 people, 24 February 1946. (Bettmann/Corbis)

of the aggregate budget. It was not until 1960 that conscription was ended, leading to a volunteer army of roughly 165,000 men, including 19,000 officers. During this time, the annual expenditure for arms was £1.6 million.

The times placed great stress on the British Army, occasionally leading to outbreaks of rebellion among the troops. For example, in 1946 at Muar Camp near Kuala Lumpur in Malaya, 258 men of the 13th Battalion Parachute Regiment, many of whom were veterans of the D-Day invasion, mutinied over living conditions. That same year, there was a Royal Air Force mutiny of nearly 50,000 men at bases in India, Ceylon, Singapore, and the Far East. The servicemen's complaints included dissatisfaction with working conditions as well as disagreement over British imperialism.

In 1946, anti-British riots broke out across India. For five days in August 1946, six British battalions skirmished with violent mobs in Calcutta, and hundreds of Indians were killed. Violence spread to Bombay, Delhi, and the Punjab region. India finally gained its independence on 15 August 1947, and six months later the last of the British soldiers departed, dramatically ending more than two centuries of British occupation. London now no longer controlled the Indian Army, reducing by half the troops it had available for colonial policing.

The Middle East also proved to be a policing problem. As Zionists worked toward establishing a Jewish homeland, British forces fought to restrict the flow of refugees from Europe to Palestine, provoking a violent response. The British 1st Infantry Division had to be reinforced by the 6th Airborne Division and the 3rd Infantry Division. Some of these reinforcements were diverted from European security duties in the Federal Republic of Germany (FRG, West Germany). Ironically, some of the rebels had been part of the British-trained Jewish Brigade Group, which during World War II had fought in Italy under the British Eighth Army.

During the Korean War (1950–1953), the postwar British Army peaked at more than 440,000 men. Sixteen battalions of British infantry participated in the fighting. Armored and artillery units also played a key role. Britain's only role in the Vietnam War that followed was to provide a jungle-warfare training team in Malaya.

In Egypt, a British presence protected the Suez Canal, an occupation that was also met with resistance. During 1950–1956, more than 50 British servicemen were killed, leading to retaliatory incidents. In March 1956, the last of the British troops left the Suez Canal zone. When Egyptian President Gamal Abdel Nasser nationalized the British-owned Suez Canal Company, the British government called up 20,000 reservists and bolstered its forces in the eastern Mediterranean. Israel, France, and Britain then combined to attack Egypt but were pressured by the United States and the United Nations (UN) to withdraw.

In 1961, Kuwait became independent and was immediately threatened by the Iraqi regime under General Abdul Kassem, leading to the deployment of British troops. The incident was a prelude to the Persian Gulf War three decades later, when British forces totaled 45,000 men. In the 1982 Falklands (Marianas) War, a British task force of 27,000 personnel arrived in the Falkland Islands on 117 ships and defeated an Argentine garrison of 12,000 men.

In the various deployments and military operations of the Cold War era, more than 3,500 British soldiers were killed and an additional 17,000 wounded. Following the end of World War II, 1968 marked the first year in which no British soldiers died in combat. The postwar tally shows that the British Army suffered 223 dead and 478 wounded in Palestine, 489 dead and 961 wounded in Malaya, 865 dead and 2,589 wounded in Korea, 12 dead and 69 wounded in Kenya, 79 dead and 414 wounded in Cyprus, 12 dead and 63 wounded in Suez, 59 dead and 123 wounded in Malaysia, 52 dead and 510 wounded in Aden, 225 killed and 777 wounded in the Falklands, and 87 dead and 1,700 wounded in the Persian Gulf.

During the Cold War, the British Army primarily tended to unrest in its former colonial holdings, problems that were directly and indirectly related to the larger struggle between the East and the West. Britain's resolve to commit troops around the world in crisis situations played a role in containing communism by limiting opportunities for Kremlin designs. By the time of the 1991 Persian Gulf War, when Britain partnered with the United States in opposing Saddam Hussein, the Soviet Union had practically reached its end as leaders of the West proclaimed a new world order.

Roger Chapman

See also

Falklands War; Korean War; Malayan Emergency; Mau Mau; North Atlantic Treaty Organization, Origins and Formation of; Persian Gulf War; Suez Crisis; United Kingdom

References

Farrar-Hockley, Anthony H. "After the War: 1945–68." Pp. 287–295 in *History of the British Army,* edited by Peter Young and J. P. Lawford. New York: Putnam, 1970.

Pimlott, John, ed. *British Military Operations, 1945–1985.* New York: Military Press, 1984.

Stanhope, Henry. *The Soldiers: An Anatomy of the British Army.* London: Hamish Hamilton, 1979.

United Kingdom, Navy

The United Kingdom's Royal Navy (RN) was gradually streamlined and downsized during the Cold War, shifting its strategic capability from that of a surface fleet to one that primarily employed submarines and antisubmarine warfare. In 1945 Britain still maintained naval bases around the world. Its domestic fleet bases were located at Portsmouth, Devonport, and Chatham. There was also a dockyard at Rosyth in Scotland. Overseas bases were situated in Malta; Ceylon; (Trincomalee); Singapore; and Simonstown, South Africa (near Capetown), with Gibraltar and Bermuda serving as dockyards. In 1954, the navy had more than 600 vessels and a regular force strength of 117,700. By 1991, its active-duty force had been downsized to 60,000. During 1950–1990 there were major reductions in the number of aircraft carriers (from 12 to 3), cruisers (from 29 to 0), destroyers/frigates (from 280 to 51), and conventional submarines (from 66 to 9).

The financial realities of waging the Cold War had a major impact on Great Britain beginning in 1951, the year after the outbreak of the Korean War, when military expenditures doubled. At that time, British troops were already in Malaya and Hong Kong in response to perceived communist threats. The RN was a major participant in the Korean War, utilizing aircraft carriers (the *Glory, Ocean, Theseus,* and *Triumph*); cruisers (the *Birmingham, Belfast, Jamaica, Kenya,* and *New Castle*); destroyers (the *Charity, Cockade, Comus, Consort,* and *Cossack*); frigates (the *Alacrity, Black Swan, Heart, Morecome Bay, Mounts Bay,* and *Whitesand Bay*); a hospital ship (the *Maine*); and other vessels. RN aircraft employed in Korea included the Sea Fury, Firefly, and Seafire.

Prior to the Korean War, the RN experienced several incidents in the Mediterranean and the Far East. In 1947, the Mediterranean Fleet had attempted to stem the tide of illegal Jewish immigrants from Europe to Palestine. In 1949, the destroyers *Saumarez* and *Volage,* during a show of force against the communists, struck mines off the coast of Albania, resulting in the loss of forty-four lives. Also in 1949, the frigate HMS *Amethyst* came under attack by Chinese communist forces when it patrolled up the Yangtze River. In 1951, the RN responded to the Anglo-Iranian oil dispute by imposing a blockade on the port of Abadan to prevent oil from being exported.

In 1956 Britain, France, and Israel carried out a coordinated attack on Egypt. During the Suez Crisis, the RN dispatched the aircraft carriers *Eagle, Albion,* and *Bulwark* to the Canal Zone. In that conflict, the *Ocean* at Port Said launched the first helicopter-borne amphibious landing in history. The Suez Crisis revealed serious shortcomings in Britain's military reach and indicated that it was no longer able to undertake major unilateral military action. Britain's military position was also affected by the hydrogen bomb. A Defence White Paper of April 1957 concluded that "the role of naval forces in total war is uncertain." Conscription came to an end that same year, and greater reliance was placed on nuclear weaponry. The same year, after successfully lobbying the United States to amend its Atomic Energy Act, British officials were able to purchase from the Americans a nuclear propulsion plant for the first British nuclear-powered submarine, HMS *Dreadnought.*

The *Dreadnought,* commissioned in 1963, represented a new strategy. From this point in the RN, traditional aircraft carriers declined in importance. HMS *Ark Royal,* the last such vessel, was decommissioned in 1978. Beginning in 1980, smaller carriers—the *Invincible, Illustrious,* and *Ark Royal*—transported helicopters and vertical-lift Sea Harrier jets. Beginning in the 1970s, a Polaris submarine fleet of four boats—the *Resolution, Repulse, Renown,* and *Revenge*—also strengthened Britain's nuclear capability. Each submarine could carry sixteen missiles armed with nuclear warheads with a striking range of 2,500 nautical miles.

Despite naval spending cuts during the 1960s and 1970s, defense costs remained high, and by the early 1980s there was pressure for an even leaner military. On 25 June 1981, Secretary of State for Defence John Nott submitted to Parliament "The United Kingdom Defence Programme: The Way Forward." This report recommended a strategic emphasis on Europe, in conjunction with North Atlantic Treaty Organization (NATO) forces, with less emphasis on global capability. Since the British Army and the Royal Air Force were already largely oriented toward West European defense, the brunt of the cuts was earmarked for the RN. Fortunately for the government of Prime Minister Margaret Thatcher, the crisis in the Falklands broke out prior to the implementation of this new approach.

In 1982, Britain went to war with Argentina over the Falkland Islands. It was Britain's first engagement with a modern navy since 1945 and proved a challenging undertaking, as it was fought 8,000 miles from the British Isles. During the Falklands War, the RN provided essential reach and support for a British expeditionary force to reconquer the islands from Argentina. In all, the United Kingdom committed 117 ships and 27,000 personnel, led by Rear Admiral John "Sandy" Woodward. On 2 May 1982, the British nuclear-powered submarine *Conqueror* torpedoed and sank the Argentine cruiser *General Belgrano.* Under Argentine Air Force attack with French-made Exocet missiles, Britain lost the Type 42 destroyers *Sheffeld* and *Coventry,* the Type 21s *Antelope* and *Ardent,* the landing ship *Sir Galahad,* and the container ship *Atlantic Conveyor.* British war dead tallied 255, with another 777 wounded. The war prompted British officials to reconsider their drastic downsizing of the RN.

In 1991, Britain began replacing the Polaris submarine-launched ballistic missiles (SLBMs) with larger Tridents. With the end of the Cold War, aside from the submarine-missiles deterrent, the RN's primary role has been antisubmarine warfare, which was aided by three antisubmarine warfare carriers lifting Sea King antisubmarine and early warning helicopters.

Roger Chapman

See also

Aircraft Carriers; Anglo-Iranian Oil Crisis; Falklands War; Hydrogen Bomb; Korean War; Missiles, Polaris; Submarines; Suez Crisis; Thatcher, Margaret; Warships, Surface

References

Armitage, M. J., and R. A. Mason. *Air Power in the Nuclear Age.* Urbana: University of Illinois Press, 1983.

Childs, David. *Britain since 1945: A Political History.* London: Routledge, 2001.

Hill, J. R., ed. *The Oxford Illustrated History of the Royal Navy.* Oxford: Oxford University Press, 1995.

Murfett, Malcolm H. *In Jeopardy: The Royal Navy and the British Far Eastern Defence Policy, 1945–1951.* Oxford: Oxford University Press, 1995.

Pimlott, John, ed. *British Military Operations, 1945–1985.* New York: Military Press, 1984.

United Nations

Multinational organization established in 1945 and designed to promote four primary objectives: collective security, international economic and cultural cooperation, multilateral humanitarian assistance, and human rights. The creation of the United Nations (UN) represented an attempt by the World War II Allies to establish an international organization more effective than the interwar League of Nations, which had failed to mitigate the worldwide economic depression of the 1930s or prevent a second world war. UN architects were heavily influenced by the belief that during the 1930s, nationalist policies, economic and political rivalries, and the absence of international collaboration to help resolve outstanding disputes had contributed substantially to the outbreak of World War II.

Even before the United States officially joined the war effort, in the early months of World War II U.S. Secretary of State Cordell Hull established a departmental planning group for the purpose of creating the UN. At a meeting off the Newfoundland coast in August 1941, American President Franklin D. Roosevelt and British Prime Minister Winston Churchill included a broad proposal for an international security system in the Atlantic Charter, which was their declaration of overall war objectives.

On 1 January 1942, the governments of twenty-six nations fighting Germany, Italy, and Japan issued the Declaration by the United Nations affirming their alliance against the Axis powers and also stating their commitment to liberal war objectives, as set forth in the Atlantic Charter, and the restoration of the principles of international law. In 1943, both houses of the U.S. Congress also passed resolutions demanding the creation of a postwar international security organization in which, they implied, their own country should take the leading role that it had abdicated in the League of

British Prime Minister Clement Atlee addressing the first meeting of the United Nations General Assembly in 1946. (Corel)

Nations. Meeting in Moscow in October 1943, foreign ministers of the four leading Allied powers—the United States, Great Britain, the Soviet Union, and China—signed the Declaration of Four Nations on General Security, committing their nations in general terms to the creation of a postwar international organization.

More specific proposals came out of the Dumbarton Oaks Conference held in Washington, D.C., from August to October 1944 in which thirty-nine nations participated. These recommendations represented a compromise between the ideas of Roosevelt and other devotees of realpolitik—that agreement between the Big Four Allied powers, "the four policemen," must be the foundation of postwar international security—and more idealistic popular visions of a world in which all powers, great and small, enjoyed equal status and protection. The Dumbarton Oaks Conference agreed to create a bipartite UN modeled on the earlier League of Nations but reserving ultimate authority to the dominant Allied states. Any peace-loving state that was prepared to accept the terms of the UN Charter would be eligible to apply for membership. All member states would be represented in the UN General Assembly, which would debate, discuss, and vote on issues that came before it. Executive authority rested with the eleven-member UN Security Council, which would have five permanent members: Britain, France, the United States, Russia, and China. The remaining Security Council representatives were

drawn from other UN states, all of which would serve two-year terms in rotation. Besides providing an international security mechanism, the UN was also expected to promote international cooperation on economic, social, cultural, and humanitarian issues.

At the February 1945 Yalta Conference, the Allies—at Soviet insistence—agreed that each permanent Security Council member should enjoy veto power over all General Assembly decisions. The Soviet Union also obtained separate representation for Belorussia (Belarus) and Ukraine. The Yalta Conference further agreed on a UN trustee system to administer both former League of Nations mandatory territories—originally colonies taken from Germany and Turkey after World War I—and areas seized from the Axis powers when the current war ended.

The Yalta Conference formally invited all Allied and most neutral powers to attend a conference that would open in San Francisco on 25 April 1945 to establish the UN. Representatives of fifty-one nations attended this gathering, which ended on 25 July 1945, and hammered out the details of the UN Charter, which accorded smaller states slightly more authority than had the original Dumbarton Oaks proposals. The charter incorporated the International Labor Organization (ILO), established under the original 1919 League of Nations Covenant. To pursue its stated nonsecurity objectives, the charter also created the United Nations Economic,

Social and Cultural Organization (UNESCO), together with an eighteen-member Economic and Social Council, a Trusteeship Council, an International Court of Justice, and the UN Secretariat, which administered the organization. By the end of 1945, all fifty-one states represented at San Francisco had ratified the UN Charter. In 1946 the body held its first session in London and in 1947 moved permanently to the United States, where its headquarters was completed soon afterward in New York City.

So vast were the mandate and responsibilities of the UN that much regarding its future role remained open when it was founded in 1945. As is not uncommon with bureaucracies, additional agencies proliferated, and its structure gradually became more complex. As former colonies won independence and large states were sometimes partitioned into smaller units, by the end of the twentieth century the membership had expanded from the original 51 member states to close to 200. As the number of members soared, the Security Council grew from 11 to 15 members, and the Economic and Social Council rose first to 27 members and eventually to 54. By the mid-1990s, the UN system embraced fifteen specialized institutions, among them the ILO, the International Monetary Fund (IMF), the World Bank Group, UNESCO, and the World Health Organization (WHO); two semiautonomous affiliates, including the International Atomic Energy Authority (IAEA); fifteen specific organizations established by and responsible to the General Assembly; six functional commissions; five regional commissions; and seventy-five special committees. By the mid-1990s, more than 29,000 international civil servants worked for the UN in its New York headquarters and its subsidiary offices in Geneva and Vienna.

The UN soon became an arena for Cold War contests and disputes in which the major powers tested their strength, while third world nations came to see the UN as a forum where, given their growing numbers, the concerns of less-developed countries could be voiced and made effective, especially in the General Assembly, which was empowered to discuss all international questions of interest to members. In the Cold War context, the UN became a venue in which the Western and communist camps contended for power. Despite its stated security role, the organization proved remarkably unsuccessful in defusing the growing tensions that, during the second half of the 1940s, rapidly came to divide the former World War II Allies such that the Western powers of Britain, France, and the United States were soon fiercely at odds with the Soviet Union.

With UN endorsement, in 1948 the Republic of Korea (ROK, South Korea) established a pro-Western and noncommunist government, while the communist Democratic People's Republic of Korea (DPRK, North Korea) failed to win UN recognition. A much greater test of strength came after the communist takeover of Mainland China in October 1949,

when the United States vetoed Soviet-backed efforts to transfer UN representation for China from the rejected Guomindang (GMD, Nationalist) government—which still controlled the island of Taiwan—to Mao Zedong's new People's Republic of China (PRC). In protest against the veto, the Soviet delegation withdrew from the UN, a boycott that was maintained for several months. Only in 1970 did the PRC win UN membership and China's Security Council seat.

When the UN was founded, it was anticipated that peacekeeping and the restoration of international security and order, if necessary by military means, would be among its major functions. Under Article 43 of the UN's charter, member states were originally expected to agree to make specified military forces available to the UN for deployment under the organization's control, for use on occasions when military intervention was required to maintain or reestablish international peace and security. In practice, no nation signed any such agreement relinquishing control of any military forces to UN authority.

The Soviet boycott permitted the United States in June 1950 to win UN endorsement for military intervention in Korea after North Korean forces invaded South Korea. Subsequent Soviet attempts later that year to veto the continuation of UN intervention in Korea were blocked when the United States persuaded the General Assembly, where it possessed a majority, to pass the Uniting for Peace Resolution, allowing the assembly to recommend measures to member states to implement the restoration of international peace and security. The Korean War was the only occasion until the 1990–1991 Persian Gulf War on which the UN itself intervened militarily to restore the status quo. In practice, the United States provided the bulk of troops involved, although other North Atlantic Treaty Organization (NATO) allies, most notably Britain and Canada, provided substantial forces, as did Australia and New Zealand. The fact that the stalemated Korean War lasted for approximately three years, despite all UN efforts at mediation, illustrated the limitations of the peacekeeping functions of the organization.

Between 1945 and 1988 the UN did, however, undertake eleven limited peacekeeping operations, deploying an Emergency Force of troops—usually from states such as Canada, Colombia, Sweden, Norway, and Pakistan that were not permanent members of the Security Council—at the request and on the territory of at least one nation involved in a conflict or crisis in efforts to maintain peace. The first such occasion was the Suez Crisis of October 1956, when British, French, and Israeli forces attacked Egypt. The UN responded to a request from Egypt's President Gamal Abdel Nasser by sending a contingent of 6,000 lightly armed personnel to oversee truce arrangements and the withdrawal of the invading forces. Although such arrangements were supposedly neutral, in practice the UN normally acted on the request of one party or the other in a dispute, and its forces often came to be identified with that side. When UN forces were dispatched to the Congo for several years in the early 1960s, they were soon perceived as working closely with Lieutenant General (and future president) Joseph Mobutu Sese Seko and against Prime Minister Moise Tshombe, a situation that soon led to increased casualties among UN forces.

Apart from such peacekeeping efforts, the UN responded to most international crises, such as the successive Arab-Israeli wars, with calls for cease-fires and truces and offers of mediation. After the failure to implement the Geneva Accords of 1954, which mandated the unification of Vietnam after nationwide elections, the UN refused to admit either the northern or southern Vietnamese states as members. From the late 1950s to the early 1970s, successive UN secretary-generals nonetheless made repeated though unavailing efforts to negotiate a peace settlement in Vietnam. The UN verbally condemned the Soviet invasions of Hungary in 1956 and Czechoslovakia in 1968 and the imposition of martial rule in Poland in 1981. Often, too, the UN embargoed the shipment of military equipment to states at war, although the effectiveness of such sanctions varied according to the willingness of member states to enforce them.

The UN General Assembly was the arena for some of the most significant pronouncements and dramatic confrontations of the Cold War. In 1953, President Dwight D. Eisenhower delivered his "Atoms for Peace" address before the assembly, calling for international cooperation to develop peaceful uses for nuclear energy. More tense occasions included those when the flamboyant Soviet leader Nikita Khrushchev openly defied the Western powers, and U.S. representative Adlai Stevenson's challenge to his Soviet counterpart in October 1962 to confirm the presence of Soviet missiles in Cuba. During the Cuban Missile Crisis, UN Secretary-General U Thant offered to mediate a settlement, an offer that President John F. Kennedy might have accepted had his own efforts proved unsuccessful. More embarrassingly for the United States, during the American-backed Bay of Pigs invasion attempt against Cuba in April 1961, Stevenson initially denied that his country was involved, a statement that he was later forced to retract. The UN generally encouraged all international efforts toward arms control and provided the arena for the negotiation of the 1968 Treaty on the Non-Proliferation of Nuclear Weapons, the 1972 Biological and Toxin Weapons Convention, and the 1992 Convention on the Prohibition of the Development, Production, Stockpiling, and Use of Chemical Weapons.

The rapid increase in UN member-states during the 1950s and 1960s, largely the result of decolonization, brought growing numbers of African and Asian representatives to the General Assembly. In 1964, African, Asian, and Latin American nations formed the Group of Seventy-Seven, whose numbers eventually grew to 120 states from third world or developing nations and who frequently voted as a bloc and constituted more than a two-thirds majority of the General Assembly. Cuba, the bête noire of successive American presidents, took a prominent role in this grouping. The group's concerns focused primarily on economic issues (including the global distribution of wealth, resources, and power), the Arab-Israeli conflict, and South Africa rather than the Cold War per se. These concerns nonetheless frequently put them at odds with the United States, while the Soviet Union endorsed most Group of Seventy-Seven positions. It was largely at the group's instigation, for example, that the UN in 1970 expelled the Republic of China (ROC, Taiwan), admitting the PRC in its place, and sought to impose international economic sanctions on countries such as Israel, Rhodesia (subsequently Zimbabwe), and South Africa that defied UN resolutions. Western moral authority within the UN was also affected by the revelation in the late 1970s that as a young man during World War II, the Austrian-born UN Secretary-General Kurt Waldheim had belonged not just to the Nazi party but also to a military unit that had committed atrocities in Yugoslavia. No secretary-general since Waldheim has been of European origin.

Faced with declining influence in the UN and from the mid-1960s finding itself on the winning side less than 50 percent of the time in General Assembly votes, from the late 1960s onward the United States became decidedly less enthusiastic toward the organization. In the mid-1970s, U.S. representative to the UN Daniel Patrick Moynihan chose to adopt more confrontational tactics, aggressively putting forward his country's position and its commitment to the values of liberty and democracy. For the rest of the 1970s his successor, Andrew Young, nominated by President Jimmy Carter, was more conciliatory, but under President Ronald Reagan UN Ambassador Jeane Kirkpatrick once again adopted a confrontational stance, fiercely defending American values and the U.S. commitment to authoritarian but noncommunist regimes and assailing the communist position around the world. In Nicaragua, the United States not only supported the Contras who sought to undermine the left-wing Sandinista government but also defied the International Court of Justice by mining the harbor of Managua, the capital. In 1985, distaste for the organization's policies, outlook, and management led the United States to withdraw from UNESCO, an action that the United Kingdom and Singapore soon emulated. Even more significantly, citing financial mismanagement and inefficiency, in 1985 the United States, which normally contributed at least 25 percent of the UN's budget, declined to pay a substantial portion of its assessed contribution, a decision reversed only in the mid-1990s.

The announcement in 1988 by Soviet President Mikhail Gorbachev that his country intended to renounce the "use or threat of force" as an "instrument of foreign policy" and to cut dramatically its military forces in Eastern Europe marked the beginning of a new era for the UN. Initially skeptical, U.S. leaders gradually came to credit Gorbachev's good faith. The Soviet Union and the United States were no longer at odds in the Security Council, and the Group of Seventy-Seven could no more rely automatically on Soviet, or subsequently Russian, support. Between 1988 and 1994, the Security Council undertook twenty peacekeeping operations, while the UN helped to bring about a settlement of the Iran-Iraq War and to facilitate Soviet withdrawal from its lengthy and fruitless intervention in Afghanistan. The UN also encouraged negotiation by the Soviet Union and the United States of wide-ranging arms control agreements that, by the mid-1990s, had massively reduced the numbers of nuclear weapons each side deployed on its own soil and elsewhere.

Although less controversial and publicized than its efforts to maintain peace and resolve international conflicts, at all times many of the UN's energies were devoted to economic, social, cultural, and humanitarian efforts, including the eradication and prevention of disease, environmental and climatic issues, human rights, women's and children's rights, immigration, education, the care of refugees, and measures to combat such transnational problems as international dealings in human beings and the narcotics trade. The UN was perhaps most successful in promoting joint international action on humanitarian, economic, social, and environmental issues that transcended national boundaries and demanded concerted international action, such as food and hunger, health, trade policies, social justice, women's rights, pollution, and other ecological concerns. The ending of the Cold

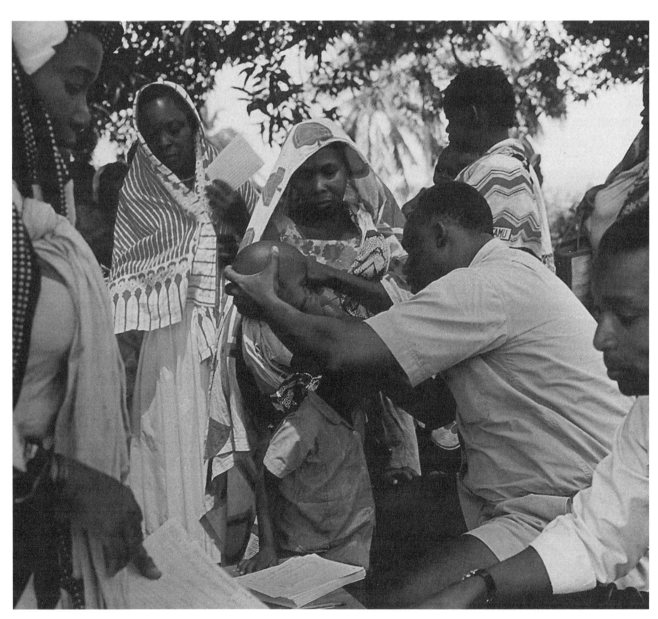

A United Nations doctor examines a baby under a mango tree, Mzizima, Uganda, 1967. (Corel)

War facilitated UN endeavors to promote such objectives by removing some of the East-West barriers to their successful implementation.

Although sometimes derided as ineffective and handicapped in international crises by its reliance upon military forces contributed by member states, the UN often provided a valuable forum for the quiet exchange of views and the promotion of humanitarian and social goals. On occasion, it also conveniently furnished a useful alternative channel of communications among powers whose diplomatic relations were otherwise limited or even nonexistent. While never as effective in terms of resolving international conflicts as its founders envisaged, the UN proved considerably more successful than its predecessor, the League of Nations, in attracting and retaining as members most of the world's major as well as minor states, whose continuing membership implicitly bestowed authority and legitimacy upon the organization's statements and actions. Although often hampered by Cold War antagonisms, during the forty-five years from 1945 to 1990 the UN played a significant role in moderating Cold War tensions and defusing at least some international crises, providing an arena in which disputes could be nonviolently resolved.

Priscilla Roberts

See also

Afghanistan War; Arab-Israeli Wars; Arms Control; Biological and Toxin Weapons Convention; China, People's Republic of; China, Republic of; Churchill, Winston; Congo, Democratic Republic of the; Eisenhower, Dwight David; Gorbachev, Mikhail; Hammarskjöld, Dag; Iran-Iraq War; Khrushchev, Nikita; Kirkpatrick, Jeane Jordan; Korean War; Lie, Trygve; Mobutu Sese Seko; Nasser, Gamal Abdel; Nicaragua; Nuclear Non-Proliferation Treaty; Reagan, Ronald Wilson; Roosevelt, Eleanor; Roosevelt, Franklin Delano; Soviet Union; Stalin, Josef; Stevenson, Adlai Ewing, II; Suez Crisis; U Thant; United States; Waldheim, Kurt; World War II, Allied Conferences

References

Firestone, Bernard J. *The United Nations under U Thant, 1961–1971.* Lanham, MD: Scarecrow, 2001.

Gaglione, Anthony. *The United Nations under Trygve Lie, 1945–1953.* Lanham, MD: Scarecrow, 2001.

Heller, Peter B. *The United Nations under Dag Hammarskjöld, 1953–1961.* Lanham, MD: Scarecrow, 2001.

Hilderbrand, Robert C. *Dumbarton Oaks: The Origins of the United Nations and the Search for Postwar Security.* Chapel Hill: University of North Carolina Press, 1990.

Lankevich, George J. *The United Nations under Javier Pérez de Cuéllar, 1982–1991.* Lanham, MD: Scarecrow, 2001.

Luard, Evan. *A History of the United Nations.* 2 vols. New York: St. Martin's, 1982–1989.

Meisler, Stanley. *The United Nations: The First Fifty Years.* New York: Atlantic Monthly Press, 1995.

Ostrower, Gary B. *The United Nations and the United States.* New York: Twayne, 1998.

Ryan, James Daniel. *The United Nations under Kurt Waldheim, 1972–1981.* Lanham, MD: Scarecrow, 2001.

Schlesinger, Stephen C. *Act of Creation: The Founding of the United Nations; A Story of Superpowers, Secret Agents, Wartime Allies and Enemies, and Their Quest for a Peaceful World.* Boulder, CO: Westview, 2003.

Simons, Jeff. *The United Nations: A Chronology of Conflict.* New York: St. Martin's, 1994.

United Nations Economic Commission for Latin America

Chartered at the sixth session of the United Nations (UN) Economic and Social Council held in February 1948, the Economic Commission for Latin America (ECLA), later changed to include the Caribbean, was established to study, report on, and recommend action concerning economic conditions and the need to promote economic development in the region. The ECLA developed economic development strategies that attempted to allow for distinctions between the center and peripheries of the international economy while advocating regionally centered programs and projects that aimed at economic reform in Latin America.

Backed primarily by the delegations of Chile, Cuba, Mexico, and Venezuela, the ECLA hoped to establish a body of economic thought and policy recommendations independent from the theory and practice currently shaped in the developed world. In the wake of World War II and in the midst of the Cold War, the backers of the ECLA believed that Latin America's traditional role in the world economy was not sustainable. Declining prices for raw materials and increasing prices for imported industrial goods meant that the region, which had relied on agricultural and mineral exports as the motors of its economies, needed to find a different path toward development.

Raúl Prebisch, an Argentine economist who had developed a pragmatic approach to economic policymaking as a result of his experiences during the Great Depression and World War II, emerged as the intellectual leader of the ECLA. In the 1950s, he and the commission recommended that Latin American governments adopt policies that artificially promoted and stimulated industrial development. Regional trade linkages and structural reforms would allow the region to develop separately and autonomously from the core areas of the international economy.

The push to integrate Latin America in economic terms represents the ECLA's most successful initiative. Beginning with efforts to create a common market in Central America in the 1960s and continuing through the Common Market of the South (Mercosur) in the 1990s, the goal of regional growth through integration remains vibrant.

The call for forced industrial growth, in part justified as a reaction to the intensification of the Cold War and the perceived need for alternative sources of industrial products, had more serious consequences, however. The ECLA in the 1950s recommended import substitution strategies that relied on high tariffs and exchange controls as a means of isolating markets and protecting fledgling industries. Artificially forcing industrialization created unanticipated economic problems. Policies that promoted industrial growth often discouraged already-established economic activities and led to falling export revenues and budget crises. Industrial promotion also encouraged explosive urban growth that taxed the ability of governments to manage material, demographic, and social changes.

In the 1960s, the commission shifted its attention to structural reform of the region's economies. This shift coincided with the creation of the Alliance for Progress that the United States promoted in the wake of the 1959 Cuban Revolution. In partnership with other inter-American agencies, the ECLA promoted land reform, food and health programs, tax reforms, and educational programs.

In recent decades, the ECLA has continued to serve as a source of statistical information and as a center for the study of the social and political impact of economic change within Latin America and the Caribbean.

Daniel Lewis

See also
Alliance for Progress; Americas; Organization of American States; United Nations

References
Cayuela, José. *ECLAC: 40 Years (1948–1988)*. Santiago, Chile: United Nations Economic Commission for Latin America and the Caribbean, 1988.

Houston, John Albert. *Latin America in the United Nations*. Westport, CT: Greenwood, 1978.

United States

The United States of America, arguably the world's most influential nation during the second half of the twentieth century, is located on the North American continent. With a 1945 population of approximately 140 million, the United States is bordered to the north by Canada and to the south by Mexico and the Gulf of Mexico. Its eastern borders are defined by the Atlantic Ocean and its western borders by the Pacific Ocean. The United States, including its territories of American Samoa and Guam in the Pacific Ocean and Puerto Rico and the U.S. Virgin Islands in the Caribbean Sea, has an area of 3.539 million square miles, making it the fourth-largest country in the world.

In World War I, the United States was a reluctant belligerent, not entering the war until April 1917, some thirty-two months after the conflict began. It emerged from the Great War in a position of preponderant economic and political strength, having been spared completely the devastation that had been wrought on the other major belligerents. Despite its putative policy of neutrality during much of the war, its economy had also benefited handsomely from the sale of war matériel and other goods to its allies, chiefly France and Great Britain. By the end of the war, in fact, New York City had supplanted London as the world's chief financial center.

At the end of World War I, U.S. President Woodrow Wilson attempted to construct a New World Order, one in which future military conflagrations would be unlikely and in which all nations would participate on a more-or-less equal footing. Wilson's internationalism policy was predicated upon three tenets. First, the postwar order was to be based upon a free-market liberal capitalist system, modeled after the United States, in which the United States would play a central role. Second, new international economic arrangements were to stress free trade, equal access to markets, and the reduction of ruinous competition. And third, international arrangements and the peace would be enforced by a supranational body known as the League of Nations—the precursor to the post–World War II United Nations (UN)—to which all nations would belong and contribute. Wilson, who referred to the League of Nations as "an alliance to end all alliances," had clearly envisioned an activist, proactive role for U.S. foreign policy. But his vision remained just that—a vision.

The U.S. Senate refused to ratify the Treaty of Versailles and by doing so refused to sanction U.S. membership in the League of Nations. Thus, the United States never participated in the body, and by the late 1920s Republican-led administrations had turned American foreign policy into one of unilateral, limited internationalism rather than multilateral internationalism. The onset of the Great Depression saw the United States become even more isolationist, so much so that Congress passed a series of Neutrality Acts to keep the nation out of a future war. Only with the obvious aggression of Nazi Germany in the late 1930s was President Franklin D. Roosevelt able to wrench his nation off the path of neutrality and isolationism, and even then it took the December 1941 Japanese attack on Pearl Harbor to bring the nation into the war, more than two years after it had begun.

World War II silenced all but the most intransigent American isolationists. The war proved that isolationism had only invited aggression and that if a third world war was to be avoided, the United States had to take the lead in international affairs, essentially filling the vast power vacuums left in the war's wake. In 1945, America was in a unique position to do just that.

Unlike all the other major World War II belligerents, the American homeland had been left entirely undamaged, and its industrial capacity, which grew exponentially throughout the war, was capable of providing much of the world's manufactured goods. While once-mighty empires such as that of the British had been brought low because of the war, the United States emerged from the war as the world's most powerful nation. Its war casualties were comparatively small, it boasted the most technologically advanced armed forces in history, and it alone possessed the atomic bomb. And although the Soviet Red Army may have had numerical superiority at war's end, the Soviet Union was no match for American economic and military power. Before World War II had ended, U.S. policymakers had already begun to plan for the postwar world, which included the establishment of the UN, another supranational organization in which the United States would, this time, play a pivotal role.

The United States took on the role of leader of noncommunist nations in the Cold War and vied with the communist powers, most prominently the Soviet Union, for influence in decolonized and third world countries. For Americans, the Cold War was a military, political, economic, and ideological contest between democracy and totalitarianism, between capitalism and communism. Yet in establishing anticommunist alliances, the U.S. government sometimes backed undemocratic governments that did not share American ideals of democracy and freedom but were anticommunist and willing to cooperate with U.S. diplomatic aims. The Cold War was the primary focus of American foreign relations and military policy for more than four decades, and as such it also influenced American politics, society, and culture.

Even before the end of World War II, American policymakers feared Soviet expansion into Western Europe and Asia. Soon after the war, deteriorating relations between East and West, the drawing of what British Prime Minister Winston Churchill termed the Iron Curtain, and the imposition of communist governments in Eastern Europe bolstered these fears. In 1947, President Harry S. Truman declared that the United States would assist any free nation in opposing takeover by hostile powers, serving as one of the earliest public announcements of the U.S. containment policy to prevent the spread of communism. This commitment, known as the Truman Doctrine, was to be the operative anticommunist policy for the duration of the Cold War, in the process making the United States the world's policeman. The Marshall Plan, also announced in 1947, represented a massive U.S. effort to rebuild Western Europe's war-torn economies and in so doing construct a citadel against Soviet encroachments in the region.

International developments in the late 1940s and early 1950s stoked Americans' fears of the global reach of communism, reinforced U.S. determination to counter it, and fueled the post–World War II defense buildup and nuclear arms race. In 1948, Congress reinstated the Selective Service Act, which until 1973 required all eligible young men to register for military service. The Soviet-led Berlin Blockade (1948–1949) fortified Americans' suspicions of communist expansionism

in Europe. In 1949, the United States entered into the North Atlantic Treaty Organization (NATO), a security pact with Canada and West European nations committing all signatories to come to the defense of any one attacked by a hostile power—implicitly understood to be the Soviet Union. This was a radical departure in U.S. foreign policy, as the nation had not been part of any permanent military alliance since the Revolutionary War in the late eighteenth century. A few months later, Americans grimly received the news of the triumph of Mao Zedong's communist forces in China, fast upon the heels of the shocking revelation that the Soviets had obliterated the U.S. atomic monopoly by exploding their first A-bomb in September.

This development led the Americans to embark on the construction of a thermonuclear—or hydrogen—bomb in January 1950, which was successfully detonated in 1952. In April 1950, Truman's National Security Council (NSC) produced a report, NSC-68, advocating a massive military buildup to prevent the spread of communism and to demonstrate U.S. determination to meet communist expansion head-on. Truman did not act on the report's recommendations until after the outbreak of the Korean War in June 1950. Within hours of the attack by the Democratic People's Republic of Korea (DPRK, North Korea), he committed U.S. troops to the fight via the UN. The Korean War lasted three years and caused the loss of nearly 37,000 American lives. Korea also forced Truman to implement the prescriptions in NSC-68, resulting in a huge military rearmament program and the permanent stationing of troops in both Asia and Western Europe.

Cold War events overseas greatly influenced American domestic politics. Although anticommunism was no stranger to the United States, it exploded after World War II. War hawks and Truman critics accused his administration of losing China to the communists and branded the Democrats as soft on communism. In February 1950, Senator Joseph R. McCarthy helped perpetuate the second American Red Scare of the twentieth century (the first one occurred in the immediate aftermath of World War I) by charging that communists had infiltrated the highest levels of the U.S. government. Although his tactics were abhorrent and his charges mostly scurrilous, McCarthy created a four-year-long anticommunist witch-hunt—subsequently dubbed "McCarthyism"—that ruined myriad careers and stifled political discourse. Simultaneously, investigations of former State Department official Alger Hiss and the atomic espionage trial of Julius and Ethel Rosenberg contributed to Americans' notions that fellow citizens might indeed be aiding a communist takeover from within the United States.

The Cold War also influenced American society and culture. Hundreds of thousands of people relied on the defense industry for employment between the 1950s and 1980s. For example, aerospace companies under contract by the U.S.

Secretary of State Dean Acheson signing the North Atlantic Treaty on behalf of the United States, 4 April 1949. (NATO Photos)

government burgeoned in southern California, stimulating a mass migration to the region. Soon, a new defense economy, or military-industrial complex, had transformed the nation by attracting millions of people from the old industrial heartland of the Northeast and Midwest to the new industrial areas of the South and Southwest. This major demographic shift resulted in a realignment of political power, moving it farther west and south. It is little coincidence that since 1964, America has had three presidents from Texas, two from California, and two from the Deep South. In the declining cities of the North, however, urban decay, deindustrialization, high unemployment, and a diminishing tax base resulted in the creation of a permanent underclass of people unable to access reputable educational opportunities or decent jobs. Military service was expected of able young men, millions of whom served overseas in hot and cold wars in the 1950s and 1960s.

U.S. civil defense authorities asked all Americans, including housewives and children, to prepare for the possibility of nuclear war by storing foodstuffs, building homemade fallout shelters, and ducking and covering in the event of atomic

attack. The Cold War shaped not only work opportunities and civic duties but also ideas about gender relations, family, and home life. For Americans, modern suburban life featuring fashionable furnishings, the latest appliances and gadgets, and a resplendently chromed automobile symbolized the superiority of the American way of life over that of communism. During the 1950s and 1960s, suburbs of cities both large and small sprang up like mushrooms in damp soil. Indeed, in American thought at the time, the ideal suburban family—with the father as sole breadwinner and the wife as dutiful homemaker and mother—had to be protected and encouraged at almost any cost. Not surprisingly, advertisements, movies, and—most famously—television promoted this alleged domestic ideal. Indeed, the family unit itself was believed to be a powerful defense against the communist subversion that Americans worried would take root in a disordered society characterized by the rejection of traditional gender roles and family arrangements. The nuclear family and an idealized home also symbolized security in an age of anxiety concerning nuclear conflict. Television sets, which

Two women volunteers demonstrate meal preparation from canned goods in an emergency fallout shelter set up at the National Canners Association convention in Chicago, 1961. (National Archives and Records Administration)

proliferated in the 1950s, occasionally broadcast programs on the evils of communism, Soviet spies, and the possibility of nuclear warfare.

Because of their nation's superpower status and its role as the leader of the anticommunist world, Americans were aware that the peoples of other nations paid attention to how they behaved at home and abroad. The excesses of McCarthyism and the trial and execution of the Rosenbergs caused those in other nations to question whether the United States actually guaranteed its citizens the constitutional rights it held up to the world as evidence of its moral authority. The civil rights movement, which gained momentum in the mid-1950s, also drew international attention to how the United States treated its African American population. The Soviets as well as U.S. allies and citizens in nonaligned nations closely followed the Montgomery Bus Boycott (1955–1956) and the attempt of nine African American students to integrate into a Little Rock, Arkansas, all-white high school in 1957. Onlookers in other nations condemned America's racist Jim Crow laws and vio-

lence against people of color and asked whether the United States could truthfully proclaim itself the beacon of democracy when it tolerated such patently unjust treatment of its own citizens.

Concerns about white Americans' conduct abroad also intensified in the 1950s. The widely read 1958 novel *The Ugly American,* by Americans William J. Lederer and Eugene Burdick, portrayed U.S. foreign service employees as boorish and ignorant of Southeast Asian languages and customs and argued that their incompetence endangered U.S. Cold War policies and even pushed potential allies toward the communist camp. To counter global negative perceptions of Americans, the U.S. government attempted to project a positive image of itself through cultural diplomacy, including informational pamphlets, student exchanges, international exhibitions, and jazz concerts.

By the dawn of the 1960s, McCarthyism was largely a thing of the past, although anticommunist policies and sentiments remained strong. In his 1960 presidential campaign, President

John F. Kennedy sharply criticized President Dwight D. Eisenhower's administration as being weak in its fight against communism. In less than three years, Kennedy's administration demonstrated a tough and bellicose (if not always successful) anticommunist posture in its botched attempt to overthrow Cuban leader Fidel Castro in the April 1961 Bay of Pigs invasion, clashes with the Soviets over Berlin in the summer of 1961, nuclear brinkmanship with the Russians over the installation of nuclear missiles in Cuba in October 1962, and the dramatic increase of U.S. military advisors assisting the Republic of Vietnam (RVN, South Vietnam). Kennedy's successor, Lyndon B. Johnson, while expanding the role of the government in protecting public welfare and promoting civil rights, sought to carry on Kennedy's tough anticommunist policies. Congress's August 1964 Gulf of Tonkin Resolution authorizing Johnson to enlarge the role of the United States in fighting the communist Democratic Republic of Vietnam (DRV, North Vietnam) provoked a massive escalation in the Vietnam War. Johnson's Vietnam War policies were expensive and divisive. By 1968, America was being torn apart by a burgeoning antiwar movement, race riots, political assassinations, and a virtual clash of cultures between the old ruling elite and the new generation of politically active college students and other young adults.

In American culture and society in the 1960s, irreverent critiques of Cold War dogma became popular. Joseph Heller's novel *Catch-22* (1961) ridiculed the armed forces as ineffectual and its missions as self-destructively irrational. Kurt Vonnegut's *Cat's Cradle* (1963) satirized the assumption that science ensured progress, portraying a nuclear scientist's invention intended to benefit the military as a threat to the existence of humankind. Among those who criticized the U.S. military engagement in Vietnam were many youths who had grown up practicing duck and cover exercises at school, reading textbooks that uncritically lauded the United States as the heroic leader in the crusade against the evils of communism, and watching films and television programs that depicted devious communists outwitted by resourceful American heroes. The counterculture movement, which influenced and was heavily influenced by anti–Vietnam War and antidraft activists, also rejected the consumerism and militarism of American society.

Despite challenges to the Cold War consensus forged in the previous decades, anticommunist attitudes persisted throughout the 1960s. Many Americans, whom President Richard M. Nixon termed "the silent majority," resented the hippies, protestors, and radicals who were seen as destroyers of the American way of life and backed conservative domestic and foreign policies. Although all the major candidates for president in 1968 had promised to remove U.S. troops from Vietnam, many Americans supported the continued air war against the Democratic Republic of Vietnam (DRV, North

Vietnam) in the early 1970s. Despite his pledge to end the war quickly, Nixon did not remove American troops from Vietnam until the beginning of his second term in 1973. Internationally, however, the Vietnam War cost the United States much of its credibility in global affairs and its claim to moral leadership in the struggle against communism. It also fueled anti-Americanism worldwide.

The 1970s saw détente between the United States and the Soviet Union, the end of the Vietnam War, and the normalization of relations with the People's Republic of China (PRC), which was recognized by President Jimmy Carter's administration in 1979. In the wake of the destructive Watergate scandal, which forced Nixon from office, Americans wrestled with the role of their nation internationally and the conduct of their government at home. The takeover of the Republic of Vietnam (ROV, South Vietnam) by the communist nationalists on the heels of the hasty American departure from Saigon in April 1975 made many Americans wonder why their nation had invested so much money, so many lives, and so many years to preserve a small, volatile nation on the other side of the world.

The costs of the war were indeed high, and ultimately the United States had not achieved its goal of preventing the reunification of Vietnam under communist rule. The disclosure of America's secret bombings in Cambodia and Laos, reports of war atrocities committed by U.S. forces, Nixon's ignominious resignation in August 1974, the fall of South Vietnam, and revelations about nefarious activities by the Federal Bureau of Investigation (FBI) and the Central Intelligence Agency (CIA) at home and abroad badly shook the American psyche. At the same time, skyrocketing oil prices, inflation, unemployment, and a stagnant economy seemed to show that the American Dream was becoming a nightmare by the end of the 1970s. The public mood turned inward, more concerned about problems at home than abroad.

Cold War tensions flared once more when Soviet forces invaded Afghanistan in December 1979 in an effort to uphold a pro-Soviet government there. President Carter had initially envisioned a foreign policy that emphasized the advancement of human rights rather than a harsh anticommunist stance entailing accelerated defense spending. The Soviet invasion, however, galvanized him to demonstrate U.S. opposition to Soviet expansionism by supporting the Afghan resistance, suspending arms limitation talks with the Soviets, placing embargoes on sales of grain and technology to Russia, reinstating registration for the draft, and boycotting the 1980 Summer Olympics in Moscow. To make matters worse, the United States was gripped by the Iran Hostage Crisis between November 1979 and January 1981, which only seemed to prove America's international weakness and Carter's inability to solve thorny foreign policy issues. Although it must be said that Carter was largely a victim of circumstances beyond

Cars lined up at a gas station in California on 9 May 1979, the first day of gas rationing following the Arab oil embargo. (UPI-Bettmann/Corbis)

his control, he nevertheless bore the brunt of Americans' frustration with a reeling economy and international crises.

Carter lost the 1980 presidential race to Ronald Reagan, who simultaneously ushered in a sometimes frighteningly militaristic anticommunism and uplifting pro-American rhetoric. In condemning the Soviet Union as an evil empire, Reagan revived in many Americans the belief in the United States as the champion of freedom and justice in the world, which appealed to those still galled by the U.S. failure in Vietnam, its loss of status in the world, and a flagging economy. In Reagan's first term as president, his administration pushed through billions of dollars of cuts to social programs, tax cuts, and major increases in defense spending.

While many Americans supported the nuclear buildup—including in 1983 Reagan's proposed Strategic Defense Initiative (SDI), nicknamed "Star Wars," a space-based system to shield the United States from incoming nuclear missiles—as necessary to counter Soviet power, others were alarmed. In June 1982, 750,000 people gathered in New York City's Central Park to protest the accelerating nuclear arms race. Apprehension over the possibility of nuclear destruction emerged in many cultural forms during the 1980s, including the controversial television movie *The Day After* (1983), which graph-

ically depicted a nuclear attack on a Midwestern city, showing the instant vaporization of humans, slow death by radiation poisoning, and the collapse of society. Popular music and literature served as additional outlets for fears of nuclear annihilation. Prince's 1983 song "1999" advocated enjoying life to its fullest as nuclear war loomed. Doug Coupland's 1991 novel *Generation X: Tales from an Accelerated Culture* depicted an unambitious group of friends in their twenties, living in the southern California desert to escape from the consumerist society of the 1980s, as deeply troubled by fears of nuclear destruction and radiation.

The mid-1980s, however, saw a rapid deceleration in Cold War tensions. The personal rapport between Reagan and Mikhail Gorbachev, who became general secretary of the Communist Party of the Soviet Union (CPSU) in 1985, inspired international optimism that perhaps the two superpowers could find solutions to their differences and step back from the nuclear abyss. Summits between the two leaders yielded an agreement in 1987 for mutual inspections of nuclear arms. Between 1989 and 1991, Reagan's successor, George H. W. Bush, and Gorbachev negotiated momentous economic and arms reduction agreements.

In the aftermath of the Cold War, those who study it continue to pursue answers to many questions. Was the Soviet Union as expansionist as American policymakers in the 1940s assumed? Might the United States have learned to coexist with communist states, or was conflict unavoidable? To what extent were pro-Soviet agents working in the United States as spies and saboteurs? Access to archival sources in the former Soviet Union as well as declassified U.S. historical documents are helping scholars to answer these questions.

Why the Cold War ended remains the subject of lively debate. Some analysts primarily credit U.S. resolve, demonstrated by a mighty (and massively expensive) defense, a steadfast opposition to communist ideology, and economic strategies that thwarted Soviet expansion over the decades. The costs to the Soviets of countering U.S. power, according to this view, contributed greatly to the demise of the Soviet Union. Other scholars give greater weight to economic and political problems inherent in the Soviet system and to Gorbachev's reforms. While Cold War triumphalists claimed that the fall of the Soviet Union proved the superiority of capitalism and democracy over communism, others pointed to U.S. failures to adhere to its own proclaimed democratic principles over the course of the Cold War, such as its covert and possibly illegal operations to help remove governments in Iran (1953), Guatemala (1954), and Chile (1973) and the subversion of the U.S. constitutional process in the Iran-Contra Affair (1984–1986).

In the early twenty-first century, remnants of the Cold War persist in U.S. foreign relations. The U.S. government still refuses to recognize the Cuban government of communist

Fidel Castro. The PRC's human rights abuses and suppression of democracy continued to trouble Americans, although Sino-American relations, especially in trade, had improved. North Korea, perhaps the last lonely outpost of the Cold War, remained intractably bellicose.

Donna Alvah and Paul G. Pierpaoli Jr.

See also

Carter, James Earl, Jr.; Civil Defense; Containment Policy; Cuba; Détente; Duck and Cover Drill; Eisenhower, Dwight David; Guatemala; International Expositions; Iran; Iran-Contra Affair; Johnson, Lyndon Baines; Kennedy, John Fitzgerald; King, Martin Luther, Jr.; Korean War; Marshall Plan; McCarthyism; Military-Industrial Complex; National Security Council Report NSC-68; Nixon, Richard Milhous; North Atlantic Treaty; Nuclear Arms Race; Race Relations, United States; Reagan, Ronald Wilson; Rosenberg, Julius; Truman, Harry S.; Truman Doctrine; Vietnam War; Vietnam War Protests

References

Buckingham, Peter H. *America Sees Red: Anti-Communism in America, 1870s to 1980s.* Claremont, CA: Regina Books, 1988.

Dudziak, Mary. *Cold War Civil Rights: Race and the Image of American Democracy.* Princeton, NJ: Princeton University Press, 2000.

Fernlund, Kevin J., ed. *The Cold War American West, 1945–1989.* Albuquerque: University of New Mexico Press, 1998.

Friedberg, Aaron L. *In the Shadow of the Garrison State: America's Anti-Statism and Its Cold War Grand Strategy.* Princeton, NJ: Princeton University Press, 2000.

Gaddis, John Lewis. *We Now Know: Rethinking Cold War History.* New York: Oxford University Press, 1997.

Judge, Edward H., and John W. Langdon, eds. *A Hard and Bitter Peace: A Global History of the Cold War.* Upper Saddle River, NJ: Prentice Hall, 1996.

Lafeber, Walter. *America, Russia and the Cold War, 1945–2002.* Updated 9th ed. New York: McGraw-Hill, 2004.

Leffler, Melvyn P. *The Specter of Communism: The United States and the Origins of the Cold War, 1917–1953.* New York: Hill and Wang, 1994.

May, Elaine Tyler. *Homeward Bound: American Families in the Cold War Era.* New York: Basic Books, 1988.

Powaski, Ronald E. *The Cold War: The United States and the Soviet Union, 1917–1991.* New York: Oxford University Press, 1998.

Schrecker, Ellen, ed. *Cold War Triumphalism: The Misuse of History after the Fall of Communism.* New York: New Press, 2004.

Sherry, Michael J. *In the Shadow of War: The United States since the 1930's.* New Haven, CT: Yale University Press, 1995.

Whitfield, Stephen J. *The Culture of the Cold War.* 2nd ed. Baltimore: Johns Hopkins University Press, 1996.

Winkler, Allan M. *Life under a Cloud: American Anxiety about the Atom.* New York: Oxford University Press, 1993.

United States, Air Force

The U.S. Army Air Forces (AAF) ended World War II as the largest and most powerful air force in the world. By the end of the conflict, the AAF comprised some 2.4 million personnel in 16 separate air forces (12 of them overseas) and 243 groups (later designated as wings). The important role played by the AAF in the war helped bring about realization of the goal long sought by its leaders of an independent air force.

The National Security Act, passed by Congress and signed into law by President Harry S. Truman in July 1947, established the U.S. Air Force (USAF) as an independent armed service. The USAF established three major combat commands in the United States: the Strategic Air Command (SAC), the Tactical Air Command (TAC), and the Air Defense Command (ADC). The concept of strategic bombardment, which the AAF had embraced in World War II, continued to receive emphasis, and under General Curtis E. LeMay, SAC became the dominant USAF command. It controlled the long-range bomber force and the nation's nuclear delivery capability. SAC also assumed responsibility for aerial tankers to extend the strike range of the bombers. SAC gained responsibility for intercontinental ballistic missiles (ICBMs) when they entered the U.S. force structure in the late 1950s.

Created in 1946, the ADC and TAC were initially merged into the Continental Air Command in December 1948 but were separated two years later. The USAF used TAC and theater commands overseas to conduct aviation missions in support of theater operations, including air superiority, ground attack (close air support and interdiction), reconnaissance, and airlift in the Military Air Transport Service (MATS). MATS demonstrated its importance during the 1948–1949 Berlin Airlift.

First Secretary of the Air Force Stuart Symington (1947–1950) and air force leaders argued for a 70-wing air force, but budget retrenchment following World War II led to aggressive force reductions, resulting in an actual force structure of 48 wings. Nonetheless, because of the perception of airpower and atomic weapons as a war-winning combination, the USAF became the dominant service in terms of funding and political support, and SAC was clearly the most influential command in the U.S. defense establishment during the 1950s. The onset of the Korean War (1950–1953) brought significant improvement and increased spending for more personnel and new aircraft, leading to a 235-wing force in 1956.

Airpower did play a key role in the Korean War. It was certainly one of the most important factors in enabling United Nations Command (UNC) personnel to stand at the Pusan Perimeter until the United States could effect its military buildup and take the offensive. Propeller-driven Boeing B-29 Superfortress bombers destroyed the industrial base of the Democratic People's Republic of Korea (DPRK, North Korea) and soon ran out of meaningful targets. U.S. airpower continued to savage North Korean and, later, Chinese supply lines and exacted a heavy toll on their ground personnel. Communist Mikoyan-Gurevich MiG-15 interceptor aircraft, initially flown by Soviet pilots, however, forced the UNC to

A U.S. Air Force North American F-86 Sabre jet launching 5-inch rockets. America's first swept-wing jet and the world's first air-superiority fighter, the Sabre played an important role in the Korean War. (U.S. Air Force)

abandon strategic daytime bombing. The Lockheed F-80 Shooting Star, the first U.S. mass-produced jet aircraft, and the more capable Republic F-84 Thunderjet proved no match for the MiG-15, although on 8 November 1950 an F-80 did shoot down a MiG-15 in the first clash between jet aircraft in history. A worthy opponent for the MiG appeared in the North American F-86 Sabre, hastily rushed to Korea. These two jet aircraft were well matched, but the F-86s racked up an impressive kill ratio thanks to superior pilot training.

Top USAF leaders nonetheless concluded that the Korean War had been an anomaly, and they continued to invest significant resources in SAC programs. SAC's first strategic bomber was the propeller-driven Boeing B-50 Superfortress, introduced in 1947. Basically a vastly improved B-29, it was certainly outclassed by jet aircraft. In 1948 the Convair B-36 Peacemaker six-engine bomber entered service. With a gross weight of 410,000 pounds, it was the world's largest aircraft. The B-36 was also the world's first intercontinental bomber and was capable of carrying up to 72,000 pounds of muni-

tions. It remained in service until 1959. The first four-engine American jet bomber was the North American B-45 Tornado. Produced beginning in 1948, it served in Korea in a reconnaissance role and was in service for a decade. The Boeing B-47 Stratojet medium bomber was one of the most important of USAF aircraft. Sleek and futuristic and the first swept-wing bomber ever in production, the B-47 entered service in 1951. Boeing's follow-on aircraft to the B-47, the B-52 Stratofortress, entered service in 1955. The Stratofortress has been in service for more than fifty years. Certainly one of the most important aircraft ever produced, it was capable of carrying a 40,000-pound payload 8,800 miles. B-52s are closely identified with the Cold War and played a leading role in the Vietnam War, even acting in support of ground operations. They are best remembered, however, for their role in the December 1972 Christmas Bombing of Hanoi and Haiphong. In 1960, SAC received the sleek Convair B-58 Hustler. In service for a decade, the large delta-configuration B-58 was capable of a speed of 1,385 mph—the world's first supersonic bomber.

THE NO-FLY ZONE WAR, 1991 – 2003

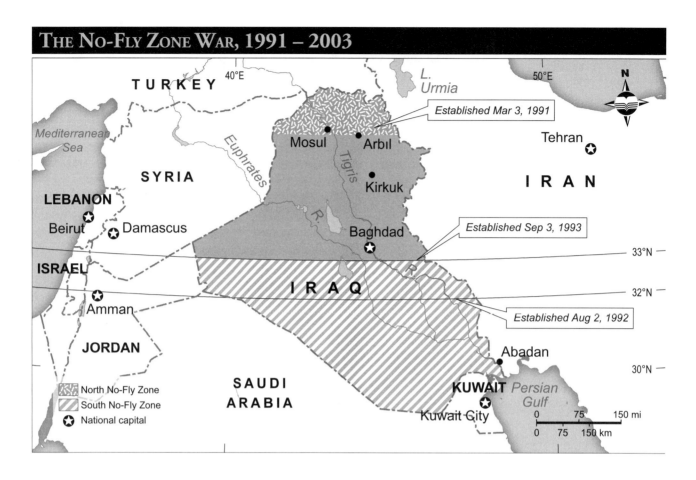

The Vietnam War saw the USAF carry out operations in direct support of ground troops but also conduct the highly publicized bombing of North Vietnam (Operations ROLLING THUNDER, LINEBACKER I, and LINEBACKER II) and the secret bombing of Laos (Operations BARREL ROLL and STEEL TIGER) and Cambodia (Operation MENU). The interdiction campaigns were frustrating in that they never could completely halt the infiltration of men and supplies by the Democratic Republic of Vietnam (DRV, North Vietnam) into the Republic of Vietnam (RVN, South Vietnam), but they certainly did make it much more difficult for the communist side in the war and kept many North Vietnamese troops and weapons out of South Vietnam. The campaigns did reveal the limitations of airpower in nonconventional warfare, however. U.S. airpower, to include the U.S. Navy and the U.S. Marine Corps, did play an important role in such battles as the action in the Ia Drang Valley, the 1968 Tet Offensive, and the siege of Khe Sanh, and certainly airpower was a key factor in North Vietnam's invasion of South Vietnam in the Spring or Easter Offensive of 1972.

In 1957, the United States launched its first ICBM, and shortly thereafter SAC also controlled nuclear-armed ICBMs. By the end of the 1960s, SAC controlled more than 1,000 ICBMs as the number of nuclear-capable bombers dwindled. The bombers and ICBMs combined with the navy's submarine-launched ballistic missiles (SLBMs) to create the triad nuclear deterrence force. Coordination in targeting and the development of the nuclear Single Integrated Operations Plan was the responsibility of the Joint Strategic Target Planning Staff, collocated at Offutt Air Force Base with SAC headquarters. SAC was disestablished on 1 June 1992, following the end of the Cold War. Its nuclear planning and command and control role continued in the Unified Command, U.S. Strategic Command, and its operational forces were dispersed to other USAF major commands: bombers and missiles to Air Combat Command (missiles later moved to Space Command) and tankers to Air Mobility Command.

In the early Cold War years, the offensive capability of SAC was complemented by extensive USAF air defense forces. The ADC was responsible for the interceptor fighters dedicated to the defense of the continental United States. The command also directed the early warning radar system and the command and control structure that coordinated all air defense resources, including resources provided by other services in an emergency. The ADC became the U.S. component of the North American Air Defense Command (NORAD), and the ADC commander normally served simultaneously as the NORAD commander as well. As space systems became increasingly important to warning and defensive operations, the USAF renamed the command the Aerospace Defense

Command in 1968. The ADC was headquartered at Ent Air Force Base, Colorado, and then at Peterson Field, Colorado. The ADC was inactivated in March 1980, and its functions were dispersed to other major commands, primarily SAC, TAC, and, eventually, Space Command.

Prominent interceptor aircraft flown by the USAF in this period included the Northrop F-89 Scorpion and the Lockheed F-94 Starfire. These aircraft entered service in 1950 and served for a decade, bringing radar intercept capabilities for night and bad weather operations. The North American F-86D Sabre of 1951 was the first USAF single-seat all-weather jet interceptor. The North American F-100 Super Sabre appeared in 1954 and served until 1979. It was the first USAF fighter to cruise at supersonic speeds and was designed as an interceptor. The Lockheed F-104 Starfighter appeared in 1958 as an interceptor but ended its career as a ground attack aircraft. The second generation of air defense systems included the McDonnell Douglas F-101B Voodoo, Convair F-102 Delta Dart, and Convair F-106 Delta Dagger interceptors.

The TAC was established in 1946 to control and train forces that would work with U.S. Army units in theater operations. TAC's primary missions were securing air superiority and providing support to the ground forces through close air support, interdiction, and reconnaissance missions. TAC was merged into the Continental Air Command in 1948. In December 1950, the USAF returned TAC to major command status, reflecting the demands of the Korean War on theater air resources. TAC was headquartered at Langley Air Force Base in Virginia. The USAF converted TAC to Air Combat Command in 1992 as part of the post–Cold War reorganization.

The F-80, F-84, and F-86 were among the first jet fighters. They were followed in the 1950s by day-fighter designs that had a secondary ground-attack role, especially the Super Sabre and the Starfighter. Over time, both the F-100 and the F-104 became primarily ground-attack platforms. In the mid-1960s, the USAF adapted the navy-designed McDonnell Douglas F-4 Phantom as a multirole aircraft to perform the air superiority and ground-attack roles. The McDonnell Douglas F-15 Eagle was the first USAF design specifically for air superiority. It entered service in 1974 and saw extensive service in the 1991 Gulf War. It also performed brilliantly for the Israeli Air Force. The General Dynamics F-16 Fighting Falcon of 1980, conceived as a lightweight multirole complement to the F-15, combined air-to-air and ground-attack capabilities.

Fighter-bomber, attack, and reconnaissance aircraft included the Thunderjet of 1947. It saw extensive service in a variety of missions during the Korean War. Reflecting the nuclear-oriented force structure of Dwight D. Eisenhower's presidency, the USAF embraced the Republic F-105 Thunderchief fighter-bomber as a supersonic nuclear weapons delivery system. In a conventional bombing role, it bore the brunt of the air war over North Vietnam.

The superb Phantom entered service in 1960 and served extensively in Vietnam, where it established an enviable combat record. The Phantom remained in service throughout the Cold War period. The General Dynamics F/FB-111 Aardvark of 1968 was the first operational combat aircraft with a swing-wing. Finally, mention must be made of the F-117A Nighthawk stealth fighter. In appearance unlike any other aircraft and making use of radar absorbent materials, the triangular-shaped F-117A appeared in 1983 and first saw action in the 1989 U.S. invasion of Panama. It also participated extensively in the Gulf War, hitting targets with great precision. Of reconnaissance aircraft, Lockheed produced perhaps the world's two best in the Cold War: the U-2 (1956) and the SR-71 (1964).

Of major USAF overseas commands, the two most important were the United States Air Forces in Europe (USAFE) and the Pacific Air Forces (PACAF). USAFE was established in August 1945 and served as the air force component of the U.S. European Command. USAF theater forces in the Pacific were initially organized as the Far East Air Forces. In 1957, the designation shifted to Pacific Air Forces. PACAF was the USAF component of the U.S. Pacific Command.

Airlift emerged as a vitally important function during World War II. This continued in the Cold War. In 1948, the Air Force Air Transport Command and the Navy Air Transport Service were merged to create MATS, which was charged with providing all necessary airlift support to the U.S. military. The USAF changed MATS to the Military Airlift Command (MAC) in 1966. MAC became the air force component to U.S. Transportation Command, the unified command responsible for moving and sustaining U.S. combat forces. In addition to military aircraft, MAC managed contracted airlift and the Civil Reserve Air Fleet (CRAF), which provided an additional surge airlift capacity in national emergencies. MAC was headquartered at Scott Air Force Base, Illinois. During the post–Cold War USAF reorganization in 1992, MAC was renamed Air Mobility Command and gained control of the tanker aircraft that had previously been assigned to SAC.

McDonnell Douglas provided a large number of transport aircraft in this period. Among these were the workhorse C-47 Skytrain (the military version of the DC-3); the C-54 Skymaster (the civilian DC-4), the first four-engine U.S. military transport; the C-74 Globemaster, at its introduction in 1945 the world's largest transport plane; the C-118 Liftmaster (the DC-6 in civilian service); the C-124 Globemaster, the USAF's first strategic cargo plane; and the C-133 Cargomaster. Lockheed also provided noteworthy Cold War transport aircraft, including the C-121 Super Constellation, the C-130 Hercules, and the C-141 Starlifter, in 1965 the world's first all-jet air transport aircraft. Lockheed's giant C-5 Galaxy entered service in 1969 and held the title as the world's largest operational aircraft for more than fifteen years. The twin-engine Fairchild C-119 Flying Boxcar entered service in 1949

A Delta launch vehicle carrying an active magnetospheric particle tracer explorer satellite lifts off from the Kennedy Space Center, 16 August 1984. (U.S. Department of Defense)

and served with distinction in Korea and in Vietnam. Tanker aircraft include the McDonnell Douglas KC-10 Extender and Boeing KC-135 Stratotanker.

The USAF was heavily involved in the development of space systems from its origin as a separate service and became the lead agency for space launches, working closely with other government agencies, especially the Central Intelligence Agency (CIA) and the National Reconnaissance Office, to develop a wide range of space-based capabilities. Initially, the development and launch of satellite systems were the responsibilities of the Air Research and Development Command (ARDC), which also dealt with aircraft and other weapons system designs. The USAF redesignated ARDC the Air Force Systems Command (AFSC) in 1961. The rapidly increasing importance of space led the USAF to establish the Air Force Space Command in September 1982. Air Force Space Command provided launch support and operational control of space platforms and became the lead agency for U.S. military space activities. It also assumed some of the ADC component functions in NORAD and in 1985 became the air force component of the U.S. Space Command.

The USAF relied on a number of supporting major commands to develop and sustain its capabilities. The Air Force Logistics Command (AFLC, Air Matériel Command until 1961) provided supply and maintenance support. In the post–Cold War reorganization of 1992, the USAF merged the AFLC and the AFSC into Air Force Matériel Command. An additional important command for the USAF was Air Training Command (ATC), the organization that provided all of the formal training for USAF personnel, including flying training for pilots and navigators and technical training for all career fields. The USAF later renamed the ATC the Air Education and Training Command.

USAF doctrinal emphasis on deep attacks in pursuit of decisive effects often placed it in conflict with the other services, which believed that airpower should be used in a support role to assist the surface forces in traditional campaigns against enemy surface forces. In addition to seeking decisive offensive victories, USAF doctrine emphasized the importance of technological dominance and the need for pursuing advanced capabilities. As the Cold War ended, USAF theater airpower and space power, developed to deter and if necessary engage Soviet power, was nonetheless highly effective in providing the foundation for victory in Operation DESERT STORM, the 1991 campaign to liberate Kuwait from Iraqi occupation.

The end of the Cold War brought a considerable decline in USAF strength. In 1987 the USAF had 171 wings, 7,245 active duty aircraft, and 607,000 personnel. By 1991 these numbers had fallen to 153 wings (115 wings by 1995), 4,710 aircraft, and 388,100 personnel. Air National Guard (ANG) and Air Force Reserve (AFR) totals experienced similar declines, from 263,000 to 181,000 personnel.

Jerome V. Martin and Spencer C. Tucker

See also

Aircraft; Aircraft Carriers; Bombers, Strategic; Missiles, Intercontinental Ballistic; Missiles, Intermediate-Range Ballistic; North American Aerospace Defense Command; Nuclear Arms Race; Nuclear Weapons, Tactical; Triad

References

Boyne, Walter J. *Beyond the Wild Blue: A History of the United States Air Force, 1947–1997.* New York: St. Martin's, 1997.

Dick, Ron. *American Eagles: A History of the United States Air Force.* Charlottesville, VA: Howell, 1997.

Frisbee, John L., ed. *Makers of the United States Air Force.* Washington, DC: U.S. Government Printing Office, 1987.

Futrell, Robert Frank. *Ideas, Concepts, Doctrine: Basic Thinking in the United States Air Force,* vols. 1 and 2. Maxwell AFB, AL: Air University Press, 1989.

Lambeth, Benjamin S. *The Transformation of American Air Power.* Ithaca, NY: Cornell University Press, 2000.

Momyer, William W. *Air Power in Three Wars.* Washington, DC: U.S. Government Printing Office, 1982.

Nalty, Bernard C., ed. *Winged Shield, Winged Sword: A History of the United States Air Force.* 2 Vols. Washington, DC: Air Force History and Museums Program, U.S. Government Printing Office, 1997.

Ravenstein, Charles A. *The Organization and Lineage of the United States Air Force.* Washington, DC: Office of Air Force History, USAF, U.S. Government Printing Office, 1986.

Trest, Warren A. *Air Force Roles and Missions: A History.* Washington, DC: Air Force History and Museum Program, U.S. Government Printing Office, 1998.

United States, Army

The U.S. Army emerged from World War II as the best-armed, most-mobile, best-equipped, best-supplied, most-educated, and highest-paid army in history. Immediately following the end of the war, President Harry S. Truman supported a measured reduction from 8.2 million to 1.5 million men, but domestic political pressures resulted in an army drawdown to fewer than 591,000 personnel in ten divisions and five regiments by June 1950. The 1947 National Security Act, designed to unify the nation's armed forces and decrease interservice rivalries, established the U.S. Air Force as independent from the army and designated the army as having primary responsibility for land-based operations.

Despite streamlining of command structure in the late 1940s, low budgets contributed to a dramatic decline in army combat effectiveness. By 1950, few of the army's ten divisions were fully capable of deployment outside the continental United States. Four understrength, poorly trained, and inadequately equipped divisions were in occupation in Japan, while 80,000 men were in Germany.

The Korean War began in June 1950. American advisors and troops rushed from Japan helped purchase just enough time to prevent Democratic People's Republic of Korea (DPRK, North Korea) forces from completely overrunning the Republic of Korea (ROK, South Korea) before substantial forces could be sent from the United States. This also presented serious difficulties, as the army was stretched thin trying to keep up its guard in Europe with the formation of the North Atlantic Treaty Organization (NATO) in 1949.

The war revealed the appalling state of the U.S. military, especially the army, which had undergone major cutbacks under Defense Secretary Louis Johnson, who favored the air force over both the army and navy. Troops were often sent into combat without proper training, and equipment was both obsolete and inadequate. The buildup in Korea was made possible only by calling up reserve and National Guard units, which also had the effect of securing experienced combat veterans. Most of the weaponry employed by the army in Korea was of World War II vintage.

Massive U.S. artillery fire and airpower helped to offset Chinese numbers. The war also saw the army carry out extensive experimentation with the helicopter for medical evacuation but also for resupply and the movement of troops. In addition, the war speeded up desegregation of the army. During the conflict, the defense budget quadrupled, and the army grew dramatically in size. By 1953, army strength stood at twenty divisions and eighteen regiments with a total of 1.5 million personnel. The Korean War also acted as a stimulus to research and development programs, which brought new

weapons into the field in the latter 1950s and early 1960s, and ensured that the United States maintained a significant military establishment. After every previous conflict, the United States had largely disarmed.

With an armistice in Korea in July 1953, the new administration of President Dwight D. Eisenhower sought to shift emphasis to nuclear deterrence in the so-called New Look policy (popularly known as "more bang for the buck"). By 1958, army strength had again decreased, this time to fifteen divisions. Under the New Look, the army prepared to use flexible but short-range nuclear munitions to offset the greater manpower of potential enemies in Europe and Asia. In the mid-1950s, the army developed the Jupiter and Nike missiles as well as artillery systems capable of firing nuclear munitions. In order to increase survivability and mobility on nuclear battlefields, the army introduced the M41, M47, and M48 tanks, reestablishing four armored divisions by 1956.

Structurally, because nuclear weapons could easily destroy concentrated groups of soldiers, the army reorganized its units into decentralized and autonomous pentomic divisions, consisting of five battle groups, that could operate independently or join together to provide mass and firepower. By 1958, the army had divided all of its infantry and airborne divisions into pentomic structures.

In the early 1960s, political events in Latin America as well as the Berlin Crises and the Cuban Missile Crisis intensified the Cold War. President John F. Kennedy's administration became concerned with combating the domino effect of encroaching communism while providing a more balanced approach to military threats. This strategy, known as flexible response, called for an increase in the army's conventional force structure to provide a nonnuclear response to future threats. It also emphasized counterinsurgency warfare.

In the 1960s, Secretary of Defense Robert S. McNamara spearheaded a wholesale reorganization of the army that consolidated redundant structures and decreased inefficiencies. Largely due to previous programs coming to fruition, the army received the M60 machine gun and the M60 tank and replaced its outdated M-1 Garand rifle with the M-14 and a few years later the M-16. The army also abandoned the pentomic division structure and established traditional three-brigade Reorganization Objective Army Divisions (ROADs), including mechanized divisions equipped with the M113 armored personnel carrier. While the army's doctrine for its ROADs centered on fighting in nonnuclear battlefields, its primary focus remained linear battles in the European theater.

As the Soviet Union and the United States approached nuclear parity, however, the army also began to prepare to counter a newly emerging threat of guerrilla-style communist insurgencies. In 1961, Kennedy significantly increased the size and scope of Special Forces units for counterinsurgency operations. Special Forces soldiers became expert in the tactics, techniques, and procedures of both defeating guerrilla movements and training indigenous soldiers, particularly as special advisors in Vietnam.

America's involvement in Vietnam, which had begun with support for the French in the Indochina War (1946–1954), rapidly escalated with the renewal of the insurgency in the late 1950s. President Kennedy sent only advisors and helicopters, but in mid-1965 his successor, Lyndon B. Johnson, introduced U.S. ground troops. The war gradually escalated, and at peak strength in early 1969 the United States had 543,400 men in Vietnam.

For the U.S. Army, the Vietnam War meant adapting to an assortment of new challenges. Enemy force capabilities ranged from squad-sized local Viet Cong units employing guerrilla tactics to well-trained North Vietnamese Army regiments and divisions supported by conventional artillery assets. The enemy could slip into local population centers and the jungle underbrush, which made locating him difficult. Additionally, enemy forces often compensated for their comparative lack of firepower by fighting at night and establishing well-placed ambushes, booby traps, and mines.

The army adapted to these challenges by employing a mixture of new tactics and new weapon systems to fight in this nonlinear battlefield. The Vietnam War also saw the United States make extensive use of the helicopter, and in August 1965 it introduced in Vietnam the 1st Air Cavalry Division,

which was entirely air mobile. Helicopter operations significantly improved the ability to mass, reinforce, and withdraw forces if necessary in remote areas not easily accessible to ground transportation.

Despite the army's overwhelming success in pitched battles with North Vietnamese regulars, the United States failed to secure victory in Vietnam. It had concentrated on big-unit actions and body counts rather than on pacification programs as measurements of success.

The army emerged from Vietnam in terrible condition. The war exacted a shocking toll on both discipline and morale. Racial problems abounded as did insubordination, and a general permissiveness led to careerism or "ticket-punching" among the officer corps and an abrogation of authority by noncommissioned officers. During the mid-1970s, all branches of the armed services, but particularly the army, suffered from underfunding and congressional and executive neglect.

The army sought an all-volunteer force. Its Volunteer Army Project (VOLAR), begun in 1970, received President Richard Nixon's warm support. He embraced the plan as a means of ending middle-class opposition to his Vietnam War policies, and he abolished the draft in 1973. The U.S. armed forces, including the army, became all-volunteer.

Recruiting standards were upgraded, and discharge programs helped to rid the army of drug users and those unsuited

A U.S. Army field training exercise involving M60 main battle tanks and AH-1 Cobra helicopters, 1974. (U.S. Department of Defense)

for military life. In 1975 the army insisted on a high school diploma for its recruits. It also began a massive educational program to eradicate perceived and actual racial discrimination. The number of African American officers increased, and promotion boards ensured that minorities were promoted equally based on percentages of numbers of those serving. Other initiatives such as barracks renovation and involving enlisted men by seeking their ideas on how to improve quality of life ended many irritants of the draft era. Another major change was allowing women increased opportunities in occupational specialties, although supposedly not in combat units. Army chief of staff General Creighton Abrams (1972–1974) and Secretary of Defense Melvin Laird (1969–1974) also did much to create a total force policy that restructured the entire army to make it impossible for political leaders to commit the army to war without mobilizing its reserve components. This was successively the case in the Persian Gulf War, the Balkans, Afghanistan, and Iraq.

As the Vietnam War faded, the army refocused its attention on what had always been considered the most significant threat: a potential Warsaw Pact invasion of Western Europe. The 1973 Arab-Israeli War convinced U.S. Army leaders that new advances in the lethality of tank munitions, artillery, and wire-guided antitank weapons created dramatic advantages for defenders in a conventional mechanized war. Technologically, these new advances required the army to modernize its antiquated equipment and develop a new tank, infantry fighting vehicle, and helicopter. Doctrinally, in 1976 the army emphasized establishing an active defense policy, an elastic strategy comprised of battle positions organized in depth that focused on firepower and attrition.

It was not until the advent in 1981 of President Ronald Reagan's administration, which focused on directly confronting Soviet capabilities in Europe, that the army received full modernization funding. The M1 Abrams Main Battle Tank, supported by the Bradley Infantry Fighting Vehicle, became the basis of maneuver warfare. In 1982, under the direction of General Donn Starry, the army adopted the AirLand Battle doctrine. Designed to deter the Soviet Union, AirLand Battle revolutionized army doctrine by shifting emphasis from defensive to offense operations and employing maneuver warfare that involved coordination of joint forces, especially close air support. Units would train to strike hard and fast to disrupt and attack the enemy's critical second-echelon forces. The U.S. Army proved the effectiveness of its training, doctrine, and equipment-modernization efforts shortly after the Cold War ended during the one hundred–hour ground offensive against Iraq in the 1991 Persian Gulf War.

At the end of the Cold War in 1991, U.S. Army strength stood at 739,594 active duty and close to 1.085 million Army Reserve and National Guard personnel.

Kelly A. Fork and Spencer C. Tucker

See also
AirLand Battle; Flexible Response; Korean War; New Look Defense Policy; Persian Gulf War; Tanks; Vietnam War; War, Operational Art of
References
Bacevich, A. J. *The Pentomic Era: The US Army between Korea and Vietnam.* Washington, DC: National Defense University Press, 1986.
Connor, Arthur W., Jr. *The Army and Transformation, 1945–1991: Implications for Today.* Carlisle Barracks, PA: U.S. Army War College, 2002.
Romjue, John L. *The Army of Excellence: The Development of the 1980s Army.* Fort Monroe, VA: Office of the Command Historian, U.S. Army Training and Doctrine Command, 1993.
———. *From Active Defense to AirLand Battle: The Development of Army Doctrine, 1973–1982.* Fort Monroe, VA: Historical Office, U.S. Army Training and Doctrine Command, 1984.
Rose, John P. *The Evolution of U.S. Army Nuclear Doctrine, 1945–1980.* Boulder, CO: Westview, 1980.
Weigley, Russell F. *History of the United States Army.* Enlarged ed. Bloomington: Indiana University Press, 1984.

United States Commander in Chief, Europe

Established on 1 August 1952, the United States Commander in Chief, Europe (USCINCEUR) is responsible for executing the military and defense policies of the United States by ensuring that combat-ready forces from the U.S. Army, Navy (including Marines), and Air Force are in the region. These forces may conduct operations alone or in concert with other countries. When originally formed, the area of responsibility included Europe from the North Cape in Norway south to the Mediterranean Sea as well as North Africa and Turkey. The area was eventually expanded to include the Middle East as far south as Saudi Arabia, east to Iran, and south to include Africa all the way to the Cape of Good Hope in South Africa.

The officer in this position also serves as Supreme Allied Commander Europe (SACEUR). Because the flag officer serving at USCINCEUR also serves as the SACEUR, the Deputy Commander in Chief, Europe (DCINCEUR), has the authority to make decisions and direct U.S. military matters for the USCINICEUR. The first USCINCEUR was General Matthew B. Ridgway, who served during 1 August 1952–11 July 1953.

Dallace W. Unger Jr.

See also
Europe, U.S. Armed Forces in; North Atlantic Treaty Organization, Origins and Formation of; Ridgway, Matthew Bunker; Supreme Allied Commander Europe
References
Leffler, Melvyn P. *A Preponderance of Power: National Security, the Truman Administration, and the Cold War.* Stanford, CA: Stanford University Press, 1992.
Paul, Roland A. *American Military Commitments Abroad.* Camden, NJ: Rutgers University Press, 1973.

United States Information Agency

American foreign information/media service agency responsible for the propagation and dissemination of anti-communist propaganda, the circulation of news and other information to Eastern bloc nations, and the arrangement of certain cultural and educational exchanges during the Cold War. The United States was the last major power to engage in permanent foreign propaganda operations in support of political and cultural objectives. This reluctance changed abruptly after the 1941 Pearl Harbor attack. In 1941 President Franklin D. Roosevelt created the Office of War Information (OWI), whose mission was to publicize American policies to overseas audiences. The agency mounted the largest overseas propaganda operation of all the major combatants, including the Voice of America (VOA) shortwave radio network as well as the establishment of information centers on all continents. These activities set the tone and organizational structure of the OWI's Cold War successor, the United States Information Agency (USIA).

The OWI was shut down shortly after the end of World War II. Its operations were drastically reduced and transferred to the Department of State. By 1948, however, Cold War concerns led Congress to authorize a sharp expansion of the program. Congress also approved the U.S. Educational and Cultural Exchange Act of 1948, which gave permanent status to an overseas information (and propaganda) effort.

In 1953, President Dwight D. Eisenhower decided to transfer the program from the State Department to the new USIA. This decision was motivated in large part by Republican campaign promises to give greater attention to propaganda operations as part of a coordinated political and military effort that would roll back the Soviet threat. The agency's budgets were later increased to provide for more VOA broadcasting facilities, including programs in more than forty languages.

Although VOA radio was the USIA's best-known operation to most Americans, the bulk of the agency's operations took place at its 275 overseas posts. Known locally as the United States Information Service (USIS), the posts were an extension of the local American embassy, although they were usually located outside the embassy building, often on a main street. The most visible USIS activity was a street-front library. In many Asian, African, and Latin American cities, these were the first open-shelf libraries from which books could be checked out and taken home. As a result, they were often so crowded with students and other information seekers that patrons had to make advanced reservations to be admitted.

USIS centers provided a wide variety of other media and cultural activities. These included a daily news file on American events, transmitted overnight from Washington and then sent in translated form to local newspapers and other media outlets. By 1960, the USIA was also the largest periodical publisher in the world, with magazines in twenty languages and twenty-two newspapers in fourteen languages. Their combined circulation at the time was 110 million copies.

The best known of the agency's publications was *America Illustrated*, published in Russian and distributed in the Soviet Union under a cultural agreement that provided for reciprocal sale of a Soviet magazine, *Soviet Life*, in the United States. Sales of *Soviet Life* languished, however, largely because of its heavy-handed propaganda approach, typically featuring happy peasants and brawny steelworkers in heroic poses as they filled their production quotas. *America Illustrated* was more eclectic, and its wide-ranging descriptions of American life made it hugely popular among Soviet readers. Each issue became a black market item, with copies resold or rented until they became too tattered to read.

The USIA was also a major producer of foreign exhibits, films, and television programs. One of its television projects was a Spanish-language soap opera, *Nuestro Barrio* (Our Neighborhood), chronicling daily life in an unnamed Latin American city. The series was popular throughout Latin American nations, where it was telecast on local stations, bringing a subtle message of American support for social and economic progress.

The majority of observers agree that the USIA's most effective operation was its management of academic and cultural exchanges to and from the United States. In 1940 there were fewer than 20,000 foreign students in American colleges and universities. By 1999, this number had risen to more than a half million. The USIA was the leading American agency in recruiting foreign students and helping process their admission to American colleges. It also played a major role in administering the best known of the exchange programs, the Fulbright scholarships, awarded to more than a quarter million American and foreign academics and students since 1947.

Another exchange effort identified up-and-coming young foreign leaders and brought them to the United States for a tour that included a personalized itinerary to visit wherever they wanted to go or to meet whomever they wanted to meet. Participants in these tours included Britain's Tony Blair and Margaret Thatcher, Egypt's Anwar Sadat, Germany's Willy Brandt, India's Indira Gandhi, and Tanzania's Julius Nyerere. More than forty participants in the program became heads of government in the years after their visits.

A definitive assessment of the USIA's effectiveness is difficult to make. Famed television journalist Edward R. Murrow, who was a director of the agency in the 1960s, once told a congressional committee that no cash register rang when someone overseas viewed the United States more positively as the result of a USIA message. The agency's role, he said, was to state the American case as clearly as possible. He also believed that USIA should participate in the early formation of foreign policy decisions, stressing the importance of overseas public opinion in implementing policy. Indeed, in the later decades of the Cold War, the agency did play an increasingly significant role in foreign policy decisions.

With the collapse of the Soviet Union in 1991 and the easing of tensions with the People's Republic of China (PRC), the USIA's role as a Cold War agency was altered. In 1999, President Bill Clinton transferred its functions to the State Department where, under the new rubric of public diplomacy, the USIA deals with the complex public-opinion challenges created by the resurgence of international terrorism.

Wilson Dizard Jr.

See also
Voice of America
References
Dizard, Wilson, Jr. *Inventing Public Diplomacy: The Story of the U.S. Information Agency.* Boulder, CO: Lynne Rienner, 2004.
Heil, Alan. *The Voice of America.* New York: Oxford University Press, 2003.
Hixson, Walter L. *Parting the Curtain: Propaganda, Culture, and the Cold War, 1945–1961.* New York: St. Martin's, 1997.
Wagnleitner, Reinhold, and Elaine Tyler May. *Here, There and Everywhere: The Foreign Politics of American Culture.* Hanover, NH: University Press of New England, 2000.

United States–Japan Security Treaty (8 September 1951)

Security and defense treaty, signed on 8 September 1951, guaranteeing U.S. defense of Japan from armed external aggression and internal insurrection. The United States–Japan Security Treaty was signed simultaneously with the Treaty of Peace with the Allied powers, which together restored full sovereignty to Japan. The Security Treaty granted the United States the right "to dispose of United States land, air, and sea forces in and about Japan" in order "to contribute to the maintenance of international peace and security in the Far East and the security of Japan against armed attack." It also stipulated that U.S. forces "may be utilized to put down large-scale internal riots and disturbances in Japan."

The United States–Japan Security Treaty differed from other defensive arrangements entered into by the American government, such as the U.S.–South Korea and the U.S.-Philippines treaties, in that Japan did not have an obligation to defend U.S. territory. This fundamental difference is explained by limitations placed on postwar Japan's military structure, which was only allowed to exercise the right of self-defense under the war renunciation clause established in the Japanese constitution of 3 May 1947. Japan's limited military

capabilities turned the Security Treaty into a rather asymmetrical agreement in that the United States would provide military protection in return for basing rights in Japan.

This asymmetry engendered Japanese criticism of the treaty, which was considered one-sided and unfair. The Japanese government was concerned about the risk of becoming involved in an American military confrontation in the Far East, despite the fact that the treaty did not obligate the Japanese to mutual defense. In addition, the "internal disturbance" clause raised Japanese suspicions that the agreement essentially retained vestigial remnants of the postwar U.S. occupation period.

After a review process in the late 1950s, Japan and the United States concluded a Treaty of Mutual Cooperation and Security on 19 January 1960. The asymmetrical nature of the original Security Treaty remained relatively unchanged in the 1960 revision, as it granted U.S. forces the use of "facilities and areas in Japan" for "the security of Japan and the maintenance of international peace and security in the Far East." However, the revision improved on the reciprocity of the Security Treaty.

First, it acknowledged Japan's obligation to maintain and develop its own capabilities to resist armed attack in conjunction with the U.S. obligation to defend Japan, recognizing that Japan now had an obligation to assist American forces in a future conflict involving Japanese territories. Second, the revised treaty introduced a consultative mechanism regarding the implementation of the agreement. Now, "the use of facilities and areas in Japan as bases for military combat operations" would be "subject to prior consultation with the Government of Japan." Third, it encouraged political and economic cooperation between the two signatories. Finally, and perhaps most important to the Japanese, the 1960 treaty eliminated the so-called internal disturbance clause and established a ten-year term for the treaty, subject to renegotiation upon notice of each party.

Takeda Yasuhiro

See also
Japan; Japan, Armed Forces; Japan, Occupation after World War II
References
Buckley, Roger. *US-Japan Alliance Diplomacy, 1945–1990.* New York: Cambridge University Press, 1992.
Olsen, Edward A. *U.S.-Japan Strategic Reciprocity: A Neo-Internationalist View.* Stanford, CA: Hoover Institution Press, 1985.
Weinstein, Martin E. *Japan's Postwar Defense Policy, 1947–1968.* New York: Columbia University Press, 1971.

United States, Marine Corps

Marines are similar to soldiers in that their primary mission is to fight on land. However, the U.S. Marine Corps (USMC) is part of the Department of the Navy and serves in close coordination with the U.S. Navy. Thus, primary Marine Corps missions are amphibious invasions, noncombatant evacuation operations (NEOs), and internal security onboard ships. Moreover, Marines have traditionally guarded U.S. embassies.

During the Cold War, the USMC fought in Korea, Vietnam, Grenada, Panama, and the Persian Gulf. They were also involved in smaller-scale operations, such as interventions in both Lebanon and the Dominican Republic, NEOs from Cyprus and Cambodia, the *Mayaguez* Incident, and Lebanon. The USMC also stood prepared to wage a third world war against the Soviet Union by reinforcing Norway and Denmark's Jutland Peninsula.

The USMC drastically downsized as part of the demobilization following World War II, going from a peak of 485,053 personnel during the war to 107,000 by the late 1940s. Some politicians, including President Harry S. Truman, wanted to disband the USMC, as they thought that amphibious operations were obsolete in the atomic age and that the army could absorb the USMC's mission. However, the performance of the USMC in Korea in 1950 quelled this debate.

Marines took part in the desperate fighting along the Pusan Perimeter. They also spearheaded the amphibious landing at Inchon that turned the tide in the war in September 1950. Marines subsequently helped liberate Seoul in bloody house-to-house fighting. General Douglas MacArthur then ordered the Marines to seize Wonsan in an unopposed amphibious assault and simultaneous drive north to the Yalu River. The drive to the Yalu, however, brought Chinese intervention, and in late November 1950, some 100,000 men of the Chinese 9th Army Group cut off the 1st Marine Division near the Changjin (Chosin) Reservoir in bitter winter weather. Despite the desperate situation, in one of the great military withdrawals in all history, the Marines fought their way south, bringing out their wounded, dead, and equipment. The USMC later participated in United Nations Command (UNC) offensives, defense against the 1951 Chinese Spring Offensive, and UNC counteroffensives.

Following the Korean War, the USMC enjoyed a period of relative calm punctuated by smaller operations. In July 1958, following a request by the Lebanese government, President Dwight D. Eisenhower sent Marines to Beirut. The Marines maintained general order there before being withdrawn in mid-October. The April 1965 Dominican Intervention saw the Marines evacuate more than 3,000 U.S. citizens during political upheaval there. Subsequently, more than 8,000 Marines and additional U.S. Army troops enforced the peace.

Marines also served as advisors to the Republic of Vietnam (RVN, South Vietnam). The USMC deployed its first operational unit, the Medium Helicopter Squadron 362, to Vietnam on 15 April 1962. The 9th Marine Expeditionary Brigade deployed to Vietnam as the first USMC ground com-

A U.S. Marine Corps combat patrol in the Republic of Vietnam (ROV, South Vietnam). (National Archives and Records Administration)

bat unit on 8 March 1965. The Marines were deployed to the northern provinces of South Vietnam. Marines played a crucial role in defeating the January 1968 Tet Offensive, especially in retaking Hue. They also held the Khe Sanh base during a prolonged siege by Democratic Republic of Vietnam (DRV, North Vietnam) troops. The Marines were active in pacification programs, especially with their innovative Combined Action Platoons. Marine units began withdrawing from South Vietnam in 1970. All USMC ground and air operations in Vietnam ceased in June 1971. The final Marine role came in April 1975, when Marine units assisted with the evacuation of Americans and South Vietnamese during the fall of Saigon to communist forces.

The early 1970s marked a period of recovery for the USMC, which had been badly bruised during the decade-long Vietnam involvement. Once again, the USMC prepared for traditional amphibious operations missions. However, Marines did evacuate U.S. citizens from Cyprus in July 1974 and from Cambodia in April 1975. Conflict with Cambodia continued with the capture of the U.S. ship *Mayaguez* and its crew on 12 May 1975. President Gerald R. Ford ordered in the Marines, who retook the ship three days later.

In 1983, President Ronald Reagan sent Marines to Lebanon to monitor the evacuation of the Palestine Liberation Organization (PLO). However, attacks on the Marines culminated in the 23 October 1983 suicide truck bombing of the office building holding the Marine headquarters. The blast killed 239 Americans, 220 of them Marines. Reagan pulled all

American forces out by late February 1984 in large part because of this devastating attack. The USMC participated in Operation URGENT FURY, the U.S. invasion of Grenada in October 1983 ordered by Reagan. During the Iran-Iraq War (1980–1988), Reagan deployed Marines to help protect oil tankers in the Persian Gulf against attack, a mission that lasted from 1986 to 1989.

Marines also participated in the 1989 Panama invasion, Operation JUST CAUSE, securing key installations, seizing critical bridgeheads, controlling vital crossroads, and processing 1,200 captured Panamanians.

When Iraqi forces invaded Kuwait on 2 August 1990, President George H. W. Bush deployed the Marines to protect Saudi Arabia from an Iraqi incursion (Operation DESERT SHIELD). During the ground offensive (Operation DESERT STORM), in an advance on Kuwait City in the Battle of Khafji, Marine units easily repulsed two Iraqi armored columns in the largest tank battle in USMC history. Two Marine brigades feigned an amphibious landing from ships in the Persian Gulf, which fixed Iraqis in eastern Kuwait and facilitated the Coalition's western envelopment. Undoubtedly, the USMC played an important role during the Cold War.

Jonathan P. Klug

See also

Dominican Republic, U.S. Interventions in; Grenada Invasion; Iran-Iraq War; Korean War; Lebanon, U.S. Interventions in; Persian Gulf War; United States Navy; Vietnam War

References

Alexander, Joseph H. *Fellowship of Valor: The Battle History of the United States Marines.* New York: HarperCollins, 1997.

———. *Sea Soldiers in the Cold War: Amphibious Warfare, 1945–1991.* Annapolis, MD: Naval Institute Press, 1995.

Kindsvatter, Peter S. *American Soldiers: Ground Combat in the World Wars, Korea, and Vietnam.* Lawrence: University Press of Kansas, 2003.

Millett, Allen R. *Semper Fidelis: The History of the United States Marine Corps.* New York: Free Press, 1991.

United States, Navy

The U.S. Navy's primary mission was, and is, to ensure the command of the seas. Command of the seas allows unfettered U.S. commerce and military sea lines of communication. Thus, the U.S. economy can continue to operate, and U.S. forces can move across the sea to foreign soil. Conversely, the U.S. Navy's command of the seas interdicts the maritime commerce and military activities by enemies of the United States. After Japan's formal surrender on the deck of the U.S. battleship *Missouri* on 2 September 1945, the U.S. Navy's mission to maintain command of the seas took many forms, from launching carrier strikes to diplomatic shows of force. During the Cold War, the navy fought in Korea, Vietnam,

Lebanon, Grenada, Panama, and the Persian Gulf; enforced a quarantine of Cuba during the Cuban Missile Crisis; and helped prevent a communist Chinese invasion of Taiwan. The navy's submarines armed with nuclear missiles, which formed one leg of the U.S. strategic triad, also played a key role. Finally, if a president needed a show of muscle, he often sent a carrier task force to impress a foreign power or intimidate a potential adversary.

The U.S. Navy drastically downsized as part of the post–World War II general demobilization, shrinking from 3 million to 1 million sailors. It also ceased construction of more than 150 warships and several thousand small craft and decommissioned 2,600 others. Nevertheless, the navy's commitments were still immense, and the American government called upon the navy frequently. A show of force to deter a possible communist coup during the Italian elections of 1948 was one of the first examples of the navy in action during the Cold War. Twenty-five percent of the aircraft that participated in the Berlin Airlift belonged to the navy. Furthermore, U.S. Navy units protected Taiwan from the threat of a communist Chinese invasion.

After World War II, many U.S. political leaders believed that a large navy was no longer necessary. Thus, the U.S. Navy continually had to fight for funding for operations and new equipment. For example, twenty-seven days after taking office, on 23 April 1949 Secretary of Defense Louis A. Johnson canceled the navy's new 60,000-ton supercarrier *United States* without consulting either the secretary of the navy or the chief of naval operations. The navy argued that it needed the new supercarriers, as existing carriers were too small to handle multiengine jet aircraft capable of delivering nuclear weapons. Johnson, a former secretary of the air force, favored the B-36 bomber, but his decision precipitated a vicious battle over the roles of the services. The navy fought back against Johnson to the extent that some senior officers went to the press. The media referred to this fight as the Revolt of the Admirals.

Despite this temporary setback, the U.S. Navy was able to start construction of four frigates and three hunter-killer submarines. It also began development of new carrier aircraft capable of delivering nuclear weapons as well as development of nuclear ship propulsion. Especially important in the latter area was the work by Captain Hyman Rickover in developing nuclear power plants for submarines.

The U.S. Navy did not have a serious or prolonged fight to gain command of the seas during the Korean War, but it did play a vital role in the conflict. Naval air and gun support slowed the Democratic People's Republic of Korea (DPRK, North Korea) drive to conquer the Republic of Korea (ROK, South Korea) and assisted in maintaining United Nations Command (UNC) forces in the Pusan Perimeter. The navy transported X Corps in the Inchon amphibious assault and provided air and naval gunfire support. The navy also cleared

The advent of nuclear weapons prompted the U.S. Navy to procure long-range aircraft capable of delivering the weapons from aircraft carriers. The North American AJ-1 Savage, pictured here in 1951, was the first U.S. Navy aircraft specifically designed for this purpose. (National Museum of Naval Aviation)

mines from Korean harbors, including Wonsan, on the eastern coast of North Korea and it made possible the withdrawal of X Corps from Hungnam and other points on the northeastern coast of Korea following Chinese entry into the war at the end of 1950. The navy continued to provide key air and naval gunfire support for ground operations until the armistice on 27 July 1953.

The performance of the U.S. Navy during the Korean War demonstrated its key role in U.S. global security operations and led to more political support and funding, including new programs under National Security Council Report NSC-68. This included Forrestal-class supercarriers, new naval aircraft, and destroyers and guided-missile cruisers. The submarine *Nautilus,* the world's first nuclear-powered warship, entered active service in early 1955. The navy began development of submarine-launched ballistic missiles (SLBMs) in 1959, and USS *George Washington* made the first operational patrol armed with SLBMs in November 1960. The navy's nuclear submarines became one-third of the U.S. strategic triad, alongside intercontinental ballistic missiles (ICBMs) and strategic bombers carrying nuclear bombs. During this

period of rebuilding, the navy also supported the Marines in the Lebanon Intervention of 1958 and in the evacuation of U.S. civilians during the Dominican Intervention of 1965.

The Cuban Missile Crisis was a signal event in the Cold War, when the United States and the Soviet Union came closest to nuclear Armageddon. In October 1962, U.S. policymakers learned that Cuba, with Soviet assistance, was building medium-range ballistic missile (MRBM) sites. After much deliberation, President John F. Kennedy ordered the navy to impose a blockade of Cuba and prevent the Soviet Union from bringing in additional supplies and missiles for the MRBM launch sites. The navy enforced the quarantine and was prepared to conduct combat operations if necessary. After Soviet leaders backed down, Second Fleet warships closely monitored the dismantling of the Cuban MRBM threat to the continental United States.

After the crisis, the Soviets began building a balanced navy due to their inability to challenge the U.S. Navy during the Cuban Missile Crisis. While the U.S. Navy tried to develop enhanced strategic capabilities in the form of an extended-range Polaris missile and an improved submarine capable of launching ballistic missiles, another threat loomed on the horizon in the form of the Vietnam War.

U.S. Navy ships were involved in intelligence gathering (DESOTO patrols) in the Gulf of Tonkin off the coast of the Democratic Republic of Vietnam (DRV, North Vietnam) when on 1 August 1964 North Vietnamese torpedo boats attacked the destroyer *Maddox*. A second alleged attack on 4 August on the *Maddox* and another destroyer, the *Turner Joy*, almost certainly did not occur. President Lyndon B. Johnson nonetheless ordered retaliatory air raids against North Vietnamese coastal targets, and the U.S. Congress passed the Tonkin Gulf Resolution, authorizing the president to use U.S. military resources as he deemed fit in Vietnam.

The U.S. Navy's involvement in Vietnam took many forms. In Operation MARKET TIME, the navy executed offshore interdiction of North Vietnamese vessels seeking to infiltrate men and supplies into the Republic of Vietnam (RVN, South Vietnam) and, in Operation GAME WARDEN, it fought the communist Viet Cong for control of South Vietnam's vital and extensive river systems. Navy aircraft provided key air support to ground troops in South Vietnam from carriers off the coast of South Vietnam (Dixie Station). The navy also provided important gunfire support to operations near the coast as well as shelled North Vietnam, and it supported amphibious operations by U.S. and South Vietnamese forces.

U.S. Navy aircraft participated in Operation ROLLING THUNDER, the air war against North Vietnam, from carriers stationed off the coast of North Vietnam (Yankee Station). Washington's goals for ROLLING THUNDER were to halt the infiltration of men and supplies into South Vietnam and to force North Vietnamese leaders to abandon their support for the communist insurgency in South Vietnam and come to the negotiating table. Although the operation exacted a considerable toll on North Vietnam, it failed to achieve its goals. The cost was also high due to the sophisticated and growing North Vietnamese air defense network. In thirty-seven months between 1965 and 1968, the navy lost 421 planes and 450 aviators. The navy also helped train personnel and then turned over substantial assets in vessels and equipment to the South Vietnamese Navy as part of the Vietnamization program.

Washington subsequently called upon the U.S. Navy to execute numerous other missions. The navy supported the evacuation of U.S. citizens from Cyprus in July 1974 and then from Cambodia and from South Vietnam in April 1975. The navy also assisted in operations to retake the *Mayaguez* and its crew when they were taken captive by the Khmer Rouge in Cambodia in May 1975.

The U.S. Navy struggled during Jimmy Carter's presidency as a consequence of the standoff between the president and Congress. Despite being a former naval officer, President Carter did not wish to expend large sums on the navy, while Congress sought to increase its funding. The election of Ronald Reagan as president in November 1980 led to a massive military buildup that revitalized the navy and saw it come close to Reagan's goal of 600 ships.

When President Reagan sent Marines into Lebanon in 1983, Arab attacks of Marine installations escalated, and the U.S. Navy provided naval gunfire support to thwart the attacks. Nevertheless, the suicide truck-bomb attack on the Marine barracks in Beirut effectively ended U.S. involvement in Lebanon in February 1984. The navy also provided key assistance in the Grenada Invasion of October 1983 and in the invasion of Panama during December 1989–January 1990.

During the Iran-Iraq War of 1980–1988, the belligerents began attacking oil tankers in the Persian Gulf. The U.S. Navy executed freedom of navigation operations to ensure U.S. access to oil from the Persian Gulf, clearly maintaining command of the sea. However, unique operational difficulties existed in a confined area such as the Persian Gulf. Iranian mines and antiship missiles were significant threats. A missile attack on USS *Stark* on 17 March 1987 killed 37 American sailors. In another major incident in the area, on 3 July 1988 the U.S. cruiser *Vincennes* mistakenly fired on an Iranian civilian jetliner, killing 290 passengers.

When Iraqi dictator Saddam Hussein's forces invaded Kuwait on 2 August 1990, President George H. W. Bush ordered the U.S. Navy to protect Saudi Arabia from potential Iraqi aggression in Operation DESERT SHIELD. Naval aircraft and gunfire assisted UN Coalition forces in significantly deterring Iraqi attacks. Navy Harpoon precision-guided missiles played a vital role in attacking Iraqi targets. Furthermore, U.S. Navy and Marine Corps aircraft made up 30 percent of the sorties flown in the resultant coalition war with Iraq, Operation DESERT STORM, that ultimately liberated Kuwait and crushed Iraqi forces.

The U.S. Navy had proven its indispensable mettle during more than forty years of Cold War tension and in countless hot wars between 1945 and 1991, when the Cold War officially ended.

Jonathan P. Klug

See also

Aircraft Carriers; Cuban Missile Crisis; Johnson, Louis Arthur; Korean War; Missiles, Polaris; Missiles, Poseidon; Missiles, Submarine-Launched Ballistic; Persian Gulf War; Submarines; Triad; United States; United States Marine Corps; Vietnam War; Warships, Surface

References

Baer, George. *One Hundred Years of Sea Power: The U.S. Navy, 1890–1990.* Palo Alto, CA: Stanford University Press, 1996.

Hagan, Kenneth J. *In Peace and War: Interpretations of American Naval History, 1775–1984.* 2nd ed. Westport, CT: Greenwood, 1984.

———. *This People's Navy: The Making of American Sea Power.* New York: Free Press, 1991.

Hartmann, Frederick H. *Naval Renaissance: The U.S. Navy in the 1980s.* Annapolis, MD: Naval Institute Press, 1990.

Howarth, Stephen. *To Shining Sea: A History of the United States Navy, 1775–1991*. New York: Random House, 1991.

Isenberg, Michael T. *Shield of the Republic: The United States Navy in an Era of Cold War and Violent Peace*, Vol. 1, *1945–1962*. New York: St. Martin's, 1993.

Uruguay

Spanish-speaking South American nation covering 68,039 square miles, equivalent in size to the U.S. state of Washington. Uruguay, with a 1945 population of 2.26 million people, is bordered by Brazil to the north, Argentina to the west, and the Atlantic Ocean to the south and east. Uruguay enjoyed prosperity and financial stability in the early Cold War era. In a sense it was a showcase, as U.S. foreign policymakers advocated that Latin American nations open their economies to free trade and investment as a means of spurring economic growth, which is what Uruguay did.

Beginning in the mid-1950s, however, falling export earnings required cuts in imports of industrial materials as well as consumer goods. Despite assistance from the Alliance for Progress, the Uruguayan economy in the 1960s was weak, and inflation became uncontrollable. With economic problems came political problems. In response to the growing power of the Tupamaro urban guerrilla movement, on 13 June 1968 the government of Jorge Pacheco Areco curtailed public liberties and implemented security measures, maintained by the government intermittently through the 1980s. The Tupamaros aimed to overthrow the government and replace it with a socialist regime in the style of Fidel Castro's regime.

With rising anti–North American sentiment in the late 1960s, Washington feared that left-wing Latin Americans would use Uruguay as a base for operations throughout South America. Uruguay, with its open political culture and society, had traditionally provided a friendly environment for such activity. However, the U.S. government maintained a degree of influence over the Uruguayan military by giving military assistance through the Civic Action Program, which was implemented in a number of Latin American nations and provided funding for the military to construct roads, schools, and other infrastructure projects in rural areas.

Until the early 1970s, U.S. officials took cordial relations with Uruguay for granted. With Salvador Allende's rise to power in Chile, however, and with the advent of guerrilla movements in the region, policymakers in Washington began to fear a leftward drift in South America. Two events in the early 1970s significantly shook U.S.-Uruguayan relations. First, the Tupamaros kidnapped two U.S. Agency for International Development (USAID) officials and killed one of them, Daniel Mittrone, in August 1970. Next, American officials feared that a left-wing coalition, the Frente Amplio (FA, Broad Front), would win the November 1971 elections. In the end, the FA fared poorly, and the traditional parties garnered the majority of the votes. Juan María Bordaberry of the Blanco Party was elected president.

During April–September 1972, a number of Tupamaros escaped from prison and assassinated military leaders. Because the General Assembly was investigating allegations of torture by the military and because the military disliked Bordaberry's choice of a civilian for defense minister, it forced Bordaberry to dissolve the Assembly in June 1973 and create a Council of State in its place that, along with the military, held effective power. Finally, the military forced Bordaberry to resign in June 1976. In July 1976 the military and Council of State appointed Dr. Aparicio Méndez president.

After 1973, Uruguay's military-controlled government became more anticommunist and pro–United States than its civilian predecessors. This thoroughly suited Washington. As was typical for U.S. relations with Latin America during the Cold War, the administrations of Presidents Richard M. Nixon and Gerald R. Ford supported Uruguay's military-controlled regime as a bulwark against communism. In part because of the revelations by the U.S. Congress of Central Intelligence Agency (CIA) activity in Cuba and Chile in the 1960s and 1970s, however, and because of human rights violations by the Uruguayan military regime—including torture, assassination, and imprisonment without trial—in September 1976 the U.S. Congress curtailed military assistance to Uruguay and other Latin American nations.

Beginning in the mid-1970s, a combination of Uruguayan religious (mainly Catholic) and secular activists worked to return Uruguay to democracy. These groups were heartened that President Jimmy Carter further reduced military assistance to a number of Latin American dictatorships.

Prodded by civilian activists, in 1980 the Uruguayan military drafted a new constitution, which was rejected in a plebiscite in November that same year. Méndez resigned in 1981, and the military appointed Gregorio Álvarez president in 1982. In 1984, military and civilian groups agreed to elections, which were held that November. Colorado Party leader Julio María Sanguinetti won the presidency and took office in 1985. In keeping with its policy toward Latin America in the 1980s, Washington supported Uruguay's transition to democracy.

James F. Siekmeier

See also

Alliance for Progress; Americas; Brazil; Carter, James Earl, Jr.; Central Intelligence Agency; Dirty War; Ford, Gerald Rudolph; Nixon, Richard Milhous; Latin America, Popular Liberation Movements in

References

Gilio, Maria Ester. *The Tupamaro Guerrillas*. Translated by Anne Edmonson. New York: Saturday Review Press, 1972.

Hudson, Rex A., and Sandra W. Meditz, eds. *Uruguay: A Country Study*. Washington, DC: U.S. Government Printing Office, Secretary of the Army, 1990.

Kaufman, Edy. *Uruguay in Transition: From Civilian to Military Rule*. New Brunswick, NJ: Transaction, 1979.

Weinstein, Martin. *Uruguay: The Politics of Failure*. Westport, CT: Greenwood, 1975.

U.S. Armed Forces in Asia

See Asia, U.S. Armed Forces in

U.S. Armed Forces in Europe

See Europe, U.S. Armed Forces in

U.S.–Republic of China Mutual Security Treaty

See Mutual Security Treaty, U.S.–Republic of China

Ustinov, Dmitry Fedorovich (1908–1984)

Soviet arms industry manager, minister of the defense industry (1953–1957), and defense minister (1976–1984). Born on 17 October 1908 in Samara, Dmitry Fedorovich Ustinov served in the Soviet Red Army during 1922–1923, attended a technical institute in Makarov, and joined the Communist Party of the Soviet Union (CPSU) in 1927. Following work as a fitter, he was selected for the Leningrad Military-Mechanical Institute, graduating in 1934 as an artillery designer. He worked for three years at the Naval Artillery Research Institute in Leningrad before moving to the Bolshevik Arms Factory, where he was director during 1938–1941.

Named people's commissar for armaments in 1941, Ustinov directed the production of small arms and artillery during World War II and oversaw the relocation of arms factories beyond the Urals during the German invasion. He remained in this post (renamed minister of armaments after the war) until 1953. He received the rank of colonel general of engineering artillery in 1944 and was named a full member of the CPSU Central Committee in 1952. Appointed minister of the defense industry in 1953, he served until 1957, when he joined the Council of Ministers, becoming deputy chairman the next year and first deputy chairman in 1963. During this time, he played a major role in the modernization of Soviet forces. Following Soviet Premier Nikita Khrushchev's ouster in 1964, Ustinov was appointed to the Defense Council and became a candidate member of the Presidium (Politburo). In 1965 he became Central Committee secretary responsible for armaments. Over the next decade, he continued his involvement in the expansion of Soviet defense production.

In April 1976 Ustinov was named defense minister following the death of Andrei Grechko and held that post until his death in 1984. As minister, Ustinov oversaw the continued growth of Soviet ground forces and the integration of air-assault helicopter brigades into the force structure, although economic decline beginning in the late 1970s would lead to a leveling off in defense procurement. He was reluctant to support détente, only grudgingly accepted the Strategic Arms Limitation (SALT) negotiations, and was a strong advocate of intervention in Afghanistan. Abandoning his traditional abstention from political battles, he supported Yuri Andropov over Konstantin Chernenko to succeed Leonid Brezhnev in November 1982 but supported Chernenko following Andropov's death in February 1984. In ill health for many years, Ustinov died in Moscow on 20 December 1984.

Steven W. Guerrier

See also
Afghanistan War; Soviet Union, Army; Soviet Union, Army Air Force; Soviet Union, Navy

References
Friedman, Norman. *The Fifty Year War: Conflict and Strategy in the Cold War*. Annapolis MD: Naval Institute Press, 2000.

Gelman, Harry. *The Brezhnev Politburo and the Decline of Détente*. Ithaca, NY: Cornell University Press, 1984.

V

Vance, Cyrus Roberts (1917–2002)

U.S. secretary of the army (1962–1964), deputy secretary of defense (1964–1967), and secretary of state (1977–1980). Born in Clarksburg, West Virginia, on 27 March 1917, Cyrus Vance graduated from Yale University in 1939 and from Yale Law School in 1942. He saw combat service in the Pacific as a naval gunnery officer during World War II, after which he joined the New York law firm of Simpson, Thacher & Bartlett, his professional base throughout his career.

Vance's first government assignment came in 1957 as special counsel to the Senate Preparedness Investigation Committee chaired by majority leader Lyndon B. Johnson. In 1961 Vance became general counsel to the Department of Defense, in which post he negotiated the release of Cuban prisoners after the abortive 1961 Bay of Pigs invasion, implemented a major restructuring of departmental organization, and modernized weapons and personnel systems.

Secretary of Defense Robert McNamara appointed Vance secretary of the army in 1962, and in that capacity he advised President John F. Kennedy to deploy federal troops to quell growing civil rights violence in the South. From January 1964 until June 1967, Vance was deputy secretary of defense, serving primarily as a troubleshooter in efforts to resolve difficulties with Panama in 1964 and the Dominican Republic in 1965 and to mediate the 1967 civil war in Cyprus.

Vance was initially a hawk on Vietnam. By mid-1966, however, he was skeptical of continued American air and ground escalation, and he left office disillusioned with American Vietnam policies. As one of the senior advisors, or "Wise Men," with whom President Johnson consulted after the communist Tet Offensive in January 1968, Vance recommended that the United States cease bombing and open peace negotiations. He then served as deputy to chief negotiator W. Averell Harriman in the fruitless 1968 Paris peace talks.

In 1971 Vance met future president and fellow Trilateral Commission member Jimmy Carter. Vance then served as a foreign policy advisor to Carter's 1976 presidential campaign and became his secretary of state. Suspicious of grand theories of geopolitical and strategic designs and of attempts to discern linkages between different aspects of foreign policy, Vance believed that the international situation no longer fit the early Cold War bipolar model. Instead, he sought to adapt U.S. diplomacy to a more complicated and less schematic world. He was strongly committed to continuing the two previous administrations' policies of arms control and détente with the communist world, but he soon clashed with Carter's assertive national security advisor, the fiercely anti-Soviet Zbigniew Brzezinski.

Vance negotiated the 1979 Strategic Arms Limitation Treaty (SALT II) with the Soviet Union, imposing ceilings on the number of nuclear missiles and delivery vehicles and banning the introduction of new missile and antimissile systems. His other major accomplishments included the negotiation of the 1977–1978 treaties returning the Panama Canal to Panamanian ownership and operation, the 1978 Camp David Accords, the full normalization in 1978 of U.S. relations with the People's Republic of China (PRC), and the conclusion of a settlement in Rhodesia (Zimbabwe) that brought black majority rule in 1979.

On other issues, however, Brzezinski undercut Vance, especially after the 1979 Soviet invasion of Afghanistan caused a dramatic cooling between the two superpowers, and Carter

One of the ablest U.S. diplomats and troubleshooters, Cyrus R. Vance is shown here during a visit to Korea in February 1968. Vance was U.S. secretary of state during 1977–1980. (National Archives and Records Administration)

increasingly favored Brzezinski's advice. In early 1980, Vance urged direct talks with the Soviets in an effort to resolve the Afghan crisis, but Carter refused. Vance's early hopes to normalize American relations with Cuba also fell victim to the deteriorating U.S.-Soviet situation and to revelations that Cuban troops were deployed in Ethiopia. After Vietnam signed a treaty of friendship with the Soviet Union in November 1978, American efforts to reopen relations with Vietnam also stalled in part due to a massive outflow of refugee boat people and because of Vietnam's failure to resolve to America's satisfaction the issue of soldiers still missing in action.

In Iran, where growing popular discontent threatened the government's stability, Vance unsuccessfully advised the autocratic Shah Mohammad Reza Pahlavi that the introduction of genuine reforms was the best means to counter growing domestic unrest. In January 1979 the shah fled Iran, and an anti-American fundamentalist Muslim regime took power. Ten months later, on 4 November 1979, Iranian students sacked the American embassy in Tehran and took fifty-three Americans hostage. Vance believed that quiet diplomacy was the best means of freeing them, but Brzezinski insisted that the United States mount a dramatic rescue. On 11 April 1980,

the National Security Council (NSC) met during Vance's absence and authorized a rescue mission, a decision that Vance unavailingly protested upon his return as foolhardy and poorly planned. In protest, he submitted his resignation on 21 April, becoming only the third secretary of state to resign over a matter of principle. Three days later the rescue mission was aborted at the loss of eight American lives.

Vance returned to his law practice and in 1983 published his memoirs. He also accepted several further diplomatic assignments from the United Nations (UN). During the 1980s he helped to mediate the Nagorno-Karabakh conflict between Azerbaijan and Armenia and a peaceful end to white rule in South Africa. In the early 1990s he helped to broker a cease-fire in Croatia. Vance died in New York City on 12 January 2002.

Priscilla Roberts

See also

Afghanistan; Afghanistan War; Arms Control; Bay of Pigs; Brzezinski, Zbigniew; Camp David Accords; Carter, James Earl, Jr.; China, People's Republic of; Cuba; Cyprus; Dominican Republic; Dominican Republic, U.S. Interventions in; Egypt; Ethiopia; Human Rights; Iran; Israel; Johnson, Lyndon Baines; Kennedy, John Fitzgerald; Khomeini, Ruhollah; McNamara, Robert Strange; Mohammad Reza Pahlavi; Panama; Panama Canal Treaties; *Pueblo* Incident; Radical Islam; Somalia; Strategic Arms Limitation Talks and Treaties; Tet Offensive; Trilateral Commission; United States Army; Vietnam; Vietnam War; Zimbabwe

References

Brzezinski, Zbigniew. *Power and Principle: Memoirs of the National Security Adviser, 1977–1981.* New York: Farrar, Straus and Giroux, 1983.

Carter, Jimmy. *Keeping Faith: Memoirs of a President.* Fayetteville: University of Arkansas Press, 1995.

Houghton, David Patrick. *US Foreign Policy and the Iran Hostage Crisis.* New York: Cambridge University Press, 2001.

Jordan, Hamilton. *Crisis: The Last Year of the Carter Presidency.* New York: Putnam, 1982.

McLellan, David S. *Cyrus Vance.* Totowa, NJ: Rowman and Allanheld, 1985.

Muravchik, Joshua. *The Uncertain Crusade: Jimmy Carter and the Dilemmas of Human Rights Policy.* Lanham, MD: Hamilton Press, 1986.

Smith, Gaddis. *Morality, Reason, and Power: American Diplomacy in the Carter Years.* New York: Hill and Wang, 1986.

Strong, Robert A. *Working in the World: Jimmy Carter and the Making of American Foreign Policy.* Baton Rouge: Louisiana State University Press, 2000.

Vance, Cyrus. *Hard Choices: Critical Years in America's Foreign Policy.* New York: Simon and Schuster, 1983.

Vandenberg, Arthur Hendrick (1884–1951)

U.S. senator and chairman of the Senate Foreign Relations Committee (SFRC) during 1947–1949. Born in Grand Rapids,

Michigan, on 22 March 1884, Arthur Hendrick Vandenberg spent one year at the University of Michigan before leaving for financial reasons. He went on to become a politically influential newspaper reporter and editor, loyal to the Republican Party. Appointed senator for Michigan in 1928, he won reelection that year and again in 1934, 1940, and 1946.

Mildly progressive domestically and predominantly isolationist on foreign policy, during the 1930s Vandenberg served on the Nye Committee that investigated the munitions industry's role in precipitating American entry into World War I. He also supported, with reservations, American membership in the World Court. Following the December 1941 Japanese attack on Pearl Harbor, he gradually moved to supporting internationalist policies, publicly renouncing isolationism in 1944. By then a prominent Republican senator, he was crucial in converting his party to internationalism. President Franklin D. Roosevelt made Vandenberg, the ranking Republican on the SFRC, a delegate to the 1945 San Francisco Conference that drew up the final United Nations (UN) Charter. Vandenberg, already suspicious of Soviet motivations, obtained the inclusion of an article permitting the creation of regional security organizations.

Vandenberg represented a large Polish constituency, and he therefore took particular interest in the agreements on Poland and Eastern Europe that Roosevelt, British Prime Minster Winston Churchill, and Soviet leader Josef Stalin concluded at the February 1945 Yalta Conference. President Harry S. Truman deliberately included Vandenberg in the U.S. delegations to postwar meetings of Big Four (U.S., Soviet, British, and Chinese) foreign ministers in New York, Paris, and London intended to resolve remaining questions from World War II, assignments that convinced Vandenberg of the impossibility of dealing with the Soviet Union. He was also a U.S. delegate to the first two sessions of the new UN General Assembly.

The Truman administration's diligent cultivation of Vandenberg proved fruitful. As chairman of the SFRC in 1947 and 1948, he worked assiduously to implement the Truman Doctrine aid program for Greece and Turkey and the Marshall Plan. The Vandenberg Resolution, introduced in 1948, paved the way for Senate approval of the creation of the North Atlantic Treaty Organization (NATO). Although ailing, Vandenberg discouraged the excesses of McCarthyism and accepted, albeit reluctantly, Truman's June 1950 decision to send U.S. troops to war in Korea. Vandenberg died in Grand Rapids on 18 April 1951.

Priscilla Roberts

See also
London Conference of Foreign Ministers; Marshall Plan; North Atlantic Treaty Organization, Origins and Formation of; Paris Peace Conference and Treaties; Roosevelt, Franklin Delano; Truman, Harry S.; Truman Doctrine; United Nations; Vandenberg Resolution; World War II, Allied Conferences

References
Caspar, Luzian Reto. *Senator Vandenberg, 1884–1951: Von Isolationismus zum Sicherheitssystem.* Zürich, Switzerland: ADAG Administration and Druck, 1979.
Hill, Thomas Michael. "Senator Arthur H. Vandenberg, the Politics of Bipartisanship, and the Origins of the Anti-Soviet Consensus, 1941–1946." *World Affairs* 138(3) (Winter 1976): 219–241.
Hudson, Daryl. "Vandenberg Reconsidered: Senate Resolution 239 and American Foreign Policy." *Diplomatic History* 1(1) (Winter 1977): 46–63.
Tompkins, C. David. *Senator Arthur H. Vandenberg: The Evolution of a Modern Republican, 1884–1945.* Lansing: Michigan State University Press, 1970.
Vandenberg, Arthur H., Jr., ed. *The Private Papers of Senator Vandenberg.* Boston: Houghton Mifflin, 1952.

Vandenberg, Hoyt Sanford (1899–1954)

U.S. Army and U.S. Air Force general and chief of staff of the U.S. Air Force (1948–1953). Born in Milwaukee, Wisconsin, on 24 January 1899, Hoyt Sanford Vandenberg—the nephew of future Michigan Senator Arthur H. Vandenberg, whose political influence probably smoothed his nephew's career—graduated in 1923 from the U.S. Military Academy, West Point, and immediately joined the U.S. Army Air Service. Selected in October 1927 as a flight instructor, until 1939 he rotated between teaching and taking advanced flying and staff courses.

In 1939 Vandenberg joined the Plans Division under Lieutenant General Henry H. "Hap" Arnold, chief of the U.S. Air Corps. Vandenberg's excellent staff work directing the rapid air force expansion consequent to the start of World War II won him promotion to colonel in 1942. In the summer of 1942 he moved to Britain to work on air support for the forthcoming North African invasion. Promoted to brigadier general that December, he accompanied Major General James Harold Doolittle to Northwest Africa as his chief of staff, flying twenty-six combat missions and attending the 1943 Quebec, Tehran, and Cairo Conferences. In August 1944 Vandenberg took command of the Ninth Air Force of more than 4,000 aircraft that provided tactical support to Allied ground forces throughout the West European theater. He was promoted to major general in March 1945.

Following staff appointments in Washington, in 1946 Vandenberg became director of the Central Intelligence Group, forerunner of the Central Intelligence Agency (CIA), substantially expanding and centralizing its activities. Promoted to full general in October 1947 and appointed the newly independent U.S. Air Force's vice chief of staff under General Carl "Tooey" Spaatz, six months later Vandenberg succeeded him. Almost immediately, the air force was confronted by the Berlin Blockade and for fifteen months sustained a massive airlift to keep West Berlin supplied. Vandenberg advocated a seventy-group air force, but President Harry S. Truman's stringent budgetary policies initially restricted him to fifty-five or fewer. Vandenberg concentrated resources on developing strategic air offensive capabilities, ably presenting air force views in the heated 1949 controversy over the U.S. Navy's strategic deterrent role, and strongly supported development of the hydrogen bomb.

When the Korean War began in June 1950, the air force quickly established air superiority in Korea and provided vital support to United Nations (UN) ground forces. The war also brought the expansion that Vandenberg had long advocated, doubling the air force to 106 wings, although he furiously protested the decision to defer for several years after his June 1953 retirement a promised further increase to his ideal 143 wings. Vandenberg died in Washington, D.C., on 2 April 1954. His indefatigable efforts to build up the air force effectively ensured the United States a Cold War strategic striking strength far surpassing that of any other nation.

Priscilla Roberts

See also

Atomic Bomb; Berlin Blockade and Airlift; Bombers, Strategic; Central Intelligence Agency; Containment Policy; LeMay, Curtis Emerson; Nuclear Weapons, Tactical; Roosevelt, Franklin Delano; Truman, Harry S.; United States, Air Force

References

Meilinger, Phillip S. *Hoyt S. Vandenberg: The Life of a General.* Bloomington: Indiana University Press, 1989.
Parrish, Noel F. "Hoyt S. Vandenberg: Building the New Air Force." Pp. 205–228 in *Makers of the United States Air Force.* Edited by John L. Frisbee. Washington, DC: U.S. Government Printing Office, 1987.
Reynolds, John. "Education and Training for High Command: General Hoyt S. Vandenberg's Early Career." Unpublished PhD diss., Duke University, 1980.
Smith, Robert. "The Influence of USAF Chief of Staff Hoyt S. Vandenberg on United States National Security Policy." Unpublished PhD diss., American University, 1965.

Vandenberg Resolution (11 June 1948)

U.S. Senate resolution named for its sponsor, Senator Arthur H. Vandenberg, that embraced internationalism and collective security. The Vandenberg Resolution, passed on 11 June 1948, was a defining moment in the diplomatic history of the United States. Confronting the growing challenges of the Cold War, the U.S. Senate, using the United Nations (UN) Charter as a model, paved the way for American membership in a defensive alliance, the North Atlantic Treaty Organization (NATO), which was formed in 1949. Vandenberg's sponsorship constituted a revolution in American foreign policy, which had traditionally eschewed military alliances, and guaranteed America's preeminence in international affairs. All the more

remarkable was Vandenberg's support, as he had been an ardent isolationist prior to World War II.

Vandenberg, a Republican from Michigan, had developed a keen interest in foreign affairs since the advent of World War II. He was a U.S. delegate to the UN Conference in San Francisco (1945) and to the meetings of the UN General Assembly in London and New York (1946); had served as American advisor during the meetings of the Council of Foreign Ministers in London, Paris, and New York (1946); was an American delegate to the Rio de Janeiro Conference that drafted the Rio Treaty on inter-American defense assistance; and, most critically, had chaired the Senate Foreign Relations Committee (SFRC) during 1947–1949.

On 11 April 1948, Secretary of State George C. Marshall and Undersecretary of State Robert M. Lovett initiated a series of conversations with Senator Tom Connally of Texas (the ranking Democrat on the SFRC) and Senator Vandenberg on the topic of the Soviet threat in general and the need for security in the North Atlantic in particular. Since March 1946, when former British Prime Minister Winston Churchill gave his "Sinews of Peace" speech (also known as the "Iron Curtain" speech) in Fulton, Missouri, relations between the Western Allies and the Soviet Union had deteriorated badly. At the same time, the Canadian government was proposing the creation of a collective defense system for the West, with the British seemingly in support. The conversations and proposals ultimately led to Vandenberg championing American involvement in a politico-military alliance.

During April 1948, Vandenberg carefully prepared a resolution based on the precepts of the UN Charter. The six major clauses of the resolution were suspension of the veto on admitting new UN members and on concerns involving the peaceful settlement of international disputes, the establishment of bilateral or multilateral agreements to secure self-defense, involvement of the United States in such agreements that were in its national interests, the reinforcement of Article 51 of the UN Charter on the right to self-defense, reaffirmation of the role of the UN to secure world peace, and the need to strengthen the UN to render it more effective in its peacekeeping operations. The third component was perhaps the most significant, as it created a constitutional basis for the United States to enter into mutual defense agreements.

The Vandenberg Resolution (Senate Resolution 239 of the 80th Congress, 2nd Session) was approved by the Senate on 11 June 1948 by a vote of 64 to 4. The Vandenberg Resolution was a significant development in the history of the Cold War, as it provided a firm basis for American involvement in NATO.

William T. Walker

See also

Connally, Thomas Terry; Marshall, George Catlett; North Atlantic Treaty; North Atlantic Treaty Organization, Origins and Formation of; Vandenberg, Arthur Hendrick

References

Gazell, James A. "Arthur H. Vandenberg, Internationalism, and the United Nations." *Political Science Quarterly* 88(3) (September 1973): 375–394.

McCullough, David. *Truman.* New York: Simon and Schuster, 1992.

Tompkins, C. David. *Senator Arthur H. Vandenberg: The Evolution of a Modern Republican, 1884–1945.* Lansing: Michigan State University Press, 1970.

Vandenberg, Arthur H., Jr., ed. *The Private Papers of Senator Vandenberg.* Boston: Houghton Mifflin, 1952.

Van Fleet, James Alward (1892–1992)

U.S. Army general and commander of the Eighth Army in Korea (1951–1953). Born in Coytesville, New Jersey, on 19 March 1892, James Alward Van Fleet graduated from the U.S. Military Academy, West Point, in 1915. He saw service in the 1916–1917 Mexican Punitive Expedition and in World War I, fighting with the American Expeditionary Forces. Between the wars he served in the infantry and as an instructor. In 1941, now a colonel, he took command of the 8th Infantry Regiment of the 4th Infantry Division, leading its assault on Utah Beach in the June 1944 D-Day Normandy invasion. Promoted to brigadier general and then to major general, during the drive against Germany Van Fleet led various divisions in heavy fighting at Metz, in the Ardennes, at Remagen, in the Ruhr, and in Austria.

After the war, Van Fleet served in the United States and Germany, and in early 1948 he became, as a lieutenant general, director of the Athens-based Joint U.S. Military and Planning Group advising the Greek government on suppressing communist rebels. Appointed to the Greek National Council, for two years he successfully directed the training and use of Greek military forces in that nation's civil war.

In April 1951 Van Fleet, now a four-star general, took command of the Eighth Army in the Korean War from General Matthew Ridgway, who had just replaced Douglas MacArthur as commander of the United Nations (UN) forces. For much of 1951, Van Fleet's troops saw fierce fighting, driving north in mid-1951 and again after peace talks stalled from August to October. Thereafter, he was restricted to maintaining frontline defensive positions, as the war became largely one of attrition and stalemate. He became increasingly frustrated when superiors repeatedly turned down his plans for major offensives, although in mid-1952 his forceful protests eventually persuaded them to authorize limited smaller operations against communist positions, assaults that proved largely fruitless. Serious ammunition shortages damaging to troop effectiveness and morale also irritated Van Fleet, although some blamed these on his prodigality with artillery barrages. He devoted much effort to reforming, rebuilding and strength-

U.S. Eighth Army commander Lieutenant General James Van Fleet, shown here visiting a regimental command post on the front lines in Korea, 17 April 1951. Eighth Army was the chief U.S. ground combat force in the Korean War. (National Archives and Records Administration)

ening the demoralized South Korean forces, who by late 1952 comprised almost three-quarters of his frontline troops.

In February 1953, shortly before the war ended, Van Fleet turned over the Eighth Army to General Maxwell D. Taylor before resigning from the army in protest in April 1953. The following month, Van Fleet published articles echoing MacArthur's assertions that had the political leaders uncompromisingly exercised American power, they could have achieved total victory in 1951. These charges delighted Republican critics but infuriated Ridgway, Taylor, and Army Chief of Staff General Joseph Lawton Collins.

In 1954 Van Fleet served as President Dwight D. Eisenhower's special envoy to the Far East. As a Defense Department consultant in the early 1960s, Van Fleet suggested that Adlai Stevenson's failure to defend the botched Bay of Pigs invasion required his dismissal as his country's UN representative. Van Fleet died in Washington, D.C., on 23 September 1992. Like many great combat soldiers, he was an inspiring battlefield leader but deficient in broader diplomatic skills.

Priscilla Roberts

See also
Bay of Pigs; Bradley, Omar Nelson; Collins, Joseph Lawton; Containment Policy; Eisenhower, Dwight David; Germany, Federal Republic of; Greece; Greek Civil War; Korea, Republic of, Armed Forces; Korean War; MacArthur, Douglas; Marshall, George Catlett; McNamara, Robert Strange; Ridgway, Matthew Bunker; Stevenson, Adlai Ewing, II; Taylor, Maxwell Davenport; United States, Army

References
Braim, Paul E. *The Will to Win: The Life of Gen. James A. Van Fleet.* Annapolis, MD: U.S. Naval Institute Press, 2001.
Hermes, Walter G. *The United States Army in the Korean War: Truce Tent and Fighting Front.* Washington, DC: U.S. Government Printing Office, 1966.
Paik, Sun Yup. *From Pusan to Panmunjom.* London: Brassey's, 1992.
Schnabel, James P. *The United States Army in the Korean War: Policy and Direction, the First Year.* Washington, DC: U.S. Government Printing Office, 1972.

Vatican City

Independent city-state and seat of the Roman Catholic Church covering 108.7 acres within the city limits of Rome, Italy, on the west bank of the Tiber River. In 1945, Vatican City had an estimated population of 800 people. Residents of Vatican City include the pope, head of the worldwide Roman Catholic Church; numerous high-ranking and support Catholic clergy; and some nuns. As head of the Church and bishop of Rome, the pope is the absolute ruler of the city-state.

Vatican City has all the attributes of an autonomous state: citizenship, currency, postage, a flag, and a large diplomatic corps. It also has its own newspaper, *L'Osservatore Romano* (The Roman Observer), broadcasting facilities, and a railroad station. The political autonomy of the Vatican is guaranteed and protected by Italy via concordat.

The city-state has a civil government for conducting day-to-day business, run by a lay governor and a council who are all appointed by and responsible to the pope. The judicial system is essentially that of the Church, relying on canon law and several courts. There is a court of first instance, dedicated to both civil and criminal cases arising in the city. Over time, an elaborate Vatican bureaucracy has developed, called the Curia Romana, with the pope as head of state in charge of temporal as well as spiritual affairs. Although his power is absolute, the pope often relies on the College of Cardinals for advice as well as for the administration of church governance.

In the twentieth century, the emergence of communist parties and governments, officially committed to an ideology fiercely opposed to religion of every kind, presented challenges for the Vatican. In the case of Soviet Russia, the fact that the great majority of the population belonged to the official Russian Orthodox Church made it relatively simple for the Vatican to keep its distance from the Bolshevik state. In a number of countries that often had a radical and anticlerical tradition, Catholic clergy broadly discouraged parishioners from joining or working with local communist parties and opposed communist politicians almost on principle. During the bitter 1936–1939 Spanish Civil War, representatives of the Catholic Church generally supported Francisco Franco's Nationalist forces against the Republican government, which received assistance from Soviet communist operatives.

As World War II progressed, the Vatican under Pope Pius XII apprehensively watched the spread of Soviet power into East European states, where there were strong national Catholic churches in Germany, Poland, Hungary, and Czechoslovakia and smaller but substantial communions in Romania, Albania, Yugoslavia, and Bulgaria. From 1945 onward, the Vatican was forced to steer a middle path in the Cold War, balancing its genuine and deep-rooted antipathy toward communism against the need to seek to protect the status of those churches under communist rule. In Eastern Europe, Church lands were often expropriated under communist-initiated land reform programs. Immediately after World War II, the Vatican took a strongly anti-Soviet line, appointing the staunchly anticommunist Hungarian nationalist Cardinal József Mindszenty as primate of Hungary in 1945, for example, and deploring the extension of communist rule well into Central Europe.

Throughout the Cold War, the Catholic Church also experienced pressure, especially from the United States, to favor the West and support its containment policies. Under Pope Pius XII, the Roman Catholic Church came out strongly against the Italian Communist Party in the 1948 elections, which hinged in part on whether Italy should align itself firmly with the Western alliance. However, by that time the Church also openly deprecated the division of Europe resulting from the containment policy, the Marshall Plan, and the North Atlantic Treaty Organization (NATO) military alliance, which threatened to isolate Catholics within the communist bloc from the remainder of the Church. In 1949, after the Romanian and Bulgarian governments effectively closed down their countries' Catholic churches and Mindszenty was arrested, convicted of treason, and imprisoned, Pius XII went so far as to threaten excommunication for Catholics who collaborated with communist regimes. In practice, by 1950 several stronger East European Catholic churches, including those in Hungary, Poland, and Czechoslovakia, reached formal or informal accommodation with the communist authorities. Even so, in the early 1950s the Czechoslovak Archbishop Josef Beran, Polish Cardinal Stefan Wyszyński, and Archbishop József Grösz of Hungary were all incarcerated. Other less prominent priests and bishops were arrested or executed, essentially because their respective governments perceived them as political threats. From the 1950s onward, the Vatican tended to employ quiet diplomacy rather than confrontational tactics

St. Peter's Basilica in the Vatican City, Rome. The dome, or cupola, was designed by Renaissance painter and sculptor Michelangelo. (iStockPhoto.com)

to secure such individuals' release and to ensure that East European Catholics could still practice their faith. Such pragmatic practices sometimes, however, exposed Vatican officials to charges that they had abandoned principle in order to cravenly appease communist regimes.

Seeking to steer a middle course and to defuse the attractions of communism, from 1949 on well-publicized Vatican pronouncements deplored the growing emphasis on materialism, especially in the Western world, and supported social justice, welfare policies, and measures designed to aid impoverished nations around the world. Vatican Council II, held from 1962 to 1965—during which the popular and outgoing Pope John XXIII died, to be replaced in 1963 by the more austere but reformist Pope Paul VI—resisted an internal Church movement to condemn communism outright, emphasized the common good, and defended the right of all individuals to enjoy access to food, shelter, medical care, and social services. The pronouncements effectively demanded that capitalism transcend the profit motive and promote the well-being of the entire community. In 1967 and 1971 encyclicals, Paul VI also criticized the asymmetries of wealth and power that existed between rich, largely Western nations and poor nations, ascribing these in part to the legacy of colonialism. Although Ngo Dinh Diem, president of Vietnam from 1955 to 1963, was

a Catholic, the Vatican refused to endorse the U.S. position in the Vietnam War, instead making repeated though unsuccessful offers of mediation. The emergence in the early 1970s of liberation theology—Catholic teachings arguing that revolution and violent resistance to state power were sometimes acceptable in the interests of social justice—emboldened some priests, bishops, and nuns in Latin America and Africa to align themselves with leftist and radical movements against authoritarian governments. The Vatican refused to endorse this stance and in the 1980s appointed conservative bishops strongly opposed to liberation theology. The Church did, however, condemn states' forcible repression via such tactics as torture, rape, and murder of opponents. The most spectacular example of the latter was the 1980 assassination while celebrating mass in his own cathedral of Archbishop Oscar Arnulfo Romero y Galdámez of San Salvador.

In Asia, the post–World War II emergence of communist states, especially the People's Republic of China (PRC) in 1949, posed particular problems for the Roman Catholic Church, whose missions—in China dating back to the late sixteenth century—were heavily tainted by association with colonialism. Mao Zedong's China had expelled virtually all foreign missionaries by late 1952, in some cases accusing them of espionage. Many noncommunist Chinese also fled, some to

Hong Kong and Taiwan, others farther afield. Some 70 percent of Chinese bishoprics were left vacant, allowing the Chinese Communist Party (CCP) to appoint self-elected and self-consecrated local bishops and establish a self-styled patriotic church independent of Vatican control. Under land reform programs, Catholic properties were often confiscated. Despite official religious toleration policies, Chinese Christians of all persuasions were viewed as a threat to communist control and were therefore liable to attract fierce persecution as rightists.

This attitude peaked during the 1966–1976 Cultural Revolution but continued sporadically thereafter. Although the officially sponsored church, the Chinese Catholics' Patriotic Association, existed, some Chinese Catholics and priests also kept in existence an underground church that maintained clandestine ties with Rome. The late twentieth century saw a great upsurge of all forms of religion in Mainland China. Some estimate that by the early twenty-first century the underground Catholic church had twice as many members as its officially sanctioned counterpart and that altogether China had 12 million Catholics.

Further complicating the situation, the Vatican maintained diplomatic relations with the Republic of China (ROC) on Taiwan, where there was a sizable Catholic community, and stated its intention to keep these intact, citing the fact that it had never broken such links with any state, even communist Cuba. The last Vatican ambassador to live in Taiwan was, however, recalled in 1971 after Taiwan's expulsion from the United Nations (UN). The PRC's move to more pragmatic polices from the mid-1970s onward brought sporadic though inconclusive negotiations between Chinese and Vatican officials, with other top Asian Catholic representatives often serving as intermediaries, aimed at a rapprochement and potential regularization of the status of the Chinese Catholic Church. These generally foundered on Chinese insistence that the Vatican cease to recognize Taiwan and refrain from any interference in what the PRC considered its own internal affairs, including human rights and the treatment of Chinese Christians—conditions that the Vatican was unwilling to meet. In 2000 Pope John Paul II infuriated the PRC government by canonizing 120 Chinese and foreign Christians martyred in China and terminating promised negotiations for a rapprochement whereby the Vatican would end the protracted standoff in China and switch diplomatic recognition from Taipei to Beijing. Although tensions rose at times as local bishops and clergy publicly criticized PRC policies, Mainland China did respect the independence of the Vatican-affiliated Catholic churches in Hong Kong and Macau after those territories returned to China in 1997 and 1999, respectively, observing the provisions for religious freedom mandated in the handover agreements previously concluded with Britain and Portugal.

In Poland, the Roman Catholic Church was the leading national institution to survive German occupation. The Church hierarchy, by tradition decidedly independent of Rome, was prepared to work with the incoming communist regime if Church rights were respected. Acquiescence nonetheless did not necessarily imply approval, as demonstrated after the 1978 election of Archbishop Karol Wojtyła of Kraków, Poland, as the first non-Italian pope in more than four centuries. The charismatic John Paul II traveled tirelessly around the world, winning new adherents to the Catholic faith in the developing world, particularly Africa and Asia, and gaining immense personal respect and authority during his twenty-six-year papacy.

On an early visit to his native Poland in 1979, John Paul II quietly encouraged the leaders of the Solidarity labor movement to stand firm and work to challenge and undermine communist rule. Such pressures contributed to the eventual collapse of communism throughout Eastern Europe and in the Soviet Union. There were rumors that John Paul II's support for the Solidarity-orchestrated strike at the Gdańsk shipyard in 1980 so infuriated the Kremlin that in 1981 on Soviet orders the Bulgarian secret service organized an assassination attempt on his life that almost succeeded.

Pope John Paul II also apologized for past Catholic implication in anti-Semitic persecution of Jews. In the early twenty-first century, the Vatican and Russia nonetheless failed to open diplomatic relations. The Russian Orthodox Church would not sanction the Catholic demand to be allowed to proselytize in Russia, and Russian nationalists resented the pope's efforts to further the collapse of the Soviet Union. John Paul II nonetheless continued his predecessors' criticisms of unfettered market forces and materialism, charging that neither communism nor capitalism could meet humanity's spiritual needs unaided.

A social conservative, John Paul II also affronted many Western liberals by deprecating the pursuit of individual—especially women's—rights and sexual freedoms. Within the Catholic Church, his appointment of growing numbers of African, Asian, and Latin American cardinals, many of conservative, fundamentalist religious views, diluted the power of American and European liberals and meant that the influence of his own outlook would probably remain strong for many years after his death in 2005.

Luc Stenger and Priscilla Roberts

See also

China, People's Republic of; Cultural Revolution; John XXIII, Pope; John Paul II, Pope; Mindszenty, József; Paul VI, Pope; Pius XII, Pope; Roman Catholic Church; Stepinac, Aloysius, Archbishop; Vatican Council II; World Council of Churches; Wyszyński, Stefan, Cardinal

References

Diskin, Hanna. *The Seeds of Triumph: Church and State in Gomułka's Poland.* New York: Central European University Press, 2001.

Dunn, Dennis J. *The Catholic Church and the Soviet Government, 1933–1949.* Boulder, CO: East European Monographs, 1977.

Ellis, Kail C., ed. *The Vatican, Islam, and the Middle East.* Syracuse, NY: Syracuse University Press, 1987.

Floridi, Alexis Ulysses. *Moscow and the Vatican.* Ann Arbor, MI: Ardis, 1986.

Giammanco, Rosanna Mulazzi. *The Catholic-Communist Dialogue in Italy: 1944 to the Present.* New York: Praeger, 1999.

Kent, Peter C. *The Lonely Cold War of Pius XII: The Roman Catholic Church and the Division of Europe, 1943–1950.* Montreal: McGill-Queen's University Press, 2002.

Kent, Peter C., and John F. Pollard, eds. *Papal Diplomacy in the Modern Age.* Westport, CT: Praeger, 1994.

Kreutz, Andrej. *Vatican Policy on the Palestinian-Israeli Conflict: The Struggle for the Holy Land.* New York: Greenwood, 1990.

Leung, Beatrice. *Sino-Vatican Relations: Problems in Conflicting Authority, 1976–1986.* Cambridge: Cambridge University Press, 1992.

Luxmoore, Jonathan, and Jolanta Babiuch. *The Vatican & the Red Flag: The Struggle for the Soul of Eastern Europe.* London: Geoffrey Chapman, 1999.

McKenna, Joseph C. *Finding a Social Voice: The Church and Marxism in Africa.* New York: Fordham University Press, 1997.

Michel, Patrick. *Politics and Religion in Eastern Europe: Catholicism in Hungary, Poland and Czechoslovakia.* Translated by Alan Braley. Oxford, UK: Polity, 1991.

Van Dee, Eugene H. *Sleeping Dogs and Popsicles: The Vatican versus the KGB.* Lanham, MD: University Press of America, 1996.

Walsh, Michael J. *Vatican City State.* Santa Barbara, CA: ABC-CLIO, 1983.

Weigel, George. *The Final Revolution: The Resistance Church and the Collapse of Communism.* New York: Oxford University Press, 1992.

Woolner, David B., and Richard J. Kurial, eds. *FDR, the Vatican, and the Roman Catholic Church in America, 1933–1945.* New York: Palgrave Macmillan, 2003.

Zmijewski, Norbert A. *The Catholic-Marxist Ideological Dialogue in Poland, 1945–1980.* Aldershot, UK: Dartmouth Press, 1991.

Vatican Council II (1962–1965)

Roman Catholic ecumenical council convened in four separate sessions during 1962–1965. On 25 January 1959, Pope John XXIII announced his intention to call an ecumenical council for the Roman Catholic Church. Serious preparations for the council began in June 1959, when the pope sought advice and suggestions from 2,600 members of the Church's hierarchy in 134 countries. On 5 June 1960, John XXIII announced the formation of various commissions to prepare the documents to be debated during council sessions. In *Humanae Salutis* (Of Human Salvation), issued on 25 December 1961, the pope formally chartered the council and announced that it would be held at St. Peter's Basilica at the Vatican. In February 1962, the Holy See set the council's opening date for 11 October 1962.

Vatican Council II opened with a public session. In his address, John XXIII declared that the council was to meet the specific needs of the present-day Roman Catholic Church. He also emphasized that work must be undertaken to achieve unity with other Christians as well as with non-Christians. The council met for the first day of work on 13 October 1962 but adjourned after an hour. A group of progressive cardinals made a motion to adjourn so that national groups at the council had an opportunity to review the lists of names selected to serve on the ten commissions that would guide debate. The first session eventually debated issues relating to the structure and purpose of the liturgy, the church's relationship with the media, and a document calling for unity with Eastern churches. The ailing John XXIII closed the first session on 8 December 1962.

During the period between the sessions, the commissions met to draft documents to be voted on in the next session. John XXIII's death on 3 June 1963 ended all work until a new pope was elected. In his first message, Pope Paul VI, John XXIII's successor, promised that the council would continue and set the opening date for the second session for 29 September 1963.

In an opening address to the second session, the new pope outlined the four primary purposes of the council: to define the Church more fully, especially the role of bishops; to renew the Church; to restore unity among all Christians; and to "start a dialogue with contemporary men."

During the second session, the council's progress stalled over the document outlining the constitution of the Church. Among the questions raised by this document were the role of laypeople, the relationship with other churches, the importance of religious orders, and the relationship between church and state. Eventually work continued, and the council approved reforms of the liturgy, including the use of vernacular languages in the mass. A document on the use of modern communications media was also approved. The session debated a document stating that the Jews were not responsible for the death of Jesus, but the document was not approved before the second session closed on 4 December 1963.

The third session opened on 14 September 1964. Early in the session, the council approved a series of documents outlining the nature of the Church and the relationship between the Church and its people. On 23 September 1964, fifteen women took their seats as auditors of the council, the first women to ever participate in a Roman Catholic ecumenical council. The session continued the debate on ecumenical issues and the role of laypeople in the Church. During the debate over the position of the Church in the modern world, the pope told the council to remove discussion on artificial contraception from its agenda. A separate commission was studying the issue, and the pope did not want the council to vote in anticipation of the commission's decisions.

According to observers at the council, the third session was the most contentious. Before the session closed on 21 November 1964, the council approved documents on the Church in the modern world, ecumenism, and the relationship with the Eastern churches.

The fourth session opened on 14 September 1965. In his opening speech Paul VI announced that he would be visiting the United Nations (UN). He also announced his intention to establish a synod of bishops to advise him, part of an effort to increase collegiality within the Church hierarchy. The debate during the fourth session was wide-ranging. Documents were approved outlining religious freedom, the role of the Church in the modern world, and the relationship with non-Christian religions. The role of women in the Church was debated, as was the significance of Christian marriage. The law governing clerical celibacy was strengthened. An attempt to include a strong condemnation of communism was defeated. The council also emphasized the role of the common good in society and defended the rights of all individuals to enjoy access to adequate food, shelter, medical care, and basic social services, pronouncements that effectively expected capitalism to transcend the profit motive and promote the well-being of the entire community. The fourth session thus ended, and Vatican Council II officially closed on 8 December 1965.

John David Rausch Jr.

See also

John XXIII, Pope; Paul VI, Pope; Roman Catholic Church

References

McCarthy, Timothy. *The Catholic Tradition: Before and after Vatican II, 1878–1993.* Chicago: Loyola University Press, 1994.

Muggeridge, Anne Roche. *The Desolate City: Revolution in the Catholic Church.* Revised and expanded ed. San Francisco: Harper and Row, 1990.

Rynne, Xavier. *Vatican Council II.* New York: Farrar, Straus and Giroux, 1968.

Wiltgen, Ralph M. *The Rhine Flows into the Tiber: The Unknown Council.* New York: Hawthorn Books, 1967.

Venezuela

South American nation covering 352,143 square miles, roughly a third larger than the U.S. state of Texas. With a 1945 population of approximately 4.25 million, the Republic of Venezuela is located on South America's northern coast and borders the Caribbean Sea to the north, Guyana to the east, Brazil to the south, and Colombia to the west. In 1830, Venezuela was proclaimed a republic. However, a string of dictatorial regimes followed that crippled the country's development. Under the government of Antonio Guzmán Blanco (1870–1888), a modern infrastructure was constructed, while foreign investment increased. During 1908–1935, Venezuela was governed by the brutal dictator Juan Vicente Gómez, who developed the nation's oil-exporting industry. Following his death, a military junta took control until the leftist Rómulo Betancourt and his Acción Democrática (AD, Democratic Action) party seized the political initiative beginning in 1945.

During 1945–1948, the reformist government in Venezuela enacted policies that hurt U.S. economic interests. However, Washington supported the regime because it seemed a bulwark against economic nationalism and communism. Because the United States became a net importer of oil in 1947, interest in Venezuela was all the more pronounced.

In 1948, conservative military leaders overthrew the populist government. With Colonel Marcos Pérez Jiménez as head of state, the Venezuelan government suppressed popular dissent and became one of Washington's staunchest regional allies. As such, the U.S. government extended substantial military and economic support. Despite Washington's backing, however, a coup toppled the regime in early 1958, and elections were scheduled for the next year. Nevertheless, the Pérez Jiménez regime cast a long shadow on Venezuelan relations with the United States. In May 1958, anti-American riots erupted when U.S. Vice President Richard M. Nixon arrived on a state visit. Angry protestors practically overturned his car. After he returned home to a triumphal greeting, Washington accelerated the process of focusing more attention on the region.

Both a majority of Venezuelans and U.S. officials hoped to put the repression of the Pérez Jiménez years behind them and welcomed the election of Betancourt of the AD in February 1959. Betancourt had cut his political teeth as a student in the late 1920s when he had actively supported the ouster of Gómez. Betancourt's reformist vision resonated with New Deal liberals in the United States.

Although U.S. President John F. Kennedy's record of supporting democracies in Latin America was spotty, Kennedy supported Betancourt because he was a moderate reformer who led an oil-rich nation and valued harmonious relations with the United States. Indeed, reformist pro-American governments seemed the best antidote for preventing the spread of Fidel Castro's brand of communism. As Betancourt's tumultuous tenure in office proceeded, the U.S. government offered increasing support as part of the Alliance for Progress, despite the implementation of state-capitalist policies. A hotline was even set up between the White House and the Venezuelan presidential residence in Caracas. Betancourt served as president until 1964.

Of particular importance to U.S. officials was the Venezuelan military. American leaders perceived strong anticommunist militaries as the only sure defense against radical or communist takeovers in Latin America, and Venezuela was no different. During Betancourt's time in office, military aid

In 1975, Puerto Miranda was the largest oil port in the Western world, capable of pumping 145,000 tons per day and receiving supertankers with a capacity of 80,000 tons. (Diego Goldberg/Sygma/Corbis)

accounted for $64.5 million of the $180.1 million in U.S. assistance. U.S. military assistance to Venezuela was critically important, because the fear of Castroism spreading to Venezuela seemed more tangible compared to the risk to the rest of the region. In 1963, the Venezuelans discovered a small cache of Cuban weapons hidden on an isolated stretch of coastline. The uncovering of this clumsy attempt to aid pro-Castro insurgents in Venezuela prompted the Organization of American States (OAS) to apply economic sanctions against Cuba. In 1966, Venezuelan officials also captured four Cuban officers who were apparently training Venezuelan guerrillas.

There was one persistent sticking point in U.S.-Venezuelan relations. From the U.S. point of view, free trade and private investment were to be the engines of economic growth in Venezuela and ultimately of pro-American stability. But from Venezuela's viewpoint, free trade translated into lower prices for oil, its principal export, and thus deteriorating terms of trade for the import of finished goods. To garner additional income from oil exports, in 1960 Venezuela helped to organize the Organization of Petroleum Exporting Countries (OPEC). Although OPEC did not register on U.S. policymakers' radar

screens until the 1970s when it burst on the world scene as a major economic player, its formation and maturation (aided by Venezuela throughout the 1960s) represented a significant challenge to U.S. influence in the world economy.

For years, Venezuela had sought a hemispheric preference for its imports to the United States, which the United States refused because worldwide oil supplies were plentiful. This preference would have allowed Venezuela to estimate the revenue flow from oil and create long-term economic development plans. Thus, once the energy crisis of the mid-1970s hit the United States, Venezuelan officials expressed little sympathy for their major purchaser of petroleum. However, because of the historically close relationship between Venezuela and the United States, Venezuela stepped up exports of oil to a grateful United States during the 1973–1974 Arab oil embargo.

Relations between the United States and Venezuela cooled somewhat with the December 1973 election of the AD's Carlos Andrés Pérez. Arguing that the industrial world had used its economic power to take advantage of third world producers of primary products, Pérez took action to garner greater income from Venezuela's sale of oil and steel. These industries were nationalized on 1 January 1975.

Expropriation with an indemnity was made possible with the run-up in oil prices starting in late 1973. The higher prices gave Venezuela the capital to offer compensation for the nationalization. Despite the AD's leftist rhetoric, Venezuela (most particularly the elite) thought it important to offer compensation to the oil companies in order to stay on good terms with them and with the United States. Cordial relations with the companies and the United States were important because the South American nation was still dependent on the United States for high-technology items, finished products, and technicians. Although the expropriated companies were not entirely happy with the settlement, they ultimately accepted Venezuela's offer of compensation.

The early 1970s marked an important turning point in contemporary Venezuelan history. With increased revenue from oil sales, Venezuela transformed itself from a relatively impoverished nation to an important contributor of foreign assistance, even donating up to 12 percent of its gross domestic product (GDP) for foreign assistance to the developing world.

As petroleum prices slid in the mid-1980s and the Latin American debt crisis reverberated around the hemisphere, Venezuela entered a time of economic and political crisis, which included rioting in 1989 and two political coups in 1992. Venezuelan relations with the United States, however, remained close during the 1980s and early 1990s. In fact, Venezuela was the only developing nation to secure F-16 fighter aircraft from the United States in the 1980s. Although Venezuela worked with Mexico, Colombia, and Panama in the Contadora Group to help resolve deepening tensions between the United States and Nicaragua, the Venezuelans downplayed their participation by playing a quiet role in the process, as the U.S. pointedly frowned upon the Contadora Group.

Lower oil prices meant that Washington officials were less concerned with U.S.-Venezuelan relations. Crises in the Middle East in the early 1990s, however, again highlighted the importance of a large Western Hemispheric source of petroleum. Even as the Cold War faded away, and in part because of the large amount of U.S. investment in the nation and the continuing importance of a close supplier of petroleum, Washington officials and Venezuela still valued close relations.

James F. Siekmeier

See also
Alliance for Progress; Americas; Betancourt, Rómulo; Castro, Fidel; Contadora Group; Organization of American States; Organization of Petroleum Exporting Countries

References
Alexander, Robert. *Rómulo Betancourt and the Transformation of Venezuela.* New Brunswick, NJ: Transaction, 1982.
Ewell, Judith. *Venezuela and the United States.* Athens: University of Georgia Press, 1996.
Levine, Daniel. *Conflict and Political Change in Venezuela.* Princeton, NJ: Princeton University Press, 1973.
Rabe, Stephen G. *The Road to OPEC.* Austin: University of Texas Press, 1982.

Venona Project

U.S. code-breaking operation that revealed extensive Soviet spying in the United States during World War II and the early years of the Cold War. Beginning on 1 February 1943, the U.S. Army Signal Security Agency—commonly known as Arlington Hall and the predecessor organization to the National Security Agency (NSA)—began a secret program to decrypt and analyze thousands of encoded messages intercepted between Moscow and its diplomatic missions in the West. This program, which underwent at least a dozen code names, came to be known finally as Venona. In the course of deciphering the encoded diplomatic communications, the analysts uncovered evidence of espionage activities by the People's Commissariat of Internal Affairs (NKVD), the Soviet intelligence agency.

Gene Graebel, a former schoolteacher, began the project, and it took two years for Arlington Hall to break into the Soviet communications. Arlington Hall's Lieutenant Richard Halleck, a Signal Corps reserve officer who had been an archeologist at the University of Chicago, discovered weaknesses in the Soviet cryptographic system, namely that the Soviets were reusing some of the encoding in many of their messages. Halleck and his colleagues, many of whom were young women, went on to break into a significant quantity of Soviet trade traffic having to do with Lend-Lease and the Soviet Purchasing Commission. Cryptanalyst Meredith Gardner (a former language instructor at the University of Akron who spent twenty-seven years on the project) then employed these breakthroughs to decipher NKVD and Soviet Army General Staff Intelligence Directorate (GRU) communications, first breaking into these in December 1946. Arlington Hall worked in close collaboration with other U.S. agencies and the British MI5 intelligence agency, which joined the effort in 1948. Information provided by defecting Soviet cryptologist Igor Gouzenko also helped.

Among Venona's revelations were confirmation of the spying activities of Klaus Fuchs, David Greenglass, Bruno Pontecorvo, and Julius and Ethel Rosenberg. Venona also contributed to the unmasking of the Cambridge Five spy ring of British communist agents.

Soviet agents were able to inform the Komitet Gosudarstvennoi Bezopasnosti (KGB) of the Venona secret in 1948, after which Soviet communications became unreadable, but much valuable information was obtained. The Venona program continued until 1980. Beginning in July 1995, the NSA made six public releases of Venona translations and related documents. The first of these dealt with Soviet efforts to secure information on U.S. atomic bomb research. The remainder are a variety of NKVD communications, most of them during World War II.

Spencer C. Tucker

See also

Cambridge Five; Espionage; Fuchs, Klaus; Gouzenko, Igor; MI5; Roosevelt, Franklin Delano; Rosenberg, Julius; White, Harry Dexter

References

Benson, Robert Louis. *The Venona Story.* Washington, DC: National Security Agency, Center for Cryptologic History, 2001.

Benson, Robert Louis, and Michael Warner. *Venona: Soviet Espionage and the American Response, 1939–1957.* Washington, DC: National Security Agency and Central Intelligence Agency, 1996.

Haynes, John Earl, and Harvey Kehr. *Venona: Decoding Soviet Espionage in America.* New Haven, CT: Yale University Press, 1999.

West, Nigel. *Venona: The Greatest Secret of the Cold War.* London: HarperCollins, 1999.

Verwoerd, Hendrik Frensch (1901–1966)

South African apartheid leader and prime minister (1958–1966). Born in Amsterdam on 8 September 1901, Hendrik Frensch Verwoerd immigrated with his family to South Africa in 1903. He attended the University of Stellenbosch, eventually earning a doctorate in social psychology in 1924. He then studied further in Germany. He returned to South Africa in 1928 to become professor of applied psychology at Stellenbosch. In 1937 he left academia to edit the Afrikaner Nationalist newspaper *Die Transvaler,* which drew him into public life.

In 1950, as an unelected member of the country's senate, Verwoerd was appointed minister of native affairs, in which capacity he systematically implemented South Africa's segregationist apartheid policies. In 1958, following the sudden death of Prime Minister J. G. Strijdom, Verwoerd was elected leader of the ruling National Party and became prime minister.

Deeply suspicious of communist influences and their potential effect on South Africa's black majority, Verwoerd set out to subdivide the country and formally separate the races into separate states. In 1961, he removed South Africa from the British Commonwealth and instituted a republic. His domestic policies and regional agenda were fiercely resisted by South Africa's majority. The resulting confrontations were indeed tragic. Of the many demonstrations, the March 1960 Sharpeville massacre was the most notorious. Sharpeville engendered the wrath of the international community

and set the stage for a campaign for sanctions against the apartheid regime led by the World Council of Churches and the Non-Aligned Movement. In 1961, Verwoerd narrowly escaped death in an assassination attempt. A second attempt was successful, however. Verwoerd was stabbed to death by Dimitri Tsafendas, a part-time parliamentary messenger, in the parliament building on 6 September 1966 in Cape Town. Tsafendas, whose mother was black, was declared insane and sent to prison. Recent work suggests that Tsafendas may have been driven to the deed by political motives.

Peter Vale

See also

South Africa

References

Barber, James, and John Barratt, eds. *South Africa's Foreign Policy: The Search for Status and Security, 1945–1988.* Johannesburg: Southern Books, 1990.

Grundy, Kenneth W. *Confrontation and Accommodation in Southern Africa: The Limits of Independence.* Berkeley: University of California Press, 1973.

O'Meara, Dan. *Forty Lost Years.* Athens: Ohio University Press, 1997.

Vienna Conference (3–4 June 1961)

Summit meeting between U.S. President John F. Kennedy and Soviet Premier Nikita Khrushchev in Vienna, Austria, on 3–4 June 1961. Shortly after Kennedy took office in January 1961, Khrushchev suggested a meeting with his American counterpart. After the embarrassing and abortive Cuban Bay of Pigs invasion in April, Kennedy's advisors were adamantly opposed to the conference, believing that Khrushchev would exploit the failed invasion either by berating the president or using it as a propaganda ploy. Kennedy rejected their advice.

Kennedy wanted the meeting to focus on a nuclear test-ban treaty and the neutralization of Laos, where a communist insurgency was threatening the government. The president believed that these agreements would be important steps toward easing Cold War tensions, which had grown more intense since the May 1960 U-2 Crisis. He also hoped that the summit might lead to a wider détente.

Khrushchev had little interest in a test ban and almost no interest in Laos, however. His primary concern was the fate of Berlin. He wanted an agreement that would stanch the flow of East Germans fleeing to the West via Berlin. His earlier attempt to pressure President Dwight D. Eisenhower into accepting a Berlin settlement by threatening to sign a peace treaty with the German Democratic Republic (GDR, East Germany), which would have given it full control of the city, had failed embarrassingly.

Following President Kennedy's death in 1963, his brother, Attorney General Robert F. Kennedy, reported that he had

U.S. President John F. Kennedy and Soviet Premier Nikita Khrushchev meet in Vienna, Austria, for their summit on 3–4 June 1961. (John F. Kennedy Library)

laid the groundwork for the summit during secret meetings with Khrushchev's conduit Georgi Bolshakov, a Soviet intelligence officer who worked undercover as a reporter. Kennedy later claimed that Khrushchev had used the correspondence to trick his brother into believing that he would limit the Vienna discussions to Laos and the test-ban treaty, which Khrushchev hinted could be verified by numerous on-site inspections. Robert Kennedy had not saved the messages, but the Soviets had. Their records verified that Khrushchev was not interested in either Laos or a nuclear test ban and that he had never agreed to on-site inspections. Instead, Khrushchev's notes to Kennedy focused on Berlin, reiterating his earlier threats.

Khrushchev's recalcitrance concerned the president. In hopes of making the summit a success, President Kennedy sent the attorney general to Bolshakov, offering concessions and assurances that he wanted a good working relationship. Shortly before leaving for Europe, the president severely injured his back, leaving him in constant pain throughout the conference. Many suggest that the president was not at

the top of his form as a result. Shortly before leaving for Vienna, Khrushchev met with his advisors, berating those who suggested that he work seriously with Kennedy and telling them that the president was weak and would buckle under his threats.

The summit had no formal agenda, allowing the two men to roam from topic to topic. Kennedy told his aides that when he broached the subject of the dangers of war through miscalculation, Khrushchev became almost uncontrollably hostile. The Soviet leader also rebuffed Kennedy's efforts to discuss the nuclear test ban, telling him that it "meant nothing" outside the context of total nuclear disarmament. Predictably, Khrushchev taunted Kennedy over Cuba. On Berlin, Khrushchev again threatened to sign a peace treaty if Kennedy did not agree to neutralize the city. Although Kennedy had been badgered, he did not back down.

The following day, Khrushchev hinted at possible future discussions concerning Laos, although no progress was made on the test ban. In his last meeting with the president that day, Khrushchev told Kennedy that he was going to give East Germany control over West Berlin's access routes, adding that if the United States used force to keep them open, there would be war. Kennedy icily replied, "Then there will be war, Mr. Chairman. It's going to be a very cold winter." Despite Kennedy's bold counterpunch, Khrushchev believed that he had sufficiently cowed the president.

Although Kennedy's aides told him that the meeting had been typical for Khrushchev, the president refused to believe it and began to prepare for war over Berlin. In a 25 July 1961 speech, Kennedy announced that he was dramatically expanding the armed forces, reinforcing Berlin, and calling for increased congressional appropriations for civil defense. The administration even advised Americans to build backyard bomb shelters.

Khrushchev soon realized that he had badly miscalculated by bullying Kennedy. Believing that Kennedy had lost control of his government to militarists, Khrushchev concluded that the only way to solve the Berlin Crisis and avoid a war was to construct the Berlin Wall. Nevertheless, largely because of Vienna, Khrushchev continued to believe that Kennedy was weak. It took the 1962 Cuban Missile Crisis to dispel that notion.

Robert Anthony Waters Jr.

See also
Bay of Pigs; Berlin Crises; Berlin Wall; Cuba; Cuban Missile Crisis; Kennedy, John Fitzgerald; Khrushchev, Nikita; Nuclear Tests; Partial Test Ban Treaty; U-2 Incident

References
Beschloss, Michael R. *The Crisis Years: Kennedy and Khrushchev, 1960–1963.* New York: HarperCollins, 1991.
Dallek, Robert. *An Unfinished Life: John F. Kennedy, 1917–1963.* Boston: Little, Brown, 2003.
Fursenko, Aleksandr, and Timothy Naftali. *"One Hell of a Gamble": Khrushchev, Castro, & Kennedy, 1958–1964.* New York: Norton, 1997.
Reeves, Richard. *President Kennedy: Profile of Power.* New York: Touchstone, 1993.

Vienna Document (17 November 1990)

Final document of the Vienna Conference on Confidence and Security-Building Measures (CSBM). Soviet General Secretary Mikhail Gorbachev's June 1986 call for a new CSBM conference to build on the agreements contained in the Stockholm Document (1986) was adopted by the Conference on Security and Cooperation in Europe (CSCE) at its Vienna follow-up meeting on 15 January 1989, after two years of preliminary discussions. Gorbachev's proposal for new talks on conventional forces in Europe had been adopted the previous day, and the two sets of negotiations were mandated to be completed at the same time.

Both negotiating sessions were to be held in Vienna, with the CSBM conference beginning on 6 March 1989, to include all thirty-five CSCE members. The talks concluded on 17 November 1990 with the adoption of the Vienna Document that same day.

Many provisions of the Vienna Document were little changed from those in the Stockholm Document. The parties to the agreement pledged to refrain from the threat or use of force, and provisions for prior notification of troop movements, observation of troop movements, and the production of annual calendars forecasting expected troop movements by each party were essentially the same, as was the area of coverage from the Atlantic to the Urals. New provisions included a single threshold of 40,000 troops for the requirement to give notice of movements two years in advance, replacing the dual threshold contained in the Stockholm Document.

The most significant changes from the 1986 agreement dealt with verification. The signatories were required to submit detailed annual reports on their armed forces, including information on manpower levels, organization, weapons systems, command structure, and location down to the regimental level. The resulting data set would support a new form of verification to supplement the inspection provisions retained from the Stockholm Document. Termed "evaluation," it provided for on-site inspections of units in garrison. Each party was required to accept one evaluation inspection per year for each sixty regiments it deployed, up to a total of fifteen visits per year. The Vienna Document enhanced European stability and lessened the chance of misunderstandings resulting from nonaggressive military activities. Subsequent negotiations brought revisions to the document in 1992 and 1994 to reflect changes in the European political situation stemming from the collapse of communism.

Steven W. Guerrier

See also
Conventional Forces in Europe Treaty; Gorbachev, Mikhail; Helsinki Final Act; Security and Cooperation in Europe, Conference on; Stockholm Document

References
Blackwell, Robert D., and F. Stephen Larrabee, eds. *Conventional Arms Control and East-West Security.* Durham, NC: Duke University Press, 1989.
MacIntosh, James. "Confidence-Building Measures in Europe." Pp. 929–945 in *Encyclopedia of Arms Control and Disarmament*, edited by Richard Dean Burns. New York: Scribner, 1993.

Vienna Meeting (15–18 June 1979)

The sole summit meeting held between President Jimmy Carter and Soviet leader Leonid Brezhnev during 15–18 June 1979 in Vienna, Austria. By signing the Strategic Arms

Limitation Treaty (SALT II) at this conference, the two leaders hoped to promote a new spirit of cooperation in U.S.-Soviet relations. Unfortunately, they achieved only a slight pause in the deteriorating relationship between the United States and the Soviet Union.

The SALT I agreement signed at the 1972 Moscow Meeting by Brezhnev and President Richard Nixon had intended only to restrain the arms race for ten years, during which time the superpowers would negotiate a more comprehensive accord. At the 1974 Vladivostok Meeting, Brezhnev and President Gerald R. Ford agreed to establish ceilings for the sum total of missiles and bombers that each side could have and the number of those that could be fitted with multiple warheads. A SALT II agreement seemed within reach. Because of the worsening international climate and the complexity of arms control talks, however, negotiations took longer than expected. They were further delayed in 1977 when Carter sought extensive arms reductions, far beyond those agreed to at Vladivostok. As a result, the treaty was not completed until 1979.

SALT II, the high point of U.S.-Soviet relations during the Carter presidency, followed the guidelines set at Vladivostok. It limited each side to 2,400 strategic launch vehicles through 1981 and then 2,250 until 1985. Limits were also placed on the number of multiple independently targeted reentry vehicles (MIRVs) on land-based missiles (820), land-based and submarine-launched missiles (1,200), and MIRV missiles and heavy bombers equipped with long-range cruise missiles (1,320). The Soviet Union still held the advantage in total throw weight and in the number of land-based missiles. The United States possessed more submarine-based weapons, cruise missiles, and forward-based systems not covered by the agreement. Each side retained vast quantities of intercontinental ballistic missiles (ICBMs), submarine-launched ballistic missiles (SLBMs), air-to-surface ballistic missiles (ASBMs), and MIRVs, but the arms race had been slowed, and the treaty called for future negotiations to achieve more significant cuts in the nuclear arsenals of both powers.

Before signing SALT II, Carter and Brezhnev discussed a variety of issues privately, without reaching any common ground. They sparred over human rights; Iran; Afghanistan; the Middle East; Southeast Asia; and Soviet adventurism in Central America, the Caribbean, and Africa. Brezhnev spent much of this time warning Carter not to threaten the Soviet Union by "playing the China card." Carter insisted that the Soviet leader understand that the Persian Gulf represented a vital interest to the United States. Each leader described what he considered provocative behavior of the other country while claiming nothing beyond a basic desire for peace. They then looked toward the future of arms control. Carter wrote twelve suggestions for a SALT III on a yellow pad and handed it to Brezhnev. Most notably, he suggested a freeze on the production of warheads and launchers, a total ban on nuclear tests, 5 percent annual reductions in strategic arms, and annual summit meetings. Neither harm nor good resulted from this overture. Carter simply demonstrated his vision of achieving further progress on arms control.

The U.S. Senate never ratified SALT II. Senator Henry "Scoop" Jackson, a Washington state Democrat, blasted the treaty as "appeasement" even before it was signed and led a determined opposition. Carter tried to save the treaty by convincing conservative senators that he was tough on defense by pushing for deployment of the MX missile and moving ahead on stationing Pershing II and cruise missiles in Western Europe to counter new SS-20 Soviet missiles. But Carter's sagging popularity and a number of mounting irritants in U.S.-Soviet relations during the fall of 1979—for example, the discovery of a Soviet brigade in Cuba and Congress's failure to grant the Soviet Union most-favored nation trade status— made Senate ratification unlikely. Carter then withdrew the treaty from Senate consideration.

Equally important, the 1979 Iranian Revolution cost the United States some of its best facilities for monitoring Soviet treaty compliance. The Soviet invasion of Afghanistan in December 1979 ended any chance of ratifying the treaty and solidified a shift in Carter's Soviet policy from one of attempting to sustain a weak policy of détente to confrontational containment. This was clearly evident by the refusal to sell U.S. grain to Moscow, the American boycott of the 1980 Moscow Olympics, and the pronouncement of the Carter Doctrine in 1980.

Although the treaty failed to gain Senate approval, both Washington and Moscow professed to abide by it up to and beyond its expiration at the end of 1985.

Dean Fafoutis

See also

Arms Control; Détente; Missiles, Cruise; Missiles, Intercontinental Ballistic; Missiles, Pershing II; Missiles, Submarine-Launched Ballistic; Moscow Meeting, Brezhnev and Nixon; Olympic Games and Politics; Strategic Arms Limitation Talks and Treaties

References

Carter, Jimmy. *Keeping Faith: Memoirs of a President.* Fayetteville: University of Arkansas Press, 1995.

Garthoff, Raymond L. *Détente and Confrontation: American-Soviet Relations from Nixon to Reagan.* Rev. ed. Washington, DC: Brookings Institution Press, 1994.

Smith, Gaddis. *Morality, Reason, and Power: American Diplomacy in the Carter Years.* New York: Hill and Wang, 1986.

Viet Minh

Indochinese Communist Party (ICP) front organization. The Viet Nam Doc Lap Dong Minh Hoi (Viet Minh, or Vietnam

Independence League) was founded by Ho Chi Minh at the Eighth Plenum of the ICP in May 1941 as a means of mobilizing the Vietnamese population into a National United Front in order to defeat both the French and Japanese. As such, the Viet Minh served a tactical rather than a strategic purpose, for the ICP's ultimate objective remained the creation of a communist-dominated government in Vietnam. Consequently, during World War II, less stress was placed on class struggle, while more emphasis was placed on working with all elements of Vietnamese society, including those normally branded as class enemies.

The leaders of the Viet Minh placed particular effort on forming and training armed guerrilla detachments. When the Japanese surrendered in August 1945, the Viet Minh was the best prepared of all resistance groups to seize power. As a result, it was at the forefront of the August Revolution that followed. On 2 September 1945 in Hanoi, Ho declared Vietnam's independence and an end to the Nguyen dynasty. Soon thereafter, the dissolution of the ICP was officially announced, which ostensibly left the Viet Minh as the sole party apparatus.

The Viet Minh led the resistance effort following the outbreak of the Indochina War in late 1946. To rebuild the strength of the National United Front, since the broad mass of the Vietnamese population had come to identify it with the communist leadership, the Viet Minh was merged into the newly created Hoi Lien Hiep Quoc Dan Viet Nam (Lien Viet Front, or League for the National Union of Vietnam) in early 1951. The basic tactical elements of the front did not change, however, as the redesignation was made chiefly to accommodate communist revolutionary theory, which dictated that such a step was required when the historical situation was radically altered. The Lien Viet Front would also be reconstituted following the signing of the 1954 Geneva Accords, when it would be replaced by the Fatherland Front.

Concurrent with the creation of the Lien Viet Front, the ICP was publicly resurrected with a new name, Dang Lao Dong Viet Nam (Vietnamese Worker's Party), in order to recognize the growing Chinese communist influence on domestic policy and to reinforce the critical importance of gaining the support of the general Vietnamese population. These changes and the reasons for them notwithstanding, popular and historical accounts of the Indochina War have usually referred to the Vietnamese resistance forces throughout as the Viet Minh.

George M. Brooke III

See also

Geneva Conference (1954); Ho Chi Minh; Indochina War; Nationalism; Vietnam

References

Duiker, William J. *Ho Chi Minh.* New York: Hyperion, 2000.

Huynh Kim Khánh. *Vietnamese Communism, 1925–1945.* Ithaca, NY: Cornell University Press, 1982.

Pike, Douglas. *A History of Vietnamese Communism, 1925–1978.* Stanford, CA: Hoover Institution Press, 1978.

Vietnam

Southeast Asian nation and the easternmost state of Indochina. Vietnam is bordered by China to the north, Laos and Cambodia to the west, and the Gulf of Tonkin and the South China Sea to the east and south. It encompasses some 127,300 square miles, slightly larger than the U.S. state of New Mexico. Vietnam's 1945 population was roughly 24.5 million. During the course of the Cold War, the population more than doubled. By 1996 it had grown to 70 million. Vietnam contains at least fifty-eight distinct national groups, but 85 percent of the population is ethnically Vietnamese, rendering the country largely culturally and ethnically homogenous. The French identified the original aboriginal inhabitants—chiefly the Thai, Muong, and Meo peoples—as Montagnards (mountain people). Other important ethnic minorities are the Chinese and the Khmer (Cambodians). In 1967, there were about 1 million Chinese in Vietnam and perhaps 700,000 Khmer.

In 938, the Vietnamese freed themselves from more than 1,000 years of Chinese rule. It remains a source of great national pride that Vietnam then maintained its independence, defeating subsequent Chinese attempts to reestablish control. Vietnam is, however, unique among countries of Southeast Asia in having adopted many Chinese cultural patterns.

The French arrived in the second half of the nineteenth century, establishing control first over southern Vietnam (Cochin China) by 1867, then expanding it to central Vietnam (Annam) and northern Vietnam (Tonkin). The French also dominated Cambodia. In 1887 Paris created the administrative structure of French Indochina. Laos was added in 1893. Technically, only Cochin China was an outright colony. The others were protectorates, but French officials made all the key decisions.

Nationalism spread in Vietnam after World War I. The French crushed the moderates, with the result that the more radical Indochinese Communist Party (ICP) took over the leadership against the French. In September 1940, the Japanese arrived. Taking advantage of the defeat of France by Germany, Tokyo sent troops and established bases in Vietnam. Japan's move into southern Vietnam in July 1941 brought U.S. economic sanctions that led to the Japanese decision to attack Pearl Harbor.

During World War II, ICP leader Ho Chi Minh formed the Vietnam Independence League (Viet Minh) to fight both the Japanese and the French. By the end of the conflict, with Chinese and American assistance, the Viet Minh had liberated

Ho Chi Minh, leader of the Viet Minh that fought against the Japanese and the French and president of the Democratic Republic of Vietnam (DRV, North Vietnam), shown here in October 1954. (Bettmann/Corbis)

much of Tonkin. The French, meanwhile, planned an insurrection against the Japanese, but in March 1945 the Japanese arrested all the French soldiers and administrators they could find. There was thus a political vacuum at the end of the war, into which Ho moved. On 2 September in Hanoi, he publicly proclaimed the independence of the Democratic Republic of Vietnam (DRV, North Vietnam).

Acting in accordance with wartime agreements, British forces occupied southern Indochina, and Nationalist Chinese forces arrived in northern Indochina. Ho was able to secure the departure of the Chinese, while the British released the French prisoners in southern Indochina and allowed them to reestablish their control there. Appeals by Ho to the Soviet Union and the United States fell on deaf ears, and Ho, forced into negotiations with the French, concluded an agreement on 6 March 1946 with French diplomat Jean Sainteny.

In the Ho-Sainteny Agreement, the French recognized the independence of North Vietnam and agreed to a plebiscite in southern Vietnam to see if it wished to join the North Vietnamese government, while Ho allowed the return of some French troops to North Vietnam to protect French interests there. The collapse of subsequent talks in France led to the outbreak of fighting in November 1946. This occurred because the French wanted to reassert control over their richest colony;

there was a long-standing mutual mistrust; and on 1 June 1946, without prior approval from Paris, French High Commissioner for Indochina Admiral Thierry d'Argenlieu issued a proclamation for an independent Republic of Cochin China.

The Indochina War lasted until 1954. The conflict was unpopular in France, and Paris never committed the resources necessary to win it. The war was lost for all practical purposes with the 1949 communist victory in China, for this gave the Viet Minh secure basing areas and supplies. In 1949, in part to win U.S. support, the French government negotiated the Elysée Agreement with ex-Emperor Bao Dai. The agreement officially granted independence to Vietnam. The new State of Vietnam was, however, a sham, completely dominated by the French until the end of the war.

With the French military defeat in the Battle of Dien Bien Phu in May 1954, the politicians in Paris shifted the blame onto the military and extricated France from the war. The July 1956 Geneva Accords granted independence to Vietnam, Laos, and Cambodia. Vietnam was to be temporarily divided at the 17th Parallel, pending national elections in two years to reunify the country.

In southern Vietnam, Catholic politician Ngo Dinh Diem took charge and brought a semblance of order. His power base rested on some 1 million northern Catholics who had relocated there after the Indochina War. In 1955 Diem staged a referendum, calling on the people of southern Vietnam to choose between Emperor Bao Dai and himself. Diem won the vote handily and proclaimed the Republic of Vietnam (RVN, South Vietnam), with himself as president. He held power until his assassination in November 1963. Claiming that he was not bound by the Geneva Accords, he refused to hold the promised elections, and U.S. President Dwight D. Eisenhower's administration supported this position. When the date for the elections passed, Viet Minh political cadres in South Vietnam resumed the armed struggle, this time against the Diem government. Diem, meanwhile, received substantial economic aid and increasing military assistance from the United States.

In North Vietnam, Ho and other leaders were not displeased with Diem's establishment of order in South Vietnam pending the national elections. North Vietnam did face serious economic problems, for while it contained the bulk of the industry, South Vietnam had most of the food. Ruthless moves against small landholders brought actual rebellion, crushed by the People's Army of Vietnam (PAVN, North Vietnamese Army) troops. When the Viet Minh began guerrilla warfare in South Vietnam, the North Vietnamese leadership voted to support this, beginning the Vietnam War. The war was extraordinarily costly to North Vietnam economically and in terms of casualties, but the desire to reunify the country overrode all other considerations. During the war, North Vietnam received substantial economic and military assistance

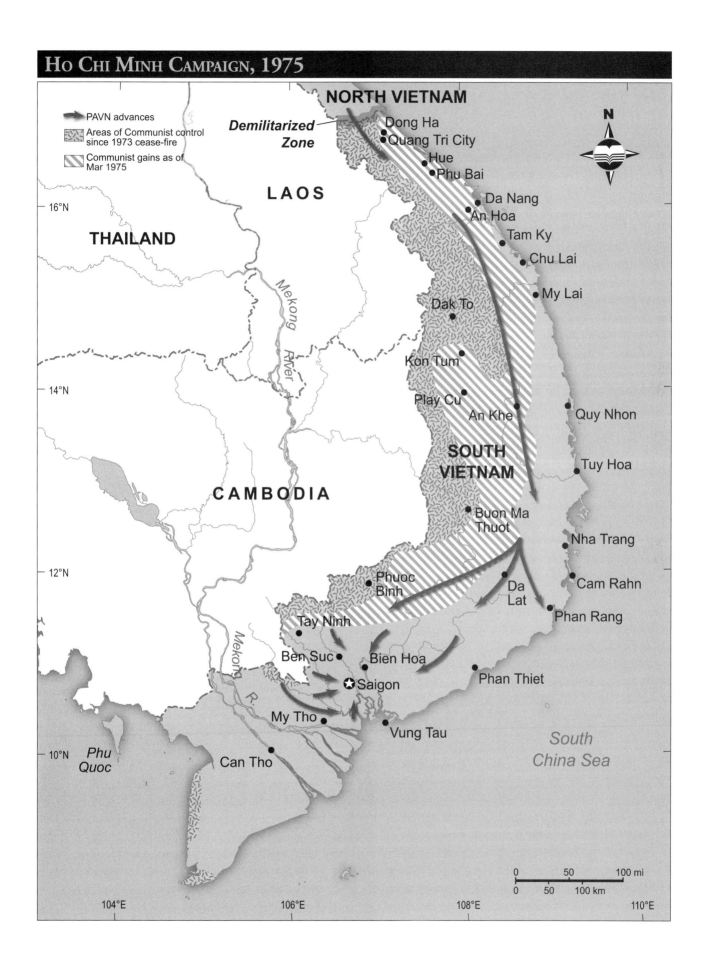

HO CHI MINH CAMPAIGN, 1975

PAVN advances

Areas of Communist control since 1973 cease-fire

Communist gains as of Mar 1975

NORTH VIETNAM

Demilitarized Zone

LAOS

THAILAND

Dong Ha
Quang Tri City
Hue
Phu Bai
Da Nang
An Hoa
Tam Ky
Chu Lai
My Lai

16°N

Dak To

Kon Tum

14°N

Play Cu
An Khe

Quy Nhon

Tuy Hoa

SOUTH VIETNAM

CAMBODIA

Buon Ma Thuot

Nha Trang

12°N

Phuoc Binh

Da Lat

Cam Rahn

Phan Rang

Tay Ninh

Ben Suc
Bien Hoa

Phan Thiet

Saigon

My Tho
Vung Tau

South China Sea

10°N

Phu Quoc

Can Tho

N

Mekong River

Mekong R.

0   50   100 mi
0   50   100 km

104°E   106°E   108°E   110°E

from the communist bloc, including China but especially the Soviet Union.

The Vietnam War raged until 1975, although U.S. forces departed in early 1973. In April 1975, PAVN forces were victorious militarily, capturing the South Vietnamese capital of Saigon. Vietnam was now reunited, but under communist rule. In April 1976, general elections occurred for a single National Assembly. It met in June and the next month proclaimed the reunified country the Socialist Republic of Vietnam (SRV) with Hanoi as its capital. Saigon was renamed Ho Chi Minh City. In September 1977, Vietnam was admitted to the United Nations (UN).

The new Vietnam faced staggering problems. These included rebuilding the war-ravaged country, knitting together the two very different halves of the country with their opposing patterns of economic development, and providing for the needs of a burgeoning population. The Vietnamese Communist Party (VCP) retained its monopoly on power. Indeed, the constitution guaranteed it as the only legal force capable of leading the state and society.

Immediately after the war, the government also carried out a political purge in southern Vietnam, although it was nothing like the bloodbath feared and so often predicted by Washington. Thousands of former South Vietnamese officials and military officers were sent to reeducation camps for varying terms, there to be politically indoctrinated and to undergo varying degrees of physical and mental discomfort, even torture. The government also undertook a program to reduce the urban populations in south Vietnam, especially in Ho Chi Minh City, by far the nation's largest metropolitan area. People had fled to the cities during the war, and perhaps one-third of the arable land lay idle. The government established so-called New Economic Areas to develop new agricultural land and return other areas to cultivation.

The government sent some 200,000 of its citizens to work in the Soviet Union and Eastern Europe. They sent home an estimated $150 million a year. Finally, the government introduced farm collectivization in south Vietnam and new regulations that governed business practices. These led to the collapse of light and medium industry. With the economy deteriorating, in 1981 the government introduced an incentive system. Peasants paid fixed rents for the use of the land and were able to sell surplus produce on the private market. Vietnam had no official ties with the United States, although both countries would have benefited economically had such a relationship been established early on.

Meanwhile, relations between Vietnam and Kampuchea (Cambodia) deteriorated, the result of traditional animosity between the two countries and Khmer Rouge persecution of its Vietnamese minority and its claims of Vietnamese territory. By 1977 there was serious fighting. The two states became proxies in the developing Sino-Soviet rivalry. Kampuchea

was a client state of China, and Vietnam was a client state of the Soviet Union.

In December 1978, PAVN forces invaded Cambodia, and ultimately there were 200,000 Vietnamese troops there. The Khmer Rouge and other resistance groups fought back, receiving military assistance from China and the United States. Ironically, it was only the Vietnamese occupation that prevented the Khmer Rouge from returning to power and continuing its genocidal policies, and it was only thanks to the Vietnamese invasion that mass killings of Cambodians by the Khmer Rouge were confirmed.

China meanwhile threatened the Vietnamese government with force to punish Hanoi for the invasion of Kampuchea and Vietnamese treatment of its Chinese minority. Indeed, the Chinese People's Liberation Army (PLA) actually invaded Vietnam briefly during February–March 1979, but this short Sino-Vietnamese War did not force the Vietnamese to quit Cambodia. That came only from the great expense of the operation and its drain on the Vietnamese economy as well as the government's attendant isolation in the international community at a time when the nation desperately needed foreign investment. The Vietnamese leadership then decided to quit Cambodia, and by September 1989 all Vietnamese troops had departed.

The Vietnamese government continued to maintain an extremely large military establishment. In the mid-1980s it had 1.2 million people under arms, the world's fourth-largest armed force. This figure did not include numerous public security personnel. Military expenditures regularly consumed up to a third of the national budget. This and a bloated government bureaucracy consumed revenues badly needed elsewhere.

By 1986 the economy was in shambles. Famine—the result of failed farm collectivization and botched currency reform—and rampant inflation took their tolls. An economic growth rate of only 2 percent a year was outstripped by a 3 percent per year birthrate, one of the highest in the world. These developments brought striking changes at the December 1986 Sixth National Communist Party Congress. Among these were material incentives, decentralized decision making, and limited free enterprise. Many of the old hard-line leadership, including Pham Van Dong and Le Duc Tho, retired. Nguyen Van Linh, a proponent of change, became party secretary and the most powerful figure in the state.

Linh had overseen the tentative steps toward a free market economy that had helped southern Vietnam remain more prosperous than northern Vietnam. His reform program, known as *Doi Moi* (Renovation), produced results. It introduced a profit incentive for farmers and allowed individuals to set up private businesses. Companies producing for export were granted tax concessions, and foreign-owned firms could operate in Vietnam and repatriate their profits with a guarantee against being nationalized. Linh rejected opposition political parties and free elections, however.

Inflation dropped dramatically, production went up, and consumerism spread. But reform was uneven, inhibited by party bureaucrats and conservatives. Most advances came in the cities rather than in the countryside, where 80 percent of the population lived.

Toward the end of normalizing relations with the United States (achieved under President Bill Clinton in 1995), in 1987 the Vietnamese government released more than 6,000 military and political prisoners, including generals and senior officials of the former South Vietnamese government. Another incentive for the Vietnamese leadership to reach out to the West was the sharp reduction in Soviet aid, which ended altogether in 1991. The conservatives, however, used the collapse of communism in Eastern Europe to halt any movement toward political pluralism.

At the end of the Cold War, Vietnam was still plagued by serious problems. PAVN influence, despite a sharp decline in its size, remained strong. Divisions between northern and southern Vietnam also remained, and one of the highest birthrates in the world ate into economic gains. Annual per capita income ($250 a year) was among the world's lowest. The central issue for the aging communist leadership was whether Vietnam could modernize using the Chinese model of economic liberalism while maintaining strict party control.

Spencer C. Tucker

See also

Cambodia; Cambodia, Vietnamese Occupation of; Dien Bien Phu, Battle of; Ho Chi Minh; Indochina War; Le Duc Tho; Ngo Dinh Diem; Pham Van Dong; Sino-Vietnamese War; Southeast Asia; Vietnam War

References

Karnow, Stanley. *Vietnam: A History.* New York: Viking, 1983.

Tucker, Spencer C. *Vietnam.* Lexington: University Press of Kentucky, 1999.

Young, Marilyn. *The Vietnam Wars, 1945–1990.* New York: HarperPerennial, 1991.

Vietnam War (1957–1975)

The Vietnam War grew out of the Indochina War (1946–1954). The 1954 Geneva Conference, ending the Indochina War between France and the nationalist-communist Viet Minh, provided for the independence of Cambodia, Laos, and Vietnam. Agreements reached at Geneva temporally divided Vietnam at the 17th Parallel, pending national elections in 1956. In the meantime, Viet Minh military forces were to withdraw north of that line and the French forces south of it. The war left two competing entities, the northern Democratic Republic of Vietnam (DRV, North Vietnam) and the

southern French-dominated State of Vietnam (SV), each claiming to be the legitimate government of a united Vietnam.

In June 1954, SV titular head Emperor Bao Dai appointed as premier the Roman Catholic Ngo Dinh Diem, whom Bao Dai believed had Washington's backing. Diem's base of support was narrow but had recently been strengthened by the addition of some 800,000 northern Catholics who relocated to southern Vietnam. In a subsequent power struggle between Bao Dai and Diem, in October 1955 Diem established the Republic of Vietnam (RVN, South Vietnam), with himself as president. The United States then extended Diem aid, most of which went to the South Vietnamese military budget. Only minor sums went to education and social welfare programs. Thus, the aid seldom touched the lives of the preponderantly rural populace. As Diem consolidated his power, U.S. military advisors also reorganized the South Vietnamese armed forces. Known as the Army of the Republic of Vietnam (ARVN, South Vietnamese Army) and equipped with American weaponry, it was designed to fight a conventional invasion from North Vietnam rather than deal with insurgency warfare.

Fearing a loss, Diem refused to hold the scheduled 1956 elections. This jolted veteran communist North Vietnamese leader Ho Chi Minh. Ho had not been displeased with Diem's crushing of his internal opposition but was now ready to reunite the country under his sway and believed that he would win the elections. North Vietnam was more populous than South Vietnam, and the communists were well organized there. Fortified by the containment policy, the domino theory, and the belief that the communists, if they came to power, would never permit a democratic regime, U.S. President Dwight D. Eisenhower's administration backed Diem's defiance of the Geneva Agreements.

Diem's decision led to a renewal of fighting, which became the Vietnam War. Fighting resumed in 1957 when Diem moved against the 6,000–7,000 Viet Minh political cadres who had been allowed to remain in South Vietnam to prepare for the 1956 elections. The Viet Minh began the insurgency on their own initiative but were subsequently supported by the North Vietnamese government. The South Vietnamese communist insurgents came to be known as the Viet Cong (VC). In December 1960 they established the National Liberation Front (NLF) of South Vietnam. Supposedly independent, the NLF was controlled by Hanoi. The NLF program called for the overthrow of the Saigon government, its replacement by a "broad national democratic coalition," and the "peaceful" reunification of Vietnam.

In September 1959, North Vietnamese Defense Minister Vo Nguyen Giap established Transportation Group 559 to send supplies and men south along what came to be known as the Ho Chi Minh Trail, much of which ran through supposedly neutral Laos. The first wave of infiltrators were native southerners and Viet Minh who had relocated to North Vietnam in

Vietnam War, 1964 – 1967

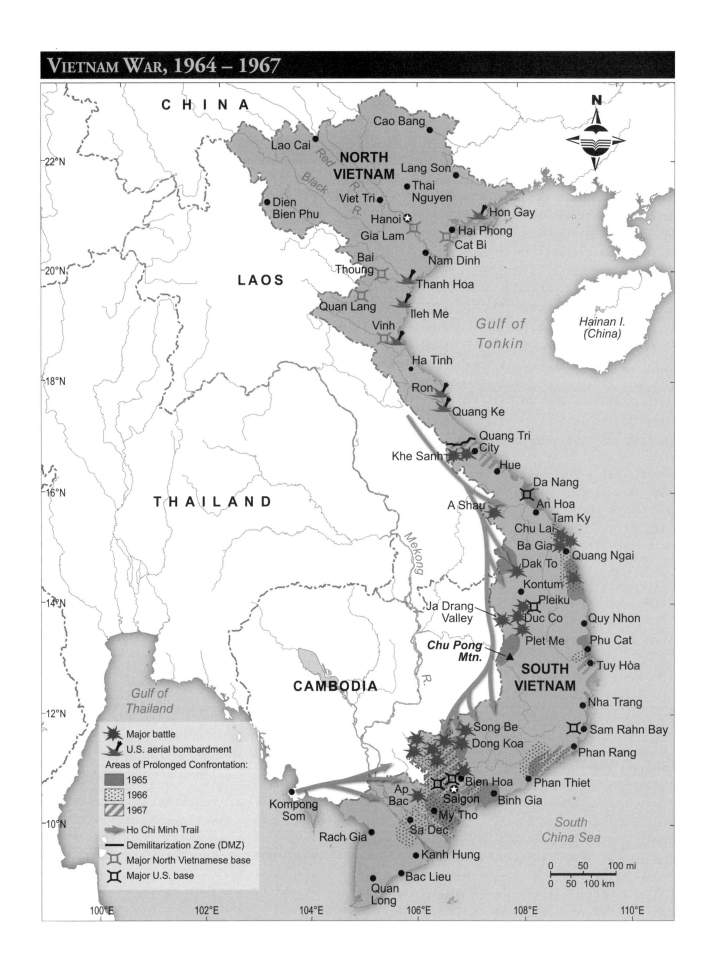

CHINA

Cao Bang

Lao Cai

NORTH VIETNAM

Lang Son

Thai Nguyen

Dien Bien Phu

Viet Tri

Hon Gay

Hanoi

Gia Lam

Hai Phong

Cat Bi

Bai Thoung

Nam Dinh

LAOS

Thanh Hoa

Quan Lang

Ileh Me

Gulf of Tonkin

Vinh

Hainan I. (China)

Ha Tinh

Ron

Quang Ke

Quang Tri City

Khe Sanh

Hue

Da Nang

An Hoa

THAILAND

A Shau

Tam Ky

Chu Lai

Ba Gia

Quang Ngai

Dak To

Kontum

Pleiku

Ja Drang Valley

Duc Co

Quy Nhon

Chu Pong Mtn.

Plet Me

Phu Cat

SOUTH VIETNAM

Tuy Hòa

CAMBODIA

Nha Trang

Gulf of Thailand

Sam Rahn Bay

Song Be

Phan Rang

Dong Koa

Kompong Som

Ap Bac

Bien Hoa

Phan Thiet

Saigon

Binh Gia

My Tho

South China Sea

Sa Dec

Rach Gia

Kanh Hung

Bac Lieu

Quan Long

Legend

- ✶ Major battle
- U.S. aerial bombardment
- Areas of Prolonged Confrontation:
  - 1965
  - 1966
  - 1967
- Ho Chi Minh Trail
- Demilitarization Zone (DMZ)
- Major North Vietnamese base
- Major U.S. base

0   50   100 mi
0   50   100 km

1954. Viet Cong sway expanded, spreading out from safe bases to one village after another. The insurgency was fed by the weaknesses of the central government, by the use of terror and assassination, and by Saigon's appalling ignorance of the movement. By the end of 1958, the insurgency had reached the status of conventional warfare in several provinces. In 1960, the communists carried out even more assassinations, and guerrilla units attacked ARVN regulars, overran district and provincial capitals, and ambushed convoys and reaction forces.

By mid-1961, the Saigon government had lost control over much of rural South Vietnam. Infiltration was as yet not significant, and most of the insurgents' weapons were either captured from ARVN forces or were left over from the war with France. Diem rejected American calls for meaningful reform until the establishment of full security. He did not understand that the war was primarily a political problem and could be solved only through political means.

Diem, who practiced the divide and rule concept of leadership, increasingly delegated authority to his brother, Ngo Dinh Nhu, and his secret police. Isolated from his people and relying only on trusted family members and a few other advisors, Diem resisted U.S. demands that he promote his senior officials and officers on the basis of ability and pursue the war aggressively.

By now, U.S. President John F. Kennedy's administration was forced to reevaluate its position toward the war, but increased U.S. involvement was inevitable, given Washington's commitment to resist communist expansion and the belief that all of Southeast Asia would become communist if South Vietnam fell. Domestic political considerations also influenced the decision.

In May 1961, Kennedy sent several fact-finding missions to Vietnam. These led to the Strategic Hamlet program as part of a general strategy emphasizing local militia defense and to the commitment of additional U.S. manpower. By the end of 1961, U.S. strength in Vietnam had grown to around 3,200 men, most in helicopter units or serving as advisors. In February 1962, the United States also established a military headquarters in Saigon, when the Military Assistance and Advisory Group (MAAG) was replaced by the Military Assistance Command, Vietnam (MACV), to direct the enlarged American commitment. The infusion of U.S. helicopters and additional support for the ARVN probably prevented a VC military victory in 1962. The VC soon learned to cope with the helicopters, however, and again the tide of battle turned.

Meanwhile, Nhu's crackdown on the Buddhists led to increased opposition to Diem's rule. South Vietnamese generals now planned a coup, and after Diem rejected reforms, the United States gave the plotters tacit support. On 1 November 1963 the generals overthrew Diem, murdering both him and Nhu. Within three weeks Kennedy was also dead, succeeded by Lyndon B. Johnson.

The United States seemed unable to win the war either with or without Diem. A military junta now took power, but none of those who followed Diem had his prestige. Coups and countercoups occurred, and much of South Vietnam remained in turmoil. Not until General Nguyen Van Thieu became president in 1967 was there a degree of political stability.

Both sides steadily increased the stakes, apparently without foreseeing that the other might do the same. In 1964 Hanoi made three decisions. The first was to send to South Vietnam units of its regular army, the People's Army of Vietnam (PAVN), known to the Americans as the North Vietnamese Army (NVA). The second was to rearm its forces in South Vietnam with modern communist-bloc weapons, giving them a firepower advantage over the ARVN, which was still equipped largely with World War II–era U.S. infantry weapons. And the third was to order direct attacks on American installations, provoking a U.S. response.

On 2 August 1964, the Gulf of Tonkin Incident occurred when North Vietnamese torpedo boats attacked the U.S. destroyer *Maddox* in international waters in the Gulf of Tonkin. A second attack on the *Maddox* and another U.S. destroyer, the *Turner Joy*, reported two days later, probably never occurred, but Washington believed that it had, and this led the Johnson administration to order retaliatory air strikes against North Vietnamese naval bases and fuel depots. It also led to a near-unanimous vote in Congress for the Gulf of Tonkin Resolution authorizing the president to use whatever force he deemed necessary to protect U.S. interests in Southeast Asia.

Johnson would not break off U.S. involvement in Vietnam, evidently fearing possible impeachment if he did so. At the same time, he refused to make the tough decision of fully mobilizing the country and committing the resources necessary to win, concerned that this would destroy his cherished Great Society social programs. He also feared a widened war, possibly involving the People's Republic of China (PRC).

By 1965, Ho and his generals expected to win the war. Taking their cue from Johnson's own pronouncements to the American people, they mistakenly believed that Washington would not commit ground troops to the fight. Yet Johnson did just that. Faced with Hanoi's escalation, in March 1965 U.S. Marines arrived to protect the large American air base at Da Nang. A direct attack on U.S. advisors at Pleiku in February 1965 also led to a U.S. air campaign against North Vietnam.

Ultimately more than 2.5 million Americans served in Vietnam, and nearly 58,000 of them died there. At its height, Washington was spending $30 billion per year on the war. Although the conflict was the best-covered war in American history (it became known as the first television war), it was conversely the least understood by the American people.

After a firefight, two soldiers of the U.S. 173rd Airborne Brigade wait for a helicopter to evacuate them and a dead companion. (National Archives and Records Administration)

Johnson hoped to win the war on the cheap, relying heavily on airpower. Known as Operation ROLLING THUNDER and paralleled by Operation BARREL ROLL, the secret bombing of Laos (which became the most heavily bombed country in the history of warfare), the air campaign would be pursued in varying degrees of intensity over the next three and a half years. Its goals were to force Hanoi to negotiate peace and to halt infiltration into South Vietnam. During the war, the United States dropped more bombs than in all of World War II, but the campaign failed in both its objectives.

In the air war, Johnson decided on graduated response rather than the massive strikes advocated by the military. Gradualism became the grand strategy employed by the United States in Vietnam. Haunted by the Korean War, at no time would Johnson consider an invasion of North Vietnam, fearful of provoking a Chinese reaction.

By May and June 1965, with PAVN forces regularly destroying ARVN units, MACV commander General William Westmoreland appealed for U.S. ground units, which Johnson committed. PAVN regiments appeared ready to launch an offensive in the rugged Central Highlands and then drive to the sea, splitting South Vietnam in two. Westmoreland

mounted a spoiling attack with the recently arrived 1st Cavalry Division (Airmobile) formed around some 450 helicopters. During October–November 1965, the 1st Cavalry won one of the war's rare decisive encounters in the Battle of Ia Drang and may have derailed Hanoi's hopes of winning a decisive victory before full American might could be deployed.

Heavy personnel losses on the battlefield, while regrettable, were entirely acceptable to the North Vietnamese leadership. Ho remarked at one point that North Vietnam could absorb an unfavorable loss ratio of ten to one and still win the war. Washington never did understand this and continued to view the war through its own lens of what would be unacceptable in terms of casualties. From 1966 on, Vietnam was an escalating military stalemate, as Westmoreland requested increasing numbers of men from Washington. By the end of 1966, 400,000 U.S. troops were in Vietnam. In 1968, U.S. strength was more than 500,000 men. Johnson also secured some 60,000 troops from other nations—most of them from the Republic of Korea (ROK, South Korea)—surpassing the 39,000-man international coalition of the Korean War.

Terrain was not judged important. The goals were to protect the population and kill the enemy, with success measured in terms of body counts that, in turn, led to abuses. During 1966, MACV mounted eighteen major operations, each resulting in more than 500 supposedly verified VC/PAVN dead. Fifty thousand enemy combatants were supposedly killed in 1966. By the beginning of 1967, the PAVN and VC had 300,000 men versus 625,000 ARVN and 400,000 Americans.

Hanoi, meanwhile, had reached a point of decision, with casualties exceeding available replacements. Instead of scaling back, North Vietnam prepared a major offensive that would employ all available troops to secure a quick victory. Hanoi believed that a major military defeat for the United States would end its political will to continue.

Giap now prepared a series of peripheral attacks, including a modified siege of some 6,000 U.S. Marines at Khe Sanh near the demilitarized zone (DMZ), beginning in January 1968. With U.S. attention riveted on Khe Sanh, Giap planned a massive offensive to occur over Tet, the lunar new year holidays, called the General Offensive–General Uprising. The North Vietnamese government believed that this massive offensive would lead people in South Vietnam to rise up and overthrow the South Vietnamese government, bringing an American withdrawal. The attacks were mounted against the cities. In a major intelligence failure, U.S. and South Vietnamese officials misread both the timing and strength of the attack, finding it inconceivable that the attack would come during Tet, sacrificing public goodwill.

The Tet Offensive began on 31 January and ended on 24 February 1968. Poor communication and coordination plagued Hanoi's plans. Attacks in one province occurred a day early, alerting the authorities. Hue, the former imperial capital, was especially hard hit. Fighting there destroyed half the city.

Hanoi's plan failed. ARVN forces generally fought well, and the people of South Vietnam did not support the attackers. In Hue, the communists executed 3,000 people, and news of this caused many South Vietnamese to rally to the South Vietnamese government. Half of the 85,000 VC and PAVN soldiers who took part in the offensive were killed or captured. It was the worst military setback for North Vietnam in the war.

Paradoxically, it was also its most resounding victory, in part because the Johnson administration and Westmoreland had trumpeted prior Allied successes, and the intensity of the fighting came as a profound shock to the American people. Disillusioned and despite the victory, they turned against the war. At the end of March, Johnson announced a partial cessation of bombing and withdrew from the November presidential election.

Hanoi persisted, however. In the first six months of 1968, communist forces sustained more than 100,000 casualties, and the VC was virtually wiped out. In the same period, 20,000 Allied troops died. All sides now opted for talks in Paris in an effort to negotiate an end to the war.

American disillusionment with the war was a key factor in Republican Richard Nixon's razor-thin victory over Democrat Hubert Humphrey in the November 1968 presidential election. With no plan of his own, Nixon embraced Vietnamization, actually begun under Johnson. This turned over more of the war to the ARVN, and U.S. troop withdrawals began. Peak U.S. strength of 550,000 men occurred in early 1969. There were 475,000 men by the end of the year, 335,000 by the end of 1970, and 157,000 at the end of 1971. Massive amounts of equipment were turned over to the ARVN, including 1 million M-16 rifles and sufficient aircraft to make the South Vietmese Air Force the world's fourth largest. Extensive retraining of the ARVN was begun, and training schools were established. The controversial counterinsurgency PHOENIX program also operated against the VC infrastructure, reducing the insurgency by 67,000 people between 1968 and 1971, but PAVN forces remained secure in sanctuaries in Laos and Cambodia.

Nixon's policy was to limit outside assistance to Hanoi and pressure the North Vietnamese government to end the war. For years, American and South Vietnamese military leaders had sought approval to attack the sanctuaries. In March 1970 a coup in Cambodia ousted Prince Norodom Sihanouk. General Lon Nol replaced him, and secret operations against the PAVN Cambodian sanctuaries soon began. Over a two-month span, there were twelve cross-border operations, known as the Cambodian Incursion. Despite widespread opposition in the United States to the widened war, the incursions raised the allies' morale, allowed U.S. withdrawals to continue on schedule, and purchased additional time for Vietnamization. PAVN forces now concentrated on bases in southern Laos and on enlarging the Ho Chi Minh Trail.

In the spring of 1971, ARVN forces mounted a major invasion into southern Laos, known as Operation LAM SON 719. There were no U.S. advisors, and ARVN units took heavy casualties. The operation set back Hanoi's plans to invade South Vietnam but took a great toll on the ARVN's younger officers and pointed out serious command weaknesses.

By 1972, PAVN forces had recovered and had been substantially strengthened with new weapons, including heavy artillery and tanks, from the Soviet Union. They now mounted a major conventional invasion of South Vietnam. Hanoi believed that the United States would not interfere. Giap had fifteen divisions. He left only one in North Vietnam and two in Laos and committed the remaining twelve to the invasion.

The attack began on 29 March 1972. Known as the Spring or Easter Offensive, it began with a direct armor strike across the DMZ at the 17th Parallel and caught the best South Vietnamese troops facing Laos. Allied intelligence misread its scale and precise timing. Giap risked catastrophic losses but hoped for a quick victory before ARVN forces could recover.

At first it appeared that the PAVN would be successful. Quang Tri fell, and rain limited the effectiveness of airpower.

In May, President Nixon authorized B-52 bomber strikes on North Vietnam's principal port of Haiphong and the mining of its harbor. This new air campaign was dubbed LINE-BACKER I and involved the use of new precision-guided munitions (so-called or smart bombs). The bombing cut off much of the supplies for the invading PAVN forces. Allied aircraft also destroyed 400–500 PAVN tanks. In June and July, the ARVN counterattacked. The invasion cost Hanoi half its force—some 100,000 men died—while ARVN losses were only 25,000.

With both Soviet and Chinese leaders anxious for better relations with the United States in order to obtain Western technology, Hanoi gave way and switched to negotiations. Finally, an agreement was hammered out in Paris that December, but President Thieu balked and refused to sign, whereupon Hanoi made the agreements public. A furious Nixon blamed Hanoi for the impasse, and in December he ordered a resumption of the bombing, dubbed LINEBACKER II but also known as the December or Christmas Bombings. Although fifteen B-52s were lost, Hanoi had fired away virtually its entire stock of surface-to-air missiles (SAMs) and now agreed to resume talks.

After a few cosmetic changes, an agreement was signed on 23 January 1973, with Nixon forcing Thieu to agree or risk the end of all U.S. aid. The United States recovered its prisoners of war and departed Vietnam. The Soviet Union and China continued to supply arms to North Vietnam, however, while Congress constricted U.S. supplies to South Vietnam. Tanks and planes were not replaced on the promised one-for-one basis as they were lost, and spare parts and fuel were both in short supply. All this had a devastating effect on ARVN morale.

In South Vietnam, both sides violated the cease-fire, and fighting steadily increased in intensity. In January 1975, communist forces attacked and quickly seized Phuoc Long Province on the Cambodian border north of Saigon. Washington took no action. The communists next took Ban Me Thuot in the Central Highlands, then in mid-March President Thieu decided to abandon the northern part of his country. Confusion became disorder, then disaster, and six weeks later PAVN forces controlled all of South Vietnam. Saigon fell on 30 April 1975, to be renamed Ho Chi Minh City. Vietnam was now reunited, but under a communist government. An estimated 3 million Vietnamese, soldiers and civilians, had died in the struggle. Much of the country was devastated by the fighting, and Vietnam suffered from the effects of the widespread use of chemical defoliants.

Saigon falls to the People's Army of Vietnam (PAVN, North Vietnamese Army), April 1975. (Francoise de Mulder/Corbis)

The effects were also profound in the United States. The American military was shattered by the war and had to be rebuilt. Inflation was rampant from the failure to face up to the true costs of the war. Many questioned U.S. willingness to embark on such a crusade again, at least to go it alone. In this sense, the war forced Washington into a more realistic appraisal of U.S. power.

Spencer C. Tucker

See also

Cambodia; Containment Policy; Domino Theory; Geneva Conference (1954); Ho Chi Minh; Indochina War; Johnson, Lyndon Baines; Kennedy, John Fitzgerald; Laos; Ngo Dinh Diem; Nixon, Richard Milhous; Vietnam

References

Karnow, Stanley. *Vietnam: A History.* New York: Viking, 1983.
Maclear, Michael. *The Ten Thousand Day War: Vietnam, 1945–1975.* New York: St. Martin's, 1981.
O'Ballance, Edgar. *The Wars in Vietnam, 1954–1960.* New York: Hippocrene, 1981.
Palmer, General Bruce, Jr. *The 25-Year War: America's Military Role in Vietnam.* Lexington: University Press of Kentucky, 1984.
Tucker, Spencer C. *Vietnam.* Lexington: University Press of Kentucky, 1999.

Vietnam War Protests

The Vietnam War protest movement brought together numerous organizations and activists with different agendas under the unifying banner of opposition to the war. Initially, this opposition came from the Old Left, a group of traditionally socialist and pacifist groups. Representative of the Old Left was the War Resisters League (WRL), founded in 1923. By 1963, the WRL focused its protests on the expanding U.S. advisory effort in Vietnam.

On 16 May 1964, the WRL sponsored a demonstration in New York City during which twelve men burned their draft cards. Soon thereafter, leadership for the antiwar movement shifted to what became known as the New Left. One of the most prominent New Left groups was the Students for a Democratic Society (SDS), formed in 1960. The SDS first focused on domestic concerns but began expressing growing concern with the military-industrial-academic establishment and the Vietnam War.

In February 1965, the United States began bombing the Democratic Republic of Vietnam (DRV, North Vietnam), providing a unifying catalyst that brought a number of groups together in opposition to the war. However, the focus of the movement shifted to college campuses. Beginning in March 1965, a series of nationwide college campus teach-ins were held, the first of them at the University of Michigan. On 17 April the SDS organized a march on Washington, D.C., in which 20,000 people participated.

As the U.S. effort in Vietnam escalated, the antiwar movement grew steadily, attracting new allies. Soon, social activists, celebrities, and musicians such as Abbie Hoffman, Timothy Leary, Allen Ginsberg, Jane Fonda, Jefferson Airplane, and others took up the antiwar cause. As the war intensified, other New Left groups such as the Catholic Peace Fellowship, the Emergency Citizens Group Concerned About Vietnam, and the National Emergency Committee of Clergy Concerned About Vietnam joined in the antiwar protests.

Martin Luther King Jr. and other civil rights leaders also began to denounce the war on moral grounds. By 1966, the antiwar movement gained strength and had formed an informal alliance with the civil rights movement. The movement received new support from former officials in the administrations of Presidents John F. Kennedy and Lyndon B. Johnson such as Arthur M. Schlesinger Jr. and John Kenneth Galbraith, who spoke out against the war. In Congress, a rising antiwar group led by Democratic Senators Wayne Morse, Mike Mansfield, and J. William Fulbright gained momentum.

As sentiment against the war grew, protests against the war took root abroad. In the Federal Republic of Germany (FRG, West Germany), numerous student-led demonstrations against the war occurred. In France, which had fought its own war in Indochina, demonstrations were reinforced by President Charles de Gaulle, who publicly declared that North Vietnam would ultimately win the war. There were antiwar protests throughout Europe, even in Great Britain, a staunch American ally. In Australia, which had sent troops to Vietnam, the antiwar movement paralleled that in the United States and grew rapidly. In communist bloc nations, students also took to the streets to protest America's war. Indeed, the international antiwar movement helped solidify and legitimize the American antiwar movement.

Back in the United States, the movement gained in strength as the number of American troops in Vietnam approached half a million. In 1967, the Spring Mobilization to End the War in Vietnam, a coalition composed of teachers, students, and Old and New Left organizations, sponsored mass demonstrations. As a result, on 15 April more than 130,000 antiwar protestors marched in New York and 70,000 protested in San Francisco. The most significant antiwar event of 1967 was October's march on the Pentagon. By then, the antiwar movement was crippling Johnson's presidency and threatening to paralyze the nation. Even some of Johnson's closest advisors began to question the war effort.

With public support for the war plummeting, Johnson fought back by overselling modest gains in the war. This set the stage for the stunning 30 January 1968 Tet Offensive debacle. By 31 January, communist forces in the Republic of Vietnam (ROV, South Vietnam) had attacked five major cities, thirty-six provincial capitals, and sixty-four district capitals. In one of the boldest attacks, a Viet Cong (VC) platoon briefly

A female demonstrator offers a flower to military police on guard at the Pentagon during an anti–Vietnam War demonstration, 21 October 1967. (National Archives and Records Administration)

penetrated the grounds of the U.S. embassy in Saigon. Although the communist forces were soundly defeated, the Tet Offensive demonstrated that Johnson had grossly overstated the war's progress, costing the government and the military the confidence of the American people. Now with fully half of all Americans opposed to the Vietnam War, the antiwar movement gained further momentum.

In March 1968, Johnson announced a halt to the bombing campaign and stood down for reelection. This did not, however, curtail the antiwar protests, which soon turned violent. Students occupied Columbia University's administration building and had to be forcibly evicted. Raids on draft boards began, during which protestors smeared blood on records and shredded files. Other demonstrations occurred at the offices and production facilities of Dow Chemical, the manufacturer of napalm. Perhaps the most widely publicized protests took place in the streets of Chicago outside the 1968 Democratic National Convention, resulting in a bloody confrontation between demonstrators and police.

During the 1968 elections, presidential candidate Richard Nixon claimed to have a plan to end the war. However, when casualties continued to mount and Nixon did not immediately scale the war back, antiwar critics turned their sights on the Nixon White House. A new round of demonstrations erupted in the fall of 1969. In October, a series of nationwide demonstrations was organized by the Vietnam Moratorium Committee (VMC). More than 100,000 people gathered in Boston Common. In November 1969, the VMC called a march on Washington, drawing some 500,000 participants. At this point, the antiwar leadership began to change. Clean-cut SDS leaders who had supported the 1968 peace candidate Eugene McCarthy were being eclipsed by movement leaders who favored more radical measures. This shift elicited a public backlash, as Americans, even those who opposed the war, became fearful and angry with the movement's radicalization.

The antiwar movement regained a measure of renewed solidarity in April 1970 when Nixon gambled that he could reduce U.S. troop strength in Vietnam by bombing communist sanctuaries in Cambodia. The result was a new round of college campus demonstrations. On 4 May 1970, Ohio National Guardsmen killed four students at Kent State University, unleashing a firestorm of student demonstrations around the country and virtually paralyzing America's college and university campuses. That same week, 100,000 people gathered to protest the killings in Washington.

The June 1971 publication of the Pentagon Papers won more converts to the movement. Nixon's decision to bomb North Vietnam in December 1972 set off a new round of protests at home and abroad. Nixon was denounced as a war criminal in Europe. Even the pope sharply criticized Nixon. This latest uproar did not substantially subside until January 1973, when the Paris Peace Accords had been signed, virtually ending America's Vietnam odyssey.

The antiwar movement revealed the sharp divisions in American society and encouraged the North Vietnamese to fight on long enough to break the back of the American war effort. The movement also greatly influenced the American political and military establishments and eroded support for both Johnson and Nixon. Finally, it is axiomatic that the movement had a significant impact on the Vietnam War's outcome.

James H. Willbanks

See also
Military-Industrial Complex; Music; Students for a Democratic Society; Tet Offensive; Vietnam War

References
DeBenedetti, Charles, and Charles Chatfield. *An American Ordeal: The Antiwar Movement of the Vietnam Era.* Syracuse, NY: Syracuse University Press, 1990.
Garfinkle, Adam. *Telltale Hearts: The Origins and Impact of the Vietnam Antiwar Movement.* New York: St. Martin's, 1997.
Halstead, Fred. *Out Now! A Participant's Account of the American Movement against the Vietnam War.* New York: Monad, 1978.
Zaroulis, Nancy, and Gerald Sullivan. *Who Spoke Up? American Protest against the War in Vietnam, 1963–1975.* Garden City, NY: Doubleday, 1984.

Vladivostok Meeting (22–24 November 1974)

Summit meeting between U.S. President Gerald Ford and Soviet General Secretary Leonid Brezhnev. The Vladivostok Meeting took place during 22–24 November 1974 and ended in a joint resolution that expressed mutual friendship and outlined future arms control measures between the United States and the Soviet Union. Vladivostok was a pivotal summit in that it not only set a working outline for the second Strategic Arms Limitation Treaty (SALT II) but also reinforced the spirit of détente that had been diminished following the 1973–1974 energy crisis and tensions in the Middle East.

Leaders from both nations and around the world initially hailed the summit at Vladivostok as a significant diplomatic success. The conference allowed Ford and Brezhnev the chance to discuss face-to-face concerns important to U.S.-Soviet relations including the situation in the Middle East, which both recognized as an intrinsically dangerous area. By far the most important issue at the Vladivostok Meeting, however, was the curtailment of the burgeoning nuclear arms race. By the end of the meeting, Ford and Brezhnev had arrived at a preliminary, nonbinding framework on which to base a future arms control agreement. The two leaders also reaffirmed their commitment to continued peaceful coexistence and détente.

The Vladivostok summit built on earlier arms control agreements, including the Anti-Ballistic Missile (ABM) Treaty and the Strategic Arms Limitation Treaty (SALT I) Interim Agreement, both signed in May 1972. The summit sought to redress inequalities in SALT I while promoting a new program to replace it when it expired in 1979. Fundamental to this was the difficult task of balancing the asymmetrical strategic forces of both sides. The draft produced at Vladivostok focused on a number of concrete issues. At the heart of the joint agreement was the overall ceiling of 2,400 placed on all nuclear delivery systems. An absolute and mutual limit of 313 heavy intercontinental ballistic missiles (ICBMs) was also part of the preliminary agreement. In addition, the talks included a ceiling on the number of multiple independently targeted reentry vehicles (MIRVs) as well as limits on the construction of new missile silos.

While these preliminary agreements received an enthusiastic response in the Soviet Union, American critics from both sides of the political spectrum pointed to several perceived flaws. On the strategic side, they noted the unfair advantage the treaty would give to the Soviet Union by excluding its intercontinental Backfire bomber. Opponents also groused about the limited ability to monitor and enforce the agreements. Other critics attacked the framework for not placing sufficiently stringent limits on the development of new weapons systems, thus shifting the nuclear rivalry into a different but equally expensive and dangerous competition for better delivery technology.

Kurt Heinrich

See also
Brezhnev, Leonid; Ford, Gerald Rudolph; Strategic Arms Limitation Talks and Treaties; Vienna Meeting

References
Blechman, Barry M., ed. *Preventing Nuclear War: A Realistic Approach.* Bloomington: Indiana University Press, 1985.
Talbott, Strobe. *Endgame: The Inside Story of Salt II.* New York: HarperCollins, 1979.
Wolfe, Thomas W. *The SALT Experience.* Cambridge, MA: Ballinger, 1979.

Vo Nguyen Giap (1911–)

Senior general in the People's Army of Vietnam (PAVN, North Vietnamese Army) during 1946–1972 and minister of defense of the Democratic Republic of Vietnam (DRV, North Vietnam) and later the Socialist Republic of Vietnam (SRV) during 1946–1986. Vo Nguyen Giap was born in An Xa, Quang Binh Province, in central Vietnam on 15 August 1911. He attended the Lycée Nationale in Hue but was labeled an agitator and expelled. He then worked for a time as a journalist, and he joined the secret Revolutionary Party for a New Vietnam.

Giap was arrested by the French in 1930 and was sentenced to two years' hard labor. Upon his release from prison, he studied at the Lycée Albert Sarraut at Hanoi, graduating in 1934. He then taught history and French at the Lycée Thuong Long. He also published a number of journals and newspapers, most of which were shut down by the authorities. In 1938 he earned a law degree from the University of Hanoi.

Giap joined the Indochinese Communist Party (ICP) in 1937. The ICP ordered him to southern China in 1940. He was forced to leave behind his wife and daughter, and in 1941 the French arrested his wife. She was subsequently tortured to death.

In China, Giap met Ho Chi Minh. Under Ho's orders, Giap returned to northern Tonkin, where he organized opposition to the French and became a leader of the Vietnam Independence League (Viet Minh), formed in 1942.

In December 1944 Giap formed thirty-four men into the Vietnam Armed Propaganda and Liberation Brigade, the beginnings of the PAVN. His troops underwent strict political indoctrination and military training. Giap was responsible for refining the rural revolutionary warfare theories of Mao Zedong that combined political and military activity into revolutionary warfare.

At the end of World War II, Giap became minister of the interior in the new North Vietnamese government formed in September 1945. He was subsequently named minister of defense with the rank of full general and command of all North Vietnamese military forces.

Giap led the Viet Minh against the French in the long Indochina War (1946–1954), in the course of which he built an army of nearly 300,000 men. He suffered heavy losses when he went over prematurely to major pitched battles against the French Army, but he achieved victory in May 1954 at Dien Bien Phu in the most important battle of the war.

Giap also led PAVN forces in fighting in the Republic of Vietnam (RVN, South Vietnam) after President Ngo Dinh Diem's refusal to hold the elections called for in 1956 by the 1954 Geneva Accords. Giap often engaged in intense debates with military commanders and political leaders over strategy. He generally cautioned patience, while others sought more aggressive action against South Vietnamese and U.S. forces. He opposed the 1968 Tet Offensive and was proven correct, as the offensive failed, producing high casualties for his own troops and no popular uprising in South Vietnam. However, the Tet Offensive also produced an unexpected psychological victory for Hanoi and led Washington to seek a way out of the war.

In 1972, Giap reluctantly ordered a massive invasion of South Vietnam in what became known as the Easter Offensive. Once again, he was proven correct when the South Vietnamese, supported by massive U.S. airpower, blunted the attack and inflicted heavy casualties on the North Vietnamese. Still, when the offensive was over, PAVN forces occupied territory that they had not previously controlled, and the subsequent 1973 peace agreement did not require their removal.

Sharp disagreements within the North Vietnamese leadership regarding Giap's military judgment led to him being stripped of his command of the PAVN, although he retained the post of minister of defense until 1986. His protégé, General Van Tien Dung, directed the final offensive in 1975 that resulted in the defeat of South Vietnam. Appointed to head the Ministry of Science and Technology, Giap opposed the 1978 Vietnamese invasion of Cambodia. In 1991 he was forced to give up his last post as vice premier in charge of family planning. After his retirement, the government designated Giap a national treasure.

James H. Willbanks

See also

Communist Revolutionary Warfare; Dien Bien Phu, Battle of; Ho Chi Minh; Indochina War; Southeast Asia; Tet Offensive; Vietnam; Vietnam War

References

Currey, Cecil B. *Victory at Any Cost: The Genius of Viet Nam's Gen. Vo Nguyen Giap*. Washington, DC: Brassey's, 1997.

Davidson, Phillip B. *Vietnam at War: The History, 1946–1975*. Novato, CA: Presidio, 1988.

Tucker, Spencer C. *Vietnam*. Lexington: University Press of Kentucky, 1999.

Van Tien Dung. *Our Great Spring Victory*. New York: Monthly Review Press, 1977.

Vo Nguyen Giap. *Unforgettable Days*. Hanoi: Foreign Language Publishing House, 1978.

Vogel, Hans-Jochen (1926–)

Federal Republic of Germany (FRG, West Germany) politician, minister for regional and city planning (1972–1974), minister of justice (1974–1981), and mayor of West Berlin (1981). Born on 3 February 1926 in Göttingen, Hans-Jochen

Vogel studied law at the University of Marburg, where he received his doctorate in 1950. That same year he joined the Social Democratic Party (SPD).

Vogel served in the Bavarian state chancellery during 1955–1958 and was head of the law division of Munich's municipal council during 1958–1960. He was also mayor of Munich during 1960–1972. In November 1972 he entered the Bundestag, where he stayed until 1981. He served again in the Bundestag during 1983–1994.

Under Chancellor Willy Brandt, Vogel became minister for regional and city planning in December 1972. In the Helmut Schmidt government, Vogel served as minister for justice during 1974–1981. The greatest challenge he faced as justice minister was the terrorist activities of the Red Army Faction, which sought to overthrow the government through the kidnapping and assassination of politicians, diplomats, and industrialists. He cooperated closely with Schmidt to crush the terrorists. By the time Vogel left office in January 1981, thirty-two people had been killed by terrorist attacks, while twenty-two terrorists had been sentenced to long-term imprisonments.

In January 1981, the Berlin House of Deputies elected Vogel governing mayor of West Berlin. After just four months, however, he was defeated in the general elections and resigned. During 1981–1983, he was SPD opposition leader in the Berlin House of Deputies. In 1983 he reentered the Bundestag, and in June 1987 a special party convention elected him SPD chairman, replacing the aging Brandt. Vogel resigned as SPD opposition leader in the Bundestag in November 1991 but retained his seat for another three years.

Bert Becker

See also
Brandt, Willy; Germany, Federal Republic of; Kohl, Helmut; Schmidt, Helmut; Weizsäcker, Richard von

References
Banchoff, Thomas. *The German Problem Transformed: Institutions, Politics, and Foreign Policy, 1945–1995.* Ann Arbor: University of Michigan Press, 1999.
Nicholls, Anthony James. *The Bonn Republic: West German Democracy, 1945–1990.* London and New York: Longman, 1997.
Vogel, Hans-Jochen. *Nachsichten: Meine Bonner und Berliner Jahre.* Munich, Germany: Piper, 1996.
Webb, Adrian. *Germany since 1945.* London and New York: Longman, 1998.

Voice of America

U.S. government global broadcasting service established in 1942. During the Cold War, the Voice of America (VOA) audience in the Soviet Union and Warsaw Pact countries grew to an estimated 52 million listeners a week. Principal languages

Baseball player Jackie Robinson with Bob Allison, Voice of America sports editor, while preparing for a special English-language interview to be heard on VOA's *In the Spotlight,* airing during 1951–1953. (National Archives and Records Administration)

beamed to that region and the Balkans over the years were Russian, Ukrainian, Polish, and English. Others included Albanian, Armenian, Azerbaijani, Bulgarian, Belarusian, Czech, Estonian, Georgian, Hungarian, Latvian, Lithuanian, Romanian, Serbo-Croatian, Slovak, Slovene, Tatar, Turkmenistani, and Uzbek.

From its inception in 1942 until the advent of multimedia in the 1990s, most VOA broadcasts were sent via shortwave with some medium-wave, or the standard AM, frequencies. Other delivery means included long-wave and occasional placement of recordings for rebroadcast by local radio outlets.

VOA Russia, which peaked at seventeen-hour broadcast days late in the Cold War, began transmissions on 17 February 1947 under the leadership of VOA Director Charles Thayer, a prominent American diplomat and Soviet affairs specialist. Programming of VOA services to the Soviet Union and Eastern Europe consisted of news, topical analyses, official U.S. policy statements, and a full range of features about life in America and the individual audience regions. A flagship program in Russian, *Events and Opinions,* was broadcast at the peak listening hour, midnight Moscow time. The offerings of it and other programs reflected American thought and ideas, democratic practices in a civil society, history, cultural developments, economic and scientific news, and music.

In English, VOA jazz impresario Willis Conover broadcast more than 10,000 programs (1955–1996). He inspired countless Russian and East European artists and others with what he called "the music of freedom."

Communist governments feared the impact of the two principal U.S. networks, VOA and Radio Free Europe/Radio Liberty (RFE/RL), and the British Broadcasting Corporation (BBC). The BBC estimated that the Soviet cost of jamming Western broadcasts was more than $900 million annually, considerably more than the combined budgets at the time of all American and British publicly funded international networks worldwide. The attempt to block incoming broadcasts, in any case, was only partially effective.

European communist governments' jamming of VOA shortwave varied with the ebb and flow of East-West tensions and crises, within and outside the target countries. Jamming ceased beginning in 1963 and commenced again after the Soviets invaded Czechoslovakia in August 1968. Jamming was again curtailed in 1974 until shortly after the Soviet invasion of Afghanistan in December 1979. Jamming of VOA finally ended in 1987 as glasnost and perestroika took hold. Other countries blocking U.S.-funded broadcasts included Bulgaria, the German Democratic Republic (GDR, East Germany), Poland, the People's Republic of China (PRC), and Cuba.

Polish President Lech Wałęsa, in assessing the influence of Western broadcasts, said in 1997: "When it comes to radio waves, the Iron Curtain was helpless. Nothing could stop the news from coming through—neither sputniks nor minefields, high walls or barbed wire. The frontiers could be closed; words could not."

Alan Heil

See also
Glasnost; Perestroika; Radio Free Europe and Radio Liberty; Wałęsa, Lech
References
Heil, Alan L., Jr. *Voice of America: A History.* New York: Columbia University Press, 2003.
Heil, Alan L., Jr., and Barbara Schiele. "The Voice Past: VOA, the USSR and Communist Europe." Pp. 98–112 in *Western Broadcasting over the Iron Curtain,* edited by K. R. M. Short. Kent, UK: Croom Helm, 1986.
Mainland, Edward, Mark Pomar, and Kurt Carlson. "The Voice Present and Future." Pp. 113–136 in *Western Broadcasting Over the Iron Curtain,* edited by K. R. M. Short. Kent, UK: Croom Helm, 1986.
Nelson, Michael. *War of the Black Heavens: The Battles of Western Broadcasting in the Cold War.* Syracuse, NY: Syracuse University Press, 1997.

Vorster, Balthazar Johannes (1915–1983)

South African apartheid leader, prime minister (1966–1978), and president (1978–1979). Born in Jamestown, South Africa, on 13 December 1915, the son of an Afrikaner sheep farmer, Balthazar Johannes "John" Vorster studied law at South Africa's Stellenbosch University, graduating in 1938. After briefly clerking for a judge, he took up practice as an attorney. During World War II he was interned for more than two years because of his pro-Nazi sympathies.

In the 1953 all-white elections, Vorster was elected to parliament on the Nationalist Party ticket. In 1961 he was appointed minister of justice and of social welfare and pensions. As such, he organized a crackdown on the rising tide of black opposition to his government's apartheid plans. His suppression methods included detention without trial and the use of anticommunist legislation to quash government opposition.

After Prime Minister Hendrik Verwoerd's 1966 assassination, Vorster became the National Party leader and prime minister. His term in office was marked by a significant shift to the Right as his government tried to cope with deepening international isolation, the threat of sanctions, and the rising anger of the black majority. In July 1971 Vorster caused an international controversy when he announced that South Africa had acquired uranium-enrichment technology. Suspicions that South Africa possessed a nuclear bomb increased in the summer of 1977, following the alleged detection by Soviet satellites of a nuclear testing facility in the Kalahari Desert. Vorster's government never provided an explanation on the nature of the facility.

Pragmatic in his approach to foreign affairs, Vorster sought to end South Africa's estrangement from its regional neighbors. In 1974, under pressure from the United States, he convinced Rhodesian Prime Minister Ian Smith to accept that minority rule would end there. In 1976, again under pressure from the Americans, Vorster agreed that South African troops should enter war-torn Angola, marking the beginning of South Africa's twenty-year involvement in the Angolan Civil War.

The Angolan war strengthened the position of the military in South African politics and weakened Vorster's party position. In 1978 he was elected president, but he was forced to resign in 1979 because of a political scandal involving allegations of misappropriation of funds. Vorster died in Cape Town on 10 September 1983.

Peter Vale

See also
Africa; Cuba and Africa; Frontline States; Namibia; South Africa; South African Destabilization Campaign
References
Barber, James, and John Barratt, eds. *South Africa's Foreign Policy: The Search for Status and Security, 1945–1988.* Johannesburg: Southern Books, 1990.
D'Olivera, John. *Vorster: The Man.* Johannesburg: Ernest Stanton, 1977.
O'Meara, Dan. *Forty Lost Years.* Athens: Ohio University Press, 1997.

Vranitzky, Franz (1937–)

Austrian banker, finance minister (1984–1986), and federal chancellor (1986–1997). Born on 4 October 1937 in Vienna, Franz Vranitzky studied international trade and commerce at the College of Commerce and graduated in 1960. In 1961 he joined the research staff of the Austrian Central Bank. In 1969 he received a doctorate in economics.

Active in Social Democratic politics since his student days, in 1970 Vranitzky became a financial advisor in the Ministry of Finance. In 1976 he was named deputy chairman of the board of directors of Creditanstalt Bankverein and in 1981 chairman of Länderbank. In 1984 Chancellor Fred Sinowatz appointed Vranitzky minister of finance. Following Sinowatz's resignation, in June 1986 Vranitzky became federal chancellor.

Vranitzky's tenure as chancellor was marked by strained Austro-American and Austro-Israeli relations over the 1986 election of Kurt Waldheim as president of Austria. Vranitzky continued Austria's policy of pursuing cordial economic and political relations with the Soviets and allowing Austria to serve as a transit point for emigrating Soviet Jews. He traveled to Moscow for a summit with Soviet leader Mikhail Gorbachev in October 1988 and oversaw Austria's hosting of the 1986–1989 Commission on Security and Cooperation in Europe (CSCE) Vienna Review Conference. In September 1989 Austria opened its borders to thousands of citizens from the German Democratic Republic (GDR, East Germany) who were trying to reach the Federal Republic of Germany (FRG, West Germany) via Hungary, thereby helping to precipitate the collapse of the East German regime.

From 1989 on, Vranitzky was increasingly preoccupied with adjusting to the implications for Austria, both positive and negative, of the collapse of communism in Eastern Europe and the Soviet Union. Large numbers of refugees and asylum seekers from the former Yugoslavia and other ex-communist states poured into the country, giving rise to a political backlash centered in Jörg Haider's Freedom Party of Austria. On the other hand, Austria stepped up its integration with Western Europe and moved out from under the constraints on its external freedom of action imposed by the 1955 Austrian State Treaty. Austria successfully negotiated entrance into the European Union (EU), which it formally joined on 1 January 1995. In addition to leading Austria's drive for EU membership, Vranitzky forged a new relationship with the North Atlantic Treaty Organization (NATO), as Austria joined the Partnership for Peace program in February 1995. Vranitzky resigned the chancellorship in January 1997. That same year, he was named special envoy of the Organization of Security and Cooperation in Europe to Albania.

John Van Oudenaren

See also
Austria; Austrian State Treaty; Waldheim Affair

References
Bischof, Günter, Anton Pelinka, and Ferdinand Karlhofer, eds. *The Vranitzky Era in Austria.* New Brunswick, NJ: Transaction, 1999.
Vranitzky, Franz. *Politische Erinnerungen* [Political Memoirs]. Vienna: Zsolnay, 2004.

VULTURE, Operation (March–April 1954)

Proposed U.S. military intervention in the Indochina War. On 13 March 1954, Viet Minh commander General Vo Nguyen Giap launched an attack on the French fortress of Dien Bien Phu established in far northwestern Vietnam on the orders of commander in Indochina General Henri Navarre. Ultimately, Giap committed to the battle some four divisions of 49,500 troops against a total French strength with reinforcements of only 13,000. Both sides recognized the importance of the battle, which took place against the backdrop of an international conference in Geneva, called to discuss Asian affairs.

In February 1954, French Army chief of staff General Paul Henri Romuald Ély and Defense Minister René Pleven undertook a fact-finding mission to Indochina. Convinced that France could not win the war there without massive military assistance, Ély traveled to Washington to meet with U.S. government officials. Arriving there on 20 March 1954, he candidly informed his American counterpart, Admiral Arthur W. Radford, of the probable fall of Dien Bien Phu and the serious consequences this would have for the Indochina War and perhaps for all of Southeast Asia.

Radford recommended that the United States consider direct military intervention, most likely in the form of airpower, should the French government so request. This was the origin of Operation VULTURE. Despite opposition from army chief of staff General Matthew B. Ridgway, Radford encouraged Ély to believe that the United States would intervene should Paris request it. After Ély's return to Paris, President Dwight D. Eisenhower did decide to send the French twenty-five additional B-25 medium bombers.

Although the military options varied, the plan revolved around an air strike by between sixty and one hundred air force B-29 bombers from the Philippines, supported by several hundred navy jet fighters flying off U.S. aircraft carriers in the Gulf of Tonkin. The option of attacking Viet Minh forces in the mountains surrounding Dien Bien Phu was abandoned because of the inadequacy of French radar. Another option called for air strikes against Viet Minh base areas and lines of communication to the Chinese border. Finally, there was discussion of possible air bursts with nuclear weapons. A Joint Chiefs of Staff (JCS) study committee concluded that three tactical nuclear bombs would be sufficient to smash the Viet Minh at Dien Bien Phu.

On 29 March, U.S. Secretary of State John Foster Dulles delivered a speech to the Overseas Press Club in New York City in which he called for "united action" to meet the communist threat in Southeast Asia. Several days later during a press conference, President Eisenhower seconded Dulles's call, although without promising direct U.S. assistance. Vice President Richard Nixon was among those urging intervention, suggesting that the United States might have to "put American boys in."

On 3 April, Dulles and Radford met with congressional leaders to solicit their support should Eisenhower decide that military intervention was necessary. The legislators set three conditions to secure congressional approval: the intervention would have to be a multinational effort, including Britain and Commonwealth nations; France would have to promise to accelerate independence for Indochina; and France would promise not to withdraw from the war should the United States become directly involved.

On 4 April, Navarre cabled Ély reporting a deterioration in conditions at Dien Bien Phu and calling for a U.S. air strike. That same night, the French government formally requested immediate U.S. intervention. On 7 April during a press conference, Eisenhower referred to the possible loss of Indochina to communism as the "falling domino principle," the first occasion in public that the administration had used the term. He again refused to commit the United States to unilateral military action, however.

Dulles then flew to London and Paris to meet with his counterparts. British Foreign Secretary Anthony Eden, while publicly supporting the principle of collective defense, refused any specific commitment. Dulles then flew on to Paris, where the French government sought to bargain regarding the European Defense Community (EDC), which the U.S. government earnestly sought. On 22 April, Dulles informed the French that without French approval of the EDC, there was no chance of U.S. intervention. Foreign Minister Georges Bidault responded that if Dien Bien Phu surrendered, France would have no interest in the EDC. Bidault said that the only alternatives were Operation VULTURE or an Indochina cease-fire. French Premier Joseph Laniel then appealed to the British government for its participation, the precondition for U.S. military intervention. Prime Minister Winston Churchill called the British cabinet into emergency session, but it decided against involvement. The British believed that the battle was too far gone and that France should seek to resolve the situation diplomatically at the Geneva Conference. Eden noted prophetically: "I am beginning to think Americans are quite ready to supplant French and see themselves in the role of liberators of Vietnamese patriotism and expulsers or redeemers

of Communist insurgency in Indo-China. If so they are in for a painful awakening."

On 7 May 1954, Dien Bien Phu surrendered. The next day, the French government entered into negotiations at Geneva to extricate France from Vietnam.

Spencer C. Tucker

See also

Bidault, Georges; Dien Bien Phu, Battle of; Dulles, John Foster; Eden, Sir Anthony, 1st Earl of Avon; Eisenhower, Dwight David; Ély, Paul; European Defense Community; Geneva Conference (1954); Navarre, Henri; Pleven, René Jean; Radford, Arthur William; Southeast Asia Treaty Organization; Taylor, Maxwell Davenport; Twining, Nathan Farragut; Vo Nguyen Giap

References

Arnold, James R. *The First Domino: Eisenhower, the Military, and America's Intervention in Vietnam.* New York: William Morrow, 1991.

Billings-Yun, Melanie. *Decision against War: Eisenhower and Dien Bien Phu, 1954.* New York: Columbia University Press, 1988.

Eden, Anthony. *Full Circle: The Memoirs of Sir Anthony Eden.* London: Cassell, 1960.

Eisenhower, Dwight D. *Mandate for Change, 1953–1956: The White House Years.* Garden City, NY: Doubleday, 1963.

Ély, Paul. *Mémoires: L'Indochine dans la Tourmente.* Paris: Plon, 1964.

Prados, John. *The Sky Would Fall: Operation Vulture, the Secret U.S. Bombing Mission to Vietnam, 1954.* New York: Dial, 1983.

Radford, Arthur W. *From Pearl Harbor to Vietnam: The Memoirs of Admiral Arthur W. Radford.* Edited by Stephen Jurika Jr. Stanford, CA: Hoover Institute Press, 1980.

Vyshinskii, Andrei Ianuarevich (1883–1954)

Soviet politician, chief prosecutor for Soviet leader Josef Stalin's show trials in the 1930s, and Soviet foreign minister (1949–1953). Born on 10 December 1883 in Odessa to a Polish family, Andrei Ianuarevich Vyshinskii fraternized with Marxists while at the University of Kiev studying law, and in 1920 he joined the Bolshevik Party. Working in the Soviet legal system, he demonstrated a talent for prosecuting alleged saboteurs and wreckers in the Shakhty Trial (1928) and the Industrial Party Trial (1930). In 1933 he became deputy prosecutor of the Soviet Union, further proving his skills in the creation and manipulation of evidence and the histrionic abuse of defendants. In the aftermath of the assassination of the Leningrad party boss Sergei Kirov in December 1934, Vyshinskii was involved in the secret trial of the Nikolayev-Kotolynov group, which was blamed for the murder.

The trial of the alleged conspirators in the assassination of Kirov led to the great show trials of 1935–1939 in which leading Bolsheviks were arrested, tortured, humiliated in court,

Soviet Foreign Minister Andrei I. Vyshinskii. (Hulton-Deutsch Collection/ Corbis)

and sentenced to death or imprisonment on the basis of fraudulent confessions. It was Vyshinskii, as chief prosecutor during 1935–1939 and faithful servant of Stalin, who dominated the trials with his wild, dramatic, vitriolic denunciations of the defendants and the use of falsified evidence. His reward was a seat in the Soviet parliament (1938) and the deputy premiership during 1939–1944.

After 1939, Vyshinskii's career was mainly in foreign affairs. He served as deputy foreign minister during 1939–1949 and then foreign minister during 1949–1953. Stalin had ousted Foreign Minister Vyacheslav Molotov after the humiliating setback of the failed Berlin Blockade (1948–1949).

Vyshinskii's tenure in office was singularly unremarkable. He made no major foreign policy decisions and was content merely to carry out Stalin's mandates. After Stalin's death in March 1953, Molotov assumed his old post, and Vyshinskii was cast aside. As a sort of consolation prize, Moscow's new collective leadership sent Vyshinskii to the United Nations (UN) in New York as a permanent Soviet delegate. There he became well known for his acerbic wit and scathing denunciations of the West and the United States in particular. Vyshinskii died in New York City on 22 November 1954.

Paul Wingrove

See also

Molotov, Vyacheslav Mikhaylovich; Soviet Union; Stalin, Josef; United States

References

Conquest, Robert. *The Great Terror*. New York: Macmillan, 1968.
Vaksberg, Arkady. *Stalin's Prosecutor: The Life of Andrei Vyshinskii*. London: Weidenfeld and Nicolson, 1990.

W

Waldheim, Kurt (1918–2007)

President of Austria and secretary-general of the United Nations (UN). Born in St. Andra-Wordern, Austria, on 21 December 1918, Kurt Waldheim entered the University of Vienna in 1937, intending to pursue a course of study that would lead to law and diplomacy, and earned a law degree in 1944. At the same time, during World War II he served as a junior officer in the German Army in the Balkans.

Waldheim entered the diplomatic service in 1945 and quickly rose through the ranks. He served as first secretary of the Austrian Legation in Paris (1948–1951) and worked in the Foreign Ministry in Vienna before being appointed as Austria's representative to the UN in 1955. Although he served only one year, the appointment marked the beginning of his long association with the UN.

After a stint in Canada (1956–1960), Waldheim again returned to Vienna, rising to the post of director-general for political affairs in 1962. Two years later, he was reappointed as Austria's representative to the UN. In 1968, he became minister for foreign affairs under Josef Klaus. Waldheim left the Austrian government in 1970 to serve as chairman of the Safeguards Committee of the International Atomic Energy Agency (IAEA). He became Austria's representative to the UN for a third time later that year.

Following an unsuccessful campaign for the presidency of Austria in 1971, Waldheim won election as secretary-general of the UN that December, succeeding U Thant. As secretary-general, Waldheim campaigned for peace around the globe. He traveled frequently to the Middle East, visited Cyprus several times, and attempted to establish peace talks among India, Pakistan, and Bangladesh. He took part in the Paris International Conference on Vietnam and presided over the opening session of the Geneva Peace Conference on the Middle East in 1973. In his second term, he negotiated, unsuccessfully, for the release of American hostages from Iran. The People's Republic of China (PRC) blocked his attempt to win a third term in 1981.

In 1986, Waldheim ran again for the post of president in Austria as the candidate of the Austrian People's Party (ÖVP). His campaign presented him as "a man the people trust" and emphasized his humanitarian role with the UN. Journalistic investigations into his background, however, uncovered evidence that he had been part of a German Army unit guilty of atrocities during World War II. Waldheim claimed that he had been on leave in Vienna when the crimes were committed and knew nothing about them.

Older Austrians rallied behind Waldheim, and he was elected president following a run-off election in June 1986. The decision proved troublesome, as the international community quickly ostracized Austria. Only the Vatican, the Soviet Union, a few nations in Eastern Europe, and some Arab states allowed Waldheim to visit as head of state. The opposition within Austria called for his resignation. Instead, the government launched its own inquiry into Waldheim's past.

The results of the investigation, released in February 1988, largely exonerated Waldheim. His response was to make a televised speech noting that the Holocaust was one of the most tragic events in history and, for the first time, admitting that Austrians had played a shameful role in it. Waldheim served the rest of his term in relative anonymity and chose not to run again in 1992. He died in Vienna on 14 June 2007.

Timothy C. Dowling

See also
Austria; United Nations; Waldheim Affair

References

Bassett, Richard. *Waldheim and Austria.* New York: Viking, 1988.

Finger, Seymour. *Bending with the Wind: Kurt Waldheim and the United Nations.* New York: Praeger, 1990.

Herzstein, Robert Edwin. *Waldheim: The Missing Years.* New York: Arbor House/William Morrow, 1988.

Pick, Hella. *Guilty Victim: Austria from the Holocaust to Haider.* London: Tauris, 2000.

Ryan, James Daniel. *The United Nations under Kurt Waldheim, 1972–1981.* Lanham, MD: Scarecrow, 2001.

Waldheim, Kurt. *Die Antwort.* Vienna: Amalthea, 1996.

———. *In the Eye of the Storm.* Bethesda, MD: Adler and Adler, 1986.

Waldheim Affair (1986)

Allegations of involvement in Nazi atrocities against Kurt Waldheim, the former secretary-general of the United Nations (UN) who was running for president of the Austrian Republic. Waldheim began his second campaign to become president of Austria in late 1985. He had run unsuccessfully in 1971 but lessened the sting of that defeat by negotiating his election as secretary-general of the UN the following year. He served two terms as secretary-general and established a reputation as a man of peace. His attempt to win a third term in 1981 was blocked by the government of the People's Republic of China (PRC), however, and Waldheim retired to Vienna. He published his autobiography in 1985.

Despite Waldheim's presence, the Austrian presidential campaign of 1986 merited little international attention until *Profil,* an Austrian news magazine, printed a series of articles alleging that Waldheim had omitted crucial details about his service in the German Army during World War II in both his autobiography and in his presidential campaign. Waldheim's account claimed that although a junior officer in a German SA unit before 1939, he had spent most of the war in Vienna recuperating from wounds and studying law. *Profil* revealed evidence that Waldheim had spent considerable time on duty in the Balkans and in Salonika, Greece. Although the magazine did not accuse Waldheim directly, it did note that his unit had murdered Yugoslav partisans and deported Jews to concentration camps during his service. Waldheim responded by saying that he had no knowledge of any atrocities and had simply "done his duty as a soldier."

The affair quickly became the focus of the presidential election. Older Austrians generally supported Waldheim, claiming that Austria was a victim of Nazi aggression and an unwilling participant in the war. Younger Austrians, however, tended to be more suspicious and called for an open discussion of Austria's Nazi past. After heated debate and a run-off election, Waldheim emerged as president of Austria in June 1986, winning 54 percent of the vote.

His presidency put Austria in the international spotlight, but in a most unfavorable way. After an investigation by the U.S. Department of Justice, Waldheim became the first head of state ever placed on a watch list of undesirable aliens and was denied entry to the United States. Many other states also treated Waldheim as persona non grata, leaving Austria isolated internationally. Only the Vatican, the Soviet Union and its satellites, and a few Middle Eastern states that had received similar treatment allowed Waldheim to visit.

Amid growing tensions, the Austrian government launched its own investigation, which largely exonerated Waldheim. Where the U.S. report had concluded that there was "a *prima facie* case that Kurt Waldheim assisted or otherwise participated in the persecution of persons because of race, religion, national origin or political opinion," these new findings found no evidence that Waldheim had participated in war crimes. At the same time, the report concluded that as a translator in the unit, Waldheim must have had knowledge of the atrocities.

Waldheim remained in office after this ambiguous finding, claiming that he did so in the best interests of the Austrian people. He also went on Austrian television to plead his case. He admitted that Austrians had played some role in the Holocaust, which he described as one of the greatest tragedies in human history, and he condemned fanaticism and intolerance in all forms. The international community remained unmoved. Whether or not Waldheim affected Austrian opinion is hard to say. He chose not to run for reelection in 1992. At the very least, Waldheim gave Austrians the chance to discuss a complicated past that had been kept under wraps for nearly fifty years.

Timothy C. Dowling

See also

Austria; United Nations; Waldheim, Kurt

References

Hazzard, Shirley. *Countenance of Truth: The United Nations and the Waldheim Case.* New York: Viking, 1990.

Herzstein, Robert Edwin. *Waldheim: The Missing Years.* New York: Arbor House/William Morrow, 1988.

Palumbo, Michael. *The Waldheim Files: Myth and Reality.* London: Faber, 1988.

Pick, Hella. *Guilty Victim: Austria from the Holocaust to Haider.* London: Tauris, 2000.

Rosenbaum, Eli. *Betrayal: The Untold Story of the Kurt Waldheim Investigation and Cover-up.* New York: St. Martin's, 1993.

Tittmann, Harold. *The Waldheim Affair: Democracy Subverted.* Dunkirk, NY: O. Frederick, 2000.

Waldheim, Kurt. *Die Antwort.* Vienna: Almathea, 1996.

Wałęsa, Lech (1943–)

Polish labor activist, Nobel Peace Prize winner (1983), and president of Poland (1990–1995). Born to a peasant family in

Lech Wałęsa led the Solidarity Trade Union movement in Poland and was later president of Poland from 1990 to 1995. (Embassy of the Republic of Poland)

the village of Popowo on 29 September 1943, Lech Wałęsa completed vocational school and from 1961 was employed as a car mechanic. During 1965–1967 he performed his mandatory service in the Polish Army.

Wałęsa then began work as an electrician in the Lenin Shipyard in Gdańsk. In December 1970, following government announcement of price increases, Wałęsa was one of the leaders in a strike at the shipyard. Arrested, he was convicted of antisocialist behavior and sentenced to a year in prison. On his release, he was elected to the new workers' council and acted as a voluntary work inspector. He also participated in various labor demonstrations and rallies.

In 1976, Wałęsa was fired from his job at the shipyard for collecting signatures on a petition to build a memorial to commemorate the 1970 casualties. He supported his family by taking temporary jobs. In 1978, together with Andrzej Gwiazda, Aleksander Hall, and other activists, Wałęsa took the lead in the organization of free, independent, noncommunist trade unions in the Baltic region. The security forces closely observed this activity. Wałęsa was often detained and arrested and could not find a permanent job.

In August 1980 Poland was struck by yet another wave of strikes. When this agitation reached Gdańsk, Wałęsa became the leader of the strike committee. As a result of the wave of strikes and negotiations with the communist government of Poland, he and the strike committee reached an agreement with the government on 31 August that allowed workers to organize their own independent, noncommunist trade unions.

This was the beginning of the Solidarność (Solidarity) trade union. One year later, in 1981, Wałęsa became president of Solidarity, which was joined by some 10 million Polish wage earners, about 70 percent of the employed population. Solidarity became a vast movement that sought sweeping social and economic changes. Although there were voices raised against the Soviet Union and Poland's membership in the Warsaw Pact, Wałęsa and the Solidarity leadership never let the union drift fully into the political arena.

On 13 December 1981, with the Soviet Union threatening military invasion, Polish General Wojciech Jaruzelski proclaimed martial law, whereupon Wałęsa and other Solidarity leaders were arrested. Released in November 1982, Wałęsa returned to work at the Gdańsk shipyard and maintained contact with underground Solidarity leaders.

Although martial law ended in July 1983, not much had changed. With many of the legal restrictions continuing in place, Wałęsa refused to collaborate with the government. In October 1983, at the time virtually under house arrest, he was awarded the Nobel Peace Prize.

In 1989, faced with no economic improvement and a steadily worsening political climate in Poland, Jaruzelski agreed to talks with Wałęsa and his colleagues. These occurred during February–April 1989, with Wałęsa leading the opposition side. The two sides reached agreement allowing semi-free national elections to be held in June 1989 that resulted in a new government under noncommunist Premier Tadeusz Mazowiecki, Wałęsa's choice.

With the collapse of communism in Eastern Europe and the end of the Cold War, Wałęsa, still head of the now-legal Solidarity labor union, traveled widely abroad and met with world leaders. In November 1989 he addressed a joint session of the U.S. Congress.

In national elections in December 1990, Wałęsa was elected president. His tenure as president was a mixed one, and his effort to make that office a strong one was only partially successful, bringing with it frequent clashes with premiers and parliament. He lost his bid for reelection in 1995. Wałęsa nonetheless remains one of the most important figures in twentieth-century Poland.

Jakub Basista

See also
Berman, Jakub; Bierut, Bolesław; Gierek, Edward; Gomułka, Władysław; Jaruzelski, Wojciech; Kania, Stanisław; Mazowiecki, Tadeusz; Michnik, Adam; Mikołajczyk, Stanisław; Poland;

Poland, Armed Forces; Rapacki, Adam; Rokossovsky, Konstantin Konstantinovich; Solidarity Movement; Światło, Józef; Wałęsa, Lech; Wyszyński, Stefan, Cardinal

References

Biskupski, M. B. *The History of Poland.* Westport, CT: Greenwood, 2000.

Craig, Mary. *Lech Walesa and His Poland.* New York: Continuum, 1987.

Kurski, Jaroslaw. *Lech Walesa: Democrat or Dictator.* Boulder, CO: Westview, 1993.

Paczkowski, Andrzej. *The Spring Will Be Ours: Poland and the Poles from Occupation to Freedom.* State College: Pennsylvania State University Press, 2003.

Wałęsa, Lech. *The Struggle and the Triumph.* New York: Arcade, 1992.

Texas, on 31 October 1993, is perhaps best remembered as being Lee Harvey Oswald's first assassination target. Oswald shot at Walker but missed as the general sat at his desk in his Dallas home on 10 April 1963.

Shawn Francis Peters

See also

John Birch Society

References

Diamond, Sara. *Roads to Dominion: Right-Wing Movements and Political Power in the United States.* New York: Guilford, 1995.

Peters, Shawn Francis. "'Did You Say That Mr. Dean Acheson Is a Pink?': The Walker Case and the Cold War." *Vietnam Generation* 6(3–4) (1995): 54–62.

Walker, Edwin Anderson (1909–1993)

U.S. Army general and controversial right-wing ideologue. Born in Center Point, Texas, on 10 November 1909, Edwin Walker graduated from the New Mexico Military Institute in 1927 and the U.S. Military Academy, West Point, in 1931. During World War II he led the so-called Devil's Brigade of commandos who fought at Anzio and in the invasion of southern France. By 1951 a colonel, Walker commanded an artillery unit in the Korean War, then commanded the Arkansas Military District. After *Brown v. Board of Education* (1954), he was tasked with desegregating Little Rock's Central High School. Although he himself adamantly opposed desegregation, he ordered his troops to protect from segregationist mobs nine African American students entering the high school. Promoted to major general in 1959, he commanded the 24th Infantry Division in Augsburg, the Federal Republic of Germany (FRG, West Germany).

In the early 1960s, Walker became embroiled in controversy after he developed a broad campaign to warn soldiers and civilians about the growing menace of communism. Its centerpiece was a propaganda program known as Pro-Blue that included everything from the scheduling of ultraconservative speakers to the distribution of voting guides, approved reading lists, and literature from the reactionary, right-wing John Birch Society. In April 1961 a U.S. Army investigation accused Walker of attempting to indoctrinate troops under his command with ultrarightist views and literature. Public pressure against him quickly mounted, with *The New York Times* and numerous other publications calling for his ouster. He resigned in November 1961, retiring as a major general.

Walker never fully capitalized on the fame generated by his brush-up with the U.S. Army. He frequently wrote and spoke on anticommunist and right-wing topics, but his only serious effort to gain elective office ended in defeat in the 1962 Texas gubernatorial primaries. Walker, who died in Dallas,

Walker, John Anthony, Jr. (1937–)

U.S. naval officer and spy. Born in Washington, D.C., on 28 July 1937, John Walker Jr. has been assessed as the most damaging Soviet spy in the United States during the Cold War. He actually headed a family of spies, including his son Michael Walker (b. 1962) and a brother, Arthur Walker (b. 1934). The other member of John Walker's espionage ring was his good friend and colleague Jerry Whitworth (b. 1939). All were members of the U.S. Navy, and their treachery involved the sale of vital navy secrets to the Soviet intelligence agency Komitet Gosudarstvennoi Bezopasnosti (KGB).

Walker graduated from high school but did not attend college. He enlisted in the navy in 1965 and was trained in electronic communications. By the date of his retirement in 1976, he had attained the rank of chief warrant officer. He served tours of duty on nuclear-powered submarines and worked shore assignments in San Diego, Norfolk, and Charleston. In the fall of 1967 he contacted the Soviet embassy in Washington, D.C., and in return for appropriate compensation offered his services to the KGB. For eighteen years he delivered to the Soviets Navy cryptological materials, including secret codes, key lists, and manuals on the internal operations of U.S. cryptographic equipment. Former KGB Major General Oleg Kalugin has estimated that Walker was paid at least $1 million during his espionage career.

Walker enjoyed the considerable income that spying offered. Thus, upon retirement he found it necessary to recruit agents to provide him with the desired information. Walker's brother, Arthur, was a retired naval lieutenant commander and worked for the VSE (Value Systems Engineering) Corporation, which provided services to the navy. Arthur was able to provide his brother with material sought by the Soviets. John Walker's son Michael enlisted in the navy in December 1982. After an assignment on the U.S. aircraft carrier *Nimitz* in January 1984, he too became a source for secret material.

Michael was placed in charge of the burn bag and could easily look for valuable documents on their way to destruction. He hid the selected material aboard ship until it could be delivered to his father. Perhaps John Walker's most valuable agent was not a family member but rather a former colleague and a senior chief radioman, Jerry Whitworth. During 1975–1979, Whitworth secured for Walker a wide range of secret material in cryptology. Whitworth's spying income was estimated to be about $330,000.

John Walker was an unscrupulous person, an accomplished liar, a heavy drinker, and a womanizer. His former wife, Barbara Crowley Walker, knew of his spying activity. Finally disenchanted by his corrupt behavior, she reported him to the Federal Bureau of Investigation in November 1984. Walker was placed under surveillance and was finally arrested while servicing a dead-drop zone in a rural area near Washington, D.C. His spy ring quickly unraveled upon his arrest. Walker and son Michael turned against Whitworth and bargained for a lighter sentence for Michael. Whitworth and Arthur Walker were left to the mercy of a judge and jury. On 7 November 1986, Michael Walker received a sentence of 25 years in prison. He was released on parole on 17 February 2000. Whitworth was given the harshest sentence: 365 years in prison and a $410,000 fine. Arthur Walker received life imprisonment coupled with a $250,000 fine. John Walker, the prime culprit and spy mastermind, received a life sentence.

Ernie Teagarden

See also
Espionage; Intelligence Collection; Komitet Gosudarstvennoi Bezopasnosti
References
Bloom, Howard. *I Pledge Allegiance: The True Story of the Walkers, an American Spy Family.* New York: Simon and Schuster, 1987.
Earley, Pete. *Family of Spies: Inside the John Walker Spy Ring.* New York: Bantam, 1989.
Hunter, Robert W., with Lynn Dean Hunter. *Spy Hunter: Inside the FBI Investigation of the Walker Espionage Case.* Annapolis, MD: Naval Institute Press, 1999.
Kneece, Jack. *Family Treason: The Walker Spy Case.* Briarcliff Manor, NY: Stein and Day, 1986.

Wallace, Henry Agard (1888–1965)

U.S. politician, New Deal administrator, and vice president of the United States (1941–1945). Henry Wallace was born on 7 October 1888 on his family's farm in Adair County, Iowa. His father was an amateur publisher whose magazine *Wallace's Farmer* became so influential that he served as agriculture secretary for Presidents Warren G. Harding and Calvin Coolidge. The younger Wallace broke with his family's Republican leanings and, as editor of the *Farmer,* endorsed Franklin D. Roosevelt for president in 1932. Wallace was sub-

sequently rewarded with his father's old job in the Department of Agriculture. For the next eight years, he was a fiercely loyal member of the New Deal elite, using the powers of the Agricultural Adjustment Administration (AAA) and the Farm Security Administrations (FSA) to shore up crop market prices and modernize small farm holdings. His visibility in office persuaded Roosevelt to choose him as his vice presidential running mate in 1940, despite the misgivings of conservative Democratic Party members who claimed that Wallace was too intellectual for the office. Such suspicions deepened during World War II as Wallace espoused an increasingly radical left-wing agenda, particularly in international matters, in which he was accused of being naïvely sympathetic toward the Soviet Union. A combination of southern Democrats and urban northeasterners prevented Wallace's renomination at the 1944 party convention, during which Senator Harry S. Truman was chosen instead. When Truman became president in April 1945, Wallace was shunted to the political sidelines with the post of commerce secretary.

Wallace refused to stay quiet, however, and soon became a leading critic of Truman's hard-line stance toward the Soviet Union, forcing the president to dismiss him in September 1946. Recognizing that his future as a prominent Democrat had ended, Wallace decided to run in the 1948 election as a third-party candidate on a platform that advocated socialist-style reform and racial integration at home and rapprochement with the Soviet Union's Eastern bloc abroad. Hawkish liberal organizations such as the Americans for Democratic Action (ADA) accused Wallace's neophyte party of being a communist front, an exaggeration but one that its leader did nothing to quash. Whether or not the Progressives were conscious fellow travelers, their opposition to the Truman Doctrine and the Marshall Plan on the grounds that they frustrated Russo-American amity was, by 1948, viewed as foolish utopianism. Wallace's national support slipped away under a barrage of criticism, and his 2.7 percent of the November 1948 vote left him in fourth place behind Strom Thurmond, a humiliating defeat that shattered the anti-Truman Left. Wallace withdrew from public life and spent his remaining years as a successful gentleman farmer. He died in Danbury, Connecticut, on 18 November 1965.

Alan Allport

See also
Americans for Democratic Action; Marshall Plan; Roosevelt, Franklin Delano; Truman, Harry S.; Truman Doctrine
References
Culver, John C., and John Hyde. *American Dreamer: The Life and Times of Henry A. Wallace.* New York: Norton, 2000.
Markowitz, Norman. *The Rise and Fall of the People's Century: Henry A. Wallace and American Liberalism, 1945–1948.* New York: Free Press, 1973.
Walton, Richard. *Henry Wallace, Harry Truman, and the Cold War.* New York: Viking, 1976.

Wang Bingnan (1906–1988)

Chinese communist politician and foreign minister of the People's Republic of China (PRC). Born in Sanyuan, Shaanxi Province, Wang Bingnan joined the Chinese Communist Party (CCP) in 1925. He enrolled at the University of Berlin in 1931 and graduated in 1935, after which he returned to China and became chief assistant to Zhou Enlai. Throughout both the Sino-Japanese War (1937–1945) and the Chinese Civil War (1946–1949), Wang assisted Zhou in handling the CCP's liaison and foreign affairs.

Following the birth of the PRC in October 1949, Wang became director of the Foreign Ministry's Staff Office, a post he held until the end of 1954, and accompanied Zhou to the Geneva Conference in April 1954. In January 1955, Wang was appointed ambassador to Poland. As a result of the Bandung Conference in July 1955, he was named the Chinese representative to the Sino-American Ambassadorial Talks, the only direct diplomatic channel between the PRC and the United States since 1949. The talks began on 1 August 1955, and initially the negotiations went smoothly on the issue of the mutual release of nationals. However, they soon deadlocked over the status of Taiwan. The talks were suspended in December 1957 when the U.S. representative U. Alexis Johnson was recalled. The ambassadorial talks were resumed in September 1958 after the Second Taiwan Strait Crisis, with Wang remaining the Chinese representative.

In April 1964, Wang was appointed vice foreign minister. His tenure, which lasted until July 1975, coincided with the ultraleftist Cultural Revolution (1966–1976), and his previous overseas service invited revisionist criticism. In 1968, he was taken into custody and imprisoned until 1972. In August 1975 he was assigned to head the Chinese People's Association for Friendship with Foreign Countries, resuming his diplomatic activity as the head of Chinese delegations to many nations until he was elected chairman of the Organizing Committee for the International Peace Year 1986. Wang died on 22 December 1988 in Beijing.

Law Yuk-fun

See also
Bandung Conference; Cultural Revolution; Geneva Conference (1954); Taiwan Strait Crisis, Second; Zhou Enlai

References
Chen, Jian. *Mao's China and the Cold War.* Chapel Hill: University of North Carolina Press, 2001.
Ma, Jisen. *The Cultural Revolution in the Foreign Ministry of China.* Hong Kong: Chinese University Press of Hong Kong, 2004.
Wilhelm, Alfred D. *The Chinese at the Negotiating Table: Style and Characteristics.* Washington, DC: National Defense University Press, 1994.

War, Operational Art of

The operational art of war consists of the body of military activities that fall between tactics and strategy. The tactical and the strategic have long been recognized as distinct levels of warfare with their own peculiar requirements and dynamics. Recognition of the operational level of war only began to evolve slowly at the start of the nineteenth century and was not fully accepted by all militaries throughout the world until the final years of the twentieth century. In the years following World War I, the Soviets fully embraced the concept of the operational art of war and for many years led the way in its theoretical development. The United States, in company with the rest of the North Atlantic Treaty Organization (NATO) countries, only accepted the operational level of war in the early 1980s, and that marked one of the key military turning points of the Cold War.

Simply stated, tactics is the art of winning battles, while strategy is the art of winning wars. The operational art focuses on winning campaigns, which are made up of battles and contribute to the winning of wars. In the late 1980s, the U.S. Army Command and General Staff College used the metaphor of a medieval flail to illustrate the relationship among the three levels of war. The handle of the flail represented strategy, the overall directing force of the weapon. The spiked ball represented tactics, the part of the weapon that delivered the actual blow. The flexible chain that connected the handle to the spiked ball represented operational art, the vital link between strategy and tactics.

The flail metaphor was a simple and effective model for introducing the concept of the operational art, but it came apart if pushed too far. The difficulty in the relationships among the three levels of warfare is that success on one level does not automatically translate into success on another level. Major General Nathanael Greene's Southern Campaign during the War for American Independence is one example where a general who lost all the battles still won the campaign. Nor does winning all the battles and even all the campaigns necessarily guarantee winning the war. The Vietnam War demonstrated that, if nothing else.

The origins of the operational level of war can be traced to the mass armies of Napoleon and his practice of marching his corps in separate approach columns and then massing his forces at the decisive point just prior to battle. During the latter half of the nineteenth century, the German Army under Count Helmuth von Moltke recognized a body of activities it called *Operativ*, which involved all of the maneuvering and preparations prior to the initiation of a battle. The first forces to arrive fixed the enemy in position, while the follow-on forces maneuvered around the enemy's flank to gain decisive tactical advantage. The Germans did not, however, identify *Operativ* as a distinct level of war-fighting. Throughout World War I, the Germans had the most advanced understanding of the operational art, although it was deeply flawed by contemporary standards. The flaws in their operational thinking would cost the German Army dearly in World War II.

In the late nineteenth and early twentieth centuries some military writers, including J. F. C. Fuller, grouped operational-level activities under a concept they called Grand Tactics. But it was the Soviet military theorists who made the most significant contributions to advancing the concept of operational art as we know it today. As early as 1907, Russian military writers were debating a concept they called *Opertika*. Following the disastrous defeat of the Red Army in the 1920 Battle of Warsaw, two opposing schools of thought emerged in the Soviet military. Marshal Mikhail N. Tukhachevsky, the Red Army front commander at Warsaw, was the leader of the annihilation school of thought. Annihilation depended upon the ability to conduct large-scale, immediate, decisive operations. It required a war industry and a large standing army. Tukhachevsky's 1924 paper "Maneuver and Artillery" had a strong influence on the Frunze Military Academy reforms of 1924–1925, and those ideas were later formalized in the Red Army's *Field Service Regulations* of 1927. Major General Aleksandr A. Svechin led the opposing school of thought. In his influential 1926 book *Strategy*, he advocated the doctrine of attrition, which relied more on Russia's traditional deep resources of space, time, and manpower. He also formally posited for the first time the concept that operations were distinct from strategy and tactics. He argued that tactics made up the steps from which operational leaps were assembled, "with strategy pointing out the path." Within a year of Svechin introducing the concept, the Soviets established a chair on the Conduct of Operations within the Department of Strategy at the Military Academy of the Red Army.

Svechin and Tukhachevsky were both eliminated in Stalin's purges of the 1930s, but their opposing theories were synthesized by Vladimir K. Triandafillov in his book *The Nature of the Operations of Modern Armies.* Published in 1929, the book is now regarded as one of the seminal works in Soviet military thought. Triandafillov was the first to introduce the planning norms that became one of the benchmarks of Soviet operational art. He also laid out the theory of successive operations and deep operations (*glubokaia operatsiia*), with the result that several successive operations were linked into a single continuous, deep operation. Thus, the point of Napoleon and line of Moltke gave way to the vector in depth, with its multiple effects—both sequentially and simultaneously—in three dimensions.

Although the operational art emerged during the interwar years in the Soviet Union as a vibrant new field of military study, many of the operational concepts associated with it were stillborn or only partially developed. The Red Army learned this hard truth and suffered accordingly during the Winter War with Finland in 1939–1940 and in 1941 during the opening months of the war with Germany. Soviet operational art only reached its highest level of development through trial and error in the crucible of World War II. Yet for all its final sophistication, the Soviets never fully developed the air and naval components of the operational art.

The widely held popular belief is that what the West called the German Blitzkrieg represented the most highly developed form of the operational art through the period of World War II. Many military analysts, however, have argued that Blitzkrieg was at best a deeply flawed expression of operational art. The keys to the operational level of war are depth and sequencing. Depth has both a temporal and a spatial component. Depth in terms of space meant that for the first time there was a recognition that the battle was not necessarily decided at the line of contact but could be carried deep into an enemy's rear area. Depth in time meant sequencing, which was the key to cumulative effects that built on the successes of one battle to the next. Unfortunately for the Germans, their military thinking from the time of Count Alfred von Schlieffen on was dominated by the concept of the battle of annihilation, what they called the *Vernichtungsschlacht.*

With its geographic position in Europe and relatively defenseless borders east and west, Germany's worst strategic nightmare was always the two-front war. To avoid this trap, German military thinking focused on conducting short wars that would be won by a single decisive battle. Thus, sequential effects and extended operations in time carried a low priority in German thinking. And since logistics is the critical enabler of any extended period of operations, the Germans never developed the robust logistics structure or the adequate logistics doctrine needed to carry them through a long war. But a long war on even more than two fronts is exactly what the Germans ended up fighting twice in a thirty-year period.

Despite their rapid movements and deep armored thrusts, the German Blitzkrieg battles of World War II were not true operational campaigns but rather were tactical maneuvers on a grand scale. Blitzkrieg did feature the innovative use of combined arms tactics aimed at achieving rupture through the depth of an enemy's tactical deployment, and it did exhibit many of the features we now associate with the operational art. But it focused far too heavily on annihilation and rapid decision by a single bold stroke.

On the tactical level of war the German army was superior to the Red Army on almost every count, yet the Soviets still beat the Germans in the end. German tactics were innovative

1406 Warnke, Paul Culliton

and flexible, and their leaders and soldiers were well trained and exhibited initiative down to the lowest levels. Soviet tactics were largely rigid, cookbook battle drills, with the soldiers and the lower-level leaders functioning as mere automatons. But the Soviets had developed a far superior concept of the operational art and especially the principles of depth and sequential effects. The Soviets became masters of striking deep into the German rear to disrupt command and control systems and the all-too-fragile German logistics system. In the end, Blitzkrieg was little more than the German Army's tactical response to Adolf Hitler's totally incoherent strategy.

Despite the flaws in what eventually became Blitzkrieg, the post–World War I German Army did have a clear, albeit imperfect, understanding of a level of war between the tactical and the strategic. Writing in 1920, General Hugo Freiherr von Freytag-Loringhoven noted that among German General Staff officers, the term *Operativ* was increasingly replacing the term *Strategisch* to "define more simply and clearly the difference from everything tactical." The 1933 edition of *Truppenführung*, the primary German war-fighting manual of World War II, distinguished clearly between tactical and operational functions. *Truppenführung*'s principal author, General Ludwig Beck, considered *Operativ* as a subdivision of strategy. Its sphere was the conduct of battle at the higher levels, in accordance with the tasks presented by strategic planning. Tellingly, when U.S. Army intelligence made a rough English translation of *Truppenführung* just prior to World War II, the term *Operativ* was translated throughout as "strategic."

Post–World War II American military doctrine focused almost exclusively on the tactical level. Although the U.S. Army and its British allies had planned and executed large and complex operational campaigns during the war, the mechanics of those efforts were largely forgotten by the early 1950s. Nuclear weapons cast a long retarding shadow over American ground combat doctrine, and the later appearance of battlefield nuclear weapons seemed to render irrelevant any serious consideration of maneuver by large-scale ground units. The Soviets, meanwhile, continued to study and write about the operational art and the operational level of war. While the U.S. military intelligence community closely monitored and analyzed the trends in Soviet doctrine, American theorists ignored or completely rejected these concepts. Because of its dominant role in NATO, America's operational blinders were adopted for the most part by its coalition allies.

In the early–to mid-1970s, American thinking began to change. The three major spurs to this transformation were the loss in Vietnam, the stunning new weapons effects demonstrated in the 1973 Middle East War, and the need to fight and win against the superior numbers of the armed forces of the Warsaw Pact. The concept of the operational level of war entered the debate when the influential defense analyst Edward

Luttwak published the article "The Operational Level of War" in the winter 1980–1981 issue of the journal *International Security*. About the same time, Colonel Harry Summers' book *On Strategy: The Vietnam War in Context* sparked a parallel renaissance in strategic thinking and the rediscovery of Clausewitz by the American military. The U.S. Army formally recognized the operational level of war with the publication of the 1982 edition of *FM 100–5, Operations,* which also introduced the concepts of AirLand Battle and Deep Battle. The operational art was first defined in the 1986 edition of *FM 100–5,* along with the concept that commanders had to fight and synchronize three simultaneous battles: close, deep, and rear. The idea was that one's own deep battle would be the enemy's rear battle, and vice versa. The close battle would always be strictly tactical, but the deep and rear battles would have operational significance.

David T. Zabecki

See also
AirLand Battle; Artillery; DePuy, William Eugene; North Atlantic Treaty Organization, Origins and Formation of; Starry, Donn Albert

References
McKercher, B. J. C., and Michael A. Hennessy, eds. *The Operational Art: Developments in the Theories of War.* Westport, CT: Praeger, 1996.
Naveh, Shimon. *In Pursuit of Military Excellence: The Evolution of Operational Theory.* London: Frank Cass, 1997.
Newell, Clayton, and Michael D. Krause, eds. *On Operational Art.* Washington, DC: U.S. Army Center of Military History, U.S. Government Printing Office, 1994.
Zabecki, David T., and Bruce Condell, eds. and trans. *Truppenführung: On the German Art of War.* Boulder, CO: Lynne Rienner, 2001.

Warnke, Paul Culliton (1920–2001)

U.S. assistant secretary of defense for international security affairs (1967–1969) and director of the U.S. Arms Control and Disarmament Agency (1977–1978). Born in Webster, Massachusetts, on 31 January 1920, Paul Warnke graduated from Yale University in 1941. During World War II he served in the U.S. Coast Guard in both the Atlantic and Pacific theaters. After earning a law degree from Columbia University in 1948, he practiced law in Washington, D.C.

In 1966 Warnke became general counsel to the Department of Defense. He was appointed assistant secretary of defense for international security affairs the following year. He firmly opposed American involvement in Vietnam. His views had a substantial impact on Secretary of Defense Robert McNamara and his 1968 successor, Clark Clifford. Originally a strong supporter of U.S. intervention, Clifford instigated new studies of the war, whose findings rapidly led him to advocate U.S. withdrawal.

When President Lyndon B. Johnson left office in 1969, Warnke joined Clifford's law practice but continued to advise Democratic presidential hopeful Edmund S. Muskie and the 1972 nominee, George S. McGovern. A strong advocate of major cuts in defense spending and freezes on the development and production of new weapons system, Warnke argued that reining in the arms race demanded that both superpowers exercise restraint. Claiming that asymmetrical nuclear balances were largely irrelevant to security, in 1975 he publicly urged that the United States should take the lead in demonstrating unilateral nuclear restraint. During the presidencies of Republicans Richard M. Nixon and Gerald R. Ford, Warnke was a prominent supporter of the protracted Strategic Arms Limitation Talks (SALT) and the SALT I and Anti-Ballistic Missile (ABM) Treaties negotiated in 1972.

Warnke's conciliatory views were anathema to the more hawkish foreign policy officials, notably Democratic Senator Henry M. Jackson and Warnke's former colleague Paul H. Nitze, clustered in the Committee on the Present Danger, founded in 1976 to press for major increases in American defense expenditures, the development of additional weapons systems, and more cautious arms control policies. In 1977 incoming Democratic President Jimmy Carter appointed Warnke director of the Arms Control and Disarmament Agency (ACDA) and chief SALT negotiator. Forty senators voted against his SALT appointment, and in office he remained a persistently controversial figure. In November 1978, with the SALT II Treaty about to seek Senate ratification, he decided to return to his law practice.

Warnke remained a special consultant on arms control to the secretary of state until 1981. Throughout the 1980s and 1990s he continued to speak and write extensively on arms control and other international issues. In 1995 he joined President William Jefferson Clinton's Advisory Board on Arms Control and Non-Proliferation Policy. Warnke died in Washington, D.C., on 31 October 2001.

Priscilla Roberts

See also

Arms Control; Carter, James Earl, Jr.; Clifford, Clark McAdams; McGovern, George Stanley; McNamara, Robert Strange; Military Balance; Nitze, Paul Henry; Present Danger, Committee on the; Strategic Arms Limitation Talks and Treaties; Vietnam War

References

Garthoff, Raymond L. *Détente and Confrontation: American-Soviet Relations from Nixon to Reagan.* Rev. ed. Washington, DC: Brookings Institution Press, 1994.

Glynn, Patrick. *Closing Pandora's Box: Arms Races, Arms Control and the History of the Cold War.* New York: Basic Books, 1992.

Herken, Gregg. *Counsels of War.* New York: Knopf, 1985.

Nolan, Janne E. *Guardians of the Arsenal: The Politics of Nuclear Strategy.* New York: Basic Books, 1989.

Talbott, Strobe. *The Master of the Game: Paul Nitze and the Nuclear Peace.* New York: Knopf, 1988.

Warsaw Pact

Politico-military alliance among the Soviet Union and its East European satellite states. The multilateral Treaty of Friendship, Cooperation, and Mutual Assistance signed on 14 May 1955 in Warsaw, Poland, formally institutionalized the East European alliance system, the Warsaw Treaty Organization, known as the Warsaw Pact. The Warsaw Treaty was identical to bilateral treaties concluded during 1945–1949 between the Soviet Union and its East European client states to assure Moscow's continued military presence on their territory. The Soviet Union, Albania, Bulgaria, Romania, the German Democratic Republic (GDR, East Germany), Hungary, Poland, and Czechoslovakia pledged to defend each other if one or more of the members were attacked.

The Warsaw Pact was created as a political instrument for Soviet leader Nikita S. Khrushchev's Cold War policy in Europe. The immediate trigger was the admission of the Federal Republic of Germany (FRG, West Germany) into the North Atlantic Treaty Organization (NATO) on 5 May 1955 and the Austrian State Treaty of 15 May 1955, which provided for Austrian neutrality and the withdrawal of Soviet troops. The creation of the Warsaw Pact sent important signals to both Eastern Europe and the West. On the one hand, the Soviet Union made clear to its satellite states that Austria's neutral status would not likewise be granted to them. On the other hand, Khrushchev allured the West with a standing offer to disband the Warsaw Pact simultaneously with NATO, contingent upon East-West agreement on a new collective security system in Europe.

The Political Consultative Committee (PCC) was established as the alliance's highest governing body, consisting of the member states' party leaders. The PCC met almost annually in one of the capitals of the Warsaw Pact states. On the military side, a unified command and a joint staff were created to organize the actual defense of the Warsaw Treaty states. Soviet Marshal Ivan G. Konev was appointed as the first supreme commander of the Warsaw Pact's Joint Armed Forces.

In its early years, the Warsaw Pact served primarily as a Soviet propaganda tool in East-West diplomacy. Khrushchev used the PCC to publicize his disarmament, disengagement, and peace offensives and to accord them a multilateral umbrella. The first concrete military step taken was the admission of the East German Army into the unified command, but not until the Berlin Crisis (1958–1961) was there a systematic militarization of the Warsaw Pact. The Soviet General Staff and the Warsaw Pact unified command prepared East European armies for a possible military conflict in Central Europe. In 1961, the Soviets replaced the old defensive strategy of

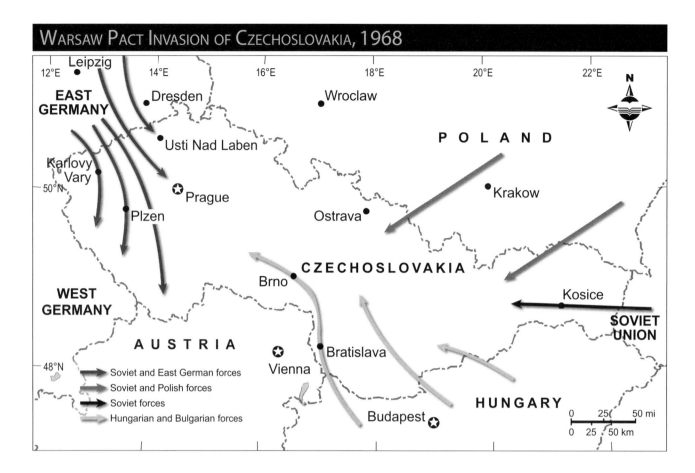

WARSAW PACT INVASION OF CZECHOSLOVAKIA, 1968

Soviet leader Josef Stalin with an offensive strategy that provided for a deep thrust into Western Europe. In the early 1960s, the Warsaw Pact began to conduct joint military exercises to prepare for fighting a nuclear war in Europe. The new strategy remained in place until 1987. Despite détente, the militarization of the Warsaw Pact accelerated under Soviet leader Leonid Brezhnev in the 1970s.

Behind the façade of unity, however, growing differences hounded the Eastern alliance. Following Khrushchev's campaign of de-Stalinization, Poles and Hungarians in the fall of 1956 demanded a reform of the Warsaw Pact to reduce overwhelming Soviet dominance within the alliance. Polish generals issued a memorandum that proposed modeling the Warsaw Pact more after NATO, while Hungary's new Communist Party leader, Imre Nagy, declared his country's neutrality and plans to leave the Warsaw Pact. In November 1956, the Soviet Army invaded Hungary and soon crushed all resistance.

In 1958, Romania demanded the withdrawal from its territory of all Soviet troops and military advisors. To cover Soviet embarrassment, Khrushchev termed this a unilateral troop reduction contributing to greater European security. At the height of the Berlin Crisis (1961), the Warsaw Pact's weakest and strategically least-important country, Albania,

stopped supporting the pact and formally withdrew from the alliance in 1968.

The Warsaw Pact was left in ignorance when Khrushchev provoked the October 1962 Cuban Missile Crisis. Only after the crisis was ended did East European leaders learn in a secret meeting that a nuclear war had been narrowly avoided. Romania reacted promptly to Moscow's nonconsultation in such a serious matter. In 1963, the Romanian government gave secret assurances to the United States that it would remain neutral in the event of a confrontation between the superpowers. In the same year, Romanian and Polish opposition prevented Khrushchev's plan to admit Mongolia into the Warsaw Pact.

In the mid-1960s the Warsaw Pact, like NATO, underwent a major crisis. The 1965 PCC meeting, convened by East Germany, demonstrated profound disagreements among Warsaw Pact allies on matters such as the German question, nuclear weapons' sharing, nuclear nonproliferation, and the Sino-Soviet split. In early 1966, Brezhnev proposed a Soviet plan to reform and institutionalize the Warsaw Pact. But resistance by Moscow's allies prevented the implementation of the scheme for more than three years.

In 1968, the Czechoslovak Crisis resulting from the Prague Spring seriously threatened the cohesion of the alliance. While

Warsaw Pact officials and generals observing military maneuvers near the Polish border, 6 April 1981. Polish Prime Minister General Wojciech Jaruzelski is second from right. To his right is General Viktor Kulikov, commander in chief of the Warsaw Pact armed forces. (Keystone/Getty Images)

the Soviet Union tried to intimidate Alexander Dubček's liberal Czechoslovak government with multilateral Warsaw Pact military maneuvers, the invading forces sent in on 20 August 1968 were mostly from the Soviet Union with token Polish, Hungarian, and East German contingents but no Romanian troops. Romania denounced the invasion as a violation of international law and demanded the withdrawal of all Soviet troops and military advisors from its territory. It also refused to allow additional Soviet forces to cross or conduct exercises on its territory.

The consolidation that resulted from the PCC session in Budapest in March 1969 transformed the Warsaw Pact into a more consultative organization. It established a committee of defense ministers, a military council, and a committee on technology. With these three new joint bodies, the Warsaw Pact finally became a genuine multilateral military alliance.

In 1976, previous informal gatherings of the Warsaw Pact foreign ministers were institutionalized into a committee of ministers of foreign affairs. In the 1970s, consultations within

Warsaw Pact bodies primarily dealt with the Council on Security and Cooperation in Europe (CSCE) process. Despite détente, preparations for a deep offensive thrust into Western Europe accelerated and intensified during numerous military exercises. In 1979, a statute on the command of the alliance in wartime was finally accepted by all but Romania after a year-long controversy.

During 1980–1981, the Solidarity Crisis in Poland heralded the end of Moscow's domination of Eastern Europe. Yet it did not pose a serious threat to the Warsaw Pact's integrity. At first, Moscow was tempted to threaten the opposition with military exercises and, eventually, military intervention. To avoid the high political costs of such a move, however, Moscow in the end trusted that the loyal Polish military would suppress the opposition on its own. The imposition of martial law by General Wojciech Jaruzelski was a major success for Moscow, as it demonstrated that the Moscow-educated Polish generals were protecting the interests of the Warsaw Pact even against their own people.

During the renewed Cold War of the 1980s, internal disputes in the Warsaw Pact increased. Romania demanded cuts in nuclear and conventional forces as well as in national defense budgets. It also called for the dissolution of both Cold War alliances and for the withdrawal of both U.S. and Soviet forces from Europe.

The issue of an appropriate Warsaw Pact response to NATO's 1983 deployment of U.S. Pershing II and cruise missiles in Western Europe, matching Soviet SS-20 intermediate-range ballistic missiles (IRBMs) aimed at West European targets, proved to be most divisive for the Eastern alliance. In 1983, East Germany, Hungary, and Romania engaged in a damage control exercise to maintain their ties with the West, which they had established during the era of détente in the 1970s.

At the time of the Warsaw Pact's thirtieth anniversary in 1985, Mikhail Gorbachev became the new Soviet leader and improved the role of Warsaw Pact consultations on the desired nuclear and conventional cuts in the Eastern alliance. At the PCC meeting in Berlin in May 1987, he changed Warsaw Pact military doctrine from offensive to defensive. In the late 1980s, however, East Germany, Bulgaria, and—in a reversal of its earlier opposition—even Romania proposed to strengthen the Warsaw Pact by improving its intrabloc political consultative functions.

After the fall of the Berlin Wall in 1989, East and West at first saw merit in keeping both Cold War alliances in place. In January and February 1991, however, Czechoslovakia, Hungary, Poland, and Bulgaria declared that they would withdraw all support by 1 July of that year. The Warsaw Pact thus came to an end on 31 March 1991 and was officially dissolved at a meeting in Prague on 1 July 1991.

Christian Nuenlist

See also
Brezhnev, Leonid; Détente; Gorbachev, Mikhail; Khrushchev, Nikita
References
Holden, Gerard. *The Warsaw Pact: The WTO and Soviet Security Policy.* Oxford, UK: Blackwell, 1989.
Jones, Christopher D. *Soviet Influence in Eastern Europe: Political Autonomy and the Warsaw Pact.* Brooklyn, NY: Praeger, 1981.
Mastny, Vojtech, and Malcolm Byrne, eds. *A Cardboard Castle? An Inside History of the Warsaw Pact, 1955–1991.* Budapest/New York: Central European Press, 2005.
Mastny, Vojtech, Sven Holtsmark, and Andreas Wenger, eds. *War Plans and Alliances in the Cold War: Threat Perceptions in the East and West.* New York: Routledge, 2006.

Warships, Surface

Although aircraft carriers and submarines drew the headlines during the Cold War, nonaviation surface ships constituted the bulk of the world's navies and conducted most naval operations. The nature, size, and armament of those ships changed gradually as the Cold War advanced. Radar and torpedo technology limitations eliminated small coastal fast-attack craft that had proven effective against ships lacking radar during World War II. The aircraft carrier and the expense of operation drove the battleships out of service by 1960 and relegated World War II–era gun cruisers to the flagship role based on their ability to carry extensive communications suites.

In fact, in Western navies, fleet surface combatants served primarily as escorts that protected the aircraft carrier. Thus, air defense and antisubmarine warfare became their dominant missions. For most U.S. Navy cruisers, that meant carrying long-range surface-to-air missiles (SAMs), but the United States was the only country that could afford to operate such ships. Thus, the unarmored general-purpose destroyer was the mainstay of the world's surface fleets for most of the Cold War. The Soviet Union was the first country to equip these units with a surface-strike capability, and that development, combined with microminiaturization technology, drove the development and missions for nonaviation surface combatants during the Cold War's final years. Of course, there were also specialized surface ships such as logistics ships, mine countermeasures, and rescue/salvage ships, which were critical to naval operations.

Having been reduced primarily to the limited roles of providing naval gunfire support for amphibious assaults and supplementing the aircraft carrier's close-in air defense, battleships became the first major surface combatants to go. Britain's last battleship, the *Vanguard,* was commissioned in 1946, but the Royal Navy scrapped eleven of its surviving pre–World War II battleships before 1949. The *Vanguard* and the four King George V–class units were decommissioned by 1957 and scrapped in 1960. Similarly, the United States decommissioned all of its pre–World War II battleships by 1948, and the remainder left service by 1960. Naval planners briefly flirted with the idea of converting the four Iowa-class units into massive air defense and nuclear missile strike platforms but abandoned the idea because of the costs involved in modifying the heavily armored hulls.

The United States briefly brought the Iowa-class battleship *New Jersey* into service for a year during the Vietnam War and then returned all four Iowa-class battleships into service in the early 1980s but spent millions of dollars modifying them with new air defense systems and surface-to-surface missiles for both antiship and land attack missions. However, the age of their operating systems and the heavy manning required to operate those systems necessitated their retirement within two years of the Soviet Union's collapse. A 1995 review determined that they were no longer cost-effective to operate and surplus to naval requirements. All are now museum ships.

Although Soviet leader Josef Stalin flirted briefly with building battleships after the war, the Soviet Union in 1956 decommissioned its two surviving battleships, initially commissioned in the 1920s, and scrapped them in 1957. France discarded its two surviving battleships as well, the *Richelieu* and *Jean Bart,* in 1959 and 1960, respectively.

The Soviet Sverdlov-class gun cruisers carried 152mm guns and were based on a blend of Italian and German World War II–era designs and technology. However, the Soviets retained them primarily as flagships and naval gunfire support platforms. Interestingly, some of the U.S. Navy's latest cruiser designs were decommissioned relatively soon after entering service. The large light cruisers *Worcester* and *Roanoke,* for example, mounted a troublesome new main armament suite and served only from 1948 to 1958. The large Des Moines–class ships were used primarily as flagships in the U.S. Sixth Fleet, with the *Newport News* serving until 1975.

The British and French simply decommissioned most of their gun cruisers. The Royal Navy discarded all of its pre–World War II cruisers by 1949, and all but two of its modern cruisers had been decommissioned by 1965. Those two, the *Lion* and *Tiger,* were converted into helicopter cruisers after

1965, retaining only one forward 6-inch gun turret. Both were reduced to reserve status by 1979 and scrapped in 1986.

The United States modified a number of its cruisers to carry heavy long-range SAMs. The first of these, the former heavy cruiser *Boston,* was recommissioned as a guided missile heavy cruiser in November 1955, carrying two Terrier SAM systems in place of its aft 8-inch gun turret. The *Canberra* followed eighteen months later.

Other cruisers were subjected to a more radical modification. The former heavy cruisers *Albany* and *Chicago* were completely converted to air defense cruisers during 1959–1964, losing all of their guns to make room for two short-range (10 nautical miles, NM) Tartar SAM systems and two long-range (80 NM) Talos SAM systems. They were also equipped with sonars and antisubmarine rockets (ASROC) to become the world's first multipurpose cruisers (capable of antisurface, antiair, and antisubmarine warfare). Several U.S. Navy light cruisers surrendered their aft 6-inch gun turrets for Talos or Terrier SAM systems.

Finally, the United States built the *Long Beach* (CGN-9) as the first cruiser designed as a guided missile platform. More importantly, upon its 9 September 1961 commissioning, it

The first nuclear-powered large combatant ship, the U.S. Navy guided missile cruiser *Long Beach,* shown under way at sea, June 1989. (U.S. Department of Defense)

became the world's first nuclear-powered surface warship. Initially completed without guns, the *Long Beach* had two single 5-inch gun mounts added in 1963 at the direct request of President John F. Kennedy, who thought it unwise to rely entirely on missiles for defense.

These conversions and decommissionings left destroyers as the workhorses for all the world's navies, including some whose missions were little more than coastal defense. The need to improve the destroyers' antiair warfare (AAW) and antisubmarine warfare (ASW) capabilities meant adding more radars, missiles, and eventually helicopters in order to increase their surveillance and attack ranges. As a result, destroyers become increasingly complex and expensive as the Cold War entered its second decade. A ship type that had averaged 2,200 tons of standard displacement in 1945 had grown to more than 7,000 tons by 1975.

In fact, among the democracies, legislative resistance to funding such expensive destroyers led to a complete reclassification of warships. The heavily modified classification system that dated back to the London Naval Limitation Treaties was abandoned completely. Now, destroyers were ships that focused on a single mission but had limited capabilities in another. Many multipurpose destroyers were then redesignated as cruisers. Ships that had once been designated as destroyer escorts (ASW-focused destroyers) became frigates, and coastal attack craft became corvettes.

Interestingly, perhaps the greatest changes in surface warship design came about because of Soviet developments in naval weaponry. Lacking the resources to build aircraft carriers during the Cold War's early years, the Soviet Union focused on developing long-range antiship missiles (ASMs) as well as SAMs for its ships. Thus, the Soviets introduced the world's first operational guided surface-launched antiship missile (SASM) into service aboard the destroyer *Bedoviy* in 1961. The North Atlantic Treaty Organization (NATO) designated the ship as a Kilden-class DDG (guided missile destroyer). Its P-1 Strela Shchuka-A (NATO designation, SS-N-1 Scrubber) cruise missile with a nuclear warhead had a range of more than 90 nautical miles (NM), far beyond the *Bedoviy*'s onboard radars and other sensors. The missile system's weight also affected the ship's handling capabilities and stability.

The Soviets then developed a smaller and shorter-ranged missile, the now famous SS-N-2 that NATO designated the Styx missile. Entering service in 1962, the Styx, with a range of 30 NM, equipped small coastal attack boats not much larger than the American PT boats of World War II. The much longer-ranged (300 NM) SS-N-3 also entered service that year when the Soviet Union's first Kynda-class cruiser entered service. As with the Kilden-class DDG, however, the *Kynda*'s command-guided missiles far outranged the ship's sensors. To support a long-range engagement, the ship required an aircraft to remain within radar range of the target and provide its location to the ship throughout the engagement. For a reconnaissance or targeting aircraft to survive an engagement that close to the carrier seemed improbable in wartime. As a result, the Soviet Union focused on starting and winning the war with the first shot: finding and targeting the aircraft carrier and then launching the attack during the war's early minutes.

Soviet technology and tactics had a profound effect on the U.S. Navy's tactical thinking and ship designs into the 1990s.

The United States had studied surface-to-surface missiles during the 1950s but abandoned them due to funding issues. It was hard to justify putting surface-to-surface missiles on surface ships after investing billions in aircraft carriers, aircraft, and SAM systems. Developing a guidance system for a surface-to-surface missile such as the then-existing Regulus missile did not seem cost-effective. More importantly, battleships and cruisers were the only units large enough to carry them. With their resources focused on aircraft carrier, aviation, and submarine technology, the West abandoned development of surface-launched antiship missiles in 1956. It was a mistake that would prove costly and embarrassing in the Cold War's third decade.

Secure in the belief that the carriers would always be there, Western intelligence agencies largely ignored the Soviet antiship missile threat. During the Vietnam War, since U.S. naval aircraft had destroyed the Democratic Republic of Vietnam's (DRV, North Vietnam) missile patrol boat force, these craft were not considered a serious problem. Certainly, they were not seen as a threat that warranted new solutions. All that changed on 21 October 1967, when a Soviet-supplied Egyptian missile patrol boat sank the Israeli destroyer *Eilat* with a single Styx missile without even leaving port. Fast coastal attack craft could no longer be taken lightly. One hit was enough to cripple, if not destroy, a $100 million unarmored warship.

The United States and France reacted swiftly, introducing high-priority programs to develop new missiles specifically designed to take out ships. The United States went a step further, developing long-range surveillance and targeting systems to support over-the-horizon engagements. Some were satellite-based, some were installed on ships, and others were installed on submarines and aircraft. All navies began to develop electronic and infrared detection and countermeasures systems to defeat these missiles' terminal guidance. Electronic warfare now encompassed more than the need to defeat an enemy's air defense systems. By 1972, a ship's electronic warfare capabilities were as critical to the ship's survival as its weapons systems.

These developments occurred parallel to the U.S. Navy's development of a global naval monitoring system driven by the Soviet Navy's first worldwide naval exercise, OKEAN-70, and the introduction of the first exercises demonstrating its

A Soviet Kynda-class guided missile cruiser under way, October 1985. (U.S. Department of Defense)

first-shot tactics. The resulting Ocean Surveillance Information System (OSIS) entered service in 1972. By the late 1970s, OSIS had taken on the additional mission of supporting rapid over-the-horizon targeting by U.S. Navy and NATO missile-equipped ships. Although the Soviets never developed a similar global oceanic monitoring capability, they did develop an extensive array of electronic air- and space-based targeting systems to support their naval units. Both sides developed increasingly complex and long-ranged antiship, air defense, and surveillance systems.

All this led to navies pursuing two completely different paths of surface warship development. Smaller navies could no longer afford oceangoing ships equipped with all of these systems. This forced them to seek smaller ships that carried weapons and sensors more suited to the missions of coastal defense, environmental protection, and patrol and control of economic exclusion zones.

The rebirth of mine warfare after the 1967 Arab-Israeli War also rejuvenated interest in mine countermeasures ships in the U.S. Navy and in Asian navies. (North Korea's and Europe's navies had never lost interest in mine warfare.)

General-purpose corvettes with limited AAW and ASW capabilities and mine countermeasures ships have become the predominant units of the world's smaller navies. Occasionally, these navies employ frigates as their flagships and on long-distance patrols, but 900–1,100-ton corvettes are these navies' workhorses. Destroyers and 10,000-ton all-purpose guided missile cruisers are found only in oceangoing navies—those whose country can afford the ships and the expensive shore facilities and ocean surveillance networks required to support their operations.

Surface ships execute the majority of naval operations, from show-the-flag and gunboat diplomacy, through disaster relief and emergency evacuation operations, to land attack and maritime transport operations. Although the combatant ships garner the headlines and are most often featured in the recruiting posters, a balanced fleet includes tankers, transports, repair and rescue ships, and even range and telemetry ships to help with the calibration of weapons systems and electronics. The Cold War saw these ships evolve from the simple, manually operated systems and uncomplicated designs of World War II to the highly automated, lightly crewed ships of today. Moreover, the Cold War's end brought new missions beyond the traditional ones of the past. Environmental and resource concerns and disaster relief are now major naval missions, and ship designs are being modified to accommodate those new missions.

Carl Otis Schuster and Dallace W. Unger Jr.

See also

Aircraft Carriers; Antiaircraft Guns and Missiles; France, Navy; Gorshkov, Sergey Georgyevich; Missiles, Cruise; Reagan, Ronald Wilson; Royal Navy; Soviet Union, Navy; Submarines; United States Navy

References

Isenberg, Michael T. *Shield of the Republic: The United States Navy in an Era of Cold War and Violent Peace,* Vol. 1, *1945–1962.* New York: St. Martin's, 1993.

Pavlov, A. S. *Warships of the USSR and Russia, 1945–1995.* Translated from the Russian by Gregory Tokar. Annapolis, MD: Naval Institute Press, 1997.

Polmar, Norman, et al. *Chronology of the Cold War at Sea, 1945–1991.* Annapolis, MD: Naval Institute Press, 1997.

Raymond, V. B. *Jane's Fighting Ships, 1950–51.* London: Jane's, 1951.

Sharpe, Richard. *Jane's Fighting Ships, 1989–90.* London: Jane's, 1990.

Sondhaus, Lawrence. *Navies of Europe, 1815–2002.* London: Pearson Education Limited, 2002.

Watson, Bruce W., and Susan M. Watson, eds. *The Soviet Navy: Strengths and Liabilities.* Boulder, CO: Westview, 1986.

Washington Summit Meeting, Nixon and Brezhnev (16–25 June 1973)

Summit meeting between U.S. President Richard M. Nixon and Soviet General Secretary Leonid Brezhnev during 16–25 June 1973. Despite growing tensions in the Middle East and in Indochina, in early 1973 the United States and the Soviet Union continued to build upon détente. Indeed, one major outcome of Nixon's 1972 visit to the Soviet Union had been the resolution to hold regular summit meetings. Although neither side's expectations of the Washington summit were as high as for the earlier Moscow meeting, the 1973 meeting nonetheless reaffirmed the U.S. and Soviet commitment to improving relations. As with the Moscow summit, daily bilateral agreements were signed, and two major agreements pertaining to the Strategic Arms Limitation Talks (SALT) were concluded.

In 1973, Nixon's domestic problems were legion. Congressional hearings on the building Watergate scandal were drawing closer to incriminating the president, and there was a dramatic increase in inflation coupled with sluggish economic growth. These economic problems only fueled growing discontent. The summit offered Nixon a respite from his domestic problems, an opportunity to divert attention from Watergate, and the chance to demonstrate the continuing success of détente.

Brezhnev gave a television address to the American people emulating Nixon's speech in Moscow a year prior. The Soviet leader spoke to the U.S. Senate Foreign Relations Committee and engaged in daily discussions with Nixon. One of Brezhnev's important goals was to further the Soviet Union's case for most-favored nation (MFN) trade status from the United States. Brezhnev viewed MFN status as a key to the continuation of détente, with the hope that it would revive a declining Soviet economy. In discussions with the Senate Foreign Relations Committee, Brezhnev conceded that the main obstacle to receiving MFN status was congressional opposition to Moscow's policy restricting Jewish emigration. Despite his eloquent plea and soft-pedaling of the emigration policy, he was not successful in making his case.

Nixon and Brezhnev discussed bilateral issues concerning agriculture, transportation, atomic energy, commercial relations, education, culture, oceanography, taxation, and air services. The two conferees reached agreements on Indochina and Europe but differed on policies concerning the Middle East. In the spirit of the 1972 Moscow Meeting, two important agreements concerning nuclear disarmament were reached. The Basic Principles of Negotiations on the Further Limitation of Strategic Offensive Arms and the Agreement on the Prevention of Nuclear War reaffirmed American and Soviet commitments to continuing SALT. Although the Basic Principles agreement was not groundbreaking, it nevertheless served as a new impetus to the continuation of détente and the SALT process. On 21 June, Nixon and Brezhnev signed the Basic Principles framework. The following day, the Agreement on the Prevention of Nuclear War was signed. Nixon's national security advisor, Henry Kissinger, pointedly revealed the importance of this document. The principal problem in the current global situation was how to prevent a nuclear war, not how to conduct one.

As the summit concluded, Nixon and Brezhnev issued a joint communiqué summarizing the intentions and outcomes of the summit. As with the previous year's Basic Principles of Mutual Relations, the document reaffirmed both parties' commitment to détente. Although there were no completely new initiatives addressed during Brezhnev's visit, it strengthened the precedent of annual summits between American and Soviet leaders. Despite mounting public criticism of the Nixon administration over the Vietnam War, the state of the American economy, and the Watergate scandal, Nixon appeared to be successfully reducing Cold War tensions. Unfortunately, technological advances in nuclear weaponry and Nixon's weakening political position prior to his last visit to Moscow in 1974 largely stalled the forward momentum of détente, a process that had been the cornerstone of both Nixon's and Brezhnev's Cold War foreign policies. The meeting also alarmed the leaders of the People's Republic of China (PRC), who feared that the two superpowers would cement an understanding on détente at the expense of the burgeoning Sino-American rapprochement.

Jonathan H. L'Hommedieu

See also

Arab-Israeli Wars; Brezhnev, Leonid; Détente; Kissinger, Henry; Moscow Meeting, Brezhnev and Nixon; Nixon, Richard Milhous; Nuclear Arms Race; Strategic Arms Limitation Talks and Treaties

References

Gorthoff, Raymond E. *Détente and Confrontation: Soviet-American Relations from Nixon to Reagan.* Rev. ed. Washington, DC: Brookings Institution Press, 1994.

Loth, Wilfried. *Overcoming the Cold War: A History of Détente, 1950–1991.* Translated by Robert F. Hogg. New York: Palgrave, 2002.

Stebbins, Richard B., and Elaine P. Adams, eds. *American Foreign Relations, 1973: A Documentary Record.* New York: New York University Press, 1976.

Stevenson, Richard William. *The Rise and Fall of Détente: Relaxations of Tensions in US-Soviet Relations, 1953–1984.* Urbana: University of Illinois Press, 1985.

Washington Summit Meeting, Reagan and Gorbachev (7–10 December 1987)

Summit meeting between U.S. President Ronald Reagan and Soviet General Secretary Mikhail Gorbachev on 7–10 December 1987. The principal agenda item for the meeting was nuclear arms reduction. The Washington Meeting showcased not only Gorbachev's new style of leadership but also the unprecedented thaw in the Cold War, which would by 1991 end upon the dissolution of the Soviet Union. The conference marked the first superpower summit on U.S. soil in fourteen years and endeavored to build upon the November 1985 Geneva Meeting, during which Reagan and Gorbachev agreed to a 50 percent mutual reduction in strategic nuclear weapons, and the Reykjavík Meeting of October 1986, which ended on a negative note over disagreements concerning Reagan's Strategic Defense Initiative (SDI). The summit in Washington saw both sides agree to eliminate an entire class of nuclear weapons (land-based intermediate-range missiles), codified by the signing of the Intermediate-Range Nuclear Forces (INF) Treaty in Moscow during Reagan and Gorbachev's final meeting together in May–June 1988.

In spite of the breakthrough in superpower relations, Reagan and Gorbachev still found themselves in disagreement on key issues during the 1987 negotiations. First, the 1972 Anti-Ballistic Missile (ABM) Treaty was interpreted differently by the Americans and the Soviets, which underscored the problems posed by SDI, colloquially referred to as "Star Wars." Gorbachev believed that SDI violated the ABM Treaty, while

Reagan tried to legitimize SDI by arguing that it fell into a category of space-based testing and development that did not violate previous agreements. Neither leader even mentioned SDI during postconference speeches to their respective nations, which may explain why the conference was deemed a success. Further, Reagan and Gorbachev failed to come to terms on regional issues in American and Soviet spheres of influence. Reagan criticized Gorbachev for turning a blind eye to the human rights record of the People's Republic of China (PRC) and also for failing to establish a timetable for the withdrawal of Soviet troops from Afghanistan. Gorbachev, in a press conference held three hours after the departure ceremony, stated that a proposal for withdrawal would be instituted as soon as the United States agreed to halt arms shipments and financial aid to insurgent forces battling Soviet troops in Afghanistan. Gorbachev also criticized Reagan over the Iran-Contra scandal and argued that the time had not yet come for the United Nations (UN) Security Council to impose sanctions on Iran for refusing to accept an earlier UN resolution demanding a cease-fire in the Iran-Iraq War.

Even if deemed a marginal success, the 1987 Washington meeting should be considered a significant turning point in Cold War history. Americans were well aware of Gorbachev's internal reforms (glasnost and perestroika) and saw his visit as powerfully symbolic, perhaps even foreshadowing the end of the Cold War. People crowded the streets to get a glimpse of Gorbachev, and many scholars indeed argue that Reagan needed the Soviet leader's cooperation in order to improve the image of the United States. Reagan had little choice but to address Gorbachev's initiatives regarding nuclear disarmament as an opportunity to divert public attention from domestic issues, such as the Iran-Contra scandal, to those that involved a dynamic new approach to foreign policy.

Whatever the ramifications of the 1987 Washington Meeting, it must be remembered not as the culmination of a process but rather as the beginning of both a new route to nuclear arms reductions and, perhaps more importantly, the end of the Cold War.

John C. Horn

See also

Anti-Ballistic Missile Treaty; Geneva Meeting, Gorbachev and Reagan; Glasnost; Gorbachev, Mikhail; Iran-Contra Affair; Moscow Meeting, Gorbachev and Reagan; Perestroika; Reykjavík Meeting; Strategic Defense Initiative

References

Fisher, Beth A. *The Reagan Reversal: Foreign Policy and the End of the Cold War.* Columbia: University of Missouri Press, 1997.

Garthoff, Raymond L. *Détente and Confrontation: American-Soviet Relations from Nixon to Reagan.* Rev. ed. Washington, DC: Brookings Institution Press, 1994.

Herrmann, Richard K. *Ending the Cold War: Interpretations, Causations, and the Study of International Relations.* New York: Palgrave Macmillan, 2004.

Lakhoff, Sanford, and Herbert F. York. *A Shield in Space? Technology, Politics, and the Strategic Defense Initiative.* Berkeley: University of California Press, 1989.

Matlock, Jack F. *Reagan and Gorbachev: How the Cold War Ended.* New York: Random House, 2004.

Washington Treaty

See North Atlantic Treaty

Watergate (1972–1974)

Far-reaching political scandal involving President Richard M. Nixon (1969–1974) that lasted from 1972 to 1974 and led to a constitutional crisis and the resignation of Nixon in August 1974. Nixon was by nature a secretive and untrusting man, and it was this mild paranoia that drove the Watergate scandal into a colossal political and constitutional crisis.

The genesis of Watergate can be traced to the leaking of the top-secret *United States–Vietnam Relations, 1945–1967: A Study Prepared by the Department of Defense,* often referred to as the Pentagon Papers, that occurred beginning in June 1971. The papers revealed highly classified—not to mention embarrassing—policy decisions made vis-à-vis the Vietnam War going back to the 1940s. By 1971, the Vietnam War had become a political nightmare for Nixon and had deeply divided the nation. The Pentagon Papers served only to heighten public distrust and discontent with the war. Nixon was livid at the leaks and vowed to get even with the man who had released the information, RAND Corporation employee Daniel Ellsberg. In fact, the first illegal break-in encouraged by the Nixon administration occurred in September 1971, when quasi-government operatives ransacked the office of Ellsberg's psychiatrist in an attempt to discredit the RAND employee. Meanwhile, the Nixon administration tried unsuccessfully to halt the publication of more sensitive information.

Now obsessed with plugging any leaks from within, Nixon's aides formed an informal committee of secret operatives whose job was to stop leaks, stonewall Federal Bureau of Investigation (FBI) probes, and retaliate against those who did leak information. The committee was fittingly called the "Plumbers."

On 17 June 1972, Washington, D.C., police arrested five men for burglarizing the offices of the Democratic National Committee, located in the Watergate complex (hence the name of the scandal). While the motive of the break-in is still unclear, one of the burglars, James W. McCord Jr., was on the payroll of the Committee to Reelect the President (CREEP).

This seemed to implicate White House involvement, although the connection would not be made in full for many months.

Officials at the White House, meanwhile, began to cover their tracks, engaging in an ever-widening cover-up that only bred more illegal activities. When questioned about the Watergate break-in, Nixon's press secretary famously dismissed it as a "third-rate burglary" of which the White House had no knowledge, and Americans believed him.

Nixon's secret taping system recorded a discussion on 23 June 1972 between the president and his chief of staff in which Nixon agreed that the Central Intelligence Agency (CIA) should be employed to block the FBI investigation into the Watergate affair. This was clear evidence that the White House was involved in the botched break-in. Nixon went on to win a landslide reelection in November 1972, and Watergate seemed all but forgotten. But the walls were about to close in beginning with the trial of the Watergate burglars in January 1973.

The five burglars pled guilty but said nothing. Indeed, CREEP had paid them hush money not to reveal anything that would implicate the president. But McCord, encouraged by the fact that he would receive leniency if he cooperated, recanted his testimony and implicated CREEP in instigating the break-in and in paying hush money to the accused. The rope was now getting tighter for Nixon, who continued to deny any involvement in the growing scandal. Congress now clamored for bipartisan hearings on the Watergate scandal, which began in May 1973 and lasted until August. The nation was riveted by the televised hearings, which revealed one bombshell after another. Perhaps as much as 85 percent of the American public viewed some or all of the hearings. The first bombshell was the realization that the White House had been directly involved in the scandal, indicated by the testimony of John Dean, Nixon's lawyer. The second was the revelation that Nixon had employed a secret taping system in the Oval Office that recorded virtually all conversations. Nixon's popularity began to plummet, and there were sporadic calls for his impeachment, even by stalwart Republicans.

As soon as the existence of the taped conversations was revealed, Archibald Cox, Watergate special prosecutor, and the U.S. Senate moved to subpoena the tapes. Nixon refused to surrender them, citing executive privilege and "national security concerns." Neither party agreed with that logic, however, and many Americans now believed that Nixon was either directly involved in the scandal or was trying to cover something up. In October 1973, when Nixon ordered Cox to withdraw his subpoena, the special prosecutor refused. The White House promptly fired him. That in turn led Nixon's attorney general and his deputy to resign in protest. A new prosecutor, Leon Jaworski, again subpoenaed the tapes. Nixon, now under immense pressure, responded by releasing selectively edited transcripts of the tapes, which pleased no one.

Worse yet, one of the tapes that the White House did release to Jaworski had an unexplained gap, which White House officials blamed on a clerical error committed by Nixon's personal secretary. In the spring of 1974, Congress continued to insist that it receive all of the contested tape recordings. Nixon stood firm.

In July 1974, the U.S. Supreme Court ruled that the Nixon administration must turn over all of the tapes requested by Congress. Meanwhile, in the House of Representatives, articles of impeachment were being prepared against the president. Nixon now had no choice but to surrender the tapes, which he knew would condemn him. On 27 July 1974, the House of Representatives passed the first of three impeachment articles against Nixon, citing him for obstruction of justice. On 29 and 30 July, respectively, two more articles of impeachment passed—one for abuse of power, the other for contempt of Congress. After being told by a delegation from his own party that he would not survive an impeachment trial in Congress, Nixon decided to resign the office of the presi-

dency on 9 August 1974. He was succeeded by his vice president, Gerald R. Ford.

Although the immediate crisis that was Watergate ended with Nixon's resignation, the episode had troubling and long-term implications for American politics and government. Many Americans rightly conflated Watergate with Vietnam. Indeed, just as U.S. policymakers led the nation into a costly, unpopular, and unwinnable war with little public discussion and no real congressional oversight, so too had the Nixon administration engaged in secretive and unsavory activities in the name of national security. As a result, Americans' trust in their politicians—and their political system—suffered a major blow. Many also talked with consternation about the unchecked powers of the presidency, which the Nixonian abuses of power so clearly highlighted. Watergate undermined the power of the Republican Party for a time and may indeed have led to the rise of President Jimmy Carter, who won the presidency in 1976 based in large part on his outsider status, personal integrity, and self-effacing manner. In the end, Watergate displayed in shocking clarity the results of the so-called imperial presidency and a national security state in which personal freedoms were subordinated to political whim and alleged public safety.

Paul G. Pierpaoli Jr.

See also
Ford, Gerald Rudolph; Nixon, Richard Milhous; Vietnam War
References
Emery, Fred. *Watergate: The Corruption of American Politics and the Fall of Richard Nixon.* New York: Touchstone, 1994.
Hoff, Joan. *Nixon Reconsidered.* New York: Basic Books, 1994.
Kutler, Stanley I. *The Wars of Watergate: The Last Crisis of Richard Nixon.* New York, Knopf, 1990.
Summers, Anthony. *Arrogance of Power: Nixon and Watergate.* London: Orion, 2001.
Woodward, Bob. *Secret Man: The Story of Watergate's Deep Throat.* New York: Simon and Schuster, 2005.

Richard Nixon boards a helicopter to depart from the White House lawn after resigning the presidency on 9 August 1974. He flashes his trademark "V for Victory" sign at this moment of disgrace. (National Archives and Records Administration)

Weathermen

American left-wing organization supportive of the worldwide struggle against alleged American imperialism that initiated terrorist attacks against the U.S. government in the late 1960s and early 1970s. The Weathermen emerged in late 1968 as one of several militant factions within the Students for a Democratic Society (SDS). Frustrated with the ineffectiveness of the anti–Vietnam War protests of the 1960s, Bernardine Dohrn, Bill Ayers, Kathy Boudin, and other members of the Weathermen called for a white revolutionary movement that would support African American militants such as the Black Panthers and developing-world revolutionaries in an international struggle against what they viewed as U.S. imperialism.

The group took its name from its first position paper, "You Don't Need a Weatherman to Know Which Way the Wind Blows," a line adopted from a Bob Dylan song. This founding statement was circulated during the last SDS convention in June 1969 in Chicago, where the Weathermen and their allies gained control of the organization.

Following Marxist-Leninist logic, the Weathermen believed that American imperialism would compel the American working class to unite in a revolutionary struggle to transform the United States into a socialist state. The Weathermen, who were mainly upper-middle-class college students, considered themselves the vanguard of the coming revolution and intended to spur workers to join the struggle. The group focused its initial recruiting efforts on white working-class youth, but most high school students opposed their militancy and refused to join the group.

As the putative vanguard group of the revolution, the Weathermen also intended to create revolutionary chaos in the United States. One of the group's first campaigns was the so-called Days of Rage that began on 8 October 1969, when the Weathermen and a few hundred supporters smashed windows and battled police in downtown Chicago. Although their attempt to bring the war home failed—a large police force quickly quelled the attack with tear gas, mace, and clubs—the group considered the melee an important inspiration for fellow white radicals. In mid-November 1969, the Weathermen precipitated a similar scuffle in Washington, D.C., where members damaged cars and windows, threw smoke bombs at the Justice Department building, and blocked streets with burning barriers until 2,000 police officers intervened.

When it became clear that their plan to bring about a revolution had failed, the Weathermen decided to continue the armed struggle as a clandestine group of terrorist cells that would attack the American government. During a meeting in Flint, Michigan, on 24 December 1969, the Weathermen, who never had more than a few hundred members, announced that they intended to go underground. In the ensuing years, small Weathermen cells initiated a wave of bombings against government buildings, military installations, and private companies that they believed supported American imperialism. On 9 June 1970, for example, the group bombed the New York City police headquarters as a response to the American invasion of Cambodia.

In December 1970, the Weathermen announced in a letter to the underground press that they had modified their ideology. They no longer considered violence their only revolutionary tool and assigned revolutionary qualities to the counterculture of the New Left. In response to criticism of the group's sexism, the Weathermen also embraced gender equality, changing the organization's name to the gender-neutral Weather Underground. Despite these tactical changes, attacks against federal buildings and private companies continued. Nevertheless, the illegal methods used by the Federal Bureau of Investigation (FBI) to prosecute members of the group led to the dismissal of charges against most of them in 1974.

That same year, the Weather Underground once more announced programmatic changes, calling upon American revolutionaries to organize for mass action clandestinely as well as publicly. As a result, the organization began to form the Prairie Fire Organizing Committee (PFOC) as an official support group. In 1976, internal factionalism led to the split of the organization into a reformist New York PFOC, or Central Committee, and a militant Bay Area Revolutionary Committee (BARC), which became the Weather Underground Organization later that year. While the Central Committee abjured violence, the BARC continued its terrorist activities. After 1977, when several leading members of the original Weathermen surrendered to federal authorities, the Weather Underground splintered into a number of separate organizations, some of which continued to advocate violence. In 1987, U.S. authorities arrested the last fugitive member of the Weathermen, Silas Bissell, and sentenced him to two years in prison.

Simon Wendt

See also
Black Panthers; Federal Bureau of Investigation; Students for a Democratic Society; Terrorism; Vietnam War; Vietnam War Protests

References
Gitlin, Todd. *The Sixties: Years of Hope, Days of Rage.* New York: Bantam, 1987.
Jacobs, Ron. *The Way the Wind Blew: A History of the Weather Underground.* New York: Verso, 1997.
Sale, Kirkpatrick. *SDS.* New York: Random House, 1973.

Wedemeyer, Albert Coady (1897–1989)

U.S. Army general and commander of American forces in China (1944–1946). Born in Omaha, Nebraska, on 9 July 1897, Albert Wedemeyer graduated from the U.S. Military Academy, West Point, in 1918 in an accelerated program and was commissioned in the infantry. Between the world wars, he served in the United States, the Philippines, and China. He attended the Command and General Staff College and was promoted to captain in 1936. His father-in-law and mentor, Colonel Stanley Embick, inspired in him a lifelong interest in strategic questions and economic issues in warfare.

From 1936 to 1938 Wedemeyer attended Kriegsakademie, the German war college, and produced a lengthy final report on the German military. This document so impressed Major General George C. Marshall, then assistant chief of staff in the War Department's General Staff War Plans Division, that in

1941, after he became chief of staff, Marshall placed Wedemeyer, now a major, in the same division. Wedemeyer contributed heavily to the War Department's Victory Plan, which governed overall planning for wartime mobilization of American manpower and industrial resources. In 1942–1943 Wedemeyer, promoted to brigadier general, served in the War Department's Operations Division, where he fervently advocated an early cross-channel invasion of Western Europe and opposed British Prime Minister Winston Churchill's alternative proposals for Mediterranean operations.

In autumn 1943 Wedemeyer, now a major general, became deputy chief of staff to the new Southeast Asia Command and helped to develop plans for future operations. He attempted unsuccessfully to resolve differences between China's Guomindang (GMD, Nationalist) president, Jiang Jieshi, and General Joseph W. Stilwell, commander of American military forces in the China-Burma-India theater and Jiang's chief of staff. In October 1944, Wedemeyer replaced Stilwell and soon developed a far less antagonistic working relationship with Jiang. Although critical of corruption and ineptitude within the Nationalist government and military, Wedemeyer, who rose to lieutenant general in early 1945, energetically helped to reorganize the Chinese Army and enhance its fighting abilities, drafting plans—never implemented—to retake southern China's coast from Japanese forces. He urged greater levels of American aid for Jiang's government and the denial of such assistance to Chinese communist leaders.

Following Japan's surrender in August 1945, Wedemeyer supervised the demobilization of Japanese troops in China and their replacement by Jiang's forces. Despite his continual criticisms of corruption and inefficiencies within the Nationalist government, Wedemeyer believed that the United States should give it staunch backing and much-expanded economic and military aid, and he expressed misgivings over Marshall's year-long 1946 effort to establish a coalition Chinese government that would include communist leaders. In April 1946 Wedemeyer left China. After Marshall sent him on a two-month fact-finding mission to China and Korea the following year, Wedemeyer repeated these recommendations while also forcefully urging the Chinese government to institute major reforms in order to survive and attract American aid. President Harry S. Truman's administration ignored Wedemeyer's advice and, deeming his report politically sensitive, for two years suppressed it.

After serving on the War Department General Staff and commanding the Sixth Army, Wedemeyer retired in 1951 to become a business executive. Active in conservative Republican politics, in his memoirs he openly condemned the Truman administration's failure to provide greater assistance to China. Wedemeyer died on 17 December 1989 in Fort Belvoir, Virginia.

Priscilla Roberts

See also
Chinese Civil War; Jiang Jieshi; Marshall, George Catlett; Truman, Harry S.

References
Cline, Ray S. *Washington Command Post: The Operations Division.* Washington, DC: Department of the Army, 1951.
Kirkpatrick, Charles E. *An Unknown Future and a Doubtful Present: Writing the Victory Plan of 1941.* Washington, DC: Center of Military History, U.S. Army, 1990.
Romanus, Charles F., and Riley Sunderland. *Time Runs Out in CBI.* Washington, DC: Department of the Army, 1959.
Stueck, William. *The Wedemeyer Mission: American Politics and Foreign Policy during the Cold War.* Athens: University of Georgia Press, 1984.
Wedemeyer, Albert C. *Wedemeyer Reports!* New York: Holt, 1958.

Weinberger, Caspar (1917–2006)

U.S. politician and secretary of defense (1981–1987). Born in San Francisco, California, on 18 August 1917, Caspar Willard Weinberger attended Harvard University, where he earned an AB degree in 1938 and a law degree in 1941. He served in the army during World War II, reaching the rank of captain. Following his discharge, he clerked for a federal judge and entered politics, winning election to the California State Assembly in 1952 and later serving as chairman of the California Republican Party.

After working in California Governor Ronald Reagan's cabinet in the late 1960s and early 1970s, Weinberger moved on to Washington, where he was director of the Federal Trade Commission (FTC) in 1970, deputy director during 1970–1972, and director during 1972–1973 of the Office of Management and Budget (OMB), and secretary of Health, Education and Welfare (HEW) during 1973–1975.

Weinberger served as an advisor to Reagan during the 1980 presidential campaign, and Reagan subsequently appointed him as secretary of defense in 1981. When Reagan nominated Weinberger, many conservative Republicans feared that given his reputation as a budget cutter, Weinberger would not support Reagan's calls for increased military spending. As director of the OMB, Weinberger had earned the nickname "Cap the Knife," and Jesse Helms, a right-wing Republican senator from North Carolina, voted against his confirmation based on those fears. However, Weinberger soon developed a reputation as one of the strongest proponents of Reagan's defense buildup.

Reagan and Weinberger identified several major goals, including nuclear arms reduction. But during Reagan's first term as president, his administration embarked upon a major buildup of nuclear weapons. Weinberger also pushed to deploy more nuclear warheads in Europe and supported Reagan's Strategic Defense Initiative (SDI) for the establishment of a

U.S. Secretary of Defense Caspar Weinberger, who directed an unprecedented peacetime buildup of U.S. military forces. (U.S. Department of Defense)

laser-guided defense system in outer space to destroy incoming ballistic missiles aimed at the United States. These and other measures were controversial and costly, but Reagan and Weinberger defended them as necessary to meet the Soviet threat. Weinberger resigned his post in November 1987, citing his wife's poor health.

In November 1992 a grand jury investigating the Iran-Contra Affair indicted Weinberger on four counts of lying to a congressional committee and the independent counsel's office and one count of obstruction of justice. During the mid-1980s the Reagan administration sold weapons to Iran in exchange for the freeing of American hostages being held in the Middle East. Some of the proceeds from the sale were illegally diverted to the Contra rebels who were fighting the communist Sandinista regime in Nicaragua. Once the story became public, Congress created a committee to investigate the affair, and an independent counsel was appointed to probe any criminal wrongdoing. Its office claimed that Weinberger had lied about his knowledge of the sale of arms to Iran. Weinberger declared his innocence and his intention

of fighting the charges, but the case never went to trial. On 24 December 1992, President George H. W. Bush issued a full and complete pardon to Weinberger and several other Reagan administration figures. Weinberger died in Bangor, Maine, on 26 March 2006.

Justin P. Coffey

See also
Bush, George Herbert Walker; Contras; Iran-Contra Affair; Nicaragua; Reagan, Ronald Wilson; Sandinistas; Strategic Defense Initiative
References
Cannon, Lou. *President Reagan: The Role of a Lifetime.* New York: Simon and Schuster, 1991.
Weinberger, Caspar W. *Fighting for Peace: Seven Critical Years in the Pentagon.* New York: Warner, 1990.
———. *In the Arena: A Memoir of the 20th Century.* Washington DC: Regnery, 1998.

Weizsäcker, Richard von (1920–)

Federal Republic of Germany (FRG, West Germany) politician, governing mayor of West Berlin (1981–1984), and president (1984–1994). Born on 15 April 1920 in Stuttgart, Richard von Weizsäcker served in the German Army on the Eastern Front during World War II and was wounded in the spring of 1945. Subsequently, he studied law and history, receiving his doctorate in law from Göttingen University in 1955.

Weizsäcker interrupted his studies in the late 1940s to serve as an assistant defense attorney during the Nuremberg Trials, where his father, Ernst von Weizsäcker, state secretary in the foreign ministry and ambassador to the Vatican during the Nazi regime, had been implicated. In 1950, the younger Weizsäcker joined the law division of a major corporation, becoming head of its economic division in 1957. During 1958–1966, he worked in the banking and chemical industries.

A member of the Christian Democratic Union (CDU) since 1954, Weizsäcker entered the Bundestag in October 1969 and served as deputy chairman of the CDU during 1973–1979. Since 1978, he had been opposition leader of the West Berlin CDU. He was elected governing mayor of West Berlin in May 1981, giving up his seat in the Bundestag. In February 1984, he resigned as mayor to run for the federal presidency. After being elected with more votes than any of his predecessors, he assumed the presidency on 1 July 1984, serving until June 1994. In October 1990 he automatically became president of the reunited Germany. As president, he was known for his integrity, high moral principles, and ability to compromise in order to reach consensus.

Bert Becker

See also
Germany, Federal Republic of

References

Nicholls, Anthony James. *The Bonn Republic: West German Democracy, 1945–1990.* London and New York: Longman, 1997.

O'Dochartaigh, Pól. *Germany since 1945.* Houndsmill, UK, and New York: Palgrave Macmillan, 2004.

Webb, Adrian. *Germany since 1945.* London and New York: Longman, 1998.

Weizsäcker, Richard von. *From Weimar to the Wall: My Life in German Politics.* Translated by Ruth Hein. New York: Broadway Books, 1999.

Welch, Robert Henry Winborne, Jr. (1899–1985)

Conservative American extremist and founder of the right-wing John Birch Society. Born in rural Chowan County, North Carolina, on 1 December 1899, Robert Welch graduated from the University of North Carolina in 1916, then attended the U.S. Naval Academy, Annapolis, during 1917–1919 and Harvard Law School during 1919–1921.

In 1922 Welch went to work as vice president of his brother's candy manufacturing company, retiring in 1956. He served on the board of directors of the National Association of Manufacturers (NAM). From this forum, he gravitated toward Republican Party politics. Through his work with NAM, he formed relationships with numerous conservative business leaders such as Texas oil magnate H. L. Hunt, the sponsor of radical right-wing groups and radio programming.

Deeply affected by the anticommunist crusade of Senator Joseph R. McCarthy and other hard-line conservatives, Welch developed a conspiratorial interpretation of U.S. politics and recent historical events. In December 1958, he and eleven other right-wing ideologues founded the John Birch Society, named after a U.S. intelligence operative executed by the Chinese communists in 1945. The society espoused the bizarre belief that the entire U.S. federal government, including President Dwight D. Eisenhower and numerous high officials such as Central Intelligence Agency (CIA) Director Allen W. Dulles and Supreme Court Chief Justice Earl Warren, were part of a vast communist conspiracy to subvert American ideals and surrender the nation to communism. Welch and his compatriots wielded considerable influence within conservative circles of the Republican Party, especially among the supporters of Arizona Senator Barry Goldwater, a fierce anticommunist and the party's 1964 presidential nominee.

Welch's John Birch Society reached its peak of influence in the early 1960s, when fears over *Sputnik 1*, the illusory missile gap, and the Cuban Missile Crisis held the nation in thrall. Welch's organization claimed between 60,000 and 100,000 members with $5 million in annual contributions during this period. The society closely guarded the anonymity of its members, behaving as secretively as the supposed conspirators it condemned. The 1960 publication of Welch's defamatory Eisenhower exposé, *The Politician,* which named the president as "a willing agent of the Soviet Union," forced a break between Birchites and most mainstream conservatives.

Welch's ideology proved a product of deeply held Cold War fears and McCarthy-era hysteria that resonated well beyond the 1950s. Welch died on 6 January 1985 in Winchester, Massachusetts. His organization survived him, focusing on the threat of "one world government," the growth of federal "socialist" powers, and alleged plans of the United Nations (UN) to take over U.S. society through the "treason" of establishment politicians.

Michael E. Donoghue

See also
Communist Fronts; Cuban Missile Crisis; Goldwater, Barry Morris; McCarthyism; Missile Gap; *Sputnik;* Walker, Edwin Anderson

References
Bennett, David H. *The Party of Fear: From Nativist Movements to the New Right in American History.* Chapel Hill: University of North Carolina Press, 1998.
Heale, M. J. *McCarthy's Americans: Red Scare Politics in State and Nation, 1935–1965.* Athens: University of Georgia Press, 1998.
Welch, Robert. *The Politician.* Belmont, MA: Self-published, 1960.

West Germany

See Germany, Federal Republic of

Western European Union (23 October 1954)

A defensive alliance formed by West European states in 1954 to establish a framework to make the controversial rearming of Germany more palatable. On 17 March 1948, the United Kingdom, France, and the Benelux countries (Belgium, the Netherlands, and Luxembourg) signed the Brussels Treaty (Treaty on Economic, Social and Cultural Collaboration and Collective Self-Defense), which created the European Union (EU). The formation of this alliance was a response to the extension of Soviet power in Central and Eastern Europe. In addition to pledging mutual support in response to an attack on any member and agreeing to integrate their air defenses and command structure, the signatories agreed to work toward European integration. The EU was superseded by the broader military alliance, the North Atlantic Treaty Organization (NATO), established in 1949.

When General Dwight D. Eisenhower was appointed NATO's first Supreme Allied Commander Europe (SACEUR) in late 1950, the members of EU merged their military organization into NATO. However, the EU continued to exist. When the Korean War broke out in June 1950, there was deep concern about the ability of the United States to fight a major war in Asia while simultaneously bearing the brunt of European defense. Thus, the rearmament of the Federal Republic of Germany (FRG, West Germany) was perceived as critical, but there were misgivings, especially in France. The French were naturally wary of a rearmed Germany on its eastern border, having been invaded from the east three times since 1870. When a proposal to integrate the West German forces into a European Defense Community was rejected by the French parliament in August 1954, British Foreign Minister Anthony Eden proposed including West Germany and Italy in the EU and changing its name to the Western European Union (WEU).

At a special conference in London in September 1954, the signatories to the Brussels Treaty and the United States and Canada agreed to invite West Germany and Italy to accede to the treaty. They did so on 23 October 1954, creating the WEU. West Germany thereby agreed to allow the WEU to exercise control over the size of its military. This concession on the part of the Germans and Britain's commitment to keep its forces in West Germany assuaged the French, who agreed to permit the entry of West Germany into NATO.

The eclipse of the WEU continued. NATO assumed its military role, the Organization for European Economic Cooperation (OEEC) replaced the EU's economic functions, and its social and cultural roles passed to the Council of Europe, which was initiated on 5 May 1949. Nevertheless, the WEU still existed and in fact played a role in the 1956 Saar settlement and continued to serve as a link between the European Economic Community (EEC) and the United Kingdom before Britain joined the European Community in 1973.

The moribund WEU was resurrected in 1984 in Rome to serve as a European counterpoint to NATO. It was viewed as a body in which European countries could consult and coordinate their responses to security issues. WEU members agreed that the foreign and defense ministers of the member states would meet twice annually to discuss the implications of ongoing crises. At a conference in The Hague in 1987, it was agreed that security issues were inseparable from the process of European integration. In effect, the WEU became the security component of the European Union (EU), which had developed from the European Community following the 1991 Treaty of Maastricht.

The WEU was expanded to include Portugal and Spain in 1990 and Greece in 1992. In 1992 Iceland, Norway, and Turkey became associate members of the WEU, and Denmark and Ireland became observers. In 1995 Austria, Finland, and Sweden became observers. In 1994 the category of associate partner was created for countries of Central and Eastern Europe that had signed the Europe Agreement with the EU. Bulgaria, the Czech Republic, Estonia, Hungary, Latvia, Lithuania, Poland, Romania, and Slovakia became associate partners in 1994, and Slovenia became an associate partner in 1996. In 1999 the Czech Republic, Hungary, and Poland became associate members.

Bernard Cook

See also
Brussels Treaty; European Defense Community; European Economic Community; European Integration Movement; European Union; North Atlantic Treaty Organization, Origins and Formation of; Organization for European Economic Cooperation

References
Cahen, Alfred. *The Western European Union and NATO: Building a European Defence Identity within the Context of Atlantic Solidarity.* London: Brassey's, 1989.
Eekelen, Willem von. *Debating European Security, 1948–1998.* Brussels, Belgium: Center for European Policy Studies, 1998.
Rees, G. Wyn. *The Western European Union at the Crossroads: Between Trans-Atlantic Solidarity and European Integration.* Boulder, CO: Westview, 1998.

Western Sahara

Northwest African region. Western Sahara covers 102,700 square miles and is bordered by Morocco to the north, Algeria to the northeast, Mauritania to the east and south, and the Atlantic Ocean to the west. Western Sahara's territory is contested, and its sovereignty remains in legal limbo. In 1945, it had an estimated population of 160,000 people. Mostly desert and sparsely populated but rich in phosphate resources, this part of Africa became a part of the Spanish Empire in 1884 and was known as the Spanish Sahara.

In the nineteenth-century European scramble for control of Africa, Spain took over the Western Sahara in 1884, primarily because of the proximity of the region to the Spanish Canary Islands and to match French claims of suzerainty in neighboring Morocco and Algeria. The Spanish and French agreed on the border between Morocco and the Spanish Sahara in negotiations conducted in 1900 and 1912. Spanish control was actually limited to coastal areas, as tribes in the interior continued to operate with considerable independence. After World War II, European empires collapsed, and decolonization swept much of the African continent. Northwest Africa was no exception, and Morocco became independent in 1956. There were also independence movements in adjacent areas, such as the bitter conflict for independence in French Algeria. The native Sahrawi of the Western Sahara began a struggle for independence before World War II that intensified in 1956.

The Spanish proved reluctant to commit the resources necessary to maintain control of the Spanish Sahara, and the

United States did not view this area as key to the larger Cold War conflict. Independent Morocco remained firmly in the Western camp, and American support for Spanish claims in the region was primarily verbal. Agitation for independence increased after the creation of the Polisario (Front for the Liberation of Saguía el Hamra and Río de Oro) in 1973. Although this was a movement rooted in communist ideology, that fact did not deter the United States from pressuring Spain to accept the recommendations by the United Nations (UN) in 1966 for a referendum to determine the future of the Spanish Sahara. Spain finally withdrew its forces in 1975 after agreements for a partition of the Spanish Sahara between Morocco and Mauritania.

Almost immediately thereafter, both Morocco and Mauritania sent troops to enforce control over their parts of the Western Sahara. The focus of Polisario then turned toward creation of a Western Sahara, independent of both Morocco and Mauritania. Both Morocco and Mauritania wanted access to the abundant phosphate deposits in the area, which were discovered in geological explorations beginning in 1949 and are among the world's largest.

In the 1970s, the issue of Western Sahara's sovereignty was relegated to the back burner of international relations, where it remains. Polisario continues to fight for independence. Mauritania has for the time being withdrawn from the conflict, but Morocco continues to press forward, as it has done since settling 350,000 Moroccans, backed by military force, in the area in 1976. The result of Moroccan policy has been the expulsion of as many as 165,000 Sahrawi natives, many of whom settled in Algeria. The UN has made repeated attempts to resolve the issue, as has the United States, but to no avail.

Daniel E. Spector

See also
Africa; Algeria; Decolonization; France; Morocco; Spain
References
Damis, John. *Conflict in Northwest Africa: The Western Sahara Dispute.* Stanford, CA: Hoover Institution Press, 1984.
Zoubir, Yahia H., and Daniel Volman, eds. *International Dimensions of the Western Sahara Conflict.* Westport, CT: Praeger, 1993.

Westmoreland, William Childs (1914–2005)

U.S. Army general, commander of U.S. forces in Vietnam (1964–1968), and U.S. Army chief of staff (1968–1972). Born in Spartanburg County, South Carolina, on 26 March 1914, William Westmoreland graduated from the U.S. Military Academy, West Point, in 1936. Commissioned a lieutenant of field artillery, he served with distinction in World War II and

the Korean War and was promoted to brigadier general in November 1952.

Promoted to major general in December 1956, Westmoreland commanded the 101st Airborne Division (1958–1960) at Fort Campbell, Kentucky. During 1960–1963, he was superintendent of the U.S. Military Academy, West Point. Promoted to lieutenant general, he returned to Fort Campbell to command the XVIII Airborne Corps in 1963. In June 1964 he was named commander of the U.S. Military Assistance Command, Vietnam (MACV), as a full general.

Westmoreland subsequently presided over the steep escalation of the Vietnam War and eventually commanded more than half a million American troops there. He embarked on an effort to seek out and engage communist forces, defeating them in a war of attrition. He had little interest in pacification programs. Westmoreland and planners in Washington never did understand the extent to which Democratic Republic of Vietnam (DRV, North Vietnam) leaders were prepared to sacrifice manpower to inflict American casualties and influence opinion in the United States. Casualty rates heavily unfavorable to the communists, taken as proof by Westmoreland that the war was being won, were nonetheless acceptable to Hanoi.

Westmoreland's overly optimistic predictions regarding the war in late 1967 helped feed public disillusionment in the United States following the heavy casualties of the January 1968 communist Tet Offensive, nonetheless lost by the communist side. Westmoreland interpreted the situation after the offensive as an opportunity and proposed the dispatch of additional troops to Vietnam. President Lyndon B. Johnson, although he sent some emergency reinforcements, denied Westmoreland's request.

In June 1968, Johnson recalled Westmoreland to Washington as chief of staff of the army. Westmoreland held that post until his retirement in July 1972, with much of his energies devoted to planning the transition to an all-volunteer force. Following retirement, he continued to speak out on the Vietnam War, published his memoirs, and ran unsuccessfully for governor of South Carolina. He remained a major and controversial figure in the postwar debate over U.S. involvement in Vietnam. Westmoreland died in Charleston, South Carolina, on 18 July 2005.

James H. Willbanks

See also
Johnson, Lyndon Baines; Tet Offensive; Vietnam
References
Furgurson, Ernest B. *Westmoreland: The Inevitable General.* Boston: Little, Brown, 1968.
Westmoreland, William C. *A Soldier Reports.* New York: Doubleday, 1976.
Zaffiri, Samuel. *Westmoreland: A Biography of General William C. Westmoreland.* New York: William Morrow, 1994.

Wheeler, Earle Gilmore (1908–1975)

U.S. Army general, chief of staff of the army during 1962–1964, and chairman of the Joint Chiefs of Staff (JCS) during 1964–1970. Born in Washington, D.C., on 13 January 1908, Earle Wheeler joined the National Guard at age sixteen and graduated from the U.S. Military Academy, West Point, in 1932. Commissioned in the infantry, during 1937–1938 he served in Tianjin, China. After training troops in World War II, from late 1944 he saw combat service in Europe as chief of staff of the 63rd Infantry Division.

From 1946 to 1949 Wheeler held various staff positions in France and Germany, and in November 1951, now a full colonel, he commanded the 351st Infantry in Trieste, Italy. From then until 1962, he alternated European and U.S. commands with Pentagon staff positions, being promoted to brigadier general in November 1952, major general in December 1955, lieutenant general in April 1960, and full general in March 1962.

In October 1962, President John F. Kennedy appointed Wheeler U.S. Army chief of staff. Almost immediately, his deft handling of racial confrontations at the University of Mississippi in Oxford impressed administration officials. In

General Earle G. Wheeler, chairman of the U.S. Joint Chiefs of Staff, 1964–1970. (U.S. Department of Defense)

July 1964, President Lyndon B. Johnson appointed Wheeler chairman of the JCS. He held this position for six years, a record that no subsequent incumbent has yet surpassed. Although he sought to enhance the bargaining power of the JCS by persuading all service heads to maintain a unanimous united front on military issues, in practice decision making often rested with Robert S. McNamara, the dominating secretary of defense.

The most controversial issue facing Wheeler was the Vietnam War, on which he consistently took a strongly hawkish line. He disliked the Johnson administration's gradual escalation of the war, an ad hoc strategy that Wheeler thought likely to prove ineffective, and unavailingly pressed political leaders to call up reserve forces to supply the manpower needed to meet American commitments in Vietnam and elsewhere. The JCS never, however, came out forthrightly to their civilian superiors to condemn the graduated response strategy and demand the application of overwhelming force against the enemy, an omission that subsequent historians have fiercely criticized. Nor did the JCS, including Wheeler, express their reservations over the Johnson administration's limited rather than full-scale air bombing campaigns.

Wheeler consistently endorsed commanding General William C. Westmoreland's requests for additional manpower. After the 1968 Tet Offensive, Wheeler urged Westmoreland to demand an additional 206,000 troops, a requirement that he apparently hoped would trigger the call-up of reserves but instead helped to precipitate the Johnson administration's March 1968 decision to open negotiations with a view to withdrawing American forces. Wheeler also supported President Richard M. Nixon's controversial 1969 decision to begin secret air strikes on communist sanctuaries in Cambodia.

After suffering several heart attacks, at least partly due to stress and frustration over Vietnam, Wheeler retired in July 1970. He died in Frederick, Maryland, on 18 December 1975. One significant legacy of his tenure as chairman of the JCS was that subsequent American military leaders came to believe that the United States should not intervene in military situations unless civilian officials were prepared to endorse the employment of forces sufficient to guarantee swift and overwhelming victory.

Priscilla Roberts

See also
Cambodia; Johnson, Lyndon Baines; Kennedy, John Fitzgerald; McNamara, Robert Strange; Nixon, Richard Milhous; Tet Offensive; Vietnam War; Westmoreland, William Childs

References
Buzzanco, Robert. *Masters of War: Military Dissent and Politics in the Vietnam Era.* Cambridge: Cambridge University Press, 1996.
Cole, Ronald H. *The Chairmanship of the Joint Chiefs of Staff, 1949–1999.* Washington, DC: Joint History Office, Office of the Chairman of the Joint Chiefs of Staff, 2000.

Korb, Lawrence J. *The Joint Chiefs of Staff: The First Twenty-Five Years.* Bloomington: Indiana University Press, 1976.

McMaster, H. R. *Dereliction of Duty: Lyndon Johnson, Robert McNamara, the Joint Chiefs of Staff, and the Lies That Led to Vietnam.* New York: HarperCollins, 1997.

Perry, Mark. *Four Stars.* Boston: Houghton Mifflin, 1989.

Webb, Willard J. *History of the Joint Chiefs of Staff: The Joint Chiefs of Staff and the War in Vietnam, 1969–1970.* Washington, DC: Joint History Office, Office of the Chairman of the Joint Chiefs of Staff, 2002.

Whisky on the Rocks Crisis (27 October 1981)

Grounding of a Soviet submarine on the Swedish coast that caused an international incident in October 1981. Throughout the 1980s, neutral Sweden was plagued by a series of Soviet submarine intrusions into its territorial waters. The most significant and public of these events was the grounding of a Soviet Whisky-class diesel-powered attack submarine inside a restricted zone located near the Swedish naval base at Karlskrona. The sub ran aground on the night of 27 October 1981 and was discovered by a Swedish fisherman as its crew was attempting unsuccessfully to extricate themselves.

When queried by astonished Swedish Navy officials, the Soviet captain declared that a "navigation error" brought the submarine to its resting place. Swedish signals intelligence, however, intercepted orders from a Soviet Kashin-class destroyer instructing the captain to concoct a cover story. Sweden formally complained to Soviet officials and asked them to apologize, pay for salvage costs, permit a Swedish salvage crew to do the job, and allow the submarine's captain to be interrogated. The Swedish ambassador to the Soviet Union was then confronted by a Soviet deputy foreign minister— and ten silent Soviet admirals behind him—who agreed to the first three demands but refused to allow the submarine captain to be questioned.

Meanwhile, a formidable Soviet naval task force assembled off the Swedish coast in international waters to intimidate the Swedish government. Six days passed. Then, a Swedish radiological survey team discovered that radiation was leaking from the Soviet sub's torpedo tube area. At that point, the Swedes concluded that the Whisky-class boat contained nuclear weapons. Sweden eventually permitted the submarine to depart after having taken full advantage of the crisis for propaganda purposes. It was later determined that the Whisky-class boat had been covertly observing classified Swedish torpedo trials off Karlskrona.

In 1982, unidentified submarine intrusions into Swedish territorial waters increased dramatically. It was assumed that they were of Soviet origin. Small submersibles, some using a tracked propulsion system, infiltrated Swedish minefields, and divers tampered with the mine suspension chains. On a number of occasions, Swedish antisubmarine forces dropped depth charges on suspected submarine contacts. The number of intrusions increased to sixty in 1983, finally tapering off to fifteen in 1986. The reasons behind this Soviet submarine activity are uncertain, although it is assumed that this was prompted by a combination of reconnaissance, intimidation, and training exercises.

Sean M. Maloney

See also
Soviet Union, Navy; Submarines; Sweden
References
Bynander, Fredrik. "Crisis Analogies: A Decision Making Analysis of the Swedish Hårsfjärden Submarine Incident of 1982." Research Report No. 29. Stockholm: Swedish Institute of International Affairs, 1997.
Leitenberg, Milton. *Soviet Submarine Intrusions in Swedish Waters, 1980–1986.* New York: Praeger, 1987.

White, Harry Dexter (1892–1948)

U.S. Treasury economist during 1934–1946 and executive director of the International Monetary Fund (IMF) during 1946–1947. Born in Boston, Massachusetts, on 9 October 1892, Harry Dexter White was the son of recent Jewish immigrants from Lithuania. After completing high school, he worked in the family hardware business, served in the U.S. Army as a first lieutenant in France during World War I, and then earned bachelor's and master's degrees from Columbia University and Stanford University and a doctorate from Harvard in 1930.

After some years of teaching, in 1934 White joined the U.S. Treasury as an economist, quickly winning the trust of Secretary Henry Morgenthau Jr., although the latter never shared White's enthusiasm for countercyclical Keynesian economic theories. In 1936 White helped to negotiate the Anglo-American currency stabilization agreement and a U.S. silver purchase accord with China. A staunch antifascist, by early 1939 he supported economic sanctions against Germany and hoped to entice the communist Soviet Union into an anti-Nazi coalition.

As Morgenthau's chief advisor during World War II, White supervised aid to Jiang Jieshi's Guomindang (GMD, Nationalist) government in China but by the war's end had concluded that the regime was too corrupt and ineffective to survive. Taking the lead in U.S. Treasury postwar planning, White helped to draft Morgenthau's abortive 1944 proposal to divide and de-industrialize Germany. White's major efforts, however, focused on creating a postwar international monetary system that would foster the revival of world trade and prevent future wars by precluding the competitive nationalist economic rivalries of the 1930s. Together with similar proposals put forward by the British economist John Maynard Keynes, White's plan for a United Nations (UN) stabilization fund and a bank for reconstruction to stimulate economic development and maintain stable international exchanges, which White drafted in 1942, laid the groundwork for the 1944 Bretton Woods Conference that established the International Monetary Fund (IMF) and the World Bank.

In early 1946, White became the IMF's first American executive director. Shortly before, Elizabeth Bentley, a former communist agent turned Federal Bureau of Investigation (FBI) informant, claimed that during the war White had passed on classified Treasury documents to Soviet agents, allegations that recently released Venona decrypts of intercepted wartime Soviet telegraphic communications appear to substantiate. In March 1947 White quietly resigned his IMF position. He testified on 13 August 1948 and denied that he had ever been either a communist or a Soviet agent after Bentley publicly told the House Un-American Activities Committee (HUAC) that White had been a Soviet operative, charges that renegade Soviet agent Whittaker Chambers repeated after White's death from a heart attack three days later, on 16 August 1948, while vacationing near Fitzwilliam, New Hampshire.

Priscilla Roberts

See also
Chambers, Whittaker; Espionage; Federal Bureau of Investigation; International Monetary Fund; Venona Project; World Bank

References
Blum, John Morton. *From the Morgenthau Diaries.* 3 vols. Boston: Houghton Mifflin, 1959–1967.
Craig, Bruce R. *Treasonable Doubt: The Harry Dexter White Spy Case.* Lawrence: University Press of Kansas, 2004.
Rees, David. *Harry Dexter White: A Study in Paradox.* New York: Coward, McCann and Geoghegan, 1973.
Van Dormael, Armand. *Bretton Woods: Birth of a Monetary System.* London: Macmillan, 1978.

White, Thomas Dresser (1902–1965)

U.S. Air Force general and chief of staff (1957–1961). Born in Walker, Minnesota, on 6 August 1902, Thomas White graduated from the United States Military Academy, West Point, in 1920. Before World War II, he served in the U.S. Army's infantry and aviation branches and in a series of attaché positions, among them duty posts in China (1927–1931), the Soviet Union (1934), Italy (1934–1937), and Brazil (1940–1942), where he was stationed when the United States entered World War II. During the war, White served in a series of senior staff positions and rose to become deputy commander of the Thirteenth Air Force and commander of the Seventh Air Force in the Pacific theater.

After the war, White first commanded the Fifth Air Force in Japan and then returned to the United States to work in several staff positions on the air force staff. In June 1953 he was named vice chief of staff and promoted to full general. In July 1957 he was elevated to chief of staff of the air force.

During his tenure at the top of the air force, White was a strong advocate of the primacy of strategic nuclear airpower and the development of modern weapons-delivery technologies. He was especially aggressive in pursuing intercontinental ballistic missile (ICBM) capabilities and military operations in space. He was responsible for inserting the term "aerospace" into air force doctrine and using the concept to claim a lead role for the air force in the military use of space. White retired in June 1961 and died in Washington, D.C., on 22 December 1965.

Jerome V. Martin

See also
Missiles, Intercontinental Ballistic; United States Air Force

References
Puryear, Edgar F., Jr. *Stars in Flight: A Study in Air Force Character and Leadership.* Novato, CA: Presidio, 1981.
Watson, George M., Jr. *Secretaries and Chiefs of Staff of the United States Air Force: Biographical Sketches and Portraits.* Washington, DC: U.S. Government Printing Office, 2001.

Whitlam, Edward Gough (1916–)

Australian Labour Party politician and prime minister (1972–1975). Born on 11 July 1916 at Kew, Victoria, Gough Whitlam was educated in the Canberra public schools. He graduated with a degree in arts and law from the University of Sydney in 1938 and served in the Royal Australian Air Force during 1941–1945, leaving the service as a flight lieutenant.

After the war, Whitlam returned to the University of Sydney to study law and was admitted to the bar in 1947. He joined the Labour Party in 1945 and entered politics in 1950 when he attempted but failed to win election to the New South Wales state parliament. In 1952 he won election to the national Parliament as a member from Werriwa, a seat he held for more than twenty years. In 1967 he became the head of the Labour Party.

Whitlam led his party to a resounding victory in 1972 and began a reform program based on his campaign platform. His ambitious program included abolishing conscription, withdrawing Australian troops from the Vietnam War, banning South African sports teams from participating in events in Australia, establishing diplomatic relations with the People's Republic of China (PRC), reforming state- and church-run schools, and negotiating aboriginal land rights. However, his reform agenda was crippled by rocketing oil prices and a stagnant economy.

Prime minister of Australia Edward Gough Whitlam, 1973. (Bettmann/Corbis)

Against a backdrop of rising unemployment and inflation, members of his party tried to secure $2 billion in overseas loans and then provided incomplete answers when this activity was discovered. The party was also handicapped by a sex scandal involving a senior Labour Party official. These events and the Australian Senate's blocking of the budget led to a showdown on 11 February 1975, when Whitlam refused to call a general election. Governor-General Sir John Kerr then dismissed the Whitlam government, and the ensuing election brought a new coalition government to power.

Following a second electoral defeat in 1977, Whitlam resigned as head of the Labour Party in 1978. During 1982–1986 he served as ambassador to the United Nations Educational, Scientific and Cultural Organization (UNESCO).

Herbert Merrick

See also
Australia
References
Patience, Allan, and Brian W. Head, eds. *From Whitlam to Fraser: Reform and Reaction in Australian Politics.* Melbourne: Oxford University Press, 1979.
Walter, James A. *The Leader: A Political Biography of Gough Whitlam.* Brisbane: University of Queensland Press, 1980.
Whitlam, Gough. *The Whitlam Government, 1972–1975.* New York: Viking, 1985.

Wilson, Charles Erwin (1890–1961)

U.S. secretary of defense (1953–1957) and president of General Motors (1941–1953). Born on 18 July 1890 in Minerva, Ohio, Charles Wilson earned an electrical engineering degree in 1909 from the Carnegie Institute of Technology. He began his business career at Westinghouse Electric Corporation, where he was involved in the engineering of military radio equipment during World War I. He joined General Motors in 1919 and eventually became its president in 1941. During World War II, he oversaw the company's massive production of military equipment.

President Dwight D. Eisenhower selected Wilson as secretary of defense in January 1953. Wilson's experience running a large corporation with significant dealings with the Department of Defense was viewed as an asset. During his nomination hearing, however, his business background led to controversy, including his initial refusal to sell his General Motors stock and a statement he made that was famously simplified to "What is good for General Motors is good for the country."

Wilson shared Eisenhower's goals of maintaining a strong defense while also reducing the defense budget and reorganizing the armed forces. This was reflected most clearly in the New Look military policy, which relied upon nuclear deterrent forces and strategic airpower in place of mass conventional forces. To implement this, Wilson gradually reduced the defense budget and shifted the defense emphasis to the U.S. Air Force, leading to tensions with the U.S. Army and the U.S. Navy. This policy transformation was most clearly seen in his 1956 decision to give the air force control over intermediate-range ballistic missiles (IRBMs) and intercontinental ballistic missiles (ICBMs) while sharply limiting the army's role in strategic missile forces.

Wilson resigned his post in October 1957 and returned to the private sector. He died in Norwood, Louisiana, on 26 September 1961.

Michael A. George

See also
Eisenhower, Dwight David; New Look Defense Policy; United States Air Force
References
Barklund, Carl W. *Men of the Pentagon.* New York: Praeger, 1966.
Geelhoed, E. Bruce. *Charles E. Wilson and Controversy at the Pentagon, 1953 to 1957.* Detroit. Ml: Wayne State University Press, 1979.
Leighton, Richard M. *History of the Office of the Secretary of Defense,* Vol. 3, *Strategy, Money, and the New Look, 1953–1956.* Washington, DC: Office of the Secretary of Defense, Historical Office, 2001.

Wilson, James Harold (1916–1995)

British Labour Party politician and prime minister (1964–1970, 1974–1976). Born into a family of modest means in Huddersfield, Yorkshire, on 11 March 1916, Harold Wilson attended Oxford University on scholarship, graduating in 1937. During World War II he worked in British economic ministries. He was elected to Parliament in the landslide Labour victory of July 1945. Briefly a junior minister, he was president of the Board of Trade during 1947–1951.

Wilson was loosely aligned with the left wing of the Labour Party, resigning from the government with the leading leftist figure, Aneurin Bevan, in protest over the rearmament budget of April 1951. Yet Wilson was pragmatic in his politics and never wholly a Bevanite. When Hugh Gaitskell succeeded Clement Attlee as Labour Party leader in December 1955, Wilson was appointed shadow (opposition) chancellor.

On the key issues that divided the party in the late 1950s—public ownership of industry and Britain's possession of the atomic bomb—Wilson was realistic although supportive of the nuclear deterrent and the North Atlantic Treaty Organization (NATO). In 1960 Wilson stood against Gaitskell for the party leadership. Wilson lost, but Gaitskell appointed him shadow foreign secretary in 1961. When Gaitskell died suddenly in January 1963, Wilson replaced him, taking his party to a slim majority in the election of October 1964.

Much of Wilson's first premiership (1964–1970) was devoted to managing a struggling economy. Wilson sought in vain to avoid a devaluation of the pound until it became inevitable in November 1967. The weakness of the pound and the need for American support may have been a factor in his lukewarm support of President Lyndon B. Johnson's Vietnam policies. Even if Wilson had wished to, however, he could offer little more than that because his party was deeply opposed to the war. Despite Johnson's pressure, Wilson refused to send British troops to Vietnam. Indeed, he tried to broker a solution to the conflict by proposing a 1965 Commonwealth peace mission. He also tried to arrange a ceasefire through Soviet leader Alexei Kosygin, with whom he met in 1966 and 1967.

Economic weakness prompted a new defense policy in July 1967, which proclaimed Britain's intention of withdrawing its forces from east of the Suez, a policy shift not welcomed by the United States. Wilson also faced an intractable problem in southern Rhodesia, where the white minority government under Ian Smith had declared the country independent of the United Kingdom. White minority rule was unacceptable to Wilson, but using force as a solution was ruled out, leaving only ineffective economic sanctions. Wilson met with Smith on two occasions (in December 1966 and

October 1968) to negotiate a settlement, but the gap between the sides was too great, and the problem remained unresolved. In October 1966 Wilson launched a second application to join the European Community. He and Foreign Secretary George Brown pressed their case with key European leaders in early 1967. Nevertheless, French President Charles de Gaulle, who had vetoed an earlier application in 1963, did so again in November 1967.

Although Labour lost the 1970 election, Wilson returned as prime minister in February 1974. While struggling with serious economic problems and the fallout from the 1973–1974 oil price shock, Wilson renegotiated the terms on which Britain had entered the European Community in 1973 and held a referendum in June 1975 on the outcome. Wilson unexpectedly resigned his post in March 1976. He later took a seat in the House of Lords as Lord Wilson of Rievaulx. Wilson died on 25 May 1995 in London.

Paul Wingrove

See also
Attlee, Clement Richard, 1st Earl; Gaitskell, Hugh; Smith, Ian Douglas; United Kingdom
References
Donoughue, Bernard. *Downing Street Diary: With Harold Wilson in No. 10.* London: Jonathan Cape, 2005.
Pimlott, Ben. *Harold Wilson.* London: HarperCollins, 1993.
Wilson, Harold. *Final Term: The Labour Government, 1974–1976.* London: Weidenfeld and Nicolson, 1979.
———. *The Labour Government, 1964–1970: A Personal Record.* London: Weidenfeld and Nicolson, 1971.
———. *Memoirs: The Making of a Prime Minister.* London: Weidenfeld and Nicolson, 1986.
Ziegler, Philip. *Wilson: The Authorized Life of Lord Wilson of Rievaulx.* London: Weidenfeld and Nicolson, 1993.

Wolf, Markus (1923–2006)

Head of German Democratic Republic (GDR, East Germany) intelligence. Born in Hechingen, Germany, on 19 January 1923, the son of communist writer and doctor Friedrich Wolf, Markus Wolf fled with his family to Moscow when Adolf Hitler came to power in 1933. Wolf eventually joined the Communist International (Comintern) and was trained as an operative. He became a member of Walter Ulbricht's group while in exile and was sent back to Berlin in 1945. Throughout the Cold War, Wolf was known as "the man without a face" because no reliable pictures of him existed.

Wolf initially worked as a journalist, but in 1953 he became one of the founding members of the new foreign intelligence service within the East German Ministry of State Security (Stasi) headed by Erich Mielke. Among Wolf's tasks was organizing teams of so-called Romeo spies (also referred to as "swallows") who seduced their targets to obtain information.

His agents successfully penetrated the office of Federal Republic of Germany (FRG, West Germany) Chancellor Willy Brandt in the early 1970s, causing an international scandal, and Wolf gained an international reputation as a spymaster. He retired in 1986 and gained a different sort of notoriety as a prominent supporter of Soviet leader Mikhail Gorbachev's policies of glasnost and perestroika.

When the East German state collapsed in 1989, Wolf was one of the first targets of scrutiny. Although he claims that the U.S. Central Intelligence Agency (CIA) offered him sanctuary, he remained in Berlin. He was subsequently arrested on charges of treason after the reunification of Germany and was tried and sentenced to six years in prison. That conviction was overturned, but he was later tried and convicted on charges of kidnapping East German citizens during the Cold War and received a two-year suspended sentence. He testified in several court cases about his activities and written several books, but he remains unapologetic. Wolf died in Berlin on 9 November 2006.

Timothy C. Dowling

See also
Brandt, Willy; Glasnost; Gorbachev, Mikhail; Guillaume, Günter; Mielke, Erich; Perestroika; Stasi; Ulbricht, Walter

References
Colitt, Leslie. *Spymaster: The Real-Life Karla, His Moles, and the East German Secret Police.* Reading, MA: Addison-Wesley, 1995.

Dennis, Mike. *The Stasi: Myth and Reality.* London: Pearson-Longman, 2003.

Reichenbach, Alexander. *Chef der Spione: Die Markus-Wolf-Story* [Chief of the Spies: The Markus Wolf Story]. Stuttgart: Deutsche Verlags-Anstalt.

Wolf, Markus. *Man without a Face: The Autobiography of Communism's Greatest Spymaster.* New York: Times Books, 1995.

———. *Spionagechef im geheim Krieg* [Espionage Chief in the Secret War]. Munich: List, 1997.

Woodstock (14–16 August 1969)

Outdoor music festival held near Woodstock, New York, on 14–16 August 1969. Billed in advance as the greatest rock concert ever, the event was perhaps the high point of the countercultural movement of the 1960s.

Neither the concert organizers nor the government officials of this small upstate New York community were prepared for the number of people who gathered for the three-day concert. Called together for a musical celebration of peace and love, the watchwords of the counterculture, individuals and groups of all descriptions poured into Woodstock from all over the United States. As the song later written by Joni Mitchell to commemorate the event suggested, most of the participants thought of themselves as coming together with other young people who were "stardust" and "golden." Observers from

John Sebastian, formerly of The Lovin' Spoonful, performs at the free Woodstock Music and Art Fair in August 1969. Perhaps 450,000 people attended the three-day affair, which is remembered as an important symbol of the liberal spirit of the 1960s. (Henry Diltz/Corbis)

outside the counterculture, however, formed an entirely different impression.

The 500,000 people who showed up for the concert quickly overwhelmed the supply of food, the provisions for sanitation, and various other health services. There was no apparent shortage of drugs or alcohol, however. Planned as a camping event, a torrential rainstorm turned the occupied 600-acre area into a huge sea of mud. In spite of these and other inconveniences, including a 20-mile-long traffic jam, the gathering ended without violence and was a huge success in the minds of most participants.

Press coverage focusing on the nudity, drug consumption, and casual sex enjoyed by many participants who often overlooked the real reason for the gathering: the music. There were well over thirty bands at Woodstock that managed to play in spite of enormous technical difficulties. The concert brought together folk, rock and roll, blues, and uncategorized musicians from the western, eastern, and southern United States as well as many groups from England. Several performers were well known when they arrived, while for others, Woodstock launched their careers. Musicians delighted their followers and made many new fans. Among the well-known musicians were Joan Baez; Sly and the Family Stone; Jefferson Airplane; the Who; the Grateful Dead; Blood, Sweat and Tears; Crosby, Stills, Nash, and Young; Santana; Jimi Hendrix; Janis Joplin; Country Joe and the Fish; and the Paul Butterfield Blues Band.

With such a diversity of artists present, the musicians coalesced into something much closer to a movement than had been the case among disorganized countercultural elements before Woodstock. A similar phenomenon occurred with most of the crowd as well. Yet in many ways, Woodstock was the last innocent celebration of the counterculture. Not long after the event, the ravages of the drug culture became more obvious with the deaths of Hendrix and Joplin (among others), who had turned in two of Woodstock's most memorable performances. At the same time, Woodstock's very success alerted recording companies and other business ventures to the massive market potential of the counterculture, whose messages of peace and love were gradually diluted by commercialization.

Spencer C. Tucker

See also

Music

References

Curry, Jack. *Woodstock: The Summer of Our Lives.* New York: Grove, 1989.

Francese, Carl, and Richard S. Sorrell. *From Tupelo to Woodstock: Youth, Race, and Rock-and-Roll in America, 1954–1969.* 2nd ed., rev. Dubuque, Iowa: Kendall Hunt, 2001.

Spitz, Bob, and Robert S. Spitz. *The Creation of the Woodstock Music Festival, 1969.* New York: Viking, 1979.

World Bank

An organization of the United Nations (UN), the aim of which is to spur economic growth and curb poverty in the developing world by providing loans, policy advice, and technical assistance. The International Bank for Reconstruction and Development (IBRD), or World Bank as it is more commonly known, came into existence in 1945. Its charter was drafted at the 1944 Bretton Woods Conference. As of 2007, 185 countries were World Bank members. Membership in the World Bank requires prior membership in the International Monetary Fund (IMF).

In July 1944, the UN convened a conference in Bretton Woods, New Hampshire, to discuss economic cooperation after the war. Concerns over monetary stability were most pressing, and thus the IMF was established at the conference. Postwar reconstruction and economic development issues were also addressed, which gave birth to the World Bank. In

December 1945, the first members signed its charter, and in 1946 the organization began its lending operations with a loan of $250 million for French postwar reconstruction. After the initial postwar reconstruction period in Europe, the second task of the World Bank, economic development, became most prominent. The World Bank used its status as a first-class debtor to pass on low-interest loan rates on funds raised on international capital markets to project countries. Among these nations were newly independent states in Africa and Asia.

Among the first World Bank signatories were Poland and Czechoslovakia. In 1950, however, the Soviets forced them to withdraw, as they considered the World Bank an instrument of U.S. economic imperialism. Since then, World Bank members have consisted largely of nations with market-oriented economies. Japan and the Federal Republic of Germany (FRG, West Germany) became members in 1952 and later were among the biggest donors of soft loans. The World Bank Charter specifically prohibits the body from interfering in the political affairs of states receiving World Bank aid and holds that only economic considerations will be used to determine need. Nevertheless, because the seat of Bretton Woods institutions (the World Bank and the IMF) was in Washington, D.C., and the World Bank maintained close relations with American-based banking institutions, politics did come into play over the years. The United States has remained the most influential World Bank member, and the president of the World Bank has always been an American.

Because the establishment of credibility in capital markets was based on World Bank recipient nations' ability to repay loans, in the first fifteen years of its existence the body focused on lending not to the poorest countries, which posed too high a risk of default, but rather to middle- or upper-middle-income countries, such as those in Latin America. This policy, however, did little to alleviate poverty. It also became problematic in terms of Cold War geopolitics. Poverty presented itself as a powerful precondition for successful communist or nationalist movements throughout the developing world. In recognition of this, in 1960 the International Development Association (IDA) was created as part of the World Bank. The aim of the IDA was to make concessional loans to the world's poorest nations, funded by contributions of member states. The two largest contributors were the United States and Japan.

During 1962–1968, under the leadership of President George Woods, the World Bank broadened its conception of economic development, which had been formerly restricted to large high-tech projects such as highways or power plants. Because earnings from these initial projects allowed increased funding, the World Bank's new lending policy included longer repayment periods, involved technical and direct assistance, and provided loans for agricultural purposes, which became a major focus of World Bank priorities.

Delegates from forty-four nations gather for a group photograph outside the Mount Washington Hotel at Bretton Woods, where a conference occurred in July 1944 to discuss programs of economic cooperation and progress after World War II. (Bettmann/Corbis)

During 1968–1981, Robert McNamara, a former Ford Motor Company chief executive officer (CEO) and secretary of defense under Presidents John F. Kennedy and Lyndon B. Johnson, served as the World Bank's president and profoundly changed the institution. During McNamara's tenure, the World Bank became involved foremost in poverty mitigation programs and increased its lending operations from $1 billion in 1968 to more than $12 billion in 1981. He also had to cope with the 1971 breakdown of the international monetary system designed at Bretton Woods, the oil price shocks of 1973–1974 and 1979–1980, and the developing world debt crisis. The first oil price shock led to the emergence of the so-called petrodollar market of Organization of Petroleum Exporting Companies (OPEC) countries. Some of these funds were borrowed by the World Bank to finance development projects, especially rural development projects in Africa. Unfortunately, the expansion of lending did not always contribute to the reduction of poverty but, on the contrary, locked many states into a vicious cycle of higher

and higher debt with no ability to pay the debt or accruing interest.

Because the World Bank raises its funds from international capital markets, it is largely independent of interventions by member governments. During the 1960s and early 1970s particularly, the World Bank witnessed active intervention by the United States to prevent lending to the Democratic Republic of Vietnam (DRV, North Vietnam) and other U.S. adversaries. This obviously politicized the World Bank. Due to successful World Bank–sponsored development projects in East Asia and Latin America, the 1980s witnessed the emergence of a consensus view of economic development based on free markets. World perception of the East Asian miracle in nations such as the Republic of Korea (ROK, South Korea), Taiwan, and Singapore was largely based on a seminal book published by the World Bank in 1993. The end of the Cold War brought a host of nations clamoring to join the World Bank, many of them in former communist bloc areas. Today, the World Bank focuses on creating sustainable economic growth by combating corruption in recipient nations and by ameliorating the situation of the poorest, most heavily indebted countries with poor growth records.

Bernhard Johannes Seliger

See also

International Monetary Fund; Organization of Petroleum Exporting Countries

References

Kapur, Devesh, John P. Lewis, and Richard Webb, eds. *The World Bank: Its First Half Century.* Washington, DC: Brookings Institution Press, 1997.

Kraske, Jochen, with William H. Becker, William Diamond, and Louis Galambos. *Bankers with a Mission: The Presidents of the World Bank, 1946–91.* New York: Oxford University Press for the World Bank, 1996.

Salda, Anne C. M. *Historical Dictionary of the World Bank.* Lanham, MD: Scarecrow, 1997.

Staples, Amy L. S. *The Birth of Development: How the World Bank, Food and Agriculture Organization, and World Health Organization Have Changed the World, 1945–1965.* Kent, OH: Ken State University Press, 2005.

World Bank. *The East Asian Miracle, Economic Growth and Public Policy.* Oxford: Oxford University Press, 1993.

World Council of Churches

Ecumenical, religious organization dedicated to world peace and the preservation of human rights. As early as 1937, religious leaders had agreed to establish a World Council of Churches (WCC), but World War II delayed the founding of the organization until August 1948, when representatives of 147 churches assembled in Amsterdam to create the WCC. Today, the WCC consists of 342 member churches in 120 countries. The WCC is the institutional expression of the modern ecumenical movement, the goal of which is to achieve Christian unity. WCC-affiliated churches are mainly Protestant (Lutheran, Reformed, Methodist, Baptist), Anglican, and Orthodox churches. The Roman Catholic Church is the only major Christian church that does not belong to the WCC.

The Cold War decided the political framework of the WCC from its start in 1948, when U.S. Secretary of State John Foster Dulles and Czechoslovak theologian Josef Hromádka argued about whether the churches should combat communism or champion such socialist ideals as class justice and equality. The WCC's first secretary-general, Willem Visser 't Hooft, partly settled the issue by advocating that the churches promote reconciliation rather than competition between East and West.

This stance changed, however, after the Third Assembly in New Delhi in 1961, when churches from former colonies in Africa and Asia and Orthodox churches from the Soviet Union and Eastern Europe entered the WCC. These over-

whelmed the older member churches and influenced WCC policy in a more anti-West direction. Philip Potter from Dominica, as secretary-general after 1964, was a voice of the former colonies. Western churches now saw themselves confronted with the indignation of developing-world and Eastern churches. Consequently, the WCC adopted the Program to Combat Racism, which proved a valuable contribution to the struggle against South Africa's apartheid government. The WCC also came to the defense of human rights in Latin America during the 1960s–1980s.

In 1975 the WCC Assembly faced a short period of Western criticism over human rights violations in Eastern Europe. However, Orthodox church officials—some of them Komitet Gosudarstvennoi Bezopasnosti (KGB) or Stasi informers—progressive Western officials, and church deputies from Africa and Asia soon stanched this criticism and concentrated on anticolonialist, antiracist, and peace programs. In Boston in 1979 the WCC announced a program to combat militarism that inspired many peace organizations throughout the world, such as Aktion Sühnezeichen in Germany and Pax Christi International.

In 1983 in Vancouver, the WCC sought to combine peace, social justice, and environmentalism into one large conciliar process. This policy bore fruit, particularly in North America, the Netherlands, and the two Germanies. In the West, it tied many loose church groups together. In East Germany it went further, stimulating protest against the regime from within the churches. The conclusion of the conciliar process took place in Seoul in 1990.

By that time, the world had changed significantly. The Cold War had all but ended, and politically driven WCC discussions had receded in importance. The WCC then had to cope with the accusations of East European dissidents and oppressed churches who believed that the WCC had not adequately defended them. Council officials were also confronted with revelations about their spying activities on behalf of communist regimes. Because of these scandals and the WCC's alleged pro-Soviet inclination, the organization lost a great deal of credibility. At the same time, Orthodox churches criticized the WCC because of its progressive positions concerning the ordination of women or the acceptance of homosexuality.

Beatrice de Graaf

See also

Anticolonialism; Human Rights

References

Bent, Ans J. van der. *Christian Response in a World of Crisis: A Brief History of the WCC's Commission of the Churches on International Affairs.* Geneva: World Council of Churches, 1986.

Besier, G., A. Boyens, and G. Lindemann. *Nationaler Protestantismus und Ökumenische Bewegung: Kirchliches Handeln im Kalten Krieg (1945–1990)* [National Protestantism and the Ecumenical Movement: Church Activism during the Cold War]. Berlin: Duncker and Humblot, 1999.

World Peace Council

Organization formally established in 1949 ostensibly to promote world peace but actually a front organization of the Soviet Union's Information Bureau of the Communist and Workers' Parties (known in the West as the Cominform). The origins of the World Peace Council (WPC), sometimes known as the World Council of Peace, are rather murky, befitting a communist front organization. Some sources trace its beginning to Poland in 1948, but 1949 is the year in which the WPC began its activities on a significant level. For the entire Cold War, the WPC was strategically located in Helsinki. Publicly, the WPC had a beneficent and worthy goal of promoting peaceful coexistence and nuclear disarmament.

Almost immediately, however, Western nations, particularly the United States, accused the WPC of having ulterior motives—that is, the advancement of Soviet foreign policy goals, disinformation, and propaganda and the infiltration of various Western peace movements. In 1950, Washington openly accused the WPC of being a front organization of the Communist Party of the Soviet Union (CPSU). The U.S. Central Intelligence Agency (CIA) allegedly had evidence that the WPC was being funded by communist bloc nations. This was proven true in 1989 when the WPC admitted to having received 90 percent of its funding from the Soviet Union. At its height in the early 1960s, the WPC may have received more than $50 million a year from Moscow. In an attempt to hide Soviet involvement, money earmarked for the WPC was heavily laundered to make it difficult to trace the source of the funding.

In 1951, the WPC was expelled from France for its fifth-column activities. Some evidence exists that the WPC helped circulate stories in 1952 about the American use of biological weapons in the Korean War, a completely bogus accusation. The WPC worked independently but also played a role in other presumably legitimate peace organizations, mainly through infiltration and co-option. One of its tenets was aggressive insistence on nuclear disarmament, and unilateral Western nuclear disarmament became one of its favorite causes. Tellingly, British philosopher and peace activist Bertrand Russell, who had spurred on the Campaign for Nuclear Disarmament (CND), denounced the WPC in 1958 (the year the CND was born) for having failed to condemn the 1956 Soviet intervention in the Hungarian Revolution.

In spite of its dubious parentage and financing, the WPC attracted many adherents. Quick to condemn U.S. foreign and military policy, the WPC organized anti–Vietnam War protests in several West European nations. The WPC was especially active in Australia, where it orchestrated massive antiwar rallies in the 1960s. At the same time, the WPC remained silent during the 1968 Soviet invasion of Czechoslovakia. The WPC lost some of its luster in the late 1960s, therefore, as the New Left came to distrust Soviet communism. Another blow to the organization came in 1966 when the People's Republic of China (PRC) withdrew from the WPC, citing the growing Sino-Soviet split.

Despite the doubts of many, the WPC continued its work and was no doubt active in the nuclear disarmament movement of the 1980s. The WPC is still in existence today, but it has been badly discredited. The end of the Cold War took away much of its mission.

Paul G. Pierpaoli Jr.

See also
Communist Fronts; Peace Movements; Russell, Bertrand; Vietnam War Protests

References
Carter, April. *Peace Movements: International Protests and World Politics since 1945.* London: Longman, 1992.

Hollander, Paul. *Political Pilgrims: Travels of Western Intellectuals to the Soviet Union, China, and Cuba, 1928–1978.* Oxford: Oxford University Press, 1981.

Sworakowski, Witold, ed. *World Communism: A Handbook, 1918–1965.* Stanford, CA: Hoover Institution Press, 1973.

World War II, Allied Conferences

During World War I (1914–1918), the Entente powers were notably unsuccessful in coordinating their strategic goals and war aims. It was not until Italy's catastrophic failure at Caporetto in November 1917 that a Supreme War Council was established, and it was a similar near-disaster on the Western Front in April 1918 that finally persuaded the British, French, and Americans to name a single Allied commander in chief. This disunity persisted into the postwar period, hindering the Versailles Treaty negotiations in 1919 and helping to prevent the establishment of a lasting peace structure.

Given such abysmal precedents, it is not surprising that British Prime Minister Winston Churchill and U.S. President Franklin D. Roosevelt placed great emphasis on maintaining a smooth working relationship among the Allied powers during World War II. This complex relationship was hammered out in a series of conferences held throughout the war, several involving direct dialogues among the various heads of government. For Churchill and Roosevelt, who prided themselves on their ability to finesse negotiations through charisma, such meetings provided a perfect medium for deal making.

The conference system produced a remarkable degree of harmony between the British and Americans. While relations with Soviet leader Josef Stalin, the third principal in the Allied triumvirate, were never so straightforward, it was at least

British Prime Minister Winston Churchill (*left*), U.S. President Franklin D. Roosevelt (*center*), and Soviet leader Josef Stalin (*right*) at the Yalta Conference. The "Big Three" met in Yalta, Crimea (in what is now the Ukraine), on 4–11 February 1945 to discuss military and political strategies for ending World War II. (Library of Congress)

possible to keep the Soviet Union committed to the fight against the Axis powers. The conferences also established workable, if far from ideal, settlements of postwar issues.

When Churchill and Roosevelt first met at Placentia Bay, Newfoundland, in August 1941, there were technically no Allied powers because there was no alliance of which to speak. The United States was still (nominally) neutral, and while the Soviet Union was engaged in a bitter fight with German forces, it was doing so neither with support from nor in coordination with the West. The Newfoundland conference was therefore more symbolic than substantive, although it did produce a powerful statement of democratic principles in the form of the Atlantic Charter. Perhaps more significantly, it led the way for the so-called Three-Power Conference in Moscow (29 September–1 October 1941), at which Churchill and Roosevelt's representatives, Lord Beaverbrook and W. Averell

Harriman, agreed to extend American Lend-Lease support to the Soviets.

After the United States entered the war in December 1941, these tentative contacts were supplanted by full-fledged diplomatic commitments. Churchill traveled to Washington in the immediate wake of the Pearl Harbor attack, and at the resulting Anglo-American conference (code name ARCADIA) during 22 December 1941–14 January 1942, the two nations negotiated the mechanisms through which they would fight the remainder of World War II together, including the Combined Chiefs of Staff Committee and joint boards to coordinate shipping, raw material usage, and industrial production. In May 1942 the two Western powers drew the Soviets closer to the new alliance system—known since January as the United Nations (UN)—via an Anglo-Soviet Treaty (26 May 1942) and a meeting between Roosevelt and Soviet Foreign

Minister Vyacheslav Molotov on 29 May 1942. These somewhat tentative steps helped reduce mutual suspicions between the liberal-capitalist and communist powers.

It should be noted, however, that the American-British relationship was not without tension. At the Second Washington Conference in June 1942, it became clear that American and British leaders had very different ideas about the conduct of the war. Although the Germany First strategy went largely unquestioned, the Americans' eagerness to launch a full-scale invasion of the European mainland as soon as possible clashed with the more cautious British proposal to restrict activities to the periphery until the Axis had been sufficiently worn down. At this stage in the war, the British view tended to predominate, as much for practical reasons as for the cogency of its appeal: the two allies simply lacked the means to launch anything more than secondary operations. It remained vital to keep the Soviets in the fight, however, hence Churchill's August 1943 visit to Moscow, an uncomfortable meeting in which the British leader had to inform Stalin that a second European front remained, for the time being, an impossibility.

The successful Allied invasion of French North Africa in November 1942 was followed by the Casablanca Conference (14–24 January 1943) at which a more confident Roosevelt declared for the first time the Allied policy of unconditional surrender. He and Churchill also approved the round-the-clock strategic bombing campaign against Germany. At a follow-up conference four months later in Washington, D.C. (11–25 May 1943), the Americans agreed to delay a cross-channel attack for another year, but they extracted from the still-skeptical British a deadline for such action of 1 May 1944. The details of this future offensive were elaborated at the first conference between the Western Allies in Quebec in August 1943, at which the top secret plans for the Manhattan Project—the atomic bomb program—were also thrashed out. By mid-1943, with the German assault on the Eastern Front finally blunted at Kursk and with Italy on the verge of collapse after the invasion of Sicily, the main issue for the alliance was not so much the defeat of the Axis but rather how and when that defeat would come.

There remained, nonetheless, great concern about the West's relationship with the Soviet Union. Might Stalin negotiate a separate peace with Germany? And what of the future map of Europe after an Allied victory? Such concerns were central to the four-power Moscow Conference (19 October–1 November 1943), at which representatives of the Big Three powers and Nationalist-controlled China ratified the unconditional surrender doctrine and agreed to the establishment of a postwar organization for global security. To solidify the still-shaky Allied relationship, Churchill and Roosevelt also suggested a personal meeting with Stalin. At the preparatory Anglo-American talks in Cairo in November 1943, Churchill

believed that he had persuaded his American colleague to take a less emphatic line on the timing of the Normandy landings. To his considerable dismay, however, Roosevelt ignored his concession in face-to-face discussions with Stalin at the Tehran Conference (28 November–1 December 1943), where he enthusiastically embraced the cross-channel invasion, Operation OVERLORD. Tehran marked the fulcrum point at which American diplomatic efforts shifted decisively toward a bilateral relationship with the Soviet Union, thereby marginalizing its weaker British ally.

By 1944, conference proceedings were dominated by the shaping of the postwar world. At Bretton Woods (1 July–15 July 1944) and Dumbarton Oaks (21–29 August 1944), the Allies drafted constitutions for the International Monetary Fund (IMF) and the UN, centerpieces of the new postwar financial and political order. Such bold declarations of idealistic principle contrasted with the rather murkier realpolitik conducted at the same time behind closed doors. At the Second Quebec Conference in September 1944, Churchill attempted, without much success, to shift the focus of the Pacific war toward the reconstitution of the British Empire in Southeast Asia. While in Moscow the following month, he made the notorious percentages agreement with Stalin that divided Eastern Europe and the Balkans into western and eastern spheres of influence. This spirit of cynicism or, from another point of view, sober realism pervaded the last meeting among Roosevelt, Stalin, and Churchill at Yalta (4 February–11 February 1945), at which the de facto division of Europe was confirmed and a number of Russo-American agreements on the future shape of East Asia were drawn up without regard for the British or Chinese.

The Allied conference era was rapidly concluding. The war against Germany was in its closing days when the delegates of the new UN met in San Francisco in April 1945 for their inaugural session. A month later President Harry S. Truman traveled to the ruins of Hitler's defeated Reich to meet Churchill, his soon-to-be replacement Clement Attlee, and Stalin at Potsdam from 17 July–2 August 1945. At Potsdam, the three partners delivered to Japan a final ultimatum for surrender and attempted to settle the disputed future of Poland, but despite the glow of certain victory, it was evident that an alliance born of expedience could not survive in the postwar environment. Potsdam marked the effective end of wartime comradeship between East and West and the beginning of forty years of Cold War.

Alan Allport

See also

Allied Control Council of Germany; Churchill, Winston; Declaration on Liberated Europe; International Monetary Fund; Lend-Lease; Roosevelt, Franklin Delano; Soviet Union; Stalin, Josef; Territorial Changes after World War II; Truman, Harry S.; United Kingdom; United Nations; United States

References

Edmonds, Robin. *The Big Three: Churchill, Roosevelt and Stalin in Peace and War.* New York: Norton, 1991.

Gardner, Lloyd C. *Spheres of Influence: The Great Powers Partition Europe, from Munich to Yalta.* Chicago: Ivan R. Dee, 1993.

Smith, Gaddis. *American Diplomacy during the Second World War, 1941–1945.* New York: Knopf, 1985.

Woods, Randall B. *A Changing of the Guard: Anglo-American Relations, 1941–1946.* Chapel Hill: University of North Carolina Press, 1990.

World War II, Legacy of

By virtually any measurement, World War II was the most devastating conflict in human history. All the world was touched by it to some degree. The war's economic and financial cost alone has been calculated at perhaps five times that of World War I. In human terms, World War II claimed half again as many military lives: 15 million versus 10 million for World War I. Total deaths from World War II, including civilians, came to 41–49 million people, a figure that would have been much higher without new sulfa and penicillin drugs and blood plasma transfusions.

When the war finally ended, vast stretches of Europe and parts of Asia lay in ruins. Whole populations were utterly exhausted, and many people were starving and living in makeshift shelters. Millions more had been uprooted from their homes and displaced. Many of them had been transported to Nazi Germany to work as slave laborers in German industry and agriculture. Transportation—especially in parts of Western and Central Europe and in Japan—was at a standstill. Bridges were blown, rail lines destroyed, and highways cratered and blocked. Ports, especially in Northwestern Europe and Japan, were especially hard-hit, and many would have to be rebuilt. Most of the large cities of Germany and Japan were piles of rubble and their buildings mere shells.

Some countries had fared reasonably well, however. Damage in Britain was not too extensive, and civilian deaths were relatively slight. Denmark and Norway escaped with little destruction. The rapid Allied advance had largely spared Belgium, although the port of Antwerp had been badly damaged. The Netherlands, however, sustained considerable destruction, and portions of the population were starving. The situation in Greece was also dire, and Poland suffered horribly from the brutal German and Soviet occupation policies and from armies sweeping back and forth across its territory.

Among major powers, the Soviet Union was the hardest hit. Its 27 million dead in the war dramatically affect national demographics to the present day. In 1959, Moscow announced that the ratio of males to females in the Soviet Union was 45 to 55. Aside from the catastrophic human costs, the Germans had occupied its most productive regions, and the scorched-earth policy practiced by both the Soviets and the Germans resulted in the total or partial destruction of 1,700 towns, 70,000 villages, and 6 million buildings, including 84,000 schools. The Soviet Union also lost 71 million farm animals, including 7 million horses. There was widespread destruction in such great cities as Kiev, Odessa, and Leningrad. Perhaps a quarter of the property value of the Soviet Union was lost in the war, and tens of millions of Soviet citizens were homeless. Simply feeding the Soviet population became a staggering task. All of this goes far to explain subsequent Russian policies, both internal and external.

Recovery efforts in Europe as well as in Asia centered for several years on the pressing problems of food, housing, and employment. As it turned out, much of the damage was not as extensive as initially thought, and many machines were still operational once the rubble was removed. In a perverse sense, Germany and Japan benefited from the bombing in that they rebuilt with the most modern infrastructure and factories.

With the end of the war, the liberated nations carried out purges of fascists and collaborators. Many were slain without benefit of trial. In France, 8,000–9,000 people were so executed, while afterward 1,500 were sentenced to death and executed following regular court procedures. The victorious Allies were determined to bring to justice the leaders of Germany and Japan, whom they held responsible for the war. Two great trials were held in Nuremberg and Tokyo. Afterward, interest in bringing the guilty to justice waned, even in the cases of those responsible for wartime atrocities. Punishment varied greatly according to nation and circumstance, and working out acceptable formulas that might punish the guilty when so many people had to some degree collaborated with the occupiers proved virtually impossible.

At the end of the war it appeared as if the idealistic, Left-leaning Resistance movements might realize their goals of new political, economic, and social institutions to implement meaningful change. Most people thought that a return to prewar democratic structures was impossible, but the bright hopes were soon dashed. Resistance leaders fell to quarreling among themselves. The fracturing of the Left, as in France and Italy, made room for the return of the old but still powerful conservative elites. The political structures that ultimately emerged from the war, at least in Western Europe, were little changed from those that had preceded it. Even so, extensive social welfare reforms were implemented throughout Western Europe, in part to compensate ordinary people in those nations for their wartime privations. In the United States, wartime rhetoric of democracy and equality encouraged African Americans, many of whom saw military service, to demand an end ro segregation and second-class status, which gave new impetus to the civil rights movement. In much of

Central and Eastern Europe, where the Soviet Union now held sway, there was significant change including land reform, although this was seldom to the real benefit of the populations involved. Soviet rule also brought widespread financial exactions in the form of war reparations to the Soviet Union and the stifling of democracy.

The war did serve to intensify the movement for European unity. Many European statesmen believed that some means had to be found to contain nationalism, especially German nationalism, and that the best vehicle for that would be the economic integration of their nations, with political unification to follow in what some called a "United States of Europe." They believed that a Germany integrated into the European economy would not be able to act unilaterally. Although steps in that direction were slow, such thinking led, a decade after the end of the war, to the European Common Market.

Asia was also greatly affected by the war. In China, the bitter prewar contest between the Chinese Guomindang (GMD, Nationalist) party and the Chinese Communist Party (CCP) resumed in a protracted civil war when Nationalist leader Jiang Jieshi sent troops into Manchuria in an effort to reestablish Nationalist control of that important region. The conflict ended in 1949 with a communist victory. To the west, British imperial India dissolved into an independent India and Pakistan in 1947.

The United States granted the Philippines delayed independence, but in other areas, such as French Indochina and the Dutch East Indies, the colonizers endeavored to continue their control. Where the European powers sought to hold on to their empires after August 1945, there would be further bloodshed. The French government, determined to maintain France as a great power, insisted on retaining its empire, which led to the protracted Indochina War and a bitter insurgency in Algeria. Fighting also erupted in many other places around the world, including Malaya and the Dutch East Indies. Even where the European powers chose to withdraw voluntarily, as in the case of Britain in Palestine and on the Indian subcontinent, there was often heavy fighting as competing nationalities sought to fill the vacuum. Nonetheless, independence movements in Africa and Asia, stimulated by the long absence of European control during the war, gathered momentum, and over the next two decades, much of Africa and Asia became independent.

One of the supreme ironies of World War II is that Adolf Hitler had waged the conflict with the stated goal of destroying communism. In the end, he had gravely weakened Europe.

South Korean soldiers patrol their side of the demilitarized zone (DMZ) along the 38th Parallel in Korea in 1990. The DMZ dividing Korea remains one of the world's flash points. (Michel Setboun/Corbis)

Rather than eradicating his ideological adversary, he had strengthened it. In 1945, the Soviet Union was one of the two leading world powers, and its international prestige was at an all-time high. In France and Italy, powerful communist parties were seemingly poised to take power. The Soviet Union also established governments friendly to it in Central and Eastern Europe. Under the pressure of confrontation with the West, these states became openly communist in the years after World War II. In 1948, the communists made their last acquisition in Central Europe in a coup d'état in Czechoslovakia. Communists also nearly came to power in Greece.

Indeed, far from destroying the Soviet Union and containing the United States, Germany and Japan had enhanced the international position of both. Western and Soviet differences meant that while treaties were negotiated with some of the smaller Axis powers, there were no big-power agreements concerning the future of Germany and Japan. Germany, initially divided into four occupation zones, in 1949 became two states: the Western-style Federal Republic of Germany (FRG, West Germany) and the communist German Democratic Republic (GDR, East Germany). Korea also had been temporarily divided at the 38th Parallel for the purposes of a Japanese surrender. Unlike Germany, which was reunited in 1990, in 2007 Korea still remained divided, another legacy of World War II.

Despite the continued importance of secondary powers such as Britain and France, the year 1945 witnessed the emergence of a bipolar world in which there were two superpowers: the United States and the Soviet Union. Added to the confrontational mix was the threat of nuclear war as both governments embarked on a new struggle, known as the Cold War.

Spencer C. Tucker

See also
Jiang Jieshi; Paris Peace Conference and Treaties; Territorial Changes after World War II

References
Black, Cyril E., et al. *Rebirth: A History of Europe since World War II.* Boulder, CO: Westview, 1992.
Calvocoress, Peter. *Fall Out: World War II and the Shaping of Postwar Europe.* New York: Longman, 1997.
Kimball, Warren F., ed. *America Unbound: World War II and the Making of a Superpower.* New York: St. Martin's, 1992.
Linz, Susan J., ed. *The Impact of World War II on the Soviet Union.* Totowa, NJ: Rowman and Allanheld, 1985.
Wheeler-Bennett, John, and Anthony J. Nicholls. *The Semblance of Peace: The Political Settlement after the Second World War.* New York: Norton, 1974.

Wörner, Manfred (1934–1994)

German politician, chairman of the North Atlantic Cooperation Council (NACC), and secretary-general of the North Atlantic Treaty Organization (NATO) during 1988–1994. Born in Stuttgart on 14 September 1934, Manfred Wörner studied at the universities of Heidelberg, Paris, and Munich, receiving a doctorate in international law in 1958. He then worked in the administration of the German state of Baden-Württemberg.

Elected to the Bundestag of the Federal Republic of Germany (FRG, West Germany) in 1965 as a Christian Democratic Union (CDU) candidate, Wörner served there until 1988. Active in defense matters, he chaired the CDU Working Group on Defense until 1976 and then was chairman of the Defense Committee of the Bundestag until 1980. He was also deputy chairman of the CDU with special responsibility in foreign policy, defense, and inter-German relations. He was an outspoken advocate of the deployment of Pershing missiles to offset the deployment of Soviet SS-20 missiles while, at the same time, urging negotiations on this matter with the Soviet Union.

In October 1982, West German Chancellor Helmut Kohl appointed Wörner defense minister, an office he held until assuming his NATO position. Wörner nearly lost his post when he publicly accused Deputy Supreme Allied Commander Europe General Günter Kiessling of homosexuality. With no proof forthcoming, Wörner offered to step down, but Kohl refused the resignation. Some have suggested that the NATO appointment was a means to remove Wörner from the German political scene.

Wörner became the seventh NATO secretary-general (in effect its chief political officer) in July 1988, the first German national to hold that post. The end of the Cold War was a time of great change for NATO, and Wörner led efforts to forge ties with Eastern Europe and urged discussions with the former Soviet Union. He was a strong advocate of a set timetable for full membership in NATO for Poland, Hungary, and the Czech Republic. His efforts to reach out to now noncommunist Eastern Europe reached fruition at the Brussels Summit in 1994, when NATO extended an invitation to all non-NATO states to join it in a Partnership for Peace program.

Wörner was also one of the first to urge that NATO assume new roles including peacekeeping operations, especially in the Balkans, where from July 1991 he publicly urged NATO intervention. He was deeply frustrated by the reluctance of most NATO leaders and their military advisors to become involved in the Balkans. As a German, he expressed an ethical compulsion to halt the ethnic cleansing there, and he also expressed the view that NATO "could not survive a second Yugoslavia." Wörner continued to press this position until his death from cancer in Brussels, Belgium, on 13 August 1994.

Spencer C. Tucker

See also
Kohl, Helmut; North Atlantic Treaty Organization, Origins and Formation of

References

Bertram, Christopher. "Manfred Wörner from Politician to Statesman." *NATO Review* 42(5) (October 1994): 31–35.

Duignan, Peter. *NATO: Its Past, Present, and Future.* Stanford, CA: Hoover Institution Press, 2000.

Schmidt, Gustave, ed. *A History of NATO: The First Fifty Years.* 3 vols. New York: Palgrave Macmillan, 2001.

Wörner, Manfred. *Change and Continuity in the North Atlantic Alliance.* Brussels: NATO Office of Information and Press, 1990.

Wu Xiuquan (1908–1997)

Chinese diplomat and vice foreign minister of the People's Republic of China (PRC). Born in Wuhan, Hubei Province, on 6 March 1908, Wu Xiuquan joined the Chinese Communist Party (CCP) as a youth and served in the Red Army—later renamed the People's Liberation Army (PLA)—as a political instructor, translator, and deputy chief of staff. In 1936 he began his diplomatic career as director of the Foreign Affairs Department.

During the Sino-Japanese War and the Chinese Civil War, Wu served on several military commissions in Northwest and Northeast China, where he was responsible for liaison and military coordination programs. After the PRC was established in 1949, he became director of the USSR and Eastern Europe Department of the Ministry of Foreign Affairs, in which capacity he accompanied Foreign Minister Zhou Enlai to Moscow in February 1950 to negotiate the Sino-Soviet Treaty. In November 1950 Wu, as the PRC's special envoy, attended a United Nations (UN) Security Council meeting in which he condemned U.S. Korean War measures in the Taiwan Strait, calling them an invasion of Chinese territory. In 1955 he became the vice foreign minister, a position he held until March 1955, when he was appointed Chinese ambassador to Yugoslavia. He returned home in late 1956 and became a member of the CCP Central Committee and in March 1959 became director of the party's International Liaison Department. He held both posts until the mid-1960s, during which time he led a number of delegations abroad, primarily to communist bloc countries.

In 1966 during the Cultural Revolution, Wu was purged from the government and imprisoned. In 1975 he returned to the public scene, first as deputy chief of the PLA General Staff. In 1980 he was named director of the Beijing Institute for International Strategic Studies and was also named vice foreign minister, in which capacities he played an active role in enhancing the PRC's international status. Wu died on 9 November 1997 in Beijing.

Law Yuk-fun

See also

China, People's Republic of; Cultural Revolution; Korean War; Sino-Soviet Treaty; Zhou Enlai

References

Garver, John W. *Foreign Relations of the People's Republic of China.* Englewood Cliffs, NJ: Prentice Hall, 1993.

Ma, Jisen. *The Cultural Revolution in the Foreign Ministry of China.* Hong Kong: Chinese University Press of Hong Kong, 2004.

Ross, Robert S., ed. *China, the United States, and the Soviet Union: Tripolarity and Policymaking in the Cold War.* Armonk, NY: Sharpe, 1993.

Wu Xueqian (1921–)

Vice premier and foreign minister of the People's Republic of China (PRC). Born on 19 December 1921 in Shanghai, Jiangsu Province, Wu Xueqian enrolled at the Jinan University in 1939, where he joined the Chinese Communist Party (CCP). Throughout the Sino-Japanese War and the Chinese Civil War, he lived in Shanghai, where he engaged in student underground work. He went on to serve the new PRC as deputy director of the International Liaison Department of the New Democratic Youth League of the CCP's Central Committee until 1953. Shortly thereafter, he became director of the International Liaison Department and simultaneously retained membership in both the New Democratic Youth League and the National Committee of the Federation of Democratic Youth. He held these posts until the mid-1960s, during which time he led a number of youth delegations abroad to foster closer ties among the PRC and other socialist nations as well Asian and African nations.

In 1967, as a result of the Cultural Revolution, Wu was relieved of all of his posts and was forced into private life. In early 1978 he reemerged publicly and resumed his former position in the International Liaison Department. From May 1982 to April 1988 he served as the PRC's foreign minister, during which time he accompanied PRC leaders on visits abroad, notably to Western Europe and North America. He also reinforced the Sino-American rapprochement begun by his predecessor. In April 1988 he became vice premier and continued his efforts to boost China's international standing. He relinquished the vice premiership in March 1993, although he retained his membership in the CCP Central Committee and Politburo, where he continues to serve.

Law Yuk-fun

See also

China, People's Republic of; Cultural Revolution

References

Garver, John W. *Foreign Relations of the People's Republic of China.* Englewood Cliffs, NJ: Prentice Hall, 1993.

Meisner, Maurice J. *Mao's China and After: A History of the People's Republic.* New York: Free Press, 1999.

Wyszyński, Stefan, Cardinal (1901–1981)

Roman Catholic prelate and prominent Polish dissident. Born on 3 August 1901 in Zuzela, Poland (then a part of the Russian Empire), Stephan Wyszyński studied at the Włocławek seminary and was ordained a priest in August 1924. He continued his studies at the Catholic University in Lublin and earned a PhD in sociology and ecclesiastical law in 1929. He then returned to Poland, where he taught at the Włocławek seminary and edited a theological review. During World War II, he served as a chaplain in the Polish underground army.

In 1946, Wyszyński was named bishop of Lublin. Two years later he became archbishop of Gniezno and Warsaw, making him primate of the Polish Roman Catholic Church. In 1953 he was named a cardinal. He was a fierce opponent of the postwar Polish government, which used Stalinist methods to seize and retain power. Nevertheless, in 1950 Wyszyński signed an agreement with the government that ostensibly allowed considerable freedom to the Roman Catholic Church in return for its tacit support of the Polish government. But Polish

Cardinal Stefan Wyszyński at the Vatican, October 1958. (Bettmann/Corbis)

authorities refused to respect the agreement. Communist officials in fact severely repressed organized religion. In 1953, Wyszyński issued a public repudiation of the government and declared an end to the Church's accommodative policies. He was subsequently arrested and imprisoned during 1953–1956.

In 1956, Wyszyński resumed his duties under the new anti-Stalinist government of Władysław Gomułka. The years after 1956 were less repressive than the early postwar years, but Wyszyński still faced constant challenges from the communist government. The cardinal maintained cordial and close relations with Rome and participated in Vatican Council II.

In 1978, when Pope John Paul II became the Roman Catholic Church's first Polish pope, the new pontiff praised Wyszyński for his steadfast commitment to human rights and thanked him for his sacrifices. In 1979, John Paul II made a triumphant pilgrimage to his native Poland, a true high point in the cardinal's life. Wyszyński was disappointed, however, when the pope's visit did not bring about any immediate change in the Polish government's policy toward the Church. Wyszyński died in Warsaw on 28 May 1981.

Jakub Basista

See also

John Paul II, Pope; Poland; Roman Catholic Church; Vatican Council II

References

Biskupski, M. B. *The History of Poland.* Westport, CT: Greenwood, 2000.

Paczkowski, Andrzej. *The Spring Will Be Ours: Poland and the Poles from Occupation to Freedom.* State College: Pennsylvania State University Press, 2003.

Y

Yahya Khan, Agha Mohammad (1917–1980)

Indian and Pakistani military leader and president of Pakistan (1969–1971). Born on 4 February 1917 in Peshawar, India (now Pakistan), Agha Mohammad Yahya Khan graduated from Punjab University and the Indian Military Academy at Dehra Dun. Commissioned in the Indian Army in 1938, during World War II he served with the British Army in North Africa, Iraq, and Italy.

Upon the creation of Pakistan in 1947, Yahya Khan co-founded the Pakistan Staff College at Quetta. He also helped to bring Muhammad Ayub Khan to power. During the Second Pakistan-India War in 1965, Yahya Khan commanded an infantry division. The following year he was appointed commander in chief of the Pakistani Army.

On 25 March 1969, civil unrest prompted Muhammad Ayub Khan, the president of Pakistan, to declare martial law. He promptly resigned after naming Yahya Khan chief martial law administrator and president. Yahya Khan moved swiftly to abolish the 1962 constitution and dissolve the National Assembly. He served as president for the next two years.

On 29 March 1970 Yahya Khan promulgated the Legal Framework Order of 1970, which functioned as an interim constitution and under which an election could be held. Then in December 1970 Yahya Khan oversaw the first free elections in Pakistani history. The Awami League led by Sheikh Mujib-ur-Rahman captured 160 out of 165 seats in East Pakistan but no seats in West Pakistan. Instead of brokering a compromise between Rahman and Zulfikar Ali Bhutto, majority leader of the West Pakistani Assembly, Yahya Khan used military force to repress the opposition in East Pakistan, and a civil war ensued. The Third Pakistan-India War (3–17 December 1971) began when India interceded. West Pakistan was defeated, and East Pakistan seceded to become Bangladesh in 1971.

Yahya Khan resigned the presidency on 20 December 1971 and was replaced by the Pakistani foreign minister Zulfikar Ali Bhutto. In 1972 Bhutto placed Yahya Khan under house arrest. Yahya Khan died on 10 August 1980 in Rawalpindi, Pakistan, after suffering a stroke.

Andrew J. Waskey

See also
Ayub Khan, Muhammad; Bangladesh; India; India, Armed Forces; India-Pakistan Wars; Pakistan; Pakistan, Armed Forces; Rahman, Mujibur

References
Basit, A. *The Breaking of Pakistan: Yahya Speaks about the Bhutto-Mujib Interaction Which Broke Pakistan.* Lahore: Liberty Publishers, 1990.

Berindranath, Dewan. *The Private Life of Yahya Khan.* New Delhi: Sterling, 1974.

Yakovlev, Alexander Nikolaevich (1923–2005)

Soviet official and member of the Politburo (1987–1990), close associate of Soviet leader Mikhail Gorbachev, and often referred to as the architect of glasnost (openness). Born in the village of Korolyovo in the Volga River region of Yaroslavl, Russia, on 2 December 1923, Alexander Yakovlev served in the Red Army in World War II. Badly wounded in fighting in 1943, after his recovery he attended Yaroslavl University, graduating with a degree in history. A member of the Communist Party of the Soviet Union (CPSU) since 1944, he worked in the party administration.

Following the relative thaw of the mid-1950s in the Soviet Union under Nikita Khrushchev, Yakovlev was one of a few Soviet citizens who were allowed to study abroad. During 1958–1959 he attended Columbia University in New York City, where he studied foreign relations.

Returning to the Soviet Union, Yakovlev rose to be head of the CPSU Department of Ideology and Propaganda during 1969–1973. In 1972 he published an article that was critical of both Soviet foreign policy and anti-Semitism. Appointed ambassador to Canada in 1973, he served in that post until 1983. He first met Gorbachev, then a member of the Politburo, when the latter visited Ottawa in the early 1980s. The two men took an immediate liking to each other and had a number of frank conversations concerning the need for reform in the Soviet Union.

When Gorbachev became the leader of the Soviet Union in 1985, he appointed Yakovlev head of the Academy of Science Institute of International Relations and the World Economy. In 1987, Gorbachev appointed Yakovlev to the Politburo with special responsibility for ideology and propaganda. Yakovlev became one of Gorbachev's principal advisors, accompanying him on trips abroad and advising him on a wide range of matters.

Yakovlev became perhaps the chief proponent of glasnost. He strongly supported freedom of the press and official recognition of past Soviet crimes. It was Yakovlev who confirmed the secret provisions of the German-Soviet Pact of 23 August 1939 concerning the division of Poland and the Baltic states between Germany and the Soviet Union.

Yakovlev favored the introduction of a multiparty system in the Soviet Union. He was much disliked by hard-liners in the Kremlin, and in August 1991 they secured his removal from the Politburo. During the coup attempt a few days later, he strongly supported the democratic movement, which was ultimately successful.

Following the collapse of the Soviet Union, Yakovlev wrote and lectured widely. He became the leader of the Party of Russian Social Democracy, and in 2002 he headed the commission that sought to rehabilitate Soviet citizens persecuted during the Stalin era. In 2000, Yakovlev attracted world attention when he announced that the Soviets had murdered Swedish diplomat Raoul Wallenberg in 1947. Wallenberg had been working to save the lives of Hungarian Jews during World War II but had disappeared in Budapest following the Soviet occupation.

In his last years, Yakovlev established and headed the International Democracy Foundation. He also lectured and wrote extensively, publishing a number of books. He was strongly critical of President Vladimir Putin's restrictions on democracy. Yakovlev died in Moscow following a protracted illness on 18 October 2005.

Spencer C. Tucker

See also
Glasnost; Gorbachev, Mikhail; Soviet Union
References
Dallin, Alexander, and Gail W. Lapidus, eds. *The Soviet System: From Crisis to Collapse.* 2nd ed. Boulder, CO: Westview, 1995.
Gibbs, Joseph. *Gorbachev's Glasnost: The Soviet Media in the First Phase of Perestroika.* College Station: Texas A&M University Press, 1999.
Yakovlev, Alexander N., and Abel G. Aganbegyan. *A Century of Violence in Soviet Russia.* Translated by Anthony Austin. New Haven, CT: Yale University Press, 1993.
———. *Perestroika, 1989.* New York: Scribner, 1989.

Yang Shangkun (1907–1998)

Politician, diplomat, and president of the People's Republic of China (PRC). Born in 1907 in Shuangjiang, Sichuan Province, Yang Shangkun enrolled at the Shanghai University in 1925 and joined the Chinese Communist Party (CCP) in 1926. In 1927 he continued his studies at the Sun Yixian University, graduating in 1930. Returning to China in 1931, he served in the Red Army as director of the Political Department. During the Sino-Japanese War and the Chinese Civil War, he served in North China, engaging in the CCP's organizational, propaganda, and liaison efforts.

Upon the establishment of the PRC in 1949, Yang became director of the General Office of the CCP Central Committee and handled the party's daily administrative affairs, a post that familiarized him with all aspects of party operations. In 1966 he was purged during the Cultural Revolution and imprisoned. In 1979 he returned to power, first as secretary and then as vice governor of Guangdong Province. In 1981 he transferred to Beijing as a Politburo member and permanent vice chairman of the Central Military Commission, in which capacities he became active in foreign affairs, leading a number of delegations abroad to promote the PRC's international standing. In 1988 he was elected the PRC's president and concurrently appointed the first vice chairman of the Central Military Commission, thus becoming the second most powerful figure in Chinese politics after Deng Xiaoping. On 4 June 1989, Yang ordered the People's Liberation Army (PLA) to crack down on the prodemocracy student demonstrators in Tiananmen Square. In 1993 he retreated from his duties. Yang died on 14 September 1998 in Beijing.

Law Yuk-fun

See also
China, People's Republic of; Cultural Revolution; Deng Xiaoping; Tiananmen Square

References

MacFarquhar, Roderick, ed. *The Politics of China: The Eras of Mao and Deng*. New York: Cambridge University Press, 1997.

Meisner, Maurice. *Mao's China and After: A History of the People's Republic*. New York: Free Press, 1999.

Yao Wenyuan (1931–2005)

Chinese writer and Communist Party official in the People's Republic of China (PRC), best known as a member of the Gang of Four. Born in Zhuji, Zhejiang Province, in 1931, Yao Wenyuan was the son of a well-known leftist writer. Yao too became a writer and a literary critic in Shanghai. As a member of the Shanghai group known as the Proletarian Writers for Purity, he became a champion of the orthodox Chinese Communist Party (CCP) literary line against liberalism. He opposed the Hundred Flowers movement and became known as "the Cudgel" for his hard-line approach (later he was dubbed "the Killer by Pen").

In November 1961 Yao published an article, "Notes on the New Historical Drama 'Hai Rui Dismissed from Office,'" first in *Wenhui bao* and then, after considerable opposition, in the *People's Daily*. The article was a critique of a play written by former vice mayor of Beijing Wu Han that was an allegory in support of former Defense Minister Peng Dehuai, who had been dismissed in 1959 by communist leader Mao Zedong for his criticism of the Great Leap Forward. In short, the play was sharply critical of Mao, and Yao's article was a defense of Mao. Believed to have been ordered by Mao, Yao's article in effect launched the Cultural Revolution in China.

Closely identified both with Mao and his wife Jiang Qing, a former Shanghai actress, in October 1966 Yao joined the Cultural Revolution Group headed by Jiang and Chen Boda that directed some of the more violent aspects of the Cultural Revolution. Together with Jiang, Wang Hongwen, and Zhang Chunqiao, Yao formed what became known as the Gang of Four. In April 1969 he became a member of both the Politburo and the Central Committee of the CCP, where he directed the regime's propaganda efforts.

Expelled from the CCP and arrested in October 1976, Yao was brought to trial with the other members of the Gang of Four and charged with responsibility for the worst excesses of the Cultural Revolution. According to the Chinese government, he also admitted forging documents that led to the purge of Deng Xiaoping, later China's leader. In October 1981 Yao received twenty years in prison, the lightest sentence of the four defendants. He was released in October 1996. He spent the remainder of his life working on a history of China. Following the death of Zhang Chunqiao in April 2005, Yao became the last surviving member of the Gang of Four. Yao died in Shanghai of diabetes on 23 December 2005.

Spencer C. Tucker

See also

China, People's Republic of; Cultural Revolution; Deng Xiaoping; Gang of Four; Jiang Qing; Mao Zedong; Peng Dehuai

References

Bonavia, David. *Verdict in Beijing: The Trial of the Gang of Four*. London: Bernett, 1984.

Daubier, Jean. *A History of the Chinese Cultural Revolution*. Translated by Richard Seaver. New York: Vintage, 1974.

Hinton, William. *Turning Point in China: An Essay on the Cultural Revolution*. New York: Monthly Review Press, 1972.

MacFarquhar, Roderick. *The Origins of the Cultural Revolution*. 2 vols. New York: Columbia University Press, 1983.

Robinson, Thomas, ed. *The Cultural Revolution in China*. Berkeley: University of California Press, 1971.

Schoenhals, Michael, ed. *China's Cultural Revolution, 1966–1969: Not a Dinner Party*. Armonk, NY: Sharpe, 1996.

Yeltsin, Boris (1931–2007)

Soviet reform politician during the last years of the Soviet Union and first elected president of Russia (1991–1999). Born on 1 February 1931 in Butka in the Sverdlovsk Oblast in the Ural Mountains, Boris Nikolayevich Yeltsin graduated from the Urals Polytechnical Institute in 1955 as a construction engineer. He joined the Communist Party of the Soviet Union (CPSU) in 1961 and worked on various construction projects in the Sverdlovsk area until 1968.

Yeltsin rose through the party ranks in the Sverdlovsk Oblast Party Committee. He was elected the region's industry secretary in 1975 and first secretary in 1976. During 1976–1985, he moved through the national ranks of the CPSU. He served as a deputy in the Council of the Union (1978–1989), a member of the Supreme Soviet Commission on Transport and Communication (1979–1984), a member of the Presidium of the Supreme Soviet (1984–1985), and chief of the Central Committee Department of Construction in 1985. The new CPSU general secretary, Mikhail Gorbachev, summoned Yeltsin to Moscow in April 1985 as part of a team of reform-minded party members.

Gorbachev asked Yeltsin to reform the Moscow City Committee. Yeltsin began to clear the city's Party Committee of corrupt officials, which endeared him to Muscovites. Eventually, he became dissatisfied with the slow pace of the perestroika reforms and openly criticized the CPSU officials. This was directed at the power base of Yegor Ligachev, who endorsed a moderate party–led reform. In 1987, Yeltsin resigned to force Gorbachev to take sides. Gorbachev needed Yeltsin to counterbalance Ligachev's growing skepticism and rejected his resignation, asking him to curb his critiques.

Boris Yeltsin, shown here campaigning for the presidency of the Russian Federation on 1 June 1991. (Reuters/Corbis)

Yeltsin ignored Gorbachev's plea. Thus, Gorbachev allowed Ligachev to continue the campaign against Yeltsin, which finally led to Yeltsin's dismissal as first secretary of the Moscow Party Committee. In 1988 Yeltsin was also expelled from the Politburo, but he remained in Moscow as the first deputy chair of the State Committee for Construction.

Yeltsin went on to win a landslide victory in the newly established Congress of People's Deputies of the Russian Soviet Federated Socialist Republic (RSFSR) in March 1989. In May 1990 he became chairman of the RSFSR. By 12 June 1990 the RSFSR, along with the other fourteen Soviet republics, had declared its independence. Yeltsin was directly elected to the newly created office of president of the now-independent RSFSR on 12 June 1991. He then demanded Gorbachev's resignation. Gorbachev refused to step down, but he did agree to sign a new union treaty in late August 1991.

Hard-line conservative forces within the CPSU tried to prevent the signing of the treaty, which would lead to the dissolution of the Soviet Union. On 19 August 1991, the conservatives dispatched troops to key positions around Moscow and held Gorbachev under house arrest. Yeltsin climbed atop one of the tanks surrounding the parliament building, denounced the CPSU coup as illegal, and called for a general strike. He and his supporters remained in the parliament

building as they rallied international support. For three days, thousands of people demonstrated in front of parliament, holding off an expected attack on the building.

The failed putsch and massive street demonstrations quickly destroyed the credibility of Gorbachev's perestroika and glasnost reforms. On 24 December 1991 the RSFSR and then later Russia took the Soviet Union's seat in the United Nation (UN) Security Council. The next day Gorbachev resigned, an act that officially dissolved the Soviet Union. Yeltsin, as president of Russia, immediately abolished the CPSU. In the meantime, he had negotiated with the leaders of Ukraine and Belarus to form the Commonwealth of Independent States as a federation of most of the former Soviet republics.

With a stagnating economy, a hostile legislature, and an attempted coup, Yeltsin was not expected to win reelection in 1996. However, he staged an amazing comeback. Despite becoming increasingly unpopular and suffering from ill health, he continued as president of Russia until 31 December 1999, when he surprisingly named Vladimir Putin acting president. Yeltsin died in Moscow on 23 April 2007.

Frank Beyersdorf

See also
Glasnost; Gorbachev, Mikhail; Ligachev, Yegor Kuzmich; Perestroika; Soviet Union

References

Braithwaite, Rodric. *Across the Moscow River: The World Turned Upside-Down.* New Haven, CT: Yale University Press, 2002.

Breslauer, George W. *Gorbachev and Yeltsin As Leaders.* Cambridge: Cambridge University Press, 2002.

Yeltsin, Boris. *Against the Grain.* New York: Summit, 1999.

———. *The Struggle for Russia.* New York: Random House, 1994.

Yemen

Middle Eastern nation located in the southern part of the Arabian Peninsula. The Republic of Yemen borders Saudi Arabia to the north, Oman to the east, the Arabian Sea and the Gulf of Aden to the south, and the Red Sea to the west. Not far off the western and southern coasts of the country are the East African nations of Eritrea, Djibouti, and Somalia. Yemen's total area encompasses 203,846 square miles and is slightly larger than twice the size of the U.S. state of Wyoming. It had an estimated 1945 population of 4.77 million people.

Since 1918, Yemen had been divided into North Yemen (Mutawakkilite Kingdom of Yemen during 1918–1962 and the Yemen Arab Republic during 1962–1990) and South Yemen (People's Republic of Yemen during 1967–1990). In 1970, when South Yemen formally declared itself a Marxist state, many hundreds of thousands of Yemenis fled north. This precipitated a virtual civil war between North and South Yemen that would endure for twenty years. Not until 1990 did the two states reconcile, forming a single state known as the Republic of Yemen. Since then, there have been several unsuccessful attempts by groups in southern Yemen to secede from the republic. The most serious secessionist move came in 1994.

As with most areas in this part of the world, Yemen's climate is characterized by torridly hot weather especially in the eastern desert regions, where rainfall is scant. The western coast has a hot and somewhat humid climate, while the mountainous regions in western Yemen are more temperate and have more rainfall. Much of the country can be characterized as a desert. Topographically, Yemen features a narrow strip of coastal plains and immediately behind them low hills that give way to high mountains. High-desert plains farther east descend to hot desert in the interior. The nation's chief resources include oil, marble, fish, minor coal deposits, gold, lead, nickel, and copper. The bulk of Yemen's arable land is located in the western part of the country and comprises less than 3 percent of the entire landmass.

Yemen's population is overwhelmingly Muslim and of Arabic descent. Arabic is the official language. Of the nation's Muslims, about 52 percent are Sunni Muslims and 48 percent are Shia Muslims. The Sunnis live principally in the southern and southeastern parts of the country. Yemen has one of the world's highest birth rates, and as a result its population as a whole is quite young. Indeed, some 46 percent of the population is age fourteen and under, while less than 3 percent is over age sixty-five. The median age is sixteen years.

Yemen is a representative republic that has a popularly elected president and a prime minister appointed by the president. The executive branch shares power with the bicameral legislature. The legal system in Yemen is a mix of Islamic law, Turkish law (a vestige of the Ottoman Empire), English common law, and local tribal dictates. Nevertheless, Islamic laws almost always take precedence in accordance with the Koran. Ali Abdullah Saleh has served as president of the Republic of Yemen since the 1990 unification. Before that, he had served as the president of North Yemen since 1978.

Recorded human habitation in the region of Yemen can be traced as far back as the ninth century BC. Yemen's strategic location on the Red Sea and the Gulf of Aden has made it an important crossroad for East-West trade as well as for trade from Asia to Africa. Around the seventh century AD, Muslim caliphs began to exert their influence over the region and gradually ceded authority to dynastic imams, who retained the caliph's theocratic government until the modern era. Over the centuries, Egyptian caliphs also held sway in Yemen. The Ottoman Empire controlled some or most of Yemen sporadically between the 1500s and 1918, when the empire crumbled as a result of World War I. Ottoman influence was most keen in northern Yemen. In southern Yemen, imams tended to control the local scene, although they were usually overseen to some extent by the central authorities in Constantinople (Istanbul).

In 1918 North Yemen won its independence from the Ottoman Empire and finally became a republic in 1962, which precipitated an eight-year-long civil war. The conflict pitted royalists in the Mutawakkilite Kingdom of Yemen against republicans. In southern Yemen until 1967, the British dominated, having established a protectorate in Aden in 1839. Soon, the British created a formal colony that incorporated Aden and southern Yemen. As such, the British had great command of the strategic waterways of the region. After World War II, however, Yemenis in the southern part of the country came to resent the British presence, and before long they had organized an anti-British insurgency with aid from the Egyptians.

Several attacks against British interests sponsored by Egypt's government under Gamal Abdel Nasser as well as by insurgents from North Yemen essentially forced the British out in 1967. The former British colony now became South Yemen. In 1970, the South Yemen government declared a Marxist state and aligned itself squarely with the Soviet Union. As a result, several hundred thousand South Yemenis fled to North Yemen, overwhelming that nation's resources. The South Yemen government did nothing to stop the mass exodus.

Before 1962, the ruling imams in North Yemen pursued an isolationist foreign policy. That country did have commercial and cultural ties with Saudi Arabia, however. In the late 1950s, the Chinese and Soviets attempted to lure North Yemen into their orbit with technological missions. By the early 1960s, North Yemen had become dependent upon Egypt for financial and technical support. Later still, the Saudis supplanted the Egyptians as the main conduit of support. During the civil war, the Saudis backed the royalists while Egypt and the Soviet Union aided the republicans. In the 1970s and 1980s, many North Yemenis found jobs in neighboring Saudi Arabia, boosting North Yemen's flagging economy.

After 1967, when South Yemen declared itself a Marxist state, it maintained tense—and sometimes hostile—relations with its conservative Arab neighbors. In addition to the ongoing conflict with North Yemen, South Yemeni insurgents engaged the Saudis in military actions first in 1969 and again in 1973. They also openly aided the Dhofar rebellion in Oman.

After the 1990 unification, the Republic of Yemen has generally pursued a pragmatic foreign policy. It is a member of the Non-Aligned Movement, is a signatory to the Nuclear Non-Proliferation Treaty, and attempted to stay impartial during the 1991 Persian Gulf War and subsequent wars in the Middle East. Its noncommittal stance in these areas, however, has not endeared it to the Gulf States or Western nations.

Yemen is among the poorest nations in the Arab world. The long civil war of 1962–1970 wrought great havoc on an already struggling economy, and the agricultural sector has been hit by periodic droughts. Coffee production, once a mainstay of northern Yemeni crops, has fallen off dramatically. The Port of Aden in southern Yemen suffered dramatic curtailments in its cargo handling after the 1967 Six-Day War and the British exit that same year. Since 1990, the return of hundreds of thousands of Yemenis from the Gulf States because of Yemen's nonalignment in the Persian Gulf War brought with it staggering unemployment. Reduced aid from other nations at this time and a brief secessionist movement in 1994 conspired to keep Yemen's economy depressed. Yemen does have significant oil deposits, but they are not of the same quality as Persian Gulf oil and thus have not brought in a windfall profit. Yemen does have major natural gas reserves, but that industry remains underdeveloped. As of 2006, the Yemeni government continues to struggle with high inflation, excessive spending, and widespread corruption.

Paul G. Pierpaoli Jr.

See also
Arab-Israeli Wars; Egypt; Middle East; Nasser, Gamal Abdel; Non-Aligned Movement; Nuclear Non-Proliferation Treaty; Persian Gulf War; Saudi Arabia; Soviet Union; Yemen Civil War
References
Dresch, Paul. *A History of Modern Yemen.* New York: Cambridge University Press, 2001.
Jones, Clive. *Britain and the Yemen Civil War.* London: Sussex Academic, 2004.
Mackintosh-Smith, Martin. *Yemen: The Unknown Arabia.* Woodstock, NY: Overlook, 2001.

Yemen Civil War (1962–1972)

Civil conflict in North Yemen (Yemen Arab Republic) lasting from 1962 until 1970 that pitted royalist forces of the Mutawakkilite Kingdom of Yemen against those seeking to establish a republic. In addition to the ongoing civil divisions in North Yemen (southern Yemen was controlled by Great Britain until 1967), the immediate catalyst of the civil war was the death of Ahmad bin Yahya in September 1962. Ahmad was the ruling imam in the region and represented the hereditary monarchy, which had controlled northern Yemen for many years. His repressive reign, which had begun in 1948, had gained few new adherents during its twenty-four-year history. Ahmad harbored visions of uniting all of Yemen but was unable to garner sufficient support to end British rule in the southern part of the country. In 1955, he had to fend off a serious coup effort instigated by two of his brothers and disgruntled army officers.

To bolster his position, Ahmad entered into a formal military pact with Egypt in 1956 that placed Yemeni military forces under a unified command structure. That same year, he also named his son Muhammad al-Badr crown prince and heir apparent and established formal ties with the Soviet Union. In 1960, Ahmad left North Yemen to seek medical treatment. In his absence, Crown Prince al-Badr began to implement several reform measures that his father had promised to implement but as yet had gone unfulfilled. Outraged that his son made such moves without his knowledge or assent, Ahmad promptly reversed the measures when he returned home. This did not, of course, endear him to his subjects, and several weeks of civil unrest ensued, which the government quashed with a heavy hand. The 1955 coup attempt and growing resentment toward Ahmad rendered the last years of his rule both paranoid and reactionary.

Ahmad died at age sixty-seven on 18 September 1962, and al-Badr then became imam. One of his first official acts was to grant a blanket amnesty to all political prisoners who had been imprisoned during his father's reign. He did so in hopes of maintaining power and keeping the kingdom's detractors at bay. But al-Badr's tactics did not stave off discord for long. On 26 September 1962 Abdullah as-Sallal, commander of the royal guard and recently appointed to that post by al-Badr, launched a coup and declared himself president of the Arab Republic of Yemen.

Al-Badr, meanwhile, managed to escape an assassination attempt and went to the northern reaches of the kingdom, where he was able to stir up support among the royalist tribes there. Within days, clashes began between royalist fighters and the republicans that soon grew into a full-scale civil war. Soliciting support from another hereditary kingdom, al-Badr gained the support of Saudi Arabia, the proximity of which to northern Yemen made it a natural ally. As-Sallal, meanwhile, rallied republican forces and had soon gained the support of Egypt. Both the Saudis and Egyptians dispatched military troops to Yemen, adding to the destructiveness of the civil conflict.

By the mid-1960s, the royalists had also enlisted the help of Iran and Jordan, while the Soviets and several other communist nations backed the republicans. From a larger perspective, the Yemen Civil War saw the more conservative Middle East regimes (e.g., Saudi Arabia, Iran, and Jordan) pitted against the more radical and Pan-Arab forces in the region, as represented by Egypt's Gamal Abdel Nasser and the Soviet Union. The conflict also became politicized along Cold War lines, as the United States, Great Britain, and other Western powers tended to side with the royalists.

On several occasions, the United Nations (UN) attempted to mediate an end to the bloodshed, but the regional and international dynamics of the struggle made this task nearly impossible. At the height of its involvement in the Yemen Civil War, Egypt, which had sent the most forces into Yemen, was fielding some 75,000 troops there. This was not only acting as a huge drain on the Egyptian treasury and military but was also stoking inter-Arab enmity. Saudi-Egyptian relations were particularly tense. It was in fact the 1967 Six-Day War and Egypt's ignominious defeat in that conflict that began to turn the tide in the civil war. After June 1967, a weakened and chastened Nasser was compelled to begin withdrawing his troops from Yemen. That same year saw the British withdrawal from southern Yemen. This presented a diplomatic opening that would ultimately lead to an end to the fighting in 1970.

By 1969, both sides in the struggle agreed that the first step to ending the war would be the withdrawal of all foreign troops from Yemeni territory. Both Egypt and Saudi Arabia agreed. The removal of foreign forces ultimately led to the 1970 compromise that allowed for the continuation of the republican government in which several key positions would be occupied by royalists. There was, however, no role for Imam al-Badr, and part of the compromise stipulated that he and his family leave the country. Al-Badr sought exile in Britain, where he lived until his death in 1996. Sadly, the Yemen Civil War left deep scars on that country's society and politics that have not yet healed. Worse yet, it is estimated that between 100,000 and 150,000 Yemenis lost their lives in the eight years of fighting.

Paul G. Pierpaoli Jr.

See also

Arab-Israeli Wars; Egypt; Nasser, Gamal Abdel; Saudi Arabia; Soviet Union; United Kingdom; Yemen

References

Dresch, Paul. *A History of Modern Yemen.* New York: Cambridge University Press, 2001.

Jones, Clive. *Britain and the Yemen Civil War.* London: Sussex Academic, 2004.

Pridham, Brian. *Contemporary Yemen: Politics and Historical Background.* London: Palgrave Macmillan, 1984.

Yoshida Shigeru (1878–1967)

Japanese diplomat and prime minister (1946–1947, 1948–1954). Born in Yokosuka, Kanagawa Prefecture, Japan, on 22 September 1878, Yoshida Shigeru graduated from Tokyo Imperial University in 1906. He entered the Ministry of Foreign Affairs and served as deputy foreign minister in 1928 and then ambassador to Italy and Great Britain during 1936–1938. During World War II, he tried to bring the war to an end with an early Japanese surrender but was arrested by the military police.

During the U.S. occupation after the war, Yoshida headed the Japan Liberal Party and served as prime minister during May 1946–May 1947 and again during October 1948–December 1954. While he was in office, the Cold War heated up, altering U.S. policy toward Japan. President Harry S. Truman's administration recognized Japan's geopolitical importance in East Asia and changed its policies to revitalize Japan's economy, retain the use of Japanese military bases, and rearm Japan. Demand for Japanese rearmament became far stronger after the outbreak of the Korean War in June 1950.

In January 1951, Yoshida held a series of talks with U.S. diplomat John Foster Dulles, assigned to negotiate a peace treaty with Japan. Dulles wanted Japan to conclude a peace treaty as a U.S. ally and to maintain adequate armed forces. Yoshida agreed to an alliance with the United States but resisted Dulles's request for rearmament. Yoshida ultimately compromised with Dulles and secretly promised to create Japanese security forces. On 8 September 1951, Yoshida signed the San Francisco Peace Treaty. That same day, he also signed the United States–Japan Security Treaty.

In October 1952, Yoshida created the National Security Forces, which succeeded the National Police Reserve established in 1950. With continuous pressure from Washington to strengthen defense forces, he transformed the National Security Forces into the Self-Defense Forces in June 1954. A few months before this, the U.S.-Japan Mutual Defense Assistance Agreement was signed, strengthening military and economic ties between the two nations. By that time the Japanese economy was flourishing, as the Korean War had pumped billions of dollars into Japanese factories.

Yoshida's diplomacy put top priority on Japanese economic development, followed by retaining defense forces at the minimum level possible. Yoshida remained a strong supporter of the Guomindang (GMD, Nationalist) government on Taiwan. In domestic matters, he increased centralization of government.

The year 1954 saw the biggest challenge to his diplomacy. The *Lucky Dragon* incident in March caused massive protests against U.S. testing of nuclear weapons. The *Lucky Dragon* was a Japanese fishing vessel that had become caught in radioactive fallout after an American nuclear test in the Pacific Ocean.

Yoshida's political power and popularity decreased during this tumultuous year, and his premiership came to end in December 1954. He died on 20 October 1967 in Oiso, Kanagawa Prefecture, Japan.

Iikura Akira

See also

Dien Bien Phu, Battle of; Japan, Armed Forces; Japan, Occupation after World War II; Korean War; Nuclear Tests; San Francisco Peace Treaty; United States–Japan Security Treaty

References

Braddick, C. W. *Japan and the Sino-Soviet Alliance, 1950–1964: In the Shadow of the Monolith.* Basingstoke, UK: Palgrave, 2004.

Dower, John W. *Empire and Aftermath: Yoshida Shigeru and the Japanese Experience, 1878–1954.* Cambridge: Harvard University Press, 1979.

Finn, Richard B. *Winners in Peace: MacArthur, Yoshida, and Postwar Japan.* Berkeley: University of California Press, 1992.

Hosoya, Chihiro, and A50 Editorial Committee, eds. *Japan and the United States: Fifty Years of Partnership.* Tokyo: Japan Times, 2001.

Schaller, Michael. *Altered States: The United States and Japan since the Occupation.* Oxford: Oxford University Press, 1997.

Ysten, Gonpo

See Panchen Lama

Yugoslavia

Former Southeast European nation. Yugoslavia, with a 1945 population of some 15 million people, covered roughly 98,000 square miles, about the size of the U.S. state of Wyoming. It was bordered by Italy, Austria, and Hungary to the north; Romania and Bulgaria to the east; Greece and Albania to the south; and the Adriatic Sea to the east.

During the twentieth century, two states bearing the name "Yugoslavia" exemplified the international standard for ethnic strife and political fragmentation. Over the course of its seventy-year history, Yugoslavia staggered from crisis to crisis, swapping one volatile form of political union for another. The Kingdom of Serbs, Croats, and Slovenes, renamed in 1929 the Kingdom of Yugoslavia (the land of the South Slavs), was created in the aftermath of World War I and disintegrated under German invasion in 1941. The Federal People's Republic of Yugoslavia, renamed in 1963 the Socialist Federal Republic of Yugoslavia, dissolved on its own in 1991 into a brutal civil war that for the first time since World War II unleashed in Europe the horrors of genocide and concentration camps.

The survival of both states depended on the political, social, and cultural harmony of the multinational, multiethnic, and multireligious population of the federation who during the Cold War lived an ostensibly peaceful life in six republics (Bosnia and Herzegovina, Croatia, Macedonia, Montenegro, Serbia, and Slovenia) and two autonomous regions (Vojvodina and Kosovo). The breakdown of relations between Orthodox Serbs and Roman Catholic Croats badly weakened the interwar Yugoslavia, making it easy prey for the Axis powers in 1941. After World War II, Josip Broz Tito and the communists subdued the interwar nationalistic tensions and put Yugoslavia on the world map as a socialist, nonaligned, self-managed alternative to Western capitalism and Soviet-style communism. In the wake of Tito's thirty-five-year benevolent dictatorship, the apparent lack of common values accentuated historical differences that were exploited by power-hungry politicians, who hastened the bloody collapse of the country in the early 1990s.

Eleven percent of Yugoslavia's 1940 population had been killed in World War II, and that conflict and subsequent resettlements completely disrupted the region's agriculture, industry, communications, and infrastructure, bringing about widespread suffering and starvation. The communist-led Partisans under Tito emerged from the war as sole rulers of Yugoslavia without significant Soviet assistance. During 1945–1948, Tito's government adopted a Soviet-style constitution that provided for a federation united under a strong central government. Meanwhile, the Yugoslav Communist Party (KPJ) adopted a Stalinist model for rapid industrial development. Through forced collectivization, nationalization, and the establishment of a strict central planning system, the government took control of virtually all of the country's wealth.

The communist regime further consolidated its grip on power by punishing wartime collaborators and eliminating political and religious opposition. The show trial and execution of Chetnik leader General Draža Mihajlović in Belgrade and the Zagreb trial and imprisonment of Archbishop Aloysius Stepinac sent strong signals to all opponents of the new regime, strengthening a siege mentality that remained a major hallmark of postwar Yugoslavia. Tito and his communist comrades recognized clearly the dangers inherent in national and religious chauvinism. To generate social tolerance, the communists introduced the brotherhood and unity concept under the national ideology of Yugoslavism as a substitute for individual ethnic nationalisms, but their efforts ultimately foundered.

Although Yugoslavia's communists began as devoted Stalinists, the image of Yugoslavia as the Soviets' staunchest ally changed dramatically in reaction to the Soviet attempt to dominate all domestic and foreign aspects of Yugoslavian affairs. In the wake of the Yugoslav-Soviet split, by 1948 Tito was seen as a hero in the West. Yugoslavia's ensuing expulsion from the Cominform (Communist Information Bureau) and Comecon (Council for Mutual Economic Assistance) led to a crisis that convinced Yugoslav leaders that a Soviet-led invasion was imminent. American and British assistance kept Tito afloat, saved the country from starvation in 1950, and contained much of Yugoslavia's trade deficit over the next decade. Yet neither Western economic aid nor U.S. military assistance resulted in Yugoslavia moving closer to the Western bloc. American officials wondered if the split with the Soviets was permanent, while Tito distrusted the United States and fretted over the Soviet reaction to American aid.

The renaming of the KPJ as the League of Communists of Yugoslavia in 1952 as well as the introduction of a new economic mechanism, workers' self-management, and market socialism of the 1960s confirmed that Yugoslavia was pursuing a unique, un-Soviet version of socialism. Yugoslavia's market socialism was based on worker-managed enterprises that used domestic and foreign forces as a management guide. Tito undoubtedly proved to be the most skillful politician in Yugoslavia's history because of his role in founding the Non-Aligned Movement, which became the keystone of the country's foreign policy during the Cold War. Yugoslavia's role in the movement stoked the competition between the Western powers and the Soviet bloc, and Tito encouraged the competition for his political gain while extracting valuable economic concessions from both sides. Despite the Yugoslav-Soviet rapprochement after Josef Stalin's death in 1953, Tito transformed one of the most isolated countries in the world into one that enjoyed reasonable diplomatic relations with more countries than any other communist regime.

During the 1960s and 1970s it appeared as if Yugoslavia's reforms were on the way to solving the most important domestic problems. Yet decentralization in 1960 in the wake of the fall of Aleksandar Ranković, the chief of the secret police who resisted reforms, did not introduce liberalization. Instead, it created deep institutional fractures, such as the introduction of a confederated system of republics with greater autonomy than before. This would ultimately result in the bloody break-up of Yugoslavia. The rise of nationalism in Croatia and elsewhere further obstructed reforms and the liberalization movement. The 1974 constitution, one of the world's longest,

aimed to provide political stability by using ethnic quotas, rotation of cadres, and the republics' right to veto federal legislation but proved to be counterproductive. Steep increases in oil prices during the mid-1970s worsened the economic situation, which had been deteriorating for decades. Economic hardships were also partially attributable to the regime's inability to successfully tackle mounting foreign debts, budget deficits, and galloping inflation.

During his last years, Tito ignored worsening economic conditions. His death in 1980 deprived the country of strong leadership capable of unifying the nation and solving its mounting problems. Anti-Serbian rioting in Kosovo only contributed to the sense of crisis. The communist system of collective rotating leadership that replaced Tito's rule was unable to cope with the mounting crises. Serbian President Slobodan Milošević exploited the situation and greatly contributed to the breakdown of the sense of community by stockpiling weaponry, abolishing the autonomous provinces, and encouraging Serbian nationalism not in an attempt to preserve Yugoslavia but rather to create a greater Serbia.

Following a decade of political inertia and deepening economic crisis, the armed conflict in Slovenia in June 1991 between the forces of the Yugoslav People's Army and the Slovenian territorial defense forces marked the beginning of the collapse of Yugoslavia. The relatively minor dispute over Slovenia's independence carried over to Croatia, which had a substantial Serbian minority who demanded Serbian annexation and feared the new nationalist Croatian government led by Franjo Tuđman. After pulling out of Slovenia, the army, strengthened by local Serbian forces, outmatched the Croats and occupied one-third of Croatian territory by December 1991. The occupied territories received the status of United Nations Protected Areas (UNPAs), and the United Nations Protection Force (UNPROFOR) replaced the Yugoslav People's Army.

This situation and sporadic fighting endured until May 1995, when the U.S.-trained Croatian Army overran the UNPA in western Slovenia. In August 1995 the Croats, in a lightning offensive, overran Serb-occupied Krajina. Both military actions received tacit approval from the West, but there was an exodus of Croatian Serb refugees who fled for fear of retaliation. The last UNPA in eastern Slovenia was peacefully reintegrated into Croatia in 1998 under the terms of the Dayton Peace Accords.

By the time the Bosnian state led by Alija Izetbegović received international recognition on 6 April 1992, Bosnian Serbs and Bosnian Croats had already formed satellite states as a part of a covert agreement between Milošević and Tuđman. Republika Srpska led by Radovan Karadžić was backed by Serbia and the Yugoslav People's Army, while Croatia supported Bosnia and Herzegovina. A three-sided ethnic war soon erupted. By the end of 1992, the Serbs controlled about

70 percent of Bosnia and laid siege to Sarajevo for three years, carrying out ethnic cleansing and torturing and murdering thousands of people in concentration camps. Croatian forces launched a war against the Muslims in May 1993 and then laid siege to the city of Mostar. The Muslims were initially poorly armed but by fighting a largely defensive war managed to hold off their opponents using equally atrocious tactics.

Peace in Bosnia was secured by the American team of negotiators led by Richard Holbrooke, who invited Tuđman, Izetbegović, and Milošević to Dayton, Ohio, to negotiate peace terms. After three weeks of intense negotiations, on 21 November 1995 the Muslim-Croat federation received control of 51 percent of the territory, while the Serbs received 49 percent. All three parties agreed to create a union in which each side would have control over its own defense, security, and taxes. The peace was enforced by 60,000 United Nations (UN) troops, reduced to a 24,000-strong international Stabilization Force (SFOR) in 1997.

The campaign of North Atlantic Treaty Organization (NATO) air strikes, led by the United States, against Serbia's atrocious Kosovo policy lasted from late March until June 1999. These strikes were precipitated by Milošević's rejection of the 1991 Rambouillet peace agreement, which stipulated that NATO forces would have unobstructed access to all of the Federal Republic of Yugoslavia to maintain peace in Kosovo. The steady suppression of the Albanian majority (90 percent of the population according to the 1991 census) erupted into an outright war with the paramilitary forces of the Kosovo Liberation Army (KLA). During 1998 and early 1999, the conflict drove from their homes more than 200,000 people, while thousands were killed. The air strikes destroyed military targets as well as factories and infrastructure throughout Serbia, including Belgrade. Milošević agreed to a peace plan on 3 June 1999 that created another international protectorate in the Balkans. A peacekeeping force, the Kosovo Force (KFOR) of 50,000 troops, was sent to ensure the safe return of refugees and maintain peace in Kosovo, which remains a part of Serbia.

The name "Yugoslavia" was officially erased from the map on 14 March 2002, when the two remaining republics that comprised the Federal Republic of Yugoslavia voted to rename the country Serbia and Montenegro.

Josip Močnik

See also

Comecon; Cominform; Djilas, Milován; Market Socialism; Milošević, Slobodan; Nationalism; Non-Aligned Movement; Soviet-Yugoslav Split; Stepinac, Aloysius, Archbishop; Territorial Changes after World War II; Tito, Josip Broz; Trieste; Tuđman, Franjo; Warsaw Pact; Yugoslavia, Armed Forces

References

Cohen, Lenard J. *Broken Bonds: Yugoslavia's Disintegration and Balkan Politics in Transition.* 2nd ed. Boulder, CO: Westview, 1995.
Djilas, Aleksa. *The Contested Country: Yugoslav Unity and Communist Revolution, 1919–1953.* Cambridge: Harvard University Press, 1991.
Lampe, John R. *Yugoslavia As History: Twice There Was a Country.* 2nd ed. Cambridge: Cambridge University Press, 2000.
Naimark, Norman M., and Holly Case, eds. *Yugoslavia and Its Historians: Understanding the Balkan Wars of the 1990s.* Stanford, CA: Stanford University Press, 2003.
Pavlovitch, Stevan K. *The Improbable Survivor: Yugoslavia and Its Problems, 1918–1988.* Columbus: Ohio State University Press, 1988.
Rusinow, Dennison. *The Yugoslav Experiment, 1948–1974.* London: Royal Institute of International Affairs, 1977.
West, Richard. *Tito and the Rise and Fall of Yugoslavia.* New York: Carroll and Graf, 1994.

Yugoslavia, Armed Forces

The large, expensive, and apparently effective armed forces of the Socialist Federal Republic of Yugoslavia were formed in 1945 from the 400,000-strong victorious, multiethnic Partisan National Liberation Army and gradually reduced to 180,000 soldiers, containing more than 100,000 conscripts, by 1990. All male citizens were subject to conscription after their seventeenth birthday, while women served as volunteers.

The Yugoslav People's Army was of colossal importance to the sovereignty of the Yugoslav state because during most of the Cold War, communist nonaligned Yugoslavia was a member of neither the Soviet bloc nor the Western bloc. Fear of a Soviet invasion was the primary factor in defense planning. President Josip Broz Tito and the Yugoslav Communist Party relied on the doctrine of total military defense, stressing brotherhood and unity ideology as well as coordination between the army and the Territorial Defense Force to safeguard and secure the regime's legitimacy.

The Yugoslav People's Army consisted of the army, air force, and navy organized into four military regions and further divided into districts that controlled draft registration, mobilization, and military facilities. The army generally controlled the large Territorial Defense Forces (more than a million strong), exercised autonomy in military matters, and exerted substantial influence within the League of Communists of Yugoslavia. In 1990 more than 100,000 army personnel belonged to the league. As with the country at large, the armed forces were beset by ethnic tensions that intensified after Tito's death in 1980.

The army contained more than half of Yugoslavia's active-duty soldiers (including conscripts) and could rapidly mobilize close to half a million trained reservists. It was comprised of infantry, armor, artillery, air defense, signal, engineering, and chemical defense corps and was organized into three military regions (Slovenia and northern Croatia; eastern Croatia, Vojvodina, and Serbia; and Kosovo and Macedonia) and ten army headquarters. The brigade was the largest operational unit.

The army operated Soviet T-34, T-54, and T-55 tanks and Yugoslav M-84 tanks, among others. It also maintained some American M-4 and M-47 tanks. Although artillery and anti-tank regiments were well equipped with Soviet, American, and domestic tactical systems, mechanized infantry brigades lacked sufficient armored combat vehicles and personnel carriers.

The air force operated more than 400 combat aircraft (including Orao-2, Super Galeb, Jastreb, and P-2 Kraguj, some armed with American AGM-65 Maverick or Soviet AS-7 and AS-9 missiles) and 200 armed helicopters (among others, Mi-8 helicopter gunships and domestic Partisan helicopters) with the support of approximately 30,000 personnel and only a few thousand conscripts. There were also nine squadrons of 130 MiG-21 fighters armed with Soviet AA-2, AA-8, SA-2, or SA-3 missiles, some of which were obsolete by the time Yugoslavia disintegrated in 1991.

The navy provided an adequate coastal defense force of more than 10,000 sailors and marines charged with protecting the country's 1,000-mile shoreline, the coastal islands, and the strategic Strait of Otranto. It had its headquarters at Split and was organized into missile, torpedo, and patrol boat brigades; a submarine division; minesweeper flotillas; and an antisubmarine warfare helicopter squadron.

Most males and females between the ages of fifteen and sixty-five participated in national defense as part of the Ter-ritorial Defense Forces. Although the Territorial Defense Forces was originally independent, the nearest army command usually exerted authority over it and its lightly armored infantry units, battalions, and regiments that were trained exclusively for defensive actions on familiar local terrain.

No form of alternative service was available for conscientious objectors, and the penalty for refusing to serve ranged from five years in prison to execution. It is indeed ironic that the same armed forces that were considered the biggest school of brotherhood and unity and one of the strongest unifying institutions guaranteeing Yugoslav statehood metamorphosed into the main instrument against it during the bloody breakup of Yugoslavia in the 1990s.

Josip Močnik

See also

Communist Revolutionary Warfare; Non-Aligned Movement; Soviet-Yugoslav Split; Tito, Josip Broz; Warsaw Pact; Yugoslavia

References

Dedijer, Vladimir, Ivan Božić, Sima Ćirković, and Milorad Ekmečić. *History of Yugoslavia.* New York: McGraw-Hill, 1974.

Dyker, David A., and Ivan Vejvoda, eds. *Yugoslavia and After: A Study of Fragmentation, Despair, and Rebirth.* London: Longman, 1996.

Gow, James. *Legitimacy and the Military: The Yugoslav Crisis.* New York: St. Martin's, 1992.

Milivojević, Marko, John B. Allcock, and Pierre Maurer, eds. *Yugoslavia's Security Dilemmas: Armed Forces, National Defence, and Foreign Policy.* Oxford, UK: Berg, 1988.

Z

Zaire

See Congo, Democratic Republic of the; Congo Civil War

Zápotocký, Antonín (1884–1957)

Czech communist politician, prime minister (1948–1953), and president of Czechoslovakia (1953). Born on 19 December 1884 in Zákolany, Bohemia, to a politically active working-class family, Antonín Zápotocký trained as a mason and joined the workers' movement and the Social Democratic Party in Kladno. He became known for his union-organizing abilities and was elected to the Kladno town council in 1911. Arrested several times for his political activities, he was drafted into the Austro-Hungarian Army, serving on various fronts during World War I.

After the war, Zápotocký returned to Kladno, resumed his activity with the Social Democrats, and wrote poetry and several novels about his involvement with the workers' movement. He received a two-year prison sentence for leading the 1920 general strike of Kladno ironworkers and miners. Released early, he became a founding member of the Communist Party of Czechoslovakia (CPCz) in 1921. He also assisted in the formation of its press and trade union movement.

In 1925 Zápotocký was elected as a deputy to the National Assembly, later serving as a senator. In 1929 he became head of the communist trade union in Czechoslovakia. After the Germans occupied Czechoslovakia in March 1939, he was arrested and interned at Sachsenhausen concentration camp until the end of World War II.

In 1945, Zápotocký joined the CPCz Politburo and became head of the Revolutionary Trade Union Organization (RTUO), the blanket union organization in Czechoslovakia. He was again elected to the National Assembly in 1946. He was instrumental in the CPCz's February 1948 coup by rallying his workers in the People's Militia to support the communist takeover. Consequently, he became a deputy prime minister and, after CPCz leader and Premier Klement Gottwald became president in June 1948, succeeded him as premier.

Under Zápotocký's leadership, Czechoslovakia became a hard-line Stalinist state that attacked organized religion, private enterprise, and civil rights while unconditionally supporting Soviet policies at home and abroad. He also played an important role in events leading up to the 1950s purges and show trials in Czechoslovakia.

In 1950 Zápotocký helped reorganize the CPCz and resigned from the RTUO after being elected to the CPCz secretariat and presidium. Upon Gottwald's death in March 1953, Zápotocký became president, holding the position until his death in Prague on 13 November 1953.

Gregory C. Ference

See also
Czechoslovakia; Gottwald, Klement

References
Korbel, Josef. *The Communist Subversion of Czechoslovakia, 1938–1948.* Princeton, NJ: Princeton University Press.
Shoemaker, M. Wesley. *Russia, Eurasian States, and Eastern Europe.* Harpers Ferry, WV: Stryker-Post, 1994.

Zhang Hanfu (1905–1972)

Vice foreign minister of the People's Republic of China (PRC). Born in Wujin, Jiangsu Province, on 7 November 1905, Zhang Hanfu studied at China's Qinghua University and also took up studies in the United States and the Soviet Union during the 1920s. Returning to China in 1929, he found work as a journalist in Shanghai. In 1938 he joined the Chinese Communist Party (CCP) and served throughout the Sino-Japanese War as editor of the CCP's wartime publications. In 1945 he accompanied Zhou Enlai, the PRC's future foreign minister, to the San Francisco conference that drafted the United Nations (UN) Charter.

During the Chinese Civil War, Zhang served in Hong Kong, where he continued his editing career. He returned to China in late 1948 and became director of the Alien Affairs Office of the Municipal People's Government in Jiangsu. Upon the establishment of the PRC in 1949, he was appointed vice foreign minister, working directly under Zhou. In December 1949, Zhang also became director of the Foreign Ministry's Committee on Foreign Treaties, where he was responsible for developing China's diplomatic relationships with Western Asian and African nations. In April 1955 he accompanied Zhou to the Bandung Conference, at which Zhou's "Five Principles for Peaceful Coexistence" were first enunciated in public.

Zhang went on to serve under Liu Shaoqi and Chen Yi, traveling with them on a number of Asian and African tours to promote the Bandung Spirit. Zhang died in Beijing on 1 January 1972.

Law Yuk-fun

See also
Bandung Conference; Chen Yi; China, People's Republic of; Liu Shaoqi; United Nations; Zhou Enlai
References
Chen, Jian. *Mao's China and the Cold War.* Chapel Hill: University of North Carolina Press, 2001.
Neuhauser, Charles. *Third World Politics: China and the Afro-Asian Peoples' Solidarity Organization, 1957–1967.* Cambridge: East Asian Research Center, Harvard University, 1968.

Zhang Wentian (1900–1976)

Chinese diplomat and vice foreign minister of the People's Republic of China (PRC) during 1955–1959. Born in Nanhui, Jiangsu Province, on 30 August 1900, Zhang Wentian joined the Chinese Communist Party (CCP) in 1925 and then enrolled at Moscow's Sun Yixian University. Upon his return to China

in 1931, he became minister of publicity for the CCP, responsible for editing the party's journals.

During the Sino-Japanese War (1937–1945), Zhang served in Yan'an, Shaanxi, as editor of party publications and president of the Institute of Marxism and Leninism. After the war, he was sent to Northeast China, where he stayed throughout the final stages of the Chinese Civil War (1947–1949), working on organizational and economic matters.

In January 1950, Zhang was transferred to Beijing to lead a delegation to the United Nations (UN) and was concurrently appointed as the PRC representative to the UN Security Council. Realizing that the PRC could not be seated in the UN, Beijing named Zhang ambassador to the Soviet Union in 1951. In April 1954 he was appointed vice foreign minister and attended the Geneva Conference held that the same month. Returning to China in early 1955, he formally assumed his ministerial duties. During his tenure, which lasted until 1959, he was responsible for the PRC's relationship with the Soviet communist bloc. In September 1959, he was relieved of his post on charges that he had developed close ties with antiparty elements. He was forced to retreat from the diplomatic front line, taking up a research fellowship in the Economic Institute, a job he held until 1965.

With the ultraleftist Cultural Revolution, Zhang was first purged and then internally exiled. He died in Wuxi, Jiangsu Province, on 1 July 1976.

Law Yuk-fun

See also
China, People's Republic of; Cultural Revolution; Geneva Conference (1954); Zhou Enlai
References
Chen, Jian. *Mao's China and the Cold War.* Chapel Hill: University of North Carolina Press, 2001.
Weng, Byron S. J. *Peking's UN Policy: Continuity and Change.* New York: Praeger, 1972.
Westad, Odd Arne, ed. *Brothers in Arms: The Rise and the Fall of the Sino-Soviet Alliance, 1945–1953.* Washington, DC: Woodrow Wilson Center Press, 1998.

Zhao Ziyang (1919–2005)

Chinese communist politician and premier of the People's Republic of China (PRC) during 1980–1987. Born in Huaxian, Henan Province, on 17 October 1919, Zhao Ziyang completed his secondary education in 1937 at Wuhan, the capital of his native province. The next year, he joined the Chinese Communist Party (CCP), becoming secretary of the Third Special District in the Hebei-Shandong Border Region, where he also fought in the Sino-Japanese War (1937–1945).

Following World War II, Zhao was responsible for rural reform work in the Hebei-Shandong-Henan Border Region.

Chinese Premier Zhao Ziyang, shown here during a meeting with U.S. President Ronald Reagan during talks at the Great Hall of the People in Beijing, 27 April 1984. (Bettmann/Corbis)

PRC's international image. In 1987 he became the general-secretary and the first vice chairman of the CCP Central Committee's Military Commission. On 19 May 1989, he visited with the student prodemocracy demonstrators in Tiananmen Square in Beijing. He begged them to depart, apologized for having arrived "too late," and warned the students that the state authorities were planning to take action against them. In June 1989, shortly after the Tiananmen Square Massacre, he was stripped of all his posts because of his support of the student demonstrators.

Zhao was then detained under house arrest in Beijing not far from the government offices where he once led China. During his long confinement, he became a powerful symbol for those who believed that the Chinese government should reassess its policies in the 3–4 June 1989 Tiananmen Square crackdown. Zhao died in Beijing on 17 January 2005, and nervous Chinese government officials strongly discouraged any public demonstrations or mourning to mark the occasion.

Law Yuk-fun

See also
China, People's Republic of; Cultural Revolution; Liu Shaoqi; Mao Zedong; Tiananmen Square

References
Chao Wei. *The Biography of Zhao Ziyang.* Translated by Chen Shibin. Hong Kong: Educational and Cultural Press, 1989.

MacFarquhar, Roderick, ed. *The Politics of China: The Eras of Mao and Deng.* New York: Cambridge University Press, 1997.

Meisner, Maurice. *Mao's China and After: A History of the People's Republic.* New York: Free Press, 1999.

Shambaugh, David L. *The Making of a Premier: Zhao Ziyang's Provincial Career.* Boulder, CO: Westview, 1984.

Zhang Liang, comp. *The Tiananmen Papers.* Edited by Andrew J. Nathan and Perry Link. Boston: Little, Brown, 2001.

During the Chinese Civil War (1946–1949), he served in his native province as the CCP's secretary of the Luoyang District. During October 1949–1965, he was assigned to Guangdong Province, holding a secretariat in the South China subbureau of the Central–South China Bureau. In mid-1965, he was promoted to the bureau level as the first secretary of Guangdong.

In October 1967, as a result of the ultraleftist Cultural Revolution, Zhao was denounced as a counterrevolutionary, a member of the landowning class, and an agent of PRC Chairman Liu Shaoqi, a rival of Mao Zedong. Thereafter, Zhao was exiled from public life, spending four years at forced labor in a factory until May 1971, when he was assigned to the Inner Mongolia Autonomous Region as the party's secretary. In April 1972 he returned to Guangdong, resuming his former posts. In 1976 he went to Sichuan, where he assumed similar positions. His successful economic modernization of Sichuan soon captured Beijing's attention.

In 1980, Zhao became premier, a post he held until 1987, during which he frequently traveled abroad to promote the

Zhdanov, Andrei Aleksandrovich (1896–1948)

Soviet political leader and his country's chief communist ideologue in the early Cold War. Born in Mariupol, Ukraine, on 14 February 1896, Andrei Zhdanov joined the Bolshevik Party in 1915. Following the Bolshevik seizure of power in November 1917, he served as a party official in several regions of the country. A close associate of Josef Stalin, Zhdanov enjoyed rapid advancement in the party hierarchy. He took the lead in developing Soviet cultural policy, helping to establish both the Union of Soviet Writers and the doctrine of socialist realism, whereby literature and art should be realistic and instructive in order to advance the communist ideal.

Following the assassination of Sergei Kirov in 1934, Stalin appointed Zhdanov to the powerful post of party boss in Leningrad. Zhdanov played a leading part in the Great Purges of the late 1930s, sending tens of thousands of suspect communists and their families to Siberia. During World War II, he took a key role in the defense of Leningrad during the long German siege of that city. Following the capitulation of Finland, which had reentered the war against the Soviet Union, he supervised reparations from that country to the Soviet Union.

Immediately after the war, Zhdanov was instrumental in the establishment of the Cominform (Communist Information Bureau) and in ensuring Soviet control over Eastern Europe. In line with this, he developed an anti-Western ideology that played on the intense patriotism roused by Soviet military accomplishments and suffering in the war to enforce discipline and stifle dissent.

In the summer of 1946, with the full support of Stalin, Zhdanov mounted an intense ideological crusade against Western influence, or bourgeois cosmopolitanism, and culture. Known as the Zhdanovshchina, it had three key elements: the glorification of Stalin, to whom all accomplishments were attributed; the achievements of the Soviet people, above all the Great Russians, in the war and in science and the arts (firsts were claimed for a variety of scientific advances); and communism. Numerous writers, artists, and scientists were sent to labor camps for failing to toe the party line.

Zhdanov, regarded by many as Stalin's heir apparent, was a heavy drinker and also suffered from heart disease. He battled a prolonged and unspecified illness for some time before his death at Valdai Heights near Moscow on 31 August 1948. Zhdanov's death precipitated a power struggle and triggered the Leningrad Affair, a sudden purge of thousands of government and party officials in and around Leningrad.

Spencer C. Tucker

See also

Cominform; Soviet Union; Stalin, Josef

References

Boterbloom, Kees. *The Life and Times of Andrei Zhadanov, 1896–1948.* Montreal: McGill-Queen's University Press, 2004.

Hahn, Werner G. *Postwar Soviet Politics: The Fall of Zhdanov and the Defeat of Moderation, 1946–53.* Ithaca, NY: Cornell University Press, 1982.

Swayze, Harold. *Political Control of Literature in the USSR, 1946–1959.* Cambridge: Harvard University Press, 1962.

Zubok, Vladislav, and Constantine Pieshakov. *Inside the Kremlin's Cold War: From Stalin to Khrushchev.* Cambridge: Harvard University Press, 1996.

Zhivkov, Todor (1911–1998)

Bulgarian Communist Party (BCP) leader and head of state during 1971–1989. Born on 17 September 1911 in Pravets, Bulgaria, Todor Zhivkov received only a modest primary education before becoming a typographer. He became politically engaged at age nineteen when he joined the clandestine Com-

munist Youth organization. He joined the BCP in 1932. During World War II, he joined the antimonarchist partisans and fought against the Bulgarian Royal Army, which was allied with Nazi Germany. At war's end, he became a member of the BCP's Central Committee and went on to serve as secretary of the Municipal Committee of Sophia, the equivalent of the city's mayor.

By the late 1940s, Zhivkov had become the protégé of Valko Tchervenkov, who at the time was the strongman of the BCP. In 1951 Zhivkov joined the BCP Politburo as his meteoric political ascendancy continued. He soon became secretary of the Politburo's Central Committee, which gave him control over much of that body as a whole. In 1954 Tchervenkov tapped Zhivkov to be first secretary of the BCP. A cunning politician, Zhivkov soon pushed his mentor aside, with Moscow's implicit blessing. From 1962 until 1971, Zhivkov functioned as the leader of the BCP and as Bulgaria's premier, which afforded him vast powers over Bulgarian affairs. He was a hard-liner with dictatorial tendencies. Even while the Soviet Union implemented de-Stalinization policies in the mid-1950s, he refused to release Bulgaria's political prisoners. Indeed, the Bulgarian gulag would not be abandoned until 1962.

In 1971 Zhivkov proclaimed himself head of state as chair of the Council of State, essentially rubber-stamping his own authority as Bulgaria's leader. He continued to rule with an iron fist, choosing to surround himself mainly with family members acting as advisors and administrators. By the mid-1980s, with significant political changes afoot in Russia, he decided to crack down on his nation's Turkish minority of some 800,000 people. His repression of the Turks led to their mass exodus, with many crossing the border into Turkey. This debacle destabilized Bulgaria's already weak economy and strained relations with Turkey and the West.

Simultaneously, Zhivkov attempted to give the impression that he, like Russia's President Mikhail Gorbachev, supported perestroika. In reality, Zhivkov implemented few meaningful reforms. By late 1989, Bulgaria was on the brink of economic collapse. On 10 November 1989, as the Berlin Wall was crumbling, he was driven from office. His rule had been brutal and his policies disastrous. In February 1991, he was put on trial for his abuses of power, convicted, and sentenced to seven years in prison. For health reasons, he was confined under house arrest. Zhivkov wrote his memoirs during imprisonment and died on 5 August 1998 in Sofia.

Luc Stenger

See also

Berlin Wall; Bulgaria; Europe, Eastern; Gorbachev, Mikhail; Gulags; Perestroika; Todorov, Stanko

References

Bankowicz, Marek. "Bulgaria—The Limited Revolution." Pp. 195–210 in *The New Democracies in Eastern Europe,* edited by Sten Berglund and Jan Ake Dellenbrant. Aldershot, UK: Edward Elgar, 1991.

Bell, John D. *The Bulgarian Communist Party from Blagoev to Zhivkov.* Stanford, CA: Hoover Institute Press, 1985.

Bokov, Georgi, ed. *Modern Bulgaria: History, Policy, Economy, Culture.* Sofia: Sofia Press, 1981.

Zhivkov, Todor. *Memoori.* Sofia, Bulgaria: "SIV" AD, 1997.

Zhou Enlai (1898–1976)

Premier and foreign minister of the People's Republic of China (PRC). Born in Shaoxing, Zhejiang Province, on 5 March 1898, Zhou Enlai traveled to France in 1920 on a work-study basis and joined the Chinese Communist Party (CCP) the following year. He returned to China in 1924 and joined the Guomindang (GMD, Nationalists) upon instructions from the Comintern as a part of an alliance called the First United Front that aimed at Chinese national unification.

The United Front broke down in mid-1927 when the GMD purged the communists from its ranks, precipitating the CCP-GMD power struggle that lasted for two decades. Zhou then joined Mao Zedong, the future chairman of both the CCP and the PRC, in the two CCP power bases at Juijin, Jiangsi Province, from 1927 to 1934 and Yan'an, Shaanxi Province, from 1935 to 1945. After the PRC's birth in 1949, Zhou became the first PRC premier and concurrently the first PRC foreign minister. Within the CCP, he took on the vice chairmanship of both the Central Committee and Central Military Committee, making him second only to Mao in rank.

Zhou's responsibilities were wide-ranging, including the restructuring of the political system, the drafting of the constitution, the implementation of mass socialization, and the launching of economic reforms such as the five-year plans and collectivization. Despite occasional differences with Mao on such matters as intervention in the Korean War and the radical Great Leap Forward economic program, Zhou always fully supported Mao. This loyalty, together with Zhou's own popularity, enabled him to remain in office and survive the Cultural Revolution, during which many senior party and government officials were purged or imprisoned.

Zhou's most notable achievements were in the diplomatic realm. Although his foreign minister post was technically transferred to Chen Yi in April 1958, Zhou remained the chief architect of the PRC's foreign policy. In his capacity as premier, he spent much of his time abroad, boosting the PRC's international standing. His diplomatic approach was flexible and pragmatic, and his liaison service can be divided into three areas: the Soviet bloc, the developing world, and the Western bloc. In pursuing Mao's lean-to-one-side policy, Zhou's first task was to build a diplomatic partnership with the Soviet Union, the first nation to accord official recogni-

Premier of the People's Republic of China (PRC) Zhou Enlai. (Bettmann/Corbis)

tion to the PRC. To reinforce Sino-Soviet ties, in January 1950 he visited Moscow and the next month secured the Sino-Soviet Treaty, which not only acknowledged Sino-Soviet solidarity but also promised Soviet aid to modernize the PRC's economy. Despite reservations as to the PRC's military readiness, he eventually supported Mao's decision to enter the Korean War in October 1950 so as to prove the PRC's faithfulness to the socialist bloc.

Zhou's interest in the developing world became readily apparent in 1953. He perceived alignment with Asian and African nations as another path to elevating the PRC's image abroad. His approach to the developing world, termed the "Five Principles of Peaceful Coexistence," was first publicized at the Bandung Conference in April 1955. He called for the mutual respect of national sovereignty and territorial integrity, mutual nonaggression, nonintervention in internal affairs, equal mutual benefits, and peaceful coexistence. These became part of the so-called Bandung Spirit, which the conference participants pledged to uphold and promote.

Zhou's policy toward the developing world soon paid off, as the new Soviet leader, Nikita Khrushchev, advocated peaceful coexistence with the West, but Sino-Soviet relations began to deteriorate. Meanwhile, Mao vituperatively attacked Khrushchev's revisionism, and by 1963 Sino-Soviet solidarity had all but disappeared. To redress the loss of the PRC's erstwhile ally, Zhou looked to the developing world, although the onset of the Cultural Revolution prevented him from forging closer ties with the Asian-African bloc.

The PRC's early alliance with the Soviet Union inevitably meant an anti-U.S. stance. Zhou's problems with the United States centered on two main issues. The first was PRC representation in the United Nations (UN). Following the PRC's birth, Zhou had demanded that Jiang Jieshi's Guomindang (GMD, Nationalist) representative to the UN be unseated and replaced with a PRC representative. America, however, blocked such an attempt. The second issue was the island of Taiwan, which Jiang's GMD still retained and to which the United States was still attached. During his tenure, Zhou frequently reiterated the PRC's sovereignty over Taiwan and harshly criticized U.S. policies toward Taiwan.

Zhou never excluded the possibility of maintaining unofficial communications with the United States. His position bore fruit after the mid-1950s, when the PRC found itself increasingly isolated diplomatically. At the Bandung Conference, Zhou initiated what later became the Sino-American Ambassadorial Talks, first held in August 1958, that provided the first direct channel for U.S.-PRC communications. Although these talks were often suspended due to the deadlock over Taiwan, Zhou did not abandon the hope of reaching an understanding with the United States with a view toward breaking his nation's diplomatic isolation resulting from the Sino-Soviet split and the Cultural Revolution. In late 1969, he proposed to Mao a normalization of Sino-American relations. Once the proposal was approved, Zhou was wholly responsible for the rapprochement that ultimately led to U.S. President Richard M. Nixon's historic trip to China in February 1972. This top-level summit laid the foundation for the formal establishment of a Sino-American diplomatic relationship, which was completed in 1979. Zhou died in Beijing on 8 January 1976. His death triggered mourning demonstrations that contributed to the overthrow of the radical Gang of Four, who succeeded Mao following his death later that year, and their replacement by the more pragmatic Deng Xiaoping, who emphasized economic development rather than communist ideology.

Law Yuk-fun

See also

Bandung Conference; Beijing Meeting; Chen Yi; China, People's Republic of; China, Republic of; Cultural Revolution; Korean War; Mao Zedong; Taiwan Strait Crisis, First; Taiwan Strait Crisis, Second

References

Chen, Jian. *Mao's China and the Cold War.* Chapel Hill: University of North Carolina Press, 2001.

Garver, John W. *Foreign Relations of the People's Republic of China.* Englewood Cliffs, NJ: Prentice Hall, 1993.

Han Suyin. *Elder Son: Zhou Enlai and the Making of Modern China.* New York: Hill and Wang, 1994.

Shao, Kuo-kang. *Zhou Enlai and the Foundations of Chinese Foreign Policy.* New York: St. Martin's, 1996.

Wilson, Dick. *Zhou Enlai: A Biography.* New York: Viking, 1984.

Zhou, Enlai. *Selected Works of Zhou Enlai.* Beijing: Foreign Languages Press, 1981.

Zhu De (1886–1976)

Chinese military leader, politician, and vice chairman of the People's Republic of China (PRC) during 1954–1959. Born in Yilong, Sichuan Province, on 18 December 1886, Zhu De went to Germany in 1922, studying in Berlin and Göttingen, and joined the Chinese Communist Party (CCP) the same year. He returned to China in 1926 and engaged in covert military activities. His two most innovative contributions were the development of the CCP's Red Army in 1927, which later became the People's Liberation Army (PLA), and the conceptualization of modern guerrilla warfare with its emphasis on control of the countryside. His military leadership and talents ensured the CCP's victories in both the Sino-Japanese War (1937–1945) and the Chinese Civil War (1946–1949). In both struggles, he commanded the CCP's armed forces.

After the birth of the PRC in October 1949, Zhu held a number of top positions, including commander in chief of the PLA, one of the vice chairmen of both the Central People's Government Council and the People's Revolutionary Council, and a member of the Standing Committee of the party's Central Committee. In September 1954 he gave up these posts and became the PRC's sole vice chairman and the first-ranking vice chairman of the National Defense Council, in political importance ranking second only to Chairman Mao Zedong. In 1955, Zhu was named one of the ten marshals of the PLA. Given his advanced age, he became less active in military affairs, participating only in important military conferences.

In foreign relations, however, Zhu became more active. During his tenure, he frequently traveled abroad on inspection tours to Moscow, Eastern Europe, and the Democratic People's Republic of Korea (DPRK, North Korea). In April 1959 he relinquished his two vice chairmanships and served as chairman of the Standing Committee of the National People's Congress, a nominal legislative body. Thereafter he seldom made public appearances until the mid-1960s, when he was persecuted during the ultraleftist Cultural Revolution (1966–1976) simply because of his military background and was perceived as a threat to Mao's leadership. Zhu died in Beijing on 6 July 1976.

Law Yuk-fun

See also

Cultural Revolution; Mao Zedong

References

Chien, Yu-shen. *China's Fading Revolution: Army Dissent and Military Division, 1967–1968.* Hong Kong: Centre of Contemporary Chinese Studies, 1969.

Joffe, Ellis. *Party and Army: Professionalism and Political Control in the Chinese Officer Corps, 1949–1964.* Cambridge: Cambridge University Press, 1965.

Zhukov, Georgi Konstantinovich (1917–1974)

Marshal of the Soviet Union and minister of defense (1955–1957). Born in a peasant family in Strelkovka, Kaluga Province, Russia, on 1 December 1896, Georgi Zhukov was conscripted into the Russian Army in 1915 and served in the cavalry during World War I. He received a severe wound in late 1916 and did not participate in the fighting in 1917. He joined the Red Army in 1918, received a commission, and rose to squadron commander during the Russian Civil War.

In 1923 Zhukov took command of a cavalry regiment and in 1930 of a brigade. He attended several service schools, including the Frunze during 1929–1930, rising steadily in rank and responsibilities. In 1933 he had charge of a cavalry division and in 1937 of a corps. He was one of the few senior officers to survive Josef Stalin's purge of the military leadership in the late 1930s. In 1938 Zhukov was appointed deputy commander of the Bialystok Military District, and in June 1939 he received command of Soviet forces battling the Japanese in Mongolia. By the end of August, he had defeated the Japanese in the Battle of Khalkin Gol.

Promoted to full general, in June 1940 Zhukov took command of the Kiev Military District. In January 1941 he became chief of the General Staff, in effect Soviet dictator Stalin's chief military advisor. Following the June 1941 German invasion of the Soviet Union, Zhukov took part in almost every major battle on the Eastern Front, earning the nickname "Stalin's Fireman." He participated in the unsuccessful defense of Smolensk in August and successfully organized the defense of Leningrad in October and of Moscow, launching the counteroffensive against the Germans there in December 1941. In the fall of 1942, Zhukov helped plan the counteroffensive that trapped the German Sixth Army at Stalingrad. Promoted to marshal of the Soviet Union and appointed deputy supreme commander of the Red Army, he helped raise the siege of Leningrad in 1943, and that July he assisted in the defense of the Kursk salient.

In the summer and autumn of 1944, Zhukov directed the great Belorussian Campaign that destroyed the German Army Group Center, and in April 1945 he personally commanded the final Soviet assault on Berlin. He was the Soviet representative at the formal German surrender of 8 May 1945, and he remained in Germany to command Soviet occupation forces there and serve as the Soviet representative on the Allied Control Commission for Germany.

In March 1946, Zhukov was recalled to the Soviet Union as commander in chief of Soviet Land Forces and deputy defense minister, but he lasted only three months in this post. In July, Stalin—no doubt jealous of Zhukov's popularity and viewing him as a potential threat—relegated Zhukov to a series of minor commands, first the Odessa Military District and in February 1948 the Ural Military District.

Following Stalin's death in March 1953, Nikita Khrushchev brought Zhukov back to the senior leadership, apparently anxious to use Zhukov's status to ensure support from the armed forces. He became first deputy minister of defense in 1953 and defense minister in February 1955. During this period, he pushed modernization of the force structure, including the integration of missiles and nuclear weapons and improving the mobility of the armed forces. He also spearheaded major revisions in doctrine and strategy to exploit advances in technology and pursued a parallel effort to professionalize the officer corps.

Zhukov organized the Soviet invasion of Hungary in 1956. In June 1957, he supported Khrushchev during an effort to oust the Soviet leader and was rewarded by appointment to the Politburo, the first professional military man to reach this top-level leadership body. Khrushchev strongly opposed Zhukov's proposed military reorganization that would reduce political influence in the armed forces and on 26 October 1957 dismissed Zhukov from his posts. He was rehabilitated after Khrushchev's fall from power in October 1964 but never again played a major role in policy making. Zhukov died in Moscow on 18 June 1974.

Jerome V. Martin and Spencer C. Tucker

See also
Khrushchev, Nikita; Soviet Union, Army; Stalin, Josef

References
Anfilov, Viktor. "Georgy Konstantinovich Zhukov." Pp. 343–360 in *Stalin's Generals,* edited by Harold Shukmnan. New York: Grove, 1993.
Chaney, Otto Preston. *Zhukov.* Rev. ed. Norman: University of Oklahoma Press, 1996.
Spahr, William J. *Zhukov: The Rise & Fall of a Great Captain.* Novato, CA: Presidio, 1993.
Zhukov, Georgi Konstantinovich. *The Memoirs of Marshal Zhukov.* New York: Delacorte, 1971.
———. *G. Zhukov, Marshal of the Soviet Union: Reminiscences and Reflections.* Translated by Vic Schneierson. Moscow: Progress Publishers, 1985.

Zia ul Haq, Muhammad (1924–1988)

Pakistani Army general, later dictator of Pakistan (1978–1988). Muhammad Zia ul Haq was born in Jullundur, Punjab (present-day India), on 12 August 1924 to a lower-middle-class family with strong Muslim beliefs. His father was an army clerical officer. Zia attended Delhi's prestigious St. Stephen's College, graduating in 1944. He then joined the British Indian Army, serving in World War II throughout Southeast Asia.

Upon British withdrawal from the subcontinent in 1947, Zia's birthplace was located in the newly independent (and predominantly Hindu) India. As with millions of other Muslims, he and his family migrated to Pakistan, settling in Peshawar, and he joined the officer corps of the Pakistani Army. After Zia received further training in the United States and steady promotions, Pakistani President Zulfikar Ali Bhutto appointed him chief of the army staff in 1976.

The following year Zia led a coup by fellow army officers, removing Bhutto from power. Over the next several years, Zia was the head of the military junta, amassing increasing power. He ruled Pakistan as its self-appointed president by disbanding parliament, increasing the power of the presidency, and imposing martial law. His assault on political opponents included the execution of Bhutto on 4 April 1979 for allegedly participating in a murder plot against his own rivals while in office.

Although a ruthless dictator, Zia was nevertheless popular among the lower classes in Pakistan. This was largely because of his reputation as a pious Muslim and his efforts at increasing the role of Islam in government, including the creation of Islamic courts. Zia was killed under mysterious circumstances in a plane crash on 17 August 1988 in Bahawalpur, Pakistan.

Brent M. Geary

See also

Afghanistan War; Bhutto, Zulfikar Ali; India-Pakistan Wars; Kashmir Dispute; Pakistan; Pakistan, Armed Forces; Radical Islam

References

Arif, Khalid Mahmud. *Working with Zia: Pakistan's Power Politics, 1977–1988.* New York: Oxford University Press, 1995.

Burki, Shahid Javed, and Craig Baxter, eds. *Pakistan under the Military: Eleven Years of Zia ul-Haq.* Boulder, CO: Westview, 1991.

Ziring, Lawrence. *Pakistan in the Twentieth Century: A Political History.* Oxford: Oxford University Press, 1997.

Zimbabwe

Landlocked nation in South-Central Africa. Zimbabwe covers 150,803 square miles, about the size of the U.S. state of Montana, and is bordered by Botswana to the west, Mozambique to the east, Zambia to the north, and South Africa to the south. In 1945 the population was about 2.5 million people, with a ratio of Africans to whites of about 16 to 1. The whites of what was then known as Southern Rhodesia, a self-governing British colony since 1923, found themselves in the 1950s incorporated by Britain into a Central African Federation with the two neighboring territories of Northern Rhodesia and Nyasaland.

Following the break-up of the federation in the early 1960s, Southern Rhodesia's whites voted in the right-wing Rhodesian Front headed by Ian Smith. It was Smith who in November 1965 unilaterally declared independence from Britain and launched the country as Rhodesia. The British government had ruled out the use of force against the settlers, who therefore got away with the illegal act. By then, a white population of some 200,000 ruled more than 4 million Africans. For a time it seemed that the settlers would be able to retain power indefinitely. As their position was increasingly challenged, Cold War involvement grew in the struggle to turn Rhodesia into an independent Zimbabwe.

In the early 1960s two major nationalist parties emerged, first the Zimbabwe African People's Union (ZAPU) under Joshua Nkomo, which developed ties with the Soviet Union, and then a rival Zimbabwe African National Union (ZANU), which was courted by the People's Republic of China (PRC). These links to communist countries were in both cases forged mainly for practical reasons and because of what the African nationalists believed to be Western support for the settler regime rather than from ideological commitment to communism.

In response to the unilateral declaration of independence, the United Nations (UN) imposed sanctions against Rhodesia, but these were flouted by South Africa, which crucially continued to supply oil by Portugal and, for a time, by the United States. In 1971, Senator Harry F. Byrd of Virginia piloted through Congress an amendment to sanction legislation that permitted the United States to import chrome ore, used for steelmaking, from Rhodesia. It was argued that because the only other source of chrome was the Soviet Union, the United States must put Cold War concerns above any antipathy to white supremacist regimes in southern Africa. In 1969 the National Security Council (NSC), under Henry Kissinger, had recommended that U.S. policy should be based on the assumption that the white settler regimes in southern Africa would remain in power for the foreseeable future. Dubbed the Tar Baby Option by its critics, this meant that the United States would give tacit support to the settler regimes.

ZAPU and ZANU had launched an armed struggle against the settler regime in the mid-1960s, and during 1967–1968 ZAPU had forged an alliance with the African National Congress (ANC) of South Africa and had sent guerrillas into Rhodesia. But until 1972 the Rhodesian regime, with South African police support, was able to contain the insurgency with relative ease. Internal feuds divided ZAPU and helped render it ineffective, but the Zimbabwe African National Liberation Army (ZANLA), ZANU's military wing, began to operate from Mozambique in the early 1970s and was there given active support by the Mozambican Liberation Front (Frelimo), which came to power at independence from Portugal in 1975.

From 1972 the liberation war began to intensify, and by the time Cuban military forces intervened in Angola in late 1975, the military wings of ZAPU and ZANU were making inroads into Rhodesia from neighboring territories. Although the Rhodesian Air Force began in the mid-1970s to bomb their camps in both Mozambique and Zambia, causing large-scale loss of life, the guerrillas increasingly operated openly in parts of rural Rhodesia, having won the support of the local people. The war dragged on and became more brutal, with both sides using terror tactics. By the time the war came to an end in 1979, more than 30,000 lives, most of them black, had been lost. There was considerable white emigration during the war, and the ratio of Africans to whites rose by the end of the decade to about 25 to 1.

By early 1976 Kissinger, now U.S. secretary of state, was concerned that unless he could bring about a negotiated settlement in Rhodesia, the war would escalate and the Cubans might become involved there as well. With Marxist regimes having come to power in Angola and Mozambique, he feared the creation of more radical pro-Soviet regimes in Africa, and he was worried that Rhodesia might be the next domino to fall. He thus traveled to Africa in April 1976 and in Zambia's capital, Lusaka, announced that the United States favored majority rule in Rhodesia. He then put pressure on Ian Smith via South African Prime Minister John Vorster, who was himself under domestic pressure, to accept the principle of majority rule, which Smith reluctantly did in October 1976 after the South Africans threatened to withdraw support from his regime. Attempts by President Jimmy Carter's administration and the British government to mediate in the conflict to produce a moderate black successor regime initially bore little fruit.

Soon after he became president, Carter pushed Congress to repeal the Byrd Amendment, which it did in March 1977, ending American violation of UN sanctions against Rhodesia. As Smith moved toward implementing a new constitution in which black Africans would take nominal power, there were many in the United States who argued that the time had come to lift sanctions. At the invitation of U.S. Senator Jesse Helms and others, Smith visited the United States in October 1978 to court support for the lifting of sanctions. Carter, however, stood firm against this and supported the British position that a settlement must include ZAPU and ZANU, which had now come together under pressure from the neighboring states in an uneasy Patriotic Front (PF).

The internal election that Smith organized and that the nationalists boycotted ushered in the majority-rule government of Abel Muzorewa. Margaret Thatcher, who became British prime minister following the Conservative Party's victory in Britain's April 1979 general election, was tempted to recognize the Muzorewa government. Instead, she invited all parties, including Smith, Muzorewa, Nkomo, and Robert Mugabe, to attend a conference at Lancaster House in London in order to reach an internationally recognized settlement. Mugabe reluctantly agreed to attend, only because Samora Machel of Mozambique threatened that if he did not, ZANU would lose its bases in his country.

British Foreign and Commonwealth Secretary Lord Carrington followed a brilliant negotiating strategy. He insisted, for example, that negotiations take place one step at a time. Thus, in the last months of 1979, the constitution for an independent Zimbabwe was agreed to, and then a process was approved for a transition to independence via a direct British presence. Mugabe in particular disliked the terms of the settlement, but Machel again put pressure on him. A British governor, Christopher Soames, was sent out to Rhodesia to oversee the holding of elections. Plots by white supremacists to assassinate Mugabe and stage a coup were foiled.

Thanks to U.S. and British diplomacy and to the cost of the war, the bitterest liberation war fought in southern Africa came to an end, and an internationally recognized, independent Zimbabwe was born. To the dismay of the British and U.S. governments, however, it was not the moderates who triumphed in the election held in early 1980 but rather Mugabe of ZANU-PF, the austere revolutionary who had served eleven years in Smith's detention centers.

Coming into office, Mugabe initially preached reconciliation, but he had never absorbed democratic norms and was prepared to act with force to suppress any opposition to his rule. Nevertheless, when Zimbabwe became independent in April 1980, the United States provided an aid package of $225 million to the new government, hoping that Mugabe's radicalism might be tempered, that Zimbabwe would remain stable and prosperous, and that it might serve as a role model for white South Africans. Whatever doubts they had about Mugabe, the Western powers had successfully prevented any significant involvement by communist countries in Rhodesia beyond the training of guerrillas and the supply of military materiél to ZAPU and ZANU.

For its first two decades after independence, Zimbabwe remained relatively stable and prosperous, although Mugabe used brutal measures in 1982, sending a brigade trained by the Democratic People's Republic of Korea (DPRK, North Korea) to stamp out opposition in southwestern Zimbabwe. More than 10,000 people are thought to have been killed in an episode that largely escaped the world's attention. Although Mugabe did not allow the ANC's armed wing to operate from Zimbabwe, his country was nevertheless the victim of a number of acts of South African aggression during the 1980s. Even as Zimbabwe moved toward becoming a de facto one-party state, the Lancaster House agreement prevented expropriation

A white Rhodesian soldier is on watch as black voters line up at a polling station at Lundi to vote in the Rhodesian election, 19 April 1979. The vote resulted in the country's first black-dominated parliament. (Bettmann/Corbis)

of land for ten years, and no moves were made to take land from whites by force until well after the end of the Cold War. In the early 1990s, Zimbabwe remained a viable state, but the rise of an effective opposition brought out Mugabe's dictatorial tendencies. By the end of the century, the country was plunging into economic ruination, with massive confiscations of white-owned farms, declining agricultural production, an AIDS epidemic, and political violence leading to rigged elections.

Christopher Saunders

See also

Africa; African National Congress; Constructive Engagement; Frontline States; Kissinger, Henry; Mozambique; Mugabe, Robert Gabriel; National Security Study Memorandum 39; Nkomo, Joshua; Smith, Ian Douglas; South Africa; Thatcher, Margaret

References

Horne, Gerald. *From the Barrel of a Gun: The United States and the War against Zimbabwe, 1965–1980*. Harare: Sapes Books, 2001.

Lake, Anthony. *The "Tar Baby" Option: American Policy towards Southern Rhodesia*. New York: Columbia University Press, 1976.

Martin, David, and Phyllis Johnson. *The Struggle for Zimbabwe: The Chimurenga War*. Johannesburg: Ravan, 1981.

Meredith, Martin. *Robert Mugabe: Power, Plunder and Tyranny in Zimbabwe*. Johannesburg: Jonathan Ball, 2002.

Stedman, Stephen. *Peacemaking in Civil War: International Mediation in Zimbabwe, 1974–1980*. Boulder, Co.: Lynne Rienner, 1991.

Tamarkin, Mordechai. *The Making of Zimbabwe: Decolonization in Regional and International Politics*. London: Frank Cass, 1990.

Zorin, Valerian Aleksandrovich (1902–1986)

Soviet diplomat. Born in Novocherkassk in the Rostov Oblast on 14 January 1902, Valerian Zorin joined the Communist Party of the Soviet Union (CPSU) in 1922. Following a decade in various party posts, he attended the Higher Communist Institute of Education, graduating in 1935. He taught and served as a party official in several posts until joining the People's Commissariat of Foreign Affairs in 1941. He served as assistant secretary-general during 1941–1942, deputy commissar during 1942–1943, and head of the Fourth (Central European) Department during 1943–1945.

In March 1945, Zorin was appointed Soviet ambassador to Czechoslovakia, where he served until the spring of 1947.

He then served as Soviet representative to the United Nations (UN) Economic Commission for Europe and later served on the Soviet delegation to the UN before returning to Moscow in November 1947 as deputy foreign minister, a post he held until 1955. He was dispatched to Prague to help oversee the February 1948 coup that installed a communist government.

From October 1952 to April 1953, Zorin was Soviet ambassador to the UN while retaining his foreign ministry post. In 1955 he was named Soviet ambassador to the Federal Republic of Germany (FRG, West Germany) before returning as deputy foreign minister the following year. Remaining in this post until 1965, he also served once again as Soviet ambassador to the UN from 1960 to 1963. During this appointment, he was involved in a now-famous exchange with U.S. ambassador to the UN Adlai Stevenson at the time of the Cuban Missile Crisis in October 1962. In 1965, Zorin was named Soviet ambassador to France, where he served until his retirement in 1971. In retirement, he served occasionally as an ambassador-at-large with responsibility for human rights issues. Elected a candidate member of the CPSU Central Committee in 1956, he became a full member in 1965. He died in Moscow on 14 January 1986.

Steven W. Guerrier

See also

Cuban Missile Crisis; Czechoslovakia; Kennedy, John Fitzgerald; Khrushchev, Nikita; Stevenson, Adlai Ewing, II; United Nations

References

Brugioni, Dino A. *Eyeball to Eyeball: Inside the Cuban Missile Crisis.* New York: Random House, 1993.

Dobrynin, Anatoly. *In Confidence: Moscow's Ambassador to America's Six Cold War Presidents, 1962–1986.* New York: Times Books, 1995.

Friedman, Norman. *The Fifty Year War: Conflict and Strategy in the Cold War.* Annapolis MD: Naval Institute Press, 2000.

Appendices

Rank Structures, Selected Cold War Militaries

All modern armies have two primary classes of soldier: officers and enlisted men. This distinction originated in the armies of ancient times. In the medieval period, the distinction was between knights and men at arms; that is, between nobility and commoners. Through the beginning of the twentieth century, the distinction between military officers and enlisted soldiers reflected the social class distinctions of society as a whole. An officer was, by definition, a gentleman. The breakdown in the old social order that began during World War I was likewise reflected in the world's armies. By the end of World War II, the distinction between officers and enlisted men had become far more a professional one than a social one.

Officers, who comprise 10–15 percent of modern armies, are further divided into three basic groups. Company-grade officers (lieutenants and captains) are responsible for the leadership of platoons and companies. Field-grade officers (majors and colonels) lead battalions and regiments. General officers command the higher military echelons and also coordinate the overall direction of an army and its military activities. It is the generals who answer directly to the political leadership of modern democracies. In some armies, the highest-level general officers hold the title of marshal. Navies also recognize three broad groups of officers, without necessarily using the army terms. In most militaries, generals and admirals are collectively called flag officers because each one has a personal flag bearing the insignia of his rank. Although women flag officers are not uncommon in the U.S. military today, the first one only appeared in the U.S. Army in the early 1970s. Female flag officers are still a rarity in most of the world's militaries.

Enlisted soldiers, sailors, and airmen are divided into two basic categories: enlisted men and noncommissioned officers (NCOs). The term used for the NCO varies from army to army—for example, *Unteroffizier* in German or *sous officier* in French—but the meaning is universal. In any army, NCOs are the backbone of the organization. They are the ones responsible for training individual soldiers and for training and leading fire teams and squads. They hold key leadership positions in platoons and companies. At the higher levels, they assist staff officers in the planning and execution of operations. In all armies, the larger majority of the enlisted ranks denote the distinctions within the NCO corps. During the Cold War, the Soviet Union and the Warsaw Pact militaries had the weakest and least professional NCO corps. The American, British, and Canadian militaries had by a wide margin the best NCO corps. The Vietnam War decimated the U.S. NCO corps, but it was painstakingly rebuilt in the 1970s and 1980s. Today, most American senior NCOs have some college education, and many have bachelor's or even master's degrees—something that would have been unthinkable as recently as the late 1950s.

NCOs include corporals, sergeants, and, in some armies, warrant officers. In most navies, the NCOs are called petty officers and, in some cases, warrant officers. Warrant officer is the most difficult to classify because its exact status varies from army to army. Most armies of the Cold War period followed the British model, in which warrant officers were the highest category of NCOs. In the U.S. military, by contrast, warrant officers were a distinct personnel class between officers and enlisted men. They were, and still are, considered to be specialist officers, highly skilled in a certain functional area (such as pilots), receiving pay equivalent to company-grade officers but without the full range of command authority and responsibilities.

In the U.S. military, warrant officers were, and still are, much closer to commissioned officers. In the British military warrant officers are clearly the most senior of the NCOs. Contrary to widely held popular belief, the rank of sergeant major does not exist in the British military. Rather, it is a position title—or an appointment, as the British call it—such as squad leader or company commander. The rank of the NCO holding the sergeant major position is always warrant officer, but he is always addressed by his position title of sergeant major. There is, then, no direct comparison between British and U.S. warrant officers, which partially explains the difficulty in correlating military ranks in any period of history.

The confusion between U.S. and British warrant officers causes problems to this day in many North American Treaty Organization (NATO) headquarters. Most armies of the Cold War had warrant officers within the British model. Italy, Poland, Greece, and Romania are among the few countries that have warrant officers within the U.S. model. The U.S. Army, Navy, and Marine Corps had four grades of warrant officer during the Cold War period, although a fifth grade was added right as the Cold War was ending. The U.S. Air Force, on the other hand, discontinued warrant officers in 1959.

While the U.S. military officer rank structure remains today essentially the same as it was in World War II, enlisted rank structures were completely revised in the late 1950s. All the services added two more enlisted pay grades, bringing the total to nine. But while the air force and navy created two new ranks at the top of their enlisted structures, the army and the marine corps added one new rank to the top and another one to the bottom. The result has been a number of anomalies. For example, a master sergeant in the army and the marine corps is a pay grade E-8, while in the air force he is an E-7, or one rank lower. The same applied to the rank of staff sergeant, which in the army and marines corps is an E-6, while it is only an E-5 in the air force.

In the late 1950s, the U.S. Army also created specialist ranks for the pay grades E-4 through E-9. In theory, specialists were not NCOs, and despite their pay grades they ranked below corporal, the lowest NCO rank. It never worked out that way in practice. A specialist 5 was, for all practical purposes, treated as an NCO, although within a given pay grade, hard-stripe NCOs always took precedence over specialists. Because the line between specialists and NCOs continued to blur, the U.S. Army eliminated the ranks of specialist 8 and specialist 9 in the late 1960s. In the subsequent years the remaining specialist ranks were eliminated, one at a time from the top down. By the end of the Cold War, only specialist 4 remained. While a specialist 4 was definitely not an NCO, a corporal (also a pay grade E-4) definitely was.

Establishing rank equivalency among armies is an inexact science at best, as the confusion over warrant officers and sergeants major illustrates. Common sense would seem to dictate that two soldiers in different armies with the exact same rank titles would be essentially equivalent. Unfortunately, that is not the case. The rank of major general provides one of the best examples. British and U.S. major generals are essentially equivalent, but they are not the same as a Soviet or Warsaw Pact general major. In the U.S. Army, major general was and is the second of the general officer ranks, whereas in the Soviet Army it was the first. Rather than simply accepting rank titles at face value, a reasonably approximate rank equivalency can only be established by considering what the holder of that rank actually did.

The problem of rank equivalency is further compounded by the fact that all armies did not have the same number of ranks, whether for officers or enlisted personnel, and sometimes even the various militaries of the same country do not have the same number of ranks. Most armies had three ranks of company-grade officer, but the Soviet and Warsaw Pact armies had four. The British Navy has no officer rank equivalent to the British Army's second lieutenant. The British Navy and the British Air Force have only one grade of warrant officer (senior NCO), but the British Army has two. The Canadian Army and Air Force, on the other hand, have three grades of warrant officer. The Norwegian military has only four enlisted ranks, the senior-most being only at the mid-level of the NATO rank-protocol list. At the most senior levels, countries such as the United Kingdom, France, Turkey, and Poland have marshals, who rank above their four-star generals. As it did during World War II, however, the Soviet Army had three levels of marshal, as did the Democratic People's Republic of Korea (DPRK, North Korea). The People's Republic of China (PRC) had two. Officer candidates had their own separate rank structures in most armies. But the ranks of cadet, midshipman, aspirant, *fahnrich*, and so on were essentially temporary training ranks. Of the eleven distinct enlisted ranks, only the Federal Republic of Germany (FRG, West Germany) had all eleven. Of the fifteen possible officer ranks, only North Korea had all fifteen.

All air forces grew from their respective armies in the first part of the twentieth century. By the Cold War, almost all air forces were independent organizations. In many countries, the rank structures for both army and air force are identical, or nearly so. The British Air Force has an officer rank structure parallel to that of the British Army but with completely different rank titles and insignia. The rank titles and insignia of U.S. Air Force officers are exactly the same as in the U.S. Army, while the enlisted rank structure is somewhat different, and the rank insignia are completely different.

Many countries during the Cold War, especially in NATO, had a fourth branch of service that may have technically been part of one of the three main services but was nonetheless distinctively separate in terms of operations, uniform, and rank structure. There were two basic types of such organizations —marines and military police. The marine corps of the United States, United Kingdom, Spain, the Netherlands, Republic of Korea (ROK, South Korea), and Republic of Vietnam (RVN, South Vietnam) were all nominally part of those countries' naval establishments. Their rank structures, and in most cases their rank insignia, were more similar to those countries' respective armies. France, Italy, Belgium, and West Germany all had national military police organizations that came under their respective ministries of defense. The German Bundesgrenzschutz (Border Police) were organized and equipped along military lines and had a specific combat role in time of war. The Bundesgrenzschutz passed to purely civilian control in 1994. The French Gendarmerie Nationale is actually a separate branch of the French military. For most of the Cold War, the Italian Carabiniere was a separate corps under the Italian Army, but after the Cold War it became a separate branch of the Italian military. As with the Bundesgrenzschutz, the Belgian Gendarmerie passed to purely civilian status in 1992.

The following tables represent an attempt to equate the various enlisted and officer ranks during the Cold War. In determining the level at which to place a given rank, the duties and responsibilities of the person holding that rank take precedence over the face value of the rank title. The tables do not include officer candidates or true warrant officers. Warrant officers as NCOs are included. Many armies also had special rank structures and designations for musicians, buglers, and pipers, which likewise are not included in the table. During the more than forty years of the Cold War period, most armies made various changes to their rank structures, and some even made complete overhauls more than once. In constructing these tables, the objective was to present a snapshot at about 1975. Even that level of precision was not completely possible. The result, then, are tables based on the best information available ranging from the late 1960s to the early 1980s.

The British Army, which describes itself as "a very tribal organization," had, and still has, a sometimes confusing number of variations on the enlisted ranks from regiment to regiment. In some cases, just the title of the rank varies, with the insignia remaining the same. Corporals and lance corporals in the British Artillery, for example, are called bombardiers and lance bombardiers. Other ranks, such as squadron quartermaster corporal, had a unique rank insignia and existed only in the Household Cavalry. For the most part, the British enlisted ranks shown in the tables are the most common.

David T. Zabecki

References

Campbell, Bert. *Marine Badges & Insignia of the World: Including Marines, Commandos, and Naval Infantrymen.* London: Blandford, 1983.

Davis, Brian L. *NATO Forces: An Illustrated Reference to Their Organization and Insignia.* London: Blandford, 1988.

Katcher, Philip. *Armies of the Vietnam War, 1962–75.* London: Osprey, 1980.

Keubke, Klaus Ulrich, and Manfred Kunz. *Militärische Uniformen in der DDR 1949–1990.* Schwerin, Germany: Atelier für Porträt- und Historienmalerie, 2003.

Rottman, Gordon L. *Warsaw Pact Ground Forces.* London: Osprey, 1987.

Wiener, Fred. *Soviet Army Uniforms and Insignia, 1945–75.* London: Arms and Armour Press, 1976.

———. *Uniforms of the Warsaw Pact.* London: Squadron/Signal Publications, 1978.

Army Forces Rank Comparison

	United States	Soviet Union	United Kingdom	West Germany	France
Officers	General of the Army	Marshal Sovetskogo Soyuza	Field Marshal		Maréchal de France
		Glavnyi Marshal Roda Voisk			
		Marshal Roda Voisk			
	General	General Armii	General	General	Général d´Armée
	Lieutenant General	General Polkovink	Lieutanant-General	Generalleutnant	Général de Corps d´Armée
	Major General	General Leitenant	Major-General	Generalmajor	Général de Division
	Brigadier General	General Maior	Brigadier	Brigadegeneral	Général de Brigade
	Colonel	Polkovnik	Colonel	Oberst	Colonel
	Lieutenant Colonel	Podpolkovink	Lieutenant-Colonel	Oberstleutnant	Lieutenant-Colonel
	Major	Maior	Major	Major	Commandant
	Captain	Kapitan	Captain	Hauptmann	Capitaine
	First Lieutenant	Starshii Leitenant	Lieutenant	Oberleutnant	Lieutenant
		Lietenant			
	Second Lieutenant	Mladshii Leitenant	Second Lieutenant	Leutnant	Sous-Lieutenant
Enlisted	Command Sergeant	Starshina	Warrant Officer Class 1	Oberstabsfeldwebel	Major
	Major Sergeant				
	Major				
	First Sergeant	Starshii Serzhant	Warrant Officer Class 2	Stabsfeldwebel	Adjudant-Chef
	Master Sergeant				
				Hauptfeldwebel	
	Platoon Sergeant		Staff Sergeant	Oberfeldwebel	Adjudant
	Sergeant First Class				
	Specialist 7				
	Staff Sergeant Specialist 6	Serzhant	Sergeant	Feldwebel	Sergent-Chef
					Maréchal-des-Logis-Chef
	Sergeant Specialist 5	Mladshii Serzhant	Corporal Bombardier	Stabsunteroffizier	Sergent Maréchal-des-Logis
	Corporal Specialist 4		Lance Corporal	Unteroffizier	Caporal-Chef
			Lance Bombardier		Brigadier-Chef
	Private First Class	Efreitor		Hauptgefreiter	Caporal
					Brigadier
	Private (E-2)			Obergefreiter	Soldat de 1ère Classe
				Gefreiter	
	Private (E-1)	Ryadovi	Private Trooper	Soldat Grenadier	Soldat de 2ème Classe
			Gunner Sapper	Kannonier	

Army Forces Rank Comparison (continued)

	Italy	Turkey	Belgium	Canada	Denmark
Officers		Maresal			
	Generale di Corpo d´Armata con Incarichi Speciali	Orgeneral	Generaal	General	General
	Generale di Corpo d´Armata	Korgeneral	Luitenant-Generaal	Lieutenant-General	Generalløjtnant
	Generale di Divisione	Tümgeneral	Generaal-Majoor	Major-General	Generalmajor
	Generale di Brigata	Tuggeneral	Brigadegeneraal	Brigadier-General	Brigadegeneral
	Colonnello	Albay	Kolonel	Colonel	Oberst
	Tenente Colonnello	Yarbay	Luitenant-Kolonel	Lieutenant-Colonel	Oberstløjnant
	Maggiore	Binbasi	Majoor	Major	Major
	Capitano	Yüzbasi	Kapitein-Commandant	Captain	Kaptajn
	Tenente	Üstegman	Kapitein	Lieutenant	Premierløjtnant
			Luitenant		Løjtnant
	Sottotenente	Tegmen	Onderluitenant	Second Lieutenant	Sekondøjtnant
Enlisted	Sergente Maggiore	Astsubay Kidemli Bascavus	Adjudant-Chef	Command Warrant Officer	Seniorsergent af 1. Grad
				Chief Warrant Officer	
		Astsubay Bascavus	Adjudant	Master Warrant Officer	Seniorsergent af 2. Grad
		Astsubay Kidemli Ustcavus			
	Sergente	Astsubay Ustcavus	1ste Sergeant-Majoor	Warrant Officer	Oversergent
		Astsubay Kidemli Cavus	1ste Sergeant	Sergeant	Sergent
		Astsubay Cavus	Sergeant	Master Corporal	Korporal
	Caporal Maggiore	Cavus	Korporaal-Chef	Corporal	Overkonstabel af 1. Grad
		Onbasi	Korporaal	Trained Private	Overkonstabel af 2. Grad
	Caporale		1ste Soldaat	Basic Private	
	Soldato	Er	Soldat	Private Recruit	Konstabel

Army Forces Rank Comparison (continued)

	Greece	Luxembourg	Netherlands	Norway	Portugal
Officers					Marechal
	Stratigos		Generaal	General	General
	Antistratigos		Luitenant-Generaal	Generalløytnant	Tenente-General
	Ypostratigos		Generaal-Majoor	Generalmajor	Major-General
	Taxiarchos		Brigade-Generaal	Oberst I	Brigadeiro-General
	Syntagmatarchis	Colonel	Kolonel	Oberst II	Coronel
	Antisyntagmatarchis	Lieutanant-Colonel	Luitenant-Kolonel	Oberstløytnant	Tenente-Coronel
	Tagmatarchis	Major	Majoor	Major	Major
	Lochagos	Capataine	Kapitein Ritmeester	Kaptein Rittmester	Capitão
	Ypolochagos	Premier Lieutenant	Eerste-Luitenant	Løytnant	Tenente
	Anthypolochagos	Lieutenant	Tweede-Luitenant	Fenrik	Alferes
Enlisted	Archilochias	Adjutant-Major	Adjudant-Onderofficier		Sargento-Mor
	Epilochias	Adjutant-Chef	Sergeant-Majoor Opperwachtmeester		Sargento-Chefe
					Sargento-Ajudante
	Lochias	Adjutant	Sergeant der 1e Klasse		Primeiro-Sargento
			Wachtmeester der 1e Klasse		
		Sergent-Chef	Sergeant Wachtmeester	Sersjant	Segundo-Sargento
	Decaneas	Premier Sergent	Korporaal der 1e Klasse	Korporal	Furriel
	Decaneas	Sergent	Korporaal	Visekorporal	Segundo-Furriel
	Ypodecaneas	Caporal-Chef	Soldaat der 1e Klasse	Primeiro-Cabo	
			Huzaar der 1e Klasse		
			Kanonier der 1e Klasse		
		Caporal			Segundo-Cabo
		Soldat de Première Classe			
	Stratiotis	Soldat	Soldaat	Menig	Soldado
		Huzaar			
		Kanonier			

Army Forces Rank Comparison (continued)

	Spain	East Germany	Poland	Romania	Czechoslovakia
Officers	Capitán General	Marschall der DDR	Marszalek Polski		
		Armeegeneral		General de Armata	Armádní Generál
	Teniente General	Generaloberst	General Broni	General Colonel	Generálplukovník
	General de División	Generalleutnant	General Dywizja	General Locotenent	Generálporucík
	General de Brigada	Generalmajor	General Brygady	General Maior	Generálmajor
	Coronel	Oberst	Pulkownik	Colonel	Plukovník
	Teniente Coronel	Oberstleutnant	Podpulkownik	Locotenent Colonel	Podplukovník
	Comandante	Major	Major	Maior	Major
	Capitán	Hauptmann	Kapitian	Capitan	Kapitán
	Teniente	Oberleutnant	Porucznik	Locotenent Maior	Nadporucík
	Alférez	Leutnant	Podporucznik	Locotenent	Porucík
	Subteniente	Unterleutnant	Chorazy	Sublocotenent	Podporucík
Enlisted	Brigada	Stabsfeldwebel	Starszy Sierzant Sztabowy	Plutonier Adjutant Sef	Nadpraporcík
		Oberfeldwebel	Sierzant Sztabowy	Plutonier Adjutant	Praporcík
				Plutonier Major	Podpraporcík
	Sargento Primero	Feldwebel	Starszy Sierzant	Plutonier	Nadrotmistr
	Sargento	Unterfeldwebel	Sierzant	Sergent Major	Rotmistr
	Cabo Primero	Unteroffizier	Plutonowy	Sergent	Rotný
	Cabo	Stabsgefreiter	Starszy Kapral	Caporal	Cetar
		Gefreiter	Kapral	Fruntas	Desátník
	Soldado Primero		Starszy Szeregowiec		Svobodník
	Soldado	Soldat	Szeregoweic	Soldat	Vojín

Army Forces Rank Comparison (continued)

	Bulgaria	Hungary	Finland	Cuba	Israel
Officers				Comandante en Jefe	
	Armeyski General	Hadseregtábornok	Kenraali	General de Ejército	
	General-Polkovnik	Vezérezredes	Kenraaliluutnantti	General de Cuerpo de Ejército	Rav Alúf
	General-Leytenant	Altábornagy	Kenraalimajuri	General de División	Alúf
	General-Mayor	Vezérörnagy	Prikaatikenraali	General de Brigada	Tat Alúf
	Polkovnik	Ezredes	Eversti	Coronel	Alúf Mishné
	Podpolknovik	Alezredes	Everstiluutnantti	Teniente Coronel	Sgan Alúf
	Mayor	Örnagy	Majuri	Mayor	Rav Séren
	Kapitan	Százados	Kapteeni	Capitán	Séren
	Starshi Leytenant	Föhadnagy	Yliluutnantti	Primer Teniente	Ségen
	Leytenant	Hadnagy	Luutnantti	Teniente	
	Mladshi Leytenant	Alhadnagy	Vänrikki	Subteniente	Ségen Mishné
Enlisted	Starshina	Fötörzsörmester	Sotilasmestari	Primer Sub-Oficial	Rav Nagád
	Starshi Serzhant	Törzsörmester	Vääpeli	Sub-Oficial	Rav Samál Bakhír
					Rav Samál Mitkadém
			Ylikersantti	Sargento de Primera	Rav Samál Rishón
	Serzhant	Örmester	Kersantti	Sargento de Segunda	Rav Samál
	Mladshi Serzhant	Szakaszvezetö	Alikersantti	Sargento de Tercera	Samál Rishón
		Tizedes	Korpraali		Samál
	Efreytor	Örvezetö		Soldado de Primera	Rav Turái
					Turái Rishón
	Rednik	Honvéd	Sotamies	Soldado	Turái

Army Forces Rank Comparison (continued)

	People's Republic of China	North Korea	South Korea	North Vietnam	South Vietnam
Officers	Zhong Hua Ren Ming	Dae Wonsu	Wonsu		Thuong Tuong
	Gong He Guo Da				
	Yuan Shuai				
	Zhong Hua Ren Ming	Wonsu			
	Gong He Guo				
	Yuan Shuai				
		Chasu			
	Da Jiang	Daejang	Taejang	Dai Tuong	Dai Tuong
	Shang Jiang	Sangjang	Chungjang	Thuong Tuong	Trung Tuong
	Zhong Jiang	Jungjang	Sojang	Trung Tuong	Thieu Tuong
	Shao Jiang	Sojang	Chungjang	Thieu Tuong	Chuan Toung
	Da Xiao	Daechwa		Dai Ta	
	Shang Xiao	Sangchwa	Taeryong	Thuong Ta	Dai Ta
	Zhong Xiao	Jungjwa	Chungryong	Trung Ta	Trung Ta
	Shao Xiao	Sojwa	Soryong	Thieu Ta	Thieu Ta
	Shang Wei	Daewi	Taewi	Dai Uy	Dai Uy
	Zhong Wei	Sangwi	Chungwi	Thuong Uy	Trung Uy
		Jungwi		Trung Uy	
	Shao Wei	Sowi	Sowi	Thieu Uy	Thieu Uy
Enlisted		Teukmu Sangsa	Wonsa	Thuong Si	Thoung Si Nhat
		Sangsa	Sangsa		Thuong Si
	Shang Shi	Jungsa	Chungsa	Trung Si	Trung Si Nhat
		Hasa	Hasa		Trung Si
	Zhong Shi	Sangkeub	Byongjang	Ha Si	Ha Si Nhat
	Xia Shi	Jungkeub	Sangbyong		Ha Si
	Shang Den Bing	Hakeub	Ilbyong	Binh Nhat	Binh Nhat
			Yibyong		Binh Nhi
	Lei Bing	Jeonsa	Mudungbyong	Binh Nhi	Trung Dinh

Naval Forces Rank Comparison

	United States	Soviet Union	United Kingdom	West Germany	France
Officers	Fleet Admiral	Admiral Flota	Admiral of the Fleet		
		Sovetskogo Soyuza			
	Admiral	Admiral Flota	Admiral	Admiral	Amiral
	Vice Admiral	Admiral	Vice-Admiral	Vizeadmiral	Vice-Amiral d'Escadre
	Rear Admiral (Upper Half)	Vitse Admiral	Rear-Admiral	Konteradmiral	Vice-Amiral
	Rear Admiral (Lower Half)	Kontr Admiral	Commodore	Flotilenadmiral	Contre-Amiral
	Captain	Kapitan Prevogo Ramga	Captain	Kapitän zur See	Capitaine de Vaisseau
	Commander	Kapitan Vtrogo Ramga	Commander	Fregattenkapitän	Capitaine de Frégate
	Lieutenant Commander	Kapitan Tret'yego Ramga	Lieutenant-Commander	Korvettenkapitän	Capitaine de Corvette
	Lieutanant	Kapitan Leitenant	Lieutenant	Kapitänleutnanent	Lieutenant de Vaisseau
	Lieutenant (Junior Grade)	Leienant	Sub-Lieutenant	Oberleutnant zur See	Enseigne de Vaisseau de 1ere Classe
	Ensign	Mladshii Leitenant	Leutnant zur See	Enseigne de Vaisseau de 2eme Classe	
Enlisted	Master Chief Petty Officer	Starshina	Warrant Officer Class 1	Oberstabsbootsmann	Major
	Senior Chief Petty Officer	Glavnyy Starshina		Stabsbootsmann	Maître-Principal
				Hauptbootsmann	
	Chief Petty Officer		Chief Petty Officer	Oberbootsmann	Premier-Maître
	Petty Officer First Class	Starshina Pervoy Stat'I	Petty Officer	Bootsmann	Maître
	Petty Officer Second Class	Starshina Vtoroy Stat'I	Leading Rate	Obermaat	Second Maître
	Petty Officer Third Class			Maat	Quartier-Maître de 1ère Classe
	Seaman Airman Fireman	Starshiny Matros	Able Seaman	Hauptgefreiter	Quartier-Maître de 2ème Classe
	Seaman Apprentice			Obergefreiter	Maître-Brevet
	Airman Apprentice				
	Fireman Apprentice				
				Gefreiter	
	Seaman Recruit	Matros	Ordinary Seaman	Matrose	Matelot

Naval Forces Rank Comparison (continued)

	Italy	Turkey	Belgium	Canada	Denmark
Officers		Büyük Amiral			
	Ammiraglio di Squadra con Incarichi Speciali	Oramiral		Admiral	
	Ammiraglio di Squadra	Koramiral	Vice-Admiraal	Vice-Admiral	Admiral
	Ammiraglio di Divisione	Tümamiral	Divise-Admiraal	Rear Admiral	Viceadmiral
	Contrammiraglio	Tugamiral	Commodore	Commodore	Kontreadmiral
	Capitano di Vascello	Albay	Kapitein-ter-Zee	Captain	Kommandør
	Capitano di Fregata	Yarbay	Fregat-Kapitein	Commander	Kommandørkaptajn
	Captiano di Corvetta	Binbasi	Korvette-Kapitein	Lieutenant-Commander	Orlogskaptajn
	Tenente di Vascello	Yüzbasi	Luitenantter-Zee 1ste Klas	Lieutenant	Kaptajnløjtnant
	Sottoenente di Vascello	Üstegman	Luitenantter-Zee	Sub-Lieutenant	Premierløjtnant
			Vaandrigter-Zee		Løjtnant
	Guardiamarina	Tegmen	Vaandrigter-Zee 2de Klas	Acting Sub-Lieutenant	Sekondløjtnant
Enlisted	Secondo Capo	Astsubay Kidemli Bascavus	Oppermeester	Command Chief Petty Officer	Seniorsergent af 1. Grad
				Chief Petty Officer 1st Class	
		Astsubay Bascavus	Eerste Meester-Chef	Chief Petty Officer 2nd Class	Seniorsergent af 2. Grad
		Astsubay Kidemli Ustcavus			
	Sergente	Astsubay Ustcavus	Eerste Meester	Petty Officer 1st Class	Oversergent
		Astsubay Kidemli Cavus	Meester	Petty Officer 2nd Class	Sergent
		Astsubay Cavus	Tweede Meester	Master Seaman	Korporal
	Sottocapo	Cavus	Kwarter Meester	Leading Seaman	Overkonstabel af 1. Grad
		Onbasi	Eerste Matroos	Able Seaman	Overkonstabel af 2. Grad
	Comune di 1a Classe		Matroos Eerste Klasse	Ordinary Seaman	
	Comune di 2a Classe	Er	Matroos	Seaman	Konstabel

Naval Forces Rank Comparison (continued)

		Greece	Netherlands	Norway	Portugal	Spain
Officers			Admiraal			Capitán General
		Navarchos	Luitenant-Admiraal	Admiral	Almirante de Armada	
		Antinavarchos	Vice-Admiraal	Viseadmiral	Almirante	Almirante
		Yponavarchos	Schout-bij-Nacht	Kontradmiral	Vice-Almirante	Vice-Almirante
		Archipliachos	Commandeur	Kommandør	Contra-Almirante	Contra-Almirante
		Pliarchos	Kapitein der Zee	Kommandør Kaptein	Capitão-de-Mar-e-Guerra	Capitan de Navio
		Antipliarchos	Kapitein-Luitenant der Zee	Orlogskaptein	Capitão-de-Fragata	Captain de Fragata
		Plotarchos	Luitenant ter Zee der 1ste Klasse	Kapteinløytnant	Capitão-Tenente	Captain de Corbeta
		Ypopliarchos	Luitenant ter Zee der 2de Klasse (Oudste Categorie)	Løytnant	Primerio-Tenente	Teniente de Navio
		Anthypopliarchos	Luitenant ter Zee der 2de Klasse	Fenrik	Segundo-Tenente	Alférez de Navio
		Simaioforos	Luitenant ter Zee der 3de Klasse	Ustskrevet	Guarda-Marinha	Alférez de Fragata
Enlisted		Archikelefstis	Adjudant-Onderofficier		Sargento-Mor	Brigada
		Epikelefstis	Sergeant-Majoor		Sargento-Chefe	
					Sargento-Ajudante	Sargento Primero
		Kelefstis			Primeiro-Sargento	
			Sergeant	Kvartermester (Konstabel I Klasse)	Segundo-Sargento	Sargento
		Dokimos Kelefstis		Ledende Menig (Konstabel II Klasse)	Sub-Sargento	Cabo Mayor
			Korporaal	Menig 1 (Konstabel III Klasse)	Cabo	Cabo Primero
		Diopos	Matross der 1e Klasse		Marinheiro	Cabo
			Matross der 2e Klasse		Primerio Grumete	Mariniero Primero
		Naftis	Matross der 3e Klasse	Menig	Segundo Grumete	Mariniero

Naval Forces Rank Comparison (continued)

	East Germany	Poland	Romania	Bulgaria	Finland
Officers	Flottenadmiral				Amiraali
	Admiral	Admiral	Amiral	Admiral	Vara-Amiraali
	Vizeadmiral	Wice Admiral	Vice-Amiral	Vitseadmiral	Kontra-Amiraali
	Konteradmiral	Kontra Admiral	Contraamiral	Kontraadmiral	Lippue-Amiraali
	Kapitän zur See	Komandor	Comandor	Kapitan I Rang	Kommodori
	Fregattenkapitän	Komandor Porucznik	Captain-Comandor	Kapitan II Rang	Komentaja
	Korvettenkapitän	Komandor Podporucznik	Locotenent-Comandor	Kapitan III Rang	Komantajakapteeni
	Kapitänleutnanent	Kapitan Marynarki	Capitan de Marina	Kapitan Leytenant	Kapteeniluutnantti
	Oberleutnant	Porucznik Marynarki	Locotenent Maior de Marina	Starshi Leytenant	Yliluutnantti
	Leutnant		Locotenent de Marina	Leytenant	Luutnantti
	Unterleutnant	Podporucznik Marynarki	Sublocotenent de Marina	Mladshi Leytenant	Aliluutnantti
Enlisted	Stabsobermeister	Starszy Bosman Sztabowy	Maistru Militar Principal	Michman	Sotilasmestari
	Obermeister	Bosman Sztabowy	Maistru Militar Classa I	Glaven Starshina	Pursimies
			Maistru Militar Classa II		
	Meister	Starszy Bosman	Maistru Militar Classa III		Ylikersantti
	Obermaat	Bosman	Maistru Militar Classa IV	Starshina I Stepen	Kersantti
	Maat	Plutonowy Bosmanmat	Sergent	Starshina II Stepen	Alikersantti
	Stabsgefreiter	Starszy Mat	Caporal		Ylimatruusi
	Obermatrose	Mat	Fruntas	Starshi Matro	
		Starszy Marynarz			
	Matrose	Marynarz	Marinar	Matros	Matruusi

Naval Forces Rank Comparison (continued)

	People's Republic of China	North Korea	South Korea	North Vietnam	South Vietnam
Officers			Wonsu		
		Chasu			
		Daejang	Taejang		Dai Tuong
	Hai Jun Shang Jiang	Sangjang	Chungjang	Do Doc	Trung Tuong
	Hai Jun Zhong Jiang	Jungjang	Sojang	Pho Do Doc	Thieu Tuong
	Hai Jun Shao Jiang	Sojang	Chungjang	Chuan Do Doc	Chuan Toung
	Hai Jun Da Xiao	Daechwa		Dai Ta	
	Hai Jun Shang Xiao	Sangchwa	Taeryong	Thuong Ta	Dai Ta
	Hai Jun Zhong Xiao	Jungjwa	Chungryong	Trung Ta	Trung Ta
	Hai Jun Shao Xiao	Sojwa	Soryong	Thieu Ta	Thieu Ta
	Hai Jun Shang Wei	Daewi	Taewi	Dai Uy	Dai Uy
	Hai Jun Zhong Wei	Sangwi	Chungwi	Thuong Uy	Trung Uy
		Jungwi		Trung Uy	
	Hai Jun Shao Wei	Sowi	Sowi	Thieu Uy	Thieu Uy
Enlisted		Teukmu Sangsa	Wonsa	Thuong Si	Thoung Si Nhat
		Sangsa	Sangsa		Thuong Si
	Hai Jun Shang Shi	Jungsa	Chungsa	Trung Si	Trung Si Nhat
		Hasa	Hasa		Trung Si
	Hai Jun Zong Shi	Sangkeub	Byongjang	Ha Si	Ha Si Nhat
	Hai Jun Xia Shi	Jungkeub	Sangbyong		Ha Si
	Shang Den Bing	Hakeub	Ilbyong	Binh Nhat	Binh Nhat
			Yibyong		Binh Nhi
	hui Bing	Jeonsa	Mudungbyong	Binh Nhi	Trung Dinh

Naval Forces Rank Comparison (continued)

	Cuba	Israel
Officers	Almirante	
	Vicealmirante	Alúf
	Contraalmirante	Tat Alúf
	Captain de Navio	Alúf Mishné
	Capitan de Fragata	Sgan Alúf
	Captain de Corbeta	Rav Séren
	Teniente de Navio	Séren
	Teniente de Fragate	Ségen
	Teniente de Corbeta	
	Alfrez	Ségen Mishné
Enlisted	Primer Sub-Oficial	Rav Nagád
	Sub-Oficial	Rav Samál Bakhír
		Rav Samál Mitkadém
	Sargento de Primera	Rav Samál Rishón
	Sargento de Segunda	Rav Samál
	Sargento de Tercera	Samál Rishón
		Samál
	Marinero de Primera	Rav Turái
		Turái Rishón
	Marinero	Turái

Air Forces Rank Comparison

		United States	Soviet Union	United Kingdom	West Germany	France
Officers		General of the Air Force		Marshal of the RAF		Maréchal de France
			Glavniy Marshal Aviatsii			
			Marshal Aviatsii			
		General	General Armii	Air Chief Marshal	General	Général d´Armée Aérienne
		Lieutenant General	General Polkovink	Air Marshal	Generalleutnant	Général de Corps Aérienne
		Major General	General Leitenant	Air Vice Marshal	Generalmajor	Général de Division Aérienne
		Brigadier General	General Maior	Air Commodore	Brigadegeneral	Général de Brigade Aérienne
		Colonel	Polkovnik	Group Captain	Oberst	Colonel
		Lieutenant Colonel	Podpolkovink	Wing Commander	Oberstleutnant	Lieutenant-Colonel
		Major	Maior	Squadron Leader	Major	Commandant
		Captain	Kapitan	Flight Lieutenant	Hauptmann	Capitaine
		First Lieutenant	Starshii Leitenant	Flying Officer	Oberleutnant	Lieutenant
			Lietenant			
		Second Lieutenant	Mladshii Leitenant	Pilot Officer	Leutnant	Sous-Lieutenant
Enlisted		Chief Master Sergeant	Starshina	Warrant Officer Class 1	Oberstabsfeldwebel	Major
		Senior Master Sergeant	Starshii Serzhant		Stabsfeldwebel	Adjudant-Chef
					Hauptfeldwebel	
		Master Sergeant		Flight Sergeant Chief Technician	Oberfeldwebel	Adjudant
		Technical Sergeant	Serzhant	Sergeant	Feldwebel	Sergent-Chef
		Staff Sergeant	Mladshii Serzhant	Corporal	Stabsunteroffizier	Sergent
		Sergeant Senior Airman		Junior Technician	Unteroffizier	Caporal-Chef
		Airman First Class	Efreitor	Senior Aircraftsman	Hauptgefreiter	Caporal
		Airman		Leading Aircraftsman	Obergefreiter	Soldat de 1ère Classe
					Gefreiter	
		Airman Basic	Ryadovi	Aircraftsman	Flieger	Soldat de 2ème Classe

Air Forces Rank Comparison (continued)

	Italy	Turkey	Belgium	Canada	Denmark
Officers		Maresal			
	Generale di Squadra Aerea con Incarichi Speciali	Orgeneral		General	
	Generale di Squadra Aerea	Korgeneral	Luitenant-Generaal	Lieutenant-General	General
	Generale di Divisione Aerea	Tümgeneral	Generaal-Majoor	Major-General	Generalløjtnant
	Generale di Brigata Aerea	Tuggeneral	Brigadegeneraal	Brigadier-General	Generalmajor
	Colonnello	Albay	Kolonel	Colonel	Oberst
	Tenente Colonnello	Yarbay	Luitenant-Kolonel	Lieutenant-Colonel	Oberstløjnant
	Maggiore	Binbasi	Majoor	Major	Major
	Capitano	Yüzbasi	Kapitein-Commandant	Captain	Kaptajn
	Tenente	Üstegman	Kapitein	Lieutenant	Premierløjtnant
			Luitenant		Løjtnant
	Sottotenente	Tegmen	Onderluitenant	Second Lieutenant	Sekondløjtnant
Enlisted	Sergente Maggiore	Astsubay Kidemli Bascavus	Adjudant-Chef	Command Warrant Officer	Seniorsergent af 1. Grad
				Chief Warrant Officer	
		Astsubay Bascavus	Adjudant	Master Warrant Officer	Seniorsergent af 2. Grad
		Astsubay Kidemli Ustcavus			
	Sergente	Astsubay Ustcavus	1ste Sergeant-Majoor	Warrant Officer	Oversergent
		Astsubay Kidemli Cavus	1ste Sergeant	Sergeant	Sergent
	Astsubay Cavus	Sergeant	Master Corporal	Korporal	
	1ere Aviere	Cavus	Korporaal-Chef	Corporal	Overkonstabel af 1. Grad
		Onbasi	Korporaal	Trained Private	Overkonstabel af 2. Grad
	Aviere Scelto		1ste Soldaat	Basic Private	
	Aviere	Er	Soldat	Private Recruit	Konstabel

Air Forces Rank Comparison (continued)

		Greece	Netherlands	Norway	Portugal	Spain
Officers					Marechal	Capitán General
		Petrarchos	Generaal	General	General	
		Antipterarchos	Luitenant-Generaal	Generalløytnant	Tenente-General	Teniente General
		Ypopterarchos	Generaal-Majoor	Generalmajor	Major-General	General de División
		Taxiarchos	Commodore	Oberst I	Brigadeiro	General de Brigada
		Sminarchos	Kolonel	Oberst II	Coronel	Coronel
		Antisminarchos	Luitenant-Kolonel	Oberstløytnant	Tenente-Coronel	Teniente Coronel
		Episminagos	Majoor	Major	Major	Comandante
		Sminagos	Kapitein	Kaptein	Capitão	Capitán
		Yposminagos	Eerste-Luitenant	Løytnant	Tenente	Teniente
						Alférez
		Anthyposminagos	Tweede-Luitenant	Fenrik	Alferes	Subteniente
Enlisted		Archisminias	Adjudant-Onderofficier		Sargento-Mor	Brigada
		Episminias	Sergeant-Majoor		Sargento-Chefe	
					Sargento-Ajudante	
		Siminias	Sergeant der 1e Klasse		Primeiro-Sargento	Sargento Primero
			Sergeant	Sersjant	Segundo-Sargento	Sargento
		Efedrossminias	Korporaal der 1e Klasse	Korporal	Furriel	Cabo Primero
			Korporaal	Vingsoldat	Segundo-Furriel	Cabo
		Yposminias	Soldaat der 1e Klasse		Primeiro-Cabo	
					Segundo-Cabo	Soldado Primero
		Anthyposminias Smintis	Soldaat	Flysoldat	Soldado	Soldado

Air Forces Rank Comparison (continued)

	Est Germany	Poland	Romania	Czechoslovakia	Bulgaria
Officers	Armeegeneral		General Comandant	Armádní Generál	General
	Generaloberst	General Broni	General Colonel	Generálplukovník	General-Polkovnik
	Generalleutnant	General Dywizja	General Locotenent	Generálporucík	General-Leytenant
	Generalmajor	General Brygady	General de Escadra	Generálmajor	General-Mayor
	Oberst	Pulkownik	Comandor	Plukovník	Polkovnik
	Oberstleutnant	Podpulkownik	Captain-Comandor	Podplukovník	Podpolknovik
	Major	Major	Locotenent-Comandor	Major	Mayor
	Hauptmann	Kapitian	Capitan	Kapitán	Kapitan
	Oberleutnant	Porucznik	Locotenent Maior	Nadporucík	Starshi Leytenant
	Leutnant	Podporucznik	Locotenent	Porucík	Leytenant
	Unterleutnant	Chorazy	Sublocotenent	Podporucík	Mladshi Leytenant
Enlisted	Stabsfeldwebel	Starszy Sierzant Sztabowy	Plutoner Adjutant Sef	Nadpraporcík	Starshina
	Oberfeldwebel	Sierzant Sztabowy	Plutoner Adjutant	Praporcík	Starshi Serzhant
			Plutoner Major	Podpraporcík	
	Feldwebel	Starszy Sierzant	Plutoner	Nadrotmistr	
	Unterfeldwebel	Sierzant	Sergent Major	Rotmistr	Serzhant
	Unteroffizier	Plutonowy	Sergent	Rotný	Mladshi Serzhant
	Stabsgefreiter	Starszy Kapral	Caporal	Cetar	
	Gefreiter	Kapral	Fruntas	Desátník	Efreytor
		Starszy Szeregowiec		Svobodník	
	Flieger	Szeregoweic	Aviator	Vojín	Rednik

Air Forces Rank Comparison (continued)

	Hungary	Finland	People's Republic of China	North Korea	South Korea
Officers					Wonsu
				Chasu	
	Hadseregtábornok	Kenraali	Kong Jun Da Jiang	Daejang	Taejang
	Vezérezredes	Kenraaliluutnantti	Kong Jun Shang Jiang	Sangjang	Chungjang
	Altábornagy	Kenraalimajuri	Kong Jun Zhong Jiang	Jungjang	Sojang
	Vezérörnagy	Prikaatikenraali	Kong Jun Shao Jiang	Sojang	Chungjang
			Kong Jun Da Xiao	Daechwa	
	Ezredes	Eversti	Kong Jun Shang Xiao	Sangchwa	Taeryong
	Alezredes	Everstiluutnantti	Kong Jun Zhong Xiao	Jungjwa	Chungryong
	Örnagy	Majuri	Kong Jun Shao Xiao	Sojwa	Soryong
	Százados	Kapteeni	Kong Jun Shang Wei	Daewi	Taewi
	Föhadnagy	Yliluutnantti	Kong Jun Zhong Wei	Sangwi	Chungwi
	Hadnagy	Luutnantti		Jungwi	
	Alhadnagy	Vänrikki	Kong Jun Shao Wei	Sowi	Sowi
Enlisted	Fötörzsörmester	Sotilasmestari		Teukmu Sangsa	Wonsa
	Törzsörmester	Vääpeli		Sangsa	Sangsa
		Ylikersantti	Kong Jun Shang Shi	Jungsa	Chungsa
	Örmester	Kersantti		Hasa	Hasa
	Szakaszvezetö	Alikersantti	Kong Jun Zhong Shi	Sangkeub	Byongjang
	Tizedes	Korpraali	Kong Jun Xia Shi	Jungkeub	Sangbyong
	Örvezetö		Shang Den Bing	Hakeub	Ilbyong
					Yibyong
	Honvéd	Sotamies	Lei Bing	Jeonsa	Mudungbyong

Air Forces Rank Comparison (continued)

	North Vietnam	South Vietnam	Cuba	Israel
Officers		Dai Tuong	General de Ejército	
	Thuong Tuong	Trung Tuong	General de Cuerpo de Ejército	
	Trung Tuong	Thieu Tuong	General de División	Alúf
	Thieu Tuong	Chuan Toung	General de Brigada	Tat Alúf
	Dai Ta			
	Thuong Ta	Dai Ta	Coronel	Alúf Mishné
	Trung Ta	Trung Ta	Teniente Coronel	Sgan Alúf
	Thieu Ta	Thieu Ta	Mayor	Rav Séren
	Dai Uy	Dai Uy	Capitán	Séren
	Thuong Uy	Trung Uy	Primer Teniente	Ségen
	Trung Uy		Teniente	
	Thieu Uy	Thieu Uy	Subteniente	Ségen Mishné
Enlisted	Thuong Si	Thoung Si Nhat	Primer Sub-Oficial	Rav Nagád
		Thuong Si	Sub-Oficial	Rav Samál Bakhír
				Rav Samál Mitkadém
	Trung Si	Trung Si Nhat	Sargento de Primera	Rav Samál Rishón
		Trung Si	Sargento de Segunda	Rav Samál
	Ha Si	Ha Si Nhat	Sargento de Tercera	Samál Rishón
		Ha Si		Samál
	Binh Nhat	Binh Nhat	Soldado de Primera	Rav Turái
		Binh Nhi		Turái Rishón
	Binh Nhi	Trung Dinh	Soldado	Turái

Special Branch Rank Comparison

	United States Marine Corps	United Kingdom Royal Marines	Federal Republic of Germany Bundesgrenzschutz	France Gendarmerie Nationale	Italy Carabinieri
Officers	General	General			
	Lieutenant General	Lieutanant-General		Général de Corps d´Armée	Generale di Corpo d´Armata
	Major General	Major-General	Generalmajor im BGS	Général de Division	Generale di Divisione
	Brigadier General	Brigadier	Brigadegeneral im BGS	Général de Brigade	Generale di Brigata
	Colonel	Colonel	Oberst im BGS	Colonel	Colonnello
	Lieutenant Colonel	Lieutenant-Colonel	Oberstleutnant im BGS	Lieutenant-Colonel	Tenente Colonnello
	Major	Major	Major im BGS	Commandant	Maggiore
	Captain	Captain	Hauptmann im BGS	Capitaine	Capitano
	First Lieutenant	Lieutenant	Oberleutnant im BGS	Lieutenant	Tenente
	Second Lieutenant	Second Lieutenant	Leutnant im BGS	Sous-Lieutenant	Sottotenente
Enlisted	Sergeant Major Master Gunnery Sergeant	Warrant Officer Class 1	Oberstabsmeister im BGS	Major	Sergente Maggiore
	First Sergeant Master Sergeant	Warrant Officer Class 2	Stabsmeister im BGS	Adjudant-Chef	
			Hauptmeister im BGS		
	Gunnery Sergeant	Colour Sergeant	Obermeister im BGS	Adjudant	Sergente
	Staff Sergeant	Sergeant	Meister im BGS	Maréchal-des-Logis-Chef	
	Sergeant	Corporal	Hauptwachtmeister im BGS	Aspirant	
	Corporal	Lance Corporal	Oberwachtmeister im BGS	Maréchal-des-Logis	Caporal Maggiore
	Lance Corporal		Grenzhauptjäger im BGS	Brigadier-Chef	
	Private First Class		Grenzoberjäger im BGS	Brigadier	Caporale
			Grenztruppjäger im BGS		
	Private	Marine	Grenzjäger im BGS	Gendarme Adjoint	Soldato

Special Branch Rank Comparison (continued)

	Belgium Gendarmerie	Netherlands Marine Corps	Spain Marine Corps	South Korea Marines	Republic of (South) Vietnam Marines
Officers		Generaal		Taejang	
	Luitenant-Generaal	Luitenant-Generaal		Chungjang	Trung Tuong
	Generaal-Majoor	Generaal-Majoor	General de División	Sojang	Thieu Tuong
	Brigadegeneraal	Brigade-Generaal	General de Brigada	Chungjang	Chuan Toung
	Kolonel	Kolonel	Coronel	Taeryong	Dai Ta
	Luitenant-Kolonel	Luitenant-Kolonel	Teniente Coronel	Chungryong	Trung Ta
	Majoor	Majoor	Comandante	Soryong	Thieu Ta
	Kapitein-Commandant	Kapitein	Capitán	Taewi	Dai Uy
	Kapitein	Eerste-Luitenant	Teniente	Chungwi	Trung Uy
	Luitenant		Alférez		
	Onderluitenant	Tweede-Luitenant	Subteniente	Sowi	Thieu Uy
Enlisted	Adjudant-Chef	Adjudant-Onderofficier der Mariniers	Brigada	Wonsa	Thoung Si Nhat
	Adjudant	Sergeant-Majoor der Mariniers		Sangsa	Thuong Si
			Sargento Primero		
	1ste Opperwachtmeester			Chungsa	Trung Si Nhat
	Opperwachtmeester	Sergeant der Mariniers	Sargento	Hasa	Trung Si
	1ste Wachtmeester	Cabo Mayor	Byongjang	Ha Si Nhat	
	Wachtmeester	Korporaal der Mariniers	Cabo Primero	Sangbyong	Ha Si
	Brigadier	Marinier ders1e Klasse	Cabo	Ilbyong	Binh Nhat
			Soldato Primero	Yibyong	Binh Nhi
	Gendarme	Marinier der 2e Klasse	Soldato Mudungbyong	Trung Dinh	

Cold War Chronology

February 1945

4–12 Yalta Conference—Big Three (United States, United Kingdom, Soviet Union) represented by Franklin Roosevelt, Winston Churchill, and Josef Stalin

May 1945

8 V-E Day (end of World War II in Europe)

June 1945

26 United Nations (UN) founding conference ends with the promulgation of the UN Charter

July–August 1945

17–2 Potsdam Conference—Big Three represented by Harry Truman, Winston Churchill (replaced by Clement Attlee during the conference), and Josef Stalin

August 1945

14 V-J Day (end of World War II in the Pacific)
17 U.S. and Soviet officials agree on 38th Parallel as the boundary line between their occupation forces in Korea

September 1945

2 Ho Chi Minh proclaims in Hanoi the Democratic Republic of Vietnam (DRV, North Vietnam)

November 1945

17 Nationalist leader Sukarno declares the Netherlands East Indies (Indonesia) independent

27 U.S. General of the Army George C. Marshall begins his mission to China to try to mediate between the Guomindang (GMD, Nationalist) and Communist Party of China (CCP) factions

January 1946

10 UN General Assembly holds its first meeting; Trygve Lie of Norway becomes first UN secretary-general
19 Iran complains to the UN Security Council that the Soviet Union is meddling in internal Iranian affairs
31 An agreement is reached in China on a new governmental structure for the country

February 1946

9 Speech by Josef Stalin stating that capitalism and communism are "incompatible"
22 George Kennan issues the "Long Telegram," the basis for the containment policy of the United States
25 Chinese Nationalists and communists agree on a program to integrate their armed forces

March 1946

5 British statesman Winston Churchill delivers his "Sinews of Peace" speech (also known as the "Iron Curtain" speech) at Westminster College in Fulton, Missouri
25 Under pressure from the West, the Soviet Union announces that it will withdraw its troops from northern Iran

1493

April 1946

18   With Marshall absent in the United States, Chinese Nationalist and communist forces clash in Manchuria

22   Merger of communist and socialist parties in Germany, creating the Socialist Unity Party (SED), in effect the new communist party

July 1946

12   The U.S. House of Representatives approves $3.75 billion loan to Great Britain

29   Opening of conference in Paris to conclude peace treaties with World War II cobelligerents of Germany

August 1946

The Nationalist and communist agreements in China collapses

September 1946

The Greek Civil War between the royalist British-backed government and Greek communist guerrillas begins

6   In an important speech in Stuttgart, U.S. Secretary of State James F. Byrnes declares the U.S. intention to restore the German economy and vows that U.S. forces will remain in Europe as long as other powers retain occupying forces there

17   In Zurich, Winston Churchill calls for the creation of a "United States of Europe"

November 1946

25   President Harry S. Truman establishes the Loyalty Commission (Presidential Temporary Commission on Employee Loyalty)

December 1946

2   The United States and Britain agree to create Bizonia by combining their occupation zones in Germany

3   The Greek government complains to the UN Security Council that the neighboring communist states are providing military support to the communist insurgency

19   Viet Minh forces attack the French in Tonkin (northern Vietnam), beginning the Indochina War

January 1947

1   Bizonia officially created

8   Marshall, having failed to bridge the wide gulf between the Nationalists and communists, leaves China

February 1947

10   Peace treaties signed with German cobelligerents of World War II: Bulgaria, Finland, Hungary, Italy, and Romania

21   British diplomats in Washington inform the U.S. State Department that Britain, hard-pressed financially, can no longer provide aid to Greece and Turkey

March 1947

4   Britain and France sign the Treaty of Dunkerque (Dunkirk) by which they pledge mutual aid in the event of a new war with Germany

12   In a speech to Congress, President Truman asks for $400 million in aid for Greece and Turkey and outlines the policy that later comes to be known as the Truman Doctrine

21   Truman issues Executive Order 9835 calling for an investigation into the loyalty of all federal employees

May 1947

8   In a speech to the Delta Cotton Council in Mississippi that is in effect a trial balloon for the later Marshall Plan, U.S. Undersecretary of State Dean Acheson discusses the economic plight of Europe and the U.S. stake in this

June 1947

5   In a speech at Harvard University, Marshall, now secretary of state, proposes an economic aid program for Europe that will later be known as the Marshall Plan

July 1947

"Sources of Soviet Conduct" by "X" (George Kennan) is published in *Foreign Affairs*

2   The Soviet Union rejects U.S. assistance under the Marshall Plan given the conditions attached, forcing its European satellites to follow suit

20   Fighting erupts in Indonesia between Dutch and nationalist forces, beginning a two-year war

26   Truman signs the National Security Act, which establishes the Department of Defense, the Central Intelligence Agency (CIA), the National Security Council (NSC), and the Joint Chiefs of Staff (JCS)

September 1947

2   Western Hemisphere states sign the Treaty of Rio, designed to establish inter-American solidarity against aggression

22–23   Communist delegates meeting in Poland establish the Communist Information Bureau (Cominform)

October 1947

18   The House Un-American Activities Committee (HUAC) begins an investigation of communism and the movie industry in Hollywood

December 1947

The Chinese Civil War between the Nationalists and the communists resumes

February 1948

25   Communist coup in Czechoslovakia—after the collapse of a coalition government, President Edvard Beneš is pressured into appointing a government dominated by the communists

March 1948

10   Czechoslovak government authorities announce the death, allegedly by suicide, of Czechoslovak Foreign Minister Jan Masaryk (a 2004 Czech Republic government investigation concludes that he had been murdered)

17   Treaty of Brussels is signed by France, Britain, Belgium, the Netherlands, and Luxembourg—forerunner to the North Atlantic Treaty Organization (NATO)

20   Soviet representatives walk out of the four-power Allied Control Council for Germany

April 1948

1   Soviet authorities in Germany impose restrictions on road and rail traffic from the Western zones of Germany into Berlin

2   The U.S. Congress establishes the Economic Cooperation Administration to oversee the Economic Recovery Program (Marshall Plan)

30   In Bogatá, Colombia, the United States and Latin American countries establish the Organization of American States (OAS)

June 1948

13   The U.S. Senate adopts the Vandenberg Resolution endorsing U.S. participation in regional defense organizations

18   The Western occupying powers introduce a new currency in their zones of Germany and Berlin

24   The Berlin Blockade begins when the Soviet Union halts all land and water traffic between the Western zones of Germany and West Berlin

26   The Berlin Airlift begins

28   Yugoslavia is expelled from the Cominform

August 1948

3   Whittaker Chambers testifies to HUAC that former State Department official Alger Hiss was a communist in the 1930s

November 1948

2   In one of the most stunning upsets in U.S. political history, Truman wins reelection as president over the favored Republican Party challenger Thomas E. Dewey

December 1948

5   Municipal elections held in the Western zones of Berlin

10   The UN General Assembly adopts the Universal Declaration of Human Rights

January 1949

22   Communist forces capture Beijing in China

25   The Soviet Union announces the creation of the Council of Mutual Economic Assistance (Comecon), the Soviet counterpart to the Marshal Plan, for its satellites of Eastern Europe

28   The UN Security Council orders the Netherlands to end military operations in Indonesia and grant it independence

February 1949

26   The government of the Netherlands agrees to grant independence to Indonesia

March 1949

25   Chinese communist leader Mao Zedong proclaims Beijing to be the capital of China

April 1949

4   NATO is established by twelve nations, including the United States

22   Nationalist forces abandon their capital of Nanjing (Nanking)

May 1949

5   Ten Western European states form the Council of Europe at Strasbourg, France

8   The Western German parliament approves the Basic Law, in effect the constitution of the Federal Republic of Germany (FRG, West Germany)

12   The Soviet Union ends the Berlin Blockade

23   West Germany is established

25   Chinese communist forces occupy Shanghai

August 1949

24   North Atlantic Treaty goes into effect following its ratification by France

29   The Soviet Union tests its first atomic bomb

October 1949

1   Mao proclaims the establishment of the People's Republic of China (PRC)

7   The German Democratic Republic (GDR, East Germany) is established

January 1950

21   Hiss is convicted of perjury

31   Truman announces that the United States will proceed with the development of nuclear fusion (the hydrogen bomb)

February 1950

9   In a speech in Wheeling, West Virginia, U.S. Senator Joseph R. McCarthy claims to have a list of 205 communist sympathizers working in the State Department

14   The Sino-Soviet Treaty of Friendship, Alliance, and Mutual Assistance signed in Moscow

April 1950

7   The National Security Council produces NSC-68, which calls for a massive military buildup

25   Truman approves NSC-68

May 1950

9   French Foreign Minister Robert Schuman proposes creation of a European coal and steel community

June 1950

25   North Korean forces invade the Republic of Korea (ROK, South Korea), beginning the Korean War

27   The UN Security Council passes a resolution sponsored by the United States calling for the defense of Korea

30   Truman approves the dispatch of U.S. ground forces to Korea

August 1950

11   In the course of a speech to the European Assembly in Strasbourg, Winston Churchill, still a private citizen, calls for the establishment of a European army, with West German participation

September 1950

15   Successful amphibious landing by American forces at Inchon, South Korea

October 1950

7   UN forces cross the 38th Parallel into the Democratic People's Republic of Korea (DPRK, North Korea)

28   Chinese communist forces launch a major intervention in the Korean War

November 1950

25–26   Chinese communist forces carry out a massive offensive against UN forces in the Korean War

December 1950

15   Truman proclaims a state of national emergency

31   Chinese communist forces cross the 38th Parallel, invading South Korea

January 1951

4   Chinese communist forces capture Seoul

10   UN forces recapture Seoul and Inchon

March 1951

29   Julius and Ethel Rosenberg are convicted of passing nuclear secrets to the Soviet Union and on 5 April receive the death sentence

April 1951

11   Truman dismisses General Douglas MacArthur as commander of UN forces in Korea, replacing him with General Matthew Ridgway

18   Delegates of West European states meeting in Paris establish the European Coal and Steel Community (ECSC)

May 1951

23   The PRC takes control of Tibet

25   Guy Burgess and Donald Maclean, British Foreign Office officials, leave Britain—later it is revealed that they had spied for the Soviet Union

June 1951

23   Soviet UN delegate Jacob Malik proposes a ceasefire in Korea and the reestablishment of the status quo antebellum

July 1951

10   Armistice talks begin at Kaesong in Korea

September 1951

8   The Treaty of San Francisco is signed between the Allied powers, associated nations (forty-nine in all), and Japan and goes into effect on 28 April 1952

27   Iran takes control of the Anglo-Iranian oil refinery at Abadan

February 1952

23   NATO authorities announces a plan to create an army of fifty divisions within a year's time

March 1952

10   Stalin proposes a reunified and neutral Germany

July 1952

21   Egyptian military officers overthrow King Farouk

October 1952

3   In waters off Australia, Britain detonates its first atomic bomb

November 1952

1   The United States tests the world's first thermo-nuclear device (hydrogen bomb)

March 1953

5   Stalin dies

6   Georgy Malenkov becomes Soviet premier and first secretary of the Communist Party of the Soviet Union (CPSU)

14   Malenkov is forced to relinquish leadership of the CPSU to Nikita Khrushchev

June 1953

17   Workers in East Berlin strike and riot against increases in work quotas and shortages of basic goods—the riots spread across East Germany and have to be put down by Soviet troops

19   Julius and Ethel Rosenberg are executed despite widespread protests against their sentence

July 1953

27   The United States and North Korea sign an armistice, ending the fighting in Korea

August 1953

19   A CIA-sponsored coup overthrows the government of nationalist Premier Mohammed Mossadegh in Iran

January 1954

12   U.S. Secretary of State John Foster Dulles enunciates the defense doctrine that will become known as massive retaliation

21   The United States launches the *Nautilus,* the world's first nuclear-powered submarine

March 1954

1   The United States explodes its first deliverable ther-monuclear bomb on Bikini Atoll in the Pacific

13   The Battle of Dien Bien Phu opens in Indochina

April 1954

22   Opening of the Army-McCarthy Hearings in Washington, D.C.

26   Beginning of the Geneva Conference on Korea and on the war in Indochina

May 1954

7   Viet Minh forces defeat the French at Dien Bien Phu following a furious two-month-long battle

June 1954

27   A CIA-sponsored coup overthrows President Jacobo Arbenz of Guatemala

July 1954

21   The Indochina War ends with the signing of agreements in Geneva, although in order to comply with a deadline imposed by French Premier Mendès-France, the document is dated 20 July

August 1954

30   The French National Assembly rejects the European Defense Community (EDC) treaty

September 1954

3   The shelling of offshore Chinese islands in the Taiwan Strait until 1 May 1955 is initiated by the PRC

8   Establishment of the Southeast Asia Treaty Organization (SEATO) with signing of documents in Manila

October 1954

3   In London, the Western Allies sign an agreement that will allow the rearmament of West Germany within NATO

December 1954

2   The U.S. Senate votes to censure Senator McCarthy

2   The United States and the Republic of China (Taiwan) sign a mutual defense treaty

February 1955

8   Malenkov resigns as premier of the Soviet Union and is replaced by Nikolai Bulganin, while Khrushchev emerges as the leader of the Soviet Union

24   Turkey and Iraq sign the Baghdad Pact

April 1955

5   Britain, Turkey, and Iraq sign the Baghdad Pact, and Iran and Pakistan join later in the year (after Iraq leaves in 1959, the name is changed to the Central Treaty Organization, or CENTO)

May 1955

5   West Germany regains full sovereignty and joins NATO as a full member on 8 May

14   The Soviet Union and its satellites form the Warsaw Treaty Organization to counter NATO

15   The Western Allies and the Soviet Union sign the Austrian State Treaty, ending the occupation of Austria

June 1955

18   Summit meeting involving Khrushchev, Dwight Eisenhower, Anthony Eden, and Edgar Faure at Geneva

August 1955

4   The U-2 spy plane makes its first overflight of the Soviet Union

December 1955

1   The Western Allies declare that despite Soviet contentions to the contrary, Berlin remains an occupied city

9   The West German government announces the Hallstein Doctrine, indicating that West Germany will no longer maintain diplomatic relations with those states that recognize the East German government

February 1956

25   Khrushchev gives his so-called secret speech to the Twentieth Party Congress of the Soviet Communist Party in which he denounces the "cult of personality built by Stalin," thus beginnings a campaign of de-Stalinization

June 1956

28   Workers riot in Poznań, Poland, against poor economic conditions and communist rule

July 1956

26   Gamal Abdel Nasser, president of Egypt, nationalizes the Suez Canal

October 1956

21   The Soviet Union accepts Władysław Gomułka as the new leader of Poland

23   The Hungarian Revolution begins

26   Representatives of seventy nations sign a document creating the International Atomic Energy Agency (IAEA)

29   The Suez Crisis begins, during which Israel, backed by Britain and France, attacks Egypt

November 1956

1   Imre Nagy announces that Hungary is leaving the Warsaw Treaty Organization

4   Soviet tanks enter Budapest to crush the Hungarian Revolution

December 1956

2   Fidel Castro and his followers land in Cuba and begin the Cuban Revolution

January 1957

5   President Eisenhower announces a new policy, later known as the Eisenhower Doctrine, that promises U.S. military aid to victims of aggression in the Middle East

March 1957

9   Eisenhower signs into law congressional legislation authorizing U.S. forces to come to the aid of Middle Eastern states

July 1957

3   Khrushchev defeats opposition to his rule and solidifies his position as leader of the Soviet Union

14   Coup in Iraq in which King Faisal and others are slain

October 1957

4   The Soviet Union launches *Sputnik I,* the world's first orbiting satellite

January 1958

1   The European Common Market and Atomic Energy Commission are established

13   British government announces that a Soviet attack on the West, regardless of the weapons employed, will evoke a British hydrogen bomb response

31   U.S. Army launches *Explorer I,* the first American artificial satellite

May 1958

Mao's disastrous Great Leap Forward (1958–1961), an attempt at rural industrialization and increased agricultural production that results in a massive famine and the deaths of perhaps as many as 30 million people, begins

July–October 1958

The United States sends troops under the Eisenhower Doctrine to protect Lebanon's pro-Western government

July 1958

29   Establishment of the National Aeronautics and
       Space Administration (NASA)

August 1958

23   Renewed shelling of Jinmen and Mazu (part of the
       Republic of China) in the Taiwan Strait by the PRC

October 1958

4   Establishment of the French Fifth Republic

December 1958

14   The Western Allies reject the Soviet demand that
       they withdraw their soldiers from West Berlin

January 1959

1   Castro takes power in Cuba

March 1959

30   Release of earlier congressional testimony by U.S.
       Chief of Naval Operations Admiral Arleigh Burke in
       which he announces the beginning of a shift in U.S.
       defense posture with a renewed emphasis on con-
       ventional forces to build up a capability to wage
       limited war

April 1959

4   The NATO Council announces its determination
       to maintain the status quo in West Berlin and the
       rights of all occupying powers to be there

July 1959

24   Vice President Richard Nixon and Khrushchev have
       the "Kitchen Debate" at a U.S. exhibition in Moscow

September 1959

15–27 Khrushchev becomes the first Soviet leader to visit
       the United States

December 1959

1   Signing of the agreement on the peaceful use of
       Antarctica, the first major postwar arms-control
       agreement

March 1960

17   Eisenhower approves a CIA plan calling for Cuban
       exiles to invade Cuba and overthrow Castro's regime

May 1960

5   Khrushchev announces that the Soviet Union shot
       down a U-2 spy plane on 1 May and captured the
       pilot, Francis Gary Powers

7   The U.S. government admits that the U-2 shot down
       over the Soviet Union had been on a surveillance
       mission

16   Eisenhower refuses to apologize for the U-2 flights,
       resulting in Khrushchev's departure from Paris and
       the collapse of the scheduled summit there

July 1960

       Civil war breaks out in the Republic of the Congo,
       which had recently received independence from
       Belgium

September–October 1960

       Khrushchev attends the UN General Assembly
       session, and Eisenhower does not offer to meet him

October 1960

19   The United States bans most trade with Cuba

December 1960

20   Establishment of the National Liberation Front
       (NLF) in the Republic of Vietnam (RVN, South
       Vietnam) by Vietnamese communists

January 1961

1   The United States breaks diplomatic relations with
       Cuba

April 1961

12   Major Yuri Gagarin of the Soviet Union becomes
       the first human to orbit Earth in space

17   Cuban exiles invade Cuba at the Bay of Pigs

May 1961

5   Commander Alan Shepard becomes the first
       American in space

15   U.S. President John F. Kennedy declares in a speech
       to Congress that the United States should achieve a
       manned flight to the moon before the end of the
       decade

June 1961

3–4   Kennedy and Khrushchev hold a summit meeting
       in Vienna

July 1961

24   Kennedy warns the Soviet Union not to interfere
       with Western access to West Berlin

August 1961

13   East German authorities close their border with the
       West and begin construction of the Berlin Wall

October 1961

26–27 Confrontation in Berlin between U.S. and Soviet tanks

February 1962

7   The United States embargoes trade with Cuba

10   The United States swaps Soviet spy Colonel Rudolf Abel for U-2 pilot Powers

20   Lieutenant Colonel John H. Glenn Jr. becomes the first American to orbit Earth in space

July 1962

1   French rule ends in Algeria following a vote in that country in favor of independence

23   The neutrality of Laos is guaranteed by accords signed in Geneva

October 1962

14   Beginning of the Cuban Missile Crisis with the discovery in a U-2 reconnaissance flight of the construction of Soviet missile bases in Cuba

22   In a speech to the American people, Kennedy announces the presence of the Soviet missile bases in Cuba and declares a quarantine on the shipment to Cuba of offensive weapons

28   Khrushchev agrees to withdraw missiles from Cuba in return for a U.S. guarantee not to invade the island

November 1962

20   Kennedy announces an end to the U.S. blockade of Cuba

June 1963

20   Establishment of a hotline between the White House and the Kremlin

26   Kennedy's speech at the Berlin Wall in which he declares, "Ich bin ein Berliner"

August 1963

5   The United States, Britain, and the Soviet Union sign a partial nuclear test–ban treaty

August 1964

2   Attack by North Vietnamese torpedo boats against the U.S. destroyer *Maddox* in international waters in the Gulf of Tonkin

7   The U.S. Congress passes the Gulf of Tonkin Resolution

October 1964

15   Leonid Brezhnev becomes first secretary of the CPSU, replacing Khrushchev

16   The PRC tests its first atomic bomb

February 1965

7   Communist forces in South Vietnam attack U.S. military installation at Pleiku

March 1965

8–9 U.S. Marines arrive in South Vietnam, the first U.S. combat troops sent there, charged with protecting U.S. bases

April 1965

28   U.S. President Lyndon B. Johnson sends Marines to the Dominican Republic

September–October 1965

30–1 A communist coup is crushed by the Indonesian Army

March 1966

9   France withdraws from NATO's military command but remains part of the alliance

June 1967

6   The Six-Day War begins between Israel and Egypt, to include Syria and Jordan

23   Johnson meets with Premier Alexei Kosygin in Glassboro, New Jersey

October 1967

21   March on the Pentagon to protest the Vietnam War

January 1968

5   Alexander Dubček becomes leader of the Czechoslovakian Communist Party (CPCz), and the Prague Spring begins two months later, in March

30   The Tet Offensive begins in South Vietnam

May 1968

10–13 The United States and North Vietnam begin peace talks in Paris

July 1968

1   The United States, the Soviet Union, and Britain sign the Nuclear Non-Proliferation Treaty (NPT)

August 1968

20–21 Warsaw Pact troops end the Prague Spring by invading Czechoslovakia

November 1968

12   Brezhnev announces the Brezhnev Doctrine in which socialist states are obligated to aid a socialist state threatened by counterrevolutionary forces

March 1969

2   Clashes erupt between the Soviet Union and the PRC along the Ussuri River

June 1969

8   The Nixon Doctrine proclaims that Asian nations will have to defend themselves with their own soldiers in the future

November 1969

17   U.S. and Soviet negotiators begin the Strategic Arms Limitation Talks (SALT)

April 1970

30   Incursion by the United States and South Vietnam into Cambodia

August 1970

12   West Germany signs a nonaggression pact with the Soviet Union

December 1970

7   West German–Polish Treaty recognizes the Oder-Neisse border

June 1971

13   *The New York Times* begins publishing the Pentagon Papers

July 1971

15   Nixon announces that he will visit the PRC in 1972

February 1972

21   Nixon begins his visit to the PRC

May 1972

26   Nixon and Kosygin sign the SALT I treaty and the Anti-Ballistic Missile (ABM) Treaty

June 1972

3   A four-power agreement between the United States, the Soviet Union, Britain, and France resolves the Berlin issue

December 1972

21   The Basic Treaty establishes mutual relations between West Germany and East Germany

January 1973

27   A Vietnam peace agreement is signed

July 1973

3   The Helsinki Conference on European security begins

October 1973

6   Egyptian forces strike across the Suez Canal, beginning what is known as the October, Yom Kippur, or Ramadan War between Egyptian and Syrian forces against Israel

November 1973

7   Congress overrides Nixon's veto of the War Powers Act

June 1974

27   Summit meeting between Nixon and Brezhnev

November 1974

23–24   President Gerald Ford and Brezhnev agree on a draft for a SALT II treaty

April 1975

17   Cambodia falls to the Khmer Rouge, and a genocidal campaign soon begins

30   Fall of Saigon and end of the Vietnam War

August 1975

1   Leaders of thirty-five nations sign the Helsinki Accords

July 1976

2   North and South Vietnam are officially united

March 1977

17   President Jimmy Carter announces that human rights will be a major focus of U.S. foreign policy

December 1978

25   Vietnam invades Cambodia

January 1979

1   The United States and the PRC open diplomatic relations

June 1979

18   Carter and Brezhnev sign the SALT II treaty (never ratified)

July 1979

17   Marxist Sandinista guerrillas seize control in Nicaragua

November 1979

4   Radical Iranian students seize the U.S. embassy in Tehran, taking seventy Americans hostage

December 1979

12   European members of NATO agree to deploy U.S. Pershing II and cruise missiles in Western Europe

27   Soviet forces seize control of Afghanistan

January 1980

3   Carter withdraws the SALT II treaty from consideration by the Senate in response to the Soviet invasion of Afghanistan

23   Carter, in a statement that later becomes known as the Carter Doctrine—a reaffirmation of the Truman and Eisenhower Doctrines and a partial repudiation of the Nixon Doctrine—announces that the United States will regard any Soviet aggression directed at the Persian Gulf as a threat to its vital interests

April 1980

7   The United States breaks off diplomatic relations with Iran

May 1980

4   President Josip Broz Tito of Yugoslavia, in power since 1945, dies

August 1980

31   Solidarity, led by Lech Wałęsa, signs an agreement with the Polish government that allows the establishment of the trade union movement

January 1981

20   American hostages held in Iran are freed

April 1981

1   The United States suspends aid to the Sandinista regime in Nicaragua

October 1981

6   President Anwar Sadat of Egypt assassinated by Muslim fundamentalist military officers

December 1981

13   The Polish government declares martial law and arrests the leaders of Solidarity

June 1982

6   Israeli forces invade southern Lebanon in an attempt to end the terrorist activities of the Palestine Liberation Organization (PLO)

November 1982

10   Brezhnev dies

March 1983

9   President Ronald Reagan calls the Soviet Union an "evil empire"

23   Reagan announces support for the Strategic Defense Initiative (SDI), popularly known as Star Wars

April 1983

18   Arab terrorists set off a bomb at the U.S. embassy in Beirut, killing sixty-three people

September 1983

1   Soviet aircraft shoot down Korean passenger jet KAL 007 in Soviet airspace

October 1983

5   Wałęsa wins the Nobel Peace Prize for his work with Solidarity

23   Arab terrorists drive a truck full of explosives into a U.S. barracks in Lebanon, killing 241 Marines

25   Invasion of Grenada by U.S. and Caribbean contingents

November 1983

23   The Soviet Union responds to the U.S. deployment of Pershing II missiles in Western Europe by walking out of the intermediate-range nuclear forces reduction talks in Geneva

May 1984

24   Congress bans further aid to the Contras in their struggle against the Sandinista regime in Nicaragua

September 1984

26   The PRC and Britain sign an agreement on the transfer of Hong Kong to the PRC in 1997

February 1985

6   Reagan announces U.S. support for all anti-communist rebels (freedom fighters) in a policy that later becomes known as the Reagan Doctrine

March 1985

11   Mikhail Gorbachev becomes general secretary of the CPSU

May 1985

20   Federal Bureau of Investigation (FBI) agents arrest naval officer John Anthony Walker Jr. as a Soviet spy

November 1985

19–21   First summit meeting between Reagan and Gorbachev is held in Geneva

April 1986

26   A major nuclear accident occurs at the Chernobyl nuclear power plant near Kiev in the Soviet Union

October 1986

11–12   Gorbachev and Reagan meet at Reykjavík, Iceland, for a second summit but fail to reach agreement on arms control

May 1987

5   Congress begins hearings on the Iran-Contra Affair

June 1987

14   Pope John Paul II makes his third papal visit to his native Poland and strongly endorses Solidarity

December 1987

8–10   Gorbachev and Reagan hold a summit in Washington, D.C., and sign the Intermediate-Range Nuclear Forces (INF) Treaty, which bans all intermediate-range nuclear missiles from Europe

May–June 1988

29–2   Reagan and Gorbachev hold a summit meeting in Moscow

December 1988

7   Gorbachev announces unilateral reductions in troop (100,000 men) and tank (10,000) strength in Europe in a speech to the UN General Assembly

January 1989

11   Hungary introduces political reforms

February 1989

15   Soviet troops leave Afghanistan

March 1989

26   The Soviet Union holds the first partially free elections in its history for the Congress of People's Deputies

May 1989

2   Hungary begins removing the barbed-wire fence along its border with Austria

June 1989

3–4   Chinese troops kill and injure thousands of pro-democracy demonstrators in Beijing's Tiananmen Square

4–18   Solidarity is victorious in Poland's first free election under communist rule

16   Imre Nagy, executed for his role in the 1956 Hungarian Revolution, is reburied with honors

August 1989

24   Poland gets its first noncommunist premier since World War II

October 1989

9   Demonstrations in Leipzig begin an expanding series of protests against the East German government

18   Egon Krenz replaces Erich Honecker as head of the East German Communist Party

25   Gorbachev publicly rejects the Brezhnev Doctrine

November 1989

9   East Germany inadvertently opens the Berlin Wall

20   More than 200,000 people demonstrate in Prague against the Czechoslovak communist regime

24   Czechoslovak communist leader Miloš Jakeš and his entire politburo resign

December 1989

2–3   President George H. W. Bush meets with Gorbachev at sea near Malta

25   A military tribunal tries and executes Romanian dictator Nicolae Ceauşescu and his wife Elena

29   Václav Havel becomes Czechoslovakia's first noncommunist president since 1948

March 1990

11   Lithuania declares its independence from the Soviet Union

13   The Congress of People's Deputies repeals Article 6 of the Soviet constitution, depriving the CPSU of its legal monopoly on political power, and the CPSU's Central Committee agrees to the change two days later

May–June 1990

30–3   Bush and Gorbachev hold a summit meeting in Washington, D.C.

July 1990

16   Meeting between Helmut Kohl, chancellor of West Germany, and Gorbachev leads to an agreement allowing German unification

October 1990

3   Germany is officially united

15   Gorbachev is awarded the Nobel Peace Prize

November 1990

21   The thirty-four members of the Conference on Security and Cooperation in Europe sign the Charter of Paris, formally ending the Cold War

July 1991

1   The Warsaw Pact formally disbands

31   Bush and Gorbachev, meeting in Moscow, sign the Strategic Arms Reduction Treaty (START I)

August 1991

19–21   Unsuccessful coup by Soviet Communist Party hard-liners

December 1991

25   Gorbachev resigns as leader of the Soviet Union

31   The Soviet Union is officially dissolved

Michael D. Richards and Spencer C. Tucker

Glossary

4-F	Draft classification given to those individuals determined to be unfit for military service
AAM	air-to-air missile
ABCCC	Airborne Battlefield Command and Control Center
ABDA	American, British, Dutch, Australian
ABL	airborne laser
ABM	antiballistic missile
Abwehr	Military intelligence (German); Germany's military intelligence branch was the Abwehrabteilung, commonly known as the Abwehr.
ACAV	Armored cavalry assault vehicle; M113 armored personnel carrier modified with two additional 7.62-mm machine guns and shielding for its main .50-caliber machine gun.
ACCS	Air Command and Control System; also Airborne Command and Control Squadron
ACG	Air Commando Group
ACV	U.S. Navy designation for an auxiliary aircraft carrier
AEW	airborne early warning
AFB	Air Force Base
AFC	Armed Forces Council
AFDD	Air Force Doctrine Document

AFMC	Air Force Material Command
AFV	armored fighting vehicle
AGM	Missile-range instrumentation ship
AIRCENT	Allied Air Forces Central Europe
AK-47	Russian-designed assault rifle, Automat Kalashnikov, manufactured throughout the communist bloc and considered to be one of the most successful infantry weapons of the twentieth century.
ALCS	airborne launch-control system
ALERT	Attack and Launch Early Reporting to Theater
amidship	The center part of the ship. This is both between the fore and aft sections and between the port and starboard sides.
amphibious warfare	Military activity that involves landing from ships, either directly or by means of landing craft or helicopters.
anyang hasham niko	Fractured American version of Korean-language *annyong hashimnigga* (hello).
AOR	area of responsibility
apartheid	Any system or practice that separates individuals within a nation by race or caste; specifically used in South Africa in the twentieth century.
APC	armored personnel carrier
APDS	armor-piercing discarding sabot

ARG/SLF	amphibious ready group/special landing force
ARM	antiradiation missile
arms race	Massive military buildup between the Soviet Union and the United States during the Cold War era.
ARPA	Advanced Research Projects Agency
ARRS	Aerospace Rescue and Recovery Service
ARV	armored recovery vehicle
ASAT	antisatellite
ASEAN	Association of Southeast Asian Nations, founded in 1967 to oppose the threat of feared communist expansionism. Members include Brunei, Myanmar (Burma), the Philippines, Indonesia, Laos, Malaysia, Singapore, Thailand, and Vietnam (admitted in July 1995).
ASM	air-to-surface missile
ASR	submarine rescue ship
ASROC	antisubmarine rocket
ASW	antisubmarine warfare
ATF	Advanced Tactical Fighter
ATGM	antitank guided missile
AWACS	Airborne Warning and Control System, a mobile long-range radar surveillance and control center for air defense.
AWOL	absent without leave
Ba Muoi Ba	A Vietnamese brand of beer (Vietnamese for "33").
ballistics	The science of projectiles, divided into interior and exterior ballistics. Its aim is to improve the design of shells/projectiles so that increased accuracy and predictability are the result. It also deals with rockets and ballistic missiles.
Baltimore Four	The Baltimore Four, activists opposed to the Vietnam War, poured human and animal blood over the files of potential draftees in 1967 in the first-ever raid on a selective service office.
battle light	Red light between decks to aid in development of night vision.
BBC	British Broadcasting Corporation
beehive round	An explosive artillery shell delivering small nail-like projectiles rather than shrapnel.
Berlin occupation zones	At the end of World War II, the Allies (the United States, Great Britain, France, and the Soviet Union) divided Berlin, Germany, into zones that each country was to occupy.
Big Four	Soviet Union, United States, Great Britain, and China
Big Three	Soviet Union, United States, and Great Britain
bipolar world	The balance of power after World War II and during the Cold War, when half of the Northern Hemisphere was controlled by the United States and capitalist democracies and the other half by the Soviet Union and communist states.
blacklist	A list of persons who are under government suspicion for possible illegal activities.
BMEWS	Ballistic Missile Early Warning System
boat people	After the Vietnam War, Vietnamese refugees by the hundreds and thousands fled their homeland on crowded fishing boats, makeshift vessels, and unseaworthy craft.
body count	The number of enemy killed, wounded, or captured during an operation.
brinkmanship	The action of escalation of a hazardous situation in an effort to force an opponent to back down.
bug out	To retreat rapidly and in panic without orders or authority when confronted with an advancing enemy and usually leaving all weapons and equipment behind; the opposite of an orderly, organized, and authorized withdrawal or relocation.
bush war	Bush wars, which are typically fought in the bush regions (wilderness areas replete with dense trees or shrubs and inhabited by people as well as wild animals) of Africa, are conflicts fought with guerrilla tactics.
CAC	Combined action company. Organized by the U.S. Marine Corps beginning in August 1965, the CACs were composed of a Vietnamese Popular Forces platoon, a Marine rifle squad, and a medical corpsman.
cai táng	Vietnamese practice of ancestor veneration. Traditionally, especially before 1954,

about three to five years after they had been temporarily buried, the remains of a dead relative would be exhumed, washed with scented alcohol, and reburied in a permanent grave. The remains might even be moved to another grave, at a site believed to bring success and luck to the dead person's descendants.

CAS	close air support
Catonsville Nine	The Catonsville Nine, a group of religious antiwar activists, led a famous protest against the Vietnam War.
CBO	combined bomber offensive
CBU	cluster bomb unit
cease-fire	A cease-fire, which occurs during times of war, may involve a partial or temporary cessation of hostilities. A cease-fire can also involve a general armistice or a total cessation of all hostilities.
CGN	guided missile cruiser with nuclear power
chaplains	Military officers who tend to the spiritual, moral, and physical needs of troops in the field and in camp; pastors in uniform.
Charlie	One of the many slang names for Communist troops; military communications code word for the letter "C"; a shortened form of Victor Charlie (VC, for Viet Cong).
Checkpoint Charlie	Border crossing point between West and East Berlin during the period of the Cold War.
cheka	political police of Russia
chicken plate	Bulletproof breastplate worn by helicopter crews.
CHICOM	Chinese communist
CHNAVADVGRP	Chief, Naval Advisory Group Vietnam (U.S. Navy)
chogey	Slang term meaning to leave an area: "cut a chogey." Originally a Korean War term that was also used in Vietnam.
Christian Democrats	Espousing such Christian values as compassion and tolerance, Christian Democrats began to form political parties in Western Europe after World War II, particularly in Germany and Italy.
CIC	Counterintelligence Corps (U.S.)
CIDG	Civilian Irregular Defense Group. Central Intelligence Agency project that combined

self-defense functions with economic programs to win the support of the civilian population. Carried out among Montagnards by U.S. Army Special Forces.

CinC	commander in chief
CINCFE	Commander in chief, Far East. Commander of U.S. forces in the Far East.
CINCMED	Commander in chief of the Mediterranean
CINCPAC	Commander in Chief, Pacific Command. Commander of U.S. forces in the Pacific, including Southeast Asia.
CINCUNC	Commander in chief, United Nations Command. Commander of United Nations military forces in Korea.
CIS	Commonwealth of Independent States
civil affairs/ military government	Those activities of a commander that embrace the relationship between the military forces and civil authorities and people in a friendly country or area (civil affairs) or occupied country or area (military government).
civilian control of the military	Civilian control of the military was established by the framers of the U.S. Constitution as an alternative to the British system in which the king alone controlled the military.
CLAA	U.S. Navy designation for an antiaircraft cruiser.
Claymore	U.S. M18 antipersonnel mine. Light, easily transported, and highly directional. Spraying more than 100 steel balls in a 40-degree arc, it could be hand-detonated or emplaced to fire electronically (command detonated).
clear and hold	Military operation used by U.S. and Republic of Vietnam troops in the pacification program in which troops encircled, captured, and searched an area, clearing it of communist forces; South Vietnamese troops then usually held the area.
containment	A primary strategy of the United States during the Cold War in which political, economic, and military force was used to prevent the spread of communism through the world.
CORDS	Civilian Operations and Revolutionary (later changed to Rural) Development Support. Organized all civilian agencies in Vietnam within the military chain of

command. Successor to the Office of Civilian Operations (OCO).

COSVN — Central Office for South Vietnam (Trung Uong Cuc Mien Nam). Communist military headquarters representing the Democratic Republic of Vietnam (DRV, North Vietnam) Lao Dong Party Central Committee in South Vietnam.

coup — Also known as a coup d'état, a coup is a sudden, decisive use of force in politics, especially in terms of a violent overthrow of an existing government by a small group, often assisted by the military.

court-martial — To subject to a military trial with a court consisting of a board of commissioned officers.

curtain fire — Artillery tactic of making a continuous wall of fire to seal off an area.

CVN — Aircraft carrier, nuclear propulsion.

DARPA — Defense Advanced Research Projects Agency

death squads — Clandestine and usually irregular organizations, often paramilitary in nature, that carry out extrajudicial executions and other violent acts against clearly defined individuals or groups of people.

D.C. Nine — On 22 March 1969, nine members of the radical Catholic Left, most of whom were Catholic priests, staged a raid on Dow Chemical offices in Washington, D.C., to protest the Vietnam War.

Defense Meteorological Satellite Program — The Defense Meteorological Satellite Program was used during the Persian Gulf War to help aircrews know which targets were clear and which were obscured by clouds or other weather phenomena.

defense perimeter — A defense without an exposed flank, consisting of forces deployed along the perimeter of a defended area.

détente — The relaxation of tension between two superpowers, through the theory of mutually assured destruction.

Dirty War — A period of strict repression during Argentina's 1976–1983 military dictatorship in which the right-wing regime contained popular opposition by brutally striking out against all alleged subversives, including leftist rebels, students, workers, and union leaders.

disarmament — The removal or drastic reduction by nation-states of major weapons.

dislocation — The displacement of populations of people from one geographic location to another, most often caused by sudden and extreme situations of a political, military, and/or economic nature.

Distant Early Warning Line — The Distant Early Warning Line, also called the DEW Line, was a chain of radar stations in the Arctic region of North America that were built during the Cold War between 1954 and 1957.

DMSP — Defense Meteorological Satellite Program

DMZ — Demilitarized zone. For example, the 5-mile-wide buffer zone along the demarcation line, just below the 17th Parallel, that was established in the 1954 Geneva Accords to provisionally divide North and South Vietnam pending elections that were to have been held in 1956. According to the Geneva Accords, there were to be no military forces, supplies, or equipment within the zone during its temporary existence.

DOD — Department of Defense (U.S.)

donut dollies — Nickname for workers in the American Red Cross Supplemental Recreation Activities Overseas (SRAO) program in Vietnam that provided a variety of recreational activities for American troops. The women were so-named because they often dispensed donuts and coffee to the troops, especially in the field. The women also assisted in hospitals and provided games and conversation in the field.

door-gunner — Soldier who fired from the open door of a helicopter, a hazardous position usually filled by volunteers.

draft evasion — The most common form of protest against the draft, or compulsory military enrollment sanctioned by the government.

Eagle Flight Special — U.S. helicopter assault force used to observe communist positions, react to emergencies, and conduct raid and ambush missions.

economic warfare — Compelling an enemy to submit either by direct action against its economic basis or indirectly through blockade or boycott.

E&E	escape and evasion
electronic warfare	The use of the electromagnetic spectrum to gain knowledge of the presence and movement of an opposing force and also to deny any opposing force the use of that spectrum.
ER/ELINT	electronic reconnaissance/intelligence
ESM	electronic support measures
espionage	Espionage, or the practice of spying to learn the secrets of other nations or organizations, has always been an important component of any military operation.
estimated position	Vessel's position advanced on the chart from a previous fixed or observed position.
ethics of war	Rules, principles, or virtues applied to warfare.
ethnic cleansing	A policy by which government, military, or guerrilla forces remove from their homes members of different ethnic communities considered to be enemies of the country.
EUSAK	Eighth U.S. Army in Korea
executive officer	The executive officer (XO) is the second in command of a vessel, squadron, etc.
FAC	Forward air controller. Low-flying spotter planes identified opposition positions and called the FAC, who in turn ordered air strikes against these positions.
fallout shelter	Structures developed to allow the users to survive a nuclear attack and its subsequent radioactive fallout.
FDC	fire direction center
FDO	fire direction officer
FEAF	Far East Air Force. Primary U.S. Air Force component serving in Korea during the Korean War.
FEC	Far East Command (today FECOM)
FECOM	Far East Command
firebase	A small artillery base used for patrol and to support ground operations, usually temporary.
firefight	A brief and violent exchange of small-arms fire between two opposing units, rather than combat action between two larger forces, during an assault.
first-strike capability	The ability of a country to launch an overwhelming surprise attack on another country.

FISCOORD	Fire support coordinator for artillery at company, battalion, or brigade level. Usually the senior artilleryman present who prepared fire plans and integrated all indirect-fire weapons.
five o'clock follies	Five o'clock follies was the derisive epithet appended by the media during the Vietnam War to daily media briefings by the Military Assistance Command, Vietnam Office of Information, at the Joint U.S. Public Affairs Office in Saigon.
flashback	A strong recurrence of memory, usually a symptom of post-traumatic stress disorder (PTSD).
flotilla	A grouping of warships, distinctive from a fleet by its smaller size.
Force Recon	The U.S. Marine Corps' elite reconnaissance element.
foreign aid	Foreign aid, the granting of assistance to other countries, may include donations of food or money, development loans, technical help, or military support.
fps	feet per second
fragging	Euphemism introduced during the Vietnam War to describe the intentional causing of friendly casualties from weapons in American hands.
freedom birds	Nickname given to the airplanes taking U.S. soldiers home after their tour of duty.
freedom schools	Freedom schools were established in the early and mid-1960s, particularly in Mississippi and Alabama, by young student civil rights activists to build awareness among African Americans as to what could be done about oppression.
friendly fire	Friendly fire describes the incidence of casualties incurred by military forces in active combat operations as a result of being fired upon by their own or allied forces.
FSB	fire support base
furlough	Any leave granted to a soldier by his superior. A soldier on furlough left his arms and accoutrements behind. He carried furlough papers detailing his leave dates, assignment, and return to duty date. Since photos were noticeably absent, such furlough papers gave a physical description of the man.

GHQ   general headquarters

glasnost   "Openness" in Russian. A policy developed by Mikhail Gorbachev of scaling back government secrecy and encouraging cooperation with the United States.

global positioning system (GPS)   A series of satellites that broadcast navigational signals by ultraprecise atomic clocks, providing accurate positioning.

GLONASS   Global Navigation Satellite System

GNSS   Global Navigation Satellite System

GPES   Ground proximity extraction system. A system whereby a long hook attached to cargo in a C-130 cargo plane would catch an arrest wire on the runway, pulling the cargo from the plane. Used during air resupply to land loads, as during the siege of Khe Sanh.

guerrilla   A type of limited warfare or a person who participates in guerrilla warfare.

gulag   A forced labor camp in the Soviet Union, often used for political prisoners.

hearts and minds   In 1965 President Lyndon B. Johnson said, "So we must be ready to fight in Vietnam, but the ultimate victory will depend on the hearts and minds of the people who actually live out there." The U.S. government tried to win the loyalty and trust of the Vietnamese through various pacification programs that included the provision of civic improvements and security from Viet Cong harassment with the objective of encouraging villagers to fight against the communists.

hegemony   The dominance of one nation over other nations, based on the dominant nation's transfer of core values and basic societal institutions, not through military conquest.

Hoa Lo Prison   The Hoa Lo Prison, nicknamed the Hanoi Hilton, was the best-known and most notorious of the camps or prisons housing U.S. prisoners of war in the Hanoi area.

hop tac   Vietnamese for "cooperation." Name of an unsuccessful 1964 pacification program concentrated around Saigon.

HQ   headquarters

HUD   head-up display

hull   Actual body of a vessel. Excludes superstructure, rigging, masts, and rudder.

HUMINT   human intelligence

hydrogen bomb   In 1950, the hydrogen bomb (H-bomb) was created under the direction of U.S. President Harry Truman in response to the growing threat of the cold war.

ICBM   intercontinental ballistic missile

ICSC   International Commission for Supervision and Control. Established at the 1954 Geneva Conference to supervise implementation of the Geneva Accords, it consisted of delegates from three countries not involved in the conflict but nonetheless representing the different points of view: India (neutralist), Canada (Western), and Poland (communist). Later, Indonesia replaced India in a revamped version of the ICSC known as the International Commission of Control and Supervision (ICCS) mandated by the 1973 Paris Peace Accords.

IDSCS   Initial Defense Satellite Communications System

intelligence community   The intelligence community comprises the government agencies charged with gathering information (intelligence) about other countries' military abilities and general intentions in order to secure U.S. foreign policy goals.

international waters   All waters apart from nations' territorial waters.

Iron Curtain   A term popularized by Winston Churchill to describe the division between the Soviet Union and its related states and the countries of Western Europe.

Iron Triangle   Area between the Thi Tinh and Saigon Rivers dominated by the Viet Cong.

IRBM   intermediate-range ballistic missile

IRPCS   International Regulations for Preventing Collisions at Sea (or Colregs by U.S. Coast Guard); internationally agreed rules of the road, designed to ensure safety at sea. Applies to all vessels on the high seas.

IVS   International Voluntary Services. A private, nonprofit organization that served as a model for the Peace Corps and that first came to the Republic of Vietnam (RVN, South Vietnam) in 1957. Funded primarily by the U.S. Agency for International Development (USAID), support also came from the RVN government during the early years. IVS workers were required to study Vietnamese and received instruction in Vietnamese culture. They signed up for a two-year stay in-country, with assignments at the village level ranging from agricultural development to the teaching of English. IVS saw its function as humanitarian and divorced from USAID political objectives. Saigon ceased approving IVS projects in 1971.

Japanese miracle	The extraordinary economic recovery and success of Japan shortly after the end of World War II.
jeep	quarter-ton truck (slang term for a general-purpose truck, or GP)
jet engine	An internal combustion engine in which hot exhaust gases generated by burning fuel combine with air, causing a rearward thrust of jet fluid and propelling an aircraft.
jihad	Islamic term that means "holy war."
JSOTF	Joint Special Operations Task Force
junta	Rule by a group of military officers who came to national power through a military coup.
JUSPAO	Joint U.S. Public Affairs Office; created in 1965 to take charge of both relations with the news media and psychological warfare operations.
JUWTF	Joint Unconventional Warfare Task Force; composed of unconventional warfare personnel from the U.S. Air Force, U.S. Army, U.S. Marine Corps, and U.S. Navy.
K rations	U.S. Army field rations
KCOMZ	Korean communications zone. In U.S. Army doctrine, a communications zone is the specified area behind the front lines where supply and administrative facilities could be established and operated to relieve the frontline commander of responsibility for functions not directly related to combat operations.
KGB	Komitet Gossudarstvennoi Bezopastnosti (Committee for State Security), the Soviet secret police.

KHz	kilohertz, or 1,000 cycles per second
KIA	killed in action
kibbutz	An agricultural settlement organized with collective principles, often in Israel.
Kit Carson scouts	Former Viet Cong or People's Army of Vietnam soldiers who were used as scouts by U.S. units.
KKK	Khmer Kampuchea Krom. Anticommunist faction, loosely allied with the Khmer Serai, seeking autonomy for Khmer Krom people living in the Mekong River Delta of South Vietnam in return for military services. During the 1960s, Khmer Krom soldiers made up numerous ethnic regular and irregular force battalions within the Army of the Republic of Vietnam (ARVN).
laws of war	International laws, enforced sometimes by nations after war and sometimes by commanders in battle, governing both the decision to engage in war and the manner of its conduct, particularly the forms of violence used, the definition of combatants, the treatment of prisoners, and the treatment of neutrals and noncombatants.
lima sites	Primitive airstrips in Laos used by U.S. forces for covert actions.
LOCs	lines of communication
LOH	Light observation helicopter (pronounced LOOCH).
long-range torpedo	Homing torpedoes having speeds up to 75 knots and ranges between 40,000 and 60,000 yards; driven by electric batteries of hydrogen peroxide engines, they leave no wake.
LORAN	long-range electronic navigation
low-intensity conflict	A system of military engagement developed during the Cold War.
M-16	U.S. assault rifle. Incurred great controversy, as early models tended to jam in combat. Troops initially preferred the M14, a magazine-fed Garand-action, U.S. rifle issued from 1957 until 1967.
MACV-SOG	Military Assistance Command, Vietnam, Studies and Observation Group
MAD	mutual assured destruction
mad minute	Strategy used by U.S. forces in an effort to force or "trip" a Viet Cong or People's

Army of Vietnam ambush or assault. Just prior to daybreak, all forces within a position would open fire into the area surrounding the position, utilizing all weapons.

martial law Temporary military governance of a civilian population when the civil government has become unable to sustain order.

massive retaliation As a result of the frustrating consequences of the Korean War, U.S. President Dwight D. Eisenhower decided to increase the production of nuclear weapons.

mayday Internationally recognized radio distress signal; may be sent only in a case of imminent danger. From French *m'aidez* (help me).

Medevac Acronym combining the words "medical" and "evacuation"; term applied to the movement of casualties from the battlefield to more secure locations for immediate medical attention.

MEO middle-earth orbit

mercenaries Hired professional soldiers who fight for a state or entity without regard to political interests or issues.

MGS Mobile Ground System

MGT Mobile Ground Terminal

MHC minehunter, coastal

MHz megahertz, or 1 million cycles per second

MIDAS Missile Defense Alarm System

MiG Alley A 6,500-square-mile airspace in northwestern Korea, site of the most intense jet aircraft combat throughout the war.

militarism The view that military power and efficiency is the supreme ideal of the state.

military base A variety of military installations can be considered military bases.

military justice The military justice system, which is responsible for disciplining members of the armed forces, operates under a code of law that is separate from civilian law.

Military Sealift Command The Military Sealift Command (MSC) is the U.S. Navy force dedicated to providing strategic mobility in support of wartime and peacetime national security objectives.

MIRACL Mid-Infrared Advanced Chemical Laser

MIRV multiple independently targetable reentry vehicle

missile gap The difference in the number of nuclear missiles between the Soviet Union and the United States.

mobilization Mobilization, in war or national defense, is the organization of the armed forces of a nation for active military service in time of war or other national emergency.

Montagnard French term for indigenous Vietnamese mountain people. Often shortened to "Yard."

mopping up Mission assigned to troops following the first assault wave; their job was to clear pockets of enemy resistance bypassed earlier.

MOS military occupational specialty

MRBM medium-range ballistic missile

mujahideen guerrilla fighters, especially in Afghanistan and Iran

mutual assured destruction The understanding that if one of the superpowers fired its nuclear arsenal at the other, the reciprocation would lead to the completion destruction of both countries.

NAG Naval Advisory Group. Former U.S. Navy section in the Military Assistance and Advisory Group, Vietnam (until May 1964). In April 1965 it became an operational naval command.

napalm Made of gasoline thickened to a gel, napalm was used by the U.S. military during World War II, the Korean War, and the Vietnam War in bombs and flamethrowers.

NASA National Aeronautics and Space Administration

NATO North Atlantic Treaty Organization

nautical mile Unit of measurement at sea, equal to 6,076 feet.

NAVSTAR Navigation Satellite Time and Ranging

NBAP Night Bomber Aviation Regiment (Soviet Union)

NLF National Liberation Front; officially National Front for the Liberation of South Vietnam (NFLSV, Viet Cong).

Nobel Prize The Nobel Foundation was established in 1900 and awarded its first annual prize in 1901.

no-fire line — U.S. fire-control measure. A designated point on a map beyond which no indirect-fire weapons or air assets could be employed without permission from the sector commander.

nonaligned movement — The nonaligned movement was initiated by many third world nations during the 1950s and 1960s in an attempt to steer a course of neutrality between the United States and the Soviet Union in the atmosphere of the Cold War. These countries felt that they had nothing to gain from entering direct alliances with either of the two superpowers, although they frequently courted both sides in attempts to gain greater amounts of economic and military assistance. The nonaligned movement first met at the Bandung Conference in Indonesia in 1955, and international meetings were held periodically over the next two decades, but the neutral nations were never able to formulate any cohesive policies because of the wide variety of member countries. With the end of the Cold War, the nonaligned movement lost any importance that it once held in international affairs.

nonproliferation — Collective term used to describe efforts to prevent the spread of weapons of mass destruction short of military means.

NORAD — North American Air Defense Command

oa — Abbreviaton for "overall," used as a descriptor of the length of a vessel; thus, a ship that is 300 feet in length (oa) measures 300 feet from the front of the bow to the end of the stern.

occupied territories — Two of the four areas seized by Israel from Arab states in the Six-Day War in 1967.

paramilitary organizations — Unofficial groups organized along military lines yet lacking the traditional role or legitimization of conventional or genuine military organizations.

Patriot missile — Built for the U.S. government by Raytheon, the Patriot tactical air defense missile system became an overnight sensation during the Persian Gulf War for shooting down incoming Iraqi Scud missiles in Saudi Arabia and Israel.

PBR — river patrol boat

peaceful coexistence — An expression that describes the act of living together without hostility, peaceful coexistence is often a foreign policy goal of nations that wish to avoid war.

perestroika — "Restructuring" in Russian; an economic policy developed by Mikhail Gorbachev to rebuild the Soviet Union.

periscope — Prismatic telescope fitted on submarines and used to observe surface vessels and other objects while the submarine is submerged.

periscope depth — Submersion of a submarine so that only its periscope is above sea level.

pinko — Slang term meaning a communist sympathizer that came into usage after World War II. A communist would be called a red.

post-traumatic stress disorder — Term developed to describe and treat stress reactions in Vietnam War veterans.

POW — prisoner of war

procurement — The act of purchasing, procurement often refers to the government's purchasing of military equipment or other supplies.

propellants — Compounds used to move a projectile from the firing device to the target.

provost marshal — chief of military police

psychological operations — The use of psychology and propaganda by military units to persuade target audiences to adopt at least some of their views and possibly to modify their behavior.

PSYOPS — psychological warfare operations

PSYWAR — psychological warfare

punji stake — A sharpened bamboo stake covered with feces or poison and placed at the bottom of a pit, underwater, or along a trail to be stepped on by troops; an effective physical and psychological weapon.

PWO — Psychological warfare officers. U.S. Army officers attached to Eighth Army headquarters who decided on suitable psychological warfare targets.

rearmament — The process a nation undertakes to rebuild its arsenal of weapons that were exhausted during a time of war or other military action.

recon — Short for "reconnaissance." Small recon patrols were used to get information about enemy troop strengths, movements, etc.; also called recce.

rest camp	Rear area for recuperation and light duties; also a sort of holding area before soldiers left on leave.
restricted fire line	U.S. fire-control measure. A designated point on a map beyond which targets could be engaged only with indirect-fire weapons or air assets with permission from tactical headquarters or when direct contact was in progress.
revetment	A makeshift bulwark to brace trench walls, usually consisting of fascines or sand bags.
ROTC	Reserve Officer Training Corps
RSFSR	Russian Socialist Federative Soviet Republic, official title of Soviet Russia.
sabotage	The destruction of military equipment in order to hinder the defense of an enemy nation.
Saigon commando	Derogatory slang term given by combat troops to soldiers assigned to rear areas. Often soldiers assigned to these billets wore the popular boonie hats and camouflage uniforms denied to frontline forces.
salient	A military position that extends into the position of the enemy.
salvo	The simultaneous firing of a number of guns.
SAM	surface-to-air missile
sanctions	Activities taken against a nation by other nations to pressure them into a change of policy. There are political, economic, and military sanctions.
satellite state	A country that is under the domination or influence of another. The term was used to describe the status of the East European states during the Cold War.
SCAP	supreme commander, Allied powers (title given to General Douglas MacArthur as head of the occupation forces in Japan)
scorched earth policy	A policy of devastating all land and buildings while advancing or retreating in order to leave nothing available to the enemy.
Seabees	U.S. Navy construction battalion.
SEAL	Sea Air Land. Elite U.S. Navy unconventional warfare teams.
SFHQ	Special Forces Headquarters
shaped charge	An explosive charge that focused its energy in a particular direction.
shrapnel	An artillery shell containing metal balls fused to explode in the air above the enemy troops; shell fragments from an exploding shell.
SIGINT	signals intelligence
SLBM	submarine-launched ballistic missile
SOF	Special Operations Forces
SOG	Studies and Observations Group. Operating out of the Military Assistance Command, Vietnam, this organization carried out clandestine operations, such as road-watch teams in Laos, in conjunction with the Central Intelligence Agency.
SOP	standing operating procedure (order to be followed automatically in specified circumstances)
sortie	One flight by one aircraft.
SRBM	short-range ballistic missile
SRV	Socialist Republic of Vietnam. North and South Vietnam reunified in 1975.
SSBN	ballistic missile submarine (nuclear).
SSN	nuclear submarine (attack)
Stavka	Russian Army Supreme Headquarters (general staff), equivalent to GHQ, OHL, and GQG in other armies
STC	Satellite Test Center
Stealth fighter	Military aircraft with unconventional shapes designed primarily to absorb incoming enemy radar beams and therefore reduce detection.
STOL	short takeoff and landing
SVAF	South Vietnamese Air Force
TAC	Tactical Air Command
TBM	tactical ballistic missile
TDY	Temporary duty; usually a six-month assignment.
teach-ins	Teach-ins, which combined protest with education, originated during the Vietnam War as a form of antiwar demonstration.
TEREC	tactical electronic reconnaissance sensor
TOA	time of arrival
toe poppers	Slang for communist antipersonnel mines designed to maim (break a foot or blow off toes).
TOT	time on target (artillery term)

tour of duty	The 365 days a soldier in the U.S. Army spent in Vietnam; for Marines the period was thirteen months.
TsAGI	Tsentral'nyi Aero-Gidrodinamicheskii Institut (Central Aerodynamics and Hydrodynamics Institute, Soviet Union)
UAV	unmanned aerial vehicle
UCAV	uninhabited combat aerial vehicle
UDT	underwater demolition team (U.S.)
USO	United Service Organizations (U.S.)
USTRANSCOM	United States Transportation Command
UXB	unexploded bomb
V/STOL	vertical/short takeoff and landing
Velvet Revolution	The intellectual-led revolt that took place in late 1989 in what was then Czechoslovakia and resulted in the ousting of the communist regime that had been in place since the end of World War II and the subsequent creation of a democratic system.
Victor Charlie	Military communications code words for VC (Viet Cong). (*See* Charlie)
Vietnamization	In 1970, President Richard Nixon used the process of Vietnamization, or the replacement of American troops with South Vietnamese troops, to transfer military responsibility to South Vietnam.
VSTOL	very short takeoff and landing
VTOL	vertical takeoff and landing
VVAW	Vietnam Veterans Against the War
wag the dog	An expression that can refer to a president's attempt to divert attention from an unpopular domestic situation by waging war or military attacks abroad.
war bride	A newly married or soon to be married woman whose husband or fiancé is serving in the military during wartime.
war crimes	Violations of the laws and customs of war entailing individual criminal responsibility directly under international law.
War on Poverty	The War on Poverty, a central component of President Lyndon B. Johnson's Great Society program, aimed to reduce and eventually to eliminate poverty in the United States.
war reparations	The demands for restitution usually imposed by the victorious party as part of the peace negotiations at the end of a war.
WIA	wounded in action
Wise Men	A select group of senior advisors to President Lyndon Johnson.
Yankee Station	An operating area off the Vietnamese coast in the South China Sea used by the U.S. Navy's Seventh Fleet Attack Carrier Strike Force (Task Force 77). Air strikes against North Vietnam were launched from Yankee Station; code name for the Gulf of Tonkin.
ZEL	zero-length launcher
zero day	Term applied to the date of an attack or a major operation.
zero hour	Term applied to the exact time of an attack, information to be kept as long as possible from the participating troops.

Selected Bibliography of the Cold War

Acheson, Dean. *Present at the Creation: My Years at the State Department*. New York: Norton, 1969.

Aldrich, Richard J. *The Hidden Hand: Britain, America, and Cold War Secret Intelligence*. Woodstock, NY: Overlook Press, 2002.

Allen, Debra J. *The Oder-Neisse Line: The United States, Poland, and Germany in the Cold War*. Westport, CT: Praeger, 2003.

Ali, S. Mahmud. *Cold War in the High Himalayas: The USA, China, and South Asia in the 1950s*. New York: St. Martin's, 1999.

Allin, Dana H. *Cold War Illusions: America, Europe, and Soviet Power, 1969–1989*. New York: St. Martin's, 1995.

Anderson, Terry H. *The United States, Great Britain, and the Cold War, 1944–1947*. Columbia: University of Missouri Press, 1981.

Appy, Christian G. *Cold War Constructions: The Political Culture of United States Imperialism, 1945–1966*. Amherst: University of Massachusetts Press, 2000.

Ball, Simon J. *The Cold War: An International History, 1947–1991*. New York: St. Martin's, 1998.

Bearden, Milt, and James Risen. *The Main Enemy: The Inside Story of the CIA's Final Showdown with the KGB*. New York: Random House, 2003.

Bell, Jonathan. *The Liberal State on Trial: The Cold War and American Politics in the Truman Years*. New York: Columbia University Press, 2004.

Berman, Larry. *Planning a Tragedy: The Americanization of the War in Vietnam*. New York: Norton, 1982.

Bernhard, Nancy E. *U.S. Television News and Cold War Propaganda, 1947–1960*. New York: Cambridge University Press, 1999.

Beschloss, Michael R. *The Crisis Years: Kennedy and Khrushchev, 1960–1963*. New York: HarperCollins, 1991.

Beschloss, Michael R., and Strobe Talbott. *At the Highest Levels: The Inside Story of the End of the Cold War*. Boston: Little, Brown, 1993.

Bills, Scott L. *Empire and Cold War: The Roots of US-Third World Antagonism, 1945–47*. New York: St. Martin's, 1990.

Borstelmann, Thomas. *Apartheid's Reluctant Uncle: The United States and Southern Africa in the Early Cold War*. New York: Oxford University Press, 1993.

———. *The Cold War and the Color Line: American Race Relations in the Global Arena*. Cambridge: Harvard University Press, 2001.

Botti, Timothy J. *Ace in the Hole: Why the United States Did Not Use Nuclear Weapons in the Cold War, 1945 to 1965*. Westport, CT: Greenwood, 1996.

Bowker, Mike. *Russian Foreign Policy and the End of the Cold War*. Brookfield, VT: Dartmouth Publishing, 1997.

Bowker, Mike, and Robin Brown. *From Cold War to Collapse: Theory and World Politics in the 1980s*. New York: Cambridge University Press, 1993.

Boyer, Paul S. *Fallout: A Historian Reflects on America's Half-Century Encounter with Nuclear Weapons*. Columbus: Ohio State University Press, 1998.

Brands, H. W. *The Devil We Knew: Americans and the Cold War*. New York: Oxford University Press, 1993.

———. *Inside the Cold War: Loy Henderson and the Rise of the American Empire, 1918–1961*. New York: Oxford University Press, 1991.

Brogi, Alessandro. *A Question of Self-Esteem: The United States and Cold War Choices in France and Italy, 1944–1958*. Westport, CT: Praeger, 2002.

Burrows, William E. *By Any Means Necessary: America's Secret Air War in the Cold War.* New York: Farrar, Straus and Giroux, 2001.

Cahn, Anne Hessing. *Killing Detente: The Right Attacks the CIA.* University Park: Pennsylvania State University Press, 1998.

Callahan, David. *Dangerous Capabilities: Paul Nitze and the Cold War.* New York: HarperCollins, 1990.

Carlton, David, and Herbert M. Levine, eds. *The Cold War Debated.* New York: McGraw-Hill, 1988.

Carmichael, Virginia. *Framing History: The Rosenberg Story and the Cold War.* Minneapolis: University of Minnesota Press, 1993.

Chafer, Tony, and Brian Jenkins. *France: From the Cold War to the New World Order.* New York: St. Martin's, 1996.

Chang Jung and Jon Halliday. *Mao: The Unknown Story.* New York: Knopf, 2005.

Chen, Jian. *Mao's China and the Cold War.* Chapel Hill: University of North Carolina Press, 2001.

Clemens, Walter C. *The Superpowers and Arms Control: From Cold War to Interdependence.* Lexington, MA: Lexington Books, 1973.

Clough, Michael. *Free at Last? U.S. Policy toward Africa and the End of the Cold War.* New York: Council on Foreign Relations Press, 1992.

Collins, Alan. *The Security Dilemma and the End of the Cold War.* New York: St. Martin's, 1997.

Craven, John P. *The Silent War: The Cold War Battle beneath the Sea.* New York: Simon and Schuster, 2001.

Crockatt, Richard. *The Fifty Years' War: The United States and the Soviet Union in World Politics, 1941–1991.* New York: Routledge, 1995.

Cronin, James E. *The World the Cold War Made: Order, Chaos and the Return of History.* New York: Routledge, 1996.

Currey, Cecil B. *Victory at Any Cost: The Genius of Viet Nam's Gen. Vo Nguyen Giap.* Washington, DC: Brassey's, 1997.

Dallas, Gregor. *1945: The War That Never Ended.* New Haven, CT: Yale University Press, 2005.

Dark, Ken R., and A. L. Harris. *The New World and the New World Order: US Relative Decline, Domestic Instability in the Americas, and the End of the Cold War.* New York: St. Martin's, 1996.

Davis, Lynn E. *The Cold War Begins: Soviet-American Conflict over Eastern Europe.* Princeton, NJ: Princeton University Press, 1974.

Defty, Andrew. *Britain, America, and Anti-Communist Propaganda, 1945–53: The Information Research Department.* New York: Routledge, 2004.

Deighton, Anne. *The Impossible Peace: Britain, the Division of Germany and the Origins of the Cold War.* New York: Oxford University Press, 1990.

Denitch, Bogdan Denis. *The End of the Cold War: European Unity, Socialism, and the Shift in Global Power.* Minneapolis: University of Minnesota Press, 1990.

Doherty, Thomas Patrick. *Cold War, Cool Medium: Television, McCarthyism, and American Culture.* New York: Columbia University Press, 2003.

Dudley, William. *The Cold War: Opposing Viewpoints.* San Diego, CA: Greenhaven, 1992.

Dudziak, Mary L. *Cold War Civil Rights: Race and the Image of American Democracy.* Princeton, NJ: Princeton University Press, 2000.

Duggan, Christopher, and C. Wagstaff, eds. *Italy in the Cold War: Politics, Culture and Society, 1948–1958.* Oxford, UK; Berg, 1995.

Dunbabin, J. P. D. *International Relations since 1945: A History in Two Volumes.* New York: Longman, 1994.

Evangelista, Matthew. *Unarmed Forces: The Transnational Movement to End the Cold War.* Ithaca, NY: Cornell University Press, 1999.

Fall, Bernard B. *Hell in a Very Small Place: The Siege of Dienbienphu.* Philadelphia: Lippincott, 1966.

FitzGerald, Frances. *Fire in the Lake: The Vietnamese and the Americans in Vietnam.* Boston: Little, Brown, 1972.

———. *Way Out There in the Blue: Reagan, Star Wars, and the End of the Cold War.* New York: Simon and Schuster, 2000.

Fordham, Benjamin O. *Building the Cold War Consensus: The Political Economy of U.S. National Security Policy, 1949–51.* Ann Arbor: University of Michigan Press, 1998.

Freedman, Lawrence. *Europe Transformed: Documents on the End of the Cold War.* New York: St. Martin's, 1990.

Freedman, Lawrence, and John Keegan. *The Cold War: A Military History.* London: Cassell, 2001.

Fried, Richard M. *Nightmare in Red: The McCarthy Era in Perspective.* New York: Oxford University Press, 1990.

Friedman, Norman. *The Fifty Year War: Conflict and Strategy in the Cold War.* Annapolis, MD: Naval Institute Press, 2000.

Gaddis, John Lewis. *The Cold War: A New History.* New York: Penguin, 2005.

———. *Cold War Statesmen Confront the Bomb: Nuclear Diplomacy since 1945.* New York: Oxford University Press, 1999.

———. *Strategies of Containment: A Critical Appraisal of Postwar National Security Policy.* New York: Oxford University Press, 1982.

———. *The United States and the End of the Cold War: Implications, Reconsiderations, Provocations.* New York: Oxford University Press, 1992.

———. *The United States and the Origins of the Cold War, 1941–1947.* New York: Columbia University Press, 1972.

————. *We Now Know: Rethinking Cold War History.* New York: Oxford University Press, 1997.

Gambone, Michael D. *Eisenhower, Somoza, and the Cold War in Nicaragua, 1953–1961.* Westport, CT: Praeger, 1997.

Garber, Marjorie B., and Rebecca L. Walkowitz. *Secret Agents: The Rosenberg Case, McCarthyism, and Fifties' America.* New York: Routledge, 1995.

Gardner, Lloyd C., Arthur M. Schlesinger, and Hans Joachim Morgenthau. *The Origins of the Cold War.* Waltham, MA: Ginn-Blaisdell, 1970.

Garthoff, Raymond L. *The Great Transition: American-Soviet Relations and the End of the Cold War.* Washington, DC: Brookings Institution Press, 1994.

————. *A Journey through the Cold War: A Memoir of Containment and Coexistence.* Washington, DC: Brookings Institution Press, 2001.

Garver, John W. *The Sino-American Alliance: Nationalist China and American Cold War Strategy in Asia.* Armonk, NY: Sharpe, 1997.

Gavin, Francis J. *The Cold War.* Chicago: Fitzroy Dearborn, 2001.

George, Alice L. *Awaiting Armageddon: How Americans Faced the Cuban Missile Crisis.* Chapel Hill: University of North Carolina Press, 2003.

Gerson, Mark. *The Neoconservative Vision: From the Cold War to the Culture Wars.* Lanham, MD: Madison Books, 1996.

Gleason, Abbott. *Totalitarianism: The Inner History of the Cold War.* New York: Oxford University Press, 1995.

Gleijeses, Piero. *Conflicting Missions: Havana, Washington, and Africa, 1959–1976.* Chapel Hill: University of North Carolina Press, 2002.

Glynn, Patrick. *Closing Pandora's Box: Arms Races, Arms Control, and the History of the Cold War.* New York: Basic Books, 1992.

Gormly, James L. *From Potsdam to the Cold War: Big Three Diplomacy, 1945–1947.* Wilmington, DE: Scholarly Resources, 1990.

Gras, Yves. *Histoire de la guerre d'Indochine.* Paris: Editions Denoël, 1992.

Gregory, Ross. *Cold War America, 1946 to 1990.* New York: Facts on File, 2003.

Grogin, Robert C. *Natural Enemies: The United States and the Soviet Union in the Cold War, 1917–1991.* Lanham, MD: Lexington Books, 2001.

Grose, Peter. *Operation Rollback: America's Secret War behind the Iron Curtain.* Boston: Houghton Mifflin, 2000.

Grossman, Andrew D. *Neither Dead nor Red: Civilian Defense and American Political Development during the Early Cold War.* New York: Routledge, 2001.

Hahn, Peter L. *The United States, Great Britain, and Egypt, 1945–1956: Strategy and Diplomacy in the Early Cold War.* Chapel Hill: University of North Carolina Press, 1991.

Halberstam, David. *The Best and the Brightest.* New York: Random House, 1972.

Hammer, Ellen J. *The Struggle for Indochina.* Stanford, CA: Stanford University Press, 1954.

Harbutt, Fraser J. *The Cold War Era.* Malden, MA: Blackwell, 2002.

————. *The Iron Curtain: Churchill, America, and the Origins of the Cold War.* New York: Oxford University Press, 1986.

Harrison, Hope M. *Driving the Soviets up the Wall: Soviet–East German Relations, 1953–1961.* Princeton, NJ: Princeton University Press, 2003.

Hastings, Max. *The Korean War.* New York: Simon and Schuster, 1987.

Henriksen, Margot A. *Dr. Strangelove's America: Society and Culture in the Atomic Age.* Berkeley: University of California Press, 1997.

Hess, Gary R. *Presidential Decisions for War: Korea, Vietnam, and the Persian Gulf.* Baltimore: Johns Hopkins University Press, 2001.

Hewison, Robert. *In Anger: British Culture in the Cold War, 1945–60.* New York: Oxford University Press, 1981.

Hill, Kenneth L. *Cold War Chronology: Soviet-American Relations, 1945–1991.* Washington, DC: Congressional Quarterly, 1993.

Hinds, Lynn Boyd, and Theodore Windt. *The Cold War As Rhetoric: The Beginnings, 1945–1950.* New York: Praeger, 1991.

Hixson, Walter L. *George F. Kennan: Cold War Iconoclast.* New York: Columbia University Press, 1989.

————. *Parting the Curtain: Propaganda, Culture, and the Cold War, 1945–1961.* New York: St. Martin's, 1997.

Hogan, Michael J. *A Cross of Iron: Harry S. Truman and the Origins of the National Security State, 1945–1954.* New York: Cambridge University Press, 1998.

————. *The End of the Cold War: Its Meaning and Implications.* New York: Cambridge University Press, 1992.

————. *The Marshall Plan: America, Britain, and the Reconstruction of Western Europe, 1948–1952.* New York: Cambridge University Press, 1987.

Horowitz, David. *Containment and Revolution.* Boston: Beacon, 1967.

Hunter, Allen. *Rethinking the Cold War.* Philadelphia: Temple University Press, 1998.

Jenkins, Philip. *The Cold War at Home: The Red Scare in Pennsylvania, 1945–1960.* Chapel Hill: University of North Carolina Press, 1999.

Jensen, Kenneth M., ed. *Origins of the Cold War: The Novikov, Kennan, and Roberts "Long Telegrams" of 1946; With Three New Commentaries.* Rev. ed. Washington, DC: United States Institute of Peace Press, 1993.

Judge, Edward, and John W. Langdon, eds. *The Cold War: A History through Documents.* Upper Saddle River, NJ: Prentice Hall, 1999.

Judt, Tony. *Postwar: A History of Europe since 1945.* London: Penguin, 2005.

Kaiser, David E. *American Tragedy: Kennedy, Johnson, and the Origins of the Vietnam War.* Cambridge: Belknap Press of Harvard University Press, 2000.

Kaledin, Eugenia. *Mothers and More: American Women in the 1950s.* Boston: Twayne, 1984.

Kanet, Roger E., and Edward A. Kolodziej. *The Cold War As Cooperation.* Baltimore: John Hopkins University Press, 1991.

Kaplan, Lawrence S. *The Long Entanglement: NATO's First Fifty Years.* Westport, CT: Praeger, 1999.

Karabell, Zachary. *Architects of Intervention: The United States, the Third World, and the Cold War, 1946–1962.* Baton Rouge: Louisiana State University Press, 1999.

Karnow, Stanley. *Vietnam: A History.* New York: Viking, 1983.

Kaufman, Burton I. *The Korean War: Challenges in Crisis, Credibility, and Command.* Philadelphia: Temple University Press, 1986.

Kelly, George A. *Lost Soldiers: The French Army and Empire in Crisis, 1947–1962.* Cambridge, MA: MIT Press, 1965.

Kent, John. *British Imperial Strategy and the Origins of the Cold War, 1944–49.* Leicester, UK: Leicester University Press, 1993.

Kim, Young Hum. *Twenty Years of Crises: The Cold War Era.* Englewood Cliffs, NJ: Prentice Hall, 1968.

Kleinman, Mark L. *A World of Hope, a World of Fear: Henry A. Wallace, Reinhold Niebuhr, and American Liberalism.* Columbus: Ohio State University Press, 2000.

Kofsky, Frank. *Harry S. Truman and the War Scare of 1948: A Successful Campaign to Deceive the Nation.* New York: St. Martin's, 1993.

Kramer, Hilton. *The Twilight of the Intellectuals: Culture and Politics in the Era of the Cold War.* Chicago: Ivan R. Dee, 1999.

Kuhns, Woodrow J. *Assessing the Soviet Threat: The Early Cold War Years.* Center for the Study of Intelligence, Central Intelligence Agency. Library of Congress Photo Duplication Service. Springfield, VA, 1997.

Kuznick, Peter J., and James Burkhart Gilbert. *Rethinking Cold War Culture.* Washington, DC: Smithsonian Institution Press, 2001.

Lacouture, Jean. *Ho Chi Minh: A Political Biography.* New York: Random House, 1968.

Lafeber, Walter. *America, Russia and the Cold War, 1945–2002.* Updated 9th ed. New York: McGraw-Hill, 2004.

Lambakis, Steven James. Winston *Churchill, Architect of Peace: A Study of Statesmanship and the Cold War.* Westport, CT: Greenwood, 1993.

Larres, Klaus. *Churchill's Cold War: The Politics of Personal Diplomacy.* New Haven, CT: Yale University Press, 2002.

Larson, Deborah Welch. *Anatomy of Mistrust: U.S.-Soviet Relations during the Cold War.* Ithaca, NY: Cornell University Press, 1997.

Latham, Robert. *The Liberal Moment: Modernity, Security, and the Making of Postwar International Order.* New York: Columbia University Press, 1997.

Lebow, Richard Ned, and Thomas Risse-Kappen. *International Relations Theory and the End of the Cold War.* New York: Columbia University Press, 1995.

Lebow, Richard Ned, and Janice Gross Stein. *We All Lost the Cold War.* Princeton, NJ: Princeton University Press, 1994.

Ledeen, Michael Arthur. *Freedom Betrayed: How America Led a Global Democratic Revolution, Won the Cold War, and Walked Away.* Washington, DC: AEI Press, 1996.

Leebaert, Derek. *The Fifty-Year Wound: The True Price of America's Cold War Victory.* Boston: Little, Brown, 2002.

Lees, Lorraine M. *Keeping Tito Afloat: The United States, Yugoslavia, and the Cold War.* University Park: Pennsylvania State University Press, 1997.

Leffler, Melvyn P. *A Preponderance of Power: National Security, the Truman Administration, and the Cold War.* Stanford, CA: Stanford University Press, 1992.

———. *The Specter of Communism: The United States and the Origins of the Cold War, 1917–1953.* New York: Hill and Wang, 1994.

Leffler, Melvyn P., and David S. Painter. *Origins of the Cold War: An International History.* New York: Routledge, 1994.

Levering, Ralph B. *Debating the Origins of the Cold War: American and Russian Perspectives.* Lanham, MD: Rowman and Littlefield, 2002.

Levine, Alan J. *The Missile and Space Race.* Westport, CT: Praeger, 1994.

Lippmann, Walter. *The Cold War: A Study in U.S. Foreign Policy.* New York: Harper and Row, 1972.

Lipschutz, Ronnie D. *Cold War Fantasies: Film, Fiction, and Foreign Policy.* Lanham, MD: Rowman and Littlefield, 2001.

Lowe, Peter. *Containing the Cold War in East Asia: British Policies towards Japan, China and Korea, 1948–1953.* Manchester: Manchester University Press, 1997.

Lucas, Scott. *Freedom's War: The American Crusade against the Soviet Union.* New York: New York University Press, 1999.

Lykins, Daniel L. *From Total War to Total Diplomacy: The Advertising Council and the Construction of the Cold War Consensus.* Westport, CT: Praeger, 2003.

Lynch, Allen. *The Cold War Is Over—Again.* Boulder, CO: Westview, 1992.

Macdonald, Douglas J. *Adventures in Chaos: American Intervention for Reform in the Third World.* Cambridge: Harvard University Press, 1992.

Maclear, Michael. *The Ten Thousand Day War: Vietnam, 1945-1975.* New York: St. Martin's, 1981.

MacShane, Denis. *International Labour and the Origins of the Cold War.* New York: Oxford University Press, 1992.

Maddox, Robert James. *The New Left and the Origins of the Cold War.* Princeton, NJ: Princeton University Press, 1973.

Maier, Charles S. *The Cold War in Europe: Era of a Divided Continent.* 3rd ed. Princeton, NJ: Markus Wiener, 1996.

———. *The Origins of the Cold War and Contemporary Europe.* New York: New Viewpoints, 1978.

Mamdani, Mahmood. *Good Muslim, Bad Muslim: America, the Cold War, and the Roots of Terror.* New York: Pantheon, 2004.

Mandelbaum, Michael. *The Ideas That Conquered the World: Peace, Democracy, and Free Markets in the Twenty-First Century.* New York: Public Affairs, 2002.

Marks, Frederick W. *Power and Peace: The Diplomacy of John Foster Dulles.* Westport, CT: Praeger, 1993.

Markusen, Ann, et al. *The Rise of the Gunbelt: The Military Remapping of Industrial America.* New York: Oxford University Press, 1991.

Marr, David G. *Vietnam 1945: The Quest for Power.* Berkeley: University of California Press, 1995.

———. *Vietnamese Anti-Colonialism.* Berkeley: University of California Press, 1971.

Marte, Fred. *Political Cycles in International Relations: The Cold War and Africa, 1945–1990.* Amsterdam: VU University Press, 1994.

Marullo, Sam. *Ending the Cold War at Home: From Militarism to a More Peaceful World Order.* New York: Lexington Books, 1993.

Mastny, Vojtech, Sven Holtsmark, and Andreas Wenger, eds. *War Plans and Alliances in the Cold War: Threat Perceptions in the East and West.* New York: Routledge, 2006.

Matlock, Jack. *Reagan and Gorbachev: How the Cold War Ended.* New York: Random House, 2004.

Matthias, Willard C. *America's Strategic Blunders: Intelligence Analysis and National Security Policy, 1936–1991.* University Park: Pennsylvania State University Press, 2001.

May, Elaine Tyler. *Homeward Bound: American Families in the Cold War Era.* New York: Basic Books, 1988.

May, Ernest R. *American Cold War Strategy: Interpreting NSC 68.* Boston: Bedford Books of St. Martin's, 1993.

McCalla, Robert B. *Uncertain Perceptions: U.S. Cold War Crisis Decision Making.* Ann Arbor: University of Michigan Press, 1992.

McGinnis, Michael D., and John T. Williams. *Compound Dilemmas: Democracy, Collective Action, and Superpower Rivalry.* Ann Arbor: University of Michigan Press, 2001.

McMahon, Robert J. *The Cold War on the Periphery.* New York: Columbia University Press, 1996.

McNair, Brian. *Images of the Enemy: Reporting the New Cold War.* New York: Routledge, 1988.

McNamara, Robert S. *Out of the Cold: New Thinking for American Foreign and Defense Policy in the 21st Century.* New York: Simon and Schuster, 1989.

Medhurst, Martin J. *Cold War Rhetoric: Strategy, Metaphor, and Ideology.* New York: Greenwood, 1990.

Medhurst, Martin J., and H. W. Brands. *Critical Reflections on the Cold War: Linking Rhetoric and History.* College Station: Texas A&M University Press, 2000.

Meyerowitz, Joanne, ed. *Not June Cleaver: Women and Gender in Postwar America.* Philadelphia: Temple University Press, 1994.

Miller, David. *The Cold War: A Military History.* New York: St. Martin's, 1999.

Miller, Lynn H., and Ronald W. Pruessen, eds. *Reflections on the Cold War: A Quarter Century of American Foreign Policy.* Philadelphia: Temple University Press, 1974.

Mitrovich, Gregory. *Undermining the Kremlin: America's Strategy to Subvert the Soviet Bloc, 1947–1956.* Ithaca, NY: Cornell University Press, 2000.

Morris, Eric. *Blockade: Berlin and the Cold War.* New York: Stein and Day, 1973.

Moulton, Harland B. *From Superiority to Parity: The United States and the Strategic Arms Race, 1961–1971.* Westport, CT: Greenwood, 1973.

Murphy, David E., Sergei A. Kondrashev, and George Bailey. *Battleground Berlin: CIA vs. KGB in the Cold War.* New Haven, CT: Yale University Press, 1997.

Nagai, Yonosuke, and Akira Iriye. *The Origins of the Cold War in Asia.* New York: Columbia University Press, 1977.

Naylor, Thomas H. *The Cold War Legacy.* Lexington, MA: Lexington Books, 1991.

Nelson, Deborah. *Pursuing Privacy in Cold War America.* New York: Columbia University Press, 2002.

Neville, John F. *The Press, the Rosenbergs, and the Cold War.* Westport, CT: Praeger, 1995.

Nichols, Thomas M. *Winning the World: Lessons for America's Future from the Cold War.* Westport, CT: Praeger, 2002.

Nincic, Miroslav. *Anatomy of Hostility: The U.S.-Soviet Rivalry in Perspective.* San Diego: Harcourt Brace Jovanovich, 1989.

Oakes, Guy. *The Imaginary War: Civil Defense and American Cold War Culture.* New York: Oxford University Press, 1994.

O'Ballance, Edgar. *The Wars in Vietnam, 1954–1960.* New York: Hippocrene, 1981.

Oberdorfer, Don. *From the Cold War to a New Era: The United States and the Soviet Union, 1983–1991.* Baltimore: Johns Hopkins University Press, 1998.

Offner, Arnold A. *Another Such Victory: President Truman and the Cold War, 1945–1953.* Stanford, CA: Stanford University Press, 2002.

O'Neill, William L. *American High: The Years of Confidence, 1945–1960.* New York: Free Press, 1986.

Ovendale, Ritchie. *The English-Speaking Alliance: Britain, the United States, the Dominions, and the Cold War, 1945–1951.* Boston: Allen and Unwin, 1985.

Painter, David S. *The Cold War: An International History.* New York: Routledge, 1999.

Parkinson, F. *Latin America, the Cold War & the World Powers, 1945–1973: A Study in Diplomatic History.* Beverly Hills, CA: Sage, 1974.

Parry-Giles, Shawn J. *The Rhetorical Presidency, Propaganda, and the Cold War, 1945–1955.* Westport, CT: Praeger, 2002.

Partos, Gabriel. *The World That Came in from the Cold: Perspectives from East and West on the Cold War.* London: Royal Institute of International Affairs, BBC World Service, 1993.

Paterson, Thomas G. *On Every Front: The Making and Unmaking of the Cold War.* New York: Norton, 1992.

———. *Soviet-American Confrontation: Postwar Reconstruction and the Origins of the Cold War.* Baltimore: Johns Hopkins University Press, 1973.

Payne, Keith B. *The Fallacies of Cold War Deterrence and a New Direction.* Lexington: University Press of Kentucky, 2001.

Peebles, Curtis. *Shadow Flights: America's Secret War against the Soviet Union: A Cold War History.* Novato, CA: Presidio, 2001.

Pessen, Edward. *Losing Our Souls: The American Experience in the Cold War.* Chicago: Ivan R. Dee, 1993.

Pierpaoli, Paul G., Jr. *Truman and Korea: The Political Culture of the Early Cold War.* Columbia: University of Missouri Press, 1999.

Pollard, Robert A. *Economic Security and the Origins of the Cold War.* New York: Columbia University Press, 1985.

Powaski, Ronald E. *The Cold War: The United States and the Soviet Union, 1917–1991.* New York: Oxford University Press, 1998.

Puddington, Arch. *Broadcasting Freedom: The Cold War Triumph of Radio Free Europe and Radio Liberty.* Lexington: University Press of Kentucky, 2000.

Reed, Thomas. *At the Abyss: An Insider's History of the Cold War.* New York: Presidio/Ballantine, 2004.

Reynolds, David. *From World War to Cold War: Churchill, Roosevelt, and the International History of the 1940s.* Oxford: Oxford University Press, 2006.

———, ed. *The Origins of the Cold War in Europe: International Perspectives.* New Haven, CT: Yale University Press, 1994.

Roberts, Geoffrey. *The Soviet Union in World Politics: Coexistence, Revolution, and Cold War, 1945–1991.* New York: Routledge, 1999.

Robin, Ron Theodore. *The Making of the Cold War Enemy: Culture and Politics in the Military-Intellectual Complex.* Princeton, NJ: Princeton University Press, 2001.

Rodman, Peter W. *More Precious Than Peace: The Cold War and the Struggle for the Third World.* New York: Scribner, 1994.

Rose, Kenneth D. *One Nation Underground: The Fallout Shelter in American Culture.* New York: New York University Press, 2001.

Rose, Lisle Abbott. *The Cold War Comes to Main Street: America in 1950.* Lawrence: University Press of Kansas, 1999.

Ross, Robert S., and Changbin Jiang, eds. *Re-examining the Cold War: U.S.-China Diplomacy, 1954–1973.* Cambridge: Harvard University Press, 2001.

Rothwell, Victor. *Britain and the Cold War, 1941–1947.* London: Cape, 1982.

Roy, Jules. *The Battle of Dienbienphu.* New York: Harper and Row, 1965.

Ryan, Henry Butterfield. *The Vision of Anglo-America: The US-UK Alliance and the Emerging Cold War, 1943–1946.* New York: Cambridge University Press, 1987.

Sainteny, Jean. *Ho Chi Minh and His Vietnam: A Personal Memoir.* Chicago: Cowles, 1972.

Samuel, Wolfgang W. E. *I Always Wanted to Fly: America's Cold War Airmen.* Jackson: University Press of Mississippi, 2001.

Saunders, Frances Stonor. *The Cultural Cold War: The CIA and the World of Arts and Letters.* New York: New Press/ Norton, 2000.

Schmidt, Gustave, ed. *A History of NATO: The First Fifty Years.* 3 vols. New York: Palgrave Macmillan, 2001.

Schrecker, Ellen, ed. *Cold War Triumphalism: The Misuse of History after the Fall of Communism.* New York: New Press, 2004.

Schulzinger, Robert D. *A Time for War: The United States and Vietnam, 1941–1975.* New York: Oxford University Press, 1997.

Schweizer, Peter. *The Fall of the Berlin Wall: Reassessing the Causes and Consequences of the End of the Cold War.* Stanford, CA: Hoover Institution Press, 2000.

———. *Reagan's War: The Epic Story of his Forty Year Struggle and Final Triumph over Communism.* New York: Doubleday, 2002.

———. *Victory: The Reagan Administration's Secret Strategy That Hastened the Collapse of the Soviet Union.* New York: Atlantic Monthly Press, 1994.

Senarclens, Pierre de. *From Yalta to the Iron Curtain: The Great Powers and the Origins of the Cold War.* Washington, DC: Berg, 1995.

Shannon, Christopher. *A World Made Safe for Differences: Cold War Intellectuals and the Politics of Identity.* Lanham, MD: Rowman and Littlefield, 2001.

Sheehan, Neil. *The Pentagon Papers As Published by the New York Times.* New York: Quadrangle, 1971.

Sibley, Katherine A. S. *The Cold War.* Westport, CT: Greenwood, 1998.

Siebers, Tobin. *Cold War Criticism and the Politics of Skepticism.* New York: Oxford University Press, 1993.

Simons, Thomas W. *The End of the Cold War?* New York: St. Martin's, 1990.

Smith, Denis. *Diplomacy of Fear: Canada and the Cold War, 1941–1948.* Toronto: University of Toronto Press, 1988.

Smyser, W. R. *From Yalta to Berlin: The Cold War Struggle over Germany.* New York: St. Martin's, 1999.

Snead, David L. *The Gaither Committee, Eisenhower, and the Cold War.* Columbus: Ohio State University Press, 1999.

Snyder, Alvin A. *Warriors of Disinformation: American Propaganda, Soviet Lies, and the Winning of the Cold War; An Insider's Account.* New York: Arcade, 1995.

Solberg, Carl. *Riding High: America in the Cold War.* New York: Mason and Lipscomb, 1973.

Stafford, David. *Spies beneath Berlin.* Woodstock, NY: Overlook Press, 2003.

Summy, Ralph, and Michael E. Salla. *Why the Cold War Ended: A Range of Interpretations.* Westport, CT: Greenwood, 1995.

Tarling, Nicholas. *Britain, Southeast Asia and the Onset of the Cold War, 1945–1950.* Cambridge and New York: Cambridge University Press, 1998.

Taubman, Philip. *Secret Empire: Eisenhower, the CIA, and the Hidden Story of America's Space Espionage.* New York: Simon and Schuster, 2003.

Theoharis, Athan G. *Chasing Spies: How the FBI Failed in Counterintelligence but Promoted the Politics of McCarthyism in the Cold War Years.* Chicago: Ivan R. Dee, 2002.

Tucker, Spencer C. *Vietnam.* Lexington: University Press of Kentucky, 1999.

VanDeMark, Brian. *Into the Quagmire: Lyndon Johnson and the Escalation of the Vietnam War.* New York: Oxford University Press, 1991.

Vo Nguyen Giap. *Dien Bien Phu.* Hanoi: Gioi, 1994.

Vogele, William B. *Stepping Back: Nuclear Arms Control and the End of the Cold War.* Westport, CT: Praeger, 1994.

Walker, Martin. *The Cold War: A History.* New York: Holt, 1994.

Weiler, Peter. *British Labour and the Cold War.* Stanford, CA: Stanford University Press, 1988.

Westad, Odd Arne. *The Global Cold War: Third World Interventions and the Making of Our Times.* Cambridge: Cambridge University Press, 2005.

———. *Reviewing the Cold War: Approaches, Interpretations, and Theory.* Portland, OR: Frank Cass, 2000.

Whitaker, Reg, and Greg Marcuse. *Cold War Canada: The Making of a National Insecurity State, 1945–1957.* Toronto: University of Toronto Press, 1996.

Whitcomb, Roger S. *The Cold War in Retrospect: The Formative Years.* Westport, CT: Praeger, 1998.

Whitfield, Stephen J. *The Culture of the Cold War.* 2nd ed. Baltimore: Johns Hopkins University Press, 1996.

Winik, Jay. *On the Brink: The Dramatic, Behind-the-Scenes Saga of the Reagan Era and the Men and Women Who Won the Cold War.* New York: Simon and Schuster, 1996.

Winkler, David F. *Cold War at Sea: High-Seas Confrontation between the United States and the Soviet Union.* Annapolis, MD: Naval Institute Press, 2000.

Wohlforth, William Curti. *The Elusive Balance: Power and Perceptions during the Cold War.* Ithaca, NY: Cornell University Press, 1993.

Woods, Randall Bennett, and Howard Jones. *Dawning of the Cold War: The United States' Quest for Order.* Athens: University of Georgia Press, 1991.

Yergin, Daniel H. *Shattered Peace: The Origins of the Cold War.* New York: Penguin, 1990.

Yohannes, Okbazghi. *The United States and the Horn of Africa: An Analytical Study of Pattern and Process.* Boulder, CO: Westview, 1997.

Young, John W. *Cold War Europe, 1945–1991: A Political History.* 2nd ed. New York: St. Martin's, 1996.

———. *France, the Cold War, and the Western Alliance, 1944–49: French Foreign Policy and Post-War Europe.* New York: St. Martin's, 1990.

———. *The Longman Companion to Cold War and Detente, 1941–91.* New York: Longman, 1993.

———. *Winston Churchill's Last Campaign: Britain and the Cold War, 1951–5.* New York: Clarendon, 1996.

Zubok, Vladislav, and Constantine Pieshakov. *Inside the Kremlin's Cold War: From Stalin to Khrushchev.* Cambridge: Harvard University Press, 1996.

Compiled by Bonnie K. Goodman

List of Editors and Contributors

Associate Editors

Gordon E. Hogg
Director, Academic Liaisons
University of Kentucky

Dr. Priscilla Roberts
Department of History
University of Hong Kong

Dr. Timothy C. Dowling
Department of History
The Virginia Military Institute

Editorial/Advisory Board

Anna Boros-McGee
Independent Scholar

Dr. Christopher Braddick
Independent Scholar

Dr. Donald Coerver
Department of History
Texas Christian University

Dr. Bernard A. Cook
Department of History
Loyola University

Dr. James Hentz
Department of International Studies
Virginia Military Institute

Dr. Hirama Yoichi
Rear Admiral, retired
Former professor
Japanese National Defense Academy

Dr. Beatrice Jansen-de Graaf
Institute for History
University of Utrecht

Dr. Kim Jinwung
Department of History
Teachers College

Dr. Law Yuk-fun
Hong Kong University Open
    Learning Institute

Shawn Livingston
Reference Librarian
W. T. Young Library

Dr. Alessandro Massignani
Independent Scholar

Dr. James I. Matray
Professor and Chair
Department of History

Dr. Malcolm Muir
Department of History
The Virginia Military Institute

Dr. Paul Pierpaoli Jr.
Independent Scholar

Dr. David Tal
Department of History
Tel Aviv University

Dr. Paul Wingrove
Department of History and Politics
The School of Humanities
University of Greenwich

Contributors

Dr. Bradley F. Abrams
Assistant Professor
History Department

Dr. Valerie Adams
Assistant Professor
Department of History

Dr. S. Mahmud Ali

Alan Allport
University of Pennsylvania

Dr. Donna Alvah
Assistant Professor and Margaret
    Vilas Chair of U.S. History
Department of History
St. Lawrence University

Dr. Elena Andreeva
Department of History
Virginia Military Institute

Asakawa Michio
Lecturer
Tokyo University of Science

Lt. Col. William J. Astore
U.S. Air Force, retired

Dewi Ball
University of Wales, Swansea

Lacie A. Ballinger
Collections Coordinator
The Sixth Floor Museum at Dealey
    Plaza

Dr. Sebastian Balta
Romania

Dr. John Barnhill
Independent Scholar

Dr. Bethany Barratt
Assistant Professor of Political
    Science
School of Policy Studies
Roosevelt University

Dr. Paul Batrop
Department of History
Deakin University

Dr. Jakub Basista
Poland

Dr. Jeffrey Bass
Assistant Professor of History
Quinnipiac University

Bob Batchelor
Independent Scholar

Dr. Bert Becker
Department of History
University of Hong Kong

Brian Behnken
University of California, Davis

Scott E. Belliveau
Department of International Studies
    and Politics
Virginia Military Institute

Dr. Mark T. Berger
International Studies Program
School of Modern Language Studies

1st Lt Robert Berschinski
Independent Scholar

Frank Beyersdorf
Heidelberg Center for American
    Studies

Dr. Günter J. Bischof
Director
Center Austria

Amy H. Blackwell
Independent Scholar

Anna Boros-McGee
Independent Scholar

Dr. Maude Bracke
Department of History
University of Glasgow

Dr. Christopher Braddick
Professor of International Political
    History
Musashi University

Christopher John Bright
Department of History
The George Washington University

Major Heiner H. Bröckermann MA
Militärgeschichtliches
    Forschungsamt MGFA

Col. Dr. George M. Brooke, III USMC
    Rtd.

Cynthia M. Brougher
Independent Scholar

Scot Bruce
Department of History
University of Nebraska-Lincoln

Dr. Lisa Miles Bunkowski
Assistant Professor
Park University

David M. Carletta
Department of History
Michigan State University

Dr. Lucia Coppolaro
HEC Department
European University Institute

Dr. Barry Carr
History Department
La Trobe University

Peter E. Carr
Independent Scholar

Dr. Roger Chapman
Instructor of History and Social
    Sciences
Lincoln Trail College

Dr. Ranjan Chhibber
Honors Program
The George Washington
    University

Pierre-Arnaud Chouvy
Geographer, Researcher at the
    Centre national de la research
    scientifique

Jonathan Alex Clapperton
Department of History
University of Victoria

Dr. Donald Coerver
Department of History
Texas Christian University

Dr. Justin P. Coffey
University of Illinois–Chicago

Dr. David J. Coles
Department of History
Longwood University

Dr. Bernard A. Cook
Department of History
Loyola University

William O. Craig
Cold War Museum

Dr. Michael Creswell
Department of History
Florida State University

Professor Phillip Deery
School of Social Sciences
Faculty of Arts
Victoria University

Dr. Bruce DeHart
History Department
University of North Carolina at
    Pembroke

LTC Louis Dimarco, USAR
CGSC, CSI

Wilson Dizard Jr.
Public Diplomacy Institute

Dr. Michael Donoghue
Department of History
Marquette University

Dr. Jérôme Dorvidal
CRESOI History Department
University of La Reunion

Dr. Timothy C. Dowling
Department of History
Virginia Military Institute

Gregory M. Duhl
Graduate Teaching Fellow
Temple University Beasley School
    of Law

Robert W. Duvall
Independent Scholar

Jaroslav Dvorak
Department of Political Science
Klaipeda University

Richard Edwards
University of Wisconsin Colleges

Dr. Jari Eloranta
Department of History
University of Jyvaskyla
Finland

Dr. Christian W. Erickson
Political Science
School of Policy Studies
Roosevelt University

Dr. Lars Ericson
Asst. Professor
President of the Swedish
    Commission for Military History
Swedish National Defence College

Dr. Dean Fafoutis
Department of History
Salisbury University

Dr. John T. Farquhar
Department of Military Strategic
    Studies
U.S. Air Force Academy

Brian K. Feltman
Department of History
Ohio State University

Dr. Gregory Ference
Department of History
Salisbury University

Dr. Richard M. Filipink Jr.
Visiting Assistant Professor
History Department
SUNY College at Fredonia

Paul Fontenoy
Curator for Maritime Research
North Carolina Maritime Museum

William E. Fork
JD Candidate (2005)
Cornell Law School

Dr. Ronald B. Frankum Jr.
Department of History
Millersville University of
    Pennsylvania

Derek Frisby
Assistant Professor
Department of History
Middle Tennessee State University

Capt. Eric Frith
Department of History
U.S. Air Force Academy

Dr. Elun Gabriel
Visiting Assistant Professor
Department of History
St. Lawrence University

Dr. Nikolas Gardner
Department of Humanities
Mount Royal College

Dr. Philipp Gassert
Assistant Professor of History
University of Heidelberg
Executive Director
Heidelberg Center for American
    Studies

Brent M. Geary
PhD Candidate
Ohio University

Michael George
Independent Scholar

Matthew Gildner
Department of History
University of Texas at Austin

Dr. Norbert Götz
Department of History
University of Greifswald

Bonnie K. Goodman
Concordia University

Jack Greene
Military History Workshop
    International

Dr. Wolf Gruner
Institute for Contemporary History
Munich-Branch, Berlin

Dr. Steven W. Guerrier
Department of History
James Madison University

Dr. Michael Hall
Department of History
Armstrong Atlantic State University

Ha Thi Thu Huong
TMC Educational Group

Dr. Glenn A. Harris
History Department
University of North Carolina at
    Wilmington

Magarditsch Hatschikjan
Germany

Melissa Hebert
International Association of Fire
    Chiefs

Dr. Alan L. Heil Jr.
Former Deputy Director
Voice of America

Kurt Heinrich
Department of History
University of Victoria

Dr. James Hentz
Department of International Studies
Virginia Military Institute

Dr. Steve Hewitt
Department of American and
    Canadian Studies
University of Birmingham

Dr. Hirama Yoichi, Rear Admiral Ret.
Former Professor
Japanese National Defense Academy

Dr. Jan Hoffenaar
Institute of Military History, RNLA

Gordon E. Hogg
Director, International Documents
    and Research Collections

Dr. Arthur M. Holst
Widener University

John C. Horn
Department of History
University of Victoria

Dr. Eric A. Hyer
Department of Political Science
Brigham Young University

Iikura Akira
Associate Professor
Josai International University

Dr. Donna R. Jackson
Research Fellow
Wolfson College

Wanda Jarzabeck
Institut Studiów Politycznych PAN

Dr. Gudni Jóhannesson
Centre for Research in the
    Humanities
Nyi Gardur
University of Iceland

A. Ross Johnson
Research Fellow
Hoover Institution
Senior Advisor, RFE/RL

Brian Madison Jones
Kansas State University
History Department

Sophia Jordan
Department of Government
Cornell University

Dr. Melissa Jordine
Department of History
California State University, Fresno

Captain Edward A. Kaplan

Dr. Cem Karadeli
Department of History
Middle East Technical University

Dr. Lawrence Katzenstein
St. Cloud State University
Minnesota

Burcak Keskin-Kozat
Department of Sociology
University of Michigan, Ann Arbor

Dr. Barbara Keys
History Department
California State University

Dr. Michael Kilburn
Assistant Professor
Law and Government
Liberal Studies
Endicott College

Dr. Kim Jinwung
Department of History
Teachers College
Kyungpok National University

Nilly Kamal
Center for Asian Studies
Faculty of Economics and Political
    Science
Cairo University

Dr. Gary Kerley
North Hall High School

Dr. Robert Kiely
Instructor
Illinois Math and Science
    Academy

Dr. Arne Kislenko
Department of History
Ryerson University

Dr. Janeen M. Klinger
Professor of National Security
Command and Staff College
Marine Corps University

Cpt. Jonathan P. Klug
U.S. Air Force Academy

Dr. Srikanth Kondapalli
Research Fellow
Institute for Defence Studies and
    Analysis
Old JNU Campus

Kosuge Margaret Nobuko
Associate Professor
Yamanashi-Gakuin University

Kotani Ken
Graduate School of Human and
    Environmental
Studies of Kyoto University

Dr. Robert O. Krikorian
Lecturer
George Washington University

Tomoki Kuniyoshi
George Washington University

Dr. Jeremy Kuzmarow
Brandeis University

Dr. Jaclyn A. Laplaca
Department of History
Kent State University, Stark Campus

Dr. Jeffrey Larsen
Senior Policy Analyst
Science Applications International
    Corporation

Takaia Larsen
University of Victoria

Dr. Mark A. Lawrence
Department of History
University of Texas at Austin

Dr. Jan Martin Lemnitzer
London School of Economics and
    Political Science

Brigitte Leucht
Centre for Postgraduate Studies
Centre for European Studies Branch
School of Languages and Area
    Studies

Lucian N. Leustean
Doctoral Candidate in Government
London School of Economics and
    Political Science

Carrie Lewis
International Documents/Research
    Collections
University of Kentucky

Dr. Daniel Lewis
History Department
California State Polytechnic
    University

Dr. Jeffrey Lewis
Undergraduate International Studies
    Program
Ohio State University

Jonathan L'hommedieu
Department of Contemporary
    History
University of Turku

Frode Lindgjerdet
Royal Norwegian Air War College

Dr. Anna Locher
Center for Security Studies and
    Conflict Research
Zurich, Switzerland

Dr. Creston S. Long
Department of History
Salisbury University

Arturo Lopez-Levy
PhD Candidate
University of Denver

Dr. David Lowe
Acting Head of the School of History,
    Heritage and Society
Faculty of Arts
Deakin University

Dr. Soo Chun Lu
Assistant Professor
Indiana University of Pennsylvania

Dr. Igor Lukes
Professor of History and
    International Relations
Boston University

Dr. Lorenz M. Lüthi
History Department
McGill University

Dr. Sean M. Maloney
War Studies Program
Royal Military College of Canada

Dr. Jerome (Jerry) V. Martin
Command Historian
U.S. Strategic Command

Dr. Richard Mason
School of Humanities
Universiti Sains Malaysia

Dr. Masuda Hiroshi
Professor, Japanese Diplomatic
    History
Toyo Eiwa Women's University

Dr. Alessandro Massignani
Independent Scholar

Dr. James I. Matray
Professor and Chair
Department of History
California State University, Chico

Dr. Jack McCallum
Texas Christian University

Michael McGregor
Independent Scholar

Dr. Jay Menzoff
Savannah Lake University

Herbert F. Merrick
Department of Joint and
    Multinational Operations
U.S. Army Command and General
    Staff College

Dr. Christopher C. Meyers
Department of History
Valdosta State University

Dr. Silviu Miloiu
Valahia University of Targoviste

Josip Močnik
Bowling Green State University

Dr. Mary Montgomery
Bejing International School
    Education Academy

Dr. A. Gregory Moore
Notre Dame College of Ohio

Dr. Malcolm Muir
Department of History
Virginia Military Institute

Mircea Munteanu
Cold War International History
    Project
Woodrow Wilson International
    Center for Scholars

Dr. Justin Murphy
Department of History
Howard Payne University

Major General Nakayma Takashi,
    Ret.
Former Professor
Japanese National Defense Academy

Dr. Lise Namikas
Lousiana State University

Nemoto Kei
Associate Professor in History and
    Peace Research
Faculty of Law
Yamanashi Gakuin University

Nenashi Kiichi
Professor
Kwansei Gakuinn University

Caryn E. Neumann
Department of History
Ohio State University

Ensign Curtis Nieboer
United States Navy

Dr. Christian U. Nuenlist
Center for Security Studies, ETH Zurich
Switzerland

Dr. Leopoldo Nuti
Professor
History of International Relations
Department du institzioni politiche
    e scienze sociali
Università Roma Tre

Dr. Matthew O'Gara
Associate Professorial Lecturer
University Honors Program
Elliott School of International Affairs
George Washington University

Dr. John Kennedy Ohl
Mesa Community College

Okada Miho
Aoyama Gakuin University

Dr. Eric Osborne
Instructor
Virginia Military Institute

Jan Van Oudenaren
European Division
Library of Congress

Dr. Andrzej Paczkowski
Instytut Studiow Politycznych
Polna 18/20

Edy Parsons
Department of History
Iowa State University

Dr. Vernon L. Pedersen
Associate Dean for Academic Affairs
    and Student Services
Montana State University, Great Falls
    COT

Dr. Maarten Pereboom
Associate Professor and Chair
Department of History
Salisbury University

Dr. Klaus Petersen
Department of History
University of Southern Denmark

Shawn F. Peters
Coordinator
University of Wisconsin–Madison
Odyssey Project
Integrated Liberal Studies
    Program

Dr. Allene Phy-Olsen
Department of English
Austin Peay State University

Paweş Piotrowski
State Hermitage Museum
St. Petersburg, Russia

Abel Polese
Hannah Arendt Institute
Dresden, Germany

Dr. Vincent K. Pollard
Lecturer, Asian Studies
University of Hawaii at Manoa

Dr. Michael J. Polley
Associate Professor
Columbia College

Francis Gary Powers Jr.
Founder
The Cold War Museum

Dr. Christopher Preble
Director of Foreign Policy Studies
The Cato Institute

Dr. Dumitru Preda
Permanent Delegation of Romania
    to UNESCO

Elizabeth Pugliese
Independent Scholar

Dr. Sarita Rai
Department of History
University of Hawaii at Manoa

Dr. Dave Rausch
Department of History/Political
  Science
West Texas A&M University

Dr. Patrick Reagan
Department of History
Tennessee Technological University

David Richards
Assistant Professor
Department of Political Science and
  Sociology
Texas Lutheran University

Dr. Michael Richards
Department of History
Sweet Briar College

Yale Richmond
Foreign Service, Retired

Dr. Jeff Roberts
Department of History
Tennessee Technical University

Dr. Priscilla Roberts
Department of History
University of Hong Kong

Dr. Peter Rollberg
Institute for European, Russian,
  and Eurasian Studies

Dr. T. Michael Ruddy
Department of History
St. Louis University

Dr. James G. Ryan
Department of History
Texas A&M University at Galveston

Mark Sanders
Reference/Outreach Services Librarian
Louisiana State University

Herschel Sarnoff
Jordan High School

Dr. Christopher Saunders
Historical Studies
University of Cape Town

Dr. Bernd Schaefer
German Historical Institute
Washington, D.C.

Cpt. Carl Otis Schuster, USN Rtd.

Dr. Bernhard Seliger
Resident Representative
Hanns Seidel Foundation
Seoul Office

Dr. Simone Selva
Department of History of Society and
  Institutions
State University of Milan

Dr. Eugene Richard Sensenig-
  Dabbous
Political Science Department
Notre Dame de Louzaire University

Bevan Sewell
De Montfort University
Leicester, United Kingdom

Dr. James F. Siekmeier
Office of the Historian
Department of State

Col. Charles Simpson, USAF Rtd.

Amrita Singh
Reader
Deshbandhu College
University of Delhi

Air Commodore Sasjit Singh, Indian
  Air Force Rtd.
Director
Centre for Strategic and International
  Studies

Dr. Udai Bhanu Singh
Institute for Defence Studies and
  Analyses
New Delhi, India

Sarah B. Snyder
Department of History
Georgetown University

Carina Solmirano
University of Denver

Dr. Appu Soman
Senior Research Fellow
Program on Global Security and
  Disarmament
University of Maryland

Nils Arne Sørensen
Syddansk Universitet
Denmark

Dr. Daniel E. Spector
United States Army Chemical Corps

John Spykerman
U.S. State Department

Robert Stacy
Independent Scholar

Cezar Stanciu
University Valahia

Steve Stein
Department of History
University of Memphis

Dr. Luc Stenger
Marseille, France

Dr. Leonard A. Steverson
Division of Business and Social
  Sciences
South Georgia College

Dr. Bernd Stöver
Universitaet Potsdam
Professur für Zeitgeschichte

Dr. Takeda Yasuhiro
Professor of International Relations
Japanese National Defense Academy

Takemoto Tomoyuki
Lecturer
Hanazono University

Takesada Hideshi
Professor
National Institute for Defense Studies

Dr. David Tal
Department of History
Tel Aviv University

Dr. Ernest (Ernie) M. Teagarden
Professor of Business (Emeritus)
Dakota State University

Dr. Samuel Totten
University of Arkansas

Dr. John Treadway
History Department
University of Richmond

Dr. Matthias Trefs
Institut fuer Politische Wissenschaft
Universitaat Heidelberg

Dr. Chris Tudda
Historian
Declassification and Publication
    Division
Office of the Historian
Department of State

Dr. Aviezar Tucker
Social and Political Theory Program
Graduate School of Social Sciences
Australian National University

Dr. Kirk Tyvela
Department of History

Dallace Unger Jr.
Colorado State University

Josh Ushay
Queensland University of
    Technology

Dr. Peter C. J. Vale
Department of Politics
Rhodes University

Dr. Mark Van Rhyn
University of Nebraska Lincoln

Dr. Tom Veve
Department of History
Dalton State College

Dr. James Voorhees
Independent Scholar

Tim Walker
Department of History
University of Texas at Austin

Dr. William T. Walker
Vice President for Academic Affairs,
    Dean of the Faculty, and Professor
    of History
Chestnut Hill College

Dr. Vernon Warren
Department of Political Science
Austin Peay State University

Dr. Andrew Jackson Waskey
Social Science Division
Dalton State College

Dr. Robert A. Waters
University of South Dakota

Dr. William Watson
Department of History
Immaculata University

Dr. Kathryn Weathersby
Senior Associate
History and Public Policy Program
Woodrow Wilson International
    Center for Scholars

Dr. Simon Wendt
John F. Kennedy Institute for North
    American Studies
Free University of Berlin

Dr. George Richardson Wilkes
Lecturer
Centre for Jewish-Christian Relations
Cambridge University

Dr. James Willbanks, LTC Ret.
Department of Joint and
    Multinational Operations
U.S. Army Command and General
    Staff College

Joseph Williams
Religion Department
Florida State University

Dr. Maurice Williams
Department of History
Okanagan University College

Dr. Warren W. Williams
United Kingdom

Brad Wineman
Department of Military History
United States Army Command and
    General Staff College

Casey Wineman
Johnson County Community College

Dr. Paul Wingrove
Department of History and Politics
School of Humanities
University of Greenwich

Dr. Anna Wittmann
Department of English
University of Alberta

Yamaguchi Satoru
Associate Professor
Osaka Gakuin University

Dr. Ronald E. Young
History Department
Georgia Southern University

Dr. Katja Wuestenbecker
Germany

Maj. Gen. Dr. David Zabecki, USAR

Dr. Sherifa Zuhur
Visiting Professor of National
    Security Affairs
Regional Strategy and Planning
    Department
Strategic Studies Institute
U.S. Army War College

Index

Page ranges for main entries appear in boldface type. Pages for documents also appear in boldface type and are followed by "Doc."